11-14

What others are saying abc

"Drs. Fazio and Cone have edited an excellent collection of articles on the dispensational heritage of the Reformation. At a time when it is generally assumed that reformed theology only gave rise to a limited form of eschatology, the contributors show that the reformer's emphasis on biblical hermeneutics eventually led to the dispensational understanding of progressive revelation. The contributors help us better understand the biblical, historical, and practical implications of the Reformation for dispensationalism today."

Dr. Ed Hindson
Founding Dean, Distinguished Professor
Rawlings School of Divinity, Liberty University

"I've been waiting a long time for a book like this. I'm especially impressed by its width and depth. It's a theological tour de force. *Forged from Reformation* cogently clarifies the continuity of dispensationalism within the stream of Reformation history. It will quickly become the go-to book for any historical defense or evaluation of dispensationalism, especially as it relates to the legacy of the Reformers."

Dr. Mark Hitchcock
Associate Professor of Bible Exposition, Dallas Theological Seminary
Senior Pastor, Faith Bible Church, Edmond, OK

"Forged from Reformation and its esteemed authors have labored to insightfully create a work celebrating both the reformation and traditional Dispensational theology. One must appreciate the labor put forth to craft such a unique book and tackle this bold thesis. This volume, comprehensive in scope, evangelical in perspective, will prove a rich and indispensable resource that no one should be without."

Dr. Joseph M. Holden
President, Veritas Evangelical Seminary

"At last, a bold declaration from biblical scholars that clearly reveals dispensationalism as the truest and most faithful herald of the Reformation legacy. Much like the posting of Luther's *95 Theses*, the publication of *Forged from Reformation* will hopefully lead to fresh discernment, sparking yet another much needed reformation and return to the faithful interpretation and exposition of Scripture."

Dr. Stephen Davey
President, Shepherds Theological Seminary

"The odometer of church history turned over a significant milestone in October 2017 when we celebrated the 500th anniversary of Martin Luther's posting of his *95 Theses* on the doors of Wittenberg Castle Church, igniting the Protestant Reformation. And while the influence of the five *solas* on the development of Protestant theology is easily recognized, their relationship to Dispensationalism is not as clearly understood. This volume, from the pens of leading dispensational scholars, helps fill in that knowledge gap. I appreciated the many insights I discovered in this volume, and I believe you will as well."

Dr. Charles Dyer
Professor-at-Large of Bible, Moody Bible Institute
Host: *The Land and the Book* radio program

"When evangelicals think of the Reformation, they rarely think of dispensationalism. This is a mistake. While it is true that the modern dispensational movement has been trans-denominational, especially in its American development, one should not be hasty to exclude a movement that stands in the direct path of the trajectory of Reformation hermeneutics. In fact, dispensationalism in many ways is the Reformation taken to its logical conclusion and the discussion is not just about eschatology as detractors sometimes posit. As a result of dispensational thought, the evangelical world has rediscovered in greater detail the Jewish perspective of the Bible. The volume *Forged from Reformation* connects the dots and allows the reader to see clearly what others overlook so readily."

Dr. Mike Stallard
Director of International Ministry, Friends of Israel
Moderator, Council on Dispensational Hermeneutics

"It is an honor to endorse *Forged from Reformation: How Dispensational Thought Advances the Reformed Legacy* ... I applaud the authors of this volume in demonstrating the importance of normative dispensational thought that furthers the Reformation on its 500th anniversary. It argues well that Reformed Theology does not own the Reformation, but that in fact dispensationalism continues the many great themes of the Reformation in establishing the Bible-centered theology it purports, its commitment to literal interpretation, its emphasis on salvation by grace through faith for the redeemed of all ages, its goal in the glory of God, and its focus on Jesus the Messiah, and His kingdom. I trust that the book will have a wide and fair hearing."

Dr. H. Wayne House
Distinguished Research Professor of Theology, Law, and Culture
Faith International University and Faith Seminary

"As a dispensationalist educated largely in Reformed institutions, I appreciate that two theological systems can exhibit significant differences and still aim at the same conclusion—the glory of God. I welcome this book because it demonstrates the differences between the dispensational and reformed approaches to interpreting Scripture, while at the same time validating that Martin Luther's Reformation in no way negates the biblical truths that define dispensationalists."

Dr. Woodrow Kroll
Director, The HELIOS Project

"Clearly the Reformation was a watershed time in the life of the Church, and this book brilliantly illuminates this crucial moment in history. But unlike some works on the Reformation, which seem to deify the reformers and ignore some of their inconsistencies, the capable authors of this book provide a helpful perspective on what took place in those critical centuries. And they convincing show that dispensational theology's taproot goes back to the Reformation ... The authors of *Forged from Reformation* provide insights into Luther, Calvin, Darby and others, showing how present day dispensational theology is a legitimate child of the reformation, but a child that has grown to be even more faithful to the spirit of reformation hermeneutics than many of the "reformed churches" of today. This book is a must read for those who think of dispensationalism as a wandering theological star out by itself in the doctrinal universe. It is a book which will bring understanding to some of the great issues facing the church today."

Dr. Paul Benware
Professor of Bible and Theology

"*Forged from Reformation* attempts to dispel the popular argument that Dispensationalism is a 19th century invention. Like the Reformation itself, Dispensationalism is not a new idea but a return to an old one. Tracing the literal straight-forward interpretation of the Bible through the Reformation and back to the Church Fathers themselves *Forged from Reformation* hopes to illustrate that Dispensationalism is the only true consistent interpretation of history and prophecy. Irenaeus was perhaps the first to actually use the word "dispensation" (from the Latin) and he himself continued the literal line of through passed down from his teacher Polycarp, the disciple of John. It is my hope that *Forged from Reformation* will thus help dispel the popular lies of Replacement Theologians and speed the return to a Biblical understanding of prophetic history."

Dr. David Criswell
Fellow at Louisiana Baptist Seminary
Author of the *Biblical Controversies* textbook series

"Nowhere is the sovereign plan of God more on display than in the dispensational program. While the Reformers made a thorough study and defense of the truths of soteriology, it did not do the same with eschatology. However, because of these truths, the Reformation's evangelical heirs regained the early church's historic stand in its formulation of dispensationalism and many of the movement's principal teachers identified themselves as Reformed. Their influence also led to the political support for Zionism, a natural application of a dispensational understanding of Israel. Although this history and its indebtedness to Reformed teaching have been obscured in the modern Reformed critique of dispensationalism, this book does a great service in restoring that inherent connection. It is my hope that it may receive a welcome reception among both Reformed thinkers and Dispensationalists, whose common roots firmly adhere to the confession *Sola Scriptura*."

Dr. Randall Price
Distinguished Research Professor of Biblical and Judaic Studies, Liberty University

"*Forged from Reformation* is an outstanding anthology addressing hermeneutics, theological method, and the critical reformational issues portraying superb dispensational scholarship. Rather than focusing on the historical and cultural milieu of social settings or church creeds, this book refreshingly focuses upon the Biblical text itself. The essays also present a wonderful blend of historical nuances and courageous commitments of our fellow believers in Christ. And in keeping with the historical dispensational emphases upon the local church and exposition, the essays are incredibly profitable for both scholars as well as for all believers in Christ. I heartily commend the book."

Dr. David Mappes
Assistant Professor, Liberty University
Director of Noble & Knowable Truth Ministries

This book is a must read for anyone who wants a greater understanding of the historical and theological relationship between Reformed theology and Dispensationalism. *Forged from Reformation* is not the predictable dog-fight between these two persuasions. Rather the authors maintain that dispensationalists have their reformed for-runners to thank for the ground-breaking work they brought to the field of hermeneutics. The contribution of Dispensationalists has been to apply those principles to the whole of Scripture. Anyone who wants to better understand the whole Bible will greatly benefit from this read."

Dr. Forrest Weiland
Director of Biblical Studies, Veritas Evangelical Seminary

"The book's two main themes, Dispensationalism and the Reformation, are two themes not often linked together. But these scholars prove they are indeed fundamentally linked. Original, insightful and helpful, I heartily commend this book!"

Dr. Les Lofquist
IFCA International Executive Director

"In *Forged from Reformation*, you will find an honest, hard-hitting, and much-needed analysis of the Protestant Reformation, written with 500 years of perspective by distinguished proponents of dispensational theology ... In these pages, you will find the thinking of dispensationalists; those who read words in literal, historical, and grammatical context. You will not find the "tour-guide view" of the reformation that points to the beautiful sights while rushing past the unsightly views. Rather, you will find words from theologians who read history like they read the Bible: literally, grammatically, and in context. The obvious truth of the reformation is that it is what it is. The blessing of this book is that it presents the reformation for what it is and not for what it is imagined to be. The reformation was a good start that brought about a better end than the reformers intended or imagined: dispensational hermeneutics and the resultant dispensational theology."

Dr. Randy White
Founder and CEO, Dispensational Publishing House, Inc.

"I enthusiastically endorse *Forged from Reformation*. The editors and contributors are men who are solidly committed to the authority and inerrancy of God's Word. They are men who endeavor to exegete Scripture following sound rules of biblical interpretation. As is stated in the introduction, "The Protestant Reformation called us back to the Word of God." The authors of this excellent volume are men who continue to follow this back-to-the-Word tradition believing that a literal/normal approach to biblical interpretation results in a dispensational understanding. May our faithful God be honored through this excellent volume!"

Dr. Gary Coombs
President, Southern California Seminary

"With contributions from top scholars among leading Christian universities and seminaries across the country, *Forged from Reformation* will give you helpful insights into the truths of Scripture which have shaped our past and still impact our lives for Christ."

Dr. David Jeremiah
Chancellor, Southern California Seminary

FORGED FROM REFORMATION

HOW DISPENSATIONAL THOUGHT
ADVANCES THE REFORMED LEGACY

FORGED FROM REFORMATION

HOW DISPENSATIONAL THOUGHT
ADVANCES THE REFORMED LEGACY

EDITED BY
CHRISTOPHER CONE AND
JAMES I. FAZIO

Southern California Seminary Press
El Cajon, California

FORGED FROM REFORMATION: *How Dispensational Thought Advances the Reformed Legacy*

©2017 Christopher Cone and James I. Fazio
Second printing with corrections, December 2017.

Published by Southern California Seminary Press
El Cajon, CA

Copyedited by Jennifer S. Ewing and Cory M. Marsh

ISBN – 978-0-9864442-3-4

Unless otherwise noted, all Scripture quotations are from The New American Standard Bible (NASB), copyright © by the Lockman Foundation, 1995.

Scripture quotations indicated (NIV) are from The Holy Bible, New International Version, copyright © by International Bible Society, 2011.

Scripture quotations indicated (NKJV) are from The Holy Bible, New King James Version, copyright © by Thomas Nelson, 1984.

Scripture quotations indicated (ESV) are from The Holy Bible, English Standard Version, copyright © by Crossway, 2011.

TABLE OF CONTENTS

Foreword *by Michael J. Vlach* vii
Contributors ix
Dedication xi
Acknowledgements xiii

INTRODUCTION

1 Forged from Reformation: How Dispensational Thought Advances
   The Reformed Legacy 3
   Christopher Cone and James I. Fazio

PART 1
HISTORICAL DEVELOPMENT

2 Dispensationalism and the Reformation 19
   Thomas Ice
3 Martin Luther: An Evaluation of the *95 Theses* 45
   Patrick Belvill
4 John Nelson Darby: The Unknown and Well Known Nineteenth
   Century Irish Reformer 81
   James I. Fazio
5 Luther Meets Darby: The Reformation Legacy of Ecclesiastical
   Independence 109
   Cory M. Marsh
6 The Doctrine of Local Church Autonomy: Its Loss, Recovery and
   Influence on Dispensationalism 145
   Kevin D. Zuber
7 How Dispensational Thought Corrects Luther's View of Israel 179
   Brian Moulton and Cory M. Marsh

PART 2
THE FIVE SOLAS OF THE REFORMATION

Sola Scriptura
8 The Protestant Reformation: An Important and Yet Incomplete
   Hermeneutical Reformation 227
   Andy Woods

9   The Protestant Hermeneutic and the Revival of Futurism 265
    Ron J. Bigalke
10 *Sola Scriptura*: Return to Literal Grammatical-Historical
    Hermeneutics..311
    Thomas S. Baurain
11 The Hermeneutical Foundations of *Sola Scriptura*: A Critical
    Examination of Luther's Christocentric Method of Interpretation .333
    James I. Fazio
12 Neither Woodenly-Literal nor Allegorical: The Dispensationalist
    Legacy of the Reformers' Doctrine of *Sola Scriptura* 353
    Jeremiah Mutie

Sola Gratia
13 How Dispensationalism Advances *Sola Gratia*....................................383
    Grant Hawley

Sola Fide
14 *Sola Fide*: Salvation is by Grace Through Faith Alone in Every
    Dispensation 423
    Glenn R. Kreider

Solus Christus
15 *Solus Christus*...465
    Paul J. Scharf

Soli Deo Gloria
16 *Soli Deo Gloria* as Pinnacle of Dispensationalism's *Sine Qua Non* 497
    Christopher Cone
17 *Soli Deo Gloria* Revealed Throughout Biblical History 525
    Luther Smith

CONCLUSION

18 *Semper Reformanda*: Always Reforming 557
    Christopher Cone

Scripture Index...569
Subject Index...577

FOREWORD

Many Christians are celebrating the 500th anniversary of the Reformation, and rightfully so. The Reformation was a needed and welcome correction to nearly a thousand years of putting tradition and human authority over the Bible. This anniversary is also cause for reflection on how Jesus' church has conducted and reformed itself in the 500 years following Martin Luther's *95 Theses* that he posted to the door of the Wittenberg Castle church. This includes an examination of the rise of dispensationalism and how this theology connects with the Reformation and its aftermath.

The editors and writers of *Forged From the Reformation* have done a great service to the church. They offer a much needed discussion of how dispensationalism relates to the Reformation. As they show in this remarkable collection of chapters from dispensational scholars, dispensationalism is truly an heir of the Reformation tradition. Not only were many of the early dispensational leaders Reformed in their theology, dispensationalism is a proud promoter and defender of the key affirmations of the Reformation—*sola Scriptura* (Scripture alone); *sola fide* (faith alone); *sola gratia* (grace alone); *solus Christus* (Christ alone); and *soli Deo Gloria* (to the glory of God alone).

History has shown that the Reformation of the sixteenth century was not a complete break with all the errors of the Roman Catholic system. Some remnants of allegorization of Scripture remained. In addition, the fog of Augustinian amillennialism, supersessionism concerning Israel and the church, and spiritualized eschatology often remained. It is in these areas that dispensationalism makes significant contributions to the Reformation ideals of *sola Scriptura* and "always reforming." As the authors of this book show, dispensationalism has clung to the core contributions of the Reformation while also bringing a better and more focused understanding of ecclesiology, eschatology, and Israel. Dispensationalism also shines light on the necessity of applying a consistent grammatical-historical hermeneutic to all areas of Scripture, including sections related to prophecy and Israel.

Clarity is a welcome thing. Fortunately, *Forged from Reformation* is a book that brings clarity to how the Reformation and dispensationalism relate to each other. I am convinced that both critics and adherents of dispensational theology will need to interact with this important work.

Dr. Michael J. Vlach
Professor of Theology
The Master's Seminary

CONTRIBUTORS

Thomas S. Baurain, Th.M., D.Min. Professor of Bible & Theology, and Seminary Director Calvary University (Kansas City, MO).

Patrick Belvill, Th.M., Th.D. President, Tyndale Theological Seminary and Biblical Institute, and Pastor of Tyndale Bible Church (Hurst, TX).

Ron J. Bigalke, M.A., M.T.S., M.Div., Ph.D. University of Pretoria, New Testament, Missions and Ethics Project, Research Associate (South Africa).

Christopher Cone, Th.D., Ph.D., Ph.D. President and Research Professor of Bible and Theology, Calvary University (Kansas City, MO).

James I. Fazio, M.Div., Th.M., D.Min. Dean of Bible and Theology, and Professor of Biblical Studies, Southern Calfornia Seminary (El Cajon, CA).

Grant Hawley. Director, Bold Grace Ministries, and Pastor of Bold Grace Fellowship (Dallas/Fort Worth, TX).

Thomas Ice, Th.M., Ph.D. Executive Director, The Pre-Trib Research Center.

Glenn R. Krieder, Th.M., Ph.D. Professor of Theological Studies, Dallas Theological Seminary (Dallas, TX).

Cory M. Marsh, M.A.B.S., M.Div., Th.M. Professor of Biblical Studies, Southern California Seminary (El Cajon, CA).

Brian Moulton, Th.M., Ph.D. Department Chair and Professor of Biblical Studies, San Diego Christian College (Santee, CA), and Professor of Biblical Studies, Southern California Seminary (El Cajon, CA).

Jeremiah Mutie, Th.M., Ph.D. Professor of Theology and Church History, Southern California Seminary (El Cajon, CA).

Luther Smith, M.A.R.S., M.A.M.F.T., Psy.D. Assistant Professor of Biblical Counseling, Calvary University (Kansas City, MO).

Paul J. Scharf, M.A., M.Div. Editor-in-chief, Dispensational Publishing House.

Andy Woods, Th.M., J.D., Ph.D. President, Chafer Theological Seminary (Albuquerque, NM), and Senior Pastor of Sugar Land Bible Church (Sugar Land, TX).

Kevin D. Zuber, M.Div., Th.M., Ph.D. Professor of Theology, Moody Bible Institue (Chicago, IL).

DEDICATION

Forged from Reformation is dedicated to our friends, Stanley Toussaint and Robert Thomas—two gracious reformers who lived well, served well, and finished well. They inspire us to carry on the legacy of truth and love, in which they so faithfully persevered.

ACKNOWLEDGEMENTS

A book such as this bears the impress of many skilled hands working together in unison. We are grateful for the talented team that we have had the privilege of working with in the formation of this project—from conception to completion.

Also, for each of the contributing authors, who have given of their time and talents to craft the chapters which serve as the content of this book, we are most appreciative.

The editorial team at SCS Press—who also managed to maintain their day-jobs as seminary librarian, academic administrator, etc.—worked tirelessly to turn a disparate collection of essays into a singular work that speaks with a clarion voice. The efforts of Jennifer Ewing and Cory Marsh nearly deserve them a place on the cover of this book (they are credited as copyeditors on the copyright page).

For the unsung efforts of Angelica Fazio—James' mother—who has served as an indefatigable editor of every written product of his hands, from the first essay in Bible College, to the final chapter of this book, James is exceedingly grateful.

For the patience of Cathy Cone—Christopher's co-heir without which his ministry would not be. To Christiana and Cara, for their patience and understanding as they gave of their time so that this project could come to fruition.

Other colleagues at Southern California Seminary who must not go overlooked include Leroy Hill, who helped to ensure the website and online presence of the book were maintained, as well as Margy Hill, who helped to coordinate the pre-sales and the book pre-release event. To the many at Southern California Seminary and Calvary University who supported this work through their own efforts and prayers.

Additionally, a tremendous debt of gratitude is owed to Dr. Gary F. Coombs, who has served as President of Southern California Seminary for twenty years. Without his steady commitment to God's Word, SCS may have gone the way of so many other theological seminaries across the nation.

Finally, a word of acknowledgement should be extended to Dr. David Jeremiah, whose influence and impact as Chancellor of Southern California Seminary must not go unnoticed. Without the leadership and support that he provides not only to SCS but to each of the ministries with which we are associated, this book would not have been possible.

Christopher Cone and James I. Fazio
General Editors

INTRODUCTION

1

FORGED FROM REFORMATION:
How Dispensational Thought Advances
The Reformed Legacy

Christopher Cone and James I. Fazio
Calvary University and Southern California Seminary

1.0 Introduction

For over 500 years Christians had celebrated All Saints' Day on November 1. It had been established by Pope Gregory IV on AD 837 as a day of remembrance for the past saints who had dedicated their lives in service to the Lord, and for those who died as martyrs. Some sources claim its roots stretch back even 500 years earlier, but no specific date or month is recorded. The celebration of All Saints' Day (or All Hallows' Day) would take many different forms; special church services would be held, along with feasts and various activities centered on remembering the lives of God's faithful men and women whose time on earth had passed. But this All Saint's Day would not come and go unnoticed, as so many had before it, because this year a German monk made it his aim to challenge long-held Christian conventions.

For Martin Luther, the posting of the *95 Theses* on the door of Wittenberg Cathedral was not part of some elaborate exit strategy from the Catholic Church. Just a month or two earlier, Luther had nailed what may be considered a far more theologically controversial work to the very same door, without stirring up much controversy at all.[1] So on All Hallows Eve, October 31, 1517, Luther tread a familiar path, up to the doors of Wittenberg Castle Church and nailed yet another long enumerated list of items for discussion. Only this time, he would garner no small attention of the Pope himself, because these theses touched a more tender spot. The *97 Theses* addressed a range of issues concerning the Church's doctrine, but the *95 Theses* dealt with the Church's coffers.

The *95 Theses* specifically addressed an abuse that many learned men within the Church were more than a little uncomfortable with, whether or not they all voiced their concern. They challenged the notion that heavenly pardons could be purchased for earthly sins that would appease God's wrath unleashed upon believers' upon death. The whole idea of it seems preposterous, but in Luther's day, it was a great social evil, and something had to be done about it; so God raised up the German Monk for such a time as this.

1.1 Why History Matters

You might be asking yourself at this point, why should I be concerned about any of this? Five hundred years later, we find ourselves living in quite a different world. The grievances of Luther's day are not compatible with our concerns today—though the same may not be said of the solutions he offered (but let's not get ahead of ourselves). In the twenty-first century everyone is buzzing along at break-neck speeds through an ever-changing world filled with technology brought upon by a rigorous study of the sciences. After all, history is about yesterday's news, and people today are more concerned about the future. In fact, most people's greatest concern seems to be for the present. As anyone who has ever sped down the highway knows, in a rapidly changing environment, the rate of travel almost demands that you keep your eyes peeled on the road ahead of you; there's no time to stop and see what's left in the rear-view mirror. We've all been told: time waits for no

---

[1] Luther's *97 Theses* offered a critical evaluation of the contemporary practice of scholastic theology with its heavy emphasis on human reason and free will. For a detailed treatment of Luther's *97 Theses* see: *Martin Luther's Theological Writings*, ed. Timothy F. Lull (Minneapolis, MN: Fortress Press, 2005).

man, and it only moves in one direction. Or does it?

What about the old adage "those who don't know history are doomed to repeat it?"[2] The church of the twenty-first century has an unprecedented vantage-point. It's been 500 years since the Protestant Reformation and nearly 2,000 years since the formation of the church. Given that amount of time, one would expect to find the church of the twenty-first century in the best of positions, with vibrant, spirit-filled assemblies stretched across the globe, as an ever-present witness that Christ has conquered sin and death and provided the solution to man's despair. Scarcely would one expect to find a pocket on earth that has not been radically transformed by the saving power of the Lord Jesus Christ and the Word of His Testimony! But things haven't developed quite like that.

A famous story has been retold (though it is doubtful that it ever truly occurred) that a monastic saint was brought before the Pope, who seeking to boast in the splendor of Rome, stretched out his arm toward the treasures amassed by the Church over centuries of dominion and conquest, and smugly exclaimed: "You see, the church can no longer say, 'Silver and gold have I none.'" The monk immediately recognized the phrase as Peter's response given to the lame man who had asked for alms outside the temple gates. Without delay, the monk retorted: "This is so. But neither can she say, 'Take up your bed and walk.'"

The monk's point is entirely valid. Despite the vast influence of the church that stretches across the globe, the same area where that story was to have taken place is now governed by secular-atheistic ideologies. The region where the seat of Christian dominance once was most pronounced is now rightly regarded as a post-Christian region. If that isn't enough, Islam is now pressing in on all sides as the fastest growing religion.[3]

---

[2] This oft-repeated saying is attributed to the 20th century Spanish philosopher, George Santayana (1863–1952).

[3] A Pew Research Center study revealed that this growth is not only seen in Muslim majority nations, but "10% of all Europeans are projected to be members of the Muslim faith by 2050...The study estimates that from 2010 to 2050 Muslims will have increased across the world by 73%, followed by Christians who are projected to grow by 35% during the same time period, and Hindus at 34%." Tricia Escobedo, "The Fastest Growing Religion? Islam," CNN.com, March 17, 2017, accessed on August 15, 2017, http://www.cnn.com/2017/03/16/world/islam-fastest-growing-religion-trnd.

What does this mean for the church today? Without feigning to speak to all that this suggests, it is safe to say that the Christian church is presently at a juncture that warrants—moreover, it demands—critical self-examination. Christians of the twenty-first century should be conducting the kind of serious self-inquiry not unlike that which the Protestant reformers conducted 500 years ago. The church of the twenty-first century is in need of another reformation.

1.2 The Legacy of the Protestant Reformation

It has been five-hundred years since Martin Luther nailed his *95 Theses* to the door at Wittenberg, fanning the flames of the Protestant Reformation. These many years later, we are no less indebted to Luther and the many who accompanied him in times of reform—who set out to return Christian thought and practice to a more biblical orthodoxy. Exemplified in the five *solas*, the Reformation represented and was spurred on by a return to biblical scholarship in the original languages, and by a more consistent application of the literal grammatical-historical hermeneutic.

Two hundred and fifty years prior to Luther's protest, Thomas Aquinas had set the tone in his *Summa Theologica* for Roman Catholic doctrine. His work was both a blessing and a curse. It was a blessing in that it provided a model for how systematic theology could be structured and communicated, and it addressed many questions that had not been previously addressed in such a systematic way. But in the absence of transparent exegesis, Aquinas had rooted his theology more in philosophical thought than in exegetical considerations. Aquinas' system of Roman Catholic theology would later be followed (at least conceptually) in the creation of the *Catechism of the Catholic Church*,[4] and thus the legacy of Catholic theology was cemented apart from exegetical emphasis. The *Catechism* itself prescribed that the Bible should be interpreted not through exegetical rigors, with consideration for the biblical text in its original languages, but that it should be read "within the living tradition of the whole Church,"[5] because "Scripture

---

[4] The *Catechism* was completed and approved under Pope John Paul II in 1992, and formally recorded the corpus of doctrine of the Roman Catholic Church.

[5] *The Catechism of the Catholic Church*, 2nd ed. (New York: Doubleday, 2003),

is written principally in the Church's heart rather than in documents and records."[6]

Erasmus, Luther, Calvin and other reformers recognized that the Scriptures *were*, in fact, documents and records, and that as such they demanded rigorous study and adherence. These leaders helped to reinfuse the Christian church with a focus on biblical authority and biblical exegesis. That renewed exegetical emphasis drew into sharp contrast accepted theological teachings and the teachings of the Bible. Reform was not necessary simply because the theology and practices were unbearable; reform was necessary because the Scripture demanded it. In particular, the reformers heeded the call in the areas where the problems were most evident—especially related to doctrines of salvation. But this soteriological focus left some important areas unrefined and in need of attention.

The formalizing of dispensational thought brought reform to eschatology and ecclesiology as well,[7] but there was still work to be done. Lewis Sperry Chafer's *Systematic* Theology, Charles Ryrie's *Dispensationalism Today*, and *Basic Theology*, along with Arnold Fruchtenbaum's *Israelology* help to remind us that the work of reform is not yet complete. There is far more to Reformation than recalibrating some doctrines; the whole thing must be examined.

The Protestant Reformation called us back to the Word of God, and shows us what that looks like, especially though not exclusively, in matters pertaining to soteriology. Dispensational thinkers have sought to exegete and apply God's Word broadly throughout every area of theology and practice. Forged from the fires of the Reformation's heightened attention to the Bible and its details, a more refined and systematic dispensational understanding has developed and continues to be shaped. Adhering to the exclusive authority of Scripture, understood through biblically-prescribed literal grammatical-historical hermeneutics, and exegeted with humility in seeking to consistently apply those hermeneutic principles, dispensational thought

---

Article 113.

[6] Ibid.

[7] Most well-known through the writings of John Nelson Darby, C.I. Scofield, J. Dwight Pentecost, and John Walvoord, though many others also contributed to these efforts.

continues to refine into a more comprehensively biblical understanding and application. This book, written by a diverse and accomplished group of dispensational scholars and practitioners, articulates in each and every chapter how, five-hundred years later, dispensational thought upholds and advances the legacy of the Reformation unlike any other theological system in Christian tradition.

1.3 Overview of this Book

This book consists of two main parts. The first part is intended to form a historical and contextual backdrop by taking a look at key issues related to the Protestant Reformation, as well as the continued development of Reformation ideals which advanced through the influence of other key historical figures. The second part of the book is laid out according to the five *solas* which defined the Reformed legacy: *sola Scriptura* (Scripture alone); *sola gratia* (by grace alone); *sola fide* (through faith alone); *solus Christus* (in Christ alone); and *soli Deo gloria* (to the glory of God alone). Each of the five *solas* have one or more chapters which demonstrate how dispensational thought advances the Reformation legacy, in some cases, even more so than current expressions of the Reformed tradition that bears the name.

1.3.1 Part One: Historical Development

In the chapter following this one, Dr. Thomas Ice, of the Pre-Trib Research Center, provides an historical introduction to the book's main two themes: dispensationalism and the Reformation. These are two themes that are not often seen together in print, and yet, the two ideas are intrinsically linked. Dr. Ice provides background to the Protestant Reformation and offers a working definition for dispensationalism as the term is used throughout this book. He surveys the development of hermeneutics down through church history and explains how dispensationalism arose in the wake of Reformed thought and how modern normative dispensationalism developed in recent centuries.

In the third chapter, Tyndale Theological Seminary President, Dr. Patrick Belvill, provides a unique evaluation of Martin Luther's *95 Theses*. In this chapter, Dr. Belvill walks through the *95 Theses*, which he groups together into categories to help the reader better understand their content and intent. Moreover, he offers a running commentary that helps frame the theses in a contemporary light, and astutely points out how their underlying doctrinal orientation is entirely compatible with dispensational thought; this is done even to the point of foreshadowing the *sine qua non* (quintessential elements) of dispensationalism as identified by the late Dr. Charles Ryrie.[8]

In the fourth chapter, Southern California Seminary's Academic Dean of Bible and Theology, Dr. James I. Fazio, offers a biographical sketch of the little known Irish clergyman from the nineteenth century, John Nelson Darby (1800–1882), who is chiefly remembered for his influence on dispensational thought. Readers may be familiar with Darby (or J.N.D. as reflected in his printed material) in name only, but few have developed a deeper acquaintance with this controversial and polemic figure who is somewhat paradoxically both well known and unknown. In his chapter Dr. Fazio demonstrates how John Nelson Darby's path bears certain parallels with Martin Luther; for example Luther who dissented broke with the Established Roman Catholic Church to begin a new Protestant tradition which later bore his name, just as the Irish clergyman broke with the Established Anglican Church to begin a new dissenting tradition which later bore his name.

The fifth chapter carries the story forward by taking a closer look at the reformation legacy of ecclesiastical independence as it was advanced by Martin Luther in the sixteenth century and again by John Nelson Darby a

---

[8] The term *sine qua non* refers to those indispensable elements without which a thing cannot be. Someone with only the faintest familiarity with dispensationalism may think that dividing history into segments, as if on a chart, is the essence of dispensational theology. Others may think that a futurist view of eschatology, replete with a secret rapture of the saints, the appearance of the antichrist, and the establishment of Christ's millennial kingdom upon the earth, is the sum-total of dispensational thought. However, neither of these are included in the *sine qua non*. Quite simply, the critical elements to dispensational thought are: (1) the distinction between Israel and the church; (2) the consistent application of a literal grammatical-historical interpretive method; and (3) the recognition of a doxological purpose in history—that is to say that all of human history presses toward an end whereby God is ultimately glorified. See Charles C. Ryrie, *Dispensationalism*, rev. and exp. ed. (Grand Rapids, MI: Moody, 1995), 38–41.

few centuries later. In this chapter, Southern California Seminary Professor of Biblical Studies, Cory M. Marsh, convincingly displays how Luther's views concerning the priesthood of every believer and his value of independent self-governing local churches were further realized through the written works and ministry of John Nelson Darby. Professor Marsh accomplishes this by considering three essential treatises of Luther: "An Open Letter [or Address] to the Christian Nobility of the German Nation," "The Babylonian Captivity of the Church," and "The Freedom of a Christian." He then proceeds to compare these against three of Darby's classic treatises: "The Nature and Unity of the Church," "The Notion of a Clergyman," and "On the Formation of Churches," and traces their influence to the latter Bible school movement in America.

The sixth chapter, by Moody Bible Institute Professor of Theology, Dr. Kevin Zuber, builds upon the theme of local church autonomy, but follows a survey approach to church history, tracing Christian thought from the earliest centuries of the church through to the present. Dr. Zuber notes the influence of such early figures as Ignatius of Antioch (c. AD 35–c. 107), Cyprian (AD 200–258), and Constantine (AD 280–337), on developing ecclesiastical thought, before stepping through the middle ages to John Calvin (1509–1564) and the Congregationalism that later emerged in New England. The chapter then culminates into present day Christian perspectives on local church autonomy—something uniquely advanced through dispensational influence.

In the seventh chapter, Southern California Seminary Professor Cory M. Marsh is joined by his colleague Dr. Brian Moulton, to tackle a highly sensitive subject concerning the tragic byproduct of anti-Semitism as it emerged in the thought of Martin Luther as a consequence of employing an inconsistent hermeneutic that includes allegory as a viable interpretive method. In this chapter, Moulton and Marsh trace the rise of anti-Semitism from the early centuries of the Church Fathers to show how Luther's outlook was influenced by a similar allegorical methodology that so many well-meaning biblical interpreters have fallen prey to over the centuries. However, before closing the chapter they don't neglect to point out how dispensational thought corrects Luther's flawed perspective of Israel by following a consistent literal grammatical-historical hermeneutic.

1.3.2 Part Two: The Five Solas of the Reformation

Chapters eight through seventeen comprise the second part of this book, and correspond directly to the five *solas* of the Reformation. A disproportionate number of chapters are dedicated to the Reformation doctrine of *sola Scriptura*, as this is the pivotal *sola* upon which all of the others hinge. Therefore, chapters eight through twelve all fall under the general heading of *sola Scriptura*.

In the eighth chapter, President of Chafer Theological Seminary, Dr. Andy Woods, takes a look at the hermeneutical revolution that took place at the time of the Reformation, and takes note of some areas that were left unfinished. Beginning with the early church, Dr. Woods traces the Alexandrian and Antiochene schools of interpretation and notes the development of the allegorical method which plunged the church into a thousand-year crisis during the period commonly referred to as the Dark Ages (c. 5th–15th centuries). He notes how the Reformation saw a resurrection of the interpretive method that was largely lost since the time of the apostolic fathers. However, like Lazarus rising out of the tomb, the reformers emerged still wearing the grave trappings in which they had been clothed. He concludes that is wasn't until the influence of dispensational thought which arose in the centuries that followed, that the hermeneutical revolution was made complete.

In chapter nine, University of Pretoria, New Testament, Missions and Ethics Project, Research Associate, Dr. Ron J. Bigalke, considers how the Protestant method of biblical interpretation reacquainted the church with the tradition of futurist premillennial eschatology which had gone overlooked for over a millennium. With the return of a literal grammatical-historical method of interpretation came a new understanding of the Scriptures that resulted in a return to the futuristic interpretation of unfulfilled prophecy and a systemization of biblical eschatology. This resulted in a return to the common view which defined the earliest centuries of the church referred to as chiliasm, millenarianism, or as it is more commonly known today, premillennialism.

In chapter ten, Dean of the Seminary at Calvary University, Dr. Thomas Baurain, elucidates how a literal—or normal—reading of the biblical text defined Protestant biblical interpretation and served as the bedrock principle for the Reformed doctrine of *sola Scriptura*. In this chapter, Dr. Baurain argues that Protestant biblical interpretation, when consistently applied, yields a dispensational theology; whereas an inconsistent application of the same normal hermeneutical method has resulted in Covenant theology. He asserts that Evangelicals today that seek to maintain the Protestant tradition would be prudent to minimize the subjectivity that comes from a haphazard application of a normal hermeneutic to Scripture, as that carries the unfortunate consequence of undermining any appeal to "Scripture alone."

In the eleventh chapter, Dean of Southern California Seminary, Dr. James I. Fazio, demonstrates that the covenantalist's inconsistent application of a literal grammatical-historical hermeneutic is not entirely without precident, as it was, in fact, modelled by the German reformer himself, Martin Luther. Dr. Fazio evaluates Luther's interpretive method by distinguishing seven principles, as articulated in Luther's own writings. Finally, he offers a critique of the internal consistency of these principles and concludes that the Christocentric-method of interpretation which Luther employed is inconsistent with all of the other principles which he affirmed in so many of his writings. On account of this defective methodology, Luther had little recourse but to create a cannon within a cannon, whereby he elevated certain Scriptures and denigrated others.

The twelfth chapter is the final entry under the heading *sola Scriptura*. In it, Southern California Seminary Professor of Theology and Church History, Dr. Jeremiah Mutie, takes a look at the two extreme sides of the hermeneutical pendulum: from Christocentric-allegory to woodenly-literal interpretation. Dr. Mutie begins by looking at contemporary Reformed and Lutheran traditions, which appeal to *sola Scriptura* but depart from a consistent literal grammatical-historical approach. Next, he turns to the Millerites to reveal the dangers of an overly literalistic, or wooden-literal tradition of hermeneutics, which overrides the normal principles governing written communication, such as literary genre, figures of speech, etc. He concludes that the consistent application of the literal grammatical-historical method, which is essential to the dispensational tradition, is the best safeguard against either extreme.

Chapter thirteen addresses the second *sola* of the Reformation: *sola*

By bru Alvn

gratia. Here, Grant Hawley of Bold Grace Publishing tackles the topic of how dispensationalism advances the Reformation doctrine of *sola gratia*. He begins the chapter by establishing a biblical understanding of grace from the Old and New Testaments before proceeding to the central role it played in the context of the Protestant Reformation and shortly thereafter. Next, he builds a case for how dispensational thought has advanced the doctrine of grace by making a healthy distinction between faith and works in the believer's sanctification. He resolves that it is the dispensationalist's understanding of the doctrine of rewards, resulting from the *bema* judgment that provides the necessary framework for dissolving the tension between God's grace in the justification and the outworking of sanctification.

In chapter fourteen Dallas Theological Seminary Professor of Historical Theology, Dr. Glenn Kreider, addresses the topic of *sola fide* and refutes a common charge leveled against dispensationalism by uninformed nondispensationalists: namely, that dispensationalism teaches multiple ways of salvation. Dr. Kreider tackles the issue head-on and flatly concludes that salvation has always been received by man exclusively as a result of God's grace through faith—in every dispensation. Dr. Kreider shows that this was no less true of Israel under the Old Covenant than it is for believers in the present dispensation.

Christ Alon

Chapter fifteen looks at the fourth *sola* of the Reformation: *solus Christus.* In it, Editor-in-Chief of Dispensational Publishing House, Paul Scharf, considers how the reformers came to view the supremacy of Christ over the church from reading the New Testament. In a style reminiscent of the author of the book of Hebrews, Scharf demonstrates the superiority of Christ above Adam, to the exclusion of Mary, the Saints, the Pope, and the entire system of priests and sacraments. Next, he goes on to reveal how dispensational thought has shone an even greater spotlight on Christ, with respect to His present ministry toward believers. He highlights how Christians have a dispensational relationship to Christ as the Head of the Body which was unprecedented in biblical history prior to Pentecost.

The penultimate two chapters address the fifth and final *sola* of the Reformation: *soli Deo gloria.* In the sixteenth chapter, President of Calvary University, Dr. Christopher Cone, considers the inseparable parallel be-

tween the fifth *sola* of the Reformation and the *sine qua non* of dispensationalism—the doxological purpose of human history. By comparing this theological distinctive against other nondispensational systems of theology, he
builds a compelling case for how dispensational thought is perhaps even
more consistent with the Reformed legacy than contemporary Reformed
theology.

In chapter seventeen, Calvary University Professor, Dr. Luther Smith,
concludes the section on *soli Deo gloria* by looking at how all of human history since the creation week declares the glory of God. Dr. Smith begins by
noting the Reformation focus on God's glory as expressed by Martin Luther, John Calvin, and in the Long and Shorter Catechism. He goes on to
demonstrate the same doxological focus as it is expressed by John Nelson
Darby, Cyrus Ingerson Scofield, Charles Caldwell Ryrie, and dispensationalism in general. In the second part of this chapter, Dr. Smith traces the
biblical narrative through seven dispensations to demonstrate that God's
glory has always been the chief end not only of man, but of all creation.

Finally, in chapter eighteen, Dr. Christopher Cone offers a conclud-
ing charge: *semper reformanda* (always be reforming)! Dr. Cone reminds us
that not only throughout church history, but in all of human history, mankind has displayed the natural—sin impacted—tendency to drift away from
God's intended purpose. Dr. Cone offers young King Josiah as a model
from the days of Israel's past, who recovered the Word of God and exhorted
the people to follow it—resulting in nationwide revival for all of Judah. It is
a familiar biblical pattern, and one worthy of being brought to our remembrance in the present day—some 500 years after the Protestant Reformation.

1.4 Conclusion

Although the occasion of this book is the influence of 500 years of
Reformation and its impact on the church today—and more specifically, an
apologetic for how dispensational thought has carried the reformer's legacy
forward—it is so much more than that. It is an appeal to you, the reader, to
stand in the same tradition of the reformers who came before us, and to
carry that same unflinching commitment to God's Word forward, in our
present generation. While this a book about history, it is not a book for the
sake of history. To the contrary, it is a book for the sake of the future. What

manner of future will that be? What legacy will you leave for those who may be looking back 500 years from now—should the Lord tarry? Even so, come Lord Jesus.

Bibliography

Catholic Church. *The Catechism of the Catholic Church*. 2nd ed. New York: Doubleday, 2003.

Escobedo, Tricia. "The Fastest Growing Religion? Islam." CNN.com, March 17, 2017. Accessed on August 15, 2017. http://www.cnn .com/2017/03/16/world/islam-fastest-growing-religion-trnd.

Luther, Martin. *Martin Luther's Theological Writings*. Edited by Timothy F. Lull. Minneapolis, MN Fortress Press, 2005.

Ryrie, Charles C. *Dispensationalism*. Rev. and exp. ed. Grand Rapids, MI: Moody, 1995.

PART 1
HISTORICAL DEVELOPMENT

2

DISPENSATIONALISM AND THE REFORMATION

Thomas Ice
Pre-Trib Research Center

2.0 Introduction

The reforms of the Protestant Reformation led the way to the eventual development of dispensationalism. This is bolstered by the fact that within the Eastern Orthodox Church there has never been a reformation nor has any form of dispensationalism arisen within its confines, at least as far as this author knows. This chapter will first look at the changes brought by the Reformation and then compare them with the characteristics of dispensationalism in order to suggest a cause-and-effect relationship leading to the rise of dispensational theology within certain Protestant traditions.

2.1 Characteristics of the Reformation

The Reformation arose as an effort to reform the Roman Catholic Church. There had been attempts to reform the Catholic Church for several hundred years before the Reformation occurred. For example, the Cluny reform that began in A.D. 910 attempted to make changes within the Catholic Church and found some success. [1] Moreover, the Gregorian Reform Movement during the eleventh and twelfth centuries had a similar

---

[1] John McManners, *The Oxford Illustrated History of Christianity* (New York: Oxford University Press, 1990), 120, 199.

impact. [2] It appears that John Wyclif (1329–84) in the fourteenth century and Jan (John) Hus (1369–1415) of the fifteenth century were both attempting to reform the Catholic Church as well. What began as a reform movement within the Roman Church lead to the excommunication of leaders in the sixteenth century resulting in the establishment of a whole new reformed church. What began as an adjective ended up becoming a new noun descriptive of the major new movement formed in the Reformation.

The five essentials of the Reformation are often expressed in Latin terms as the five *solas*. (1) *Sola Scriptura*, "Scripture alone," as set against the authority of the Catholic Church and its magisterium. (2) *Sola gratia*, "Grace alone," salvation is totally based upon the unmerited favor or grace of God alone. (3) *Sola fide*, "Faith alone," is the only means by which a person may receive God's gracious gift of salvation. Human works are totally excluded. (4) *Solus Christus*, "Christ alone," as set against the mediatorial claim of the Church of Rome that salvation can only come through their church and saints. (5) *Soli Deo gloria*, "to the glory of God alone," is the only proper motive that one can live for. [3] Another Latin phrase reformers spoke of in relation to the Roman Church is *Ecclesia semper reformanda est*, "the church must always be reformed." The reformers argued that the Catholic Church resisted reform within leading to the split of the church and therefore true churches should be every reforming and open to reforms. Is it possible that today some within the Reformed Church have adopted the Catholic position of "no reform" as they have locked down into the creeds of the sixteenth and seventeenth centuries?

2.2 What is Dispensationalism?

Dispensationalism is a cluster of items joined together to form a system of thought. [4] Just as terms like Calvinism, Arminianism, Anglicanism,

---

[2] McManners, *Oxford Illustrated History of Christianity*, 201–3.

[3] See E. Fahlbusch et al., eds., *The Encyclopedia of Christianity* (Grand Rapids, MI: William B. Eerdmans, 2005), 4:531–32.

[4] This author does not believe that the many formulations of progressive dispensationalism are a valid expression of dispensationalism since it co-mingles at some points Israel and the church. Charles Ryrie believed that progressive dispensationalism

Catholicism, or Lutheranism are historical labels that represent, not a single idea, but a group of items joined together to form a multifaceted scheme, so is dispensationalism. Dispensationalism is a term that arose in church history to label certain Christians who believe a group of certain things that are taught in the Bible. A vital distinction to note is that dispensationalism is a system of theology and not a hermeneutic as some today label it. The reason it is not a hermeneutic is because dispensationalists follow the grammatical-historical hermeneutic (the protestant hermeneutic) most consistently. Following the grammatical-historical hermeneutic results in an exegesis that then yields the theology of dispensationalism.

Dispensationalists are those who believe the following things:

1 – The Bible is God's inspired, inerrant (i.e., without any errors) revelation to man. Scripture provides the framework through which to interpret history (past and future). God's written Word tells us of His plan for His creation, and this will surely come to past.

2 – Since the Bible is God's literal Word of His plan for history, it should be interpreted literally and historically (past and future). The grammatical-historical hermeneutic or the protestant hermeneutic is consistently applied to all of Scripture, from Genesis to Revelation.

3 – Since the Bible reveals God's plan for history, then it follows that there is an ebb and flow to His plan. Therefore, God's plan includes different dispensations, ages, or epochs of history through which His creatures (man and angels) are tested. This view has sometimes been called "periodization." Therefore, God is instructing His creatures through the progress of history, as His creation progresses from a garden to a city.

4 – Since all humanity fell into sin, each person must individually receive God's provision of salvation through the death of Christ by

---

went beyond the boundaries of dispensationalism. See Charles C. Ryrie, *Dispensationalism*, rev. and exp. ed. (1995; repr., Chicago, IL: Moody Press, 2007), 209–10, 248. The first edition of Ryrie's work was published in 1965 under the title: *Dispensationalism Today*.

believing the gospel. Thus, Jesus Christ is the only way to a relationship with God and the forgiveness of one's sin.

5   - Because of mankind's fall into sin, Scripture teaches that all humanity is naturally rebellious to God and the things of God. This is why only genuine believers in Christ are open to the teachings of the Bible. Thus, salvation through Christ is a prerequisite to properly understanding God's Word.

6   - God's plan for history includes a purpose for the descendants of Abraham, Isaac, and Jacob—that is Israel. This plan for Israel includes promises that they will possess the physical land of Israel, will have a seed, and will be a worldwide blessing to the nations. Many of the promises to national Israel are still future; therefore, God is not finished with the nation of Israel.

7   - God's plan from all eternity also includes a purpose for His church; however, this is a temporary phase that will end with rapture. After the rapture, God will complete His plan for Israel and the Gentiles.

8   - Jesus Christ is the central hero in history, as He glorifies the Father in many ways—including through His kingly and salvific works.

9   - The New Testament does not reinterpret the Old Testament; instead the New is a fluid continuation of the Old as it begins to be fulfilled. The New reveals the hidden aspects of God's single plan for history now called the church.

10 - The church does not replace Israel; instead both entities have always been part of God's single decree or plan for history. The two people of God complement each other in the outworking of the God's plan. God is glorified through both Israel and the church.

In a nutshell, Christians who believe like this are known throughout Christendom as dispensationalists. I am a dispensationalist! We believe that it is the same as saying I believe what the Bible literally teaches. Millions of Christians throughout the world are dispensationalists. In fact, the word "dispensation" occurs four times in the King James Version of the Bible (1 Cor 9:17; Eph 1:10, 3:2; Col 1:25).[5]

2.3 A Definition of Dispensationalism

Among the chief spokesmen for dispensationalism is the late Dallas Theological Seminary professor, Dr. Charles Ryrie. Many know Ryrie through his books and articles, but he is best known for his popular *Ryrie Study Bible*. Ryrie's book, *Dispensationalism* is the reference point to gain an understanding of dispensationalism.

"The central idea in the word *dispensation* is that of managing or administering the affairs of a household,"[6] notes Ryrie. According to Ryrie, "*a dispensation is a distinguishable economy in the outworking of God's purpose.*" In addition to a *definition* of a dispensation, he notes if "one were *describing* a dispensation, he would include other things, such as the ideas of distinctive revelation, testing, failure, and judgment."[7] He summarizes dispensationalism as follows:

> Dispensationalism views the world as a household run by God. In His household world God is dispensing or administering its affairs according to His own will and in various stages of revelation in the passage of time. These various stages mark off the distinguishably different economies in the outworking of His total purpose, and these different economies constitute the dispensations. The understanding of God's differing economies is essential to a proper interpretation of His revelation within those various economies.[8]

Who is a dispensationalist? Essentials are needed in order to evaluate a theology and determine whether one is or is not a dispensationalist. What are the essentials that characterize a dispensationalist? Ryrie has stated what

---

[5] Calling attention to the KJV here is merely to point out that the King James accurately translates the Greek word οἰκονομία (*oikonomia*) as "dispensation" while others English translations do not. This is not to be taken as an endorsement for what is known as King James Onlyism.

[6] Ryrie, *Dispensationalism*, 30.

[7] Ibid., 33.

[8] Ibid., 34–35.

he calls the three *sine qua non* or essentials of dispensationalism.

The essence of dispensationalism, then, is the distinction between Israel and the church. This grows out of the dispensationalist's consistent employment of normal or plain or historical-grammatical interpretation, and it reflects an understanding of the basic purpose of God
in all His dealings with mankind as that of glorifying Himself through
salvation and other purposes as well.[9]

Simply put, dispensationalism is a theology derived from the consistent literal interpretation of the entire Bible. There is no special hermeneutic, only the consistent application of the Protestant hermeneutic
known as the grammatical-historical interpretative approach and the corre-
lation into theological conclusions we label as dispensationalism. This characteristic of dispensationalism is recognized by some of those opposed to
our consistently literal hermeneutic as noted by Oswald Allis:

> Literal interpretation has always been a marked feature of Premillen-
> nialism; in Dispensationalism it has been carried to an extreme. We
> have seen that this literalism found its most thoroughgoing expression
> in the claim that Israel must mean Israel, that it cannot mean the
> Church, that the Old Testament prophecies regarding Israel concern
> the earthly Israel, and that the Church was a mystery, unknown to the
> prophets and first made known to the apostle Paul. Now if the princi-
> ple of interpretation is adopted that Israel always means Israel, that it
> does not mean the Church, then it follows of necessity that practically
> all of our information regarding the millennium will concern a Jewish
> or Israelitish age.[10]

2.4 Hermeneutics in the Early Church

During the first two hundred years of the early church two competing
schools of interpretation arose. One was the Syrian School of Antioch that
championed literal and historical interpretation and the other was in North

---

[9] Ryrie, *Dispensationalism*, 48.

[10] Oswald T. Allis, *Prophecy and the Church* (Phillipsburg, NJ: Presbyterian and
Reformed Publishing, 1947), 244.

Africa at Alexandria, Egypt, which advocated an allegorical or spiritual hermeneutic. Bernard Ramm says, "The Syrian school fought Origen in particular as the inventor of the allegorical method, and maintained the primacy of the literal and historical interpretation."[11] Clement of Alexandria (150–215) and his disciple Origen (185–254) developed the allegorical approach to biblical interpretation in the early third century.

"The fundamental criticism of Origen, beginning during his own lifetime," notes Joseph Trigg, "was that he used allegorical interpretation to provide a specious justification for reinterpreting Christian doctrine in terms of Platonic philosophy."[12] Origen believed that "Proverbs 22:20 authorizes interpreters to seek a three-fold meaning in each passage of Scripture: fleshly, psychic and spiritual." Since Origen believed that "the spiritual meaning belongs to a higher order of ideas than the literal,"[13] he was attracted to the spiritual or allegorical meaning of the text. Ronald Diprose explains the implications of an allegorical interpretation as follows:

> He motivated this view by appealing to the principle of divine inspiration and by affirming that often statements made by the biblical writers are not literally true and that many events, presented as historical, are inherently impossible. Thus only simple believers will limit themselves to the literal meaning of the text.[14]

---

[11] Bernard Ramm, *Protestant Biblical Interpretation: A Textbook of Hermeneutics*, 3rd ed. (Grand Rapids, MI: Baker Book House, 1970), 49.

[12] Joseph W. Trigg, Introduction to *Allegory and Event: A Study of the Sources and Significance of Origen's Interpretation of Scripture* by R. P. C. Hanson (Louisville, KY: Westminster John Knox Press, 2002), vi.

[13] Ronald E. Diprose, *Israel in the Development of Christian Thought* (Rome: Instituto Biblico Evangelico Italiano, 2000), 87. Frederic Farrar explains further: "The Bible, he [Origen] argued, is meant for the salvation of man; but man, as Plato tells us, consists of three parts—body, soul, and spirit. Scripture therefore must have a threefold sense corresponding to this trichotomy. It has a literal, a moral, and a mystic meaning analogous to the body, to the soul, to the spirit . . . But of two of these three supposed senses Origen makes very little use. To the moral sense he refers but seldom; to the literal sense scarcely at all." Frederic W. Farrar, *History of Interpretation* (1886; repr., Grand Rapids, MI: Baker Book House, 1961), 196–97.

[14] Diprose, *Israel in the Development*, 87–88.

The bottom line of interpretation for the Syrian School at Antioch is their assertion that "the literal was plain-literal and figurative literal." By this, they meant that "a plain-literal sentence is a straightforward prose sentence with no figures of speech in it. 'The eye of the Lord is upon thee,' would be a figurative literal sentence."[15] Such an approach had a tremendous impact on one's view of Bible prophecy, as R. H. Charles notes: "the Alexandrians, who, under the influence of Hellenism and the traditional allegorical school of interpretation which came to a head in Philo, rejected the literal sense of the Apocalypse, and attached to it a spiritual significance only."[16]

Such an interpretative approach leads to a downgrade of the modern state of Israel as prophetically significant, which also has roots in Origen and the allegorical hermeneutic. [17] Diprose notes as follows:

> An attitude of contempt towards Israel had become the rule by Origen's time. The new element in his own view of Israel is his perception of them as "manifesting no elevation [of thought]". It follows that the interpreter must always posit a deeper or higher meaning for prophecies relating to Judea, Jerusalem, Israel, Judah and Jacob which, he affirms, are "not being understood by us in a 'carnal' sense."
>
> In Origen's understanding, the only positive function of physical Israel was that of being a type of spiritual Israel. The promises were not made to physical Israel because she was unworthy of them and incapable of understanding them. Thus Origen effectively disinherits physical Israel.[18]

The allegorical approach to Israel usually ends up treating Israel the same way Origen had done. Such a view often leads to disinheriting physical Israel and replaces her with what they regularly call "spiritual Israel," which is the church. "Origen likens Israel to a divorced wife in whom an unseemly thing had been found," notes Diprose. Origen says, "And a sign that she

---

[15] Ramm, *Protestant Biblical Interpretation*, 49.

[16] R. H. Charles, *Studies in the Apocalypse* (Edinburgh: T & T Clark, 1913), 11.

[17] For more on this aspect, see Brian Moulton and Cory M. Marsh's chapter, "How Dispensational Thought Corrects Luther's View of Israel" in the current volume.

[18] Diprose, *Israel in the Development*, 89; emphasis in original.

has received the bill of divorce is this, that Jerusalem was destroyed along with what they called the sanctuary."[19] Norman Geisler notes: "ideas do have consequences, and the typological-allegorical idea has had severe consequences in the history of the church. Denying a literal fulfillment of God's promises to Israel have led to anti-Semitism."[20] Geisler concludes that those "who replace literal Israel with a spiritual church, nullify the literal land and throne promises, thus opening the door to Liberalism and cultism."[21]

Although the Syrian school had great influence the first few centuries, the Alexandrian school eventually won out, as Jerome and Augustine were advocates of the allegorical approach in the area of Bible prophecy. Henry Preserved Smith concludes concerning Augustine that "with his endorsement allegory may fairly be said to have triumphed."[22] Their influence paved the way for the dominance of allegorical interpretation during much of the Middle Ages, especially when it came to Bible prophecy. Augustine developed a dual hermeneutic. On the one hand, he tended to interpret the Bible literally, but when it came to eschatology he interpreted that spiritually or allegorically.

2.5 Medieval Christendom

The Middle Ages were a time that was primarily dominated by an allegorical method of interpretation. Since Origen in Alexandria taught that the spiritual is the deeper or real meaning of a text, why deal with the inferior literal meaning of a passage when one can see so much more in the spiritual realm. One of the beliefs that became dominant, especially in late-Medieval times, was the belief that every sentence in the pages of Scripture has to be understood as referring to Christ, also known as the Christological hermeneutic. This erroneous interpretive dictum was based upon a misapplication of Luke 24:44, which says, "Now He said to them, 'These are My

---

[19] Diprose, *Israel in the Development*, 90.

[20] Norman L. Geisler, "Review of Hank Hanegraaff's *The Apocalypse Code*," Norman Geisler.com, accessed September 11, 2017, http://normangeisler.com/a-review-of-hanegraaff-apocalypse-code/.

[21] Ibid.

[22] Henry Preserved Smith, *Essays in Biblical Interpretation* (Boston: Marshall Jones Company, 1921), 58.

words which I spoke to you while I was still with you, that all things which are written about Me in the Law of Moses and the Prophets and the Psalms must be fulfilled.'" This passage does not say that every word or sentence in the Old Testament must refer to Jesus, the Messiah, but instead it says Jesus is the one being referenced in the Old Testament when it speaks of the Messiah. For example, a Christological interpretation would mean that a clearly historical passage like 1 Chronicles 26:18, which says, "At the Parbar on the west there were four at the highway and two at the Parbar," would have to be interpreted as referring to Christ. This sentence is not speaking about Christ, but through allegorical alchemy it was explained in some kind of Christological way. "During these nine centuries we find very little except the 'glimmerings and decays' of patristic exposition," notes Frederic Farrar. "Much of the learning which still continued to exist was devoted to something which was meant for exegesis, yet not one writer in hundreds showed any true conception of what exegesis really implies."[23]

When one studies the interpretive trends of the Middle Ages, it is realized what bearing this has for today. Beryl Smalley, a Medieval scholar who specializes in Medieval views of biblical interpretation suggests that "they subordinated scholarship meanwhile to mysticism and to propaganda."[24] "Again the crisis was reflected in biblical studies. The speculation of Joachim signified a new wave of mysticism."[25] "Revolution and uncertainty have discouraged biblical scholarship in the past and stimulated more subjective modes of interpretation," she contends. "Conditions today are giving rise to a certain sympathy with the allegorists. We have a spate of studies on medieval 'spirituality.'"[26] It seems in modern times the overall trends of

---

[23] Farrar, *History of Interpretation*, 245–46.

[24] Beryl Smalley, *The Study of the Bible in the Middle Ages* (1964; repr., Notre Dame, IN: University of Notre Dame Press, 1982), 358.

[25] Ibid., 359.

[26] Ibid., 360. Traditionally non-literal interpretation has been an old garment that has been labeled "spiritualizing." In this approach the words of the author are clothed with some deeper spiritual sense. With this method of interpretation, the words of the Old Testament prophets are often explained away. A more recent and "fashionable" term is *sensus plenior*. Use of this concept involves finding a "fuller meaning" that the author did not clearly intend. The "layered look" is also finding its way into the evangelical community as some are returning to the multiple meanings of the

both secular society, and too many evangelicals are moving away from literal interpretation into the shadowy darkness of non-literal hermeneutics.

Historians have noticed that culture cycles back-and-forth between rationalism and mysticism over the years.[27] Since the 1960s, American culture has definitely moved in the direction of and is now firmly dominated by a mystical worldview. Biblical Christianity is not based on reason or mysticism as its starting point for truth; instead, it is built upon revelation or God's Word. When mysticism dominates a culture's mindset then it predisposes one hermeneutically toward mysticism and non-literal interpretation. It is into just such an American evangelical climate that we see a resurgence of a non-literal approach to Bible prophecy.

Dr. John Walvoord was asked some years ago: "What do you predict will be the most significant theological issues over the next ten years?" His answer includes the following: "the hermeneutical problem of not interpreting the Bible literally, especially the prophetic areas. The church today is engulfed in the idea that one cannot interpret prophecy literally."[28]

Walt Kaiser suggested about thirty-five years ago that the church is "now going through a hermeneutical crisis, perhaps as significant in its importance and outcome as that of the Reformation."[29] He notes, "the meaning of the text lies in its subject matter, rather than in what an author meant by that text."[30] Kaiser explains further:

---

text once held by the Schoolmen of the Middle Ages. Bruce Waltke suggests a fourfold approach: historical, typical, anagogical, and moral. See Bruce K. Waltke, "The Schoolmen's Hermeneutics Reconsidered" (paper presented at the Northwest Regional meeting of the Evangelical Theological Society, April 1993).

[27] Robert C. Walton, *Chronological and Background Charts of Church History* (Grand Rapids, MI: Zondervan, 1986), chart 78.

[28] "An Interview: Dr. John F. Walvoord Looks at Dallas Seminary," *Dallas Connection* 1, no. 3 (Winter 1994), 4.

[29] Walter C. Kaiser Jr., "Evangelical Hermeneutics: Restatement, Advance or Retreat from the Reformation?" *Concordia Theological Quarterly* 46 (1982), 167. Kaiser believes that the present-day crisis finds its historical roots in the writings of liberal existentialists like Friedrich Schleirmacher (1768–1834), Wilhelm Dilthey (1833–1911), Martin Heidegger (1889–1976), Rudolf Bultmann (1884–1976), and Hans Georg Gadamer (b. 1900). Ibid.

[30] Ibid., 167.

The process of exegesis of a text is no longer linear but circular—one in which the interpreter affects his text as much as the text (in its subject matter) somehow affects the interpreter as well. Clearly, there is a confusion of ontology with epistemology, the subject with the object, the "thereness" of the propositions of the text with the total cultural and interpretive "baggage" of the interpreter.[31]

It appears to this author that when biblical Christianity breaks down in a given area it usually descends into and locks down into some form of mysticism; thus losing its bibliocentric focus. This was the situation in the late Middle Ages when the Reformation was sparked by the Holy Spirit and has produced the last 500 years of a more biblical culture within Protestantism and a much more biblically vibrant Christianity. That era appears to be coming to an end in the United States as the church clearly is sinking into an overall swamp of mysticism, shifting away from a bibliocentric focus. Of course, as with any general overall trend there are pockets of exception still pursuing a biblical focus.

2.6 The Reformation

It was not until the dawning of the Reformation that biblical interpretation began to return to the sanity of literal interpretation. The Reformation could not have occurred if the reformers did not have the confidence that they knew what God's Word was saying. Ramm observed that "The tradition of the Syrian school...became the essential hermeneutical theory of the Reformers."[32] He points out that in Europe "there was a hermeneutical Reformation which preceded the ecclesiastical Reformation."[33] Thus, demonstrated once again in history is that one's interpretive method precedes and produces one's exegesis and when logically applied, their theological beliefs. Luther and Calvin generally returned the church to literal interpretation. Had they not done this, Protestantism would have never been born and reformation would have never taken place. Luther said, "The literal sense of Scripture alone is the whole essence of faith and of Christian

---

[31] Kaiser, "Evangelical Hermeneutics," 167.
[32] Ramm, *Protestant Biblical Interpretation*, 51.
[33] Ibid., 52.

theology."[34] Calvin said, "It is the first business of an interpreter to let his author say what he does, instead of attributing to him what we think he ought to say."[35] Calvin clearly believed the goal of interpretation of the Bible was to learn what the author intended,[36] which is the focus of literal interpretation. Both reformers made a clear break with the prevailing allegorical approaches that had dominated the Catholic Church. However, like most people, Luther and Calvin did not always follow their own theory, but they and like-minded reformers turned the hermeneutical tide in the right direction.

The flourishing of millennialism and a belief in a future return of the Jews to their land often go hand in hand. This is evident as the second generation reformers begin to fade. Thus, to date, this writer has not been able to find any reformers who supported the restoration of the Jews back to their land in Israel. Development of such views must await the post-reformation era. "Neither Luther nor Calvin saw a future general conversion of the Jews promised in Scripture; some of their contemporaries, however, notably Martin Bucer and Peter Martyr, who taught at Cambridge and Oxford respectively in the reign of Edward VI, did understand the Bible to teach a future calling of the Jews."[37] It appears that toward the end of the Reformation there was some movement toward a belief in the conversion of the Jews, which would then grow into the belief of a national restoration of the Jews to their land and the rise of premillennialism.

In the 1560s, Theodore Beza, Calvin's successor at Geneva, influenced the English and Scots exiles who produced the famed Geneva Bible. A note on Romans 11:15 and 26 in the Geneva Bible taught that the Jews would be converted in the end times.[38] "The first volume in English to expound this conviction at some length was the translation of Peter Martyr's Commentary upon Romans, published in London in 1568," says Daniel

---

[34] Martin Luther quoted in Ramm, *Protestant Biblical Interpretation*, 54.

[35] John Calvin quoted in Ramm, *Protestant Biblical Interpretation*, 58.

[36] For support of this observation see David L. Puckett, *John Calvin's Exegesis of the Old Testament* (Louisville, KY: Westminster John Knox Press, 1995), 13.

[37] Daniel Gruber, *The Church and the Jews: The Biblical Relationship* (Springfield, MO: General Council of the Assemblies of God, 1991), 301–2.

[38] Gruber, *The Church and the Jews*, 302.

Gruber. "The probability is strong that Martyr's careful exposition of the eleventh chapter prepared the way for a general adoption amongst the English Puritans of a belief in the future conversion of the Jews."[39] This view was then adopted by such great Puritan theologians as William Perkins, Richard Sibbes, Thomas Goodwin, William Strong, William Bridge, George Gillespie and Robert Baillie—to name but a few.[40]

Crawford Gribben tells us:

> This latter-day conversion of the Jews to the Christian faith was to become a staple component of subsequent puritan eschatology, but is an expectation absent from the writings of the earlier Reformers. Calvin's understanding was that the passage which appeared to teach the latter-day conversion of the Jews—Romans 9–11—only referred to 'spiritual Israel', not Jews but the elect of all ages, places, and nationalities.[41]

However, it is important to note that the Reformation in many ways prepared the way for the later rise of premillennialism and a future for the Jews. "It marked the end of the medieval era and the beginning of the modern time."[42] The main gift of the Reformation was that of the Bible in the language of the people. "The reformation opened men's eyes to the Scriptures," notes Gruber. "Its entire thrust was to turn away from the traditions of men which had nullified the Word of God, and to examine the Word itself."[43]

Gruber declares: "Views which were 'un-Lutheran' and 'un-Calvinistic,' but thoroughly Biblical, began to emerge from the Reformation."[44] "Since Wyclif's time," notes Barbara Tuchman, "the New Learning had re-

---

[39] Gruber, *The Church and the Jews*, 302.

[40] Ibid., 302.

[41] Crawford Gribben, *The Puritan Millennium: Literature and Theology, 1550–1682* (Dublin: Four Courts Press, 2000), 39–40.

[42] James A. Saddington, "Prophecy and Politics: A History of Christian Zionism in the Anglo–American Experience, 1800–1948" (PhD diss., Bowling Green State University, 1996), 32.

[43] Gruber, *The Church and the Jews*, 299.

[44] Ibid., 300.

vived the study of Greek and Hebrew, so long ignored in the Latin-dominated Middle Ages."[45] Michael Pragai lucidly points out:

> The growing importance of the English Bible was a concomitant of the spreading Reformation, and it is true to say that the Reformation would never have taken hold had the Bible not replaced the Pope as the ultimate spiritual authority. With the Bible as its tool, the Reformation returned to the geographic origins of Christianity in Palestine. It thereby gradually diminished the authority of Rome.[46]

Thus, it would come to be that the provision of the Bible in the language of the people would become the greatest spur to the rise of premillennialism, setting the stage for a later development into dispensational premillennialism. Having the Bible in the native tongue of the people allowed them read and become familiar with it—especially the Old Testament. It was in this rich soil that over time yielded a crop of Christian Zionism. From a widespread belief in the conversion of the Jews by the end of the Reformation period, it was a short step to the widely held view in the restoration of Israel to her covenant land among post-Reformation Puritans, and which developed into an Israel/church distinction. It was a short step from a near consensus belief in the conversion of the Jews by the end of the Reformation period to the widely held view among post-Reformation Puritans in the restoration of Israel to her covenant land and the rise of a clear picture of Israel followed later by an Israel/church distinction.

Thus it is apparent, the process that moves one toward a dispensational theology begins with a proper understanding of Israel's role in God's plan for history. Once one sees a future time of conversion and blessing for national Israel, then it causes one to have to think about how such a view relates to the church. Since God makes specific promises to both people groups, the only way to reconcile matters in a non-contradictory way is to see a distinction between the church and Israel. This will begin to occur

---

[45] Barbara W. Tuchman, *Bible and Sword: England and Palestine from the Bronze Age to Balfour* (New York: Ballantine Press, 1956), 93.

[46] Michael J. Pragai, *Faith and Fulfilment: Christians and the Return to the Promised Land* (London: Vallentine, Mitchell, 1985), 10.

when one becomes convinced that the unfulfilled promises to national Israel will be fulfilled in the future.

2.7 The Post-Reformation

During the post-Reformation period many Protestants began to slowly
cast off a thousand years of allegorical interpretation of the Bible, especially
in the area of Bible prophecy, as they began to widen the scope of their
biblical studies. They applied literal interpretation first in issues relating to
the doctrine of salvation and then began to apply it increasingly to the entire
Bible. In the early 1600s there was a return to premillennialism because
some started applying a more literal hermeneutic to Revelation 20.[47] At the
same time, many Protestants began to see that there was a literal future for
national Israel,[48] which was spearheaded by reading the premillennialism of
the early church fathers[49] and for the English-speaking world the notes in

---

[47] Jeffrey K. Jue documents how Joseph Mede and a host of many others among
the English began adopting a millennialist view of eschatology. Jue says, "By the mid-
seventeenth century the most popular eschatological position in England was millenarianism." *Heaven upon Earth: Joseph Mede (1586–1638) and the Legacy of Millenarianism*
(Dordrecht, Holland: Springer, 2006), 4.

[48] Jue notes that, "the majority of New England puritans held to the doctrine of
a future national conversion of ethnic Jews." *Heaven upon Earth*, 191. "The doctrine of
the national conversion of the Jews was an integral part of the eschatology of the New
England settlers." Jue, *Heaven upon Earth*, 193. "Virtually all seventeenth- and early
eighteenth-century millennialists on both sides of the Atlantic agreed that even though
the Jews were still languishing in their Diaspora, Jehovah had not forgotten his chosen
people and would, in due time, restore them to their once-elevated position among the
nations." Reiner Smolinski, *The Threefold Paradise of Cotton Mather: An Edition of "Triparadisus"* (Athens, GA: The University of Georgia Press, 1995), 21.

[49] Wallis tells us: "The rediscovery of the last five chapters of Irenaeus about 1570
may have contributed to Alsted's formulation of premillennialism, since he and others
used the writers of the ancient church. We may feel that the intensive Bible study of
the Reformation, combined with the knowledge of antiquity, was beginning to swing
the pendulum back to the primitive premillennialism of Irenaeus which had been rejected by Augustine." Wilber B. Wallis, "Reflections on the History of Premillennial
Thought," in *Interpretation and History: Essays in Honour of Allen A. MacRae*, ed. R. Laird
Harris, Swee-Hwa Quek, and J. Robert Vannoy (Singapore: Christian Life Publishers,
1986), 229. Early Puritan Joseph "Mede observed a similarity between Patristic chiliasm

the Geneva Bible.[50]

Even though literal interpretation was being restored in Christian scholarship during the Reformation and post-Reformation periods, it still took a while for biblical interpreters to more consistently rid themselves of the medieval allegorical influences. For the influential Puritan theologian William Perkins, "the medieval four-fold sense was reduced to a two-fold or double-literal sense."[51] This would be similar to Augustine's dual hermeneutic. However, most Protestant Bible interpreters were increasingly moving toward a more consistent use of the literal hermeneutic and functioning within that framework so the historical, grammatical, contextual method was labeled the Protestant hermeneutic.[52]

While biblical interpretation by the 1600s tended to agree in theory that literal interpretation is the right way to handle Scripture, it still took a couple hundred years to work that out into every area of Bible interpretation, especially when it came to dealing with Bible prophecy. Even though premillennialism had been restored, it was still dominated to a large extent by the blend of literal and allegorical interpretation that is known as *historicism*, which calculated time within a contrived day/year theory. Thus, 1260 days from Daniel and Revelation really referred to 1260 years. This is in no way consistent with literal interpretation!

---

and his own millenarianism especially the writings of the Ante-Nicene Fathers. However, in the early sixteenth century any appeal to the Ante-Nicene Fathers' views on the Apocalypse was discouraged for fear of encouraging their chiliasm." Jue, *Heaven upon Earth*, 110.

[50] In a note on Romans 11:25, The Geneva Bible says, "The blindness of the Jews is neither so universal that the Lord hath no elect in that nation, neither shall it be continual for there shall be a time wherein they also (as the Prophets have forewarned) shall effectually embrace that which they do now so stubbornly for the most part reject and refuse." *The 1599 Geneva Bible* (White Hall, WV: Tolle Lege Press, 2006), 1155. This note also believes the Old Testament Prophets taught a future for Israel as well.

[51] Jue, *Heaven upon Earth*, 199.

[52] Bernard Ramm has entitled his presentation of literal interpretation or the historical, grammatical, and contextual method as Protestant Biblical Interpretation in his book with that title. Bernard Ramm, *Protestant Biblical Interpretation: A Textbook of Hermeneutics*, 3rd ed. (Grand Rapids, MI: Baker Book House, 1970).

A likely factor that contributed to the rise of modern dispensationalism was the rise of essays on the history of redemption in the 1700s. An example of this is seen in Jonathan Edwards' (1703–1758) "A History of the Work of Redemption" given in 1739.[53] Such works began to assess the entirety of biblical history and how each era or dispensation moved God's plan of redemption forward. Such periodization prepared the way for the eventual development of the various dispensations with the ideas of distinctive revelation, testing, failure, and judgment. It was during the post-Reformation era that history was not just viewed as "redemptive history" but the history of redemption that was increasingly real history, not just ideas preceding the Christian era. Just such an approach is how dispensationalists view history.

It was not until the late 1700s and early 1800s that some biblical interpreters began becoming more consistent in applying a literal hermeneutic. Wilber Wallis tells us that, "a consistent futurism, which completely removes the necessity for calculating the times, did not emerge until the early nineteenth century."[54] In general, the Evangelical church, especially in the English-speaking world, returned to the premillennial futurism of the early church. The futurism of the early church was not developed and systematized to any great degree; however, they were clearly futurists. Now Protestants would apply the literal method and develop it beyond the beginning stage of the early church. As Wallis notes, the views of Irenaeus (c. 185) contained the basics of the literal and futurist understanding of Bible prophecy as seen in modern dispensationalism.[55] The important point to note here is that as interpreters became more consistent in applying a literal hermeneutic to the entire Bible, especially to biblical prophecy, it undoubtedly yielded a futurist view of prophecy. "We have returned to Irenaeus' conception of the futurity of Daniel's seventieth week," says Wallis.[56]

---

[53] Jonathan Edwards, "A History of the Work of Redemption, containing the Outlines of a Body of Divinity, including a View of Church History, in a Method Entirely New," in *The Works of Jonathan Edwards*, 2 vols. (1834; repr., Edinburgh, Scotland: Banner of Truth Trust, 1974), 1:532–619.

[54] Wallis, "Reflections," 229.

[55] Ibid., 232–34.

[56] Ibid., 234.

2.8 Modern Dispensationalism

Modern dispensationalism was birthed out of the Calvinistic wing of Protestantism in Great Britain and within North America as well. Therefore, dispensationalism was a development within the Reformed tradition as a rival to replacement theology. As Protestant Reformed theology continued development during the post-Reformation era, the multiple factors that led to the rise of dispensational, premillennial, pretribulationism coalesced by the early 1800s in Great Britain and in various places across the European continent. These views developed even more strongly in the United States after the Civil War under the leadership of primarily Presbyterians.

In concert with the Calvinist impulse to view history theocentricly, the author believes dispensational premillennialism provides the most logical eschatological ending to God's sovereign decrees for salvation and history. Since dispensational premillennialists view both the promises of God's election of Israel and the church as unconditional and something God will surely bring to pass, such a belief is consistent with the Bible and logic. A covenant theologian would say Israel's election was conditional and temporary. Many Calvinists are covenant theologians who think individual election within the church is unconditional and permanent. They see God's plan with Israel conditioned upon human choice, while God's plan for salvation within the church is ultimately a sovereign act of God. There is no symmetry in such logic. Meanwhile, dispensational premillennialists see both acts as a sovereign expression of God's plan for history, which is a logically consistent application of the sovereign will of God in human affairs.

The first to systematize modern dispensationalism into a distinct theology was the Irishman, John Nelson Darby (1800–1882). Historian David Bebbington notes the role of Darby's attempt to apply a consistently literal hermeneutic to Scripture:

> Historicists found it hard to be thoroughgoing advocates of literal interpretation....Futurists did not suffer from this handicap. Consequently, they shouted louder for literalism—and, among the futurists, the dispensationalists shouted loudest of all. J. N. Darby was contending as early as 1829 that prophecy relating to the Jews would be ful-

filled literally. As his thought developed during the 1830s, this principle of interpretation became the lynchpin of his system. Because Darby's opinions were most wedded to literalism, his distinctive scheme enjoyed the advantage of taking what seemed the most rigorist view of scripture. Conversely, the preference for the literal over the figurative approach to biblical exposition drew growing popular support from the advance of millenarianism. The rising prestige of biblical literalism in turn reinforced the strong convictions about scripture propounded by Haldane and his circle.[57]

Samuel H. Kellogg, an early American dispensationalist who was a Presbyterian minister, missionary, and educator wrote of the logic between Calvinism and "modern, futurist premillennialism," which was in that day (1888) essentially dispensational. "But in general," notes Kellogg, "we think, it may be rightly said that the *logical* relations of premillennialism connect it more closely with the Augustinian than with any other theological system."[58] His use of "Augustinian" is the older term for Calvinism. Kellogg points out the different areas in which Calvinism and premillennialism are theologically one. "Premillennialism logically presupposes an *anthropology* essentially Augustinian. The ordinary Calvinism affirms the absolute helplessness of the individual for self-regeneration and self-redemption."[59] He continues, it is "evident that the anthropological presuppositions on which premillennialism seems to rest, must carry with them a corresponding *soteriology*."[60] Kellogg reasons: "the Augustinian affinity of the premillennialist eschatology becomes still more manifest. For nothing is more marked than the emphasis with which premillennialists constantly insist that . . . the present dispensation is strictly elective."[61] "In a word," concludes Kellogg, "we may say that premillennialists simply affirm of the macrocosm what the

---

[57] David Beddington, *Evangelicalism in Modern Britain: A History from the 1730s to the 1980s* (Grand Rapids, MI: Baker Book House, 1989), 88–89.

[58] Samuel H. Kellogg, "Premillennialism: Its relations to Doctrine and Practice," *Bibliotheca Sacra* 45, no. 178 (Apr 1888), 253.

[59] Kellogg, "Premillennialism," 254.

[60] Ibid., 257.

[61] Ibid., 258–59.

common Augustinianism affirms only of the microcosm."[62]

This is not to say that dispensationalism and Calvinism are synonymous. It is merely to point out that it is consistent with certain elements of Calvinism, which provide a partial answer as to why dispensationalism sprang from the Reformed womb. C. Norman Kraus contends:

> There are, to be sure, important elements of seventeenth-century Calvinism in contemporary dispensationalism, but these elements have been blended with doctrinal emphasis from other sources to form a distinct system which in many respects is quite foreign to classical Calvinism.[63]

Nevertheless, dispensationalism did develop within the Reformed community and most of its adherents during the first 100 years were from within the Calvinist milieu. Kraus concludes: "Taking all this into account, it must still be pointed out that the basic theological affinities of dispensationalism are Calvinistic. The large majority of men involved in the Bible and prophetic conference movements subscribed to Calvinistic creeds."[64] This is why the Reformation paved the way for the eventual development of dispensationalism.

Only the Western church, dominated by Roman Catholicism, had a Reformation, which steered the Reformed wing of Protestantism toward a more literal hermeneutic, a revival of premillennialism, futurism, and a future for national Israel. The most popular form of such a theology is known for almost the last two hundred years as dispensationalism.

2.9 Conclusion

Rather than a wholesale opposition to Reformed or Calvinistic theology, this author personally believes that if the system of theology called dispensationalism is rightly understood then it still logically makes sense only within a theocentric and soteriologically Calvinist theology. After all, dis-

---

[62] Kellogg, "Premillennialism," 256.

[63] C. Norman Kraus, *Dispensationalism in America: Its Rise and Development* (Richmond, VA: John Knox Press, 1958), 59.

[64] Ibid.

pensationalism teaches that it is *God* who is ruling His household, as administered through the various dispensations of history. However, the reality is that dispensationalism, or elements of dispensationalism (i.e., pretribulationism, futurism, etc.), have been disseminated throughout a wide diversity of Protestant traditions. Dispensationalism is best seen as a system of theology that views God as the Sovereign ruler of heaven and earth; man as a rebellious vice-regent (along with some angels); Jesus Christ as the hero of history in saving some by His Grace; history as a lesson in the outworking of God's glory being displayed to both heaven and earth. Dispensationalism is a theology that is properly derived from biblical study and truly lets God be God. *Maranatha!*

Bibliography

"An Interview: Dr. John F. Walvoord Looks at Dallas Seminary." *Dallas Connection* 1, no. 3 (Winter 1994).

Allis, Oswald T. *Prophecy and the Church.* Phillipsburg, NJ: Presbyterian and Reformed Publishing, 1947.

Beddington, David. *Evangelicalism in Modern Britain: A History from the 1730s to the 1980s.* Grand Rapids, MI: Baker Book House, 1989.

Charles, R. H. *Studies in the Apocalypse.* Edinburgh: T & T Clark, 1913.

Diprose, Ronald E. *Israel in the Development of Christian Thought.* Rome: Instituto Biblico Evangelico Italiano, 2000.

Edwards, Jonathan. "A History of the Work of Redemption, containing the Outlines of a Body of Divinity, including a View of Church History, in a Method Entirely New." In *The Works of Jonathan Edwards*, 1:532–619. 2 vols. 1834. Reprint, Edinburgh, Scotland: Banner of Truth Trust, 1974.

Fahlbusch, E., J. M. Lochman, J. Mbiti, J. Pelikan, and L. Vischer, eds. *The Encyclopedia of Christianity.* 5 vols. Grand Rapids, MI: William B. Eerdmans, 2005.

Farrar, Frederic W. *History of Interpretation.* 1886. Reprint, Grand Rapids, MI: Baker Book House, 1961.

The 1599 Geneva Bible. White Hall, WV: Tolle Lege Press, 2006.

Geisler, Norman L. "Review of Hank Hanegraaff's *The Apocalypse Code.*" Norman Geisler.com. Accessed September 11, 2017. http://norman geisler.com/a-review-of-hanegraaff-apocalypse-code/.

Gribben, Crawford. *The Puritan Millennium: Literature and Theology, 1550–1682.* Dublin: Four Courts Press, 2000.

Gruber, Daniel. *The Church and the Jews: The Biblical Relationship.* Springfield, MO: General Council of the Assemblies of God, 1991.

Jue, Jeffrey K. *Heaven upon Earth: Joseph Mede (1586–1638) and the Legacy of Millenarianism*. Dordrecht, Holland: Springer, 2006.

Kaiser, Walter C., Jr. "Evangelical Hermeneutics: Restatement, Advance or Retreat from the Reformation?" *Concordia Theological Quarterly* 46, no. 2–3 (Apr–Jul 1982): 167–180.

Kellogg, Samuel H. "Premillennialism: Its relations to Doctrine and Practice." *Bibliotheca Sacra* 45, no. 178 (Apr 1888): 234–274.

Kraus, C. Norman. *Dispensationalism in America: Its Rise and Development*. Richmond, VA: John Knox Press, 1958.

McManners, John. *The Oxford Illustrated History of Christianity*. New York: Oxford University Press, 1990.

Pragai, Michael J. *Faith and Fulfilment: Christians and the Return to the Promised Land*. London: Vallentine, Mitchell, 1985.

Puckett, David L. *John Calvin's Exegesis of the Old Testament*. Louisville, KY: Westminster John Knox Press, 1995.

Ramm, Bernard. *Protestant Biblical Interpretation: A Textbook of Hermeneutics*. 3rd ed. Grand Rapids, MI: Baker Book House, 1970.

Ryrie, Charles C. *Dispensationalism*. Rev. and exp. ed. 1995. Reprint, Chicago, IL: Moody Press, 2007.

Saddington, James A. "Prophecy and Politics: A History of Christian Zionism in the Anglo–American Experience, 1800–1948." PhD diss., Bowling Green State University, 1996.

Smalley, Beryl. *The Study of the Bible in the Middle Ages*. 1964. Reprint, Notre Dame, IN: University of Notre Dame Press, 1982.

Smith, Henry Preserved. *Essays in Biblical Interpretation*. Boston: Marshall Jones Company, 1921.

Smolinski, Reiner. *The Threefold Paradise of Cotton Mather: An Edition of "Triparadisus."* Athens, GA: The University of Georgia Press, 1995.

Trigg, Joseph W. Introduction to *Allegory and Event: A Study of the Sources and Significance of Origen's Interpretation of Scripture*, by R. P. C. Hanson. Louisville, KY: Westminster John Knox Press, 2002.

Tuchman, Barbara W. *Bible and Sword: England and Palestine from the Bronze Age to Balfour*. New York: Ballantine Press, 1956.

Wallis, Wilber B. "Reflections on the History of Premillennial Thought." In *Interpretation and History: Essays in Honour of Allan A. MacRae*, edited by R. Laird Harris, Swee-Hwa Quek, and J. Robert Vannoy. Singapore: Christian Life Publishers, 1986.

Walton, Robert C. *Chronological and Background Charts of Church History*. Grand Rapids, MI: Zondervan, 1986.

3

MARTIN LUTHER:
An Evaluation of the *95 Theses*

Patrick Belvill
Tyndale Theological Seminary and Biblical Institute

3.0 Introduction

An examination of church history, from the second century forward, reveals that two streams of theological progress have always existed. On the one hand there is that stream which seeks to keep the interpretation of Scripture in God's hands, by maintaining a normal-literal hermeneutic, as evidenced early on by the School of Antioch.[1] On the other hand, there is a second stream which desires to give man control over God's Word, as evidenced by the School of Alexandria, which promoted the allegorical hermeneutic.[2]

As the Christian church developed, the Alexandrian school held sway with their interpretive influence until the church itself became the final arbiter of faith and practice, replacing the Bible in this respect.[3] The church's

---

[1] Gordon H. Johnson, "Hermenuetics, Antiochan School," in *Dictionary of Premillennial Theology*, ed. Mal Couch (Grand Rapids, MI: Kregel Publications, 1996), 145.

[2] Ibid., 144.

[3] "Emperor Valentinian III, in an edict in A.D. 445, recognized the supremacy of the bishop of Rome in spiritual affairs. What the bishop would enact was to be 'law for all.'" Earle E. Cairns, *Christianity through the Centuries* (Grand Rapids, MI: Academie Books, 1981), 158.

interpretive method continued to move in this direction until it became what Christopher Cone has referred to as "the canonical dogmatic herme-neutic."[4] Those who held to a more normal-literal hermeneutic became mar-ginalized, and at points in history were excommunicated as heretics[5] or killed.

However, not all within the church proper were totally satisfied with papal interpretations and practices over the centuries, and prior to 1517, other attempts had been made at reformation. In the fourteenth century, John Wycliffe, a "Yorkshireman who attended Oxford University, receiving the doctorate of theology (1372),"[6] first succeeded in convincing the English government to seize all of the lands owned by the Roman Catholic Church in an effort to eliminate immoral clergymen. Then, in 1379, Wycliffe turned his sights on the dogma of the Roman Catholic Church itself. Ac-cording to church historian Earle Cairns:

> He attacked the authority of the pope in 1379 by insisting in writing that Christ and not the pope was the head of the church. He asserted that the Bible instead of the church was the sole authority for the be-liever and that the church should model itself after the pattern of the New Testament. To support these beliefs, Wycliffe made the Bible available to the people in their own tongue.[7]

Wycliffe lost much of his support when he attacked the Roman Cath-olic doctrine of transubstantiation. He was forced out of Oxford, and re-turned to his home, where, following his death, his body was exhumed and burnt as a heretic.[8]

However, Wycliffe's teachings did not die with him. He influenced a Bohemian pastor named John Hus, an ordained priest and rector of the

---

[4] Christopher Cone, *Prolegomena, Introductory Notes on Bible Study and Theological Method* (Ft. Worth, TX: Tyndale Seminary Press, 2007), 147.

[5] An example being the Waldenses in the twelfth century.

[6] Robert Close, "Wycliffe, John (c.1329–1384)," in *The New International Diction-ary of the Christian Church*, ed. J. D. Douglas (Grand Rapids, MI: Zondervan, 1978), 1064.

[7] Cairns, *Christianity through the Centuries*, 252.

[8] Close, "Wycliffe, John," 1064.

Bethlehem Chapel in Prague.[9] Hus began to preach the ideas of Wycliffe and thus caught the attention of the Pope who ordered him to attend the Council of Constance in Baden, Germany.[10] At this council, Hus, as well as the teachings of Wycliffe, were condemned as heretical. Hus was removed from the priesthood and burned at the stake on July 6, 1415.[11]

Sixty-nine years after the death of Hus, into a world spiritually dominated by the Roman Catholic Church (with its desire to control the belief of all Christians and occasional opposition rising) Martin Luther was born.

3.1 The Growth and Schooling of Luther

Martin Luther (or Martin Ludher) came into this world on November 10, 1483. His father, Hans Ludher, came from peasant stock. He was a miner and later a mine owner.[12] According to Wengert, "in 1518, Martin changed the spelling of his name to Luther as a theological play on the Greek word, *eleutherius*, which means 'the free one.'"[13] As to religion, Luther grew up in a very conservative religious atmosphere—one in which the care of one's soul was greatly emphasized. Reformation historian Robert Godfrey states:

> The church told Martin Luther that the soul is a precious thing and that the salvation of the soul was difficult to accomplish. The church advised that anyone who wanted to be serious about his soul and about salvation should become a monk because the life of a monk was precisely the life of giving oneself over to the salvation of one's soul.[14]

Luther's family had enough money to send him to school, which they did for their own social advancement as much as for Luther's benefit. As he

---

[9] Matthew Spinka, "Hus, Jan (1373–1415)," in *The New International Dictionary of the Christian Church*, ed. J. D. Douglas (Grand Rapids, MI: Zondervan, 1978), 492.

[10] Cairns, *Christianity through the Centuries*, 252.

[11] Spinka, "Hus, Jan," 493.

[12] Timothy J. Wengert, *Martin Luther's 95 Theses: With Introduction, Commentary, and Study Guide* (Minneapolis, MN: Fortress Press, 2015), xxi.

[13] Ibid., xxi.

[14] W. Robert Godfrey, *Reformation Sketches: Insights into Luther, Calvin, and the Confessions* (Phillipsburg, NJ: P&R Publishing, 2003), 7.

grew, he attended a Latin school in the town of Mansfield, the school of the Brethren of the Common Life in Magdeburg. He then moved on to school in Eisenach, where he received the additional lessons in Latin he would need to qualify for entrance into university.[15]

In 1501, Luther matriculated at the University of Erfurt, where he entered a strictly regimented program of education meant not only for the completion of a Bachelor of Arts degree but also for completion of the Master's degree. This program included Aristotelian philosophy, interpreted according to the scholasticism of William of Occam.[16] According to Heinrich Boehmer:

> The 'Modernists,' or Occamists, differed from the Thomists and Scotists chiefly in their flat denial that human reason can attain certain knowledge of the supersensuous realities of faith. But they denied this only to emphasize more strongly that in its dogmas the church possesses an absolute infallible knowledge of these realities and that it is consequently necessary, not only on moral and religious but also on scientific grounds, implicitly to accept and obediently to believe these dogmas, no matter how absurd or contradictory they might appear.[17]

However, Cairns notes the following regarding Luther's education: "William had taught that revelation was the only guide in the realm of faith; reason was the guide to truth in philosophy. Thus Luther's philosophical studies at Erfurt made him aware of the need of divine intervention if man were to know spiritual truth and to be saved."[18] One other important area of Luther's education was the study of logic, especially considering the changes in his thought process later in life regarding the supersensuous realities of faith. Boehmer explains:

> As far as the world of sensuous and inner experience is concerned the Occamists did not dispute its accessibility to the human faculty of perception. But when they refused to attribute the character of evidence

---

[15] Cairns, *Christianity through the Centuries*, 288–289.

[16] Heinrich Boehmer, *Road to Reformation: Martin Luther to the Year 1521* (Philadelphia: Muhlenberg Press, 1946), 25.

[17] Ibid., 25.

[18] Cairns, *Christianity through the Centuries*, 289.

or science to the perceptions which man can gain in this way, they did so only because they recognized logic as the sole science in the strict sense of the word, and not because they believed that correct perceptions were impossible in this sphere of experience. On the basis of Aristotle, therefore, they taught these second-class sciences just as thoroughly as they did logic.[19]

Logic may be seen as the study of reasoning. It attempts to differentiate good reasoning from bad reasoning. Its realm is declarative statements, propositions which may be considered either true or false.[20] It is the literal nature of such a pursuit that would influence Luther's scriptural analysis in the future.

Luther completed his Bachelor of Arts degree around 1502/1503, and was awarded his Master of Arts degree in February, 1505. As a requirement of his university education, Luther had to remain at the school for an additional two years as a teacher in the arts program from which he graduated. However, this time could also be spent in advanced studies for himself. Luther's father desired that his son pursue a law degree, so in May of 1505, Luther began his studies in law.

Something, however, was troubling Luther during this period—a cause which has never been definitely identified. As a result, about a month after he had started his study of the law, Luther took a leave of absence to visit family. About ten days later, on his journey back to school, Luther was caught in a large thunder storm. Apparently, a lightning bolt struck close enough to him that he was thrown from his horse by the air pressure,[21] at which point he immediately offered up a prayer for safety to St. Anna—the patron saint of miners—and vowed that if he survived, he would become a monk.

As a fervent Catholic, upon returning to school, Luther set forth to keep his vow; he sold most of his schoolbooks, gave the money to the poor, and entered the mendicant order of the Augustinian Hermits in Erfurt. An

---

[19] Boehmer, *Road to Reformation*, 25–26.

[20] Steward Shapiro, "Classical Logic," Stanford Encyclopedia of Philosophy, accessed July 14, 2017, https://plato.stanford.edu/entries/logic-classical/.

[21] Boehmer, *Road to Reformation*, 33.

excellent student, he was ordained as a priest about two years later, and went on to earn a doctorate in 1512 from the University of Wittenberg. Luther functioned faithfully as both a priest caring for his flock, and a Roman Catholic university lecturer. Boehmer contends that his earlier education still impacted his views on faith:

> The views and doctrines which Luther was expounding, however, still breathed the old Erfurt spirit. The fact that he no longer spoke of two, but of only one chief cause of redemption, and the fact that he no longer admitted the validity of free will but only of grace would indicate, as his deductions elsewhere show, a departure from the Occamist tradition in form but not in substance.[22]

Those in charge of Luther's monastery noted the intellect of this young monk and encouraged him to focus on scriptural and theological studies, which he gladly did. It does appear, however, that his studies led him to some profound conclusions, primarily in the areas of authority and salvation.[23]

In the area of authority, the medieval Roman Catholic Church held to four sources, the Scriptures, tradition, reason, and the pope. Although the Church held that there was no tension between these four sources of authority, Luther's studies and experience told him different. As Godfrey reveals,

> His confidence first began to waiver in reason as an authority. Luther later in his life would make one of his famous hyperbolic statements when he said that reason was a whore. What he meant was not that one should never reason or that reason was not useful in conducting the affairs of this life. Rather, what he meant was that when one reflects on spiritual things, when one thinks about theology, reason will only lead you astray. Reason gets you nowhere. *One has to find truth through revelation* was Luther's ultimate conclusion.[24]

Eventually, through study and even through debate (with Johannes Maier

---

[22] Boehmer, *Road to Reformation*, 55.
[23] Godfrey, *Reformation Sketches*, 7.
[24] Ibid., 8.

von Eck), Luther reduced his list even further. Godfrey further noted: "Luther came to realize clearly that Scripture alone must be our authority."[25]

During this same period, Luther was also struggling with his understanding of righteousness and salvation. As a devout Roman Catholic monk, Luther embraced the teachings on salvation that the Church had developed over centuries to help in their control of, not only individuals, but also of nations. Salvation was something that one had to earn by keeping the commandments of the Bible along with additional commandments of the Church. Even doing this did not guarantee eternal salvation; however, without this continuous effort by the believer, all hope would be lost.

With the image of God cast as an eternal Judge rather than as a loving Father, Luther also found his view of righteousness skewed in favor of judgment. In describing Luther's difficulty, Alister McGrath quotes Luther from his *Works*:

> I had certainly wanted to understand Paul in his letter to the Romans. But what prevented me from doing so was not so much cold feet as that one phrase in the first chapter: "the righteousness of God is revealed in it" (Romans 1:17). For I hated that phrase, "the righteousness of God", which I had been taught to understand as the righteousness by which God is righteous, and punishes unrighteous sinners.[26]

As a result, although Luther considered himself a model monk, he did not believe that he was continually pleasing God with his works. In fact, after much angst over his inability to please God, Luther actually confessed to hating God for setting an impossible standard for mankind to meet.

Trusting that it was his understanding of the Church's teaching which must be wrong, Luther set about to study the Scriptures even more diligently. No one knows for sure when the change actually occurred in Luther. Some think it was "'the tower experience', on account of a later (and somewhat confused) personal recollection of Luther, which seems to imply that his breakthrough took place in a tower of the Augustinian monastery."[27]

---

[25] Godfrey, *Reformation Sketches*, 10.

[26] Alister E. McGrath, *Reformation Thought: An Introduction* (Oxford, UK: Blackwell, 1993), 95.

[27] McGrath, *Reformation Thought*, 94.

Whenever it did actually take place, the change in Luther's perspective of Scripture was incredible and would foster a return to a more literal approach to biblical interpretation. Luther wrote:

> At last, as I meditated day and night on the relation of the words "the righteousness of God is revealed in it, as it is written, the righteous person shall live by faith", I began to understand that "righteousness of God" as that by which the righteous person lives by the gift of God (faith); and this sentence, "the righteousness of God is revealed", to refer to a passive righteousness, by which the merciful God justifies us by faith, as it is written, "the righteous person lives by faith". This immediately made me feel as though I had been born again, and as though I had entered through open gates into paradise itself. From that moment, I saw the whole face of Scripture in a new light....And now, where I had once hated the phrase, "the righteousness of God", I began to love and extol it as the sweetest of phrases, so that this passage in Paul became the very gate of paradise to me.[28]

Now, while Luther was going through these struggles, he was still functioning as a priest and teacher. As such, he supported the Church's practice of selling indulgences. In fact, Wengert asserts that Luther himself once confessed:

> I once believed that the merits of Christ were actually given me through indulgences and, proceeding in this foolish notion, I taught and preached to the people that, since indulgences were such valuable things, they should not fail to treasure them, and should not consider them cheap or contemptible.[29]

However, Luther's continued study of Scripture started to give him doubts about this Church practice. By the year 1517, Luther's concern was

---

[28] Martin Luther, *Works*, WA 54:185–86, in McGrath, *Reformation Thought*, 95. WA is the abbreviation for the German language edition: *Weimarer Ausgabe*.

[29] Martin Luther, "Proceedings at Augsburg (1518)," in *The Roots of Reform*, ed. Timothy J. Wengert, trans. Suzanne Hequet, vol. 1, *The Annotated Luther*, ed. Hans J. Hillerbrand, Kirsi I. Stjerna, and Timothy J. Wengert (Minneapolis, MN: Fortress Press, 2015), 164, quoted in Wengert, *Martin Luther's 95 Theses*, xxiii–xxiv.

that the sale of indulgences was "cheapening" the price the Lord paid on the Cross. While he was not yet questioning the intention of the Church, he came to believe that individuals were purchasing indulgences with the intention of "sidestepping" the punishment of God for sin, seeing them as an alternative for true contrition of the heart. No longer was a heartfelt belief in the cross of Christ necessary for forgiveness of all sins, now that forgiveness could be bought by anyone for mere money.

Luther would, however, also develop other concerns regarding indulgences. In 1515, Pope Leo X authorized a new indulgence. It was known as Peter's Indulgence, and its purpose was to raise money for the rebuilding of St. Peter's Basilica in Rome. However, this indulgence had a second intent of which Luther was not aware in 1517: "Money raised was also to help Albrecht von Brandenburg, the newly named Archbishop of Mainz...pay off his debt for purchasing his archiepiscopal office and for being given permission to hold more than one bishopric."[30]

3.2 Johann Tetzel and the Sale of Indulgences

Pope Leo X appointed a Dominican Friar, Johann Tetzel, to preach this indulgence, as Tetzel had proven to be very successful in achieving good results. Tetzel was not permitted (by Frederick the Elector of Saxony) to preach in Wittenberg where Luther was based. However, many from Wittenberg traveled to other areas of Germany where Tetzel was permitted to speak, and many purchased indulgences from him, taking them back to Wittenberg where Luther became aware of his activities. Tetzel was such a salesman that he not only sold indulgences for those to whom he spoke, he also sold indulgences for their dead relatives, a totally unorthodox practice for which he was later severely chastised.

At this time, however, Luther was deeply involved in his studies of Church law, or Canon law, regarding indulgences. He was also influenced by a Renaissance movement sweeping across Europe known as "humanism," the study of which favored the recovery and use of the most ancient evidence and sources for any field of study, rather than just trusting the authorities of the current day. As a result, Luther started seeking out ancient

---

[30] Luther, "Proceedings at Augsburg," xxiv–xxv.

literature in his areas of study as well as using the ancient language texts; this included the Greek texts which had been discovered, in addition to the Greek New Testament compiled by Erasmus of Rotterdam. In studying these ancient documents, Luther made a life-changing discovery:

> His study of indulgences in canon law led him to the conclusion that in the ancient and early-medieval church indulgences and the penalties that they lifted were strictly ecclesiastical ones, having nothing directly to do with punishments for sin meted out by God. This meant for him that later papal decrees, which assumed the pope had authority to lift God's punishment for sin, had misconstrued the nature of indulgences and needed to be revised in light of the clear testimony of canon law, the ancient church fathers, and Scripture.[31]

Luther found further support for his evolving view of forgiveness and indulgences in Erasmus' biblical commentary on Matthew 4:17. In his Vulgate, Jerome had translated the Greek verb, μετανοεῖτε (*metanoeite*), as "do penance," referring to the sacrament of penance. However, Erasmus correctly translated this Greek verb rendering it as "Return to a right mind."[32] Thus, the correction of this Roman Catholic "proof text" for doing penance, coupled with Luther's research and discovery regarding the history of indulgences, motivated his resolve to propose formal discussion and debate regarding reformation to the doctrines of the Roman Catholic Church concerning indulgences.

3.3 Associated Texts

In doing an in-depth study of Luther's *95 Theses*, one should be aware of three additional documents which shed light on his work and add context. The first document is known as the *Summary Instruction*. When Rome would issue an indulgence to be offered, it included a set of instructions for the clerics who would be offering the indulgence for purchase. These in-

---

[31] Luther, "Proceedings at Augsburg," xxxii.

[32] Erasmus, *Annotationes in Novum Instrumentum* (Basel, Froben, 1516), 241, quoted in Wengert, *Martin Luther's 95 Theses*, xxxiii.

structions detailed the benefits which could be received from the indulgence as well as the permissible language to be used by the salesman in offering the indulgence. In other words, he could not offer more than was detailed in the *Summary Instruction.*

As previously noted, the particular indulgence, which prompted Luther to write his *95 Theses*, was known as "Peter's Indulgence." It was proclaimed by Pope Leo X in 1515 to be preached in the Germanic lands to raise money to help rebuild St. Peter's Basilica in Rome. Since it was to be preached in the Germanic lands, the duty of writing the *Summary Instruction* was given to the highest church authority in those lands, the Archbishop of Mainz, who in turn gave the assignment to his theological faculty.

Even though the preaching Peter's Indulgence was not permitted in Wittenberg, members of Luther's church, venturing into areas where they could purchase this indulgence, returned to Wittenberg and told Luther of Tetzel's "sales pitch." Luther obtained a copy of the official *Summary Instruction,* confirming the actual details of what was being offered, and saw that Tetzel was making spiritual promises from this indulgence that were far beyond the official scope approved by the pope. This revelation added to Luther's desire for reformation of the indulgence system.

The second document of import is Luther's letter directly to the Archbishop of Mainz, Albrecht of Brandenburg. Today, scholars debate whether or not Luther actually nailed a copy of his theses to the door of the church in Wittenberg. Assuming that he actually did, this would have brought him an audience of local scholars to discuss his points. It appears though that Luther wanted a wider German audience. On October 31, 1517, Luther wrote a letter to the Archbishop of Mainz alerting him to his concerns regarding indulgences and addressing just a few of the topics contained in the *95 Theses.* Along with the letter, Luther enclosed a copy of the *95 Theses* for consideration by the Archbishop. Upon receipt of the package and the reading thereof, Albrecht turned it over to his theological faculty and had them send a copy to Rome. It does not appear that Luther initially wanted this discussion to go beyond the Germanic bishopric, but thanks to the Archbishop, the audience would now include the See of Rome.

The third document of importance is the *Explanations of the Ninety-Five Theses,* which Luther started writing in 1517, but did not publish until 1518.

In his *Explanations*, Luther expanded on most of the points contained in the *95 Theses* giving fuller explanations of what he believed. He did it, citing the Holy Scriptures as his primary authority, only referring to the traditions of the Church or its ecclesiastical councils if the point in question was not addressed by Scripture. This adherence to the primacy of Scripture, over and above that of Church doctrine, councils and traditions, speaks to a nascent dispensational mindset with Luther's evolving acceptance (to some degree) of a literal-grammatical-historical hermeneutic.

3.4 The *95 Theses*

The reader may be surprised at the notion that Luther's *95 Theses* reflect a proto-dispensational mindset. It would be irresponsible and disingenuous to claim that Martin Luther anticipated dispensational theology in all of its nuances. Neither is it the claim of this author that Luther subscribed to a dispensational division of history—though he, indeed, fought vociferously for the distinction between the former and present dispensations, using the terms "Law" and "Grace" or "Law and Gospel." Nevertheless, a thorough consideration of the *95 Theses* will serve to reveal the nascent dispensational mindset that emerged from Luther's appeal to a literal grammatical-historical hermeneutical method.

Beginning with the first four theses[33] dispensational thought is reflected in Luther's thoughts regarding the nature of repentance:

1. When our Lord and Master Jesus Christ said, "Repent" [Matt. 4:17], he willed the entire life of believers to be one of repentance.
2. This word cannot be understood as referring to the sacrament of penance, that is, confession and satisfaction, as administered by the clergy.
3. Yet it does not mean solely inner repentance; such inner repentance is worthless unless it produces various outward mortifications of the flesh.

---

[33] Martin Luther, "Explanations of the Ninety-Five Theses," in *Luther's Works*, ed. Helmut T. Lehmann, vol. 31, *Career of the Reformer I*, ed. Harold J. Grimm, trans. Carl W. Folkemer (Philadelphia, PA: Muhlenberg, 1958), 83–252. Subsequently referenced as, *Explanations* or "Explanations."

4. The penalty of sin remains as long as the hatred of self, that is, true inner repentance, until our entrance into the kingdom of heaven.

The first thesis refers to Jesus' words in Matthew 4:17. However, when Jerome wrote the Vulgate, he translated the Greek word μετανοεῖτε (*metanoeite*) which means "to change one's mind" to the Latin *pœnitentiam agite* which was interpreted by the Catholic Church as "do penance." Luther points out this error in his *Explanations* saying,

> Nevertheless, I shall prove the thesis for the sake of those who are uninformed, first from the Greek word *metanoeite* itself, which means "repent" and could be translated more exactly by the Latin *transmentamini*, which means "assume another mind and feeling, recover one's senses, make a transition from one state of mind to another, have a change of spirit"; so that those who hitherto have been aware of earthly matters may now know the spiritual, as the Apostle says in Rom. 12 [:2], "Be transformed by the renewal of your mind." By this recovery of one's senses it happens that the sinner has a change of heart and hates his sin.[34]

Thus, theses two through four explain why the Roman Catholic interpretation is in error. Thesis two explains that the word "repentance" cannot mean the Catholic sacrament of penance since this deals with an external, vocal confession and remission of sin without any knowledge as to the inward repentance of the individual. Thesis three states that true inward repentance will have an outward manifestation, and thesis four confirms that this process will continue, in the true believer, throughout one's life. When Luther refers to the "hatred of self" he is speaking of the attitude of the believer as he grows in his knowledge of God. Reformed Scholar Stephen J. Nichols offers the following insight:

> In his *Explanations* he clarifies his meaning of hating the self: "True sorrow must spring from the goodness and mercies of God, especially from the wounds of Christ, so that man comes first of all to a sense of

---

[34] Luther, "Explanations," 31:84.

his own ingratitude in view of divine goodness and thereupon to hatred of himself and love of the kindness of God. Then tears will flow
and he will hate himself from the very depths of his heart, yet without
despair. Then he will hate sin, not because of the punishment but
because of his regard for the goodness of God; and when he has perceived this he will be preserved from despair and will despise himself
most ardently, yet joyfully."[35]

So, from the very first thesis, Luther takes his stand, not only for the primacy of Scripture, but also for its correct interpretation as being literal
and grammatical and taken from the original language text. The reader
will be reminded here that the normal grammatical-historical interpretive
method is a bedrock of dispensational thought, or as dispensational theologian Charles C. Ryrie has called it, a *sine qua non* (without which not).[36]

Thesis five contains Luther's main premise and is the beginning of a
section (through thesis twenty), detailing his thoughts on the limits of the
pope's power to grant indulgences:

5. The pope neither desires nor is able to remit any penalties except
those imposed by his own authority or that of the canons.
6. The pope cannot remit any guilt, except by declaring and showing
that it has been remitted by God; or, to be sure, by remitting guilt
in cases reserved to his judgment. If his right to grant remission in
these cases were disregarded, the guilt would certainly remain un-
forgiven.
7. God remits guilt to no one unless at the same time he humbles
him in all things and makes him submissive to his vicar, the priest.
8. The penitential canons are imposed only on the living, and, according to the canons themselves, nothing should be imposed on
the dying.
9. Therefore the Holy Spirit through the pope is kind to us insofar
as the pope in his decrees always makes exception of the article of

---

[35] Stephen J. Nichols, *Martin Luther's Ninety-Five Theses* by Martin Luther, ed.
Stephen J. Nichols (Phillipsburg, P&R Publishing, 2002), 24.
[36] Charles C. Ryrie, *Dispensationalism*, rev. and exp. ed. (1997; repr., Chicago, IL:
Moody Publishers, 2007), 47.

death and of necessity.

10. Those priests act ignorantly and wickedly who, in the case of the dying, reserve canonical penalties for purgatory.

11. Those tares of changing the canonical penalty to the penalty of purgatory were evidently sown while the bishops slept [Matt. 13:25].

12. In former times canonical penalties were imposed, not after, but before absolution, as tests of true contrition.

13. The dying are freed by death from all penalties, are already dead as far as the canon laws are concerned, and have a right to be released from them.

14. Imperfect piety or love on the part of the dying person necessarily brings with it great fear; and the smaller the love, the greater the fear.

15. This fear or horror is sufficient in itself, to say nothing of other things, to constitute the penalty of purgatory, since it is very near the horror of despair.

16. Hell, purgatory, and heaven seem to differ the same as despair, fear, and assurance of salvation.

17. It seems as though for the souls in purgatory fear should necessarily decrease and love increase.

18. Furthermore, it does not seem proved, either by reason or Scripture, that souls in purgatory are outside the state of merit, that is, unable to grow in love.

19. Nor does it seem proved that souls in purgatory, at least not all of them, are certain and assured of their own salvation, even if we ourselves may be entirely certain of it.

20. Therefore the pope, when he uses the words "plenary remission of all penalties," does not actually mean "all penalties," but only those imposed by himself.

In thesis five, Luther starts defining the limits of the pope's power regarding the remission of sin. By saying that the pope's power was limited to penalties that he himself imposed, Luther removed the power of the pope from penalties listed in Scripture as well as Church canon law. In his *Explanations* Luther states, "He seems, therefore, to remit only those which are

imposed concerning fasts, prayers, alms giving, and other works and disciplines, some for seven years, some for less, some for more."[37]

Furthermore, Luther stated that the only way the pope did remit any
sin was through prayer and not through the sale of indulgences. In this one
thesis, Luther declares the sovereignty of the Scriptures over the power of
the pope and declares void the promises made by Johann Tetzel in his sale
of indulgences, which included full remission for any anticipated time in
purgatory, as stated in the *Summary Instruction.*[38]

Theses six and seven deal with the "guilt" of sin and its remission. It
is important to note that in medieval Roman Catholic theology, a distinction was made between the "guilt" of sin and the "penalty" of sin. The belief
was that God alone could forgive the "guilt" of sin, but other means, such
as indulgences, could affect the "penalty" of sin. However, as seen in the
Summary Instruction, as well as the eyewitness reports on the presentations
made by Tetzel, this distinction was sometimes overlooked. Thesis seven
also affirms Luther's belief in the role and authority of the local priest. As
his theology evolved Luther moved "toward advocating the priesthood of
all believers."[39]

Thesis eight deals with another abuse within the indulgence system.
Luther here references the "penitential canons," ancient texts which dealt
with penalties to be imposed on sinners in the hopes of reconciliation. However, he makes clear that these documents affirm the church only has control over a church member while he is alive and that no requirement should
be placed on that member when he is facing death. As evidence, in his *Explanations,* Luther cites Romans 7:1-2. This abrogates the teaching that an
indulgence could be purchased on behalf of dead family members, to lessen
their time in purgatory. This theme of Luther's dealing with abuses of penance and indulgences continues through thesis thirteen.

In theses fourteen through twenty-six, another theme starts, that being
Luther's focus on purgatory to point out indulgence abuse by promising the
total remission of sins, as promoted by Tetzel, and stated in the *Summary
Instruction.* It is true that, at this point in his faith, Luther still believed in

---

[37] Luther, "Explanations," 31:92.
[38] Wengert, *Martin Luther's 95 Theses,* 35n28.
[39] Nichols, *Martin Luther's Ninety-Five Theses,* 24.

purgatory as a place for Catholics to pay the required punishment for their sins. But as seen in his *Explanations* he still used Scripture, literally interpreted, to support his statements made regarding the limits of the pope's power in this area.

21. Thus those indulgence preachers are in error who say that a man is absolved from every penalty and saved by papal indulgences.

22. As a matter of fact, the pope remits to souls in purgatory no penalty which, according to canon law, they should have paid in this life.

23. If remission of all penalties whatsoever could be granted to anyone at all, certainly it would be granted only to the most perfect, that is, to very few.

24. For this reason most people are necessarily deceived by that indiscriminate and high-sounding promise of release from penalty.

25. That power which the pope has in general over purgatory corresponds to the power which any bishop or curate has in a particular way in his own diocese or parish.

26. The pope does very well when he grants remission to souls in purgatory, not by the power of the keys, which he does not have, but by way of intercession for them.

Theses twenty through twenty-two speak in particular of Luther's view regarding the limitation of the pope's power. Although, in thesis twenty-one Luther lays the blame at the door of the indulgence salesmen, in essence he is saying that the pope does not possess the power to issue an indulgence that may remove all of the penalties from sin and guarantee salvation to the purchaser. Then, in thesis twenty-two, Luther clearly states one of the limitations placed on the power of the pope based on the canons of the Church itself. This, of course, references back to thesis eight, in which Luther supported his claim, not only from canon law, but also from Romans 7:1-2.

Theses twenty-five and twenty-six introduce a positive view of the pope's power by Luther. However, this power is not exclusive to the pope. Luther will maintain that once the earthly life of an individual has ended and his eternal, spiritual life has begun, the only power the pope has is that of intercessory prayer, as do any of his subordinates; this is the pope's power "in a general way over purgatory." Luther expresses it this way in his *Explanations*:

> The pope has absolutely no authority over purgatory, nor does any other bishop. If, however, he does have some authority, he certainly has only the same kind in which his subordinates also share.
>
> Moreover, this is an authority by which the pope and any Christian who so wishes can intercede, pray for, fast, etc. on behalf of departed souls – the pope in a general way, the bishops in a particular way, and the Christian in an individual way.[40]

In thesis twenty-six, Luther's reference to "the power of the keys" is speaking of the Roman Catholic interpretation of Matthew 16:16-19 from which they derive their doctrine of apostolic succession. When Luther states that the pope does not possess the power of the keys, he is careful to say, "in this case." Luther, at this point, is not denying power to the pope, he is simply limiting it to the realm of temporal life. Luther has already stated that the pope has no more power in the realm of purgatory than any other Christian, So, here he is just clarifying his view in terms of the source of power recognized by the Roman Catholic Church by which the pope governs.

In theses twenty-seven through thirty-five, Luther focuses on the dangers involved in believing the claims made by the indulgence salesmen, dangers which could include eternal damnation.

27. They preach only human doctrines who say that as soon as the money clinks into the money chest, the soul flies out of purgatory.
28. It is certain that when money clinks in the money chest, greed and avarice can be increased; but when the church intercedes, the result is in the hands of God alone.
29. Who knows whether all souls in purgatory wish to be redeemed, since we have exceptions in St. Severinus and St. Paschal, as related in a legend.
30. No one is sure of the integrity of his own contrition, much less of

---

[40] Luther, "Explanations," 31:156-57.

having received plenary remission.

31. The man who actually buys indulgences is as rare as he who is really penitent; indeed, he is exceedingly rare.

32. Those who believe that they can be certain of their salvation because they have indulgence letters will be eternally damned, together with their teachers.

33. Men must especially be on their guard against those who say that the pope's pardons are that inestimable gift of God by which man is reconciled to him.

34. For the graces of indulgences are concerned only with the penalties of sacramental satisfaction established by man.

35. They who teach that contrition is not necessary on the part of those who intend to buy souls out of purgatory or to buy confessional privileges preach unchristian doctrine.

Thesis twenty-seven is a reference to a sales phrase which made Johann Tetzel famous. Nichols' explains,

> Luther refers to Tetzel's marketing jingle. The phrase was rather catchy in German:
>
> *Solbald das Geld in Kasten klingt,*
> *Die Seel' aus dem Fegfeuer springt.*
> As soon as the money in the chest rings (klinks)
> A soul from purgatory springs.[41]

Thesis twenty-nine refers to legends regarding two popes in which they both hoped for more time to be spent in purgatory in order to gain greater glory in heaven. When the Greek verb μετανοέω (*metanoeō*) is translated as "repent," its literal meaning "to change one's mind" is often linked to the act of contrition or remorse for what was done. This is common in Protestantism as well as Roman Catholicism. This is what Luther is addressing in theses thirty and thirty-one where he considers the truly pious Catholic and how indulgences actually work against true piousness in the individual. Luther explained it this way:

---

[41] Luther, in Nichols, *Martin Luther's Ninety-Five Theses*, 30.

Again I speak in their sense in order that they may see the presumptu-
ousness, indeed the contradiction, of their unrestrained preaching.
When they cry that indulgences are profitable for so many people and
yet confess that there are so few who walk the narrow way, they do not
even blush or give attention to what they are saying. But this is not
surprising. They have not assumed the office of teaching contrition
and the narrow way [Matt. 7:14]. Therefore I advance the opinion
that, if only a few are contrite, nevertheless many, indeed everybody
in the whole church could be set free from the punishments of the
canons, as they actually are now, simply by abolishing the canons.[42]

In thesis thirty-four Luther reiterates (now, in relation to the pope's pardons) the point he made in theses five and twenty: the fact that only God
can forgive the guilt for sins. The pope's ability is limited to man-made
canon law and limited to a person's temporal life.

Thesis thirty-five speaks to one of the most deceitful aspects of indulgence sales (from Luther's perspective): the fact that the salesmen were
teaching that no μετάνοια (*metanoia*, repentance), no change of mind, regarding sin was necessary when the individual was buying his soul out of purgatory. In explaining his view on this, Luther reveals that his thought process
is moving away from the Roman Catholic authorized interpretation of
Scripture and moving toward a literal-grammatical hermeneutic. Luther
states,

Indeed, I believe there is a big difference between redeeming souls and
the remission of punishments. In the remissions of punishment one
receives good, but in the redemption of souls one does good. Moreover, the wicked man can receive good, but by no means can he do
good. And the work of the wicked man cannot be pleasing to God if
the man himself is not pleasing to God, as Gen. 4[:4] says: "The Lord
had regard for Abel and his offering." It is contrary to Scripture for
anyone to pity another rather than his own soul, and for anyone to
pluck out the speck from his brother's eye rather than the beam from
his own eye [Matt. 7:3]. And it is altogether contrary to Scripture for
a servant of the devil to redeem a child of God and do this even in the

---

[42] Luther, "Explanations," 31:179.

name of God himself.[43]

In theses thirty-six through forty-one, Luther moves toward a more positive approach stating the benefits possessed by all Christians, the mind-set they should possess, and cautions regarding indulgences.

36. Any truly repentant Christian has a right to full remission of penalty and guilt, even, without indulgence letters.
37. Any true Christian, whether living or dead, participates in all the blessings of Christ and the church; and this is granted him by God, even without indulgence letters.
38. Nevertheless, papal remission and blessing are by no means to be disregarded, for they are, as I have said [Thesis 6], the proclamation of the divine remission.
39. It is very difficult, even for the most learned theologians, at one and the same time to commend to the people the bounty of indulgences and the need of true contrition.
40. A Christian who is truly contrite seeks and loves to pay penalties for his sins; the bounty of indulgences, however, relaxes penalties and causes men to hate them – at least it furnishes occasion for hating them.
41. Papal indulgences must be preached with caution, lest people erroneously think that they are preferable to other good works of love.

In thesis thirty-six, Luther stands against the clear teaching of the Roman Catholic Church, that they can affect the penalty of sin in a Christian's life through indulgences. Then, in thesis thirty-eight, Luther draws a clear distinction between the remission of sin and the remission and participation in the benefits of the church, stating that the benefits of the church are granted, by the pope, because of divine remission (that given by God to true believers). In other words, the pope only rules over and controls those aspects of Christian practice that the Church itself has created.

As previously stated in thesis six, the pope only recognizes the divine remission of guilt given by God to believers. The pope in no way performs,

---

[43] Luther, "Explanations," 31:186–87.

governs, or limits that remission. Thus, in thesis thirty-nine Luther basically declares his difficulty and that of any Bible-based Catholic theologian of his time: How can one emphasize the need for a believer to be sorry for his sins in order to obtain remission from God, when at the same time, that one is supposed to be recommending the purchase of indulgences which are purported to accomplish the same remission, only without the contrition?

In theses forty-two through fifty-one Luther continues his positive theme with a summary of what he believes "Christians should be taught." In his defensive rebuttal to Luther's work, Johann Tetzel adopted this phrase to begin each of his statements.

42. Christians are to be taught that the pope does not intend that the buying of indulgences should in any way be compared with works of mercy.

43. Christians are to be taught that he who gives to the poor or lends to the needy does a better deed than he who buys indulgences.

44. Because love grows by works of love, man thereby becomes better. Man does not, however, become better by means of indulgences but is merely freed from penalties.

45. Christians are to be taught that he who sees a needy man and passes him by, yet gives his money for indulgences, does not buy papal indulgences but God's wrath.

46. Christians are to be taught that the buying of indulgences is a matter of free choice, not commanded.

47. Christians are to be taught that, unless they have more than they need, they must reserve enough for their family needs and by no means squander it on indulgences.

48. Christians are to be taught that the pope, in granting indulgences, needs and thus desires their devout prayer more than their money.

49. Christians are to be taught that papal indulgences are useful only if they do not put their trust in them, but very harmful if they lose their fear of God because of them.

50. Christians are to be taught that if the pope knew the exactions of the indulgence preachers, he would rather that the basilica of St. Peter were burned to ashes than built up with the skin, flesh, and bones of his sheep.

51. Christians are to be taught that the pope would and should wish to give of his own money, even though he had to sell the basilica of St. Peter, to many of those from whom certain hawkers of indulgences cajole money.

Luther addresses a few themes in this section all under the instruction of what should be taught to Christians. Thus, these are not just his own personal thoughts regarding the validity of indulgences, but mandates from a teacher of God's Word regarding that which every Roman Catholic (here described as "Christians"), should know.

Luther's first theme is the superiority of good works over indulgences (theses forty-two through forty-five), ostensibly for the purpose of lessening one's time in purgatory. Next, Luther describes the limited value of indulgences (theses forty-six through forty-nine), since they only affect failures against church canon law and cannot be used for the dead in purgatory.[44] As always, Luther supports his views directly from a literal, grammatical interpretation of Scripture, such as this reasoning for thesis forty-seven:

The Apostle says: "If anyone does not provide for his relatives, and especially for his family, he has disowned the faith and is worse than an unbeliever" [I Tim. 5:8]. But there are many who have neither bread nor proper clothing and yet, led astray by the din and noise of the preachers of indulgences, rob themselves and bring about their own poverty in order to increase the wealth of the indulgence sellers.[45]

Lastly, Luther defends the spiritual focus and intent of the pope. All throughout this work (theses five, nine, twenty-six, forty-one, forty-two), Luther has maintained the innocence of the pope, placing the blame for erroneous teaching on the indulgence salesmen (and, by extension, the writers of the *Summary Instruction*). Here, in theses fifty and fifty-one, Luther continues this view of the pope, imbuing it with a greater humility than was warranted for his current pontiff. Luther based his view on the historic accounts of Saint Ambrose and Saint Polinus of Nola, both of whom made

---

[44] In his *Explanations*, Luther stated, "In my opinion indulgences are the most worthless of all possessions of the church and ought to be granted only to its most worthless members." Luther, "Explanations," 31:207.

[45] Luther, "Explanations," 31:204.

great sacrifices on behalf of others.[46] In theses fifty-two through fifty-five, Luther can be seen magnifying the Word of God as well as the Gospel message.

52. It is vain to trust in salvation by indulgence letters, even though the indulgence commissary, or even the pope, were to offer his soul as security.

53. They are enemies of Christ and the pope who forbid altogether the preaching of the Word of God in order that indulgences may be preached in others.

54. Injury is done the Word of God when, in the same sermon, an equal or larger amount of time is devoted to indulgences than to the Word.

55. It is certainly the pope's sentiment that if indulgences, which are a very insignificant thing, are celebrated with one bell, one procession, and one ceremony, then the gospel, which is the very greatest thing, should be preached with a hundred bells, a hundred processions, a hundred ceremonies.

Luther begins this group of theses by directly contradicting the claims put forth in the official *Summary Instruction* regarding the efficacy of the Peter's Indulgence, thus putting himself in direct opposition to the See of Rome. Thesis fifty-three refers to a common practice of that time period when an indulgence salesman came to town. All of the other churches would be closed so that all of the Roman Catholics in the town could go to the church in which the indulgence was being preached. In thesis fifty-four Luther was actually including himself, since he was a priest who would teach during a church service, but who also had to spend some of that time, on occasion, speaking in support of indulgences which were being sold in his area. Thesis fifty-five speaks of another common practice when the indulgence salesman came to town. Wengert explains,

According to contemporary accounts and pictures, he would have been met at a town's gates by all the important government and church officials, who would have processed to the town's main church

---

[46] Cf. Luther, "Explanations," 31:208.

where the papal coat-of-arms and the papal bull decreeing this indulgence would be prominently displayed, while all the organs and bells in the town's churches sounded. All other preaching would be halted so that the citizenry had opportunity to give full attention to Tetzel and the indulgences he had to offer.[47]

Theses fifty-six through sixty-eight deal with a concept known as the "treasures of the church." Nichols explains this concept:

> The phrase "treasures of the church" refers to the medieval Roman Catholic teaching that the surplus merits of Christ and the saints are kept in a heavenly treasury. This explains why Roman Catholics pray to and appeal to saints, especially Mary. In Luther's day the pope could withdraw from this treasury and apply these excess and unused merits to those who fell short and needed more. The withdrawal of merits usually came by way of financial contributions to the church.[48]

Luther carefully examines these "treasures" to show the error of the Roman Catholic Church in its interpretation of this concept, and then compares the true "treasure" to the false "treasure" of indulgences.

56. The treasures of the church, out of which the pope distributes indulgences, are not sufficiently discussed or known among Christians.
57. That indulgences are not temporal treasures is certainly clear, for many indulgence sellers do not distribute them freely but only gather them.
58. Nor are they the merits of Christ and the saints, for, even without the pope, the latter always work grace for the inner man, and the cross, death, and hell for the outer man.
59. St. Laurence said that the poor of the church were the treasures of the church, but he spoke according to the usage of the word in his own time.
60. Without want of consideration we say that the keys of the church, given by the merits of Christ, are that treasure;

---

[47] Wengert, *Martin Luther's 95 Theses*, 2.
[48] Nichols, *Martin Luther's Ninety-Five Theses*, 36.

61. For it is clear that the pope's power is of itself sufficient for the remission of penalties and cases reserved by himself.
62. The true treasure of the church is the most holy gospel of the glory and grace of God.
63. But this treasure is naturally most odious, for it makes the first to be last [Matt. 20:16].
64. On the other hand, the treasure of indulgences is naturally most acceptable, for it makes the last to be first.
65. Therefore the treasures of the gospel are nets with which one formerly fished for men of wealth.
66. The treasures of indulgences are nets with which one now fishes for the wealth of men.
67. The indulgences which the demagogues acclaim as the greatest graces are actually understood to be such only insofar as they promote gain.
68. They are nevertheless in truth the most insignificant graces when compared with the grace of God and the piety of the cross.

In theses fifty-six through sixty-one Luther analyzes varying views on the "treasures of the church," showing why each view is incorrect. Then, in thesis sixty-two, Luther takes his stand: "the true treasure of the church is the most holy gospel of the glory and grace of God." Notice here Luther's carefully chosen words. First, the treasure is the "most holy gospel," stating that the revelation of the death, burial and resurrection of Jesus Christ is the most valuable treasure given to the church. It is in fact not only the most valuable treasure given to the church, but to all of mankind. One important point to be made here is that in Luther's mind, this position of the church stands in strong contradistinction from Israel. Such a strong distinction between Israel and the church is another bedrock or *sine qua non* of dispensational thought.[49] This then serves as the second core distinctive of dispensational thought evidenced in Luther's *95 Theses*. The first being Luther's appeal to a literal grammatical-historical interpretive method, and the second being the recognition of a strong distinction between Israel and the church.

---

[49] Ryrie, *Dispensationalism*, 47.

Next, Luther clarifies that this "gospel" is directly related to the "glory and grace of God." At this point, the third *sine qua non* of dispensationalism becomes apparent in Luther's thought. The dispensationalist's application of a consistently literal grammatical-historical hermeneutic will result in the primary focus of Scripture being the glory of God, and His resultant grace explains the sacrifice of Christ. Another way of looking at it would be that the true treasure of the church is the "good news" of the glory and grace of God. Once again, the central theme is first the "glory of God," which dispensationalists maintain results from a consistent application of a literal grammatical-historical hermeneutic. Although this was a nascent biblical view for Luther, his words give evidence that he was beginning to adopt this hermeneutic, and along with it, certain derived dispensational convictions which it yields.

On the basis of Luther's revelation in thesis sixty-two, thesis sixty-three points to the sinful carnality of man which makes this good news unattractive. Then he follows this in theses sixty-three through sixty-eight with a description of how indulgences actually play into this carnality, providing solutions for both the Roman Catholic laity and the Roman Catholic Church leadership through the use of money. In explaining his views further, Luther maintains his application of a literal-grammatical use of Scripture in this expansion of thesis sixty-five:

> The Apostle said, "I seek not what is yours but you" [II Cor. 12:14]. And Christ said, "I will make you fishers of men" [Matt. 4:19]. This sweet word directs as it attracts the will; indeed, it makes a man surrender his will to Christ. Hence St. Peter, portrayed as a fisherman in the city [of Rome], says, "For my ship I steer the Church, all the regions of the world are my sea, the Scripture is my net, man is the fish."[50]

Theses sixty-nine through eighty deal with the question of proper oversight of indulgence salesmen by the hierarchy of the Roman Catholic Church.

69. Bishops and curates are bound to admit the commissaries of papal

---

[50] Luther, "Explanations," 31:232–33.

indulgences with all reverence.

70. But they are much more bound to strain their eyes and ears lest these men preach their own dreams instead of what the pope has commissioned.

71. Let him who speaks against the truth concerning papal indulgences be anathema and accursed;

72. But let him who guards against the lust and license of the indulgence preachers be blessed.

73. Just as the pope justly thunders against those who by any means whatsoever contrive harm to the sale of indulgences.

74. But much more does he intend to thunder against those who use indulgences as a pretext to contrive harm to holy love and truth.

75. To consider papal indulgences so great that they could absolve a man even if he had done the impossible and had violated the mother of God is madness.

76. We say on the contrary that papal indulgences cannot remove the very least of venial sins as far as guilt is concerned.

77. To say that even St. Peter, if he were now pope, could not grant greater graces is blasphemy against St. Peter and the pope.

78. We say on the contrary that even the present pope, or any pope whatsoever, has greater graces at his disposal, that is, the gospel, spiritual powers, gifts of healing, etc., as it is written in 1 Cor. 12[:28].

79. To say that the cross emblazoned with the papal coat of arms, and set up by the indulgence preachers, is equal in worth to the cross of Christ is blasphemy.

80. The bishops, curates, and theologians who permit such talk to be spread among the people will have to answer for this.

In the above theses, Luther makes it clear that he believes indulgences to have value and that they should not be impugned. This view was further defined and supported earlier in theses five, six, twenty, twenty-one, and forty-one (for example). According to Wengert, "In later writings, Luther attributes the statements in theses 75, 77, and 79 directly to Johann Tetzel, who categorically denied ever saying these things. See *Against Hanswurst*

(1541), LW 41:231-35."[51] However, even in his defense of what he determined to be the "proper" sale of indulgences, Luther applied the Scriptures in a literal-grammatical manner. For example, in explanation of thesis sixty-nine, Luther pointed to Romans 13:2 seeing it as a reference to the pope as being the "authority" spoken of in this verse. Later, in his explanation of thesis seventy-four, Luther does include secular powers as being part of the "authority" spoken of in Romans 13:1-7.

In theses seventy-eight and seventy-nine, Luther once again asserts the primacy of the gospel and the cross of Christ, as being greater than the blessings promised by indulgences. In further explanation Luther states, "Must the souls who are redeemed by the blood of Christ be entrusted to these men? The cross of Christ gives life to the whole world by the destruction of sin."[52]

Back in thesis seventy-two, Luther stated, "But let him who guards against the lust and license of the indulgence preachers be blessed." Much of this list of theses has concerned itself with the license taken by Tetzel and others regarding their outlandish offers made regarding this indulgence. Such teaching generated many pertinent questions among the laity considering their purchase. Some of these will now be addressed in theses eighty-one through ninety-one.

81. This unbridled preaching of indulgences makes it difficult even for learned men to rescue the reverence which is due the pope from slander or from the shrewd questions of the laity,

82. Such as: "Why does not the pope empty purgatory for the sake of holy love and the dire need of the souls that are there if he redeems an infinite number of souls for the sake of miserable money with which to build a church? The former reasons would be most just; the latter is most trivial."

83. Again, "Why are funeral and anniversary masses for the dead continued and why does he not return or permit the withdrawal of the endowments founded for them, since it is wrong to pray for the redeemed?"

---

[51] Wengert, *Martin Luther's 95 Theses*, 23.
[52] Luther, "Explanations," 31:243.

84. Again, "What is this new piety of God and the pope that for a consideration of money they permit a man who is impious and their enemy to buy out of purgatory the pious soul of a friend of God and do not rather, because of the need of that pious and beloved soul, free it for pure love's sake?"

85. Again, "Why are the penitential canons, long since abrogated and dead in actual fact and through disuse, now satisfied by the granting of indulgences as though they were still alive and in force?"

86. Again, "Why does not the pope, whose wealth is today greater than the wealth of the richest Crassus, build this one basilica of St. Peter with his own money rather than with the money of poor believers?"

87. Again, "What does the pope remit or grant to those who by perfect contrition already have a right to full remission and blessings?"

88. Again, "What greater blessing could come to the church than if the pope were to bestow these remissions and blessings on every believer a hundred times a day, as he now does but once?"

89. "Since the pope seeks the salvation of souls rather than money by his indulgences, why does he suspend the indulgences and pardons previously granted when they have equal efficacy?"

90. To repress these very sharp arguments of the laity by force alone, and not to resolve them by giving reasons, is to expose the church and the pope to the ridicule of their enemies and to make Christians unhappy.

91. If, therefore, indulgences were preached according to the spirit and intention of the pope, all these doubts would be readily resolved. Indeed, they would not exist.

In thesis ninety-one it is once again evident that Luther is holding the pope blameless of all of the abuse being done in his name, yet Luther makes pointed criticism of the pope and his power in theses eighty-six through eighty-nine under the guise of questions from the laity. The question stated in thesis eighty-seven is previously addressed in theses six, thirty-seven and thirty-eight. Thesis eighty-nine is a grave accusation that makes evident the mercenary attitude of Rome. The pope would actually suspend the efficacy of previously purchased indulgences in order to force the laity to purchase the current indulgence on sale. Regarding this, Wengert adds, "This objection was already in the imperial complaint (*gravamina*) of 1511. Both Leo X's bull proclaiming the Peter's Indulgence (31 May 1515) and the *Summary Instruction* did this very thing."[53] Luther himself was most appalled by this action of the pope. In his explanation for this thesis he states:

> This disturbs and displeases me most of all and, I confess, to a great degree, for this suspending of earlier letters and indulgences is the only reason that indulgences have become worthless. I cannot deny that everything which the pope does must be endured, but it grieves me that I cannot prove that what he does is best. Although, if I were to discuss the intention of the pope without becoming involved with his mercenary hirelings, I would say, briefly and with confidence, that one must assume the best about him.[54]

Theses ninety-two through ninety-five serve as Luther's conclusion and summary to his disputation.

92. Away then with all those prophets who say to the people of Christ, "Peace, peace," and there is no peace! [Jer. 6:14]
93. Blessed be all those prophets who say to the people of Christ, "Cross, cross," and there is no cross!
94. Christians should be exhorted to be diligent in following Christ, their head, through penalties, death, and hell;
95. And thus be confident of entering into heaven through many tribulations rather than through the false security of peace [Acts 14:22].

Thesis ninety-two is a direct condemnation of indulgence salesmen who promise "forgiveness through money" without repentance. While thesis ninety-three may be seen as a poetic answer to thesis ninety-two; without explanation it may appear hard to understand. As Wengert reports, Luther gave greater insight into this statement in a letter from 23 June 1516 to Michael Dressel:

---

[53] Wengert, *Martin Luther's 95 Theses*, 25–26.
[54] Luther, "Explanations," 31:250.

Are you ignorant, most honorable father, that God... places his peace in the midst of no peace, that is, in the midst of all trials? . . . Therefore, that person whom no one disturbs does not have peace – on the contrary, this is the peace of the world. Instead, that person whom everyone and everything disturbs has peace and bears all of these things with quiet joy. You are saying with Israel, 'Peace, peace, and there is no peace'; instead say with Christ, 'Cross, cross, and there is no cross.' For as quickly as the cross ceases to be cross so quickly you would say joyfully [with the hymns], 'Blessed cross, among the trees there is none such [as you].'[55]

3.5 Conclusion

Although Luther's spiritual and theological movement toward a new hermeneutical paradigm began some years earlier, the sale of the Peter's Indulgence by Rome moved him to state his disputation in writing. Despite the narrow focus of his topic from the *95 Theses* themselves and, more so, from his *Explanations* published a year later, a nascent form of the dispensationalist's literal grammatical-historical interpretative method can be seen. This hermeneutic, which had been violently suppressed by the developing Roman Catholic Church, came to him from the apostles, through the school at Antioch, and found its way forward through select groups of believers who were condemned as heretics by the established Church. There was also unanticipated support offered by the humanist school of thought developed during the Renaissance period—the principle of seeking out the original evidence and source material for any field of study, rather than depending on current interpretation.

Thus, Luther studied deeply the ancient Hebrew, Aramaic and Greek texts of Scripture. When faced with differences from Roman Catholic doctrine, Luther chose to follow the Scriptures using a literal grammatical-historical hermeneutic which forms the basis of dispensational thought.

The *95 Theses* was just the beginning of Luther's disputation with the Roman Catholic Church and began his journey toward the development of

---

[55] Wengert, *Martin Luther's 95 Theses*, 26.

a more literal, biblical theology. Although the focus of the *95 Theses* is specifically regarding indulgences—their efficacy and sale—Nichols makes this observation regarding Luther's closing thesis: "Luther's closing statement underscores that he does not wholly understand justification by faith. By his own admission it would be another two years before his personal theological breakthrough and his recovery of this essential doctrine."[56]

And although Luther wrote these theses in order to promote discussion and debate on the indulgence topic among German Roman Catholic theologians (Luther did not send his theses to the pope), by the time of his *Explanations* the following year, Luther saw the greater need and wrote the following:

> The church needs a reformation which is not the work of one man, namely, the pope, or of many men, namely the cardinals, both of which the most recent council [Fifth Lateran Council, 1512-1517] has demonstrated, but it is the work of the whole world, indeed it is the work of God alone. However, only God who has created time knows the time for this reformation. In the meantime we cannot deny such manifest wrongs. The power of the keys is abused and enslaved to greed and ambition. The raging abyss has received added impetus. We cannot stop it. "Our iniquities testify against us" (Jer. 14:7), and each man's own word is a burden to him (cf. Gal. 6:5).[57]

---

[56] Nichols, *Martin Luther's Ninety-Five Theses*, 46. Nichols's commenatry aside, the exact date of Martin Luther's "tower experience," that is, his full realization of justification by grace thought faith, is disputed by scholars. Several events and persons are known to have influencd Luther's thoughts on the matter which make plotting a specific moment in time difficult to prove. Dates ranging from 1514-18 have been offered due in large part to Luther not cleary expressing his personal belief in the doctrine until he officially published *Of the Threefold Righteousness of Christ* in 1518. See Carl S. Meyer, "Luther, Martin (1483-1546)," in *The New International Dictionary of the Christian Church*, ed. J. D. Douglas (Grand Rapids, MI: Zondervan, 1978), 609; and, R. W. Heinze, "Luther, Martin (1483-1546)," in *Evangelical Dictionary of Theology*, ed. Walter A. Elwell (Grand Rapids, MI: Baker, 1984), 665-66.

[57] Luther, "Explanations," 31:250.

Bibliography

Boehmer, Heinrich. *Road to Reformation: Martin Luther to the Year 1521.* Philadelphia: Muhlenberg Press, 1946.

Cairns, Earle E. *Christianity through the Centuries.* Grand Rapids, MI: Academie Books, 1981.

Cone, Christopher. *Prolegomena, Introductory Notes on Bible Study and Theological Method.* Ft. Worth, TX: Tyndale Seminary Press, 2007.

Couch, Mal, ed., *Dictionary of Premillennial Theology.* Grand Rapids, MI: Kregel Publications, 1996.

Douglas, J. D., ed., *The New International Dictionary of the Christian Church.* Grand Rapids, MI: Zondervan, 1978.

Godfrey, W. Robert. *Reformation Sketches: Insights into Luther, Calvin, and the Confessions.* Phillipsburg, NJ: P&R Publishing, 2003.

Heinze, R. W. "Luther, Martin (1483–1546)." In *Evangelical Dictionary of Theology*, edited by Walter A. Elwell, 665–667. Grand Rapids, MI: Baker, 1984.

Luther, Martin. "Explanations of the Ninety-Five Theses." In *Luther's Works*, edited by Helmut T. Lehmann. Vol. 31, *Career of the Reformer I*, edited by Harold J. Grimm, translated by Carl W. Folkemer, 77–253. Philadelphia, PA: Muhlenberg, 1958.

———. *Martin Luther's Ninety-Five Theses.* Edited by Stephen J. Nichols. Phillipsburg, P&R Publishing, 2002.

McGrath, Alister E. *Reformation Thought: An Introduction.* Oxford, UK: Blackwell, 1993.

Meyer, Carl S. "Luther, Martin (1483–1546)." In *The New International Dictionary of the Christian Church*, edited by J. D. Douglas, 609–611. Grand Rapids, MI: Zondervan, 1978.

Ryrie, Charles C. *Dispensationalism.* Rev. and exp. ed. 1995. Reprint, Chicago, IL: Moody Publishers, 2007.

Wengert, Timothy J. *Martin Luther's 95 Theses: With Introduction, Commentary, and Study Guide*. Minneapolis, MN: Fortress Press, 2015.

4

JOHN NELSON DARBY:
The Unknown and Well Known
Nineteenth Century Irish Reformer

James I. Fazio
Southern California Seminary

4.0 Introduction

Five hundred years after Martin Luther first posted his *95 Theses* in Wittenberg, Germany, Protestants across the globe look back upon that contentious act as the event which profoundly changed not only the Christian church, but the entire world. Nevertheless, Christians today are not so naïve as to think that the Reformation occurred in a single day, nor do they suppose that it can be attributed to a solitary person, let alone a single act. Without question, the ideas which fueled the Reformation began much earlier than October 31, 1517. In previous centuries, Peter Waldo (c. 1140–c. 1205), John Wycliffe (c. 1320s–1384) and Jan Hus (1369–1415) all preached against Roman Catholic abuses, including transubstantiation, purgatory, and indulgences.[1] Each of these men were condemned as heretics and enemies of the church, though centuries later, their ideas were carried forward in the Protestant Reformation.

---

[1] Hus wrote his *Six Errors*, in which he criticized the corruption of the clergy, and fixed it to the door of his church. Afterward, on February 22, 1418, these were condemned in Council and by the Bulls *Inter Cunctas* and *In eminentis*. Nevertheless, Hus' ideas would go on to influence the German Reformer a century later.

Just as the Reformation did not begin with the German reformer, so also it did not end with him. In fact, the Reformation continued long after the death of both Martin Luther (d. 1546) and John Calvin (d. 1564). No single date is agreed upon by historians as the end of the Reformation, though several have been offered. Some have pointed to the Peace of West-phalia, wherein a series of treaties ended the Thirty Years War (1618–1648) and allowed Calvinism to be freely exercised. Others have placed it in the mid-eighteenth century, around the time of the First Great Awakening (1730–1755). However, some have maintained that the Reformation has never truly ended; rather it continues on to the present day.

This chapter will suggest that the ideas which began to coalesce in the minds of the sixteenth century reformers continued into the centuries that followed, and were in fact most pronounced in the far-reaching ministry of one who may well be among the most overlooked and underappreciated figures in church history: the unknown and well known nineteenth century Irish reformer, John Nelson Darby (1800–1882).

4.0.1 The Second Reformation in Ireland

Skeptical readers may balk at the idea that an Irishman who lived some two to three hundred years after the German and Swiss Reformation launched should be referred to as a reformer. This chapter will aim to demonstrate that his ideas were, in the main, right in line with advancing Reformation principles. Nevertheless, it should be disclosed that the notion of John Nelson Darby as an eighteenth century Irish reformer is not some novel idea contrived in the mind of the author. The period and location in question—Ireland in the 1820s—has been remembered in history as the "Second Reformation."[2] In effect, this term refers to a period of about fifty years—1820s–1860s—when Ireland was stricken with poverty and famine. By capitalizing on the harsh conditions confronting the Irish peasants, zealous Protestants, sometimes referred to as "Biblicals" or "New Reformers" made in-roads converting the beleaguered Roman Catholic population.[3]

---

[2] For a more detailed discussion on this point, see Irene Whelan, *The Bible War in Ireland: The 'Second Reformation' and the Polarization of Protestant-Catholic Relations, 1800–1840* (Madison, WI: University of Wisconsin Press, 2005).

[3] See also, Desmond Brown, *Protestant Crusade in Ireland, 1800–70: A Study of*

This period of Irish history directly corresponds to the years in which Darby served as a clergyman and Protestant Dissenter of the Established State Church of Ireland. Moreover, Darby's seemingly effective ministry converting Catholics, his vehement criticisms of Roman Catholicism, as well as his dissenting stance which put him in constant tension with the mainline position of "moderates" within the Church of Ireland, all serve to indicate that John Nelson Darby on all accounts fits the description of a "New Reformer" within the "Second Reformation." Despite all this, the suggestion put forth in this chapter is that Darby stood in a tradition much more akin to the German reformer Martin Luther than most realize. This chapter will endeavor to make this connection.

4.1 Unknown and Well Known

In a recently released book by distinguished historian Donald Akenson, the author leads off with the following question: "If you were asked to name, in order, the four most influential (post-biblical) figures in the formation of present-day Protestantism, who would they be? The primary bone of contention would be for number 1: Martin Luther or John Calvin? Almost certainly number 3 would be John Wesley."[4] Who then, does Akenson propose as a candidate for the fourth most influential figure of present-day Protestantism? None other than John Nelson Darby.

So who is John Nelson Darby? Many readers may be entirely unacquainted with the name, while others may have some vague familiarity, but would be hard-pressed to supply any kind of concrete association with which to affix it. A third group may even recognize the name as one which some voice from the past may have even cautioned against. So, who exactly is this unknown figure, and how is it that one so significant to Protestant thought, today, could be so shrouded in mystery?

A quick consultation with the *Dictionary of Major Biblical Interpreters* may be helpful in answering this question—though only partially. That is to say that it will help to answer why he is so shrouded in mystery, but it will

---

Protestant-Catholic Relations between the Act of Union Disestablishment (Toronto, ON: University of Toronto Press, 1978).

[4] Donald Harman Akenson, *Discovering the End of Time: Irish Evangelicals in the Age of Daniel O'Connell* (Chicago, IL: McGill-Queen's University Press, 2016), 1.

not help to inform the reader as to who he is, because his name is not found among the hundreds of entries of "major biblical interpreters" which are the subject of that book.[5] How is it that someone who could be—at least in one historian's estimation—among the top four influential figures in the formation of present-day Protestantism be entirely overlooked in a 1106 page dictionary covering hundreds of major biblical interpreters? The aim of this chapter is to resolve the paradox of how the Irish reformer of the nineteenth century can be simultaneously unknown and well known.

4.1.1 Darby's Early Years and Conversion

Born on November 18, 1800, John Nelson Darby was the youngest son and second to last child in a family of nine children. His father, John Darby Sr., was a wealthy Irishman who had moved to England, where he operated a successful business in London. In 1784, he married Miss. Anne Vaughan, a native of England and daughter to a rich merchant who owned plantations in the New World.

At age 14, Darby graduated from Westminster in England, and moved to Ireland to attend Trinity College in Dublin. He attended there from 1815 to 1819. In 1819, upon finishing college, he began studying law at King's Inn before transferring to Lincoln's Inn, where he completed his studies. On January 21, 1822, Darby was called to the Irish Bar, though he never professionally practiced law. It so happened that during that time (1820–1821), his life trajectory changed—Darby was eternally impacted by the Gospel of Jesus Christ.[6] It is uncertain whether he was influenced by his

---

[5] It should be observed that Darby's name is buried among a handful of other entries, including F. F. Bruce, where it references: "the New Translation of John Nelson Darby." W. W. Gasque, "Bruce, F(redrick) F(yvie) (1910–1991)," in *Dictionary of Major Biblical Interpreters*, ed. Donald K. McKim (Downers Grove, IL: InterVarsity Press, 2007), 237–42. Later in that volume, in an entry on C. I. Scofield, Darby's name is mentioned in passing: "The anthropological distinction of Jew, Gentile, and the church of God, involving a heavenly (church) and earthly (Jew) dichotomy of their character and destiny, characterizes Scofield's thought, echoing J.N. Darby." S. R. Spencer, "Scofield, C(yrus), I. (1845–1921)," in *Dictionary of Major Biblical Interpreters*, ed. Donald K. McKim (Downers Grove, IL: InterVarsity Press, 2007), 906–10.

[6] There is some debate as to when exactly this event took place. Looking back on his conversion some years later, Darby wrote in the marginal notes of his Greek New

older brother, Christopher Lovett, who was, himself, a clergyman with the Church of Ireland, or through his relationship with the local bishop Rev. Robert Daly, whom he had interacted with while attending Trinity College. However, it was not likely due to any single person or act.[7] Still, the young Irishman did not immediately find peace, but continued to wrestle with the Scriptures in the years that followed,[8] spending a good deal of time in Psalm 88, in particular.[9]

Despite the time and expense that went into his legal education, rather than practice law, Darby decided to follow in the footsteps of his older brother, Christopher Lovett; he entered vocational ministry as a clergyman for the Established Church of Ireland.[10] Ironically, a dear friend of his later life by the name of William Kelly remarked: "[Darby] used to say that three classes, from their antecedents, are apt to make bad brothers; clergymen, lawyers, and officers. He himself was a brilliant exception, though a lawyer first, and a clergyman afterward."[11] On August 7, 1825, Darby was ordained as a deacon in the Calary District. He was evidently a good minister, as within half a year's time he was ordained a priest in Christ Church Cathedral, Dublin, on Sunday, February 19, 1826.

Testament next to 2 Timothy 3: "[I] loved Christ, I have no doubt sincerely and growingly since June or July, 1820, or 1821, I forget which." Max S. Weremchuk, *John Nelson Darby: A Biography* (Neptune, NJ: Loizeaux Brothers, 1992), 204.

[7] Weremchuk has concluded: "Darby's conversion took place, as he himself testified, through the reading of God's Word alone and not with the help of any man." Weremchuk, *John Nelson Darby*, 34.

[8] In his own words, looking back on this time of his life, Darby wrote: "experience has to be passed through after conversion. In my own case, I went through deep exercise of soul before there was a trace of peace, and it was not till after six or seven years that I was delivered." John Nelson Darby, *Letters of J. N. D.*, ed. William Kelly, vol. 2, *1868–1879* (London: Stow Hill Bible and Tract Depot, n.d.), 310.

[9] Concerning this, one biographer wrote: "Mr. Darby said that for these seven years he practically lived in the 88th Psalm, his only ray of light being in the opening words, 'O Lord God of my salvation.'" W. G. Turner, *Unknown and Well Known: A Biography of John Nelson Darby*, ed. E. N. Cross (London: Chapter Two, 2006), 17.

[10] Darby had four surviving brothers, three of whom followed their father's path as secular businessmen; whereas, Christopher Lovett and John Nelson entered the ministry in 1817 and 1825 respectively. Akenson, *Discovering the End of Time*, 127.

[11] Weremchuk, *John Nelson Darby*, 196.

4.1.2 Darby's Ministry as a Clergyman

The Calary district, in which Darby carried out his duties as a minister of the Church of Ireland, was known primarily for two things: poverty[12] and Roman Catholicism.[13] It's been reported that among these two populations, Darby's ministry was effective. Darby assumed the life of an ascetic and was embraced as a true friend to the poor, being himself often mistaken for one, on account of his meager diet and humble appearance.[14] Darby took his ministry among the poor seriously, and was careful not to appear in any form more advantaged than they—despite hailing from a family of the upper-class gentry. In one account retold by W. Blair Neatby, Darby reported that he: "fasted in Lent so as to be weak in body at the end of it; ate no meat on week-days—nothing till evening on Wednesdays, Fridays, and Saturdays, then a little bread, or nothing; observed strictly the weekly fasts too."[15] Externally, this served his ministry well, currying him favor with the local Roman Catholics. Speaking to this point, one biographer has reported:

> All this served to give his frame the appearance of a monk of La Trappe, so much had it been wasted away...One can be sure that such a man greatly excited the poor Romanists in the area, who looked upon him as a genuine saint of the ancient breed. The stamp of heaven seemed clear to them in this frame so wasted by austerity, so superior to worldly pomp—in this man who shared in all their needs.[16]

---

[12] "J. C. Philpot, who was in the same area for a short time, wrote of having 'seen and talked with the poor peasants in their smoky, miserable cabins, and been almost horrified by the spectacle of Irish misery.'" Weremchuk, *John Nelson Darby*, 42.

[13] Calary at that time was reported as "containing between 2,500 and 2,800 souls, of whom slightly more than 600 were Protestants [thus, the remainder would have been Catholic]" Akenson, *Discovering the End of Time*, 41.

[14] "[Darby] endeared himself to the poor by his sympathy and devotedness...Every evening almost he was found to be teaching the peasantry in the cabins scattered amid the bogs in the remote country outskirts of the wide country parish he served, seldom returning to his own humble lodging before midnight." Turner, *Unknown and Well Known*, 18–19.

[15] William Blair Neatby, *A History of the Plymouth Brethren* (London: Hodder and Stoughton, 1901), 14.

[16] Weremchuk, *John Nelson Darby*, 42.

Darby's ministry among the impoverished Catholics in Calary at that time was reportedly quite effective. It has been repeated by Darby and others that during that period of Irish history, often referred to as "the Second Reformation," Catholics were converting to Protestantism in droves.[17] Brethren biographer Marion Field has attributed at least some of Darby's effectiveness to the fact that, "Darby was a superb linguist and he preached to the villagers in Gaelic, their native language; this pleased them as the Irish Roman Catholic priests suppressed Gaelic and insisted that English should be spoken."[18]

However, Darby was not able to maintain this feverish pace for long, as he suffered a debilitating injury while riding on horseback in October of 1827.[19] Biographers have suggested that Darby was flung down from his horse, though this may have been slightly mythologized—perhaps as a parallel of Luther's startling conversion story.[20] At any rate, his recovery lasted for a number of months, during which time he clung to his Scriptures, giving special attention to the early church as revealed in the Book of Acts.[21]

---

[17] Darby reported that "Roman Catholics were passing over to Protestantism many hundreds in the week." John Nelson Darby, *Collected Writings of J. N. Darby*, ed. William Kelly, vol. 20, *Ecclesiastical No. 4* (London: Stow Hill Bible and Tract Depot, n.d.), 288. Elsewhere, William Kelly reported the number to be as high as "600 to 800 a week." John Nelson Darby, *Collected Writings of J. N. Darby*, ed. William Kelly, vol. 1, *Ecclesiastical No. 1* (London: Stow Hill Bible and Tract Depot, n.d.), 1. However, these numbers were likely exaggerated and should by no means be attributed to Darby's direct ministry, as the entire population of Calary at the time was reported to contain no more than 2,533 inhabitants, all together. Samuel Lewis, *A Topographical Dictionary of Ireland* (London: S. Lewis, 1837), 1:242.

[18] Marion Field, *John Nelson Darby: Prophetic Pioneer* (Godalming, Surrey: Highland Books, 2008), 32. Akenson, however, has cautiously questioned the reliability of this claim.

[19] Weremchuk, *John Nelson Darby*, 47.

[20] Some have painted a dramatic image whereby Darby was flung from his horse when it shied, violently. Field, *John Nelson Darby*, 39. Weremchuk, *John Nelson Darby*, 47. Turner, *Unknown and Well Known*, 19. However, Akenson has offered a more modest and likely account, whereby Darby's leg was smashed against a doorpost when his horse eagerly bolted to return to the inside of its stable. Akenson, *Discovering the End of Time*, 228.

[21] Though he may well have been influenced by his reading of Thomas Scott's

Darby's discontentment with the state of the church grew, as he longed for a church experience that matched what he found modelled in the pages of Scripture.[22]

Not long afterwards, Darby had taken up the pen to direct a private concern to the Archbishop of Dublin and to other fellow members of the Anglican clergy who had affixed their name to a petition to the state to afford Protestants certain protections.[23] In this letter, Darby outlined the distinct domains of the church and the state and argued that it was impossible for the Christian minister to claim protection from the state and remain an unshackled servant of Jesus Christ. The Archbishop and other members of the clergy were not sympathetic to Darby's concerns, which only further increased the tension between Darby's perspective of the Church and the majority position of those who maintained governance in the Established Church.

4.1.3 The Pathway of Dissent

Darby rose from his sickbed, with a renewed vision of the church, as well as of his own position with respect to it. He had no intention at that time of renouncing his association with the Church of Ireland, but rather continued down a path that would ride the fringe of the mainstream channels of the Established Church as a Protestant Dissenter. Although Darby would later become known as the founder of the Plymouth Brethren—also referred to as Darbyism—he was not in actuality pioneering new territory.

Essays on the Most Important Subjects in Religion at this time, if the marginal notes written in his Greek New Testament next to 2 Timothy 3 are rightly understood: "I think Scott's essays gave a strong determination to my thoughts at one time, while my mind was working upon it."

[22] Later, looking back on this period, Darby wrote: "The careful reading of the Acts afforded me a practical picture of the early church, which made me feel deeply the contrast with its actual present state, though still as ever, beloved by God." John Nelson Darby, *Letters of J. N. D.*, ed. William Kelly, vol. 3, *1879–1882* (London: Stow Hill Bible and Tract Depot, n.d.), 298.

[23] Many years later, this letter was published under the title: "Considerations Addressed to the Archbishop of Dublin and the Clergy who Signed the Petition to the House of Commons for Protection," in *Collected Writings of J. N. Darby*, ed. William Kelly, vol. 1, *Ecclesiastical No. 1* (London: Stow Hill Bible and Tract Depot, n.d.), 1–19.

Decades earlier, a number of disenfranchised Anglicans had pursued a similar path by seceding from the Established Church in a course not very dissimilar from Darby's. In his book *Anglican Evangelicals*, historian Greyson Carter has taken note:

> As early as 1794, Alderman Hutton opened his home in Luson Street, Dublin, one evening a week, 'wishing to afford the fashionable folk in the south portion of the city an opportunity of hearing the Gospel'...Around the same time, Wilmott House, a large family home outside Dublin, was opened to preachers from the Established Church, the Methodists, the Moravians, and other evangelical bodies. The Scottish evangelical James Alexander Haldane, who visited Dublin in 1804, was a first-hand witness to this Evangelical effervescence. In his memoir we find mention of several small religious gatherings meeting at this time throughout the city closed to those not sharing their particular views and receiving the Lord's Supper at an hour when it was not publicly administered in the parish churches. Impressed by the effectiveness of this development, Haldane exported it back to Scotland where he undertook to establish a similar movement.[24]

"House meetings" or "drawing-room meetings," as they came to be called, crept-up all across the British Isles, but nowhere were they more pronounced than in Ireland. The purpose of these meetings was to provide a place for like-minded believers from diverse Protestant denominations to meet together for Bible-reading and for the breaking of bread around the Lord's Table. This may seem a strange practice to today's readers—seeing as how this is generally the purpose of the gathering of local churches. However, in the days of these early Protestant dissenters, this was not the case. The Church of England/Ireland at that time was a State church, and as such, its population consisted of the entirety of the population, whether saved or unsaved.

British historian David Bebbington describes this problem well in his book *Evangelicalism in Modern Britain*: "the Church of England was intertwined with the state. The monarch was the supreme head of the church.

---

[24] Grayson Carter, *Anglican Evangelicals: Protestant Secessions from the Via Media, c. 1800–1850* (Eugene, OR: Wipf and Stock, 2001), 197.

Theoretically, all his subjects in England and Wales belonged to it. The bishops of the Church of England sat at the right in the House of Lords. Parliament exercised as much authority in spiritual matters as in temporal affairs."[25] For this reason, frustrated Protestants who desired something more than a social club had to look outside the church (or rather, they looked for a remnant from within) to form a nucleus of saints with which to gather, on common ground.

More than thirty years before Darby's discontentment led him to break bread with a few brothers, eventually leading to the formation of "the Darbyites," another Trinity College alumnus, Thomas Kelly, preceded him. Kelly, too, was a lawyer, turned-Anglican clergy, turned-Protestant Dissenter. Kelly seceded from the Church of Ireland as early as 1803. Those who met in the simple house-meetings which he set-up became known as "the Kellyites."[26] Within a year of Kelly's secession, a fellow clergyman by the name of John Walker followed suit. John Walker, the sometimes-friend, and other-times, rival of Kelly, was of a feistier disposition. Whereas Kelly did not allow his secession from the Established church prevent him from maintaining fellowship with those believers who remained within,[27] Walker took a decidedly different approach. When Walker seceded from the Established Church in 1804, he formally announced his resignation of fellowship as well. The house-meetings that followed lead to the formation of "the Walkerites," who were chiefly remembered as separatists of the most divisive manner.[28] Over the course of time, Darby's orientation toward ministry, and that of "the Darbyites" came to reflect the positions of both of the groups mentioned above.

None of this is intended to take away from Darby's contribution to the development of Protestantism. Rather, it is intended to show that such sweeping changes do not occur in a vacuum, in a single moment in time, or on account of a single human agent. Nevertheless, like Luther before him, Darby was afforded a platform that he was able to effectively utilize in order

---

[25] David W. Bebbington, *Evangelicalism in Modern Britain: A History from the 1730s to the 1980s* (New York: Routledge, 1989), 17.

[26] Carter, *Anglican Evangelicals*, 72–73.

[27] Ibid., 75.

[28] Ibid., 86–87.

to bring about sweeping reform within the Protestant church.

4.1.4 Darby's Effort to Reform from Within

Against this backdrop, in 1828, Darby took up the pen a second time, but this time he determined to address a broader audience than before—as many as had an ear to hear. Darby's first public tract was published: "Considerations on the Nature and Unity of the Church of Christ."[29] In it, Darby advocated not for ecumenism, but for the simple gathering together of redeemed brothers and sisters as one in Christ. Additionally, he strongly condemned the fracturing of the saints that results from denominationalism as anti-Christian.

If that did not do enough to stir up controversy among members within his own denomination, then surely the next tract that he released later that year could not go unnoticed. Darby's second controversial publication intended for public dissemination bore the condemnatory title: "The Notion of a Clergyman: Dispensationally the Sin Against the Holy Ghost."[30] In it, Darby asserted that the substitution of a humanly appointed office in place of the divinely appointed church of God results in the following: (1) it assumes the authority of God, (2) it undermines the appointment of Christ, and (3) it must therefore be concluded that it despises the ministry of the Holy Spirit.

It should be noted at this point that each of these three publications of Darby was produced while he was still a functioning clergyman within the Established Church. As such, they should be regarded as sincere efforts toward reform, rather than an aim to tear down from a position of opposition. In this regard, Darby's writings up to this point could be viewed in some ways as similar to Luther's nailing of the 95 *Theses* to the doors of Wittenberg. They were presented for public discourse among as many as might be inclined to ponder the suitability of the emperor's new clothes.

---

[29] John Nelson Darby, "Considerations on the Nature and Unity of the Church of Christ," in *Collected Writings of J. N. Darby*, ed. William Kelly, vol. 1, *Ecclesiastical No. 1* (London: Stow Hill Bible and Tract Depot, n.d.), 20–35.

[30] John Nelson Darby, "The Notion of a Clergyman: Dispensationally the Sin Against the Holy Ghost," in *Collected Writings of J. N. Darby*, ed. William Kelly, vol. 1, *Ecclesiastical No. 1* (London: Stow Hill Bible and Tract Depot, n.d.), 36–51.

Just as in Luther's case, the goal was not to oppose the Established Church, but rather to correct its course from within.

4.1.5 The Beginnings of the Brethren

Darby followed a path similar to the Irish Protestant dissenters spoken of above. In the winter of 1827–28, he began to meet with four other men outside of the Established Church—J. G. Bellet, Dr. Cronin, Mr. Hutchinson, and Mr. Brooke—for the purpose of mutual fellowship in the breaking of bread. Due to the prominence of these men, and the respected positions which each one held, others began to take notice. In time, more were added, so that before long, Mr. Hutchinson's home proved to be an unsuitable meeting place for the number that had amassed on Sunday mornings.

Nevertheless, Darby did not renounce his association with the Church of Ireland. Even after writing the two polemic tracts mentioned above, he took up the pen in 1831 in an effort to openly defend the historic Reformed position of the church against Arminian heterodoxy. He did this by responding to remarks from the Regius Professor of Divinity at Oxford, Edward Burton, who had issued an official university statement affirming Arminian principles. Burton had done so as a reply to a public sermon preached earlier by Henry Bulteel who, according to Mark Stevenson, "boldly rebuked the Established Church for its departure from the Calvinism of The Thirty Nine Articles."[31] Darby argued vigorously from the writings of the Professors at Cambridge and Oxford, and others from the sixteenth century, defending Calvinism by demonstrating that the mainstream Protestant doctrine at the time of the reformers was pronouncedly in agreement with the position of

---

[31] Mark R. Stevenson, *The Doctrines of Grace in an Unexpected Place: Calvinistic Soteriology in Nineteenth-Century Brethren Thought* (Eugene, OR: Pickwick, 2017), 119.

John Calvin.[32] In his refutation, Darby affirmed predestination and effectual calling,[33] insisting that these were the main Protestant positions during the sixteenth century.[34] Moreover, Darby affirmed the reformers' view of the depravity of man appealing to support from Luther's famous book: *Bondage of the Will*.[35]

The significance of this point is that Darby was an equal opportunity offender. He had little regard for whom he might offend by his writings, nor did he consistently target the same audience. In fact, during the period between writing "The Notion of a Clergyman" and "The Doctrine of the Church of England," Darby took up the pen to refute the positions of fellow premillennialists, with whose interpretation of prophetic language he begged to differ.[36]

Darby has been characterized by some as a curmudgeon who loved nothing more than to stir up controversy with anyone unfortunate enough to fall in his crosshairs. However, as one biographer has pointed out: "this judgment is not quite fair, since for him the important thing was the error, and not the person who had to be dealt with."[37] Neither was it his custom

---

[32] This historical fact is in complete contrast to John Gerstner's and R. C. Sproul's portrayal of dispensationalism as having only "spurious" ties to Calvinism. See John H. Gerstner, *Wrongly Dividing the Word of Truth: A Critique of Dispensationalism* (Morgan, PA: Soli Deo Gloria, 2000), ix-xi, 115-67, 244-66; and R. C. Sproul, *What is Reformed Theology: Understanding the Basics* (Grand Rapids, MI: Baker, 1997), 192-95.

[33] John Nelson Darby, "The Doctrine of the Church of England at the Time of the Reformation Itself, of Scripture, and of the Church of Rome, Briefly Compared with the Remarks of the Regius Professor of Divinity," in *Collected Writings of J. N. Darby*, ed. William Kelly, vol. 3, *Doctrinal No. 1* (London: Stow Hill Bible and Tract Depot, n.d.), 3.

[34] Ibid., 4-19.

[35] Ibid., 26-27; cf. Stevenson, *Doctrines of Grace*, 74-80.

[36] John Nelson Darby, "Reflections upon the Prophetic Inquiry and the Views Advanced in It," in *Collected Writings of J. N. Darby*, ed. William Kelly, vol. 2, *Prophetic No. 1* (London: Stow Hill Bible and Tract Depot, n.d.), 1-31. Also, John Nelson Darby, "On 'Days' Signifying 'Years' in Prophetic Language," in *Collected Writings of J. N. Darby*, ed. William Kelly, vol. 2, *Prophetic No. 1* (London: Stow Hill Bible and Tract Depot, n.d.), 32-42.

[37] Weremchuk, *John Nelson Darby*, 182.

to prolong a matter, but rather to expose the error and move on.[38] However, Darby possessed the tenacity common to so many of the reformers, to take a stand for the truth, as he understood it, despite the threat of conflict or controversy.

In just over one year from their first gathering, a man by the name of Mr. Parnell (who sometime later took on the name Lord Congleton) hired a large auction room for the Brethren's use on Sundays for the Lord's Table. Darby persisted in sharing his unique insight of the Scriptures with those to whom he ministered. This led to the publishing of more pamphlets: "Separation from Evil, God's Principle of Unity," "Grace, the Power and Unity of Gathering," "Ecclesiastical Independency," "Churches and the Church," and other such works, whose primary concern centered on the church. Up to this point, prophecy and eschatology were still developing issues for Darby, and not one of primary significance to him, as is evidenced by the titles and subject matters of so many of his publications up to this point. Indeed, this is noteworthy considering modern critics of Darby virtually ignore the spectrum of his theology choosing rather to focus solely on his eschatology or systematizing of dispensationalism.[39]

The main principles which distinguished these early Brethren were surprisingly not very dissimilar from those which are commonly held by Evangelicals today: (1) they appealed to the authority of Scripture, being primarily interpreted through a literalistic reading of the biblical text; (2) they believed that the church was properly understood as a spiritual body defined by the regeneration of the Holy Spirit, rather than by some external-temporal citizenship; (3) they disparaged denominationalism as generally factional and divisive among members of the church whom Christ has united by His Spirit; and, (4) they shared an expectation concerning the coming of Christ and the fulfillment of apocalyptic prophecy that was futuristic, as opposed to the amillennial expectations that were common to

---

[38] In his own words he expressed the following words in a letter dated 1863: "I have written enough in a controversial shape, because the truth is fully out. For disputation I have no taste." John Nelson Darby, *Letters of J. N. D.*, ed. William Kelly, vol. 1, *1832–1868* (London: Stow Hill Bible and Tract Depot, n.d.), 348.

[39] E.g., Millard J. Erickson, *Christian Theology*, 2nd ed. (Grand Rapids, MI: Baker, 2007), 1168; Gerstner, *Wrongly Dividing*, 13, 22.

the Catholic Church—and which had been more-or-less uncritically inherited by the first generation of protestants who broke with her, including Lutherans, Anglicans, etc.

4.1.6 Developing Emphasis on Biblical Prophecy

In 1831, a widow of considerable means, by the name of Lady Theodosia Powerscourt, opened her palatial estate to the Irish Evangelicals who had been meeting in various capacities throughout the surrounding area. The custom was an emerging one, as she had seen it modeled in Surrey, England, at the estate of Henry Drummond in 1826.[40] Lady Powerscourt had long maintained a robust interest in biblical prophecy and was eager to provide a venue where local expositors could gather with the intended purpose of discussing their understanding of unfulfilled prophetic events. So, in October of 1831, Lady Powerscourt decided to bring this tradition to Ireland, with the help of her good friend, the local Anglican bishop, Rev. Robert Daly, who chaired the event.[41]

The response to this conference met, if not exceeded, Lady Powerscourt's expectations. It had no doubt been her intention to make an annual tradition of this from the start; and so it came as little surprise when in the following year, Lady Powerscourt opened her estate again to local Protestant biblical interpreters. Thus, began the tradition of the Irish Prophecy Conferences, which continued in the years that followed.[42] During these years, Darby's attention turned toward prophecy, as he became a primary force in the successive conferences. These meetings provided a platform for Darby to discuss a plethora of ideas related to the unfulfilled prophecies of the Bible, with like-minded—and some not so like-minded—individuals.[43]

---

[40] Field, *John Nelson Darby*, 90–93.

[41] Akenson, *Discovering the End of Time*, 382.

[42] The following year (1833) Lady Powerscourt hosted the conference at her estate for the final time, before Dublin became the host-site for the 1834–1836 conferences. Akenson, *Discovering the End of Time*, 379.

[43] To say that conflict erupted in those meetings would be an understatement. The Powerscourt Conferences became something of a colosseum for rhetorical repartee. The agenda did not provide a list of speakers, but rather a list of questions/topics to be discussed among any/all in attendance. Rev. Robert Daly chaired the first two

One recurring theme in some of those meetings centered on the place of the sign gifts in the church, which had begun emerging in some of the house-gatherings in England. Edward Irving, who had been a major player in the early Drummond Prophecy Conferences in Albury, became known for his charismatic preaching. One historian has described Irving as: "tall and handsome, authoritarian, and with a powerful gift for oratory, he possessed an intense pulpit passion."[44] Irving's passion excited both the minds and the hearts of the Scottish and English women who listened to him, some of whom responded by breaking out in ecstatic utterances in response to his passionate preaching.[45] Irving did not condemn this behavior, and in time, it followed him, until "the Irvingites" became known for their demonstrative, ecstatic and indistinguishable "prayer-language" or "tongues-speaking" in their house meetings, in addition to other sign-gifts which served to signify that the end of the world had come to Ireland.

Word of these manifestations had piqued Darby's attention, so that in 1830 he traveled to Scotland to investigate the matter first-hand. He walked away from the experience not the least bit impressed by what he saw, and chalked it up to excessive emotionalism, for which he had no particular fondness.[46] Subsequently, he was well-prepared to tackle the issue when it arose in the Powerscourt conference of 1832, and several Irvingites were present for the discussion.[47]

Ultimately, the topic of the sign-gifts in the church was just one small matter in the overall schedule of the Powerscourt Conferences. Others included the future restoration of Israel, the interpretation of prophetic years, such as those presented in Daniel and Revelation, the nature of the rapture of the saints, and the character of the future millennium on the earth. The common thread that all of these topics centered on was the premillennial

---

meetings, but the conflict became too great for him. He stepped out after the second Powerscourt Conference, and did not return to chair the third one, even though he still served as Bishop and remained a close friend to Lady Powerscourt, in whose home all three conferences were held. Akenson, *Discovering the End of Time*, 410–14.

[44] Carter, *Anglican Evangelicals*, 172.
[45] Akenson, *Discovering the End of Time*, 403.
[46] Ibid., 403.
[47] Ibid., 405.

return of Christ, which was generally assumed by all who attended—despite that this was not the official position of the Anglican Church.[48] However, Grayson Carter put it well when he said, "perhaps the most salient feature of the Irish prophetic conferences was the dominance and theological dogmatism of John Nelson Darby."[49]

In the years that followed, Darby's involvement in the conferences increased, along with the development of his dispensational view of the Scriptures, which regarded Israel and the church as two distinct peoples of God, each with their own respective programs and prophetic timetables. By the time of the last conference in 1836, Darby had worked out a fairly robust understanding of the outworking of the end-times, complete with a pretribulation rapture of the church, followed by a literal seven-year tribulation period on earth, culminating in a literal one-thousand-year reign of Christ on the earth. This scheme is generally recognized today by the term dispensational-premillennialism—a system which Darby played an indispensable role in shaping.

4.2 Darby's Legacy of Dispensational-Premillennialism

The dispensational scheme of Darby bore an impact on his contemporaries: Dwight L. Moody, Harry H. Ironside, and James H. Brookes. Brookes may have well been the one who introduced Cyrus Ingerson Scofield to dispensational theology.[50] Later, Scofield would embed his own slightly modified version of Darby's dispensational framework into the study notes of the premier American study Bible, which came to be known as *The Scofield Reference Bible* published by Oxford University Press in 1909. This Bible would bear a profound influence on shaping American Fundamentalism in the twentieth century.

It the following years, Scofield became a significant influence on Lewis Sperry Chafer, who would not only go on to write the first multi-volume systematic theology from a thoroughly dispensational perspective, but he

---

[48] Akenson, *Discovering the End of Time*, 407–8.

[49] Carter, *Anglican Evangelicals*, 210.

[50] Carl E. Sanders II, *The Premillennial Faith of James Brookes: Reexamining the Roots of American Dispensationalism* (New York: University Press of America, 2001).

would become the founder and president of Dallas Theological Seminary—the first distinctly dispensational school. These influences would serve to cement dispensational-premillennialism as an enduring fixture in churches all across North America, up until the present day.

It cannot be denied that Darby's teaching has gone on to shape much of what is today considered as "the fundamentals" of the evangelical faith. In addition to his advocacy of a dispensational perspective of human history, and his significant contribution to the church's present-day understanding of biblical prophecy, Darby also gave much consideration to the reformation doctrines of the literal grammatical-historical hermeneutic and the priesthood of every believer. Despite all of this, Darby would not go on to be remembered in the history with all charity and fondness as the critical pioneering agent behind dispensational-premillennialism. The reason for this is because Darby was at once a highly polemic and polarizing figure.

4.3 Division Among the Dissenters

In the years following the Prophecy Conferences, Darby became a speaker of some international renown, making visits to French-speaking Switzerland as well as frequent trips to North America. Akenson notes that "in late August 1837, Darby moved his personal mission to the Continent. This connection with Switzerland 'was significant as it opened up a new field of endeavor at a time when Darby's notoriety as a separatist had rendered him *persona non grata* in Ireland.'"[51]

At one point during his travels, a disputation arose among the brethren in Switzerland, and Darby was petitioned concerning the dispute. The charity expressed in his response at that time was quite revealing:

It is my joy and my privilege to find myself in the midst of brethren who know one another in Christ, and to rejoice in the blessedness of brotherly communion in all the weakness in which it may be found at present; but I could not recognize an assembly that does not receive all the children of God because I know that Christ receives them. I see

---

[51] Timothy Stunt, *From Awakening to Succession: Radical Evangelicals in Switzerland and Britain, 1815–1835* (Edinburgh: T and T Clark), 304, quoted in Akenson, *Discovering the End of Time*, 485.

the Church in ruins: I follow my conscience according to the light that I have received from the word, but I desire to bear with the weakness or lack of light that I may find in other Christians, and do all that I can to unite those who love the Lord.[52]

By the point at which Darby penned these words, his chief operation in the British Isles had relocated from Ireland to Plymouth, England.[53] It so happened that during that period when Darby was travelling internationally, a colleague by the name of Benjamin Willis Newton, with whom Darby had experienced some conflict prior to his departure,[54] had taken a position of prominence within the Plymouth assembly. Returning from his travels in 1843, Darby discovered that the Plymouth Assembly was being dominated by the personality of a single brother: Benjamin Newton. Darby would have none of it.

On top of this injury, Newton had published a book just a few years prior, in which he presented a somewhat different futurist interpretation of unfulfilled biblical prophecy than Darby's. In it, Newton was critical of Darby's prophetic end-time expectations, though they agreed on a number of parts.[55] A year after Darby's return, Newton published another book advancing more of those same ideas, titled: *Thoughts on the Apocalypse*.[56] In ad-

---

[52] Darby, *Letters*, 1:34.

[53] The assembly, which met at this location in Plymouth, would become the defining assembly for the movement, which history would remember as "the Plymouth Brethren," despite that it did not originate in Plymouth but rather in Dublin.

[54] Akenson notes that the seeds of conflict had already been sewn between Darby and Newton by the close of the 1833 Powerscourt Conference: "Benjamin W. Newton 'complained bitterly that the conference had been organized in such a way as to 'control' private judgment.' Newton refused to attend any of the later Irish conferences and concentrated instead on becoming the parental figure in the Plymouth assembly." Akenson, *Discovering the End of Time*, 435. In the following year (1834), Newton held a competing prophecy conference in Plymouth at the same time, and even discussed some of the very same topics, as the principle one held in Dublin which Darby attended. Field, *John Nelson Darby*, 130.

[55] One critical distinction was that Newton anticipated a post-tribulation rapture as opposed to Darby, who held firmly to a pre-tribulation rapture.

[56] Benjamin W. Newton, *Thoughts on the Apocalypse* (London: J. B. Rowe, 1844).

dition to projecting a futurist interpretation of biblical prophecy that differed with Darby's, Newton also advanced ideas concerning Christ's sinless nature with which Darby took strong exception.[57]

Thus, Darby found not only ecclesiastical grounds to take up issue with Newton, but doctrinal as well. Before long, the two were embroiled in conflict in a way that would leave an indelible scar on the testimony of unity among the Brethren—the very principle upon which the early assemblies were founded. In the following years, all attempts to bring the affair to an end fell flat. By 1845, separation seemed inevitable, and on Sunday, December 28,[58] there was not one, but two assemblies which convened in Plymouth for the breaking of bread—an act which served to commemorate Christ's unity among the Body.

At that point Darby and Newton found themselves with horns locked, neither one able to escape the conflict with their pride fully intact. Within a few years, when both independent assemblies persisted, Darby felt the need to bring the issue to a head, not by an act of contrition, but by doubling-down on his position concerning Newton's heresies. This happened in 1848, when two associates from the Plymouth assembly visited Bristol and broke bread with the brethren at Bethesda. When word of this got back to Darby, he demanded that Bethesda judge matters pertaining to Plymouth. The Brethren at Bethesda insisted that they would not close fellowship to the men from Plymouth. Concerning this point, a Brethren historian has observed:

> While the church at Bethesda continued to do what Darby himself had done at the first, that is, to maintain the independence of each congregation and its right to receive any individual whom it had reason to believe was born again and sound in faith and conduct, Darby had shifted from that ground and adopted the "catholic" position of an organized body of churches, excluding all outside their own circle,

---

[57] Newton held to the view concerning Christ's ability to sin that, though Christ was sinless He could have sinned (pecability), whereas Darby insisted that Christ could not have sinned (impeccability).

[58] Field, *John Nelson Darby,* 139.

and subject to one central authority, in this case himself and the meeting in London with which he was associated.[59]

When excommunication of the individual did not deal the decisive blow that Darby had intended, he went so far as to renounce those who would not make a decisive judgment concerning the matter.[60] However, this redoubled effort of Darby's proved even less fruitful than the first. Many among the brethren who were otherwise sympathetic to Darby, felt that he went too far in excommunicating an entire assembly simply because they would not close off fellowship to those who had been Newton's associates. One biographer has noted: "Darby's authoritarian behavior did not have the result he expected. Although he had firmly rejected the 'Notion of a Clergyman', some felt he was behaving more like a Pope."[61]

Needless to say, many of the churches that Darby had been so instrumental in setting up—like Bethesda—were more interested in following the teaching of Scripture, rather than the edicts of any man. The result of this yielded two distinct lines of Brethren, both of which have persisted to the present day. Those who accepted Darby's stand would eventually come to be known as "Exclusive Brethren," whereas those with a mind to pursue open fellowship with all Brethren were known as "Independent," and "Neutral," and afterward, "Open Brethren."[62]

4.4 Darby's Broad-Reaching Influence on Protestantism

By the end of his life, at age 81, Darby had done far more to shape Protestantism than any could have realized at that time. Certainly, his accomplishments were many, since he ministered throughout much of Europe and in virtually the entire English-speaking world. Near the time of his passing, Brethren historian Andrew Miller gave the following report: "In a

---

[59] Edmund Hamer Broadbent, *The Pilgrim Church: Tracing the Pathway of the Forgotten Saints from Pentecost to the Twentieth Century* (1931; repr., Grand Rapids, MI: Gospel Folio Press, 1999), 392–393.

[60] Field, *John Nelson Darby*, 143.

[61] Ibid., 144.

[62] Ibid., 150.

list of meetings which they publish annually for the convenience of Brethren who may be travelling, they give the addresses of 523 in England, 48 in
Ireland, and 75 in Scotland. There are also a goodly number on the Continent of Europe, in Australia and New Zealand, in the West Indies, in Can-
ada, and in the United States."[63] In addition to the churches he was personally instrumental in setting up, Darby had a major personal impact on many
notable Bible teachers, including D. L. Moody and C. I. Scofield. Among
his most noteworthy accomplishments, however, was his written ministry,
which included translations of the Old and New Testaments into French,
German, and English.

It is not just the Exclusive and Open Brethren who owe a debt to
Darby for his influence on shaping the tradition in which they stand. Congregationalists, Presbyterians, Baptists, and virtually all American Fundamentalism which would emerge on the scene in the twentieth century
would be indebted to Darby, in one way or another, for the ideas which he
helped put into practice. Akenson, who had proposed that John Nelson
Darby may be a contender for the fourth most influential figure on Protestantism after Luther, Calvin, and Wesley, concluded:

> Darby's central ideas became the ideological core of North American
> evangelicalism in the first half of the twentieth century...quietly, al-
> most silently, the theology of John Nelson Darby became the clenched
> fist within the America evangelical glove. His method of hyper-close
> Bible study; his insistence upon literalism in the reading of biblical
> texts, while permitting the rearrangement of the scriptures to show
> God's original intention; his assertion that humankind was inevitably
> a failure and, crucially, his making all this balance on the any moment
> return of Jesus in the secret-Rapture provided both an explanation of
> why the world was in such a mess and a formulation of sure promise
> for the future.[64]

---

[63] Andrew Miller, *Miller's Church History* (1874; repr., Addison, IL: Bible Truth
Publishers, 1980), 1184–1185.

[64] Akenson, *Discovering the End of Time*, 485-86.

4.5 Conclusion

In many ways the life of the Irish reformer, John Nelson Darby, bears many similarities to the German reformer, Martin Luther. Although separated by more than two hundred years, and operating in different countries, both men's lives took similar paths, full of unexpected bends, high mountain peaks, and low valleys, with each one parting company with fellow-travelers at critical forks in the road. Both men were dogged and resolute, firmly bent on the task that they felt the Lord had entrusted to them. While Darby made tremendous strides in his lifetime, the same "party-spirit" which divided Martin Luther from Ulrich Zwingli and the Swiss reformers effected Darby's life as well. In a similar vein to how the German reformer, at the end of his life, came to reflect the very thing which he fought so avidly against, so Darby's obstinate stand contrasted the founding principle which energized his early ministry.

Subsequently, in 1882, when Darby went to be with the Lord, the rift between himself and Newton had not been mended. Although one can see many evidences today of how effectively God used Darby to impact the Protestant world, one cannot help but notice the terrible blemish to the present day that was also left on both the Brethren and dispensational theology.

Newton vs Darby Beef

Darby wrote the following commendation of Luther's ministry, in 1854, in the preface to the German Translation of the New Testament:

> When God at the beginning of the sixteenth century caused His light to break forth on the world deeply sunk in darkness, Martin Luther was the instrument specially chosen by Him to spread the truth in Germany. This labourer, full of faith, occupied himself principally with the work with which God had entrusted to him. To gain this object he used the Bible, which he himself translated for this end. Others followed him in this, in in various lands, some of whom were even compelled to forfeit their lives in attaining the object of their holy zeal. Far be it from us to despise the toil and labour of love of these blessed instruments in the Lord's hand! Surely God Himself has

not despised them, and many lands have enjoyed for these three centuries the fruit of their labours.[65]

It may well be that these same words, or some very similar, could be
spoken concerning the influence of the instrument specially chosen by God
to spread the truth in the nineteenth century, beginning in Ireland and
reaching to the ends of the earth. Today, over one-hundred and fifty-years
later, at a little plot in Bournemouth, England, there stands a gravestone in
Wimbourne Road Cemetery, which reads:

John Nelson Darby
"As unknown and well known."
Departed to be with Christ
29th April 1882.
Aged 81.
II Cor. V. 21.

Beneath that, a simple prayer of Darby's is engraved:

Lord, let me wait for Thee alone.
My life be only this.
To serve Thee here on earth unknown,
Then share Thy heavenly bliss.
J.N.D.

It would seem as though the Lord has seen fit to answer this humble
prayer of the nineteenth century Irish reformer.

---

[65] John Nelson Darby, "Preface to the German Testament," in *The Collected Writings of J. N. Darby*, ed. William Kelly, vol. 13, *Critical No. 1* (London: Stow Hill Bible
and Tract Depot, n.d.), 167.

Bibliography

Akenson, Donald Harman. *Discovering the End of Time: Irish Evangelicals in the Age of Daniel O'Connell.* Chicago, IL: McGill-Queen's University Press, 2016.

Bebbington, David W. *Evangelicalism in Modern Britain: A History from the 1730s to the 1980s.* New York: Routledge, 1989.

Broadbent, Edmund Hamer. *The Pilgrim Church: Tracing the Pathway of the Forgotten Saints from Pentecost to the Twentieth Century.* 1931. Reprint, Grand Rapids, MI: Gospel Folio Press, 1999.

Brown, Desmond. *Protestant Crusade in Ireland, 1800–70: A Study of Protestant–Catholic Relations between the Act of Union Disestablishment.* Toronto, ON: University of Toronto Press, 1978.

Carter, Grayson. *Anglican Evangelicals: Protestant Secessions from the Via Media, c. 1800–1850.* Eugene, OR: Wipf and Stock, 2001.

Darby, John Nelson. *Collected Writings of J. N. Darby.* Edited by William Kelly. Vol. 1, *Ecclesiastical No. 1.* London: Stow Hill Bible and Tract Depot, n.d.

———. *Collected Writings of J. N. Darby.* Edited by William Kelly. Vol. 20, *Ecclesiastical No. 4.* London: Stow Hill Bible and Tract Depot, n.d.

———. "Considerations Addressed to the Archbishop of Dublin and the Clergy who Signed the Petition to the House of Commons for Protection." In *Collected Writings of J. N. Darby,* edited by William Kelly. Vol. 1, *Ecclesiastical No. 1,* 1–19. London: Stow Hill Bible and Tract Depot, n.d.

———. "Considerations on the Nature and Unity of the Church of Christ." In *Collected Writings of J. N. Darby,* edited by William Kelly. Vol. 1, *Ecclesiastical No. 1,* 20–35. London: Stow Hill Bible and Tract Depot, n.d.

Darby, John Nelson. "The Doctrine of the Church of England at the Time of the Reformation Itself, of Scripture, and of the Church of Rome, Briefly Compared with the Remarks of the Regius Professor of Divinity." In *Collected Writings of J. N. Darby*, edited by William Kelly. Vol. 3, *Doctrinal No. 1*, 1–43. London: Stow Hill Bible and Tract Depot, n.d.

———. "Preface to the German Translation." In *Collected Writings of J. N. Darby*, edited by William Kelly. Vol. 13, *Critical No. 1*, 167–186. London: Stow Hill Bible and Tract Depot, n.d.

———. *Letters of J. N. D.* Edited by William Kelly. Vol. 1, *1832–1868*. London: Stow Hill Bible and Tract Depot, n.d.

———. *Letters of J. N. D.* Edited by William Kelly. Vol. 2, *1868–1879*. London: Stow Hill Bible and Tract Depot, n.d.

———. *Letters of J. N. D.* Edited by William Kelly. Vol. 3, *1879–1882*. London: Stow Hill Bible and Tract Depot, n.d.

———. "The Notion of a Clergyman: Dispensationally the Sin Against the Holy Ghost." In *Collected Writings of J. N. Darby*, edited by William Kelly. Vol. 1, *Ecclesiastical No. 1*, 36–51. London: Stow Hill Bible and Tract Depot, n.d.

———. "On 'Days' Signifying 'Years' in Prophetic Language." In *Collected Writings of J. N. Darby*, edited by William Kelly. Vol. 2, *Prophetic No. 1*, 32–42. London: Stow Hill Bible and Tract Depot, n.d.

———. "Reflections upon the Prophetic Inquiry and the Views Advanced in It." In *Collected Writings of J. N. Darby*, edited by William Kelly. Vol. 2, *Prophetic No. 1*, 1–31. London: Stow Hill Bible and Tract Depot, n.d.

Erickson, Millard, J. *Christian Theology.* 2nd ed. Grand Rapids, MI: Baker, 2007.

Field, Marion. *John Nelson Darby: Prophetic Pioneer.* Godalming, Surrey: Highland Books, 2008.

Gasque, W. W. "Bruce, F(redrick) F(yvie) (1910–1991)." In *Dictionary of Major Biblical Interpreters*, edited by Donald K. McKim, 237–242. Downers Grove, IL: InterVarsity Press, 2007.

Gerstner, John H. *Wrongly Dividing the Word of Truth: A Critique of Dispensationalism*. Morgan, PA: Soli Deo Gloria, 2000.

Lewis, Samuel. *A Topographical Dictionary of Ireland*. Vol 1. London: S. Lewis, 1837.

Miller, Andrew. *Miller's Church History*. 1874. Reprint, Addison, IL: Bible Truth Publishers, 1980.

Neatby, William Blair. *A History of the Plymouth Brethren*. London: Hodder and Stoughton, 1901.

Newton, Benjamin W. *Thoughts on the Apocalypse*. London: J. B. Rowe, 1844.

Sanders, Carl E., II. *The Premillennial Faith of James Brookes: Reexamining the Roots of American Dispensationalism*. New York: Univeristy Press of America, 2001.

Spencer, S. R. "Scofield, C(yrus), I. (1845–1921)." In *Dictionary of Major Biblical Interpreters*, edited by Donald K. McKim, 906–910. Downers Grove, IL: InterVarsity Press, 2007.

Stevenson, Mark R. *The Doctrines of Grace in an Unexpected Place: Calvinistic Soteriology in Nineteenth-Century Brethren Thought*. Eugene, OR: Pickwick, 2017.

Sproul, R. C. *What is Reformed Theology: Understanding the Basics*. Grand Rapids, MI: Baker, 1997.

Turner, W. G. *Unknown and Well Known: A Biography of John Nelson Darby*. Edited by E. N. Cross. London: Chapter Two, 2006.

Weremchuk, Max S. *John Nelson Darby: A Biography*. Neptune, NJ: Loizeaux Brothers, 1992.

Whelan, Irene. *The Bible War in Ireland: The 'Second Reformation' and the Polarization of Protestant–Catholic Relations, 1800–1840*. Madison, WI: University of Wisconsin Press, 2005.

5

LUTHER MEETS DARBY:
The Reformation Legacy of Ecclesiastical Independence

Cory M. Marsh
Southern California Seminary

5.0 Introduction

While the battle cry of the Reformation concerned issues directly majoring on soteriology, ecclesiology was affected only incidentally.[1] Yet, issues raised during this period would quickly alter assumed ecclesiastical convictions resulting most notably in the individual church member's prerogative to interpret Scripture, and regard himself as a Spirit-led priest under the authority of Christ alone. As such, the Pope and his Roman Church were quickly found to be obstructing the New Testament's portrayal of local, self-governing assemblies. With this serving as a backdrop, this chapter will examine the impact left on the clergy/laity divide resulting from the recovery of Scripture's ultimate authority and the Christian's right to interpret it. The argument advanced throughout is that with the recovery and development of *sola Scriptura* and the Priesthood of Believers, papal authority was

---

[1] James Orr, *The Progress of Dogma* (London, UK: Hodder and Stoughton, 1901), 43–64, Kindle, traces the historical progression of Christian theology and labels the Reformation era as "the soteriological period" and "the period of controversies on the application of redemption (justification)." It appears Orr assumed that ecclesiology was a doctrine still in progress as he never devotes a specific chapter to its development in contrast to other key doctrines.

transferred to Spirit-filled laity which would later result in the rebirthing of local, autonomous churches. A spotlight is thus shown on the furtherance of the Reformation's legacy concerning ecclesiastical independence and individual Bible interpretation, principles that would in turn influence American evangelicalism.

5.0.1 Context and Method

Of all the sixteenth century reformers, it is Martin Luther (1483–1546) who stands out as the premier fountainhead to challenge Rome's clerical abuses. Yet, his protest did not remain in 16th century Germany. Luther's calling-to-task the Catholic Church's captivity of Western Christianity was picked up again three centuries later by another commanding reformer dealing with almost identical issues in the United Kingdom—the Anglican clergyman, turned pioneer of modern dispensationalism, John Nelson Darby (1880–1882). With a focused interaction of Luther's three most controversial treatises published targeting the Catholic Church in 1520, the methodology used here will be to analyze and compare his manifesto with Darby's three most controversial treatises targeting the Established Church in the 19th century. It will be shown that identical notions of both Scripture and ordained clergy held by Luther and Darby—though separated by time and geography—are what connect these two reforming giants. Moreover, it will be suggested that Darby simply extended the mantle of Luther's reforms to their ecclesiastical conclusions. Finally, certain key New Testament texts will be interspersed throughout the chapter giving Scripture its due authoritative honor—a technique exemplified by both men.

5.2 Background to Martin Luther's Rise

As the focus here is limited to specific beliefs held by Luther concerning Scripture and the clergy reflected in selected writings, a detailed personal biography lies outside the scope of this chapter.[2] What can be said, however,

---

[2] Three excellent biographies on Luther commended to the reader are: Rolland Bainton, *Here I Stand: A Life of Martin Luther* (New York, NY: Meridian, 1995); Michael A. Mullet, *Martin Luther* (London: Taylor & Francis, 2004), accessed February 9, 2017, EBSCOhost eBook Collection; and Carl R. Trueman, *Luther on the Christian Life: Cross*

is that Martin Luther was much like the sons of Issachar who "had understanding of the times" (1 Chron 12:32, ESV). He was a man with the depth of conviction that could only be matched by his passion for all things Christ and Scripture. Luther's sensitivity to his own personal sin as a monk in the Augustinian cloister of Erfurt has been well documented. Additionally, his personal conversion regarding the doctrines of repentance, justification, and faith alone while lecturing through the Psalms, Romans, and Galatians (1513–17) have received much attention.[3]

Luther lived in Germany during a time when the collective resentment toward Rome had been bubbling for centuries. Immorality, financial abuses and various wars traced directly to Catholic popes and clergy—a group Luther coined "Romanists"—had left a rotten stench of hypocrisy which wafted across all of Europe. Rome's captivity over the laity, highlighted in the selling of indulgences and the profiteering of personal masses, made the Catholic Church a lucrative industry; yet, it also left the citizens of Germany primed and ready for someone to rise up and lead a complete overhaul of the blatant corruption caused by dishonest clergy supposedly working for God. "It was according to this projection," Mullet observes, "the gross corruption, the spiritual and practical despotism of Rome, built up over centuries of accumulated enslavement, that gave Luther his epic historical importance as a herald of freedom."[4] It is within this context that the German laity found a liberating hero in Martin Luther.

5.2.1 Luther's Distinct Contribution

Other would-be reformers preceded Luther, even in Germany.[5] Yet,

---

and Freedom (Wheaton, IL: Crossway, 2015). The author acknowledges his dependence on these three works for major parts of this chapter.

[3] See Bainton, *Here I Stand*, 42–50, 67; Mullet, *Martin Luther*, 52–55.

[4] Mullet, *Martin Luther*, 5.

[5] This historical fact is often overshadowed by Luther's monumental involvement; yet, it is important to note that many Germans before Luther had already publically decried the corruption of the Roman papacy and clergy. In this sense, Luther, especially in his "Open Letter," was not much different than those before him and thus joined an existing national consensus for social, political, and ecclesial reform. Examples include: Ulrich Wiest's widely distributed and scathing poem, "The Insolence of

while Martin Luther may have been one link in a chain of German protestors against Roman abuses, he did distinguish himself above all others
through his masterful use of Scripture to justify each of his major com-
plaints. Reformation historian Rolland Bainton points out: "The Scriptures
assumed for Luther an overwhelming importance, not primarily as a source
book for antipapal polemic, but as the one ground of certainty."[6] Thus, for
Luther, *sola Scriptura* was more of a presupposition which he carried into all
arguments, rather than a doctrine in need of explanation. His constant appeals to Scripture above all things Rome is how Luther fleshed out this principle. It was Scripture's supreme authority to which Luther appealed while
dismantling the clergy's stronghold over the laity, as well as calling the pope
to task for his claim of exclusive authority in interpretation of the Word of
God.

5.3 Luther's Three Treatises

Nestled between his *95 Theses*, officially called the "Disputation on the
Power of Indulgences" (October 1517), and his *Bondage of the Will* (December 1525), Martin Luther wrote three rapid-fire tracts which confirmed that
a split with the Roman Catholic Church was all but inevitable. "These three
works, taken together," Church historian Carl Trueman notes, "perhaps
represent Luther's most sustained and positive vision of what reformation
should be."[7] It was in the ink spent on writing these three treatises in the
fall of 1520—works that Luther produced in the wake of his Leipzig debates
with his Catholic adversary, Johannes Maier von Eck, in 1519—that Martin

---

Ecclesiastical Princes" (1450); Erasmus' "Praise of Folly," (1509, 11); Sebastian Brant's
"The Ship of Fools," (1494) and "On the Inevitable Fall of the Holy Roman Empire"
(1504). Two solid works showcasing this pre-Reformation German attitude against
Rome are Gerald Strauss, *Manifestations of Discontent in Germany on the Eve of the Refor-
mation: A Collection of Documents Selected, Translated, and Introduced* (Bloomington, IN:
Indiana University, 1971), esp. 3–63; 223–227; and Thomas A. Brady, Jr., "The Holy
Roman Empire's Bishops on the Eve of the Reformation," in *Continuity and Change:
The Harvest of Late Medieval and Reformation History*, ed. Robert J. Bast and Andrew C.
Gow (Leiden, The Netherlands: Brill, 2000), esp. 20–47.

[6] Bainton, *Here I Stand*, 288.

[7] Trueman, *Luther on the Christian Life*, 43.

Luther most fully developed his reformation doctrines concerning the Scriptures and the laity. It is also in these three treatises where Luther's insistence on the ultimate and divine authority of the Bible and the non-ordained Christian's right to interpret it had dealt the most crushing blow to the Roman Catholic Church—which had been monopolizing all things religious and secular. To this Mullet adds, "More and more Luther was being driven back on his central focus on a reliable arbiter to hear and adjudicate his cause, the word of God in Scripture."[8]

5.3.1 The Open Letter

The first of the three treatises Luther wrote was in his native tongue called, "An Open Letter [or Address] to the Christian Nobility of the German Nation Concerning the Reform of the Christian Estate," published on August 18, 1520. Luther, a master of communication and its promotion through the still developing print media, chose not to write this tract in Latin, unlike his *95 Theses*. This was because Latin, a language in which Luther was fluent, was the written speech used by Catholic scholastics and professional theologians. However, by writing his "Open Letter" in the language of the German people, Luther fanned into flame the laity's national consciousness and seething resentment toward Rome—that old foe, now under the guise of the Holy See, which had re-birthed the Pharisaic image of exploitation and taxation from over 800 miles away.

Luther's "Open Letter" consisted mainly of a three-point manifesto, which he built to destroy the corresponding Catholic hedges he termed "Romanist Walls." These three walls were religious dogmas the Catholic

---

[8] Mullet, *Martin Luther*, 98. Mullet directed these words specifically toward Luther's stance on Rome's concilliar tradition, which often erred, but was still used to decide on various religious dogma as well as secular affairs. As a response to the Western Schism (1378–1417), ecumenical councils called by representatives of the Catholic Church militant were officially recognized as "supreme authority" at the Council of Constance 1414–18. They were later overturned by popes Julius II and Leo X at the Fifth Council of the Lateran (1512–17) thereby re-establishing the supreme authority of the papacy. This last decision took place a mere seven months before Luther posted his *95 Theses* which began his reformation career.

Church had erected to keep itself impenetrable from any non-ordained subservient who dared question its divine authority. Thus, being a patriotic
German only helped serve Luther's protest against Rome's stronghold of
the Western world as he appealed to his nation's "Christian Estates."[9] In
the preface of his "Open Letter" addressed to his friend and fellow academic, Nicholas Von Amsdorf, Luther wastes no time appealing to Scripture as he regards himself as almost prophet-like: "The time to keep silence
has passed," Luther thundered, "and the time to speak is come, as Ecclesiastes says."[10] He then goes on to make plain his intention of Reform in the
Address, arguing from the clergy to the laity, "in the hope that God may
deign to help His Church through the efforts of the laity, since the clergy,
to whom this task more properly belongs, have grown indifferent."[11] And,
just in case his sentiments toward "the Romanists" were not fully known,
Luther adds: "We must be sure that in this matter we are dealing not with
men, but with princes of hell, who can fill the world with war and bloodshed, but whom war and bloodshed do not overcome."[12] With such words
directed at the papacy in Rome, Luther now saw the Reformation akin to
Esau and Jacob's troubled relationship. If Esau was Rome, then Jacob was
the divinely-called protests of Luther, for as the Scripture says: "Jacob I
loved, but Esau I hated" (Rom 9:13).

5.3.2 The Three Romanist Walls

While the latter half of the "Open Letter" lists 27 specific reform proposals which Luther offered as the cure against Rome's abuses, the core of
his manifesto consists of a three-pronged attack destroying, what he termed,
the "Romanist Walls":

First, when pressed by the temporal power, they [the Romanists] have

---

[9] The "Christian Estates" to which Luther addressed included Germany's terri-
torial and civic rulers of all classes—from Emperor Charles V to the lesser, yet vitally
important, *Reichsritter* (Imperial Knights). Cf, Mullet, *Martin Luther*, 102.

[10] Martin Luther, "An Open Letter to the Christian Nobility of the German Nation Concerning The Reform of the Christian Estate," in *Three Treatises*, rev. James
Atkinson, trans. Charles M. Jacobs (Philadelphia, PA: Fortress, 1960), 9.

[11] Ibid.

[12] Ibid., 12.

made decrees and said that the temporal power has no jurisdiction over them, but, on the other hand, that the spiritual is above the temporal power. Second, when the attempt is made to reprove them out of the Scriptures, they raise the objection that the interpretation of the Scriptures belongs to no one except the pope. Third, if threatened with a council, they answer with fable that no one can call a council but the pope.[13]

In Luther's mind, these three Roman barriers could never withstand the crushing blow of Scripture. Solomon wrote, "A wise man scales the city of the mighty and brings down the stronghold in which they trust" (Prov 21:22), and thus Luther set out to dismantle the pope's unbiblical fortifications with a relentless appeal to the biblical Text. The timing was just right as the Catholic tradition was emerging from medieval thought more familiar with Aristotelian scholastics than Scripture. Consequently, Luther's appeal to the Word of God—not the word of Aquinas—left the Romanists seeing stars.[14]

The first two walls of Rome protected the Catholic Church's supposed authority over any individual believer, and the pope's exclusive right to interpret the Scriptures.[15] Using key texts found in 1 Corinthians 12; 1 Peter 2; and Revelation 1, 5, and 20, among others, Luther argued that every believer is a priest under Christ (not the pope), and that he or she has every right to challenge the pope's interpretation. Appealing to John 6:45—"they

---

[13] Luther, "Open Letter," 13.

[14] One month before posting his *95 Theses*, Luther caused a storm among the faculty at the University of Wittenberg with his *Disputation of Scholastic Theology* (September 1517). This tract essentially dethroned Aquinas who was the Catholic Church's bridge to Aristotle for the previous 250 years. By doing this, Luther almost single-handedly reformed the university's curriculum by returning it to an emphasis on the biblical languages. Thus a case can be made that the Protestant Reformation really began with this reform inside academia. Cf. Trueman, *Luther on the Christian Life*, 41; Bainton, *Here I Stand*, 45.

[15] While papal infallibility was not decreed official by the Catholic Church until the late 19th century First Vatican Council under Pius IX, it was nonetheless a widely held "unofficial" belief of Rome for centuries leading up to that time.

will all be taught of God"—Luther presupposes Biblical authority over fallible popes and cardinals and makes a salient observation:

> Thus it may well happen that the pope and his followers are wicked men, and no true Christians, not taught of God, not having true understanding. On the other hand, an ordinary man may have true understanding; why then should we not follow him? Has not the pope erred many times? Who would help Christendom when the pope errs, if we were not to believe another, who had the Scriptures on his side, more than the pope?[16]

Luther, in challenging the papacy's stronghold over the laity, was reminiscent of Paul's upbraiding of the Corinthian church that was showing signs of pride hindering orderly, encouraging worship: "Or was it from you that the word of God came?" Paul rhetorically quipped, "Or are you the only ones it has reached?" (1 Cor 14:36, ESV). This passage had clear application concerning the papacy. While the apostle instructed the Corinthians to share in their teaching and understanding of God's revelation (vv.29–32), the priesthood of the individual Christian was something kept under lock and key by the Romanists.

However, even the powers of Rome with its control over Western Christianity could not shut the mouth of a man of whom it was said, "was not concerned to philosophize about the structure of Church and state, [but rather] his insistence was simply that every man must answer for himself to God."[17] It was this deep-rooted faith fleshed out in works (cf. James 2:14–26) that placed Luther head and shoulders above his fellow German protestors—those who had only managed to bounce off the three walls of Romanism. In contrast, Luther penetrated these walls with a battering ram armed with details of 1 Peter 2:5–9 which describe the church in terms of "a spiritual house" and "a royal priesthood"; understanding that every believer had the Holy Spirit's anointing so that "[they] have no need that anyone should teach [them]" (1 John 2:27).

"Therefore," Luther remarked concerning the pope's shackling of Scripture, "it is a wickedly invented fable, and they cannot produce a letter

---

[16] Luther, "Open Letter," 21.
[17] Bainton, *Here I Stand*, 109.

in defense of it, that the interpretation of Scripture or the confirmation of its interpretation belongs to the pope alone."[18] Luther maintained the Christian laity had every right to read and interpret the Bible, and to do so joyfully, in faith, with full accountability before his Lord. Thus, Luther added: "We should not allow the Spirit of liberty, as Paul calls Him, to be frightened off by the fabrications of the popes, but we ought to go boldly forward to test all that they do or leave undone, *according to our interpretation of the Scripture, which rests on faith* [emphasis added], and compel them to follow not their own interpretation, but the one that is better."[19]

While the third wall dealing with the pope's exclusive right to call a council was certainly important, it is the first two that warranted the most attention here. This is because, quite simply in Luther's words, "The third wall falls of itself when the first two are down."[20] Appealing to the Scripture's divine authority, Luther summed up his assault on the third wall with: "They have no basis in Scripture for their contention that it belongs to the pope alone to call a council or confirm its actions."[21] Moreover, remaining consistent with his focus on the believer's own priestly authority, Luther ended this third Romanist Wall with: "Therefore, when necessity demands, and the pope is an offense to Christendom, the first man who is able should, as a faithful member of the whole body, do what he can to bring about a truly free council."[22]

5.3.3 The Babylonian Captivity

Following his "Open Letter" to the German nobility by two months, Luther published "The Babylonian Captivity of the Church" on October 6, 1520. If the first treatise came across as cordial (that is to say, cordial for Luther), this second treatise made his intention against the Roman Catholic

---

[18] Luther, "Open Letter," 21.

[19] Ibid., 23.

[20] Ibid.

[21] Ibid.

[22] Ibid., 24. Luther not only had a command of Scripture to prove his points, but also of church history. Here he added: "Even the Council of Nicea—the most famous of all—was neither called nor confirmed by the Bishop of Rome, but by Emperor Constantine, and many other emperors after him did the like."

Church perfectly clear: Rome had forfeited any spiritual virtue that may still be hanging on and had even gone so far as to become the pagan whore of old, Babylon. The translator to the work, A. T. W. Steinhausser, explains, "The reference is clear from the contents of the document: just as the Jews were carried away from Jerusalem into captivity under the tyranny of the Babylonian Empire, so in Europe the Christians have been carried away from the Scriptures and made subject to the tyranny of the papacy."[23] In this work, Luther's polemical tone turned even more aggressive as he left little doubt that reform from within the Catholic Church was impossible, and that separation was the only solution (cf. 2 Cor 6:17). An introductory remark in his preface made plain where his thoughts on the papacy now were: "I know for certainty," remarked Luther, "that the papacy is the kingdom of Babylon and the power of Nimrod, the mighty hunter [Gen 10:8–9]."[24]

Unlike his other two treatises, "The Babylonion Captivity of the Church" was written solely in the theological language of the church so as not to confuse who Luther intended as the target audience. Mullet asserts, "It was a Latin work by a Churchman, addressed in the first instance to other Churchmen throughout Christendom and signaling the author's utter rejection of the Roman Church as Babylon—and Antichrist."[25] Throughout this second treatise, Luther continued his notion of the legitimacy of *sola Scriptura* and the priesthood of believers with a special focus on Rome's seven sacramental pillars.[26]

With his hand guided by an acute understanding of Scripture, Luther

---

[23] A. T. W. Steinhausser, foreword to "The Babylonian Captivity of the Church," in *Three Treatises*, by Martin Luther, rev. Fredrick C. Ahrens and Abdel Ross Wentz, trans. A. T. W. Steinhausser (Philadelphia, PA: Fortress, 1960), 116.

[24] Martin Luther, "The Babylonian Captivity of the Church," in *Three Treatises*, by Martin Luther, rev. Fredrick C. Ahrens and Abdel Ross Wentz, trans. A. T. W. Steinhausser (Philadelphia, PA: Fortress, 1960), 124.

[25] Mullet, *Martin Luther*, 110.

[26] Later codified at the Council of Trent (1545–63), the seven sacraments being: Baptism; Eucharist; Confirmation; Marriage; Ordination (holy orders); Penance; and Extreme Unction (anointing of the sick).

reduced the seven so-called sacraments to two or three: the Eucharist; baptism; and penance, as these were the only three with biblical support.[27] Yet, it is also here where Luther delivers the death knell to the clergy/laity divide prized by the pope and his cardinals. It was specifically the supposed "ordained clergy" of Rome that Luther found the most troubling. Their moral scandals, profiteering of the masses, and withholding the Eucharist cup from the laity turned Luther into a Protestant "son of thunder." In Luther's developmental thinking, the "sacraments" of Rome were nothing more than man's attempt of power and control under the (always-successful) guise of religion and guilt.[28]

Railing against ordained clergy, Luther thundered: "They have sought by this means [sacrament of ordination] to set up a seed bed of implacable discord, by which clergy and laymen should be separated from each other farther than heaven from earth to the incredible injury of the grace of baptism and to the confusion of our fellowship in the gospel."[29] Thus, Luther found utter disdain for a corrupt clergy that held captive non-ordained Christians creating an impassable us/them chasm. "Of this sacrament," Luther boldly stated, "the church of Christ knows nothing; it is an invention

[27] Cf. Mullet, *Martin Luther*, 113; Bainton, *Here I Stand*, 67. It is fascinating to read Luther's thinking as it develops in "The Babylonian Captivity." One notable reason is his thoughts on "penance" turns into what evangelicals understand as "repentance." Luther's doctrine of repentance came earlier from his "glowing discovery" through Erasmus' Greek New Testament that the Latin of Matthew 4:17, *penitentiam agite* (do penance) was a mistranslation of the Greek μετανοεῖτε (*metanoeîte*, repent or be penitent), lit: "change your mind." Because repentance is found so prominently in Scripture, Luther considered it a legitimate "sacrament" unlike the other four. Yet, he seems to refine his thinking as he moves on questioning if it is indeed a sacrament or not—finally deciding on the latter (cf. Luther, "Babylon Captivity," 258).

[28] The sacramental system seems to have originated in Dionysius' Ecclesiastical Hierarchy (Syria, ca. AD 500) which mentions six sacraments and became an authority to which clergy appealed. These six were developed into seven by Peter Lombard (12th century) and was made official Catholic dogma at the Council of Florence in 1439. It is worth noting that it was the Council of Constance (1414–18) that sanctioned withholding the cup from laity—a practice the Bohemian reformer, John Huss, hated and he was ultimately burned at the stake in 1415 for disputing it a hundred years before Luther's time.

[29] Luther, "Babylonian Captivity," 244.

of the church of the pope."[30]

By Luther's time, the Roman Church had long practiced something they invented called *charactere indelebili* or indelible [sacramental] character whereby a priest once ordained, would hold the rights of that office for life. He would become tenured, in a manner of speaking, so that he could never be displaced of his office and could only move up through the hierarchy to the rank of bishop.[31] An ordained priest, therefore, whose character could never be accused of malicious behavior, even when deserving of the accusation, had free reign as to how he conducted his affairs—whether on official business for the church or personal. To this monopolizing of "holy priests," Luther pointed out that the only difference between an ordained priest and the average Spirit-filled believer was that of office, not character: "According to what the Scriptures teach us, what we call the priesthood is a ministry. So I cannot understand at all why one who has once been made a priest cannot again become a layman; for the sole difference between him and the layman is his ministry."[32] It is in the "sacrament of ordination," that Luther exposed Rome's destructive impact on the true priesthood of all believers (cf. 1 Pet 2:5; Rev 1:6).

"Let everyone," railed Luther, "who knows himself to be a Christian, be assured of this, that we are all equally priests....And therefore this 'sacrament' of ordination, if it be anything at all, is nothing else but a certain rite whereby one is called to the ministry of the church."[33] It is worth noting that Luther's protests birthed in germinal form a plea for what would later become local autonomous churches that chose their own pastors. On this, Bainton observers, "The repudiation of ordination as a sacrament demolished the caste system of clericalism and provided a sound basis for the priesthood of all believers....At this point, what the priest does any Christian may do, *if commissioned by the congregation* [emphasis added], because all

---

[30] Luther, "Babylonian Captivity," 237.

[31] While the doctrine of *charactere indelebili* was practiced for at least a thousand years before Luther, it was dogmatically defined and officially recognized at the Council of Trent (1545–63).

[32] Luther, "Babylonian Captivity," 249.

[33] Ibid., 248.

Christians are priests."[34]

5.3.4 The Christian's Freedom

Luther rounded out his insistence on Scripture's supreme authority and the priesthood of all believers in his final work of the Three Treatises called "The Freedom of a Christian." Published in November 1520, this tract was not only the shortest of the Three, but it was also published in both Latin and German since it was meant for a wider dissemination.[35] This fact alone demonstrates Luther's disdain for the clergy/laity divide as he wanted all Christians to enjoy their definitive position in Christ. It also showcases Luther's remarkable grasp of the opportunities afforded by the printing press in 16th century Europe.

In Luther's mind, since all Christians are justified by faith alone in Christ alone—a truth extrapolated from Scripture alone—then all Christians deserve to know how to live their lives to the glory of God alone (not the pope). Hence, his much more congenial treatise on the Christian's freedom in Christ. With a showering of other passages from Scripture proving the individual Christian's liberty, Luther most prominently based his argument using two from the apostle Paul: Romans 13:8 and 1 Corinthians 9:19. In the first, Paul writes, "Owe no one anything, except to love each other, for the one who loves another has fulfilled the law" (Rom 13:8, ESV); in the second, the apostle penned, "For though I am free from all, I have made myself a servant to all, that I might win more of them" (1 Cor 9:19, ESV).

With these two verses as the backdrop, Luther blankets his tract in wonderful paradox: "A Christian is a perfectly free lord of all, subject to none. A Christian is a perfectly dutiful servant of all, subject to all."[36] Mullet expresses Luther's words this way: "A royal priesthood, true Christians have the dignity and perfect freedom of the sons of God and, having freedom,

---

[34] Bainton, *Here I Stand,* 107.

[35] "The Freedom of a Christian" first appeared in Latin as Luther had sent it, along with a personal attachment, to Pope Leo X (who was probably incensed to be instructed by a lowly German monk!). After he had produced the Latin version, Luther re-wrote and published it in German, which is the more widely read version.

[36] Martin Luther, "The Freedom of a Christian," in *Three Treatises,* rev. Harold J. Grimm, trans. W. A. Lambert (Philadelphia, PA: Fortress, 1960), 277.

voluntarily exchange it for willing service of their neighbours."[37] That the pope and clergy have no inherent authority over the individual Christian is obvious in this work. The believer is free to enjoy his life under the authority of Jesus Christ alone, and is to use that freedom joyfully in the service of others (cf. Gal 5:13). The harsher words from Luther had already been spent. His dismantling of the papacy's incarceration of the laity was relentlessly proven in the "Open Letter to the German Nobility," and "The Babylonian Captivity of the Church." Now, Luther fleshed out the implications from both works in "The Freedom of a Christian," as ethical living under Christ to the glory of God took center stage. No longer was the pope to monopolize all Bible interpretation. No longer was ordained clergy to be glorified to a holy status above the laity. Each believer had the same Spirit for interpretation of Scripture (1 Cor 6:19; 1 John 2:27), and each believer was accountable to no one but the Lord Himself (Rom 14:7–8). Joyful freedom in the edification of one another was to be the Christian's primary duty (1 Cor 12; Eph 4). As Luther himself made clear ending his three treatises: "Behold, from faith thus flow forth love and joy in the Lord, and from love a joyful, willing, and free mind that serves one's neighbor willingly and takes no account of gratitude or ingratitude, of praise or blame, of gain or loss. For a man does not serve that he may put men under obligations."[38]

5.3.5 The Result of the Three Treatises

With the completion of his three treatises of 1520, Martin Luther had become Germany's premier heavyweight. To the corrupt, unbiblical papal system in Rome, he had delivered a collective knockout punch with these three works. The Roman Catholic Church would survive, of course, but it would never be the same. Luther had exposed too much. He had proven too aptly from the Scriptures. The tables were now turned, and the Catholic Church was on the defense against this former monk who was proven scriptural but ironically considered heretical. Now that these treatises were making their way throughout Europe, Rome forged their own view of this Ger-

---

[37] Mullet, *Martin Luther*, 115.
[38] Luther, "Freedom of a Christian," 304.

man reformer rocking the boat of medieval Catholicism. According to Mullet, "Martin Luther was being identified primarily as the author of published printed literary works, the first leader of the heresy of the new age of print, and capable of infinite harm against the peace of the Church and the primacy of the Holy See."[39] Yet, the vast gulf fixed between the priesthood of the papacy, and the priesthood of believers was now bridged by Luther's manifesto—the former unable to withstand the scrutiny of God's Word.

Western Christianity was now freed from its Roman captor. Principles associated with *sola Scriptura* had exposed the pope as an unnecessary appendage to the Spirit-filled believer's interpreting the Bible for himself. Christians were to submit to Jesus Christ alone—the Chief Shepherd of the church (1 Pet 5:4)—as Scripture made clear. The papacy was obstructing this truth for too long, and the time to rise up had come (cf. Eccl 3:7). This would have far reaching implications affecting ecclesiology, as the Reformation would continue furthering the cause of a church broken off from the establishment while centered on the Scriptures; a church, of course, unhindered by professionally corrupt clergy who boasted in their life-long "holy orders." In an incredible act of Providence, these very issues would resurface in Europe three centuries later as one man picked up Martin Luther's fight against a new, yet similar opponent, on an island nation across the English Channel. Enter John Nelson Darby...

5.4 Background to John Nelson Darby's Rise

Because this next reformer is both "unknown and well known," perhaps a little more space is warranted for his background.[40] When addressing

[39] Mullet, *Martin Luther*, 115.

[40] The phrase "As unknown and well known" is carved into J. N. Darby's gravestone at Bournemouth, England. The number of biographies written on Darby are far less than Luther. And, as is the case with many biographies of influential (or controversial) people, many things written on Darby are questionable. That said, three notable works used for this particular section and commended to the reader are: Max S. Weremchuck, *John Nelson Darby: A Biography* (Neptune, NJ: Loizeaux, 1992); W. G. Turner, *Unknown and Well Known: A Biography of John Nelson Darby*, ed. E. N. Cross (London, UK: Chapter Two, 2006); and Marian Field, *John Nelson Darby: Prophetic Pioneer* (Godalming, UK: Highland, 2008).

the Greeks at Mars Hill, Paul the Apostle declared that "God made from one man every nation of mankind to live on all the face of the earth, having determined allotted periods and the boundaries of their dwelling place" (Acts 17:26, ESV). That God is sovereign over every person's place and every event in history is not only dramatic throughout Scripture's metanarrative, but can also be traced to those living in modern times. And, nowhere does this ring truer than in the lives of Martin Luther and John Darby.

Much like Luther's appointed place in 16th century Europe, God likewise had His hand on the island nations forming the United Kingdom at the turn of 19th century Europe. "An Act for the Union of Great Britain and Ireland" was passed resulting in a new Western power called, "the United Kingdom of Great Britain and Ireland." This global power-move fueled by both political and religious motives occurred in the year 1800—the very year of John Nelson Darby's birth. With this act, the Church of England, which in Ireland was called the Church of Ireland, became known simply as the Established Church. As God would have it, almost the identical issues Martin Luther protested against the Catholic "Romanists," Darby would pick up again and call to task the kingly church of England—and carry them even further. This time ecclesiology was directly on the table of reforms, and John Nelson Darby would be the new champion to carry on Reformation principles in Europe. And, as God would have it, it was this latter reformer—often referred to as "the father of modern dispensationalism"[41]—who would have a distinct impact on American evangelical ecclesiology.

5.4.1 A Brief Biography of J. N. Darby

John Nelson Darby, whose family legacy was thoroughly Irish, was born in Westminster, London on November 18, 1800. The eighth child to John and Anne Darby, John Nelson was baptized as an infant 15 weeks later at the towering St. Margaret's Church in London.[42] As a young teenager,

---

[41] For a comprehensive treatment refuting the popular notion that dispensational thought was originated in the 19th century by J. N. Darby, see William C. Watson, *Dispensationalism Before Darby: Seventeenth-Century and Eighteenth-Century English Apocalypticism* (Silverton, OR: Lampion, 2015).

[42] It is interesting that throughout his life, Darby supported pedo-baptism which

Darby enrolled at Trinity College in Dublin at 14 years old. Trinity was the reputable Anglican school in Ireland known for its rigor in mathematics and classical languages and literature. Graduating in 1819 with a BA with the highest honors in classics at age 18, Darby would also win the school's prestigious classical gold medal.[43] His gifting in languages would later prominently play out in his ministry, as he would become fluent in Latin, Hebrew, Greek, French, German, Italian, and, for the most part, Dutch. How many other dialects Darby would pick up is known only to Darby. Case in point, "While visiting New Zealand," reports Weremchuck, "[Darby] learned the native language, Maori, and was able to preach in it."[44] Besides the many hymns and commentaries on Scripture he would write, perhaps Darby's remarkable gift of languages would bear the most fruit with his literal translation of the Bible's Hebrew and Greek into English, French, and German.[45] His motivation for languages was always centered on reaching people with the gospel and instructing them in the Scriptures—something he was adamant they could do on their own without being reliant on man-appointed clergy.

---

put him at odds with most of his own Plymouth Brethren and the countless people his theology influenced. It seems to be the one lingering Anglican/Catholic ritual he could never shake. However, Darby thought more highly of peace and gospel unity among Christians than he did on baptizing children. Writing to a fellow Christian in 1852, Darby, as quoted in Weremchuck, *John Nelson Darby*, 203, stated: "What I think on the baptism of infants...I care much more for the peace of the church than any opinion on that. I have never tried to persuade anybody. I believe that everyone must act according to his own conscience."

[43] Cf. Weremchuck, *John Nelson Darby*, 30–31. The parallels are interesting in Luther's and Darby's young academic lives. Both entered college as young teenagers (Luther at 15, Darby at 14), and both had aspirations to be lawyers. However, one notable difference can be seen in how they each performed academically. Darby graduated head of his class *summa cum laude* winning the coveted "gold medal" in classics, while Luther graduated in the less-than-half bottom tier of his class with no awards earned.

[44] Ibid., 164.

[45] Turner adds, "Darby did not feel such a need for a new translation in English, because he considered the King James Version to be adequate for most purposes, and he encouraged his followers to continue to use it. But, he decided to produce a highly literal English version for study purposes." Turner, *Unknown and Well Known*, 143–44.

5.4.2 Darby the Lawyer

Like Calvin and Luther before him, Darby originally trained for a career in law but surpassed them both in actually securing a short legal vocation after being admitted to Lincoln's Inn in 1819/20. Lincoln's Inn was the most prestigious of London's schools for those called to the Bar. Because J. N. Darby was virtually born in the Anglican Communion, he had an awareness of Christ, but one that was dry of any true flavor throughout his teenage years (contra. Ps 34:8). This began to haunt him. Devoid of any intimate relation with the true Vine (John 15:1, 5), Darby was a branch desperately seeking purpose for his life, and rest for his soul. He even toyed with the idea of becoming a Roman Catholic, a taboo that would put him in the minority of a nation where practically every citizen at the time held life-long associations with the Established Church. Yet, while at Lincoln's Inn, he began reading his dusty New Testament and finally got to chapters nine and ten of Hebrews which convinced him that the Catholic Mass, with its suggestion of the perpetual sacrifice of Christ, was indeed heretical.[46] This discovery was the first for Darby who would live a life consistently rejecting Catholic dogma, and promoting Reformation principles. Christ would soon grab hold of Darby at 21 while he worked as a "barrister" (a British courtroom lawyer). He was converted through simply reading the Scriptures on his own. Hence, the private interpretation of Scripture, which Luther so ably defended, Darby would always hold dear. For him, it was personal.

Likewise, in the same vein as Luther, Darby would hold the Bible as the ultimate authority under heaven, and would have occasional "glowing discoveries" and "great recoveries." Resembling Martin Luther's sensitive conscious, the more Darby read the Bible, the more he became convicted of his unworthiness of salvation—and it weighed heavy on his soul. "He felt that Christ was the only Savior," relates Weremchuck, "but was not able to say that he possessed Him, or that he was saved by Him. He looked for proofs of regeneration in himself, something that can never give peace."[47] Darby continued on as an aspiring lawyer, but with a view toward delving

---

[46] Cf. Field, *John Nelson Darby*, 26.
[47] Weremchuck, *John Nelson Darby*, 36.

back into his childhood faith wrought in the Established Church—an institution which held sway over England and Northern Ireland. Much like prereformation Europe that hardly kept a distinction between church and state, England was dominated by its own state church since King Henry VIII founded Anglicanism, and it did all it could to stamp out any Catholic influence. This even included a sworn commitment from England and Ireland's brightest lawyers. In fact, as Weremchuck points out, "Part of the oath [Darby] had to take when called to the Irish Chancery Bar contained the vow to prevent the further growth of popery."[48]

5.4.3 Darby the Clergyman

After Darby came to Christ through reading His Word, he desperately craved relief for a soul that wanted nothing but Jesus. Wrestling with this in prayer, and through the advice of others, John Darby decided to leave his law career for ministry and was later ordained a deacon in the Established Church in 1825. In the following year, Darby was ordained an Anglican priest in the famed Christ Church Cathedral in Dublin. Like Martin Luther's father whose chief desire was for his son to practice law, Darby's father was not pleased with his son's decision either. He even disinherited him over it.[49] Just like Luther who did the monkish rituals in constant desperation to ease his conscience, so did Darby, who was known, to fast for weeks at a time—even to the point of severely jeopardizing his health. Also like Luther, he would tremble at taking the elements of the Lord's Supper, always being sure he was approved to do so by a more senior clergy member. In 1826, Darby took up a pastoral position in the country village of Calary, Ireland, being the only clergy of the town. It was during this time of concentrated ministry, that he fell in love with pastoring Christ's sheep.[50] It was

---

[48] Weremchuck, *John Nelson Darby*, 36.

[49] Ibid., 38.

[50] Unfortunately, Darby has too often portrayed as an esoteric, divisive figure devoid of any love or humility. This characterization is incredibly unbalanced. While it is wise (and realistic) not to portray any man as consistently Christ-like in all of his endeavors, a case must be made for Darby's tender pastoral heart. In fact, the village people of Calary got together and wrote a beautiful letter of commendation for their beloved pastor dated March 28, 1829, expressing their sincere gratitude and affections

also during this time, that Darby saw the inconsistencies of the established institutionalized version of the church. "His soul was still not eased while a priest," observes Weremchuck, "because he was beginning to feel that the style of work was not in agreement with what he read concerning the church and Christianity."[51]

Ironically, the Protestant Anglican clergy of Darby's day held too many similarities with the Roman Catholic clergy of Luther's day. It seems the squid of Romanism had far reaching tentacles with its habit of turning the church into a lucrative industry. The ordained clergy, as Darby began to notice, seemed to hold no true convictions for the people God put under their care. Like the clergy that surrounded Luther, they had no true knowledge of or from the Scriptures. Everything they appealed to was ritualistic as passed down to them from the Anglican hierarchy. According to Weremchuck:

> The clergy were, as a whole, careless in giving out the bread of life to the flocks who had been committed to their care and keeping. At best they preached a carnal and soul-benumbing morality, and trafficked with souls of men by receiving money for discharging the pastoral office in parishes where they did not so much as look on the faces of the people more than once a year.[52]

Thus, Darby began to hold the ordained clergy of the Established Church in contempt. Once again, Christ and His Word were not the authority; bishops were. Once again, an impassable gulf was fixed between the Christian laity and the ordained priesthood. This period in Darby's life was much like Luther's in that it took serving as an ordained member of the establishment to see how far it had fallen from the Scriptures.[53] And, if Scripture really did come with God's ultimate authority, then it is only toward God through Christ alone that man must give an account. No bishop, priest, pope, or king can act as a substitute.

---

for "Dr. and Rev'd. Mr. Darby" for his unceasing love and care toward them (cf. Field, *John Nelson Darby*, 45; Weremchuck, *John Nelson Darby*, 217–18).

[51] Weremchuck, *John Nelson Darby*, 44.

[52] Ibid., 40.

[53] Cf. Ibid., 61; Turner, *Unknown and Well Known*, 26.

It was the Book of Acts with its portrayal of the early church that had a particular affect on Darby's ecclesiastical beliefs, as Acts ran contrary to what he was used to seeing around him. As such, it would be Darby's conviction of *sola Scriptura* that would lead directly to his beliefs concerning ecclesiology. The Christian was not accountable to any "ordained" man, but to Christ. The Christian, as a member of Jesus' body, really did have freedom—one that was highlighted in serving one another in God's love. The church of God was not a business set up like a corporation, or one that lorded different stages of ordained holiness over the Lord's sheep (cf. Matt 20:26–28). It was here, while serving as the "curate of Calary," that Darby "saw that membership in Scripture was not membership of an association organized and formed by man...but membership of Christ—a hand, foot etc. (1 Cor 12:18, 20.)."[54] Darby would eventually leave the Church of England and Ireland, being unable to find a justification for any national church structure in Scripture.[55] What he did find in the New Testament, however, were local autonomous fellowships making up the whole Body of Christ.

5.5 Darby's Three Treatises

Darby was not an innovator. He was a studious and brilliant disciplinarian who consistently carried forth Luther's exposures of the establishment in papal Rome to the kingly-state establishment in England and Ireland. And like Luther before him, Darby wrote voluminously.[56] In what

---

[54] Weremchuck, *John Nelson Darby*, 60.

[55] Cf. Turner, *Unknown and Well Known*, 23.

[55] Due to space limitations, much more can be said concerning this period in Darby's life. Perhaps the most important event would be Darby's "great recovery" after a serious horse riding accident that occurred one evening on his way to a parishioner's home. It was his recovery in Dublin which gave him the concentrated time he needed in the Scriptures that lead him to leave (yet never "officially") the Established Church in 1828, and later found the Plymouth Brethren in 1831.

[56] Darby's literary achievements are truly remarkable. In addition to his literal translations of the Bible into English, German, and French (and possibly Dutch, yet the extent of his involvement is unknown), as well as his five volume biblical commentary, *The Synopsis of the Bible*, Darby wrote 34 volumes of doctrine and theology later collected and edited by William Kelley (1821–1906). Moreover, he wrote the seven

follows, three of John Nelson Darby's influential tracts dealing directly with notions of Scripture and clergy will be analyzed in light of Luther's three above. This comparison will show the furthering of Luther's legacy by Darby into what would become a movement of ecclesiastical independence led by Spirit-filled laity, which would later directly influence American evangelicalism.

5.5.1 The Nature and Unity of the Church

John Nelson Darby published his first major work in Dublin in 1828 called "Considerations on the Nature and Unity of the Church of Christ." This tract of less than 20 pages had a massive impact on those trying to understand what the church was before both Catholicism and Anglicanism had corrupted its organic form. Darby's main contention in this work was that Christ always has His true church in the world—even when it seems she has all but apostatized. Neither pope, king, nor demon could ever thwart Jesus' promise in Matthew 16:18 that He would build His church. Like the 7000 Israelites whom the Lord kept from bowing the knee to Baal (1 Kings 19:18), Jesus still has and is yet building His faithful remnant. This even includes Christians in the Established Church or in the various dissenting groups that had protested since the Reformation. As Darby saw it, the church in its pure form is united in faith in the gospel of Jesus Christ. Whether the Christian be an Anglican, Methodist, Baptist, or Independent—the nature and unity of the church is forged together by faith in the gospel. This was so obvious to Darby from the Scriptures, he thought of it as a presupposition to Protestantism: "I am supposing here, of course," wrote Darby, "that the great truths of the gospel are the professed faith of the churches, as they are in all the genuine Protestant churches."[57]

Darby certainly recognized God's hand upon the Reformation

---

volume *Notes and Comments on Scripture*, the two volume *Notes and Jottings*, three volumes of letters, and 27 different hymns (at least the ones that were published) called *Spiritual Songs* (cf. Turner, *Unknown and Well Known*, 77–91; Weremchuck, *John Nelson Darby*, 164–70; Field, *John Nelson Darby*, 168–85).

[57] John Nelson Darby, "Considerations on the Nature and Unity of the Church of Christ" in *The Collected Writings of J. N. Darby*, ed. William Kelley, vol. 1, *Ecclesiastical No. 1* (Winschoten, Netherlands: Heijkoop, 1971), 20.

sparked by Luther, but he also made it clear that the Reformation did not root out the lingering problems of holy hierarchy still obstructing the laity from enjoying the true church. "Such indeed," remarked Darby,

> however blessed as we are all bound most thankfully, to acknowledge the Reformation to have been, was not the case: it was much and manifestly mixed with human agency . . . there was much of the old system which remained in the constitution of the churches, and which was in no way the development of the mind of Christ, by setting up the light and authority in the word.[58]

Commenting on Darby's sentiments, Turner states:

> The Reformation was seen as a great light in this growing darkness, and most certainly a work of God in which the truth of justification by faith alone shone brightly. Yet Darby thought the movement overlooked much Scriptural teaching regarding the church and substituted the opinions and the preferences of the leaders of the time. These leaders sought the favor and protection of the world, while Roman Catholicism had always sought to control the world.[59]

While the Reformation's *sola Scriptura* cry may have, for the most part, overlooked ecclesiology, Darby was sure to apply it directly to the doctrine of the church. Drawing on language he no doubt borrowed from Luther, Darby asserted: "These observations are in some measure applicable to all the great national Protestant bodies since the outward form and constitution became so prominent a matter, which was not the case originally while deliverance from Babylon was in question."[60] If the pope and clergy of Catholicism were obstructing the New Testament's vision for the church, so were the bishops and priests of Anglicanism. It was each believer's repentant-faith in Jesus Christ that gave the true church its hope and unity.

Darby recognized that a true unity in anything worthy of the gospel, the church being the premier example, was not bound together by uniform ritual prescribed by an ordained overlord. Rather, it was by the church's

---

[58] Darby, "Considerations on the Nature," 1:21.
[59] Turner, *Unknown and Well Known*, 78.
[60] Darby, "Considerations on the Nature," 1:22.

true profession in Christ and unity in the Spirit. This truth transcends all denominational lines and state-controlled religion. Darby contended: "The bond of communion is not the *unity* of the people of God, but really (in point of fact), their *differences*."[61] It was the manifest *differences* among Christians that shows the real beauty of the church's unity—something difficult to see when kept under the bondage of the Established Church, whatever its form.[62] At certain points in history, a separation from the established form of Christianity is necessary. Even New Testament history has shown that believers are prone to remain in one place if not given an obvious reason to scatter with the gospel message (cf. Acts 11:19). Too often, Christians are more ready to give an answer for the hope of their denominational tie than for their hope in Christ. To them, Darby would rebuke: "So far as men pride themselves on being Established, Presbyterian, Baptist, Independent, or anything else, they are antichristian."[63]

Believers owe their loyalties to the Christ of Scripture, not an institution. Thus, Darby saw the true church as full of independent fellowships that moved freely about the world in obedience to the Great Commission. For Darby, it is only when believers take the Word of God outside of their comfort zone that they truly fulfill their duty of witnessing. Sometimes, that means having to shake a complacent state church that has monopolized the Faith. "Our duty as believers," according to Darby—who understood the Bible as the Christian's supreme authority—"is to be witnesses of what we believe."[64] On this, Martin Luther and John Darby could not be more united.

5.5.2 Notion of a Clergyman

If Martin Luther's "The Babylonian Captivity of the Church" was his most aggressive polemic against the Catholic Church, then John Nelson Darby's "The Notion of a Clergyman" was certainly his harshest critique

---

[61] Darby, "Considerations on the Nature," 1:22.

[62] This is one reason why Darby's own Plymouth Brethren movement was genuinely in line with Darby's ecclesiastical convictions and thoroughly biblical. Ecclesiastical separation, when deemed necessary, is something the apostle Paul taught (cf. Rom 16:17; 2 Thess 3:14–15; Titus 3:10–11).

[63] Darby, "Considerations on the Nature," 1:31.

[64] Ibid., 1:28.

against the Established Church. Darby's sentiments are quickly picked up in the tract's unsubtle subtitle: "Dispensationally the Sin Against the Holy Ghost."[65] However, rather than this treatise being about an individual committing the blasphemy of the Holy Spirit (cf. Matt 12:31–32)—a misunderstanding the Anglican clergy would take it for—Darby's issue was with the Established Church substituting a man-made system for the actual gifting and leading of the Holy Spirit. Hence, it was the notion of a clergyman which Darby found to be in error. For Darby, the ordained clerical scheme in his day was as corrupt a system as the Romanists had made centuries earlier which called for Luther's reforms. And like Luther, Darby called to task a clerical system that lorded their position over the laity. Weremchuck explains, "Christendom now appeared to be a set of human ecclesiastical systems, all of which had no right claim to be *the* church of God, because there were true Christians in all of them."[66]

However, Darby took it a step further than Luther in that he did not merely see corruption within the clergy as being problematic; he saw the entire concept of the clergy as problematic. Darby did not hold back in calling it a sin because he saw the concept of an ordained clergy as an invented system devoid of any biblical warrant—one that substituted man for God:

> The statement which I make is this, that I believe the notion of a Clergyman to be the sin against the Holy Ghost in this dispensation. I am not talking of individuals willfully committing it but that the thing itself is such as regards this dispensation, and must result in its destruction: the substitution of something for the power and presence

---

[65] The actual publication date of Darby's "The Notion of a Clergyman" is little hazy as he pulled it from publication after he sent it to the printer. Yet, it had to follow his "Considerations on the Nature and Unity of the Church of Christ," per his own remarks calling attention to it in the preface. In the preface to the only available version (as collected by W. Kelley), Darby explains that the tract was originally leaked to influential clergy members in the Established Church before publication, and he was persuaded not to publish it at the time. Darby, who always remained warm toward his former church, never wanting to unnecessarily offend any of his Anglican clergy friends, conceded to hold off on publication until it could be read for its doctrine sake and not for shock value.

[66] Weremchuck, *John Nelson Darby*, 82.

of that holy, blessed, and blessing Spirit, by which this dispensation is charcaterised [sic], and by which the unrenewedness [sic] of man, and the authority of man holds the place which alone that blessed Spirit has power and title to fill, as that other Comforter which should abide forever.[67]

Because the Established Church vehemently opposed any Spirit-led movement that might expose their cracks, similar to the Romanists during Luther's time, J. N. Darby saw his state church as another resurrected form of the Pharisaical system—a system that Stephen the martyr rebuked as "stiff-necked, uncircumcised in heart and ears, always resisting the Holy Spirit" (Acts 7:51). With this Scripture and others on his mind, Darby contended:

> The sin against the Holy Ghost was the ascribing to the power of evil that which came from the Holy Ghost: and such is the direct operation of the idea of a Clergyman. It charges the testimony of the Lord Jesus Christ, which the Spirit gives by the mouth of those whom He chooses, whom they are pleased to call laymen, and the righteousness of conduct which flows from the reception of that testimony, with disorder and schism.[68]

Like Luther before him, Darby sought to destroy the wall dividing the clergy and laity. Yet, Darby took Luther's attacks further in condemning the entire concept of the clerical system. If the authority of the clergy is derived from man and not God, Darby argued, it follows that any form of church that is not of the Holy Spirit must be shelved as evil.

In this tract, Darby leans on 1 Corinthians 14:33 which teaches that God is not the author of confusion, but of peace and order. Thus, if the church truly exists in Spirit-indwelt fellowships, and in forms other than just the Establishment, these fellowships are the work of the Spirit and are not to be charged with divisiveness, confusions, or schisms. This must have carried added weight coming from a man who was technically still an or-

---

[67] John Nelson Darby, "The Notion of a Clergyman: Dispensationally the Sin Against the Holy Ghost," in *The Collected Writings of J. N. Darby*, ed. William Kelley, vol. 1, *Ecclesiastical No. 1* (Winschoten, Netherlands: Heijkoop, 1971), 38.
[68] Ibid., 1:39.

dained Anglican clergyman. Yet, Darby could not overlook the clergy's insistence that a man must be approved and ordained by senior clergy in order to administer or receive Communion, or even to preach the Word of God to common folk. As to the latter, Darby came to the same conclusion from the Scriptures as John Wesley did a century earlier, that it was not necessary to be ordained in order to preach and serve God in ministry.[69] With this, Darby realized that the notion of ordained clergy bars even preachers of the New Testament, as "St. Paul, perhaps the greatest preacher of all time, would not have been allowed to preach from the pulpit of the Established Church because he had not been ordained!"[70]

For Darby, then, this notion of ordained clergy is the sin against the Holy Spirit in the present dispensation—whether in Protestant or Catholic circles: "If a Protestant clergyman has title to this, or whatever title to respect he has," asserted Darby, "the Roman Catholic priest has the same."[71] Either way, for Darby the use of the term "clergy" as it was used in the Catholic and Established Church "is precisely the sign of *the substitution of ministers in the place of the Church of God.*"[72]

5.5.3 Formation of Churches

Originally written in French and published in Switzerland around 1840, Darby produced a tract called "On the Formation of Churches" addressing the problem of presumption among well-intended church planters. It is here in this essay where Darby's undergirding dispensationalism takes center stage helping shape his ecclesiology. It also here that Darby picked up the ecclesiastical ball where Martin Luther and other reformers had left it, since it was the building of national churches that were the monuments left in their wake. Commenting on this, Darby wrote:

---

[69] Cf. Field, *John Nelson Darby*, 43.

[70] Ibid., 42. It is interesting to note that Darby had originally defended the idea of "apostolic succession." However, he changed this view to the more inclusive "divinely appointed ministry" while diligently studying the New Testament during his convalescence in Dublin. Ironically, this time of recovery was due to the horse riding accident Darby incurred while ministering as a *clergyman* in Calary.

[71] Darby, "Notion of a Clergyman," 1:42.

[72] Ibid., 1:46.

Nationalism—in other words, the dividing of the church into bodies—consisting of such and such a nation, is a novelty, not above three centuries old, although many dear children of God are found dwelling in it. The Reformation did not directly touch the question of the true character of God's church....It did not re-establish the church in its primitive powers. On the contrary, it placed it in general under subjection to the state in order to free it from subjection to the Pope; because it regarded the papal authority as dangerous, and looked upon all the subjects of a country as Christians."[73]

Darby's main thesis in "On the Formation of Churches" was that the church in this dispensation, that is, from Pentecost (Acts 2) to rapture (1 Thess 4:17), is "ruined." As both Jesus and Paul promised that the latter times will go from bad to worse, it is in vain that Christians should ever attempt to reconstruct the church in its purest form, whether by vote or by a single charismatic leader. Consistent with the previous dispensations marked by man's failure, the present church age also bears the blemish.

For Darby, both the Roman Catholic and Established Church had proven that the church of God on earth has failed in this dispensation to keep the "unity of the Spirit in the bond of peace" (Eph 4:3). He also recognized those who dissented from their national church to form their own churches had done so, even if well intended, in the mere power man: "Those who have been endeavouring [sic] to form churches seem, though meaning well," relates Darby, "to have entirely forgotten our need of power as well as direction."[74] The power and direction of which Darby spoke is found only in the God of Scripture. For a man to try and form a church alone, armed with only his discernment while isolated from other churches, in Darby's estimation, was an evil as gross as the notion of ordained clergy.

Darby was trying his best to get across to fellow ministers that they should at least consider the possibility of presumption when they judge in full confidence that they can succeed in restoring the primitive church when

---

[73] John Nelson Darby, "On the Formation of Churches," in *The Collected Writings of J. N. Darby*, ed. William Kelley, vol. 1, *Ecclesiastical No. 1* (Winschoten, Netherlands: Heijkoop, 1971), 140.

[74] Ibid., 1:148.

other churches failed in their attempts. Darby realized the years since the church's birth had proven how much ruin man can bring upon it. This could be seen as early as the letters of rebuke addressed to the seven churches in Revelation 2–3. "I have written from a desire," states Darby, "that there should be less presumption and more diffidence in what we undertake to do: and that we should feel more deeply the ruined condition to which we have reduced the Church."[75]

Lest anyone think that Darby was against independent and local Spirit-led fellowships, on the contrary, it was that very thing he saw as Scriptural: "This truth of the gathering together of God's children is in Scripture seen realised [sic] in various localities, and in each central locality the Christians resident therein composed but one body: Scripture is perfectly clear on that head."[76] The Scriptures were plain that the true church of God already exists in fellowships all over the world, and are united by their faith in Christ and obedience to His Word. Darby understood this from Jesus' promise that He is in the midst of any gathering of at least two or three believers meeting in His name (cf. Matt 18:20). "The thought," Weremchuck clarifies, "was not to seek to be a church alongside many other churches, nor assume to be *the* church, but the thought was to give expression to an already existing unity, the only one God recognizes, the unity of the body of Christ, the one true church."[77] Rather than relying on man-appointed clergyman to lead these expressions of the church, Darby fully recognized that God gives them pastors and teachers, wherever a Spirit-filled gathering may be found. Understanding this from Ephesians 4, Darby exhorts: "It is plainly our duty to desire pastors and teachers to take the care of such congregations, and that God did raise up such a church as we see it in the world."[78] What Darby held in contempt was any notion of "independence" that was more akin to cultish-esoteric-isolation. That a man, totally independent of other fellowships, could ever form a church in order to restore it to perfection was ludicrous in Darby's estimation.[79] Finally,

[75] Darby, "On the Formation of Churches," 1:149.
[76] Ibid., 1:141.
[77] Weremchuck, *John Nelson Darby*, 82.
[78] Darby, "Formation of Churches," 1:141.
[79] It is worth pondering how much of Joseph Smith's Mormonism was on

much like Luther who had closed his "Open Letter" with a point-by-point proposal of reform, Darby closes his "On the Formation of Churches" with a point-by-point manifesto of his vision of the church as he understood it from the New Testament. Most germane to the purposes here are points four, five, and six:

> (4) The necessity of ordination in order to administer the Lord's Supper nowhere appears in the New Testament; and it is clear that it was to break bread Christians came together on the Lord's day (Acts 20:7; 1 Cor. 11:20–23); (5) A commission from man to preach the gospel is unknown to the New Testament; (6) The choosing of presidents and pastors by the assembly is all together unwarranted by the New Testament.[80]

5.5.4 The Result of the Three Treatises

Darby's writing and teaching ministry had an impact all over the world. Unlike Martin Luther who remained within the confines of Germany, even dying in the same town in which he was born, Darby ministered all over the Western hemisphere. While he would later be remembered more for his teachings on eschatology congruent with his dispensationalism, it was his beliefs regarding ecclesiology that really drove him. As his three treatises have shown, Darby was a churchman at heart first, rather than a prophecy expert.[81] "With Darby," observed Sweetnam and Gribben, "eschatology followed on from church doctrine. It was ecclesiological concern that led to Darby's rethinking of prophecy."[82]

Darby's mind when he was writing of independent, isolated church formation done in order to singlehandedly "restore the pure church." Joseph Smith (1805–44) was a contemporary of Darby, and Darby makes mention of Mormons in some of his letters and essays when ministering in America. Interestingly enough, Smith had appointed "Independence" Missouri as the new Zion for Mormonism.

[80] Darby, "Formation of Churches," 1:152.

[81] Indeed, Darby wrote four separate volumes on Ecclesiology, each volume ranging from 10–30 separate essays, which were later collected and edited by his friend, William Kelley. These are in addition to the hundreds of other writings, including hymns, from Darby that most often touched on ecclesiastical matters.

[82] Mark Sweetnam and Crawford Gribben, "J. N. Darby and the Irish Origins of

John Darby's disdain for a professionalized, corrupt clergy that kept the laity under bondage from the beauties of Scripture was matched only by Martin Luther three hundred years prior. And, it was Darby's relentless traveling, preaching, and writing ministry concerning the church that would bear a subtle, yet, enduring impact on American evangelicalism. Indeed, his treatises and preaching concerning ecclesiastical independency had a peculiar impact on the United States, where he visited at least a half dozen times. Sweetnam and Gribben acknowledge, "Though his name is not widely known, and the details of his life are unfamiliar to many, even to many of those whom he influenced the most, he has been one of the most important shapers of evangelical thought throughout the last two hundred years."[83]

5.5.5 The Unique Legacy of Darby

What is perhaps the most unique contribution of Darby's legacy in America, besides his eschatology which became overly sensationalized by those who came after him, was his influence concerning local, independent assemblies of believers. Rejecting any form of state church or denominational loyalties, Darby emphasized Spirit-filled gatherings that were led by pastors and teachers gifted from God. However, he was not looking for fame or notoriety as a pioneer, he was merely acting consistent with what he thought the Bible taught: "Darby wasn't seeking to be the progenitor of a new movement," reports Sutherland, "That came about as a result of his uncompromising positions on the doctrines of scripture."[84] And, as Darby held tightly to *sola Scriptura*, there was absolutely no room in his ecclesiology for a professional clergy that was nowhere to be found in the New Testament.

Darby saw the church of God as existing in the world through its countless, autonomous, Christian gatherings based on Jesus' promise in

---

Dispensationalism," *Journal of the Evangelical Theology Society* 52, no. 3 (September 2009): 573, accessed February 10, 2017, Galaxie Theological Journal Library Online.

[83] Ibid., 569.

[84] Winston Terrance Sutherland, "John Nelson Darby: Scholarship that Influenced the Bible College Movement," *Christian Higher Education* 9, no. 3 (July–August 2010): 276, accessed February 6, 2017. Academic Search Complete.

Matthew 18:20. And, in so doing, he was more consistent with New Testament ecclesiology, and reached further than even Luther was willing to go. The great reformers who heroically freed the church from its bondage to the Pope and the Roman Catholic clergy got no further than replacing it with a State or National Church: "This was true of Luther, who fastened a State Church upon Germany. Zwingli, who fastened a State Church upon Switzerland. John Knox, who fastened a State Church upon Scotland. Henry VIII, who fastened a State Church upon England."[85] By further carrying the Reformation recovery of *sola Scriptura* and the priesthood of all believers, John Nelson Darby left an un-repairable crack in the Established Church's wall of clericalism. A state church was no church.

In America, he had a distinctly unique impact. By emphasizing separation from corrupt ecclesiastical institutions, Darby almost single-handedly influenced what would become the Bible School movement resulting in thousands of local, non-denominational churches. Several times Darby was invited by D. L. Moody to participate in evangelistic and teaching campaigns. While they eventually had a falling out over predestination vs. free-will, Darby being labeled an "extreme Calvinist" by Moody,[86] Moody nonetheless highly revered Darby's dispensationalism, and especially, his literal hermeneutics and separatist ecclesiology free of denominations. Moody Bible Institute was later founded in 1886 as a non-denominational ministry training school that graduated gospel workers who went on to pastor independent, autonomous churches. Many other Bible schools, colleges and seminaries then followed. "Darby's 'stepchildren'," as Marion Field calls them, "are supported by certain Non-Denominational Bible Schools; Dallas Theological Seminary and Moody Bible College [sic] are examples."[87] To these could be added Grace College and Theological Seminary, Northwestern College, Grand Rapids Baptist Seminary, Western Seminary, Denver Seminary, Trinity Evangelical Divinity School, Biola University and Talbot

---

[85] "Forword [sic]," *Central Bible Quarterly* 4, no. 2 (Summer 1961): 2, accessed January 9, 2017, Galaxie Theological Journal Library Online.

[86] Cf. Turner, *Unknown and Well Known*, 34–35; Weremchuck, *John Nelson Darby*, 143–44.

[87] Field, *John Nelson Darby*, 210.

School of Theology, Southern California Seminary, The Master's University and Seminary, Calvary University, Philadelphia College of the Bible (now Cairn University), Multnomah Bible College/Biblical Seminary, William Tyndale College, and still others.[88] Hence, there is little doubt that Darby's teaching influenced American evangelicalism through the Bible College and Bible conference movements of the late 19th–early 20th centuries. These schools trained men to fill independent churches that needed qualified, Spirit-filled leadership. "Darby and the Bible college Movement," states Sutherland "paved the way to fill that need. As a natural consequence, their brand of theology proved part and parcel of the germinating movement."[89] Indeed, it was Darby's dispensationalism that drove his passion for the local church and its need for qualified pastor-teachers.

5.6 Conclusion

This chapter comes full circle—from the thunders of Martin Luther against Scripture being kept the exclusive property of the pope, along with his protests against an artificial clergy/laity divide in Rome, to John Nelson Darby's picking back up the same arguments against the Established Church in England and Ireland. Yet, it was the later reformer who most consistently carried out the Reformation legacy of *sola Scriptura* and the priesthood of all believers as it relates to ecclesiology. Rather than being solely a prophecy expert, Darby's dispensationalism formed him into a remarkable churchman who was zealous for Christ and Scripture. If Lutheranism is the legacy of Luther, local autonomous, self-governed assemblies are the legacy of Darby. Both were born out of each man's haunting conviction that Scripture is the supreme authority under heaven—and every Christian is free to read it for himself and obey it.

Therefore, this chapter has demonstrated that the Protestant Reformation's insistence of *sola Scriptura*, and its proper interpretation by the individual believer, led to its unforeseen development of modern-day ecclesiology. By way of analysis, tracing a literary connection between two reforming fountainheads—Martin Luther and John Nelson Darby—a justification

---

[88] Cf. Sutherland, "John Nelson Darby," 272.
[89] Ibid., 281.

has been provided for the modern day, local independent church as a mode of governance faithful to principles initiated by the Reformation; and, as such, was shown to be an accurate reflection of New Testament ecclesiology as well. In so doing, it has been demonstrated that without the Reformation's recovery of *sola Scriptura* spearheaded by Martin Luther, Rome would still retain its unlawful captivity of the Western church by holding the laity under lock and key—an identical battle later fought by John Nelson Darby in the United Kingdom. While Luther and Darby may have been separated by time and nation, their place in history as instruments in God's sovereign hand is indeed remarkable, and worthy of study, reflection and thanksgiving.

Bibliography

Bainton, Rolland. *Here I Stand: A Life of Martin Luther.* New York, NY: Meridian, 1995.

Brady, Thomas, A., Jr. "The Holy Roman Empire's Bishops on the Eve of the Reformation." In *Continuity and Change: The Harvest of Late Medieval and Reformation History*, edited by Robert J. Bast and Andrew C. Gow. Leiden, The Netherlands: Brill, 2000.

Darby, John Nelson. "Considerations on the Nature and Unity of the Church of Christ." In *The Collected Writings of J. N. Darby*, edited by William Kelley. Vol. 1, *Ecclesiastical No. 1*, 1–19. Winschoten, Netherlands: Heijkoop, 1971.

———. "On the Formation of Churches." In *The Collected Writings of J. N. Darby*, edited by William Kelley. Vol. 1, *Ecclesiastical No. 1*, 138–155. Winschoten, Netherlands: Heijkoop, 1971.

———. "The Notion of a Clergyman: Dispensationally the Sin Against the Holy Ghost." In *The Collected Writings of J. N. Darby*, edited by William Kelley. Vol. 1, *Ecclesiastical No. 1*, 36–51. Winschoten, Netherlands: Heijkoop, 1971.

Field, Marian. *John Nelson Darby: Prophetic Pioneer.* Godalming, UK: Highland, 2008.

"Forword [sic]." *Central Bible Quarterly* 4, no. 2 (Summer 1961): 2. Accessed January 9, 2017. Galaxie Theological Journal Library Online.

Luther, Martin. "An Open Letter to the Christian Nobility of the German Nation Concerning the Reform of the Christian Estate." In *Three Treatises*, revised by James Atkinson, translated by Charles M. Jacobs, 7–112. Philadelphia, PA: Fortress, 1960.

———. "The Babylonian Captivity of the Church." In *Three Treatises*, revised by Fredrick C. Ahrens and Abdel Ross Wentz, translated by A. T. W. Steinhausser, 113–260. Philadelphia, PA: Fortress, 1960.

Luther, Martin. "The Freedom of a Christian." In *Three Treatises*, revised by Harold J. Grimm, translated by W. A. Lambert, 261–317. Philadelphia, PA: Fortress, 1960.

Mullet, Michael A. *Martin Luther*. London: Taylor & Francis, 2004. Accessed February 9, 2017. EBSCO*host eBook Collection*.

Orr, James. *The Progress of Dogma*. London, UK: Hodder and Stoughton, 1901. Kindle.

Steinhausser, A. T. W. Foreword to "The Babylonian Captivity of the Church." In *Three Treatises*, by Martin Luther, revised by Fredrick C. Ahrens and Abdel Ross Wentz, translated by A. T. W. Steinhausser. Philadelphia, PA: Fortress, 1960.

Strauss, Gerald. *Manifestations of Discontent in Germany on the Eve of the Reformation: A Collection of Documents Selected, Translated, and Introduced*. Bloomington, IN: Indiana University, 1971.

Sutherland, Winston Terrance. "John Nelson Darby: Scholarship that Influenced the Bible College Movement." *Christian Higher Education* 9, no. 3 (July–August 2010): 271–85. Accessed February 6, 2017. Academic Search Complete.

Sweetnam, Mark and Crawford Gribben. "J. N. Darby and the Irish Origins of Dispensationalism." *Journal of the Evangelical Theology Society* 52, no. 3 (September 2009): 569–578. Accessed February 10, 2017. Galaxie Theological Journal Library Online.

Trueman, Carl R. *Luther on the Christian Life: Cross and Freedom*. Wheaton, IL: Crossway, 2015.

Turner, W. G. *Unknown and Well Known: A Biography of John Nelson Darby*. Edited by E. N. Cross. London, UK: Chapter Two, 2006.

Watson, William C. *Dispensationalism Before Darby: Seventeenth-Century and Eighteenth-Century English Apocalypticism*. Silverton, OR: Lampion, 2015.

Weremchuck, Max S. *John Nelson Darby: A Biography*. Neptune, NJ: Loizeaux, 1992.

6

THE DOCTRINE OF LOCAL CHURCH AUTONOMY:
Its Loss, Recovery and Influence on Dispensationalism

Kevin D. Zuber
Moody Bible Institute

6.0 Introduction

The doctrine of the church or ecclesiology, one of the distinct categories of systematic theology, was not often a matter of speculative or theoretical theological reflection until the time of the Reformation. Until then those who spoke or wrote about the church—the Early Church Fathers and early apologists[1]—either only mentioned the church in passing or they sought to address some specific issue or problem in the church. The idea of "the church" was more or less simply assumed to be understood by everyone, everywhere who was a part of "the church." Even the very brief allusion to "the holy catholic church" in the so-called *Apostle's Creed* reflects this general assumption—all those who made this confession would have been expected to understand (more or less) the referent behind the words.

The matter of church authority came up early in the early church and it was addressed (indirectly) by Ignatius of Antioch (c. 35–c. 107). Ignatius wrote seven letters to various churches: In them, he mentions the "bishop" (at this stage in history, just the "pastor" of a local church) and "elders"

---

[1] See Maxwell Staniforth, trans., *Early Christian Writings* (New York: Penguin, 1968).

(presbyters), and he instructs the churches to respect and obey their "bishop."[2] Later, one of the few early church works devoted to directly addressing the issue of the church per se was written by the church father Cyprian of Carthage (c. AD 200–258). His best-known work was titled *The Unity of the Church*; it was a polemic to counter the schismatic Novatians.[3] He reasoned that there was only one church, and any who broke away from it could not be saved; the Latin phrase *extra ecclesiam nulla salus*, "outside the church there is no salvation" is attributed to Cyprian. His arguments and his uses of the Latin term *ecclesiam* indicate that the idea of "the church" was something all his readers would readily understand. Cyprian argued that it was the bishops[4] who spoke for and represented the church; thus, where there were authoritative bishops, there was "the church." It must be noted, however, that Cyprian's purpose in writing was to marshal arguments to counter the schismatics; he did not intend to write, nor did he produce, a thorough articulation of a formal ecclesiology. What he believed about the polity, organization, administration and function, even the nature of the church must be gleaned from his polemical arguments. And this is true of most of the early church writings; that is, what the "early church" thought about the church must be discerned from statements and arguments employed for purposes other than articulating a formal ecclesiology.

However, since the reformers were separating from the Roman Catholic Church, they found it necessary to reflect on, and articulate, a more or less formal ecclesiology in order to demonstrate that: (1) the Roman Catholic Church had fallen away from the biblical teaching on the church; and

---

[2] Michael W. Holmes, ed. and trans., *The Apostolic Fathers: Greek Texts and English Translations*, 3rd ed. (Grand Rapids, MI: Baker, 2007), 166–261. For instance, Ignatius writes to the Ephesians: "The bishops appointed throughout the world are in the mind of Christ. Thus, it is proper for you to run in harmony with the mind of the bishop, as in fact you are doing." Ignatius, "The Letter of Ignatius to the Ephesians," 3.2–4.1, in *The Apostolic Fathers*, ed. and trans. Holmes, 184–87.

[3] The Novatians were an early sect (c. AD 250) that were quite strict and held that baptized believers who had lapsed—given up or renounced the faith under persecution—should not be readmitted to the communion of the church.

[4] By this time the office of "bishop" was that of one who holds oversight and authority over a large city or town, or even over a region or district and all the churches therein. See more on this point at footnotes 19 and 20.

(2) they were recovering the true biblical picture of "the church." While Luther wrote extensively on the church, he never produced work specifically addressing ecclesiology.[5] Calvin, on the other hand, dedicated the fourth book (IV) of the *Institutes* to the subject *Of the Holy Catholic Church*, and it begins with a discussion "of the True Church." This set the precedent for future Protestant theologies to consider the nature, function, organization and ministry of the church. Indeed, most of the major Protestant confessions considered it essential to include a statement about the church. For example, the *Belgic Confession* (1561) lists these as the marks of the true church:

> The church engages in the pure preaching of the gospel; it makes use of the pure administration of the sacraments as Christ instituted them; it practices church discipline for correcting faults. In short, it governs itself according to the pure Word of God, rejecting all things contrary to it and holding Jesus Christ as the only Head.[6]

Similarly, *The Westminster Confession of Faith* (1646) devotes seven of its thirty-three chapters to defining the church and delineating its functions and nature.[7] Much of the focus of these Protestant theologies and statements is directed at correcting the errors of the Roman Catholic Church's teaching on the church and recovering a more biblical understanding of the nature and practice of the "true church."

---

[5] "Luther's view of the church and its ministry are both grounded in the Word of God, the promise of the gospel. The church exists wherever the Word of God is proclaimed, and the church is a spiritual community oriented to and shaped by this Word in its life by the power of the Holy Spirit." Cheryl M. Peterson, "Martin Luther on the Church and Its Ministry," in *Oxford Research Encyclopedia of Religion*, ed. John Barton, Oxford University Press, March 2017, accessed July 10, 2017, http://religion.oxfordre.com/view/10.1093/acrefore/9780199340378.001.0001/acrefore-9780199340378-e-362.

[6] See "Belgic Confession," Christian Reformed Church, accessed July 10, 2017, https://www.crcna.org/welcome/beliefs/confessions/belgic-confession.

[7] See "The Westminster Confession of Faith," Center for Reformed Theology and Apologetics, accessed July 10, 2017, http://www.reformed.org/documents/wcf_with_proofs/. Chapters XXV to XXXI cover the definition of the church, the sacraments, discipline and the relations of the church.

6.0.1 Definition

One of the fruits of the reformers' renewed and biblical focus on the church is the doctrine of local church autonomy.[8] This doctrine may be defined in terms of "church authority" and it affirms that the spiritual leaders in the local church (elders, pastors, deacons) "operate under the authority of Christ, the Chief Shepherd" and so "they represent the highest level of spiritual authority in the local church and are answerable to Him (1 Pet. 5:2–4)."[9] Because Christ is the Head of the church (Eph 1:22; 4:15) He is the ultimate authority but He has appointed ("And He gave . . ." Eph 4:11) gifted men to serve the church—to "lead and feed" the flock (cf. Acts 20:28; 1 Pet 5:2) as "under-shepherds."[10] Concerning this point, John MacArthur and Richard Mayhue have observed, "Consequently, each local assembly ought to be governed by its own elders (cf. Titus 1:5), without coercion from external hierarchical authorities or parachurch organizations."[11] To this, they've added, "As the God-ordained leaders of the church, the elders ought to determine matters of policy, membership, and discipline as they prayerfully look for guidance from the Scriptures (cf. Acts 15:19–31; 20:28; 1 Cor. 5:4–7; 1 Pet. 5:1–4)."[12] In addition, since every member of the Body of Christ (cf. 1 Cor 12:12, 27) is in contact to the Head through the indwelling Spirit (cf. 1 Cor 6:19, 12:7, 11), it has been noted that "the entire membership is charged with the responsibility of maintaining order (1 Cor. 14:40)" and the "whole church also bears the responsibility for purity in doctrine

---

[8] According to Merriam-Webster.com, the English term "autonomy" is used in three ways: 1. The quality or state of being self-governing—especially the right of self-government; 2. Self-directing freedom and especially moral independence; 3. a self-governing state." Merriam-Webster, s.v. "autonomy," accessed July 10, 2017, https://www.merriam-webster.com/dictionary/autonomy. Thus, "local church autonomy" would indicate "the right of the local church to be self-governing."

[9] MacArthur and Mayhue, *Biblical Doctrine*, 768.

[10] The designations of "bishop; overseer" (*episkopos*), "elder" (*presbyteros*) and "pastor; shepherd" (*poimen*) (cf. Acts 20:17, 28; 1 Tim 3:1–2; 5:17; Titus 1:6–9; 1 Pet 5:1–4) all "refer to the same office of church leadership." MacArthur and Mayhue, *Biblical Doctrine*, 759.

[11] MacArthur and Mayhue, *Biblical Doctrine*, 768.

[12] Ibid., 768–69.

and practice. Contending for the faith is the duty of all the 'sanctified' (Jude 1, 3)."[13]

In short, a careful study of the relevant New Testament teaching gives no indication that there was to be an office, or as D. A. Carson has put it: "a bishop, for instance," that "exerted authority over several congregations."[14] While the gospel to be preached by all the churches must be the same gospel as that preached by the apostles (see Gal 1), and the doctrine to be taught in each church was "the faith which was once for all handed down to the saints" (Jude 3; see admonitions to "hold fast" to right doctrine—1 Thess 5:21; Rev 2:25), each New Testament congregation was to be "autonomous."

With such an apparently clear picture of "local church autonomy" coming from the teaching of the apostles, it is incumbent upon believers to ask, "What happened?" Why did the church move away from that doctrine to develop the hierarchical system of the Roman Catholic Church that necessitated the recovery of that doctrine by the reformers? And, in the interests of the work of which this chapter is a part, it might be asked: "What role, if any, did the recovery of local church autonomy have on the development and teaching of dispensationalism?" Answering these questions is the

---

[13] Robert L. Saucy, *The Church in God's Program* (Chicago: Moody, 1972), 117. Many evangelical theologies, attempting to articulate the relevance of the New Testament teaching, make the distinction between the "universal church" and the "local church." MacArthur and Mayhue explain: "The universal church includes all genuine Christians throughout the entirety of the church age. They are members of 'the assembly of the firstborn who are enrolled in heaven' (Heb. 12:23)." MacArthur and Mayhue, *Biblical Doctrine*, 747. At times this is called the "invisible" church—not as something other than the "visible" church but in the sense of the "true church" as over the "mixed church." That is, the "universal church" is made up of only genuine, fully regenerated believers while the "visible church" (seen in the membership of local churches) has both genuine, fully regenerated believers and those who are "tares" (cf. Matt 13:24–30) or those who merely make a profession of faith. However, the terminology of "invisible" and "visible" has been used in a variety of ways by the reformers themselves and their spiritual descendants and this tends to make the designation somewhat unclear, even problematic. See the discussion by Louis Berkhof, *Systematic Theology* (1938; repr., Grand Rapids, MI: Eerdmans, 1996), 565–66; also Saucy, *Church in God's Program*, 17.

[14] Donald A. Carson, "Church, Authority in the," in *Evangelical Dictionary of Theology*, ed. Walter A. Elwell, 2nd ed. (Grand Rapids, MI: Baker, 2001), 250.

intention of this chapter.

6.1 Early Church Indications

As noted above the early church did not devote much thought to issues of ecclesiology as a matter of mere theoretical or academic reflection.
They did consider the organization, government or polity of the local
church as a practical matter to be addressed to meet existential concerns.
For instance, as reflected in the book of Acts, as the apostles went into areas
like Lystra, Iconium, and Pisidian Antioch (cf. Acts 13:14, 14:21), they
preached the gospel, planted churches, and they recognized the need for
local leadership to continue the work; thus, they "appointed elders for them
in every church" (Acts 14:23). These "elders" were charged with the task of
continuing the work begun by the apostles by building on the foundation
of the teaching of the apostles (cf. Eph 2:20). Later on, likely patterned after
the role of the "godly men" who were chosen to serve and assist the apostles
in Acts 6, the office of deacon was added to assist the elders (cf. Phil 1:1, 1
Tim. 3:8ff).

The elders were charged by Paul to "shepherd the church of God"
(Acts 20:28, 1 Pet 5:2), and be about the work of "exercising oversight"
while "proving to be examples to the flock" (1 Pet 5:2-3). At times, as the
recognized leaders of the local churches, they were called on as a group to
"debate" and come to a consensus on doctrinal matters that affected the
whole (universal) church (see Acts 15:6-7, 22, 23). The "Jerusalem Council"
should not be construed as the commencement or establishment of a
church hierarchy made of "bishops." Rather this council: (1) was called and
presided over by the apostles themselves; (2) was an *ad hoc* gathering of those
who were like minded in "the faith" and in essential agreement on matters
of gospel-doctrine; (3) apparently held no votes nor did they pass resolu-
tions, rather, they came to a consensual agreement (being instructed by the
apostles); and (4) made no decisions regarding local church practice that
were to be imposed on other local congregations—instead, the members of
the council appealed to the local assemblies on certain matters having to do
with maintaining a good testimony before the Jews (cf. Acts 15:19-21).
There is nothing there to suggest that the "Jerusalem Council" was intended
to serve as a pattern for the later development of a "church hierarchy."

Beyond the New Testament itself, other indications from the early church (though sparse) seem to confirm that it was assumed that the local congregations would by themselves (on their own authority) take up the task of "appointing elders in every church." For example, *The Didache*, or "Teaching of the Twelve," is probably a late first or early second century collection or composite work made up of early fragments giving mostly moral instruction to the churches (purportedly from the Twelve Apostles, though it is actually an anonymous work).[15] One section offers instructions on "church order" and has this: "Therefore appoint (*cheirotonesate*, appoint) for yourselves bishops and deacons, worthy men of the Lord, men who are humble and not avaricious and true and approved, for they carry out for you the ministry of the prophets and teachers" (*Did.* 15.1).[16] It is significant that the term used here: "Therefore χειροτονήσατε (*cheirotonesate*, appoint) for yourselves bishops and deacons, worthy men of the Lord, men who are humble and not avaricious and true and approved, for they carry out for you the ministry of the prophets and teachers" (*Did.* 15.1).[17] It is significant that the term used here—χειροτονέω (*cheirotoneō*, appoint)—is the same word used in Acts 14:23: "When they [Paul and Barnabas] χειροτονήσαντες (*cheirotonesantes*, appointed) (πρεσβυτέρους, *presbyterous*, elders) in every church." Apparently, the early church continued the practice of the apostles when each local church appointed its own local church leaders.

This picture is consistent with that of Ignatius of Antioch, c. AD 35–c. 107) who wrote a series of letters[18] in which "he speaks habitually of a single elder (or pastor) in each church, [along with] a body of presbyters [elders], and a company of deacons."[19] Shelley observes that the precise

---

[15] See Holmes, *Apostolic Fathers*, 334–338.

[16] Ibid., 366, 367.

[17] Ibid.

[18] Ibid., 166–271.

[19] Bruce L. Shelley, *Church History in Plain Language*, 4th ed. (Nashville, TN: Thomas Nelson, 2013), 76. For instance, in *The Letter . . . to the Magnesians*, Ignatius refers to "Demas, your godly bishop (*episkopou*)" and to "the council of presbyters (*presbuterio*) (2.2); and also he writes, "Indeed, it is right for you also not to take advantage of the youthfulness of your bishop (*episkopo*) but to give him [note the singular] all the respect due him . . . just as I know that the holy presbyters (*presbuterous*) likewise have

mechanism that resulted in this pattern is unknown: "No one seems to know just how the single pastor assisted by the elders and deacons, became the widespread pattern within the churches, but we know it did."[20] Furthermore, this basic pattern varied widely in its particular or local applications— "not all [churches] administered affairs in the same way."[21] This is a good indication that the early church operated with a fairly large degree of local church autonomy.

Nineteenth century church historian, Lyman Coleman, concluded that the churches of the late first and early second century were "separate and independent bodies, competent to appoint their own officers and administer their own government without reference or subordination to any central authority or foreign power."[22] This observation supports the notion that the early church operated with a fairly high measure of "local church autonomy."

6.1.1 Later and Medieval Developments

It is difficult to accurately assess how soon into the second century that high measure of "local church autonomy" began to recede, but the historical indications are that it happened rather quickly. Again, the precise reasons or mechanisms of this development are not entirely clear. What is clear is that the early church had to deal with serious and existential matters of false teaching and persecution and that both problems required a robust leadership to address them. As noted before, when controversy arose, men like Cyprian of Carthage exerted (or at least, attempted to) a measure of authority and expertise (in both doctrinal and administrative matters) to resolve conflicts and answer false teachers that were influencing the church. In the words of Louis Berkhof, "The early Church Fathers, in combating these sectaries [i.e. those who were dividing the church into various "sects"],

---

not taken advantage of his youthful appearance . . . ." (3.2, 5). Holmes, *Apostolic Fathers*, 202-5.

[20] Shelley, *Church History*, 76.

[21] Ibid., 77.

[22] Lyman Coleman, *Ancient Christianity Exemplified in the Private, Domestic, Social and Civil Life of the Primitive Christians* (Philadelphia, PA: Lippincott, Grambo, 1853), 95, accessed July 10, 2017, https://archive.org/details/ancientchristian00cole.

emphasized ever increasingly the episcopal institution of the church."[23] In other words, the church leaders, like Cyprian, needed to assert their authority as bishops—in the sense that office had come to be understood as officials over a region or district of churches—in order to deal with schism and heresy. [24] As Berkhof summarizes, "[Cyprian] regarded the bishops as the real successors of the apostles." In Cyprian's view, the bishops "together formed a college called the episcopate, which as such constituted the unity of the church. The unity of the church was thus based on the unity of the bishops."[25] In effect, where there were functioning bishops, there was the church—and nowhere else. Thus, Shelly observed, "by the late second century . . . the unchallenged leader in church affairs was the bishop"[26] and the roll of the local congregations was diminished.

After the legalization of the church by Constantine and the *Edict of Milan* in AD 313, the surprising growth of the church also contributed to the increasing authority of the bishops. One source reports: "The growth of the church in the third century had so increased the responsibilities of the bishop, at least in the cities and larger towns, that it was no longer possible for him to know all his flock."[27] It seems that the church had come to the conclusion that each locality, whether city or town, must have a single bishop, for the sake of unity and oversight. Thus, when the congregation(s) grew too large for one man to provide oversight, "presbyters," or "priests," along with other functionaries (also called "deacons") were appointed to

---

[23] Berkhof, *Systematic Theology*, 558.

[24] See David F. Wright, "What the First Christians Believed," in *Eerdmans Handbook to the History of Christianity*, ed. by Tim Dowley (Grand Rapids, MI: Eerdmans, 1977), 117. Wright describes the situation as one where a single "bishop" would have charge over a group of "presbyters" and other minor functionaries in the church. By about AD 250 the bishop "gradually emerged as the undisputed leader of the Christian community" over the other local church leaders. See also Philip Schaff, *History of the Christian Church*, vol. 2, *Ante-Nicene Christianity AD 100–325* (1910; repr., Grand Rapids, MI: Eerdmans, 1979), 132ff, see "The Origin of the Episcopate," and especially the section on "Cyprianic Episcopacy," 150.

[25] Berkhof, *Systematic Theology*, 558.

[26] Shelley, *Church History*, 77.

[27] Richard A. Todd, "Clergy, Bishops and Pope," in *Eerdmans Handbook to the History of Christianity*, ed. Tim Dowley (Grand Rapids, MI: Eerdmans, 1977), 187.

assist the bishop. Eventually, the "presbyters" came to function as "local pastors and shepherds of the flock," and the roll of the "bishops" was to give oversight over the "presbyters." In turn, the bishops began to recognize the authority of the more prominent bishops—i.e. of the ones appointed over important urban centers—in order to resolve disputes between bishops). This eventually developed into a "formal hierarchy" of bishops. [28] In time, due largely to the prominence and importance of the city of Rome itself, the bishop of Rome was recognized as having an authority that superseded that of most other bishops of large cities and regions.[29]

Thus, from the time of Augustine,[30] and indeed through the whole of the Middle Ages, the church held to Cyprian's view of the "episcopacy." Berkhof observes: "The system of *doctrine* [concerning the church] developed by Cyprian and Augustine was fairly complete and needed but few finishing touches to bring it to its final development."[31] "But," he adds, "if there was very little development of the *doctrine* of the Church, the Church itself actually developed more and more into a close-knit, compactly organized, and absolute hierarchy."[32] In sum, the church of the Middle Ages completed the shift from the autonomy of the local church enjoyed by the early church to the hierarchical episcopacy of Cyprian and Augustine.

---

[28] Todd, "Clergy, Bishops and Pope," 187.

[29] Ibid., 190. By the fifth century the pressure of the attacks by the Huns and other "barbarians" (and other factors) had so weakened the imperial powers that Leo I (bishop of Rome from AD 440 to 461) took over many of the functions of the civil government. It was Leo who negotiated with Attila the Hun to spare the city of Rome in AD 452. Also, it was Leo who elevated the position of the bishop of Rome from "first among equals" to "the one who speaks in the place of Peter." See: *Encyclopaedia Britannica*, s.v. "Saint Leo I," accessed July 10, 2017, https://www.britannica.com /biography/Saint-Leo-I. The other prominent fifth century bishop of Rome was Gelasius I (bishop of Rome from AD 492–96). Gelasius "completed the papal theory of the Middle Ages." Cf. Todd, "Clergy, Bishops and Pope," 193.

[30] Berkhof, *Systematic Theology*, 559. Berkhof notes that Augustine was a "Churchman" who adhered "to the Cyprianic idea of the Church" and Augustine held that "the true church is the catholic church, in which apostolic authority is continued by episcopal succession." Thus, Augustine, "prepared the way for the Roman Catholic identification of the Church and the Kingdom of God." Ibid.

[31] Ibid.; emphasis added.

[32] Ibid.

6.2 Blending Church and State

Another assault on the local church autonomy that had been enjoyed in the early church came in the form of an increasing involvement of the state in church matters. After Constantine (AD 280–337) converted to Christianity in AD 311–12, he wanted to bring an end to the persecution of Christians—which he did by issuing the *Edict of Milan* (AD 313). Constantine became something of a patron of the church; he had a number of basilicas built, and he supported the church with legal reforms and appointed Christian men to important roles in the government. When he became ruler over the whole empire (east and west) in AD 324, it was said that he "was dismayed to discover . . . his new territories were split over a 'theological trifle.'"[33] He wanted to bring a measure of unity to the church, which meant ending the ongoing debates over Arianism. To that end, he called a general assembly of the bishops to a council at Nicaea in AD 325.

Beyond the obvious importance of this council to the doctrinal integrity of the church (by producing the quintessential affirmation of the Trinity in the Nicene Creed AD 325), this council had a tremendous impact on the church. The very existence of this council also had a profound effect on the waning notion of local church autonomy. First, by the very act of calling this council together, Constantine assumed (and established) the right of the secular power to involve itself in a magisterial way into the affairs of the church: "The Emperor called it, influenced its decision-making and used his civil power to give its decrees virtually the status of imperial law."[34] And second, this council elevated the role of the bishops still further. In addition to the well-known creed, the council "issued twenty 'canons' [in effect rules and regulations] regulating various aspects of the church's life."[35] These "canons" were the first steps taken toward the formulation of the complete (and comprehensive) "canon law"[36] of the Middle Ages. They also placed

---

[33] David F. Wright, "Councils and Creeds," in *Eerdmans Handbook to the History of Christianity*, ed. Tim Dowley (Grand Rapids, MI: Eerdmans, 1977), 157.

[34] Ibid., 160.

[35] Ibid.

[36] "Canon law is the body of laws and regulations made by or adopted by ecclesiastical authority, for the government of the [church] and its members. The word *adopted* is here used to point out the fact that there are certain elements in canon law

more practical administrative and operational power in the hands of the bishop over the local presbyters and congregations.

A major development in church and state relations came in the opinion of Gelasius I, who developed the theory of "the two powers" (or "two swords") which argued that God had placed power in two realms—the secular power (emperor) and the church (bishops). In a late 5ᵗʰ century letter to Emperor Anastasius, Gelasius wrote, "There are two powers, august Emperor, by which this world is chiefly ruled, namely, the sacred authority of the priests and the royal power. Of these that of the priests is the more weighty, since they have to render an account for even the kings of men in the divine judgment."[37] This opinion, which drew on the ideas of both Ambrose and Augustine, was in essence a "political theory for the church" and sought "to define the relationship between secular and spiritual authority." "There were two institutions of authority in the world: the prelates exercising spiritual power, and the kings and emperors holding royal power."[38] In effect Gelasius' opinion (1) (theoretically) separated the church and the state and yet it (2) sought to elevate the power of the church over the state. Cantor notes, the "battle to enforce this claim was a long and hard one, and in the end only met with limited success."[39]

The Gelasian theory set the stage for a millennium long struggle between the Roman Catholic Church and the secular powers of medieval Europe that would take many forms and involve many popes and kings—which

---

borrowed by the Church from civil law or from the writings of private individuals who as such had no authority in ecclesiastical society." Auguste Boudinhon, "Canon Law," in *The Catholic Encyclopedia*, ed. Charles G. Herbermann, vol. 9. (New York: Robert Appleton, 1910), accessed July 10, 2017, http://www.newadvent.org/cathen /09056a.htm. "Canon law in the Western churches after 1054 developed without interruption until the Reformation of the 16th century." Peter J. Huizing and Ladislas M. Orsy, "Canon Law," *Encyclopaedia Britannica*, October 7, 2013, accessed July 10, 2017, https://www.britannica.com/topic/canon-law.

[37] James Harvey Robinson, *Readings in Modern European History* (Boston, MA: Ginn, 1905), 72.

[38] Norman F. Cantor, *The Civilization of the Middle Ages* (New York: HarperCollins, 1993), 86–87.

[39] Ibid., 87.

would lead quite beyond the scope of this chapter[40] In the course of this struggle, Pope Gregory VII (AD 1015–1085) developed Gelasius' view into the doctrine of papal superiority over the secular power.;[41] Much later, the *Magna Carta*, which the barons and nobles of medieval England forced on King John in AD 1215, put limitations on the power of the king over church affairs, among other civil limitations on royal power.[42] So the struggle between the secular powers (emperors and kings) and ecclesiastical powers (archbishops and popes) teetered back-and-forth for centuries.

The point of all this is that the effect of the struggle—regardless of whether the church or state was in ascendancy—was to greatly diminish the idea of "local church autonomy." Whichever power dominated—imperial crown or papal mitre—the local church in the Middle Ages found itself under the authority of greater power.

6.3 Reformation Recovery: Local Church Autonomy over Ecclesiastical Hierarchy

Of the magisterial reformers, it was Calvin who wrote most clearly on the matters of ecclesiastical authority. Calvin devoted the fourth book of the *Institutes* to the doctrine of the church—"Book Fourth. Of the Holy Catholic Church."[43] On the significance of Calvin's background in this

---

[40] See Cantor, *The Civilization of the Middle Ages*, 396ff. For instance: the Investiture Controversy—a power struggle between Pope Gregory VII (AD 1072–85) and Henry IV, Holy Roman Emperor (AD 1056–1106) over who had the right to appoint (invest) the lower level and local clergy to their churches and positions in the church; the (infamous) conflict between Henry II of England (AD 1154–1189) and Thomas Becket (c. AD 1119–1170); the conflict between King John (AD 1166–1216) and the English nobility that resulted in the *Magna Carta* (AD 1215); the conflict between Pope Boniface VIII (c. AD 1230–1303) and Philip IV (the Fair) of France (AD 1268–1314) over Philip's taxing of the clergy; and the conflict between the Guelphs (those sympathetic to the papacy) and Ghibellines (those sympathetic to the German [Holy Roman] emperors; this conflict played out in Italy in the thirteenth and fourteenth centuries. See Cantor, *Civilization*, 405. See also G. R. Evans, *The Roots of the Reformation* (Downers Grove, IL: IVP Academic, 2012), 109–124.

[41] See Evans, *Roots of the Reformation*, 112–13.

[42] See Cantor, *Civilization of the Middle Ages*, 454–56.

[43] John Calvin, *The Institutes of the Christian Religion*, trans. Henry Beveridge

area, Philip Schaff writes, "Calvin was a legislator and the founder of a new system of church polity and discipline. He had a legal training, which was of much use to him in organizing the Reformed Church at Geneva."[44] Schaff notes that while Calvin was concerned about the order and organization of the church, this was always "in subordination to sound doctrine and the inner spiritual life."[45] Schaff listed and explained the resulting principles of the Calvinistic system of church polity: "1. *The autonomy of the Church, or its right of self-government under the sole-headship of Christ.*"[46] For Calvin, the "right" and best form of church government would be to have Christ Himself "rule and reign in the church" and that the church's government "should be exercised and administered solely by his word."[47] However, since He Himself "does not dwell among us in visible presence" He "uses the ministry of men by making them, as it were, his substitutes."[48] Thus, "Calvin vests the self-government in the Christian congregation, and regards all the ministers of the gospel, in their official character, as ambassadors and representatives of Christ."[49]

The second principle of the "Calvinistic system of church polity" that Schaff notes is "2. *The parity [of equal status] of the clergy as distinct from a jure divino [by divine law] hierarchy whether papal or prelatical.*"[50] In other words, all "ministers of the gospel" are equal in status; no one of them should be thought of as having a higher status from the others. Calvin dismissed the hierarchical system that stretched back to Cyprian and Augustine. Calvin held that the titles "bishops (overseers) and presbyters (elders)" were referring to the same office.[51] Calvin believed that it was the responsibility of the

---

(Grand Rapids, MI: Eerdmans, 1989), 279; hereafter simply cited with book, chapter and section, thus: *Institutes,* 4.1.1.

[44] Philip Schaff, *History of the Christian Church,* vol. 8, *The Swiss Reformation* (1910; repr., Grand Rapids, MI: Eerdmans, 1979), 466.

[45] Ibid.

[46] Schaff, *History of the Christian Church,* 8:467.

[47] Calvin, *Institutes,* 4.3.1.

[48] Ibid.

[49] Schaff, *History of the Christian Church,* 8:467.

[50] Ibid., 8:469.

[51] "Calvin maintained, with Jerome, the original identity of bishops (overseers) and presbyters (elders); and in this he has the support of the best modern exegetes and

local congregation to select these ministers. Schaff goes on to explain, "After quoting with approval two passages from Cyprian, he concludes that the apostolic and best mode of electing pastors is by the consent of the whole people; yet other pastors ought to preside over the election, 'to guard the multitude from falling into improprieties through inconstancy, intrigue, and confusion.'"[52] So Calvin concludes, "We see, then, that ministers are legitimately called according to the Word of God, when those who may have seemed fit are elected on the consent and approbation of the people."[53]

The third principle of the "Calvinistic system of church polity" observed by Schaff is "*β/The participation of the Christian laity in Church government and discipline.*"[54] He comments: "In the Roman Church the laity are passive, and have no share whatever in legislation. Theirs is simply to obey the priesthood. Luther first effectively proclaimed the doctrine of the general priesthood of the laity, but Calvin put it into an organized form, and made the laity a regular agency in the local congregation, and in the synods and Councils of the Church."[55] Thus, "Strict discipline [was] to be exercised jointly by ministers and lay-elders, with the consent of the whole congregation."[56]

The following observation by Peterson sums up Calvin's principles,

---

historians." Schaff, *History of the Christian Church*, 8:469. Schaff cites Calvin's commentary on Philippians 1:1 in support of this point. See Calvin, *Institutes*, 4.4.3.

[52] Schaff, *History of the Christian Church*, 8:468; Calvin quotes Cyprian twice to the effect that the selection (ordination) of a leader (as in the case of Levitical priests and of Matthias in Acts 1 and the deacons in Acts 6:2) should "be in the presence of the people, before the eyes of all, and be approved as worthy and fit by public judgment and testimony [Cyprian, Lib. i. Ep. 3]." And the selection should "not take place, unless under the consciousness of the people assisting, so that the ordination was just and legitimate which was vouched by the testimony of all." Calvin, *Institutes*, 4.3.15. Those quotes are not meant to endorse Cyprian's system—indeed, they seem to run counter to Cyprian's main thrust of investing all church authority in the bishops.

[53] Calvin, *Institutes*, 4.3.15.

[54] Schaff, *History of the Christian Church*, 8:470.

[55] Ibid., 8:470–71.

[56] Schaff, *History of the Christian Church*, 8:470–71. In *Institutes*, 4.4.11 to 5.2, Calvin explains how this system of selecting/electing their ministers/bishops changed from the system practiced by the early church to the "corrupt tyranny" of the Papacy.

and draws a sharp contrast to Cyprian's earlier view: "Luther's view of the church and its ministry are both grounded in the Word of God, the promise of the gospel. The church exists wherever the Word of God is proclaimed, and the church is a spiritual community oriented to and shaped by this Word in its life by the power of the Holy Spirit."[57] Cyprian had emphasized the bishop as the central factor in identifying the function of the local church, whereas Calvin and Luther turned the focus to the Word of God.

6.4 Church and State Reform

Agreement on the relation between church and state was something largely characteristic of the reformers. With the exception of a few voices, the magisterial reformers such as Calvin and Luther viewed both the church and state as distinct entities, yet equally under the sovereign rule and purpose of God.

6.4.1 Calvin

Calvin's teaching on the relation of the local church to the secular authority seems to be a combination of his ideal desire to see Christ rule over all and the more pragmatic realization that the depravity of man and the need for public order require a fairly strong form of civil government.[58] Schaff observed: "[Calvin] aimed at the sole rule of Christ and his Word both in Church and State, but without mixture and interference."[59] Contrary to a popular misconception, Calvin did not seek to establish a "theocracy" in Geneva; however, he actually might be considered "one of the key fathers" of the principle of "church-state separation."[60]

Calvin viewed both the church and the state as divinely established

---

[57] Peterson, "Martin Luther on the Church."

[58] Calvin, *Institutes*, 4.20.1, 2.

[59] Schaff, *History of the Christian Church*, 8:471.

[60] Robert Joseph Renaud and Lael Daniel Weinberger, "Spheres of Sovereignty: Church Autonomy Doctrine and the Theological Heritage of the Separation of Church and State," *Northern Kentucky Law Review* 35, no. 1 (2009): 74. "In theory, Calvin made a clearer distinction between the spiritual and secular powers than was usual in his age, when both were inextricably interwoven and confused." Schaff, *History of the Christian Church*, 8:471.

institutions, each with certain powers that had been given by God[61] and both having generally the same objective—the well-being of the constituents. The two were to work together but each had its own sphere, as Renaud and Weinberger observed, asserting: "Calvin believed in a separation of jurisdictions of church and state."[62] E. William Monter affirms this, stating: "According to Calvin, there is a unity of purpose for the church and state but there is also a distinction of purpose. For where the state supports[63] the church, the church does not obstruct the state."[64] To this, Schaff adds: "The one has to do with the spiritual and eternal welfare of man, the other with the affairs of this present, transitory life."[65] Calvin united the two powers:

> as closely as their different functions would admit. His fundamental idea was, that God alone is Lord on earth as well as in heaven, and should rule supreme in Church and State. In this sense he was theocratic or christocratic. God uses Church and State as two distinct but co-operative arms for the upbuilding of Christ's kingdom. The law for both is the revealed will of God in the Holy Scriptures. The Church gives moral support to the State, while the State gives temporal support to the Church.[66]

"Calvin believed that an independent church [should be] supported and reinforced by a godly civil magistrate;"[67] however, as Renaud and Weinberger clarify, "when Calvin speaks of the cooperation of church and state, he does not speak of subordination of one to the other. Calvin believed that the church and state coexisted as two forms of government separated from one another by God, but both under God and subject to His law-Word."[68]

---

[61] Calvin, *Institutes*, 4.20.5, 6.

[62] Renaud and Weinberger, "Spheres of Sovereignty," 74.

[63] In the sense of "supports the aims and purposes"—Calvin is not thinking here of the financial support of the state or the sanctioning of an official "state-church."

[64] E. William Monter, "The Consistory of Geneva," in *Enforcing Morality in Early Modern Europe* (London 1987), 467-84, quoted in George J. Gatgounis II, "The Political Theory of John Calvin," *ChurchMan*, 110, no. 1 (1996): 61.

[65] Schaff, *History of the Christian Church*, 8:472.

[66] Ibid.

[67] Renaud and Weinberger, "Spheres of Sovereignty," 75.

[68] Ibid.

Schaff adds a significant point when he notes that Calvin's view of the civil government "was based upon the sovereignty of the Christian people and the general priesthood of believers" in distinction from the papal system of hierarchy.[69] However, he was distrustful of full-fledged democracy and preferred a form of civil government that was "a blend of aristocracy and democracy."[70]

6.4.2 Luther

Luther's views on the relation of the church and state were similar to those of Calvin.[71] Luther spoke in terms of "two kingdoms"—in language similar to that of Gelasius, but with a very different application. Historian Arthur Monahue observed: "For Luther, the relationship between the two kingdoms was parallel rather than hierarchical."[72] Neither of these two kingdoms were subordinated to the other. Moreover, Renaud and Weinberger add, the "two kingdoms, the state and the church, were recognized [by Luther] as having distinct jurisdictions. Neither could claim supremacy over the other, for both were equals before God."[73]

6.4.3 Post-Reformation

In point of fact, the history of church-state relations after Calvin and Luther proved to be much less ideal than either of them envisioned. The rise of nation-state churches—a primary example being the Anglican Church—virtually ensured the domination of a civil-ecclesiastical hierarchy over the local church or independent groups that chose (for one reason or another) to dissent from the nation-state church. Anabaptists in Europe not only objected to infant baptism but had a "growing conviction about the

---

[69] Schaff, *History of the Christian Church*, 8:473.

[70] Garry Z. Cole, "John Calvin on Civil Government," *Western Reformed Seminary Journal* 16, no. 2 (2009): 22.

[71] Renaud and Weinberger, "Spheres of Sovereignty," 76.

[72] Arthur P. Monahan, *From Personal Duties towards Personal Rights: Late Medieval and Early Modern Political Thought, 1300-1600* (Montreal, QC: McGill-Queen's University Press, 1994), 201, quoted in Renaud and Weinberger, "Spheres of Sovereignty," 76.

[73] Renaud and Weinberger, "Spheres of Sovereignty," 76.

role civil government should play in the reformation of the church."[74] The Anabaptists in Switzerland were unwilling to wait for the civil authorities to act to initiate reforms (which they deemed necessary to bring the church more in line with Scripture) and simply began to engage in ecclesiastical practices that they believed were more in line with how they viewed the New Testament church. For that they were severely persecuted.[75] However, they continued to advocate for a "congregational view of church authority."[76]

Likewise, the arguably incomplete Reformation in England went through the turbulence of the Tudor succession crisis (particularly in the era of Bloody Mary [AD 1547–48]) and reached an uneasy compromise during the reign of Elizabeth I with the Elizabethan Religious Settlement (AD 1558). During this period the Puritans continued to advocate for greater "purity" in the church (by which they meant greater devotion and adherence to New Testament models for the church) but were met with resistance from the civil authorities. Iain Murray defined a Puritan as "a man ready to suffer not only for the gospel but for Christ's right to rule the church by His own authority."[77] The Puritans (and later the Separatists) "wanted the Reformed pattern of church government, [led] by elders and synods, with stricter discipline."[78] Neither Elizabeth nor her successor, James I, was willing to accede to these Puritan views. Some of them persisted, however, even to the point of separating from the Anglican Church in a radical attempt to initiate more local church autonomy: "This step marked the beginning of the English Independent of Congregationalist movement," observed Sprunger."[79] Not finding acceptance in England, these Puritans searched for a place to worship: "The Separatist movement was initially illegal in England, and many of its adherents were persecuted by the state and its church.

---

[74] John H. Yoder and Alan Kreider, "The Anabaptists," *Eerdmans Handbook to the History of Christianity*, ed. Tim Dowley (Grand Rapids, MI: Eerdmans, 1977), 399.

[75] Yoder and Kreider, "The Anabaptists," 401–02.

[76] Ibid., 401.

[77] Iain Murray, "Richard Baxter, The Reluctant Puritan?" in *Advancing in Adversity* (Thornton Heath, Surrey: Westminster Conference, 1992), 1, quoted in Renaud and Weinberger, "Spheres of Sovereignty," 80.

[78] Keith L. Sprunger, "Puritans and Separatists," *Eerdmans Handbook to the History of Christianity*, ed. Tim Dowley (Grand Rapids, MI: Eerdmans, 1977), 388.

[79] Ibid., 389.

Often labeled as traitors, many Separatists fled England for more tolerant lands. One such group left England for Holland in 1608, and in 1620 some of them, the Pilgrims, famously settled at Plymouth, Massachusetts."[80]

The Pilgrims who settled at Plymouth, Massachusetts, in 1620 were English separatists and congregational in their ecclesiastical convictions. Glen Moots noted,

> In church governance, Puritans rejected formal and extensive hierarchy as 'Popish.' Instead, Puritan churches favored a Congregational or Presbyterian structure that gave congregations varying degrees of autonomy and emphasized the leadership of ruling and teaching elders within the local church. [...] The Puritans' emphasis on congregational autonomy and personal religious experience has led many to see them as a source of the democratic spirit in American politics."[81]

In 1658, a group of the Congregationalists met to draw up a confession that was patterned after the *Westminster Confession of Faith*, but would reflect their own views on the church. Known as the *Savoy Declaration*,[82] the key paragraphs of this declaration are a clear assertion of local church autonomy:

> 3. Those thus called (through the ministry of the Word by his Spirit) he commandeth to walk together in particular societies or churches, for their mutual edification, and the due performance of that public worship, which he requireth of them in this world.

> 4. To each of these churches thus gathered, according to his mind declared in his Word, he hath given all that power and authority, which is any way needful for their carrying on that order in worship and discipline, which he hath instituted for them to observe, with

---

[80] *Encyclopaedia Britannica*, s.v. "Separatist," accessed July 10, 2017, https://www.britannica.com/topic/Separatist.

[81] Glen Moots, "Puritanism," First Principles: ISI Web Journal, March 5, 2012, accessed July 10, 2017, http://www.firstprinciplesjournal.com/articles.aspx?article=399&loc=r.

[82] See "A Declaration of Faith and Order [Savoy Declaration (1658)]," Creeds of Christendom, accessed July 10, 2017, http://www.creeds.net/congregational/savoy/. See Sprunger, "Puritans and Separatists," 389.

commands and rules for the due and right exerting and executing of that power.

5. These particular churches thus appointed by the authority of Christ, and entrusted with power from him for the ends before expressed, are each of them as unto those ends, the seat of that power which he is pleased to communicate to his saints or subjects in this world, so that as such they receive it immediately from himself.

6. Besides these particular churches, there is not instituted by Christ any church more extensive or catholic entrusted with power for the administration of his ordinances, or the execution of any authority in his name.

7. A particular church gathered and completed according to the mind of Christ, consists of officers and members. The Lord Christ having given to his called ones (united according to his appointment in church-order) liberty and power to choose persons fitted by the Holy Ghost for that purpose, to be over them, and to minister to them in the Lord.[83]

6.5 Congregationalism in New England

This "congregationalism" found its strongest expression in the Colonial era churches of New England. Historian Harry S. Stout explains that "New England's mission began with the church."[84] Stout goes on: "The Puritan founders [of New England] devoted so much of their creative energies to the church because the entire New World experiment hung on its design."[85] The driving motivation for the founders of the Colonial churches of New England was, according to Stout, "that the churches be pure according to the pattern of the New Testament apostolic church."[86] Two errors

---

[83] "A Declaration of Faith and Order," 2.3–7; from the section titled: "The Institution of Churches, and the Order Appointed in Them by Jesus Christ."

[84] Harry S. Stout, *The New England Soul: Preaching and Religious Culture in Colonial New England* (1986; repr., New York: Oxford, 2012), 15.

[85] Ibid.

[86] Stout, *New England Soul*, 16.

had to be avoided. First, the church must be independent of coercion by the civil authority.

The venerable John Cotton gave expression to this conviction in a sermon in 1645: "The power of the keys [cf. Matt. 16:19] is far distant from the power of the sword [i.e. civil authority] and though one of them might need the help of the other, when they go astray, and administered, the one of them doth not intercept [supersede] but establish the execution of the other."[87] This distinction between the church and civil authorities was "formally codified in *The Cambridge Platform* of 1649...the civil magistrates ordinarily were forbidden to 'meddle' in the selection and appointment of church officers, in the administration of church discipline, or in the determination of correct doctrine. Nor...regulate the preaching of the Word and administration of the sacraments. These crucial functions were left to the church alone."[88]

The second error to be avoided was the error of placing "administrative control in the hands of a national board (the episcopacy) or presbyters (the presbytery)." The New England Puritans had experienced a long and unpleasant history with such hierarchical bodies; "this too posed the threat of tyranny of the few over the faithful—which the Puritans knew from painful experience" in England.[89] According to Stout:

> Studying the origins of the New Testament, the founders [of New England's Puritan churches] concluded that the church was nothing more (or less) than a local assembly (*ecclesia*) of God's people gathered out of synagogues and pagan temples to hear the gospel proclaimed in their midst. Any ruling authority outside of the individual congregation was by definition not a part of the church and hence in competition with it. For God's Word to function freely, and for each member to feel an integral part of the church's operations, each congregation

---

[87] John Cotton, *The Way Of The Churches Of Christ In New-England* (London: Matthew Simmons, 1645), 19, quoted in Daniel J Ford, *In the Name of God, Amen: Rediscovering the Biblical and Historic Covenants* (St. Louis, MO: Lex Rex Publishing, 2003), 230, quoted in Renaud and Weinberger, "Spheres of Sovereignty," 81. This clearly reflects the view of Calvin.

[88] Stout, *New England Soul*, 16–17.

[89] Ibid., 17.

must be self-sufficient, containing within itself all the offices and powers necessary for self-regulation.[90]

This congregational form of government was based on the "covenant theology" in which the Puritans had been steeped from their early days in England.[91] Stout explains: "Churches were nothing more than local covenants whereby people voluntarily 'joined' themselves to one another and God in a visible assembly; there was no need for some higher agency or authority beyond local church officers."[92] Once the church was formed, the matter of maintaining the New Testament ideals—in church affairs and in the lives of the individual members depended upon pastors to "preach the Word." As summed up by Stout: "The selection of rulers was left solely to the consent of the brethren [the individual members of the congregation], but once ordained, congregations were expected to 'become subject, *and most willingly* [to] submit to their ministry in the Lord, whom they have so chosen.'"[93] This became known as "The Congregational Way" or "The New England Way"[94] but it had much in common with the "way" of the reformers (and Calvin in particular) before them.

---

[90] Stout, *New England Soul*, 17.

[91] Ibid. In a 1636 sermon preached to the Salem church, John Cotton "defended the principle of church covenanting...'That which doth make a people a joined people with God, that doth [also] make a church—[and] what is that? The covenant of grace doth make a people, a joined people with God, and therefore a Church of God.'" Stout, *New England Soul*, 17.

[92] Ibid.

[93] "The Cambridge Platform (1648)," in *The Creeds and Platforms of Congregationalism*, ed. Williston Walker (New York: Scribner, 1893), 214, quoted in Stout, *New England Soul*, 19.

[94] Ibid., 19ff. Stout points out, however, that this "Way" was never "absolute" in that the churches depended on the coercive power of the civil government to enforce its prescriptions (such as mandatory church attendance and open contempt of religious principles). Also, the "unofficial episcopacy" of the New England Congregational churches could force a non-conformist of a different stripe to comply or be expelled (as in the case of Roger Williams). Ibid., 19–20. See *Encyclopaedia Britannica*, s.v., "Roger Williams," accessed July 10, 2017, https://www .britannica.com/biography/Roger-Williams-American-religious-leader.

6.6 American Disestablishmentarianism

By the time of the American Revolution, these congregationalistic and Calvinistic views of the relationship of the civil government and the church (or religion) came to be the prevailing opinion of many (although not everyone based these views in Calvinistic convictions). Although there had been attempts to bring the civil government into the affairs of the church—such as the bill introduced in the Virginia House of Delegates in 1784 ("A Bill Establishing a Provision for Teacher of the Christian Religion")—men like James Madison prevented such intrusions: "Madison said the proposed bill was objectionable precisely because 'it implies that either the Civil Magistrate is a competent judge of religious truth, or that he may employ religion as an engine of civil policy.'"[95] Madison's argument may not be from Calvin but the separation of civil and ecclesiastical authority "is right in line with Reformation theology."[96] Hence by the time of the writing of the First Amendment to the U.S. Constitution, what we have come to know as Jefferson's wall of separation between church and state had become the law of the land.

6.6.1 James Henley Thornwell

The Calvinistic distinction between the powers—ecclesial and civil— was employed by at least one notable Southern Presbyterian theologian in a way not envisioned by Calvin. James Henley Thornwell (1812–1862) was a southern Presbyterian from South Carolina. He was an ardent supporter both of the Confederacy and the institution of slavery. Thornwell developed a view of the church as both a "spiritual body" and as an assembly "organized as a *court* of Jesus Christ."[97] In his view, the individual Christian as a member of the "spiritual body" may be allowed the right to discuss civil

---

[95] James Madison, "Memorial and Remonstrance against Religious Assessments (1785)" in *American Political Writing During the Founding Era, 1760-1805*, ed. Charles S. Hyneman and Donald S. Lutz (Indianapolis, IN: Liberty Press, 1983), 634, quoted in Renaud and Weinberger, "Spheres of Sovereignty," 83.

[96] Ibid.

[97] James Henley Thornwell, *The Collected Writings of James Henley Thornwell*, edited by John Adger and John Girardequ (Richmond, VA: Presbyterian Committee of Publications, 1871), 4:472.

matters, but as a part of the "*court* of Jesus Christ" one had no right to pass judgment on purely civil matters. Thornwell held that the church and the state had concerns in divergent areas or "provinces" of concern and that these areas did not sufficiently overlap so as to allow one to pass judgment on the matters involving the other. He wrote, "The provinces of the Church and the State are perfectly distinct, and the one has no right to usurp the jurisdiction of the other. . . . They are as planets moving in different orbits."[98] Thornwell often referred to *The Westminster Confession* to the effect that "synods and councils are to handle or conclude nothing but that which is ecclesiastical and are not to intermeddle with civil affairs that concern the commonwealth."[99]

But the underlying reason for Thornwell's position was slavery. Thornwell argued that the Bible did not forbid slavery, that the arguments against slavery were made in terms which only made slavery applicable as a civil matter and hence those arguments could not be used in the church— "the court of Jesus Christ." Thornwell argued that while individual Christians may choose to join and endorse certain societies for reform, the church could not require its members to join such societies, nor could it endorse the reforms (abolition) advocated by those societies. The separation of church and state provided the southern slave owners a position from which to justify the resistance to abolition.

6.6.2 James Hall Brookes

Another nineteenth century Presbyterian pastor and theologian, James Hall Brookes (1830–1897), also spoke of the church as a "spiritual body" but in a way, and for a purpose very different from that of Thornwell.[100] James Brookes was a dispensational-premillennialist, who was also a popular preacher and prolific author in the second half of the nineteenth century. After a brief pastorate in Dayton, Ohio, Brookes was called to the Second Presbyterian Church in St. Louis, Missouri, in 1858. After the Civil

---

[98] Thornwell, *Collected Writings*, 4:449.

[99] Ibid., 4:474–75.

[100] Carl E. Sanders II, *The Premillennial Faith of James Brookes* (New York: University Press of America, 2001), 37ff. "Brookes fought courageously for the doctrine of a spiritual church throughout the decade" of the 1860's. Ibid., 38.

War broke out he refused to advocate for (or even pray for victory for) either side—North or South. Because some in his congregation were advocates of the Southern cause, Brookes resigned from the Second Presbyterian Church and accepted a call from Walnut Street Presbyterian Church (which, in fact, had been started by the Second Presbyterian Church under Brookes' ministry).[101] He remained at that church for the rest of his ministry life.

According to his biographer, "Brookes opposed the mixing of religion and politics."[102] Before, during and after the war Brookes "held firmly that the affairs of God and the affairs of Caesar should be unalterably separated."[103] For Brookes the fact that the church was a "spiritual body" meant that it stood apart from the power and jurisdiction of the civil authority and that the church should not "dabble in the mudpool of politics."[104] Brookes' use of the view of the church as a spiritual body was intended to prevent the church from becoming mired in the debate over slavery and from becoming an advocate for either side of the issue. While he held some "sympathies with the South,"[105] there was no doubt that submission to the government was the "biblical responsibility" of a Christian citizen; that "resistance to the established government was sinful, whatever one might think of that government."[106] In spite of "any Southern sympathizers in the congregation, his commitment to the spirituality of the church during the Civil War was absolute."[107] And while others advocated the concept of a "spiritual church" in order to silence critics (of slavery) in the church, Brookes' "commitment to the idea was not a ruse for fostering rebellion" or surreptitiously taking sides in the conflict.[108] All through the war and the several controversies in

---

[101] Sanders, *Premillennial Faith*, 44.

[102] Ibid., 41.

[103] David Riddle Williams, *James Brookes: A Memoir* (St. Louis, MO: Presbyterian Board of Publishers, 1897), 96, quoted in Sanders, *The Premillennial Faith of James Brookes*, 41.

[104] Ibid, 42.

[105] Timothy Demy, "James Hall Brookes," Pre-Trib Research Center, accessed July 10, 2017, http://www.pre-trib.org/articles/view/james-hall-brookes.

[106] Sanders, *Premillennial Faith*, 43.

[107] Ibid., 43.

[108] Ibid.

the Presbyterian ranks that followed (particularly in Brookes' own Missouri),[109] Brookes "focused on the spirituality of the church."[110] For Brookes, the "spirituality of the church" meant the church did not have "sectional sympathies," did not engage in politics, and did not have a "political requirement for ministry or membership."[111] The church was, according to Brookes, "'a kingdom not of this world.'"[112]

However, Brookes' doctrine of the spirituality of the church picked up a different nuance in his teaching after the end of hostilities (North vs. South and southern-Presbyterian vs. northern-Presbyterian). For Brookes, according to Sanders, the "spirituality of the church" was a theme that was tied to the "heavenly calling" of the church. The church has a "heavenly calling" in distinction from the "earthly calling" of the civil government. This "heavenly calling" of the church was most clearly understood in contrast to the "earthly calling" of the nation of Israel.[113] Brookes expressed differences between Israel and the church as follows:

> Israel has an earthly calling but the church a heavenly one...Israel, as a corporate body, was given a tract of land and promises of earthly blessings. The church, on the other hand has no land but a heavenly hope and not promise of material blessings in this life. The second difference was that they were to obtain their respective inheritances by different means. Israel was commanded to take possession of the land with the sword...The church must put up its swords, love its enemies and not resist evil. [The final difference is] the Holy Spirit now unites believers to Christ to be the body of Christ with Christ as the living head.[114]

In Brookes' teaching, the two concepts: the "spirituality of the church"

---

[109] Sanders gives a clear but brief summary of these controversies and Brookes' roll in them; Ibid., 44–50.

[110] Ibid., 50.

[111] Ibid.

[112] James Hall Brookes, *Argument of James Hall Brookes* (St. Louis, MO: George Knapp, 1866), 7, quoted in Sanders, *Premillennial Faith*, 50.

[113] Sanders, *Premillennial Faith*, 51.

[114] Ibid., 51–52.

and the "heavenly church" are closely related and "strongly emphasize the distinctiveness of the church and divorce the church from the world and earthly concerns. They leave no room for political questions in the church."[115] As the church was distinct from Israel, the church must be distinct from any civil government; there must be a separation of the (temporal) state and the "spiritual church." Furthermore, the twin doctrines of the "spirituality of the church" and the "heavenly church" indicate that the church must avoid the "errors" of the "State-Church establishments of Europe."[116]

In sum, with Brookes it may be said that the Reformation doctrine of the autonomy of the church from church-state entanglements (as expressed in his views on the "spirituality of the church") contributed to his premillennial and dispensational distinction between Israel and the church. As Sanders suggests, "For Brookes, the distinction between church and state found in [the views of other Presbyterians] was superseded by a distinction between Israel and the church. The premillennial focus on the ethnic identity of the Jewish people and the future fulfillment of promises, including land, for that ethnic group complemented the church/state separation that Brookes held long before he embraced premillennialism."[117]

6.6.3 Dispensational Theologians (Chafer and Walvoord)

James Brookes had a continuing influence within dispensational thought, further carrying the Reformation recovery of ecclesiastical independence. Most contemporary, American dispensational theologians have adopted the Reformation principle of local church autonomy—if not directly, then at least in the basic concepts—thanks in large part to Brookes. Yet, rather than focusing on Brooke's rigid state/spiritual distinction, his progenitors have decided to echo Calvin's emphasis of church polity. For instance, in discussing "the order of the church," Lewis Sperry Chafer and John F. Walvoord, are emblematic of contemporary dispensational thought in emphasizing that "the concept of church order relates to those who have

---

[115] Sanders, *Premillennial Faith*, 55.

[116] James Hall Brookes, *Israel and the Church* (New York: Fleming H. Revell, n.d.), 10–11, quoted in Sanders, *Premillennial Faith*, 56.

[117] Sanders, *Premillennial Faith*, 57.

authority in the local church and provide leadership for it. [118] The local church in the New Testament included those designated as bishops and elders who were the responsible leaders of the local church."[119] They point out that the titles "bishop," "overseer," and "elder" "seem to have been used in [an] identical sense in the early church (Titus 1:5, 7)."[120] Chafer and Walvoord also affirm local church autonomy by noting that "in the early church it seems as these churches matured appointment [of the elders] was by the church itself, and such appointment was recognition of their spiritual qualities which qualified them for places of leadership (Acts 14:23; 20:28; Titus 1:5; 1 Pet. 5:2)."[121] This appears to be very much in line with the view of local church autonomy as outlined by Calvin. Chafer and Walvoord provide only a small sampling of those dispensational theologians and preachers who have upheld both the New Testament truth and the Reformation recovery of local church autonomy.

Dispensationalists may very well be found in churches that are structured around denominational policies, such as the Presbyterianism pioneered by John Calvin. Indeed, many of the system's early leaders represented the broad spectrum of evangelicalism manifested in its differing denominations. However, the Reformation principle of local church autonomy finds its most advanced legacy in the countless number of non-denominational churches that are enveloped in dispensational theology.[122] As such, not only is its recovery by the reformers a doctrine to which dispensa-

---

[118] Lewis Sperry Chafer, *Major Bible Themes: 52 Vital Doctrines of the Scripture Simplified and Explained*, rev. John F. Walvoord (Grand Rapids, MI: Zondervan, 1974), 266ff. Walvoord acknowledges that the revised edition is substantially different from Chafer's 1926 work; in effect this was a virtually new work with "about seventy-five percent of the work" being new. This accounts for the practice of referring to "the author(s)" when citing this work.

[119] Ibid., 268.

[120] Ibid.

[121] Ibid. The author(s) also note, however, that the practice of "a single pastor as the elder and other officials who assist him in spiritual matters as deacons...does not seem to be based on biblical practice." Ibid., 268.

[122] For more on this aspect see Cory M. Marsh, "Luther Meets Darby: The Reformation Legacy of Ecclesiastical Independence" in the current volume.

tionalism has consistently upheld—it is a doctrine that finds its most recognizable expression within dispensational thought and practice.

6.7 Conclusion

The recovery of "local church autonomy" by the reformers is one of the many great legacies to celebrate on the occasion of the 500th Anniversary of Luther's bold attack on indulgences. Many of the abuses Luther sought to reform began with and were perpetuated by the corrupt and unbiblical hierarchy that had ruled the church for centuries. As Christians we can be thankful to the Lord Jesus Christ and His Spirit for placing us in the Body of Christ (1 Cor 12:13). As Protestants, we can be grateful that the Lord raised up men like Luther and Calvin and others to recover the New Testament truth of local church autonomy. We can also be grateful to those who stood up to the incomplete reformations in Europe and England (the Anabaptists, the Puritans and Separatists, the early Congregationalists) for consistently calling the church at large to greater fidelity to New Testament truth. And as dispensationalists, we can be grateful to those theologians and pastors who have maintained in their theologies, and so in our schools and churches, the commitment to the autonomy of the local church.

Bibliography

"Belgic Confession." Christian Reformed Church. Accessed July 10, 2017. https://www.crcna.org/welcome/beliefs/confessions/belgic-confession.

Berkhof, Louis. *Systematic Theology.* 1938. Reprint, Grand Rapids, MI: Eerdmans, 1996.

Boudinhon, Auguste. "Canon Law." In *The Catholic Encyclopedia*, edited by Charles G. Herbermann. Vol. 9. New York: Robert Appleton Company, 1910. Accessed July 10, 2017. http://www.newadvent.org/cathen/09056a.htm.

Calvin, John. *The Institutes of the Christian Religion.* Translated by Henry Beveridge. 1 vol. ed. Grand Rapids, MI: Eerdmans, 1989.

Cantor, Norman F. *The Civilization of the Middle Ages.* New York: HarperCollins, 1993.

Carson, Donald A. "Church, Authority in the." In *Evangelical Dictionary of Theology*, edited by Walter A. Elwell, 249–251. 2nd ed. Grand Rapids, MI: Baker, 2001.

Chafer, Lewis Sperry. *Major Bible Themes: 52 Vital Doctrines of the Scripture Simplified and Explained.* Revised by John F. Walvoord. Grand Rapids, MI: Zondervan, 1974.

Cole, Garry Z. "John Calvin on Civil Government." *Western Reformed Seminary Journal* 16, no. 2 (2009): 18–23.

Coleman, Lyman. *Ancient Christianity Exemplified in the Private, Domestic, Social and Civil Life of the Primitive Christians.* Philadelphia, PA: Lippincott, Grambo, 1853. Accessed July 10, 2017. https://archive.org/details/ancientchristian00cole.

"A Declaration of Faith and Order [Savoy Declaration (1658)]." Creeds of Christendom. Accessed July 10, 2017. http://www.creeds.net/congregational/savoy/.

Demy, Timothy. "Brookes, James Hall." In *Dictionary of Premillennial Theology*, edited by Mal Couch, 64–65. Grand Rapids, MI: Kregel Publications, 1996.

———. "James Hall Brookes." Pre-Trib Reseach Center. Accessed July 10, 2017. http://www.pre-trib.org/articles/view/james-hall-brookes.

Evans, G. R. *The Roots of the Reformation*. Downers Grove, IL: IVP Academic, 2012.

Gatgounis, George J., II. "The Political Theory of John Calvin." *ChurchMan* 110, no. 1 (1996): 60–75.

Holmes, Michael W., ed. and trans. *The Apostolic Fathers: Greek Texts and English Translations*. 3rd ed. Grand Rapids, MI: Baker, 2007.

Huizing, Peter J., and Ladislas M. Orsy. "Canon Law." *Encyclopaedia Britannica*, October 7, 2013, Accessed July 10, 2017. https://www.britannica.com/topic/canon-law.

MacArthur, John, and Richard Mayhue. *Biblical Doctrine*. Wheaton, IL: Crossway, 2017.

Moots, Glen. "Puritanism." First Principles: ISI Web Journal, March 5, 2012. Accessed July 10, 2017. http://www.firstprinciplesjournal.com /articles.aspx?article=399&loc=r.

Peterson, Cheryl M. "Martin Luther on the Church and Its Ministry." In *Oxford Research Encyclopedia of Religion*. Edited by John Barton. Oxford University Press, March 2017. Accessed July 10, 2017. http:// religion.oxfordre.com/view/10.1093/acrefore/9780199340378.001. 0001/acrefore-9780199340378-e-362

Renaud, Robert Joseph, and Lael Daniel Weinberger. "Spheres of Sovereignty: Church Autonomy Doctrine and the Theological Heritage of the Separation of Church and State." *Northern Kentucky Law Review* 35, no. 1 (2009): 67–102.

Robinson, James Harvey. *Readings in European History*. Boston, MA: Ginn, 1905.

Sanders, Carl E., II, *The Premillennial Faith of James Brookes*. New York: Univeristy Press of America, 2001.

Schaff, Philip. *History of the Christian Church*. 8 vols. 1910. Reprint, Grand Rapids, MI: Eerdmans, 1979.

Shelley, Bruce L. *Church History in Plain Language*. 4th ed. Nashville, TN: Thomas Nelson, 2013.

Sprunger, Keith L. "Puritans and Separatists." In *Eerdmans Handbook to the History of Christianity*, edited by Tim Dowley, 388–389. Grand Rapids, MI: Eerdmans, 1977.

Staniforth, Maxwell, trans. *Early Christian Writings*. New York: Penguin, 1968.

Stout, Harry S. *The New England Soul: Preaching and Religious Culture in Colonial New England*. 1986. Reprint, New York: Oxford, 2012.

Thornwell, James Henley. *The Collected Writings of James Henley Thornwell*. Edited by John Adger and John Girardequ. 4 vols. Richmond, VA: Presbyterian Committee of Publications, 1871.

Todd, Richard A. "Clergy, Bishops and Pope." In *Eerdmans Handbook to the History of Christianity*, edited by Tim Dowley, 187–195. Grand Rapids, MI: Eerdmans, 1977.

"The Westminster Confession of Faith." Center for Reformed Theology and Apologetics. Accessed July 10, 2017. http://www.reformed.org /documents/wcf_with_proofs.

Wright, David F. "Councils and Creeds." In *Eerdmans Handbook to the History of Christianity*, edited by Tim Dowley, 156–178. Grand Rapids, MI: Eerdmans, 1977.

———. "What the First Christians Believed." In *Eerdmans Handbook to the History of Christianity*, edited by Tim Dowley, 96–121. Grand Rapids, MI: Eerdmans, 1977.

Yoder, John H., and Alan Kreider. "The Anabaptists." In *Eerdmans Handbook to the History of Christianity*, edited by Tim Dowley, 399–403. Grand Rapids, MI: Eerdmans, 1977.

7

HOW DISPENSATIONAL THOUGHT CORRECTS LUTHER'S VIEW OF ISRAEL

Brian Moulton and Cory M. Marsh
San Diego Christian College and Southern California Seminary

7.0 Introduction

Although the pages of the Old and New Testaments reveal the Jewish people to be God's chosen people, for the past two thousand years of church history, they have been regarded by many as God's accursed people. Despite the post-Second World War emphasis of dispensational thinkers on the importance of Israel in God's prophetic program much of the church's past has unfortunately displayed strong contempt for the Jewish people. This hatred ultimately fueled the animosity of anti-Semites[1] who found justification for their disdain toward Israel in the writings of prominent churchmen, not least of whom included the great German reformer himself, Martin Luther. Along with that came a thorough-going rejection of the notion that God would ever fulfill His covenants and earthly promises to Israel as He had revealed them to Moses and the Prophets throughout the pages of the Hebrew Scriptures. Whether because the majority of Jews refused to em-

---

[1] Although the etymology of the word "anti-Semitism" suggests hostility toward all peoples of Semitic descent, the predominant usage, and that which will be reflected in this chapter, refers solely to the Jewish people.

brace Jesus as their Messiah, or because the Gentile church sought to validate itself before the Roman Empire, the net result was a growing disdain among Christians and ultimately, the entire world, toward the Jewish people and scorn toward any thought of God fulfilling His promises to a future Jewish nation.

With an increasing disregard for Scripture's clear testimony concerning God's unconditional election of Israel and His sovereign hand upon the people He chose, the church began to hold the Jewish race in contempt as early as the second century. Remarkably, despite the many scriptural statements regarding national Israel's future salvation and restoration, which dispensationalists have been quick to point out, the first several centuries saw the church move away from the Bible's testimony ratifying promises made to Israel in favor of something altogether foreign to the pages of Scripture. As is common when hate gets injected into the lifeblood of any movement, the anti-Semitism present in the early church grew to a festering cancer over the centuries. This would have lasting affects even on Martin Luther who had originally publically promoted friendly evangelistic efforts toward Jews in Germany. However, Luther later yielded to familiar anti-Jewish rhetoric which unfortunately tarnished the image of this otherwise great reformer.

This chapter seeks to demonstrate that the origin for anti-Jewish sentiments in the church can be traced to faulty hermeneutics that allegorized key texts intended for Israel, which were fallaciously misapplied to the church. This abandonment of a normative interpretation of Scriptures containing God's promises made to Israel became an acceptable hermeneutical practice that gave sway to resentment toward the Jewish nation. Moreover, it will be shown that despite Martin Luther's heroic reforms against papal Rome's abuses—which ironically included his promotion of literal biblical hermeneutics—he also succumbed to allegorizing tendencies that replaced Israel with the church. Luther's default to this familiar hermeneutical blunder did much to justify and fan into flame a seething hatred for the Jewish people—something undeniably evident in Luther's latter writings. However, the chapter will also highlight that dispensationalism's insistence on a consistently literal, grammatical-historical interpretation has been influential in reducing the strong anti-Semitism which had infiltrated the church, and has vigorously sought to correct Martin Luther's views concerning Israel.

7.1 The Bible, the Jews, and National Israel

The Bible has much to say about the Jews and the nation of Israel. In an act of remarkable grace, God chose Israel without condition to be His special nation on earth. Deuteronomy 7:6-8 reads:

> For you are a holy people to the Lord your God; the Lord your God has chosen you to be a people for His own possession out of all the peoples who are on the face of the earth. The Lord did not *set His love on you nor choose you* because you were more in number than any of the peoples, for you were the fewest of all peoples, but *because the Lord loved you and kept the oath* [emphasis added] which He swore to your forefathers, the Lord brought you out by a mighty hand and redeemed you from the house of slavery, from the hand of Pharaoh king of Egypt.

Israel was given a series of unilateral covenants through which God would bless the world. For example, God initiated the Abrahamic promise and Covenant which pledged land, seed and blessing for Israel, with eventual blessing to the whole world (Gen 12:1-3, 15:12-21). The specific boundaries of the "holy land," as it came to be known, were determined in Genesis 15:18-21. According to these texts and the remainder of the Old Testament, the holy land was deeded to the Jews as a permanent possession. Additionally, the Davidic Covenant promised a distinctly Israelite house, throne and kingdom (2 Sam 7:11-16). This would be a kingdom centered in Jerusalem of the same land described to Abram in Genesis 15, one to be ruled by a future Davidic king. That Davidic ruler, as the New Testament reveals, is the Lord Jesus Christ, a truth made explicit in the birth narratives of Luke 1-2. Moreover, the New Covenant was promised to national Israel reconfirming spiritual blessings subsumed under the Abrahamic Covenant to be fulfilled in a future dispensation or "latter days" (cf. Jer 30:24). This בְּרִית חֲדָשָׁה (*bryt, ḥădāšâ*, New Covenant)[2] is explicitly outlined in Jeremiah

---

[2] It is only here in Jeremiah 31 that the phrase בְּרִית חֲדָשָׁה appears in the Hebrew Scriptures. The feminine singular adjective חֲדָשָׁה stems from the Hebrew verbal root

31:31–34:

> 'Behold, days are coming,' declares the LORD, 'when I will make a new covenant with the *house of Israel* and with the *house of Judah,* not like the covenant which I made with their fathers in the day I took them by the hand to bring them out of the land of Egypt, My covenant which they broke, although I was a husband to them,' declares the LORD. 'But this is the covenant which I will make with the house of Israel after those days,' declares the LORD, 'I will put My law within them and on their heart I will write it; and I will be their God, and they shall be My people. They will not teach again, each man his neighbor and each man his brother, saying, "Know the LORD," for *they will all know Me,* from the least of them to the greatest of them,' declares the LORD, 'for I will forgive their iniquity, and *their sin I will remember no more*' [emphasis added].

Dispensationalists understand that all of these statements are distinctly Jewish in scope; none of them have been fulfilled to date. Among others, it is obvious that there has never been a time that *everyone* of Jewish decent on earth has intimately known the Lord. Indeed, even modern day Israel is largely uninclined toward their ancient Abrahamic faith.[3] This

---

חָדַשׁ meaning "renew" or "repair" which is found only in the Piel and Hitpael stems (cf. 1 Sam 11:14; Psa 103:5, respectively). Its adjectival form, as at Jeremiah 31:31, expresses the uniqueness of the noun it modifies, בְּרִית (covenant)—amplifying this particular בְּרִית as it relates to the other unilateral God-to-Israel covenants: Abrahamic (Gen 15:18, 17:11); Land (Deut 29–30); and Davidic (2 Sam 7; cf. Psa 89). BDB states that the בְּרִית refers to a "prophetic covenant, a divine promise through a series of prophets to establish a new constitution," and that the בְּרִית חֲדָשָׁה in Jeremiah 31:31, most undoubtedly carries with it "new institutions and precepts." Francis Brown, S. R. Driver, and Charles Briggs, "1447, בְּרִית [bryt]" in *Brown Driver Briggs Hebrew and English Lexicon* (Oxford, UK: Clarendon, 1907), 1447, BibleWorks; cf. Ludwig Koehler and Walter Baumgartner, *The Hebrew and Aramaic Lexicon of the Old Testament* (Leiden, The Netherlands: Brill, 2000), 454, 2698, BibleWorks.

[3] Some estimates report that currently 70% and upward of the Jewish population in Israel today are non-practicing Jews, including rampant atheism. On the lack of pious, individual devotional life among modern Israelis, see Gary M. Burge, *Whose Land?*

weighty promise of the New Covenant cannot be shifted to the church so as to suggest some manner of present-day fulfillment, as Reformed theologians are inclined to do.[4] While the church benefits from the shed blood of Christ which ratified the New Covenant, that fact does not equal the fulfillment of this covenant with the church in the present age. The words of the New Covenant refer directly to a substantial salvation of national Israel with a permanent remission of sins. The covenants, during the church age, still belong to Israel (Rom 9:4; note the present tense, "to whom *belongs...the* covenants," NASB).[5]

Israel was given numerous prophecies in the Old and New Testaments which detail her prominent role on the earth in the future. These include: national repentance (Zech 12:10); worship of the King (Ezek 46:1–15); the saved righteous ones entering the kingdom (Matt 25:37); peace, worldwide disarmament (Isa 2:4, 19:23–25; Zech 8:4–5); prosperity with enormous harvests (Amos 9:13–14); the full knowledge of God (Isa 11:9); longevity of life (Isa 65:20); soaring populations (Jer 30; Ezek 47; Zech 10); an immense government in which the Jewish Messiah rules (Isa 9:6–7, 2:1–4); David serving as vice-regent (Jer 30:9; Ezek 34:23–24); as well as the church co-reining with the Jewish Messiah, Jesus Christ (Rev 5:10, 20:4). Additionally, this will be a period in which Israel is marked with holiness (Zech 14:20–21); healing (Isa 29:18, 35:5–6); justice (Isa 11:4; Psa 72:12–13); and, an absence of oppression (Isa 14:3–6, 42:6–7). Animals during this time will no longer be ferocious (Isa 11:6–9); Jerusalem will be called a city of truth (Zech 8:3); and finally, the end of the times of the Gentiles will have come (Dan 7:13–15). A thousand-year kingdom on earth, such as is described by

---

Whose Promise? What Christians Are Not Being Told About Israel and the Palestinians (Cleveland, OH: Pilgrims, 2003), 133, 162–163.

[4] Progressive dispensationalists have to a large extent followed this very same pattern of the Reformed theologians and in so doing have deviated from the consistent application of the literal, grammatical-historical hermeneutic which serves to define dispensational thought. In this regard, the progressive dispensationalist reflects a deviant position that is not characteristic of normative dispensationalism.

[5] Although the verb is missing in the Greek text, but heavily implied, the NASB correctly supplies the present tense "belongs" in its translation of the original construction: "οἵτινες εἰσιν Ἰσραηλῖται ὧν...αἱ διαθῆκαι" (whom are Israelites whose [is]...the covenants).

the Apostle John (Rev 20:1–7) will provide plenty of time for all of these blessings to be realized literally in Israel and throughout the world. There are no natural interpretive reasons to apply these physical and spiritual promises to anyone other than national Israel. The slightest change in meaning of these Israelite referents has drastic consequences that utterly violate the plain meaning of the language used by God to communicate His thought to man.

Among the promises God gave to Abram, the federal head of the Jewish people, God specified: "And I will bless those who bless you, *And the one who curses you I will curse*. And in you all the families of the earth will be blessed" (Gen 12:3, emphasis added). God has never taken lightly the ill treatment of Israel by other nations. He "curses" those who curse or bring harm to Israel. Indeed, as the psalmist says the "Lord scoffs at them" (Psa 2:4). Moreover, Zechariah 2:8 refers to the Jews as the "apple" of God's eye, a metaphor intimately connecting them to Him: "For thus says the LORD of hosts, 'After glory He has sent me against the nations which plunder you, for he who touches you, touches the apple of His eye.'" The "apple" corresponds to the pupil of the eye. Both the pupil and the entire eye itself are sensitive to any outside contact, even the very slightest scuff. As such, this passage vividly relates how severely God is discomforted by any action against Israel—the very apple of His eye.

In continuity with the Old Testament, the New Testament directly teaches the continuation of Israel after the church age. For example, Matthew describes a future kingdom for Israel as promised by Christ: "Jesus said to them, 'I assure you: In the regeneration, when the Son of Man sits on His glorious throne, you who have followed Me will also sit on twelve thrones, judging the twelve tribes of Israel'" (19:28). It appears that "the regeneration" is a reference to the future kingdom in Israel that will appear with Christ after the church age, a time when Jesus and His disciples will take their places on literal, earthly thrones.[6] Thus, the prophecy of Zechariah 14:1–9 will be fulfilled in that coming day.

---

[6] See Michael G. Vanlaningham, "Matthew," in *The Moody Bible Commentary*, ed. Michael Rydelnik and Michael Vanlaningham (Chicago, IL: Moody, 2014), 1489; and David H. Stern, *Jewish New Testament Commentary* (Clarksville, MD: Jewish New Testament Publications, 1992), 60.

The Book of Acts also shows the expectation of a literal kingdom for Israel: "So when they had come together, they asked Him, 'Lord, at this time are You restoring the kingdom to Israel?' He said to them, 'It is not for you to know times or periods that the Father has set by His own authority'" (Acts 1:6–7). This exchange between the risen Christ and His disciples is especially noteworthy as Jesus had spent the previous forty days teaching them specifically about the kingdom (v. 3). If ever He sought the opportunity to disclose that the church would replace Israel in any way, this would be the prime moment. Yet, remarkably, Jesus offered no such hint at the possibility. The fact that the disciples asked Jesus about restoring the kingdom to Israel flows naturally given the context that He had spent the previous forty days "speaking of things concerning the kingdom of God" (v. 3). A normal interpretation of this language leads one to infer the disciples asked this question because they believed the same promises of a future restoration of Israel as was commonly taught by both the Hebrew prophets and Jesus Himself. While some confusion was still present in the disciples, Jesus did not rebuke any of them at this point. Instead, He affirmed that the restoration of geo-political, national Israel was in God's timetable—an event still awaiting the future (v. 6). The disciples anticipated it, though the church, as recorded in Acts 2, was about to begin. The point here is, rather than denying a future to national Israel, Jesus continually acknowledged it throughout His earthly ministry and afterward.

7.2 Allegory and Anti-Semitism

As early as the extra-biblical *Epistle of Barnabas* in the second century, anti-Semitism found its first foothold in the church. Composed most likely in Alexandria around A.D. 135, this letter took extreme license in its interpretation of Old Testament passages by allegorizing vital texts. Church historian Everett Ferguson reveals that this was done in order to argue that any biblical covenant found in the Hebrew Scriptures "belong[ed] to the latter people (Christians) and no longer to the Jews."[7] Replacement ideas like this

---

[7] Everett Ferguson, *Church History: The Rise and Growth of the Church in Its Cultural, Intellectual, and Political Context*, vol. 1, *From Christ to Pre-Reformation* (Grand Rapids, MI: Zondervan, 2013), 50.

can be inferred by the epistle's various chapter titles, which, among others, include: "Antichrist is at hand: let us therefore avoid Jewish errors," "The new covenant, founded on the sufferings of Christ, tends to our salvation, but to the Jews' destruction," and "Christians, and not Jews, [are] the heirs of the covenant."[8]

The *Epistle of Barnabas* and other early extra-biblical writings would go on to spiritualize Jewish biblical institutions such as circumcision, sacrifices, the Temple, and the Sabbath by twisting their literal meaning in order to refer distinctly to New Testament Christian practices.[9] Historian Joraslav Pelikan has pointed out that, "Virtually every major Christian writer of the first five centuries either composed a treatise in opposition to Judaism or made this issue a dominate theme in a treatise devoted to some other subject."[10] While Pelikan's assessment may be guilty of overstating the case, his point is nonetheless worthy of reflection.

Either the fact that Jesus and all the original Christians and known New Testament authors were Jewish seemed to escape these early church writers, or their Jewishness was severely downplayed in order to find deeper "spiritual" meanings for them. Christianity's obvious indebtedness to ancient Judaism was explained away by redefining what the term "Israel" (along its various institutions) meant. As more Gentiles entered its fold, it seems the early church refused to bear any semblance of their Jewish roots. "What was offensive about Christianity in the eyes of Gentiles was," observed Pelikan, "what it had inherited from Judaism."[11] The very concept of a "Jewish-Christian" was one that some early church Fathers dismissed as a group of heretics due to their devotion to distinctly Jewish customs.[12] By redefining the Bible's portrayal of national Israel and misapplying it to the church, resentment toward the Jewish people was given its structural war-

---

[8] See *Epistle of Barnabas*, chap. 4, 5, 13.

[9] Cf. Ferguson, *Church History*, 1:45–46.

[10] Joraslav Pelikan, *The Christian Tradition: A History of the Development of Doctrine*, vol. 1, *The Emergence of the Catholic Tradition (100-600)* (Chicago, IL: University of Chicago, 1975), 15.

[11] Ibid., 1:14.

[12] Ferguson, *Church History*, 1:45–46.

rant by way of abandoning a consistent literal interpretation. This allegorizing practice continued from century to century sowing seeds of anti-Semitism along the way, increasing in stream up through the Reformation. Specifically, it was this hermeneutical error to which Martin Luther, the otherwise champion of literal interpretation, defaulted when confronted with
Scripture's promises to national Israel.

7.2.1 A Needed Balanced Portrayal

There is little doubt that God used Martin Luther to expose the abuses
of papal Rome. His early literary works and disputations targeting the Catholic Church were undeniably vital to the Protestant Reformation. Luther's
mastery of Scripture and boldness in challenging the Roman clergy inspired
countless others in his wake to keep *sola Scriptura* and the priesthood of all
believers as principal weapons in their argumentative arsenal. On this,
Christian scholar A. Skevington Wood is as accurate as he is simple in describing Luther's priority: "The Bible, of course, was central in the reforming policy of Martin Luther."[13] Indeed, Luther's heroic stance on the Word
and God and his courage that helped spark the Reformation are featured
prominently in the current work. However, Luther was only a man, and
thus, prone to err.

Biographical accounts, by their very nature, risk temptations of uncritical hagiographic portrayals or otherwise unfair vilification. Often times in-
spiring men are elevated to legendary status at the expense of any shortcom-
ings they may possess, while other men are caricatured as undeserving of
any adulation. Such portrayals are often due either to emotive ties, or in
some cases, denominational loyalties. While the former is, in a sense, understandable as people naturally gravitate toward positive qualities in a figure as large as Luther, the latter less permissible. For example, one cannot
help but wonder how much of Lutheran scholar Carl Meyer's sentiments
smack more of party loyalty than unbiased research.[14] Writing for the his-

---

[13] A. Skevington Wood, *The Principles of Biblical Interpretation: As Enunciated by
Irenaeus, Origen, Augustine, Luther and Calvin* (Grand Rapids, MI: Zondervan, 1967), 72.

[14] See Carl S. Meyer, "Luther's Alleged Anti-Semitism," *Concordia Theological*

torically Lutheran *Concordia Theological Monthly*, Meyer displays inconsistencies in a desperate attempt to excuse Martin Luther of his anti-Jewish rhetoric.[15] According to Meyer, Luther's hate for the Jews is at most only "alleged." As hopeful as Meyer may be, his exoneration of Luther is in direct contrast to the reformer's of own shameful, published anti-Jewish statements.

Therefore, in keeping with this book's theme of detailing how dispensational thought advances the Reformed legacy, Martin Luther, for all his good, must likewise be exposed for his bad. It is here that the troublesome "Jewish question" comes to the fore. Scholars representing the broad spectrum of Christian theology have wrestled with the obvious distinctions between the Old and New Testaments since the days of Marcion. Reflections of continuity vs. discontinuity in the Bible have been well documented.[16] The issue is a magnet for controversy as it directly touches on God's plan(s) for Israel and the church. While that topic lies outside the scope of this chapter, one thing should be kept in mind as Luther's most appalling statements are considered below: When it comes to the sensitive issue regarding

---

Monthly 32, no. 11 (November 1961): 692–696, accessed August 16, 2017, ATLA Religion Database with ATLASerials.

[15] For example, Meyer lists several events of Jewish expulsions in medieval Europe ending with "they may not have been known to Luther" (693). This in itself is a remarkable statement given Luther's mastery of church history—something to which he regularly appealed when challenging papal abuses (e.g., his *Address to the Christian Nobility of the German Nation* and *The Babylonian Captivity of the Church*, both published in 1520). Meyer then switches his appeal to Luther's ignorance of history with "Luther reacted unfavorably to such treatment of the Jews" (Ibid.) before going on to heavily suggest that Luther was opposed to any destroying of Jewish writings—an impossibility given the Reformer's own words, as shown below in his *On the Jews and Their Lies*.

[16] The best treatment on the matter, in the opinion of this author (Cory), is John S. Feinberg, ed., *Continuity and Discontinuity (Essays in Honor of S. Lewis Johnson, Jr.): Perspectives on the Relationship Between the Old and New Testaments* (Wheaton, IL: Crossway, 1998). For two important treatments focusing on implications of the issue, see James M. Hamilton Jr., "Old Covenant Believers and the Indwelling Spirit: A Survey of the Spectrum of Opinion," *Trinity Journal* 24, no.1 (Spring 2003): 37–54; and Ramesh P. Richard, "Soteriological Inclusivism and Dispensationalism," *Bibliotheca Sacra* 151, no. 601 (January 1994): 85–108.

national Israel and the continuance of the Jewish race, since the Reformation period, it has historically been dispensationalists, more than any other Christian group, who have brought the church back to the literalness of Scripture's promises and covenants given by God to national Israel. Because of the dispensational insistence of a consistently literal, grammatical-historical interpretation of the Bible, they have without a doubt done the most to expose and correct Luther's anti-Semitic views.

7.3 Background to Martin Luther's "On the Jews and Their Lies"

Three years before Luther died, he penned a scathing diatribe revealing his hateful stance concerning the Jewish people and their promised nation. Two others would follow, but this particular work entitled *On the Jews and Their Lies* (1543) was undoubtedly his harshest of the three. This latter work of Luther was so drastically different from his Jewish-sympathetic tract *That Jesus Christ Was Born a Jew* (1523), published twenty years earlier, has been the topic of much debate. While several explanations for Luther's radical mood change have been offered, one cannot dismiss the fact that a great part of the answer lies in his inconsistent hermeneutics. That Luther's own increasing allegorical hermeneutical method of replacing "Israel" with the "church" played a major part in his latter thoughts concerning the Jews, in the estimation of some, cannot be ignored. According to the editors of *Luther's Works* (LW) American edition who penned the introduction to the treatise, among other groups in which he found disagreement, Luther "grew fearful of what he regarded as a misinterpretation and exaggeration of Old Testament motifs on the part of chiliastic [premillennialist] radicals."[17] Thus, Luther sought to allegorize any and all blessings promised to national Israel to keep from a supposed "misinterpretation and exaggeration" of those who read the Bible literally and understood it to teach a future, literal kingdom for Israel.

While anti-Semitism had been coursing the veins of church history

---

[17] Helmut T. Lehmann and Franklin Sherman, introduction to "On the Jews and Their Lies," by Martin Luther in *Luther's Works*, ed. Helmut T. Lehmann, vol. 47, *The Christian in Society VI*, ed. Franklin Sherman, trans. Martin H. Bertram (Philadelphia, PA: Fortress Press, 1971), 126.

since the earliest centuries of the church, Luther's contemporaries found his vitriol toward all things Jewish distasteful. As the editors of *On the Jews and Their Lies* (LW) have pointed out: "Melanchthon and Osiander are known to have been unhappy with its severity. Henry Bullinger, in correspondence with Martin Bucer, remarked that Luther's views reminded him of those of the Inquisitors."[18] Critiques of Luther from his peers are important to note given the propensity to characterize the entire medieval period as anti-Semitic. While hatred for the Jewish people no doubt existed in those times—as it has, unfortunately, in every period—restraint should nonetheless be employed so as not to cast this label onto every person living during a specific era. That said, Luther is still to be held responsible for his own anti-Jewish remarks published in the last three years of his life. While various reasons have been proffered in an effort to help audiences today better understand the cause of his statements, they are, in the end, simply inexcusable.

7.3.1 Martin Luther's "On the Jews and Their Lies" (1543)

With the above historical context in place, Luther's published comments in the twilight of his years speak for themselves as to his views concerning the Jews and national Israel. Therefore, an extensive sampling of Luther's own pen without interruptive commentary is what follows. In "On the Jews and Their Lies," Martin Luther stated:

> What shall we Christians do with this rejected and condemned people, the Jews? Since they live among us, we dare not tolerate their conduct, now that we are aware of their lying and reviling and blaspheming. If we do, we become sharers in their lies, cursing, and blasphemy. Thus we cannot extinguish the unquenchable fire of divine wrath, of which the prophets speak, nor can we convert the Jews. With prayer and the fear of God we must practice a sharp mercy to see whether we might save at least a few from the glowing flames. We dare not avenge ourselves. Vengeance a thousand times worse than we could wish

---

[18] Lehmann and Sherman, introduction to "On the Jews and Their Lies," 47:123.

them already has them by the throat.[19]

Despite Luther's seemingly tolerant position of not seeking vengeance, he then proposes a list of actions against the Jews:

First, to set fire to their synagogues or schools and to bury and cover with dirt whatever will not burn, so that no man will ever again see a stone or cinder of them. This is to be done in honor of our Lord and of Christendom, so that God might see that we are Christians, and do not condone or knowingly tolerate such public lying, cursing, and blaspheming of his Son and of his Christians. ...

Second, I advise that their houses also be razed and destroyed. For they pursue in them the same aims as in their synagogues. Instead they might be lodged under a roof or in a barn, like the gypsies. This will bring home to them the fact that they are not masters in our country, as they boast, but that they are living in exile and in captivity, as they incessantly wail and lament about us before God.

Third, I advise that all their prayer books and Talmudic writings, in which such idolatry, lies, cursing, and blasphemy are taught, be taken from them.

Fourth, I advise that their rabbis be forbidden to teach henceforth on pain of loss of life and limb. ...

Fifth, I advise that safe-conduct on the highways be abolished completely for the Jews. For they have no business in the countryside, since they are not lords, officials, tradesmen, or the like. Let them stay at home . . . . If you great lords and princes will not forbid such usurers the highway legally, some day a troop may gather against them, having learned from this booklet the true nature of the Jews and how one should deal with them and not protect their activities. For you, too, must not and cannot protect them unless you wish to become participants in all their abominations in the sight of God.[20]

---

[19] Martin Luther, "On the Jews and Their Lies," in *Luther's Works*, ed. Helmut T. Lehmann, vol. 47, *The Christian in Society IV*, ed. Franklin Sherman, trans. Martin H. Bertram (Philadelphia, PA: Fortress, 1971), 268.

[20] Ibid., 47:268–70.

In brief, dear princes and lords, those of you who have Jews under your rule—if my counsel does not please you, find better advice, so
that you and we all can be rid of the unbearable, devilish burden of
the Jews, lest we become guilty sharers before God in the lies, the blasphemy, the defamation, and the curses which the mad Jews indulge in
so freely and wantonly.[21]

Luther continued to justify the above actions by a series of grotesque
descriptions which vilifies the Jewish people, and making Christians appear
longsuffering:

I have read and heard many stories about the Jews which agree with
this judgment of Christ, namely, how they have poisoned wells, made
assassinations, kidnaped children, as related before. I have heard that
one Jew sent another Jew, and this by means of a Christian, a pot of
blood, together with a barrel of wine, in which when drunk empty, a
dead Jew was found. There are many other similar stories. For their
kidnaping of children they have often been burned at the stake or
banished (as we already heard). I am well aware that they deny all of
this. However, it all coincides with the judgment of Christ which declares that they are venomous, bitter, vindictive, tricky serpents, assas-
sins, and children of the devil, who sting and work harm stealthily
wherever they cannot do it openly. For this reason I should like to see
them where there are no Christians. The Turks and other heathen do
not tolerate what we Christians endure from these venomous serpents
and young devils. . . . next to the devil, a Christian has no more bitter
and galling foe than a Jew. There is no other to whom we accord as
many benefactions and from whom we suffer as much as we do from
these base children of the devil, this brood of vipers.[22]

7.3.2 No Vacuum, Ancient Terms Set

The obvious question upon reading these is: What led Martin Luther

---

[21] Luther, "On the Jews and Their Lies," 47:274–75.
[22] Ibid., 47:277–78.

to utter such ghastly statements against God's unconditionally elected people, the very apple of God's eye?[23] How could he, with this treatise, allow himself to be so turned against the very people whom Scripture describes as "belonging to the Lord" and bearing an honorable name (Isa 44:5)? The same Martin Luther who so championed the book of Romans in his earlier university lectures had now disregarded Paul's strong advocacy for Israel in Romans 9–11. It is, however, helpful to point out that Luther's stance against the Jews did not occur in a vacuum.

As noted earlier, an anti-Semitic streak persisted in the church for over a thousand years leading up to the Reformation. Historian Carl Trueman has helpfully pointed out: "The church as a historical entity always addresses the present in terms set by her past."[24] This helps clarify why Luther and others of the period held such contemptuous views toward Jews: the tracks of anti-Semitism in the church had long since been laid down leading straight to the Reformation church.

This by no means absolves Luther from his unapologetically vile statements regarding the Jewish people; he is personally accountable for all of them. Yet, it is equally important to keep in mind that by Luther's day, unguarded hermeneutical subjectivism leading to a belief that the church had replaced Israel had a long and storied past.

The irony of Luther's (and other reformers') hermeneutical method is difficult to miss. While he unabashedly promoted the importance of literal hermeneutics in his appeal to *sola Scriptura*, he did so by emphasizing Scripture's grammar while neglecting to remain consistent with the text's historicity. As Wood observed: "Although [Luther] urges the primacy of the lit-

---

[23] For an interesting five-point offering of Luther's multi-understanding of the word "Jew," see Kirsi I. Stjerna's essay, "The Jew in Luther's World" in *Martin Luther, the Bible, and the Jewish People: A Reader*, ed. Brooks Schramm and Kirsi I. Stjerna (Minneapolis, MN: Fortress, 2012), 32–33.

[24] Carl R. Trueman, "Reading the Reformers after Newman," in *The People's Book: The Reformation and the Bible*, ed. Jennifer Powell McNutt and David Lauber (Downers Grove, IL: InterVarsity, 2017), 196. While Trueman's words were directed specifically at the church's development of doctrine, his point is nonetheless applicable regarding anti-Semitism in the church, as well as any other controversial position within the church's history.

eral sense, it cannot be said that to *sola Scriptura* he adds the further principle of *sola historica sentential* [historical sense alone]."[25] By employing this
unbalanced hermeneutical method, Luther was guilty of dismissing Scripture's prophecies concerning a national Israel to be fulfilled in a literal, historical setting. If one disregards the Bible's *literal-historical* fulfillment of
prophecy—which serves as assurance for its objectivity—it becomes much
simpler to finagle any of the text's grammar to one's liking.

More will be said later, but suffice to say it is no trivial matter that
dispensationalism has consistently offered a balanced emphasis to Scripture's history as well as its grammar. The faulty un-balanced interpretive
methodology helped grow anti-Jewish sentiments into the familiar norm in
which men like Luther wrote. However, these methodological "terms" had
been set long before the celebrated reformer; indeed, there existed an extensive history leading up to him.

7.4 Anti-Semitism by Allegory in Early Church Fathers

Among the earliest church Fathers were those who both gave birth to
and sustained Christian anti-Semitism. Some of these early writers, as will
be demonstrated, were inconsistent in their hermeneutical treatment on
matters pertaining to Israel and the church. Allowing the latter to swallow
up the former, they erroneously used Scripture to denounce the very nation
Scripture promotes. Indeed, it is this hermeneutical blunder—a replacing of
Israel with the church—that would set in motion Luther's later stance
against the Jewish people.[26]

While each of the following examples provide their own uniqueness,
one common theme running through all of them is undeniable: an abandonment of any literal interpretation of Scripture's positive statements concerning national Israel. Remarkably, whatever benevolence Scripture
granted toward Israel, these early Christian writers chose to spiritualize and
apply solely to the church. Conversely, any of Israel's curses were left to

---

[25] Wood, *Principles of Biblical Interpretation*, 80.

[26] For one of the better treatments on this subject the reader is directed to Michael Vlach, *Has the Church Replaced Israel? A Theological Evaluation* (Nashville, TN:
B&H, 2010).

literal, national Israel. As mentioned earlier, with allegory comes a re-interpretation of key concepts; this then becomes the leading culprit of dismantling Scripture's distinction between the nation of Israel and the church.
This is an error which dispensational thought and method have vigorously
sought to correct.

7.4.1 The Epistle of Barnabas (c. A.D. 70–135)

The blatant use of allegory in *The Epistle of Barnabas* has already been
broached above. Yet, a few direct examples are warranted here. For instance,
in the epistle's depiction of the Old Testament's familiar phrase for historical Israel as "a land flowing with milk and honey" (Deut 26:9; Jer 32:2, et
al.), "Barnabas" (a pseudonym) ignores Scripture's literal-historical usage
and applies it directly to the church. After quoting Psalm 22:22—a text from
David concerning his adoration of God in the Jewish assembly—the author
emphasized *the church* as the true referent of the land for Israel: "*We then*,
are they whom He has led into the good land [emphasis added]."[27]

The epistle also appears to reason that the Jews were deemed as carnal,
having no ability to understand the hidden messages in their own Scriptures. The Jews were apparently not as sophisticated as the epistle's author,
who creatively assigns allegorical meanings to numbers in the Old Testament as well as to the Greek letters of Jesus' initials in order to arrive at
fanciful conclusions. As a result of his creative interpretive method, the epistle's author suggests the Jews had forever forfeited their claim to the covenants made with them by God and revealed in Scripture. The translators to
the work add: "The author proceeds to deny that the Jews had any further
interest in the promises."[28]

"Barnabas's" replacement of the word Israel for the church runs directly counter to Paul's argument in Romans which states that during the
times of the Gentiles, the covenants are still valid for Israel: "For I could
wish that I myself were accursed, separated from Christ for the sake of my

---

[27] "The Epistle of Barnabas," in *The Ante-Nicene Fathers: Translations of the Writings
of the Fathers Down to A.D. 325*, ed. Alexander Roberts and James Donaldson, vol. 1,
The Apostolic Fathers with Justin Martyr and Irenaeus (Grand Rapids, MI: Eerdmans,
1981), 141.

[28] Ibid., 1:141n15.

brethren, my kinsmen according to the flesh, who are Israelites, to whom belongs the adoption as sons, and the glory and the covenants and the giving of the Law and the temple service and the promises" (9:3–4).

It is worth noting that Paul's defense of national Israel and the continuance of the Jewish race in chapters 9–11 of Romans is a vital text of Scripture to which dispensational thought has relentlessly called attention.[29] Because Paul so adamantly insists that Israel refers to a literal-historical nation in this passage, so do dispensationalists. Dispensational scholar David Olander is representative of the tradition: "In Romans 9–11, there is a very evident flow in the text of chapter 9 concentrating upon the history of Israel with their God ordained privileges, chapter 10 with present Israel, and chapter 11 both present and future Israel."[30] Paul is clear that God will never abandon His chosen nation (Rom 11:1), and that to Israel belongs the covenantal promises (9:4). To this Olander confirms, "The covenanted kingdom program of God has always been with Israel and *never* with the church."[31] In a Christian academic culture that elevates allegory while unfairly scoffing at literal fulfillment—dispensational theology has virtually been alone in upholding the literal hermeneutic which Romans 9–11 demands.[32]

7.4.2 Justin Martyr (A.D. 100–165)

In Justin's *Dialogue with Trypho, a Jew*, he suggests that since the Jews

---

[29] E.g., see the treatments of Romans 9–11 within Lewis Sperry Chafer, *Systematic Theology*, vols. 1, 3–7 (Dallas, TX: Dallas Seminary, 1948); Henry Clarence Thiessen, *Lectures in Systematic Theology* (Grand Rapids, MI: Eerdmans, 1963), 28, 297–518; Alva J. McClain, *The Greatness of the Kingdom: An Inductive Study of the Kingdom of God* (Winona Lake, IN: BMH, 2007), 297–463; J. Dwight Pentecost, *Things to Come: A Comprehensive Study in Biblical Eschatology* (Findlay, OH: Dunham, 1959), 69–536.

[30] David Olander, "God's Sovereign Choice of Israel: The Holy Root of Romans 11:16–17," *Journal of Dispensational Theology* 19, no. 58 (Winter 2015): 253.

[31] Ibid., 254; emphasis in original.

[32] In his widely influential textbook, George Ladd called attention to preterism (a highly allegorical interpretive eschatology) as being the predominant view in New Testament scholarship. His comments written forty years ago are still valid today as it relates to non-dispensational academic theology. George E. Ladd, *A Theology of the New Testament* (Grand Rapids, MI: Eerdmans, 1979), 621.

crucified Jesus Christ, they were forever removed from the plan of God; the church had now taken her seat permanently. Next to *Barnabas*, this work is perhaps the first encounter in church history with supersessionism[33] or what became known as replacement theology.[34] Justin taught specifically that God's covenants with Israel were no longer valid, and that the church is the true spiritual Israel: "Even so, we, who have been quarried out from the bowels of Christ, are the true Israelitic [*sic*] race."[35]

Moreover, Justin suggested that the Jews were deserving of punishment for killing the Messiah and would thus be exiled and persecuted as divine justice would demand. To the charge, Justin lays no blame on Gentiles (contra. Acts 4:27); rather, Jews and Jews alone are guilty of crucifying Christ, while gentile Christians are among their victims: "But the highest pitch of [Jewish] wickedness lies in this, that [they] hate the Righteous One, and slew Him; and so treat those who have received from Him all that they are and have, and who are pious, righteous and humane."[36] The hermeneutical replacement of Israel for the church in *Dialogue with Trypho* is telling as Justin inconsistently applied only positive promises to the church while leaving all condemnatory statements for literal Israel. Ronald Diprose observed:

---

[33] Supersessionism is "From the Latin *super* (on, upon) and *sedere* (to sit). Thus, supersessionism is the view that the Church has permanently taken the seat of Israel, or, in other words, has replaced her and thus all promises given to that nation are now applied solely to the Church. Another view is that 'Israel' in the OT always referred to the Church." Cory M. Marsh, "Kingdom Hermeneutics and the Apocalypse: A Promotion of Consistent Literal Methodology," *The Journal of Ministry and Theology* 20, no. 2 (Fall 2016): 88.

[34] There is virtually no difference of meaning between "supersessionism" and "replacement theology" other than some prefer to use one term over the other. Michael J. Vlach, *Has the Church Replaced Israel?*, states, "I have no trouble with the designation *replacement theology* because with the supersessionist view there is a taking away or transferring of what national Israel was promised to another group" (10); and "The supersessionist approach defangs the OT and does not allow the Hebrew Scriptures to speak to the issues they address such as God's plans for the nation Israel" (96).

[35] Justin Martyr, "Dialogue of Justin, Philosopher and Martyr with Trypho, the Jew," in *The Ante-Nicene Fathers: Translations of the Writings of the Fathers Down to A.D. 325*, ed. Alexander Roberts and James Donaldson, vol. 1, *The Apostolic Fathers with Justin Martyr and Ireneaus* (Grand Rapids, MI: Eerdmans, 1981), 267.

[36] Ibid., 1:268.

"The tendency to Christianize the Old Testament is evident throughout the Dialogue....The people of Israel are correspondingly held in contempt."[37]

7.4.3 Clement of Alexandria (A.D. 150–215)

Clement, the esteemed teacher of Origen, is perhaps the first academic to teach an allegorical hermeneutical method. The Catechetical School at Alexandria would be Clement's legacy which did much to promulgate a non-literal interpretation of Scripture.[38] In his treatise *The Instructor*, Clement took extreme license with his interpretation of "Israel" assigning to it multiple meanings. In one place Clement bypassed a literal understanding and wrote, "wherefore also Israel means, 'he that sees God'—that is, he that understands God."[39] Later, Clement quotes Ezekiel's words in a promise of blessing given to national Israel (18:5–9) and offers the subsequent explanation, "These words contain a description of the conduct of Christians, a notable exhortation to the blessed life, which is the reward of a life of goodness—everlasting life."[40] Clement goes on in the *The Instructor* to suggest that since Israel had forfeited their place in God's covenants, the true Israel is now the church.[41]

Like Justin Martyr before him, Clement of Alexandria appears oblivious to the dual-responsibility of both Jew and Gentile in the death of Christ (cf. Acts 4:27). Moreover, in Clement's allegorical system, he bore no mind to the words of Isaiah 53:10, that "it pleased the Lord to bruise Him." Understanding this literally, the death of Jesus Christ should cause no permanent rage to people of any kind, Jew or Gentile, because ultimately His death was the perfect fulfillment of God's predetermined will (cf. Acts 4:28).

---

[37] Ronald E. Diprose, *Israel and the Church: The Origins and Effects of Replacement Theology* (Downers Grove, IL: InterVarsity, 2000), 75.

[38] Cf. Patrick Belvill's chapter, "Martin Luther: An Evaluation of the *95 Theses*" in the current volume.

[39] Clement of Alexandria, "The Instructor," in *The Ante-Nicene Fathers: Translations of the Writings of the Fathers Down to A.D. 325*, ed. Alexander Roberts and James Donaldson, vol. 2, *Fathers of the Second Century: Herma, Tatian, Athenagoras, Theophilus, and Clement of Alexandria (Entire)* (Grand Rapids, MI: Eerdmans, 1981), 229.

[40] Ibid., 2:233.

[41] Ibid.

7.4.4 Hippolytus of Rome (A.D. 170–235)

A significant teacher in the third century, Hippolytus was a student of Irenaeus. In a scathing diatribe foreshadowing Martin Luther's *On the Jews and Their Lies*, Hippolytus wrote a tract called, "Expository Treatise Against the Jews." In it, he affirmed a literal meaning for Israel when describing their "present condition" of a "myriad of troubles," and yet applied Scripture's statements of forgiveness solely to "the Gentiles, because it is the time for favour with Gentiles."[42] To the Jews, Hippolytus declared, "Surely you have been darkened in the eyes of your soul with a darkness utter and everlasting."[43] He further detailed that they were to live neither "four hundred and thirty years as in Egypt, nor seventy as in Babylon, but...always."[44]

Like the allegorizers who preceded him above, Hippolytus was guilty of the same inconsistent term-switching of biblical statements for national Israel: the good was applied to the church, the bad was applied solely to the Jewish nation. Indeed, the inconsistency of literal interpretation is a trait binding all of these anti-Jewish works. The point of these specific examples is that any swapping of Scripture's intended meaning for "Israel" tends to wreak havoc on one's theology.

7.4.5 An Early Growing Trend

This unfortunate trend of hostility continued through the third, fourth, fifth centuries, and beyond. Space limits the extent of the present treatment, but early Christian interpreters following Alexandrian allegory yielding anti-Jewish sentiments were multiplied. From the second century onward, the point is clear enough: neglecting a consistent literal hermeneutical method, in favor of allegorizing "Israel," is a common theme behind some of the worst anti-Jewish sentiments in church history.

---

[42] Hippolytus, "The Expository Treatise Against the Jews" in *The Ante-Nicene Fathers: Translations of the Writings of the Fathers Down to A.D. 325*, ed. Alexander Roberts and James Donaldson, vol. 5, *Fathers of the Third Century: Hippolytus, Cyprian, Caius, Novatian, Appendix* (Grand Rapids, MI: Eerdmans, 1981), 219.

[43] Ibid., 5:220.

[44] Ibid.

For instance Cyril of Alexandria (A.D. 375–444) commented on Romans 9, saying: "God chose Israel for himself from the beginning...But the Israelites fell because they were proud, wicked, and, worst of all, murderers of their Lord. Therefore, they perished, for they were rejected and abandoned and excluded from God's company, placed even behind the Gentiles and cut off from the hope promised to their ancestors.[45] Cyril's commentary appears to be radically divergent from Paul's emphatic response to any notion of God rejecting his people: μὴ γένοιτο (*me genoito*, "By no means!") (Rom 11:1).[46] This forceful negation is captured well by Greek grammarian Daniel Wallace who translates the Pauline phrase, "*You should never conclude such as thing! God forbid that you should think so! No way!*"[47]

Likewise, teacher of the noted fourth century expositor John Chrysostom, Diodore of Tarsus (died c. 394), made his allegory explicit by substituting Israel for an exclusively Gentile church: "Because the promises which had been given to the Jews had been transferred to the Gentiles, Paul wanted to avoid the charge that God had lied about his promises."[48] Diodore, like so many others, never explained why only blessings promised to national Israel were transferred to the "Gentiles" (i.e., church), and not the corresponding curses (e.g., Deut 28:15–68). His is a remarkable case, given that, in addition to instructing Chrysostom, Diodore also taught Theodore of Mopsuestia—the very founder of the Antiochene School noted for its "literalistic school of exegesis," which directly challenged the hermeneutics of

---

[45] Cyril of Alexandria, "Explanation of the Letter to the Romans," quoted in Gerald Bray and Thomas C. Oden, eds., *Romans*, Ancient Christian Commentary on Scripture, New Testament 4 (Downers Grove, IL: InterVarsity Press, [2005]), 238–39.

[46] Andreas Köstenberger et al. describes this particular Greek optative construction as "expressing abhorrence" and that 14 out of the 15 New Testament occurrences of μὴ γένοιτο are found in Paul's writings. Andreas J. Köstenberger, Benjamin L. Merkle, and Robert L. Plummer, *Going Deeper With New Testament Greek: An Intermediate Study of the Grammar and Syntax of the New Testament* (Nashville, TN: B&H, 2016), 207–8.

[47] Daniel B. Wallace, *Greek Grammar beyond the Basics: An Exegetical Syntax of the New Testament* (Grand Rapids, MI: Zondervan, 1996), 482; emphasis in original.

[48] Diodore, "Pauline Commentary from the Greek Church," quoted in Gerald Bray and Thomas C. Oden, eds., *Romans*, Ancient Christian Commentary on Scripture, New Testament 4 (Downers Grove, IL: InterVarsity Press, [2005]), 239.

his mentor.[49]

While more examples can be offered, it should be clear that insipient replacement theology, justified by its non-literal hermeneutic, became the seed and force behind Christian anti-Semitism. The Old Testament promises made distinctly for Israel gradually became the possession of the church. God's specially chosen nation was now rejected and cursed forever, according to this error, and Israel was solely responsible for killing Jesus—the only hope for the Jewish people. As the church became less Jewish and more Gentile in its constituency, the allegorical reading of both Old and New Testament prophecies was rapidly taking shape. As a result, the literal meaning of both Old and New Testament passages concerning Israel had begun to change—and devolved through the passage of time up to Luther.

7.5 A Literal Future for Israel Present in the Earliest Christians

While the above examples demonstrate the tendencies of allegorization and anti-Semitism in some of the early church Fathers, there also existed those who interpreted Scripture literally and thus saw a future kingdom to be established in national Israel. Far from novel, a literal transitional kingdom was an early Christian belief carried over from the Hebrew Scriptures and ancient Judaism. Among those who advocated this position were Papias and Polycarp (1st–2nd cent.), Irenaeus (2nd cent.), Lactantius (3rd cent.), Victorinus of Pettau (4th cent.), and still others. Though their *consistency* in applying a literal hermeneutic lacked regularity, they nonetheless interpreted many Old Testament prophecies concerning Israel at face value. Indeed, it is the very notion of consistency that would later highlight the hermeneutics of dispensational theology.

Despite the early Christian writers who slipped anti-Jewish sentiments into their works, these other teachers did in fact hold out for a future national Israel. This was based on their interpretive method that elevated the text's *sensus literalis* (literal sense)—to include its *historica sentential* (historical sense). Thus, to be established at the second advent of Christ, Israel's future entailed a literal transitional kingdom which was promised throughout the Scriptures (e.g., Isa 2:2–4, 9:6–7, 14:1–2; Jer 3:17, 33:14–18; Zech 14:1–9;

---

[49] Diodore, "Pauline Commentary," 390, cf. 383.

Matt 19:28; Rev 20:2–7). As such, the historical fulfillment of these promises regarding a future literal kingdom on the earth—with Israel's Messiah ruling in literal Jerusalem—was not lost on many of the earliest apostolic fathers. To be sure, the literal sense of Scripture, particularly of Old Testament texts, was the sense most highly esteemed by the first Christians.

One Old Testament text quoted or alluded to by New Testament authors more than any other is Psalm 110:1: "Sit at my right hand, until I make your enemies your footstool." The messianic undertones of this psalm are difficult to miss. "Every Christian scholar would agree," observed Old Testament scholar Leslie Allen, "concerning the canonical value of the psalm [110] as a messianic promise."[50]

This specific Old Testament prophecy gave the earliest church saints an understanding as to why Jesus would delay His second coming; it also clarified for them the need for a future transitional kingdom. Traditionally labeled a "royal psalm," Old Testament scholar Michael Grasanti explained that Psalm 110 anticipates "an anointed king who belongs to the line of David" as well as his "coming in conquest."[51] As a clear *messianic* prophecy, Psalm 110:1 presents a time gap before the Messiah would establish His earthly rule. New Testament scholar Alexander Stewart observed: "The earliest Christians were keenly aware that Jesus's life, death, and resurrection did not lead to the restoration of the kingdom to Israel and their expected utopian future (Acts 1:6). A future return of Jesus was needed to lead to the final and full fulfilment of God's promises, kingdom, and new creation."[52] According to Stewart, therefore, the idea of a literal, temporary and transitional kingdom was one inherited from Jewish belief; it was not a Christian invention: "Many of these expectations involved a messianic agent, and

---

[50] Leslie C. Allen, *Psalms 101–150*, Word Biblical Commentary 21 (Waco, TX: Word, 1983), 84.

[51] Michael A. Grasanti, "The Book of Psalms," in *The World and the Word: An Introduction to the Old Testament*, ed. Eugene Merrill, Mark F. Rooker, and Michael A. Grasanti (Nashville, TN: B&H, 2011), 517.

[52] Alexander E. Stewart, "The Temporary Messianic Kingdom in Second Temple Judaism and the Delay of the Parousia: Psalm 110:1 and the Development of Early Christian Inaugurated Eschatology," *Journal of Evangelical Theological Society* 59, no. 2 (June 2016): 255.

some included that God's messianic agent would begin a transitional period of rule on earth which would bridge the gap between this evil age and the future age to come."[53]

Although lacking a uniform eschatology, these early Christians nevertheless believed that Jesus Christ would establish His kingdom on earth after the Times of the Gentiles and before the eternal state. Moreover, this future kingdom would have literal Jerusalem as its locus in literal Israel, in fulfillment of key prophecies such as Zechariah 14:6–9.

While various samples of the names offered above can be presented demonstrating an early belief in the literalness of a coming millennium in national Israel[54], one early Christian theologian will suffice given his revered standing in church history: the bishop of Lugdunum in ancient Gaul, Irenaeus.

7.5.1 Irenaeus (A.D. 130–202)

The testimony of Irenaeus is significant since he was a student of Polycarp, who in turn was taught by none other than the beloved apostle John. Thus, an unbroken line exists between Irenaeus and the latest of New Testament authors. This is especially pertinent when one considers that it was John who penned Revelation 20:2–7, the most explicit biblical passage regarding a literal thousand year kingdom after Christ's return. Employing a literal understanding of texts in Genesis, Daniel, Matthew, and Revelation, Irenaeus wrote:

---

[53] Stewart, "The Temporary Messianic Kingdom," 268. Remarkably, Stewart, who is not a dispensational-premillennialist, goes on to say: "One result of this study is that the pre-Christian Jewish idea of a temporary messianic kingdom cannot be used uncritically as support for a literal future earthly millennium" (269). While his point is well taken, as scholarship demands a detailed (critical) investigation of the evidence, Stewart's comments still bear the all too familiar academic disdain for dispensational thought—regardless of the very evidence that he masterfully presents throughout his essay.

[54] For more examples of early premillennial Christian literalists, see Andy Woods's "The Protestant Reformation: An Incomplete Hermeneutical Reformation" in the current volume; and, Roy B. Zuck, *Basic Bible Interpretation: A Practical Guide to Discovering Biblical Truth* (Colorado Springs, CO: David C. Cook, 1991), 233–35.

But when this Antichrist shall have devastated all things in this world, he will reign for three years and six months, and sit in the temple at Jerusalem; and then the Lord will come from heaven in the clouds, in the glory of the Father, sending this man and those who follow into the lake of fire; but bringing in for the righteous the times of the kingdom, that is, the rest, the hallowed seventh day; and restoring to Abraham the promised inheritance, in which kingdom the Lord declared, that 'many coming from the east and from the west should sit down with Abraham, Isaac, and Jacob.'[55]

Later, Irenaeus made clear when these things would take place: "The predicted blessing, therefore, belongs unquestionably to the times of the kingdom, when the righteous shall bear rule upon their rising from the dead."[56] Further, lest anyone be led into assuming the authority of Irenaeus's literal interpretation of a future kingdom in Israel rested with him alone, he ended by appealing to apostolic authority for his view: "As the elders who saw John, the disciple of the Lord, related what they had heard from him, how the Lord used to teach in regard to these times."[57]

It is Irenaeus's connection to the apostle John that gave his voice such prominence. If the future kingdom in Israel was one to be understood figuratively, it seems Irenaeus would be among the first to posit such an idea. Yet, there is no such evidence from his pen. Instead, Irenaeus bears witness to a literal hermeneutic that sees biblical promises of a future kingdom in Israel fleshed out in real space and time. Thus, while allegory no doubt existed in the early centuries, and even flourished up through the medieval period, there likewise always existed a remnant of interpreters who remained faithful to literal methodology—the necessary hermeneutic imbedded in Scripture's perspicuity.[58]

---

[55] Irenaeus, "Irenaeus Against Heresies," in *The Ante-Nicene Fathers: Translations of the Writings of the Fathers Down to A.D. 325*, ed. Alexander Roberts and James Donaldson, vol. 1, *The Apostolic Fathers with Justin Martyr and Ireneaus* (Grand Rapids, MI: Eerdmans, 1981), 560.

[56] Ibid., 1:562.

[57] Ibid., 1:562–63.

[58] For more on the literal-grammatical interpretation being necessitated by the doctrine of the perspicuity of Scripture, see the chapter, "Neither Woodenly-Literal nor

7.6 Return to Martin Luther's Hermeneutics

Initially Luther seemed repulsed by the anti-Jewish spirit of Christians in his day. Often, during the first decade of his teaching ministry, 1513–1523, Luther condemned the persecution of the Jews and recommended a more tolerant policy toward them based on the spirit of brotherhood. In his earlier tract *That Jesus Christ was Born a Jew* (1523) he expressed the need to deal kindly with Jews and to seek their conversion to Christianity.[59] But when the Jews around him did not respond to the Jesus of Christianity, he turned back to the familiar waters of anti-Semitism.[60] As touched on earlier, many have seen this refusal of Luther's Jewish audience to embrace Jesus as their Messiah as the sole or pivotal reason for his hateful turn toward the Jewish people. While acknowledging the merit of that assessment, the more specific argument advanced throughout the chapter is that it was Luther's abandonment of a consistently literal hermeneutic that underlied his anti-Jewish stance. In other words, an inconsistent interpretive methodology gave Luther his scriptural warrant to justify his hate.

Luther's spiritualizing of a literal, future kingdom for Israel was a comfortable tendency for him long before he penned his latter anti-Jewish tracts.

Allegorical" by Jeremiah Mutie in the current volume.

[59] Luther went so far as to add, "If I had been a Jew and had seen such dolts and blockheads govern and teach the Christian faith, I would sooner have become a hog than a Christian." Martin Luther, "That Jesus Christ as Born a Jew," in *Luther's Works*, ed. Helmut T. Lehmann, vol. 45, *The Christian in Society II*, ed. and trans. Walter I. Brandt (Philadelphia, PA: Fortress, 1962), 200.

[60] Church historian Johannes Wallmann prefers the term "anti-Judaism" rather than "anti-Semitism" when speaking of Luther's latter disdain for all things Jewish. Cf. J. Wallmann, "Luther on Jews and Islam," in *Creative Biblical Exegesis: Christian and Jewish Hermeneutics through the Centuries*, ed. Benjamin Uffenheimer and Henning Graf Reventlow, Journal for the Study of the Old Testament, supp. ser. 59 (Sheffield, UK: JSOT Press, 1988), 150ff, accessed August 28, 2017, EBSCO*host* eBook Collection. According to Wallmann, it was more the erroneous *theological system* of the Jews that Luther resented, rather than the people themselves. While Wallmann's point is worthy of consideration, the dichotomy he places between Jews and Judaism is far too rigid in this author's (Cory) opinion. Jews have always historically and culturally been directly tied to a Judaic system for their identity—even Christ-following Jews who adhere to their system termed *Messianic Judaism*.

His allegorical tendencies were present even in his earlier literature that in turn helped validate his growing resentment for the Jewish people. Ironically, his refusal to accept literal fulfillment for Israelite promises presents itself in Luther's Jewish-friendly *That Jesus Christ was Born a Jew.* For example, interpreting the prophecy of Shiloh and the coming kingdom in purely spiritual terms, while discarding all of its literal intention (Gen 49:10), Luther explained:

> Thus, the kingdom of our Lord Jesus Christ squares perfectly with this prophecy. For there was a hegemony among the Jews until he came. After his coming, however, it was destroyed, and at the same time he began the eternal kingdom in which he still reigns forever. That he was of the tribe of Judah is unquestionable. *Because as regards his person he was to be an eternal king, it could not be that he should govern in a temporal and secular sense, because what is temporal will pass away.* [emphasis added][61]

For Luther, any notion in the text of a future transitional kingdom ruled by Christ was to be understood in a non-literal, non-temporal (i.e., non-historical) sense. He then followed this up with a dismissal of any literal meaning for the coming Davidic King and kingdom: "So now he [Christ] lives and reigns, and holds the exalted office of binding his foal to the vine and washing his garments in the red wine; that is, he governs our consciences with the holy gospel."[62] While his spiritualizing of key Old Testament prophecy here is certainly Christ-centered and gospel saturated viz., "Christo-centric" it is still not keeping with the original text's literal sense.[63] As such, Luther's replacing of a literal interpretation with one that sees *only* a spiritual reign of Jesus, opens the door to spiritualizing any Old Testament prophecy at the interpreter's will. With this error always comes a dismissal of any future literal kingdom in Israel.

Approximately 15 years after the release of *That Jesus Christ was Born a*

---

[61] Martin Luther, "That Jesus Christ as Born a Jew," 45:219.

[62] Ibid.

[63] For a specific critique of Luther's Christocentric hermeneutic, see James I. Fazio, "The Hermeneutical Foundations of *sola Scriptura*: A Critical Examination of Martin Luther's Christocentric Method of Interpretation" in the current volume.

Jew, Martin Luther published *Against the Sabbatarians* in 1538. Unlike his earlier tract that took a sympathetic stance concerning the Jews, this latter work progresses toward a more anti-Jewish tone, foreshadowing the more infamous works that would be published several years later. For example, in *Against the Sabbatarians,* Luther declared: "It is evident that [God] has forsaken [Jews], that they no longer be God's people, and that the true Lord, the Messiah, must have come fifteen hundred years ago."[64] In order to arrive at Luther's conclusion, one must entirely disregard God's literal promise to Jeremiah that "Israel will [n]ever cease to be a nation before [Him]" (Jer 31:36). This dismissal of God's promise to national Israel in Jeremiah is precisely what Luther does. The English translator to Luther's treatise, Martin Bertram, provides a telling comment regarding the reformer's allegorical hermeneutic—a methodology that unquestionably lent support for his resentment toward the Jewish people: "The implication here is that since the advent of the Messiah, these promises find their fulfillment in Christ's kingship and in the church as the New Israel, rather than in the Jewish people. This is a fundamental tenet in Luther's view of the relationship of Christianity and Judaism, and of course had long been part of the Christian tradition."[65] Thus, for Luther, both Christ and the church had forever fulfilled any promises given to national Israel viz., prophecies that solely promised blessings. Bertram also called attention to what has been demonstrated so far—this hermeneutical blunder had been in place for many years prior to Luther. These were indeed familiar terms.

After publishing *On the Jews and Their Lies* 1543, Luther produced his final anti-Semitic treatise called *On the Last Words of David.* It is in this commentary on 2 Samuel 23:2–7 that Luther's allegorical hermeneutics takes center stage. Rather than seeing any literal fulfillment of the future Davidic kingdom in Israel, Luther opts for a novel fulfillment framed in purely Christian ideas. Specifically, it was verse five of the Davidic passage that Luther found it most troubling to accept as literal: "Truly, is not my house so with God? For He has made an everlasting covenant with me." These

---

[64] Martin Luther, "Against the Sabbatarians," in *Luther's Works,* vol. 47, *The Christian in Society IV,* ed. Franklin Sherman and Helmut T. Lehmann, trans. Martin H. Bertram (Philadelphia, PA: Fortress, 1971), 96–97.

[65] Martin H. Bertram, "Against the Sabbatarians" by Martin Luther, 47:72n10.

words of course point back to the Davidic Covenant in 2 Samuel 7, namely verse 13: "He shall build a house for My name, and I will establish the throne of his kingdom forever." Because the physical nation of Israel was no longer relevant by Luther's time, a change of language was needed that took God's promise to David as something other than literal. Thus, Luther swapped any referent pertaining to future Israel for the church and concluded: "Holy Scripture, in particular, the New Testament informs us about this house. It is *the holy Christian church*, which extends to the ends of the earth [emphasis added]."[66] As such, Luther reasoned, there could be no future period of blessing for national Israel: "Nor can this refer to a transitory, temporal, and earthly kingdom."[67] Rather than exposing the text's literal meaning through biblical exegesis, Luther approached the text with allegory in mind and produced what scholar John Slotemaker sees as a distinct genre he termed, "polemical exegesis." Writing for the *Harvard Theological Review*, Slotemaker observed, "On the Last Words of David reframes this pericope by developing a trinitarian reading that emphasizes the messianic dimensions of the text and simultaneously de-emphasizes a Jewish understanding of the eternality of God's promise or covenant with the Jewish nation and people."[68]

It is important to highlight that Luther's rejection of any future literal kingdom in Israel, one in which Christ rules from David's throne in Jerusalem, is what connects all of his anti-Jewish works. His abandonment of a consistently literal, grammatical-historical hermeneutic not only fanned into flame Luther's growing hostility toward all things Jewish, but provided him the structure by which to justify it.

The covenants which God promised to Israel were given new spiritual

---

[66] Martin Luther, "Treatise on The Last Words of David," in *Luther's Works*, ed. Jaroslav Pelikan and Hilton C. Oswald, vol. 15, *Notes on Ecclesiastes, Lectures on the Song of Solomon, Treatise on the Last Words of David*, trans. Martin H. Bertram (Philadelphia, PA: Fortress, 1972), 282.

[67] Ibid., 15:289.

[68] John T. Slotemaker, "The Trinitarian House of David: Martin Luther's Anti-Jewish Exegesis of 2 Samuel 23: 2–7," *Harvard Theological Review* 104, no. 2 (2011): 235, accessed August 16, 2017, ATLA Religion Database with ATLASerials.

meanings, with the church as God's new replacement. Slotemaker concluded: "Luther had to find a way to exegete this passage that reinterpreted
the covenant and the covenant partners....This, in short, was a continual
'Christianization' of this passage by Luther, as he was clearly uncomfortable
with the theological implications of an eternal covenant with the Jews."[69]
Thus, Luther's allegorical method—borrowed from so many others preceding him—unfortunately tarnishes the legacy of the man who earlier so courageously defended his interpretations against papal Rome. With allegory,
comes inconsistency and faulty conclusions. Indeed, it is this very danger,
resulting from abandoning a literal, grammatical-historical hermeneutic,
that dispensationalists have done much to expose and correct.

7.7 Two Vital Caveats

Much has been said demonstrating the connection between allegory
and anti-Semitism. That the former, as a hermeneutical method, can result
in the latter is undeniable as demonstrated throughout the chapter. From
the *Epistle of Barnabas* to Martin Luther, institutions and promises which
God gave to Israel were transferred to the church by Christian writers who
were not satisfied with a text's original, single-meaning—one that demanded
national Israel as its referent.[70] The resulting anti-Semitism existed in direct
contrast to how the Bible describes God's favor on Israel and the Jewish
race. Scripture is adamant that they are a chosen nation, the apple of His
eye, and the people by which the Son of God was made manifest. That said,
it is incumbent at this point to offer two vital caveats that may go unnoticed
if not made explicit: (1) Allegory does not necessitate anti-Semitism; and (2)
At no point in biblical history (past or future) are Jewish people favored by
God merely because they are Jews.

---

[69] Slotemaker, "The Trinitarian House," 254.
[70] For solid treatments defending an author's single-intended meaning, see E. D.
Hirsch, *Validity in Interpretation* (New Haven, CT: Yale, 1967), esp. 1–67; and, Robert
L. Thomas, *Evangelical Hermeneutics: The New Versus the Old* (Grand Rapids, MI: Kregel,
2002), esp. 141–60.

7.7.1 Allegory Does Not Necessitate Anti-Semitism

Concerning this first point, while a relationship has undoubtedly been present, a vital distinction must still be made between a hermeneutical method, and an anti-Semitic Christian. The latter is entirely dependent on the former for justification, while the former in no way necessitates the latter. In other words, a Bible interpreter can adhere to non-literal methodology while never accepting conclusions that would justify hostility toward Jews. It goes without saying there exists today a myriad of brilliant Christian scholars in the covenantal tradition who reject a consistently literal hermeneutic, and yet would condemn any form of anti-Semitism as ardently as dispensationalists do. These fellow brothers and sisters simply believe that opting for non-literal fulfillment, when deemed warranted, is part of a robust hermeneutical methodology with much to offer.

For example, Kenneth Gentry, who is a Christian Reconstructionist (a form of Covenant theology) has no qualms whatsoever promoting a non-literal meaning for Israel that would yield a supersessionist conclusion: "Reconstruction thought does hold to supersession: we believe that the international Church has superseded for all times national Israel as the institution for the administration of divine blessing to the world."[71] However, Gentry also makes plain that his school of thought does not support anti-Semitism: "I know of no published Reconstructionist who disdains or seeks to persecute Jewish people. In fact, our view of history holds that one day the Jews will be blessed of God."[72] The reader must decide for himself if there in fact lies a logical link between supersessionism (dependent on an allegorical method) and ant-Semitism. Nonetheless, while most dispensationalists would agree that the allegorical method can lend itself to anti-Semitic conclusions, the method itself does not demand it. Ultimately, the blame for anti-Semitism lies with a darkened heart (cf. 1 John 4:20–21).

---

[71] Kenneth L. Gentry, "Reformed Anti-Semitism?" Chalcedon, June 13, 2005, accessed August 31, 2017, https://chalcedon.edu/resources/articles/reformed-anti-semitism.

[72] Ibid. Covenantalists like Gentry are known to support a future salvation for Jewish people *en masse*, while rejecting a *national* salvation or restoration for the nation Israel. This false dichotomy is inevitable due to their inconsistent hermeneutical methodology that disregards Scripture's clear promises to literal Israel.

7.7.2 Jewish People Are Not Favored Because They Are Jews

As for the second caveat, both John the Baptist and Jesus were clear regarding those who took refuge in their Jewish lineage as a means of obtaining God's favor (Luke 3:7-9; John 8:31-47). This in direct harmony with Moses' point to the stiff-necked nation well over a thousand years prior (Deut 7:6-8; cf. 9:6). God's love for Israel is due entirely to His grace and original covenant with Abraham. Much to their shame, there have been times when dispensationalists have over emphasized God's love for Israel and the Jewish people at the expense of their desperate need for His mercy and redemption. Jewish people share an undeniable link with Gentiles in that both groups are saved only by God's grace through faith in Jesus Christ alone (Eph 2:8-9; cf. Rom 9:16, 31-32). Indeed, it is the need for faith in the Lord that provides a continuous thread through all the distinct economies disclosed in Scripture.[73] Dispensational scholar Charles Ryrie best represented the system's position on salvation for *all* peoples in *all* times when he lucidly explained: "The *basis* for salvation in every age is the death of Christ; the *requirement* for salvation in every age is faith; the *object* of faith in every age is God; the *content* of faith changes in the various dispensations."[74] Far from teaching a salvation by works or two-ways of salvation (both unfair critiques repeatedly given by non-dispensationalists), Ryrie's assessment of dispensational thought on salvation most accurately reflects the nature of Scripture's progressive revelation.

It is also worth noting that the modern state of Israel is not the fulfillment of God's unilateral covenants with her. Modern Israel is a nation marked by unbelief and, often times, indifference to God's moral commands as outlined in Scripture (cf. Deut 28:15-68). While it cannot be denied that there have been some adherents of dispensational thought who have promoted the idea that modern Israel (established in 1948) is proof of covenant fulfillment, that position is not supported by dispensational scholarship—rather, it has been advanced by those whose eschatology is governed

---

[73] For a detailed analysis, see Glenn Kreider's chapter "*Sola Fide*: Salvation is by Grace Through Faith Alone in Every Dispensation" in the current volume.

[74] Charles C. Ryrie, *Dispensationalism*, rev. and exp. ed. (Chicago, IL: Moody, 1995), 115. Other than *basis*, all emphases are in the original.

more by the reading of newspaper headlines than by the reading of Scripture. Contrary to such empty speculation, God has not given modern Israel unbridled carte blanch freedom in all its political affairs. [75] Any teaching that suggests the modern state of Israel is a fulfillment of the Abrahamic Covenant is proof of sloppy exegesis and theology on the individual's part, not of prophetic fulfillment. Furthermore, this belief is in no way a defining element of dispensationalism. Quite simply: modern Israel is *not* biblical Israel.

7.8 The Needed Dispensational Correction

What has been advanced throughout the chapter is that hiding beneath Martin Luther's resentment toward the Jewish people was a structural hermeneutic that allowed for re-interpretation of key biblical texts. This re-interpretation was one that erroneously swapped national Israel for the church—a hermeneutical maneuver disparaged by all normative dispensationalists. As expressed earlier, the tendency among Reformation scholars has been to focus on Luther's culture, his health, or his anger over the lack of Jewish-Christian converts as reasons for his anti-Semitism. The notion that Luther's disparaging of the Jewish people may be largely attributed to his inherited non-literal biblical hermeneutics of Old Testament prophecies regarding Israel has not received the attention it deserves. Nevertheless, it is a theory that is bolstered by a wealth of historical support, and thus merits further consideration. Recently, scholars have begun to inquire into Luther's interpretation of Scripture as it relates to "the Jewish question." The importance of Luther's inconsistent hermeneutics as a main option to consider for his anti-Jewish sentiments is becoming more widely accepted. For example, in addition to the editors of *On the Jews and Their Lies* (LW) who earlier affirmed Luther's hermeneutics as a cause for his views, Lutheran

---

[75] Two contrasting, yet illuminating, studies on modern Israel and its place in the covenant are Gary M. Burge, *Whose Land? Whose Promise? What Christians are not being Told about Israel and the Palestinians* (Cleveland, OH: Pilgrims, 2013), already mentioned; and Shadi Khalloul, "Theology and Morality: Is Modern Israel Faithful to the Moral Demands of the Covenant in Its Treatment of Minorities?" in *The New Christian Zionism: Fresh Perspectives on Israel and the Land*, ed. Gerald R. McDermott (Downers Grove, IL: InterVarsity, 2016), 281–301.

scholar Brooks Schramm has suggested:

> Luther was indeed constrained by ideas, images, and superstitions regarding the Jews and Judaism that he inherited from medieval Christian tradition, but the engine in the development of his theological thought as it relates to the Jews is his biblical hermeneutics, in particular his Old Testament hermeneutics. . . . Just as 'the Jewish question' is a central, core component of his thought, so biblical interpretation—and especially Old Testament interpretation is the primary arena in which claims Jews and Judaism are formulated and developed....Luther's anti-Judaism is predominately biblically based and biblically driven, rather than culturally or socially based.[76]

Schramm's assessment of Luther highlights the vital role hermeneutics plays in one's theology. Indeed, everything doctrinal boils down to the hermeneutics employed to expose the doctrine. It is for this reason that Dispensational thought emphasizes the Reformation principle of *sola Scriptura* to the extent it does, along with the accompanying principle of consistent application of literal grammatical-historical interpretation—without which, any appeal to Scripture is nearly meaningless.

To be sure, dispensationalists interpret figures of speech and understand symbols and such in any biblical text. Much has been written on this by dispensationalists over the years. But, they do so never divorcing the direct statements of Scripture from literal, historical and geographical realities when the texts speak plainly of such actualities. The consistently literal hermeneutics employed by normative dispensationalists demands that a text has a single meaning which is never abrogated. This is especially key when dealing with Old ~~~~~~ rophecies. The New Testament may at times ex~~~~~~ ginal Old Testament meaning is never abolished ~~~~~~ as a fixed, single meaning as intended by its auth~~~~~~ dispensational approach to hermeneutics. "If an au~~~~ meaning is not represented by a text in a manner that is reproducible by the interpreter," observed Nathan Hoff, "then it is not possible

---

[76] Brooks Schramm, "Martin Luther, the Bible, and the Jewish People," in *Martin Luther, the Bible, and the Jewish People*, 4.

that one can claim to have understood the Author/author's meaning."[77]
With the dispensational insistence on keeping biblical promises made to
national Israel as truly referring to national Israel, there is absolutely no
warrant whatsoever for the anti-Semitic views of Martin Luther—and so
many other Christians before him and after. To the latter, it is no small
coincidence that Luther's dismissal of national Israel was also adopted by
leaders in Nazi Germany to justify their horrific treatment of the Jews. In
addition to the repeated appeals to Luther made by the Führer himself, the
founder of the anti-Semitic Nazi newspaper *Der Stürmer*, Julius Streicher,
boldly testified at his Nuremberg trial: "Dr. Martin Luther would very probably sit in my place in the defendants' dock today, if this book [*The Jews and
Their Lies*] had been taken into consideration by the Prosecution."[78]

In contrast to Luther, and those who likewise amalgamate Scripture's
distinction between Israel and the church, dispensationalists have endeavored to call attention to and correct this hermeneutical error. Tommy Ice
has called attention to the contribution dispensational thought has made
to keep Israel and the church distinct: "The church will not be substituted
for Israel if the grammatical-historical system of interpretation is consistently used because there are no indicators in the text that such is the case."[79]
It is the consistent grammatical-historical approach to Scripture which Ice
promotes that sets dispensationalism apart from alternative theologies. Between the text's grammar and the historical context the interpreter is provided guardrails to keep from careening off to subjective conclusions—any
racist notion assumed to come from the text being the worst example. The
dispensationalist's consistent application of a literal, grammatical-historical
hermeneutic guards against the error of replacing Israel with the church, as

---

[77] Nathan Hoff, "Meaning and Text-Tokens: An Examination of the Relation-
ship between the Biblical Text and its Meaning," in *The Theory and Practice of Biblical
Hermeneutics: Essays in Honor of Elliot E. Johnson*, ed. H. Wayne House and Forrest
Weiland (Silverton, OR: Lampion, 2015), 13.

[78] Raul Hilberg, *The Destruction of the European Jews* (New York: Harper & Row,
1961), 689–90.

[79] Thomas D. Ice, "Dispensational Hermeneutics," in *Issues in Dispensationalism*,
ed. Wesley R. Willis and John R. Master (Chicago, IL: Moody, 1994), 32.

well as the anti-Semitism that has historically been the result of such interpretation.

7.9 Conclusion

If we are to fully appreciate Luther's career as a reformer guided by his unwavering stance on *sola Scriptura*, then we must consider that along with his correct doctrine also came errors. In other words, Luther's appeal to Scripture alone, in one sense, was an appeal to his particular interpretation of it. Seen in this light, it is ironic that Luther's theological errors came primarily from his commitment of keeping the Bible first. As shown throughout the chapter, the basis of one's theology lies in one's hermeneutical method. With that, there is little doubt that Luther's allegorical tendency emerges from the gloomy shadows of his hate toward the Jewish people, particularly that of exchanging national Israel for the church, making it the number one felon responsible for his shameful views.

When the interpreter allegorizes Scripture by rejecting its plain meaning—in search of a more "spiritual" or "internal" meaning—then all objectivity is lost and one can make the Bible say whatever one wishes it to say. It is clear that anti-Semitism became a legitimized doctrine of the church through the use of an allegorical hermeneutical method—a method which allowed Bible interpreters to scrub Israel from prophecy, and substitute her covenanted place with the church—which continued down the pathway of Jewish persecution from slander to murder. With the dawn and development of replacement theology in the second through fifth centuries, the foundation for anti-Semitism was determined and the Jews became public enemy number one.

However, as has also been demonstrated, dispensationalism's insistence upon a consistently literal, grammatical-historical hermeneutic fully counters anti-Semitism, and brings the church back to God's literal promsies given to national Israel. By consistently emphasizing a biblical text's grammar—as well as its history—Martin Luther's views on Israel are exposed and corrected. As readers reflect on 500 years of Reformed legacy stemming from Luther's historic igniting of what became the Protestant Reformation, it is apropos that the church should reflect on his and the other reformers' principles to which they risked their own lives. Chief among these was their adherence to *sola Scriptura*—a vital doctrine to which dispensational thought has remained consistently faithful, and has done much to advance throughout its history.

Bibliography

Allen, Leslie C. *Psalms 101–150*. Word Biblical Commentary 21. Waco, TX: Word, 1983.

Brown, Francis, S. R. Driver, and Charles Briggs. *Brown Driver Briggs Hebrew and English Lexicon*. Oxford, UK: Clarendon, 1907. BibleWorks.

Burge, Gary M. *Whose Land? Whose Promise? What Christians Are Not Being Told About Israel and the Palestinians*. Cleveland, OH: Pilgrims, 2013.

Chafer, Lewis Sperry. *Systematic Theology*. 8 vols. Dallas, TX: Dallas Seminary, 1948.

Clement of Alexandria. "The Instructor." In *The Ante-Nicene Fathers: Translations of the Writings of the Fathers Down to A.D. 325*, edited by Alexander Roberts and James Donaldson. Vol. 2, *Fathers of the Second Century: Herma, Tatian, Athenagoras, Theophilus, and Clement of Alexandria (Entire)*, 207–296. Grand Rapids, MI: Eerdmans, 1981.

Cyril of Alexandria. "Explanation of the Letter to the Romans." Quoted in Gerald Bray and Thomas C. Oden, eds. *Romans*. Ancient Christian Commentary on Scripture, New Testament 4. Downers Grove, IL: InterVarsity Press, [2005].

Diodore. "Pauline Commentary from the Greek Church." Quoted in Gerald Bray and Thomas C. Oden, eds. *Romans*. Ancient Christian Commentary on Scripture, New Testament 4. Downers Grove, IL: InterVarsity Press, [2005].

Diprose, Ronald E. *Israel and the Church: The Origins and Effects of Replacement Theology*. Downers Grove, IL: Intervarsity, 2000.

"The Epistle of Barnabas." In *Ante-Nicene Fathers: Translations of the Writings of the Fathers Down to A.D. 325*, edited by Alexander Roberts and James Donaldson. Vol. 1, *The Apostolic Fathers with Justin Martyr and Ireneaus*, 133–149. Grand Rapids, MI: Eerdmans, 1981.

Ferguson, Everett. *Church History: The Rise and Growth of the Church in Its Cultural, Intellectual, and Political Context.* Vol. 1, *From Christ to Pre-Reformation.* Grand Rapids, MI: Zondervan, 2013.

Feinberg, John S., ed. *Continuity and Discontinuity (Essays in Honor of S. Lewis Johnson, Jr.): Perspectives on the Relationship Between the Old and New Testaments.* Wheaton, IL: Crossway, 1998.

Gentry, Kenneth L. "Reformed Anti-Semitism?" Chalcedon. June 13, 2005. Accessed August 31, 2017. https://chalcedon.edu/resources/articles/reformed-anti-semitism.

Grasanti, Michael A. "The Book of Psalms." In *The World and the Word: An Introduction to the Old Testament,* edited by Eugene Merrill, Mark F. Rooker, and Michael A. Grasanti, 512–26. Nashville, TN: B &H, 2011.

Hamilton, James H., Jr. "Old Covenant Believers and the Indwelling Spirit: A Survey of the Spectrum of Opinion." *Trinity Journal* 24, no. 1 (Spring 2003): 37–54.

Hilberg, Raul. *The Destruction of the European Jews.* New York: Harper & Row, 1961.

Hippolytus. "The Expository Treatise Against the Jews" in *The Ante-Nicene Fathers: Translations of the Writings of the Fathers Down to A.D. 325,* edited by Alexander Roberts and James Donaldson. Vol. 5, *Fathers of the Third Century: Hippolytus, Cyprian, Caius, Novatian, Appendix,* 219–221. Grand Rapids, MI: Eerdmans, 1981.

Hirsch, E. D. *Validity in Interpretation.* New Haven, CT: Yale, 1967.

Hoff, Nathan. "Meaning and Text-Tokens: An Examination of the Relationship between the Biblical Text and its Meaning." In *The Theory and Practice of Biblical Hermeneutics: Essays in Honor of Elliot E. Johnson,* edited by H. Wayne House and Forrest Weiland, 11–32. Silverton, OR: Lampion, 2015.

Ice, Thomas D. "Dispensational Hermeneutics." In *Issues in Dispensationalism*, edited by Wesley R. Willis and John R. Master, 29–50. Chicago, IL: Moody, 1994.

Irenaeus. "Irenaeus Against Heresies." In *The Ante-Nicene Fathers: Translations of the Writings of the Fathers Down to A.D. 325*, edited by Alexander Roberts and James Donaldson. Vol. 1, *The Apostolic Fathers with Justin Martyr and Ireneaus*, 309–567. Grand Rapids, MI: Eerdmans, 1981.

Justin Martyr. "Dialogue of Justin, Philosopher and Martyr with Trypho, the Jew." In *The Ante-Nicene Fathers: Translations of the Writings of the Fathers Down to A.D. 325*, edited by Alexander Roberts and James Donaldson. Vol. 1, *The Apostolic Fathers with Justin Martyr and Ireneaus*, 194–270. Grand Rapids, MI: Eerdmans, 1981.

Khalloul, Shadi. "Theology and Morality: Is Modern Israel Faithful to the Moral Demands of the Covenant in Its Treatment of Minorities?" In *The New Christian Zionism: Fresh Perspectives on Israel and the Land*, edited by Gerald R. McDermott, 281–301. Downers Grove, IL: InterVarsity, 2016.

Koehler, Ludwig, and Walter Baumgartner. *The Hebrew and Aramaic Lexicon of the Old Testament*. Leiden, The Netherlands: Brill, 2000. Bible-Works.

Köstenberger, Andreas J., Benjamin L. Merkle, and Robert L. Plummer. *Going Deeper With New Testament Greek: An Intermediate Study of the Grammar and Syntax of the New Testament*. Nashville, TN: B&H, 2016.

Ladd, George E. *A Theology of the New Testament*. Grand Rapids, MI: Eerdmans, 1979.

Luther, Martin. "Against the Sabbatarians." In *Luther's Works*. Vol. 47, *The Christian in Society IV*, edited by Franklin Sherman and Helmut T. Lehmann, translated by Martin H. Bertram, 57–98. Philadelphia, PA: Fortress, 1971.

Luther, Martin. "On the Jews and Their Lies." In *Luther's Works*, edited by Helmut T. Lehmann. Vol. 47, *The Christian in Society IV*, edited by Franklin Sherman, translated by Martin H. Bertram, 121–306. Philadelphia, PA: Fortress, 1971.

———. "That Jesus Christ as Born a Jew." In *Luther's Works*, edited by Helmut T. Lehmann. Vol. 45, *The Christian in Society II*, edited and translated by Walter I. Brandt, 195–229. Philadelphia, PA: Fortress, 1962.

———. "Treatise on the Last Words of David." In *Luther's Works*, edited by Jaroslav Pelikan and Hilton C. Oswald. Vol. 15, *Notes on Ecclesiastes, Lectures on the Song of Solomon, Treatise on the Last Words of David*, translated by Martin H. Bertram, 265–352. Philadelphia, PA: Fortress, 1972.

Marsh, Cory M. "Kingdom Hermeneutics and the Apocalypse: A Promotion of Consistent Literal Methodology." *The Journal of Ministry and Theology* 20, no. 2 (Fall 2016): 84–105.

McClain, Alva J. *The Greatness of the Kingdom: An Inductive Study of the Kingdom of God.* Winona Lake, IN: BMH, 2007.

Meyer, Carl S. "Luther's Alleged Anti-Semitism." *Concordia Theological Monthly* 32, no. 11 (November 1961): 692–696. Accessed August 16, 2017. ATLA Religion Database with ATLASerials.

Olander, David. "God's Sovereign Choice of Israel: The Holy Root of Romans 11:16–17." *Journal of Dispensational Theology* 19, no. 58 (Winter 2015): 253–68.

Pelikan, Joraslav. *The Christian Tradition: A History of the Development of Doctrine.* 5 vols. Chicago, IL: University of Chicago, 1975.

Pentecost, J. Dwight. *Things to Come: A Comprehensive Study in Biblical Eschatology.* Findlay, OH: Dunham, 1959.

Richard, Ramesh P. "Soteriological Inclusivism and Dispensationalism." *Bibliotheca Sacra* 151, no. 601 (January 1994): 85–108.

Ryrie, Charles C. *Dispensationalism*. Rev. and exp. ed. Chicago, IL: Moody, 1995.

Schramm, Brooks, and Kirsi I. Stjerna, eds. *Martin Luther, the Bible, and the Jewish People: A Reader*. Minneapolis, MN: Fortress, 2012.

Slotemaker, John T. "The Trinitarian House of David: Martin Luther's Anti-Jewish Exegesis of 2 Samuel 23: 2–7." *Harvard Theological Review* 104, no. 2 (2011): 233–254. Accessed August 16, 2017. ATLA Religion Database with ATLASerials.

Stern, David H. *Jewish New Testament Commentary*. Clarksville, MD: Jewish New Testament Publications, 1992.

Stewart, Alexander E. "The Temporary Messianic Kingdom in Second Temple Judaism and the Delay of the Parousia: Psalm 110:1 and the Development of Early Christian Inaugurated Eschatology." *Journal of Evangelical Theological Society* 59, no. 2 (June 2016): 255–70.

Thiessen, Henry Clarence. *Lectures in Systematic Theology*. Grand Rapids, MI: Eerdmans, 1963.

Thomas, Robert L. *Evangelical Hermeneutics: The New Versus the Old*. Grand Rapids, MI: Kregel, 2002.

Trueman, Carl R. "Reading the Reformers after Newman." In *The People's Book: The Reformation and the Bible*, edited by Jennifer Powell McNutt and David Lauber, 188–204. Downers Grove, IL: InterVarsity, 2017.

Vanlaningham, Michael G. "Matthew." In *The Moody Bible Commentary*, edited by Michael Rydelnik and Michael Vanlaningham, 1449–1514. Chicago, IL: Moody, 2014.

Vlach, Michael J. *Has the Church Replaced Israel? A Theological Evaluation*. Nashville, TN: B&H: 2010.

Wallace, Daniel B. *Greek Grammar beyond the Basics: An Exegetical Syntax of the New Testament*. Grand Rapids, MI: Zondervan, 1996.

Wallmann, Johannes. "Luther on Jews and Islam." In *Creative Biblical Exegesis: Christian and Jewish Hermeneutics through the Centuries*, edited by Benjamin Uffenheimer and Henning Graf Reventlow, 149–60. Journal for the Study of the Old Testament, Supp. Ser. 59. Sheffield, UK: JSOT Press, 1988. Accessed August 28, 2017. EBSCOhost eBook Collection.

Wood, A. Skevington. *The Principles of Biblical Interpretation: As Enunciated by Irenaeus, Origen, Augustine, Luther and Calvin*. Grand Rapids, MI: Zondervan, 1967.

Zuck, Roy B. *Basic Bible Interpretation: A Practical Guide to Discovering Biblical Truth*. Colorado Springs, CO: David C. Cook, 1991.

PART 2
THE FIVE SOLAS OF THE REFORMATION

Sola Scriptura
[Scripture Alone]

8

THE PROTESTANT REFORMATION:
An Important and Yet Incomplete Hermeneutical Reformation

Andy Woods
Chafer Theological Seminary

8.0 Introduction

This October marks the 500 year anniversary when the church reformer, Martin Luther (A.D. 1487–1546), nailed his *95 Theses* to a cathedral door in Wittenberg, Germany. When Luther did so, on October 31, 1517, it is doubtful that he could have anticipated the far-reaching influence and impact of his protest. The monk's decisive action set off a chain reaction all around Europe and ultimately the known world, restoring the church to some of its most cherished, foundational doctrines.

Yet, when the story of the Protestant Reformation is told, the subject must be approached with candor and intellectual honesty. The great contributions of the Protestant reformers to the Christian faith notwithstanding, the Protestant Reformation really represented a mixed bag. As much as the reformers are appreciated today, their revolution can only be described as partial, at best. The great contribution of the Protestant Reformation to Christianity involves the restoration of a hermeneutic. While the Protestant reformers selectively applied this hermeneutic to some of the Bible, a more comprehensive revolution would have to await subsequent generations, who took the reformers' hermeneutic and applied it to the totality of God's Word. The purpose of this chapter is to tell the story of that revolution.

8.1 The Literal Hermeneutic of the Early Church

Concerning the interpretation of Old Testament prophecy, even a casual perusal of the New Testament demonstrates that its biblical characters and writers interpreted these prophecies in a literal sense (Matt 19:28, 26:29; Luke 19:17, 19; Rom 11:25–27; Rev 5:10, etc.). Thus, it is not surprising to discover that Christianity's second generation after the apostolic age also followed a literal approach when interpreting Bible prophecy. In fact, what rose to prominence in early church history was the school at Syrian Antioch, which interpreted prophetic subjects in a literal manner. This school represented the mindset of the apostles since apostolic succession can be traced from Antioch. After all, it was at Antioch the early believers in Jesus began to multiply exponentially and were first called "Christians" (Acts 11:25). Antioch also became the beachhead from where the Apostle Paul launched his three missionary journeys into predominately-Gentile territory (Acts 13:1–3, 14:26, 15:35–41, 18:22–23).

This school of Antioch taught a literal approach to prophecy that indicated that the kingdom of God would not materialize upon the earth until the King, Jesus Christ, first returns physically. While this perspective is called premillennialism today, it was known as *chiliasm* then. This word *chiliasm* comes from the Greek word χίλιοι (*chilioi*) meaning "thousand" and is taken from the six-fold description of the duration of Christ's kingdom (sometimes called the millennium) depicted in Revelation 20:1–10. The School at Antioch exercised such great influence over early Christianity, that virtually all of its most influential leaders were noted *chiliasts*. In fact, in that day, one's embracement of *chiliasm* was viewed as a test to determine one's orthodoxy.

Note the words of respected church father Justin Martyr (A.D. 100–160) in his *Dialogue with Trypho*: "But I and every other completely orthodox Christian feel certain that there will be a resurrection of the flesh, followed by a thousand years in the rebuilt, embellished, and enlarged city of Jerusalem as was announced by the prophets Ezekiel, Isaiah, and the others."[1] The predominance of *chiliasm* amongst the earliest adherents of Christianity has also been observed by reputable historians. Church historian Philip Schaff

---

[1] Justin Martyr, *Dialogue with Trypho*, chap. 80.

summarizes the millennial views of the early church fathers:

> The most striking point in the eschatology of the ante-Nicene age [A.D. 100–325] is the prominent chiliasm, or millenarianism, that is the belief of a visible reign of Christ in glory on earth with the risen saints for a thousand years, before the general resurrection and judgment. It was indeed not the doctrine of the church embodied in any creed or form of devotion, but a widely current opinion of distinguished teachers, such as Barnabas, Papias, Justin Martyr, Irenaeus, Tertullian, Methodius, and Lactantius.[2]

Likewise, Edward Gibbon (1737–1794), who authored the renowned work *The History of the Decline and Rise and Fall of the Roman Empire*, observes the tendency among the early church fathers toward *chiliasm*:

> The ancient and popular doctrine of the Millennium was intimately connected with the second coming of Christ. As the works of the creation had been finished in six days, their duration in their present state, according to a tradition which was attributed to the prophet Elijah, was fixed to six thousand years. By the same analogy it was inferred, that this long period of labor and contention, which was now almost elapsed, would be succeeded by a joyful Sabbath of a thousand years; and that Christ, with the triumphant band of the saints and the elect who had escaped death, or who had been miraculously revived, would reign upon earth till the time appointed for the last and general resurrection...The assurance of such a Millennium was carefully inculcated by a succession of fathers from Justin Martyr, and Irenaeus, who conversed with the immediate disciples of the apostles, down to Lactantius, who was preceptor to the son of Constantine. Though it might not be universally received, it appears to have been the reigning sentiment of the orthodox believers; and it seems so well adapted to the desires and apprehensions of mankind, that it must have contributed in a very considerable degree to the progress of the Christian

---

[2] Philip Schaff, *History of the Christian Church*, vol. 2, *Ante-Nicene Christianity AD 100–325* (1910; repr., Grand Rapids, MI: Eerdmans, 1976), 614.

faith.[3]

With such a well-entrenched belief within earliest Christianity concerning a literal interpretation of prophecy and a yet future earthly kingdom of Christ, when did the Christian world begin to shift on this vital hermeneutical issue?

8.2 The Alexandrian Allegorical Eclipse

In speaking to the Ephesian elders at Miletus at the conclusion of his third missionary journey, the Apostle Paul warned of false teaching that would soon enter the church following the passing of the apostolic generation. In Acts 20:29–30, Paul predicted, "I know that after my departure savage wolves will come in among you, not sparing the flock; and from among your own selves men will arise, speaking perverse things, to draw away the disciples after them." Such a doctrinal departure soon began to emerge as the influence of the Antiochene school was soon eclipsed by the influence of the school of Alexandria, Egypt, located in North Africa. Interestingly, while apostolic succession can be traced back to the school at Antioch, there is no apostolic succession traceable to Alexandria.

8.2.1 Allegorization and its Dangers

What made the Alexandrian school different from the Antiochene school was its introduction of allegorization as a method for interpreting Scripture, especially Bible prophecy. Allegorization involves using the literal meaning of the biblical text only as a vehicle for introducing a higher spiritual meaning, which is only clear to the one doing the allegorizing. For example, Philo (25 B.C.–A.D. 50), an influential allegorizer, who lived during the time of Christ, saw the four rivers depicted in Genesis 2:8–10 (the Pishon, Gihon, Euphrates, Tigris) as not just four literal rivers in the Garden of Eden but also representing four parts of the human soul.

A more common example of modern allegorization entails noting the spiritual meaning of the various gates of the wall surrounding the City of Jerusalem as recorded in Nehemiah 3. Interpreters following the allegorical

---

[3] Edward Gibbon, *History of Christianity* (New York: Eckler, 1916), 141–44.

approach seek to convince their audiences that the "sheep gate" (Neh 3:1) represents Christ, who is the lamb of God (John 1:29). The "fish gate" (Neh 3:3) represents evangelism since Jesus commanded His disciples to become fishers of men (Matt 4:19). The "water gate" (Neh 3:26) represents the Holy Spirit, which is frequently analogized to water (John 7:37–39). The "east gate" (Neh 3:29) represents Christ's second advent, which is analogized to lighting coming from the East (Matt 24:27). While interesting to contemplate, such an interpretation cannot be sustained from a plain reading of Nehemiah 3. Rather, it can only be sustained as the interpreter embraces allegorical interpretation.

J. Dwight Pentecost, identifies three basic problems associated with the allegorical method of interpretation: (1) the biblical text itself is not being interpreted; rather, what controls the interpretive process is an idea emanating from outside the text in question and is in turn foisted upon it; (2) the authority in interpretation is no longer the biblical text; rather the allegory foisted upon the text emanating from the interpreter's own mind becomes the authority; and, (3) since allegories and their meanings are unique to the subjective imagination of each allegorist, one is left without any basis by which to test the conclusions of the allegorical interpreter.[4] Despite these significant problems associated with allegorical interpretation, the Alexandrian school rose to prominence over the Antiochene School in terms of influence. Consequently, the Bible began to be wildly allegorized within Christendom, especially as biblical texts related to the subject of Bible prophecy and the kingdom of God.   RESULT

8.2.2 Causes of the Shift into Allegorism

What caused the Christian church to progressively reject the traditional, literal approach as espoused by Antioch and instead embrace the allegorical method as outlined by Alexandria? At the risk of oversimplification, there were likely a multiplicity of factors involved. First, the allegorical approach met the need for immediate relevance and application in Christian preaching and teaching. When the text is allegorized it can be used to

---

[4] J. Dwight Pentecost, *Things to Come: A Study in Biblical Eschatology* (1958; repr., Grand Rapids, MI: Zondervan, 1964), 5–6.

meet virtually any emotional, spiritual, or psychological need in the listener or reader. After all, who wants to listen to a boring sermon on the gates around the wall of Jerusalem in Nehemiah 3, when it is much more interesting and exciting to learn about the "true" spiritual significance of these mundane gates, such as evangelism, the Holy Spirit, the second advent, etc...? Bernard Ramm explains:

> But citing verses in the Old Testament, in themselves frequently very obscure, as if superior to verses in the New, revealed no understanding of the significance of historical and progressive revelation for hermeneutics...They considered the Old (especially) and the New Testaments filled with parables, enigmas, and riddles. The allegorical method alone sufficed to bring out the meaning of these parables, enigmas, and riddles.[5]

Second, the allegorical method became increasingly more tenable as Bible interpreters became susceptible to merging human philosophy into the process of biblical interpretation. Ramm notes the influence that Greek philosophy had over the mind of Philo who was a well-known allegorizer:

> The outstanding Jewish allegorist was Philo...He was a thoroughly convinced Jew. To him the Scriptures (primarily in the Septuagint version) were superior to Plato and Greek philosophy...Yet, he had a great fondness for Greek philosophy, especially Plato and Pythagoras. By a most elaborate system of allegorizing he was able to reconcile for himself his loyalty to his Hebrew faith and his love for Greek philosophy.[6]

Ronald Diprose similarly observes the influence of Greek upon other prominent allegorizers of the Alexandrian school:

> Clement of Alexandria (c. 155–c. 220) was unashamedly a Christian Platonist and as such he quoted from Plato, and indeed from other philosophers, with the same ease the He quoted from the Hebrew Scriptures and the New Testament. Moreover, he interpreted the Bi-

---

[5] Bernard Ramm, *Protestant Biblical Interpretation: A Textbook of Hermeneutics*, 3rd rev. ed. (Grand Rapids, MI: Baker, 1970), 30.
[6] Ibid., 27.

ble in light of Platonic concepts...His dependence upon Plato is further evident in a speculative passage in which the Jews feature as "helpers" while the Christians are considered "fit to rule." Origen continued the Alexandrian tradition of interpreting the Bible in a way which harmonized with Greek philosophy.[7]

3 Third, a related influence was that Alexandria, Egypt, was a hotbed for gnostic dualism, which taught that while the spiritual world was inherently good, the physical world was evil. The physical world, in and of itself, is obviously not evil since God pronounced all of creation "very good" (Gen 1:31) following His work in the six-day creation week. Such a dualistic belief system wreaked havoc on numerous Christian doctrines, such as Christ's incarnation. Those influenced by gnostic thought reasoned that Christ could not have come in a body, given the inherent evil associated with the physical world. Such dualism, in turn, led to cerinthianism, or the idea that Jesus was never the Christ but rather merely became the Christ when the Spirit of Christ came upon Him at His baptism and left Him prior to His crucifixion (1 John 2:22). A preoccupation with gnostic dualism also led to docetism. This name comes from the Greek verb *dokeō* which means "to seem" or "to appear." According to this errant belief, Christ never actually possessed a physical body but rather only "seemed" or "appeared" to possess one (1 John 4:2–3).

In addition to Christology, gnostic dualism also had a deleterious impact upon eschatology, which is the branch of Christian theology relating to what the Scripture reveals concerning the future. Since they believed that the physical world is inherently evil, gnostic philosophers reasoned that the various biblical prophecies relating to eating and drinking in a yet future earthly kingdom (Matt 8:11, 26:29; Luke 13:29) were obviously not meant to be taken literally, and that they therefore must be spiritualized. Thus, Renald Showers well summarizes the influence of gnostic dualistic philosophy behind Augustine's allegorical interpretation of the kingdom:

> The...factor in his change of view was the influence of Greek philosophy upon his thinking. Before his conversion Augustine was deeply

---

[7] Ronald E. Diprose, *Israel in the Development of Christian Thought* (Rome: IBEI, 2000), 157–58.

immersed in the study of this philosophy, much of which asserted the inherent evil of the physical or material and the inherent goodness of the totally spiritual. This philosophy continued to leave its mark up on him even after his conversion. It prompted him to reject as carnal the pre-millennial idea of an earthly, political Kingdom of God with great material blessings. He believed that, in order for the Kingdom of God to be good, it must be spiritual in nature.[8]

In his classic work, *The City of God*, Augustine himself acknowledges the impact his gnostic dualistic presuppositions had upon his interpretive decision to spiritualize the biblical prophecies predicting the arrival of God's earthly kingdom:

> And this opinion would not be objectionable, if it were believed that the joys of the saints in that Sabbath shall be spiritual, and consequent on the presence of God; for I myself, too, once held this opinion. But, as they assert that those who then rise again shall enjoy the leisure of immoderate carnal banquets, furnished with an amount of meat and drink such as not only to shock the feeling of the temperate, but even to surpass the measure of credulity itself, such assertions can be believed only by the carnal. They who do believe them are called by the spiritual Chiliasts, which we may literally reproduce by the name Millenarians.[9]

4   A fourth factor leading the church to embrace the allegorical method of interpretation was the decline in Jewish believers within the church's ranks. The early chapters of the book of Acts reveal the universal Jewish composition of the early church. In fact, there were no Gentile converts into the church until the salvation of Cornelius (Acts 10–11). However, following Paul's first missionary journey into Southern Galatia, this ethnic pattern dramatically changed as the Gentiles become the predominant Christian converts and the majority of the Jews rejected the Gospel message

---

[8] John Ankerberg and Renald Showers, *The Most Asked Prophecy Questions* (Chattanooga, TN: ATRI, 2000), 326.

[9] Augustine, *The City of God*, trans. Marcus Dods (New York: Random House, 1950), 10.7.719.

(Acts 13:45, 48). By the time Paul wrote his epistle to the Romans, the Gentile Christians were in such numerical ascendancy over their Jewish counterparts that Paul had to instruct these Gentile believers not to be arrogant on account of Israel's apparent spiritual hardening (Rom 11:13, 17–21).

Given the Jewish familiarity with not only the content but also with a proper understanding of the Hebrew Bible, or the Old Testament, it is doubtful that the church would have ever embraced the allegorical method of interpretation espoused by the Alexandrian school had they retained their majority status within the church. However, the Gentile Christians, coming out of pagan backgrounds, were not so similarly educated. Thus, they were vulnerable to the suggestion that the Old Testament could be spiritualized, allegorized, and consequently marginalized.

Fifth, Constantine's *Edict of Milan* (A.D. 313), which granted religious toleration to Christianity within the Roman Empire, also played a significant role in the church's embracement of the allegorical Alexandrian method of interpretation. With the stroke of a pen, Christianity went from a persecuted status within Rome to a protected and even elevated status. Prior to this point in time, going all the way back to the reign of Nero, Christianity had face the horrific reality of daily persecution at the hands of Rome. Now, thanks to Constantine, the tide had suddenly turned. Such an abrupt transition from persecution to tolerance and even elevation had indeed convinced many within the church that the kingdom of God had now come. This new-found belief caused them to allegorize many of the terrestrial kingdom promises related to national Israel into present spiritual kingdom realities. Showers again explains:

> That new view became known as Amillennialism. Several things prompted this change in Augustine. First, the political situation of the Church in the Roman empire had changed radically around the period of his life. By his time the Roman persecution of the Church had stopped, and the state had made itself the servant of the Church. As the Roman empire crumbled, the Church stood fast, ready to rule in the place of the empire. It looked as if Gentile world dominion was being crushed and that the Church was becoming victorious over it. Under these circumstances Augustine concluded that Premillennialism was obsolete, and that it did not fit the current situation. In the

place of it he developed the idea that the Church is the Kingdom of the Messiah foretold in such Scriptures as Daniel 2 and 7 and Revelation 20. In his book, *The City of God,* he became the first person to teach the idea that the organized Catholic (Universal) Church is the promised Messianic Kingdom and that the Millennium began with the first coming of Christ.[10]

This convergence of factors led to the ascendancy of the Alexandrian method of interpretation within Christendom.

8.2.3 Prominent Allegorizers

Several prominent allegorical interpreters arose out of the Alexandrian school. One such interpreter was Origen (A.D. 185–254). According to Diprose:

> Origen was also influenced by the example of Philo, a first-century Alexandrian Jew who had interpreted the Old Testament Scriptures allegorically in order to make them harmonize with his Platonism. Allegorism played an important part in Origen's theory of interpretation and, as he was the first biblical scholar to work out "a complete hermeneutical theory," his work was destined to exert great influence on the Christian approach to the Hebrew Scriptures, for centuries to come...Origen is remembered for his philosophical speculation as the allegorist *par excellence* among Biblical interpreters.[11]

Reference has also already been made to Augustine (A.D. 354–430) and his influential work, *The City of God.* By influential, it is not to mean in the positive sense but rather in the negative sense. Because *The City of God* was the first major written systematization and exposition of amillennialism in church history, it is perhaps also the most influential book in church history. This work, more than any other, cast an allegorical spell over the church which, as will be explained later, took Christendom well over a millennium to crawl out from under.

The City of God wildly allegorized the biblical passages dealing with the

---

[10] Ankerberg and Showers, *Most Asked Prophecy Questions,* 325.

[11] Diprose, *Israel in the Development,* 86–87.

future earthly reign of Christ. For example, the "first resurrection" (Rev 20:4-6) was reinterpreted to refer to regeneration rather than a future, physical, bodily resurrection.[12] Regarding the millennial binding of Satan in the abyss (Rev 20:1-3), Augustine indicated that the abyss was not a literal place.[13] He also taught that the binding of Satan merely "means his being more unable to seduce the Church."[14] Concerning the future thousand year reign of Christ along with His saints (Rev 20:4), Augustine wrote, "the saints reign with Christ during the same thousand years, understood in the same way, that is, of the time of His first coming"[15] and "Therefore the Church even now is the kingdom of Christ, and the kingdom of heaven. Accordingly, even now His saints reign with Him."[16]

8.2.4 Disdain for Chiliasm

So entrenched had become the Alexandrian method of interpretation that the church began to view the earlier chiliasm as the product of the less enlightened and less intelligent. Note the words of Eusebius (A.D. 260-340) as he critiqued the *chiliastic* work of Papias (A.D. 60-130):

> To these belong his statement that there will be a period of some thousand years after the resurrection of the dead, and that the kingdom of Christ will be set up in material form on this very earth. I suppose he got these ideas through a misunderstanding of the apostolic accounts, not perceiving that the things said by them were spoken mystically in figures. For he appears to have been of very limited understanding, as one can see from his discourses.[17]

In fact, chiliasm itself began to be viewed as a mere fable rather than the product of a careful study of the biblical text. Such a telling statement attributed to Jerome (A.D. 347-420) reads as follows:

---

[12] Augustine, *The City of God*, 10.6.717.

[13] Ibid., 10.6.720.

[14] Ibid., 10.8.722.

[15] Ibid., 10.9.725.

[16] Ibid., 10.9.725-26.

[17] Eusebius, *Ecclesiastical History*, 3.39.12-13.

How must we understand what the Saviour says in Matthew: "But I say to you, I will not drink again of this fruit of the vine until that day when I drink it new with you in the Kingdom of my Father"? (Matth. 26. 29). This passage is the origin of a certain fable of a thousand years, in which they say that Christ will reign in the flesh and will drink that wine which he has not drunk since that time until the end of the world...For the kingdom of God isn't food and drink, but justice, joy and peace in the Holy Spirit (Rom. 14. 17).[18]

In sum, the ascendancy of the Alexandrian school of interpretation in lieu of the prophetic literalism espoused by Antioch was accomplished through the combination of several factors as well as through the influence of several prominent Alexandrian theologians. Such an eclipse relegated chiliasm, which had dominated Christian thinking in its first two generations, into a minority status. This eclipse even caused chiliasm to be viewed with suspicion, as the product of the less enlightened, and even as a mere fable. What impact did this new paradigm shift have upon Christ's church?

8.3 The Dark Ages

The ascendancy of the Alexandrian school plummeted the church into a time often referred to as the Middle Ages or even "The Dark Ages."[19] During this era, the study of end times prophecy was rendered all but obsolete. This era dominated church history for well over a millennium: from the fourth to the sixteenth century. Showers describes this era as follows:

> Augustine's allegorical amillennialism became the official doctrine of the church, and Premillennialism went underground. Some aspects of Premillennialism were even branded as heretical. The Roman Catholic Church strongly advocated and maintained Augustine's Amillennial view throughout the Middle Ages. During that span of time occasionally pre-millennial groups formed to challenge the doctrine and political power of the major part of organized Christendom, but they

---

[18] Jerome, "Letter 120 (Ad Hedibiam). To Hedibia, on Biblical Problems (Excerpts)," The Tertullian Project, accessed May 20, 2017, http://www.tertullian .org/fathers/jerome_letter_120.htm

[19] Pentecost, *Things to Come*, 25–26.

were not able to restore Premillennialism to its original position as the accepted, orthodox view of the Church.[20]

During this era, only one church existed within Christendom—the Roman Catholic Church. Because of the dominance of the allegorical method of interpretation (in which, as noted previously, the subjective interpretation of the allegorist can never be tested), only the clergy were deemed qualified to read and allegorically interpret Scripture. Such a sharp clergy-laity distinction had the net effect of removing the Bible from the common man. In fact, throughout Europe the Bible was typically chained to the pulpits of most churches. Thus, the Scripture was only accessible to the priests. This problem was further compounded by widespread illiteracy among the population, which made the Bible all the more inaccessible to the masses. In the fourth century, Jerome translated the Scriptures into Latin in order to make them accessible to the common man. The Roman Catholic mass continued to be read and conducted in Latin up to time of Luther, even though it was no longer a language understood by most people. Thus, although many regularly went to mass, they were unable to understand what was being communicated.

Such biblical illiteracy made the people vulnerable to spiritual deception and manipulation. The sale of indulgences was common throughout the era. The people did not have access to the Scripture to ascertain if Purgatory was even a biblical concept. Thus, the church authorities routinely told them that they could purchase deceased relatives out of Purgatory by paying the right monetary sum to the church. In fact, Johann Tetzel, a friar during the time of Martin Luther, infamously quipped, "when the coin in the coffer rings the soul from Purgatory springs." The practice of the sale of indulgences was condoned by both the church, as well as the existing political authorities, since they served as a convenient source of fund raising necessary to subsidize the church's various building projects, such as the refurbishment of Saint Peter's Basilica in Rome. In addition, due to the inaccessibility to the Scripture, God's future promises to the Jewish people were not available to serve as a natural defense or bulwark against the anti-Semi-

---

[20] Ankerberg and Showers, *Most Asked Prophecy Questions*, 327–28.

tism of the day. Thus, rampant Jew hatred continued unabated and unchallenged.[21] Due to these pitiful conditions, the church was in dire need of theological rescue.

8.4 The Contribution of the Protestant Reformers

The Protestant Reformation became the tool that God used to redirect the church, which was then experiencing the "Dark Ages," back to the solid foundation of His eternal Word.

8.4.1 The Reformers Embrace Literal Interpretation

The Protestant reformers rescued the church from the Alexandrian allegorical method of interpretation and its consequences that were experienced in the Middle Ages through an application of a literal hermeneutic to some selective areas of Scripture, such as ecclesiology and eschatology. For example, William Tyndale (A.D. 1494–1536) asserted, "The Scripture hath but one sense, which is the literal sense."[22] Luther also wrote that the Scriptures "are to be retained in their simplest meaning ever possible, and to be understood in their grammatical and literal sense unless the context plainly forbids."[23] Calvin wrote in the preface of his commentary on Romans "it is the first business of an interpreter to let the author say what he does say, instead of attributing to him what we think he ought to say."[24]

Because of their adherence to literal interpretation, both Calvin and Luther condemned the allegorical method of interpretation. Luther denounced the allegorical approach to Scripture in strong words. He said: "Allegories are empty speculations and as it were the scum of Holy Scripture."

[21] Michael L. Brown, *Our Hands Are Stained with Blood: The Tragic Story of the "Church" and the Jewish People* (Shippensburg, PA: Destiny Image, 1992), 7–17.

[22] William Tyndale, "Obedience of a Christian Man," in *Doctrinal Treatises and Introductions to Different Portions of the Holy Scriptures*, ed. Henry Walter (Cambridge: Cambridge University Press, 1848), 304.

[23] Martin Luther, *Luther's Works*, vol. 6, *Lectures on Genesis 31–37*, 509, quoted in Roy B. Zuck, *Basic Bible Interpretation: A Practical Guide to Discovering Biblical Truth* (Colorado Springs, CO: Victor, 1991), 45.

[24] John Calvin, preface to *Commentary on Romans*, quoted Zuck, *Basic Bible Interpretation*, 47.

LUTHER

"Origen's allegories are not worth so much dirt," "To allegorize is to juggle the Scripture." "Allegorizing may degenerate into a mere monkey game." "Allegories are awkward, absurd, inventive, obsolete, loose rags."[25] Calvin similarly rejected allegorical interpretations. He called them "frivolous games" and accused Origen and other allegorists of "torturing scripture, in every possible sense, from the true sense."[26]

Reformers Martin Luther and John Calvin, both students of the law in their formative educational years,[27] rejected the use of church tradition as a guide for spiritual truth and instead advocated returning to Scripture alone, or *sola Scriptura*, as the source of Christian belief and practice. To put this into legal terms, Luther and Calvin rejected the case law approach as a guide to Scripture.[28] The case law method places more emphasis on studying what legal authorities have said about a given legal source than on studying the legal source itself. Thus, both reformers recognized the value of knowledge of biblical Hebrew and Greek since a return to Scripture inevitably required knowledge of the original languages of Scripture.

8.4.2 Blessings of the Reformation

The reformers also did not want to see the biblical ignorance of the common man exploited for financial purposes, as had been the case with the sale of indulgences. Consequently, the reformers laid stress on the idea that the people no longer had to go through an intermediary, such as a priest, in order to receive and understand God's Word. They need not do

---

[25] Martin Luther, *Comm. in Gen.*, iii., xv., xxx, quoted in Frederic W. Farrar, *History of Interpretation* (1886; repr., Grand Rapids, MI: Baker, 1961), 328.

[26] John Calvin, *Commentary on Galatians*, iv.22, quoted in James D. Wood, *The Interpretation of the Bible: A Historical Introduction* (London: Duckworth, 1938), 92, quoted in Zuck, *Basic Bible Interpretation*, 47.

[27] Alan W. Gomes, *Reformation and Modern Theology and Historical Theology Survey Course Syllabus* (La Mirada, CA: Biola Bookstore, 1999), 23; Justo L. Gonzáles, *The Story of Christianity: The Reformation to the Present Day* (San Francisco, CA: Harper Collins, 1985), 62; Dave Hunt, *What Love Is This? Calvinism's Misrepresentation of God*, 4th ed. (Bend, OR: Berean Call, 2013), 40.

[28] John Eidsmoe, *Christianity and the Constitution: The Faith of Our Founding Fathers* (Grand Rapids, MI: Baker, 1987), 402.

so since they were already priests themselves (Rev 1:6). This notion, often called "the priesthood of all believers," also meant that the Scripture had to be both accessible and understandable to the clergy and laity alike. This new theological emphasis explains why prominent reformers, like Tyndale and Luther, set out to translate the Scriptures into the languages of the common man of their day (just as Jerome had accomplished in the fourth century with his Latin Vulgate).

The privilege inherent in "the priesthood of all believers" theological construct also meant that literacy was necessary so that the common man could both read and understand the Bible. Thus, the Reformation introduced great advances in public education to erase illiteracy. Luther valued education built upon a biblical foundation. After all, it was Martin Luther himself, who warned:

> I am afraid that the schools will prove the very gates of hell, unless they diligently labor in explaining the Holy Scriptures and engraving them in the heart of the youth. I advise no one to place his child where the Scriptures do not reign paramount. Every institution in which men are not unceasingly occupied with the Word of God must become corrupt.[29]

It is doubtful that public education would have ever become what it is today had it not been for the reformers' influence. In fact, the first public school system in America was founded in 1642 in Massachusetts by those who had escaped religious persecution in Europe and thus were the direct beneficiaries of the Reformation.[30] Its founding charter was expressed in the *Old Deluder Satan Law*:

> It being one chief project of that old deluder, Satan, to keep men from the knowledge of the Scriptures, as in former time...It is therefore ordered...that after the Lord hath increased the settlement...they

---

[29] Martin Luther, "An Open Letter to the Christian Nobility of the German Nation Concerning The Reform of the Christian Estate," in *Luther's Works*, ed. Helmut T. Lehmann, vol. 44, *The Christian in Society I*, ed. and rev. James Atkinson, trans. Charles M. Jacobs (Philadelphia, PA: Fortress, 1966), 207.

[30] For more on Separatists and church autonomy, see Kevin Zuber's chapter "The Doctrine of the Local Church" in the current volume.

shall...appoint one within their town, to teach all such children to read...they shall set up a grammar school to instruct youths.[31]

This law's allusion to the "former time" was, of course, an explicit reference to the pre-Reformation dark ages when the Scripture remained inaccessible to the masses. So as not to repeat the historical nightmare of the "Dark Ages" that was largely undone by the reformers, America from its inception stressed literacy so that everyone could read the Bible for themselves.[32]

8.4.8 *The Five Solas*

The Protestant reformers, through their diligent application of the literal, grammatical-historical method of interpretation to certain parts of the Scripture, restored to the church five important doctrines that had been lost to the church for over a millennium due to excessive allegorization during the "Dark Ages." These five doctrines are sometimes called the five *solas*. *Sola* is a Latin word meaning "alone" or "by itself." They are: (1) *sola gratia*, or salvation by grace alone; (2) *sola Christus*, or salvation by Christ alone; (3) *sola Scriptura*, or spiritual teaching that is based upon the Scripture alone; (4) *sola fide*, or salvation by faith alone; and (5) *sola Deo gloria*, or salvation is accomplished to the glory of God alone.

Thus, looking back upon the Reformation, there is much to be grateful for in terms of both the doctrinal and societal progress that it introduced. The reformers dedicated their lives to this task thereby making these gains realizable. In some cases, reformers, like Tyndale and even precursors to the Reformation, like John Huss (A.D. 1369–1415), paid the ultimate price of martyrdom so that subsequent generations could enjoy these fruits of Protestantism. In all of this Christians can rejoice. Yet, what the Protestant Reformation accomplished should not be overstated.

8.5 The Reformers' Incomplete Revolution

Despite their emphasis upon literally interpreting some aspects of Scripture, Luther and Calvin did not go far enough in applying a literal

---

[31] *Church of the Holy Trinity v. U.S.*, 143 U.S. 457, 467 (1892).

[32] David Barton, *Original Intent: The Courts, the Constitution, and Religion*, 3rd ed. (Aledo, TX: Wall Builder Press, 2000), 80.

hermeneutic to all areas of divine truth.

8.5.1 The Reformers' Selective Literalness

When it came to the issue of what Scripture reveals concerning origins, the reformers, to their credit, generally employed the same literal approach that they had used in order to reclaim the five *solas*.[33] Luther noted:

> We know from Moses that the world was not in existence before 6,000 years ago...He calls "a spade a spade," i.e., he employs the term "day" and "evening" without allegory, just as we customarily do... we assert that Moses spoke in the literal sense, not allegorically or figuratively, i.e., that the world, with all its creatures, was created within six days, as the words read. If we do not comprehend the reason for this, let us remain pupils and leave the job of the teacher to the Holy Spirit.[34]

John Calvin similarly asserted:

> And they will not refrain from guffaws when they are informed that but little more than five thousand years have passed since the creation of the universe...Must we pass over in silence the creation of the universe? No! God's truth is so powerful, both in this respect and in every other, that it has nothing to fear from the evil speaking of wicked men.[35]

Although the reformers were literal in their approach to protology (the doctrine of beginnings), Christology (the doctrine of Christ), soteriology (the doctrine of salvation), and bibliology (the doctrine of the Scripture), other doctrines, such as ecclesiology (the doctrine of the church) and eschatology (the doctrine of the end) were treated in an entirely different matter. Regarding the selective literalness of Luther, Roy B. Zuck observes:

---

[33] For further historical evidence demonstrating the reformers' belief in literal Genesis, see Joel R. Beeke, "What Did the Reformers Believe About the Age of the Earth," in *The New Answers Book 4: Over 30 Questions on Creation/Evolution and the Bible*, ed. Ken Ham (Green Forest, AR: Master Books, 2013), 101–10.

[34] Martin Luther, *Luther's Works*, vol. 1, *Lectures on Genesis 1–5*, ed. Jaroslav Pelikan, trans. George V. Schick (St. Louis: Concordia, 1958), 3, 6.

[35] John Calvin, *Institutes of the Christian Religion*, 3.21.4.

Though Luther vehemently opposed the allegorizing of Scripture, he too occasionally allegorized. For instance, he stated that Noah's Ark is an allegory of the Church.

For Luther, Bible interpretation is to be centered in Christ. Rather than allegorizing the Old Testament, he saw Christ frequently in the Old Testament, often beyond what is legitimately provided for in proper interpretation.[36]

In fact, Calvin seems to have ignored much of God's prophetic Word. Despite having written commentaries on every book of the New Testament, in addition to not writing commentaries on the little books of 2 and 3 John, Calvin failed to write a commentary on the Book of Revelation.[37] When Calvin was not ignoring eschatological biblical texts, he seemed preoccupied with employing the Alexandrian and Augustinian method of interpretation to these texts. Notice Calvin's spiritualizing treatment of Christ's thousand-year earthly kingdom described in Revelation 20:1–10 and the contempt in which he viewed those who rejected his allegorical interpretation of eschatology:

> But Satan has not only befuddled men's senses to make them bury with the corpses the memory of resurrection; he has also attempted to corrupt this part of the doctrine with various falsifications...Now their fiction is too childish either to need or to be worth a refutation. And the Apocalypse, from which they undoubtedly drew a pretext for their error, does not support them. For the number "one thousand" [Rev. 20:4] does not apply to the eternal blessedness of the church but only to the various disturbances that awaited the church, while still toiling on earth...Those who assign the children of God a thousand years in which to enjoy the inheritance of the life to come do not realize how much reproach they are casting upon Christ and his Kingdom.[38]

The reformers' retention of the allegorical method of interpretation in the area of biblical eschatology is also evident in the way they took the

---

[36] Zuck, *Basic Bible Interpretation*, 45.

[37] Ibid., 47.

[38] Calvin, *Institutes*, 3.25.5.

prophecies aimed at a future Babylon and the antichrist and redirected them so as to make it seem as if these prophecies were instead speaking of the Roman Catholic Church. Such an interpretation was advanced at the expense of the literal sense of these passages. Note Luther's prophetic application to the Pope:

> No man can believe what an abomination the papacy is. A Christian does not have to be of low intelligence, either, to recognize it. God himself must deride him in the hellish fire, and our Lord Jesus Christ, St. Paul says in II Thessalonians 2 [:8] "will slay him with the breath of his mouth and destroy him by his glorious coming." I only deride, with my own weak derision, so that those who now live and those who will come after us should know what I have thought of the pope, the damned antichrist, and so that whoever wishes to be a Christian may be warned against such an abomination.[39]

Calvin similarly redirected the prophecies concerning Babylon and the antichrist against the Pope and the Roman Catholic Church:

> However, when we categorically deny to the papists the title of *the* church, we do not for this reason impugn the existence of churches among them. Rather, we are only contending about the true and lawful constitution of the church, required in the communion not only of the sacraments (which are the signs of profession) but also especially of doctrine. Daniel [Dan 9:27] and Paul [2 Thess 2:4] foretold that Antichrist would sit in the Temple of God. With us, it is the Roman pontiff we make the leader and standard bearer of that wicked and abominable kingdom. The fact that his seat is placed in the Temple of God signifies that his reign was not to be such as to wipe out either the name of Christ or of the church. From this it therefore is evident that we by no means deny that the churches under his tyranny remain churches. But these he has profaned by his sacrilegious impiety, afflicted by his inhuman domination, corrupted and well-nigh killed by

---

[39] Martin Luther, "Against the Roman Papacy, an Institution of the Devil," in *Luther's Works*, vol. 41, *Church and Ministry III*, ed. Eric. W. Gritsch (Philadelphia, PA: Fortress Press, 1966), 273–74.

his evil and deadly doctrines, which are like poisoned drinks. In them Christ lies hidden, half buried, the gospel overthrown, piety scattered, the worship of God nearly wiped out. In them, briefly, everything is so confused that there we see the face of Babylon rather than that of the Holy City of God.[40]

8.5.2 The Lingering Catholic Influence on the Reformers

Because the reformers were primarily concerned with soteriological issues, they failed to apply the same literal interpretation that they used to interpret soteriology to the areas of ecclesiology and eschatology. Consequently, the reformers left untouched (and even carried into their new Reformed theology) Alexandrian and Augustinian amillennialism. Showers explains, "The Lutheran, Reformed, and Anglican Reformers rejected premillennialism as being 'Jewish opinions.' They maintained the Amillennial view which the Roman Catholic Church had adopted from Augustine."[41] Barry Horner similarly notes:

> The inheritance from the Augustinian tradition that modern Europe received, notwithstanding the opposition of Melanchthon and others to Luther's excesses, resulted in a continuance of an eschatology that upheld the essentially anti-Judaic thesis, namely, the transference of blessings, formerly promised to Israel, to the Christian church for it's fulfillment. . . . On a much larger scale the reformed movement maintained its allegiance to Augustinian eschatology, which essentially found authoritative expression in the writings of Francis Turretin (1623–1687) who studied at Calvin's academy in Geneva and later taught there for 30 years. His monumental *Institutes of Elenctic Theology* became the epitome of reformed doctrine. Not surprisingly, his quotations of Augustine are copious, even far exceeding references to Calvin. Consequently, Turretin's eschatology is almost predictable. . . . Of course such a mass incorporation into the church is to the exclusion of any perpetuation of Jewish identity. In classic Augustinian fashion, there is token recognition of Jewish individuality for a time,

---

[40] Calvin, *Institutes*, 4.2.12.
[41] Ankerberg and Showers, *Most Asked Prophecy Questions*, 328.

though any form of Jewish restoration was considered to be a gross form of chiliasm. Turretin's *Institutes* became the central textbook for systematic theology in American Ivy League colleges during the later half of the 18th century. It is not surprising that the early theologians of Princeton Theological Seminary highly esteemed this most influential legacy, and of course it's eschatology.[42]

Despite the reformers' doctrinal progress in select areas, it is simply a matter of historical naïveté to assume that the reformers made a clean break with Roman Catholicism back in the sixteenth century. On the contrary, as Roman Catholics themselves who had even initially sought to remain within the Catholic church, they dragged many vestiges of Roman Catholicism with them into their infant and newly developing Reformed theology. In addition to the retention of Augustinian amillennialism, there were other Roman Catholic holdovers as well.[43] One such holdover related to the Roman Catholic practice of infant baptism, Luther considered infant baptism a sacrament and therefore a means of grace. He believed that "such sacraments could generate faith; and hence baptism could generate faith of an infant."[44] Still another holdover related to the doctrine of consubstantiation, which appears to be a slight modification of the doctrine of transubstantiation. Caner explains, "Luther denied the doctrine of Transubstantiation, rejecting any molecular change of the elements. Consubstantiation, a term never employed by Luther, is used to explain his view that the body and blood are present 'in, with, and under' the bread and wine."[45]

Yet another carryover related to the Roman Catholic church's view

[42] Barry E. Horner, *Future Israel: Why Christian Anti-Judaism Must Be Challenged*, NAC Stuides in Bible and Theology (Nashville, TN: Baker, 2007), 155–60.

[43] For a comprehensive treatment of those aspects of Roman Catholic theology carried over into Reformed theology by the Protestant reformers, see Jeremy Edmondson, "Free Grace is Returning to Scripture as Our Sole Authority," in *Free Grace Theology: 5 Ways It Magnifies the Gospel*, ed. by Grant Hawley (Allen, TX: Bold Grace, 2016), 1–29.

[44] Alister E. McGrath, *Reformation Thought: An Introduction* (Grand Rapids, MI: Baker, 1995), 179.

[45] Emir Caner, "Balthsar Hubmaier and His Theological Participation in the Reformation: Ecclesiology and Soteriology," *Faith and Mission* 21, no. 1 (2003): 42.

that it was the sole representative of the kingdom of God upon the earth. This Romanist failure to distinguish between God's earthly kingdom program for Israel and his pilgrimage and heavenly identity of the church carried over into Calvin's Geneva. Here, Calvin sought to reconstruct a society through the imposition of the Mosaic Law, "which he tried to imitate as much as possible in his new Christian republic in Geneva."[46] This social experiment resulted in dire societal consequences:

> A measure of legalism became apparent in Geneva, as the consistory put the lives of church members under continuous review and applied discipline to offenders. Church attendance was compulsory. Eating fish on Fridays was forbidden, as were attendance at theaters, dancing, cardplaying, and criticism of pastors. All heretical teaching was deemed subversive and subject to penalties under criminal law. Flagrant infractions could lead to banishment, imprisonment, and in extreme cases death. Judicial torture was common procedure.[47]

Perhaps the greatest blight upon Calvin's Geneva involved the execution of Michael Servetus in 1553 under Calvin's watch. Servetus was executed merely for holding the doctrine of the Trinity in question.[48] Apparently, placing government's power of the sword simultaneously into the hands of the church proved too great a temptation for church authorities to abuse political power against not actual criminals but rather mere theological objectors. The tyrannical nightmare in Geneva well demonstrates the failure of the reformers to apply literal interpretation to ecclesiology, which would have led them to a consistent Israel–church distinction.

Finally, it must be pointed out that some of the vitriolic anti-Semitism of the Middle Ages also found its way into the Reformation movement. After all, it was the respected and revered church reformer Martin Luther who, late in his life, and frustrated at the Jews unwillingness to receive Christ on the basis of faith alone, wrote a nearly eighty-page scathing tract

---

[46] Salo W. Baron, "Calvin, John," in *Encyclopedia Judaica*, ed. Cecil Roth (Jerusalem: Keter Publishing, 1971), 5:66.

[47] James Edward McGoldrick, "Introducing John Calvin: The Reformer's Preparation," *Reformation and Revival* 10, no. 4 (2001): 21.

[48] Hunt, *What Love Is This*, 67–87.

against the Jewish people entitled, *The Jews and Their Lies*. This tract contains numerous anti-Semitic rants, such as the following excerpt:

> First, their synagogues should be set on fire....Secondly, their homes should likewise be broken down and destroyed....Thirdly, they should be deprived of their prayer books and Talmuds....Fourthly, their rabbis must be forbidden under threat of death to teach any more...Fifthly, passport and traveling privileges should be absolutely forbidden to the Jews....Sixthly, they ought to be stopped from usury (charging interest on loans....Seventhly, let the young and strong Jews and Jewesses be given the flail, the ax, the hoe, the spade, the distaff, and spindle, and let them earn their bread by the sweat of their noses....We ought to drive the rascally lazy bones out of our system....Therefore away with them....To sum up, dear princes and nobles who have Jews in your domains, if this advice of mine does not suit you, then find a better one so that you and we may all be free of this insufferable devilish burden—the Jews.[49]

Although some claim that the same level of anti-Semitic vitriol is not found in the work of John Calvin as is found in the later writings of Luther,[50] such a claim is without merit.[51] For example, note how Calvin's correction of distinguished Jewish scholar Rabbi Barbinel in Calvin's commentary on Daniel 2:44 laid bare the true intentions of the reformer's heart toward the Jewish people.

> But here he [the rabbi] not only betrays his ignorance, but his utter stupidity, since God so blinded the whole people that they were like restive dogs. I have had much conversation with many Jews: I have never seen either a drop of piety or a grain of truth or ingenuousness—nay, I have never found common sense in any Jew. But this fellow,

---

[49] Brown, *Our Hands Are Stained*, 14–15. For Luther's complete tract, see Martin Luther, *The Jews and Their Lies* (1852; repr., York, SC: Liberty Bell, 2004).

[50] Michael J. Vlach, *Has the Church Replaced Israel? A Theological Evaluation* (Nashville, TN: Broadman & Holman, 2010), 57.

[51] For multiple examples of clear anti-Semitism found in Calvin's writings, see Andrew D. Robinson, "The Error of Replacement Theology, Part Eleven: Calvin's Unreformed Theology," *Prophetic Witness Magazine* 14, no. 221 (October 2014): 4–8.

who seems so sharp and ingenious, displays his own impudence to his great disgrace.[52]

8.5.5 Reasons for the Reformers' Inconsistency

With these aforementioned Catholic hangovers remaining, we might ask why did the Protestant reformers not also reform the church in these other areas as well? Several possibilities can be given. Perhaps they were fatigued. They had already sacrificed greatly, and in some cases ultimately, in order to achieve what they did. To require them to take on any more beyond their monumental achievements would have been unrealistic, to say the least. Also, perhaps these other doctrinal areas involving ecclesiology and eschatology were not their focus. Their primary battle with the Roman Catholic hierarchy was soteriological in nature. Any other theological subject matter was simply outside their narrow purview.

While we can be thankful for what the reformers did accomplish, this much is certain: their hermeneutical revolution was incomplete. Much ground remained to be conquered. Thus, it would be up to future generations to take the reformers' interpretive methodology and apply it to the totality of Scripture.

8.6 The Error of Reformed Theology Today

A significant weakness of the Reformed movement is that it assumed that there was no further hermeneutical progress to be made following the Protestant Reformation. Consequently, the movement took the progress accomplished by the reformers and essentially froze it into various creedal statements, such as the Westminster Confession. Thus, today, Reformed theology remains in a fossilized state, having enshrined the progress of the Reformation along with its failures to apply its methodology to the full counsel of God's Word. Today the Reformed movement can be characterized as Protestant in the areas of soteriology and bibliology; yet it retains a significant dose of Alexandrian, Augustinian Roman Catholicism in the ar-

---

[52] John Calvin, "Daniel 2:44–45," in *Commentary on the Prophet Daniel*, trans. Thomas Myers, 1:185. Logos Bible Software.

eas of ecclesiology and eschatology. In other words, Reformed theology today is largely a mixed bag. It represents a tradition that is Protestant in many of its beliefs while being unequally yoked to a Roman Catholic eschatology. Jeremy Edmondson summarizes:

> The goal of the Reformation was to point Christianity back to the Scriptures. The noble intentions of the Reformers called for the Bible as the supreme authority for believers everywhere. For this we rejoice! But if the Reformation and its resulting creeds are exalted to the standard of measuring orthodoxy, does it not defeat the very purpose for which it was intended?[53]

8.6.1 Zechariah 14:4

Allegorization of eschatological biblical texts is a common practice among Reformed interpreters. In other words, it is common for Reformed exegetes to apply a literal hermeneutic to much of the Bible while employing an allegorical method upon eschatological biblical texts. For example, David Reagan makes the following legitimate criticism of postmillennialist Loraine Boettner's handling of Zechariah 14:4.

> Let me give you a classic example of spiritualization taken from the writings of a theologian by the name of Loraine Boettner. It has to do with his interpretation of Zechariah 14:1–9. That passage says that in the end times Jerusalem will be surrounded by enemy forces and will be ready to fall to them when the Lord will suddenly return to the Mount of Olives. When His feet touch the Mount, it will split down the middle. The Lord will then speak a supernatural word that will instantly destroy all the enemy forces. And on that day, the Lord will become King over all the earth. In his commentary on this passage, Boettner completely spiritualized it. He argued that the Mount of Olives stands for the human heart. The enemy forces symbolize the evil in this world that surrounds and attacks the heart. The Lord's return represents what happens when a person accepts Jesus as Lord and Savior. Thus, when Jesus comes into a person's heart, their heart (the

---

[53] Edmondson, "Free Grace is Returning," 3.

Mount of Olives) splits in contrition, and all the evil influences in the person's life are defeated, and Jesus becomes king of that person's heart. That's what I call an exercise in imagination![54]

8.6.2 Preterism

Other examples of prophetic allegorical spiritualization are all too common within the Reformed community. R. C. Sproul exemplifies such an interpretive approach through his advocacy of partial preterism. This theological system holds that most of Scripture's unfulfilled prophecies found their realization in A.D. 70. Sproul claims he adheres to the preterist interpretation because of the various texts found in the New Testament that seem to indicate that Christ would return within the life span of His original audience (Rev 1:1, 1:3, 3:11, 22:6–7, 22:10, 22:12, 22:20). Thus, Sproul embraces a theological system that maintains that Christ came back invisibly in the form of the Roman armies in A.D. 70.[55]

However, to reach such a conclusion Sproul must reject the plain language of Scripture by wildly allegorizing Revelation's prophecies. Such excessive allegorization is necessary in order to fit Scripture's predicted global events into the local event of A.D. 70. For example, Revelation predicts that the entire sea will be turned to blood (Rev 16:3), half of the world's population will be destroyed (Rev 6:4; 9:15), and the greatest earthquake in human history will occur (Rev 16:18). How can these prophesied global events have been fulfilled in the local Jewish War of A.D. 70? The ordinary import of Revelation's words and phrases makes it impossible to argue that most of the book's contents have already been fulfilled in a past, local event. Thus, in order for the preterist system to work, the plain language of the text must be abandoned and allegorized. The point is that the preterist system only becomes viable to the extent that the interpreter rejects the plain meaning of Revelation's language regarding global judgment. Thus, Sproul must allegorize Revelation's plain language communicating global judgments in order to teach that most of the Bible's prophecies were fulfilled in the first

---

[54] David Reagan, "The Beginning and the Ending," *The Lamplighter* 32, no. 5 (September–October 2011): 1, accessed April 19, 2017, http://christinprophecy.org/articles/the-beginning-and-the-ending/.

[55] R. C. Sproul, *The Last Days According to Jesus* (Grand Rapids, MI: Baker, 1998).

century.

8.6.3 *Allegorization in the Apocalypse*

Other examples of Reformed interpreters who routinely allegorize Revelation's plain meaning are those who insist that the New Jerusalem of Revelation 21–22 must be understood symbolically on account of the city's large size. Apparently, a city 1500 miles long, wide and high (Rev 21:16) is simply too big for many interpreters to grasp. Consequently, they begin to allegorize these dimensions.[56] According to Swete, "Such dimensions defy imagination and are permissible only in the language of symbolism."[57] Similarly, Barnes concludes, "Of course, this must preclude all idea of there being such a city literally in Palestine...this cannot be understood literally; and the very idea of a literal fulfillment of this shows the absurdity of that method of interpretation...this cannot be taken literally; and an attempt to explain all of this literally would show that that method of interpreting the Apocalypse is impracticable."[58] Moreover, Grant notes that there is "no clearer proof...that all is figurative. Such a height is simply out of harmony with the constitution of our world."[59] The issue to these interpreters is not what Scripture plainly reveals according to the ordinary import of Revelation's words and phrases but rather the imposition of a free-wheeling allegorical approach that routinely spiritualizes prophetic texts.

8.6.4 *Ezekiel's Millennial Temple and Sacrifices*

Most Reformed interpreters also reflexively and instinctively allegorize the predictions of the millennial temple and sacrifices as depicted in Ezekiel 40–48. Preterist Gary DeMar adheres to such an approach when he notes, "The Book of Hebrews was written to show beyond a shadow of a doubt

---

[56] The following list was originally compiled in Paul Lee Tan, *The Interpretation of Prophecy* (Winona Lake, IN: BMH, 1974), 285–86.

[57] Henry Barclay Swete, *The Apocalypse of St. John* (London: Macmillan, 1907), 289.

[58] Albert Barnes, *Notes on the New Testament* (Grand Rapids, MI: Kregel, 1968), 1722.

[59] P. W. Grant, *The Revelation of John* (London: Hodder and Stoughton, 1889), 593.

that the entire Old Covenant system–with its priest, sacrifices, ceremonies, and temple–has been done away with in Christ."[60] DeMar's solution to this apparent contradiction is to allegorize Ezekiel 40-48. He maintains, "The prophecy of Ezekiel's temple is a picture of the restored covenant community that returned to the land after the exile. The vision should not be projected 2500 years into the future into some earthly millennial kingdom where sacrifices will be offered *for atonement* in the presence of the crucified Christ."[61]

However, by allegorizing in this manner, DeMar ends up rejecting the plain import of Ezekiel 40-48. Nowhere does Ezekiel even hint at the notion that his description of the temple and its sacrifices are to be understood non-literally. In fact, the opposite seems to be the case. Ezekiel goes to great lengths to record the minute details of the millennial temple. The people involved as well as the geographical notations are discussed with great specificity. Moreover, the revelatory angel instructs Ezekiel to record all of the minute details of the temple vision so that he might declare them to the House of Israel. Such instruction would be meaningless if the details of the vision are not to be understood plainly. In addition, Ezekiel employs a formula to inform his readers when he is speaking non-literally. He explains that a particular item is symbolic and then interprets the symbols for the reader. For example, in Ezekiel 37, the prophet explains that the valley of dry bones is symbolic and then he interprets this symbol as the House of Israel. No such formula is employed in Ezekiel 40-48.

Whether dealing with Christ's earthly return as depicted in Zechariah 14:4, Revelation's global language, the dimensions of the New Jerusalem found in Revelation 21-22, or Ezekiel's millennial temple and sacrifices (Ezek 40-48), a common trend is found to exist among Reformed interpreters. They consistently employ an allegorical method of interpretation to biblical prophetic texts. They do so despite the fact that they would not use such methodology elsewhere in Scripture. In fact, Reformed theologians themselves concede this very fact and admit that it is the dividing line be-

---

[60] Gary DeMar, *Last Days Madness*, 4th rev. ed. (Powder Springs, GA: American Vision, 1999), 97.
[61] Ibid., 98.

tween Reformed theology and premillennialism. Note the words of amille-
narian Albertus Pieters:

> The question whether the Old Testament prophecies concerning the
> people of God must be interpreted in their ordinary sense, as other
> Scriptures are interpreted, or can properly be applied to the Christian
> church, is called the question of spiritualization of prophecy. This is
> one of the major problems in biblical interpretation, and confronts
> everyone who makes a serious study of the Word of God. It is one of
> the chief keys to the difference of opinion between Premillenarians
> and the mass of Christian scholars. The former reject spiritualization,
> the latter employ it; and as long as there is no agreement on this point
> the debate is interminable and fruitless.[62]

Such an inconsistent approach represents the partial hermeneutical restoration accomplished by the Protestant Reformation and now carried on by
its spiritual descendants in today's Reformed theology.

8.7 Dispensationalism and the Completed Revolution

Dispensationalists should be credited for completing the hermeneutical revolution begun by the Protestant reformers. The reformers deserve
credit through the employment of the right methodology, a literal interpretation, to some of the Bible.

8.7.1 Consistent Literal Interpretation

As has been demonstrated, Reformed theology continued to allow
much allegorization of the Scripture, especially as it related to ecclesiology
and eschatology. Dispensationalists, on the other hand, as it came into its
own roughly two centuries after the Reformation, took the Reformation

---

[62] Albertus Pieters, "The Spiritualization of Prophecy," *The Leader* 27, no. 49
(September 5, 1934), 3, quoted in G. H. Hospers, *The Principle of Spiritualization in Hermeneutics* (East Williamson, NY: The Author, 1935), 5, quoted in John F. Walvoord,
The Millennial Kingdom: A Basic Text in Premillennial Theology (Findlay, OH: Dunham,
1959), 128. Please note: the original citation in Hospers was inaccurate; the citation
here was verified by Russell L. Gasero, Archivist of the Reformed Church in America.

hermeneutic that was used to rescue certain doctrines during the Reformation era, and applied this same hermeneutic to the totality of Scripture.

Examples of consistent literal interpreters of the Bible include such luminaries as John Nelson Darby (1800–1882), Sir Robert Anderson (1841–1918), Cyrus Ingerson Scofield (1843–1921), William Eugene Blackstone (1841–1935), Henry Allen Ironside (1876–1951), and Lewis Sperry Chafer (1871–1952). When such a consistent application of literalism is followed (taking into account figures of speech when they are textually conspicuous), what rapidly re-merges is premillennialism or the very *chiliasm* initially espoused by the Antiochene school of interpretation that dominated the life of the church for its first two centuries. Just as the reformers demonstrated that literalism was the essential prerequisite necessary to restore the *five solas* to Christendom, dispensationalists demonstrated that literalism was also an essential prerequisite to restore premillennialism and pre-tribulationalism (the belief that the rapture will occur before the future tribulation) to Christendom.

What makes dispensationalism unique as a theological system is not merely its emphasis upon a literal, grammatical-historical hermeneutic. Many theological systems, such as Reformed theology, selectively incorporate this hermeneutic. Rather, dispensationalism remains unique in its insistence on consistently applying this literal hermeneutic to the totality of biblical revelation. Thus, Ryrie includes consistent literal interpretation in his *sine qua non* ("without which there is nothing") of dispensational theology when he says, "the distinction between Israel and the church is born out of a system of hermeneutics that is usually called literal interpretation."[63] Notice that dispensationalism does not have as its starting point the Israel–church distinction that is then read back into the Bible. Rather, it has as its starting point a consistent literal approach to Scripture. This approach causes the interpreter to recognize that Israel and the church are unique. Ryrie is clear that the system known as dispensationalism did not originate from forcing a theological grid upon the biblical text. Rather it arose when interpreters became committed to a consistent use of the literal, grammatical-historical hermeneutic.

---

[63] Charles C. Ryrie, *Dispensationalism*, rev. and exp. ed. (Chicago: Moody Press, 1995), 40.

8.7.2 Literalism's Restoration of Important Doctrines

For example, if the same literal, grammatical-historical hermeneutic that is used to interpret other sections of Scripture is applied to biblical prophecy, then the interpreter will naturally see a future tribulation period and a subsequent earthly kingdom of Christ (otherwise known as *chiliasm* or premillennialism). They will also see a clear distinction between Israel and the church. When it is understood that God has separate programs for Israel and the church, such theology acts as a natural deterrent against the heavenly and pilgrim church from claiming Israel's earthly promises through the Alexandrian-Augustinian allegorical method of interpretation. Such a belief prevents the church from seeing itself as the kingdom of God upon the earth as the reigning New Israel and from misapplying Israel's Law of Moses to itself, as was done in Calvin's Geneva.

The Israel–church distinction also helps the church to see that God is not finished with Israel but, rather, has a special end time plan for her that will play out nationally. Comprehending this future for Israel acts as a restraint necessary to curb anti-Semitic impulses among the Gentile-dominated church in the present. The Israel–church distinction also assists the church in understanding that she will not be in Israel's tribulation period leading to her conversion (Jer 30:7). Thus, the Israel–church distinction furnishes the proper foundation for embracing a pre-tribulation rapture.

These aforementioned concepts are restored to the church only through a consistent literal application to the whole Bible. However, if literalism is never applied to biblical ecclesiological and eschatological texts, these important concepts, just like the five *solas* prior to the Protestant Reformation, will remain dormant. Although none of these concepts were retrieved by the Protestant reformers or are found in today's Reformed theology, the reformers are still owed a debt of gratitude since they introduced the correct literal interpretive methodology by which these dispensational distinctions could be restored to their rightful place alongside the revered ideas of the Reformation.

8/8 Conclusion

As the 500 year anniversary of Martin Luther nailing the *95 Theses* to the cathedral door in Wittenberg, Germany, is celebrated, let us rejoice in the fact that this event was used by God to trigger what is now known as the Protestant Reformation. However, at the same time, let us not idolize the reformers based upon the faulty assumption that the Reformation instantaneously cured all the ecclesiastical ills introduced by the Alexandrian-Augustinian allegorical method of interpretation of the fourth century. The Reformation did introduce doctrinal progress. But perhaps more importantly, it also reignited the flame of literal interpretation that would be used by subsequent generations to restore doctrinal wholeness and health to Christ's church.

Bibliography

Ankerberg, John, and Renald Showers. *The Most Asked Prophecy Questions.* Chattanooga, TN: ATRI, 2000.

Augustine. *The City of God.* Translated by Marcus Dods. New York: Random House, 1950.

Barnes, Albert. *Notes on the New Testament.* Grand Rapids, MI: Kregel, 1968.

Baron, Salo W. "Calvin, John." In *Encyclopedia Judaica*, edited by Cecil Roth, 5:66-67. Jerusalem: Keter Publishing, 1971.

Barton, David. *Original Intent: The Courts, the Constitution, and Religion.* 3rd ed. Aledo, TX: Wall Builder Press, 2000.

Beeke, Joel R. "What Did the Reformers Believe About the Age of the Earth." In *The New Answers Book 4: Over 30 Questions on Creation/Evolution and the Bible*, edited by Ken Ham, 101-10. Green Forest, AR: Master Books, 2013.

Brown, Michael L. *Our Hands Are Stained with Blood: The Tragic Story of the "Church" and the Jewish People.* Shippensburg, PA: Destiny Image, 1992.

Calvin, John. *Commentary on the Prophet Daniel.* Translated by Thomas Myers. Vol. 1. Logos Bible Software.

Caner, Emir. "Balthsar Hubmaier and His Theological Participation in the Reformation: Ecclesiology and Soteriology." *Faith and Mission* 21, no. 1 (2003): 32-61.

DeMar, Gary. *Last Days Madness.* 4th rev. ed. Powder Springs, GA: American Vision, 1999.

Diprose, Ronald E. *Israel in the Development of Christian Thought.* Rome: IBEI, 2000.

Edmondson, Jeremy. "Free Grace is Returning to Scripture as Our Sole Authority." In *Free Grace Theology: 5 Ways It Magnifies the Gospel*, edited by Grant Hawley, 1-29. Allen, TX: Bold Grace, 2016.

Eidsmoe, John. *Christianity and the Constitution: The Faith of Our Founding Fathers*. Grand Rapids, MI: Baker, 1987.

Farrar, Frederic W. *History of Interpretation*. 1886. Reprint, Grand Rapids, MI: Baker, 1961.

Gibbon, Edward. *History of Christianity*. New York: Eckler, 1916.

Gonzáles, Justo L. *The Story of Christianity: The Reformation to the Present Day*. San Francisco, CA: Harper Collins, 1985.

Grant, P. W. *The Revelation of John*. London: Hodder and Stoughton, 1889.

Horner, Barry E. *Future Israel: Why Christian Anti-Judaism Must Be Challenged*. NAC Studies in Bible and Theology. Nashville, TN: Baker, 2007.

Hunt, Dave. *What Love Is This? Calvinism's Misrepresentation of God*. 4th ed. Bend, OR: Berean Call, 2013.

Jerome. "Letter 120 (Ad Hedibiam). To Hedibia, on Biblical Problems (Excerpts)." The Tertullian Project. Accessed May 20, 2017. http://www.tertullian .org/fathers/jerome_letter_120.htm.

Luther, Martin. "Against the Roman Papacy, an Institution of the Devil." In Luther's Works, edited by Helmut T. Lehmann. Vol. 41, *Church and Ministry III*, edited by Eric. W. Gritsch, 257–376. Philadelphia, PA: Fortress Press, 1966.

———. *The Jews and Their Lies*. 1852. Reprint, York, SC: Liberty Bell, 2004.

———. *Luther's Works*. Vol. 1, *Lectures on Genesis 1–5*, edited by Jaroslav Pelikan, translated by George V. Schick. St. Louis, MO: Concordia, 1958.

———. "An Open Letter to the Christian Nobility of the German Nation Concerning The Reform of the Christian Estate." In *Luther's Works*, edited by Helmut T. Lehmann. Vol. 44, *The Christian in Society I*, edited and revised by James Atkinson, translated by Charles M. Jacobs, 115–217. Philadelphia, PA: Fortress, 1966.

McGoldrick, James Edward. "Introducing John Calvin: The Reformer's Preparation." *Reformation and Revival* 10, no. 4 (2001): 15–34.

McGrath, Alister E. *Reformation Thought: An Introduction.* Grand Rapids: Baker, 1995.

Pentecost, J. Dwight. *Things to Come: A Study in Biblical Eschatology.* 1958. Reprint, Grand Rapids, MI: Zondervan, 1964.

Ramm, Bernard. *Protestant Biblical Interpretation: A Textbook of Hermeneutics.* 3rd rev. ed. Grand Rapids, MI: Baker, 1970.

Reagan, David. "The Beginning and the Ending." *The Lamplighter* 32, no. 5 (September–October 2011): 3–10. Accessed April 19, 2017. http://christinprophecy.org/articles/the-beginning-and-the-ending/.

Robinson, Andrew D. "The Error of Replacement Theology, Part Eleven: Calvin's Unreformed Theology." *Prophetic Witness Magazine* 14, no. 221 (October 2014): 4–8.

Ryrie, Charles C. *Dispensationalism.* Rev. and exp. ed. Chicago: Moody Press, 1995.

Schaff, Philip. *History of the Christian Church.* 8 vols. 1910. Reprint, Grand Rapids, MI: Eerdmans, 1976.

Sproul, R. C. *The Last Days According to Jesus.* Grand Rapids, MI: Baker, 1998.

Swete, Henry Barclay. *The Apocalypse of St. John.* London: Macmillan, 1907.

Tan, Paul Lee. *The Interpretation of Prophecy.* Winona Lake, IN: BMH, 1974.

Tyndale, William. "Obedience of a Christian Man." In *Doctrinal Treatises and Introductions to Different Portions of the Holy Scriptures,* edited by Henry Walter, 127–344. Cambridge: Cambridge University Press, 1848.

Vlach, Michael J. *Has the Church Replaced Israel? A Theological Evaluation.* Nashville, TN: Broadman & Holman, 2010.

Walvoord, John F. *The Millennial Kingdom: A Basic Text in Premillennial Theology.* Findlay, OH: Dunham, 1959.

Zuck, Roy B. *Basic Bible Interpretation: A Practical Guide to Discovering Biblical Truth.* Colorado Springs, CO: Victor, 1991.

9

THE PROTESTANT HERMENEUTIC AND
THE REVIVAL OF FUTURISM

Ron J. Bigalke
University of Pretoria

9.0 Introduction

Biblical eschatology can be divided into two categories: *personal eschatology* and *general eschatology*. Personal eschatology addresses the subjects of death, hell, and resurrection. General eschatology addresses the timing of events such as the tribulation and millennium.[1] Whereas there is generally slight disagreement among evangelicals concerning personal eschatology, significant differences persist among evangelicals when it comes to general eschatology. The primary reason for such dissimilarities comes down to one's usage or disregard of a consistent and literal grammatical-historical interpretation of biblical prophecy. Of course, interpretative differences are certainly true concerning the timing of prophetic fulfillment and the mean-

---

[1] Millennialism (chiliasm) "is the belief of a visible reign of Christ in glory on earth with the risen saints for a thousand years, before the general resurrection and judgment. It was indeed not the doctrine of the church embodied in any creed or form of devotion, but a widely current opinion of distinguished teachers." Philip Schaff, *History of the Christian Church*, vol. 2, *Ante-Nicene Christianity From the Death of John the Apostle to Constantine the Great A.D. 100-325* (1858; repr., Peabody, MA: Hendrickson Publishers, 1996), 614.

ing of the millennium. Knowledge of the various theological systems of prophetic timing fulfillment provides understanding of the logic and tenets of the various views that seek to provide meaning to the millennium. If the basic characteristics of preterism, historicism, idealism, and futurism are understood, then it is not difficult to understand a specific perspective regarding the millennium. Furthermore, the views of prophetic timing are more foundational as to what a person believes Scripture reveals concerning the millennium.

The fundamental differences among various millennial systems arise from one's hermeneutic. Both pre-Christian and early Christian interpretation was distinctively literal as opposed to being allegorical, which is why the early church was premillennial.[2] Indeed, premillennialism "is the oldest of the various millennial views"[3] (this is a point that has not merely been observed by dispensationalists). The reformed church historian Philip Schaff has noted in his classical work: "The most striking point in the eschatology of the anti-Nicene age is the prominent chiliasm, or millenarianism, that is the belief of a visible reign of Christ in glory on earth with the risen saints for a thousand years, before the general resurrection and judgment."[4]

Indeed, it was not until the time of Origen, whose views were formative in establishing a non-literal method of interpretation, that the church fathers deviate from premillennialism. Augustine then systematized the non-literal method of interpretation, which is the prevailing doctrine of Roman Catholicism, and was adopted (with variations) by the majority of the Protestant reformers (in addition to many other Augustinian doctrines). As a consequence of non-literal interpretation, premillennialism became the minority view amidst the medieval church until after the reformers revived the literal method of interpreting the Bible.

---

[2] Ron J. Bigalke, "Historical Survey of Biblical Interpretation," *Journal of Dispensational Theology* 14, no. 42 (August 2010): 35–50.

[3] John F. Walvoord, *The Millennial Kingdom* (1959; repr., Grand Rapids, MI: Zondervan, 1976), 7.

[4] Schaff, *History of the Christian Church*, 2:614.

9.1 The Timing of Prophetic Fulfillment

Prior to proceeding further, it is prudent to explain the meanings of the terms "tribulation" and "millennium." For instance, the word "tribulation," as used in the Bible, is not a technical term; it can refer to general suffering (John 16:33; Acts 14:22; Rom 5:3, 12:12), to the seven years of Daniel's seventieth week (Jer 30:7–9; Dan 9:24–27, 12:1), or to the second half of that week: the "great tribulation" (cf. Matt 24:21). When used in this final sense, it refers to the last half of Daniel's seventieth week as the great tribulation, while Matthew 24:8 uses "beginning of sorrows" in reference to the first half.[5]

The word "millennium" is derived from the Latin *mille* ("thousand") and *annum* ("year") in reference to the statement in Revelation 20:4 ("and they came to life and reigned with Christ for a thousand years"). As demonstrated in the quote by Schaff, in the previous section, the early church referred to the millennium by the Greek term, χίλια (*chilia, thousand*). Throughout the history of the church, there have been three primary views concerning the nature of the thousand years: (1) amillennialism, (2) postmillennialism, and (3) premillennialism. Interpretative differences are the reason for the three views, such as whether to understand "thousand" in Revelation 20 as literal or symbolic. How one understands the millennium will also influence views concerning the details of eschatology. Directly influencing one's view of the millennial kingdom is how one understands the fulfillment of biblical prophecies to occur.

There are four possible views concerning the timing of prophetic events: preterism (past), historicism (present), idealism (timeless), and futurism (future). Preterism is the view that the majority of prophetic events have already been fulfilled. Historicism equates the current church age with the time of the tribulation; therefore, prophetic events are regarded as being

---

[5] Daniel's seventieth week does not relate to God's purpose for the church. The tribulation will come upon a world that is in rebellion against God (Rev 15:1, 16:1–21, 19:15) and will reveal Satan's nature (12:7–12). During the tribulation, national Israel will be brought to faith and repentance in the Messiah, which is in preparation for the millennial kingdom (Jer 30:7–9; Zech 12:9–14:5; Rev 19:1–6); it will also be a time of profound evangelism (Matt 24:14; Rev 6:9–11, 7:1–17, 11:2–14, 12:13–17, 13:7, 14:1–5, 12–13).

fulfilled throughout the church age. Idealism is the view that the Bible does not specify a time (chronology) for the fulfillment of prophetic events. Recognizing that approximately 300 prophecies were fulfilled literally in regards to the first coming of Christ, futurism believes that the remaining prophecies associated with the Lord's second coming will also be fulfilled literally in an eschatological period.

As previously stated, significant disagreement unfortunately exists among evangelicals in regards to general eschatology. However, the interpretative differences are certainly not due to lack of clarity in Scripture; but rather, they exist mainly because of one's application or rejection of a consistent and literal interpretation of biblical prophecy. The most natural interpretation of unfilled biblical prophecies leads to a pretribulational and premillennial expectation. Disagreements exist due to inconsistency in biblical interpretation (of course, this could be said about so many doctrines of the Bible). How one understands the timing of prophetic fulfillment also influences an understanding of the meaning of the millennium. One's understanding of prophetic fulfillment relates to an understanding of the meaning of the millennium (which is why all the views concerning the timing of prophetic fulfillment could be consistent with postmillennialism, but not with amillennialism and premillennialism).

9.2 The Theological System of Historicism

Historicism is the view that the timing of Bible prophecy occurs during the entirety of the church age (this view will be given extra attention principally because it was the dominant view of the reformers, as it was inherited from the Roman Catholic Church). Whereas preterism, historicism, and futurism all interpret general eschatology as unfolding certain historical events, historicists differ from the other two views by believing that prophetic books and texts of the Bible are entirely symbolic in form. Therefore, major Bible prophecies are interpreted in a non-literal manner according to the belief in fulfillment during the entire course of church history. Historicists will agree with both preterists and futurists that Christ did bring judgment upon Israel in AD 70. Historicists and futurists will differ with preterists in believing that the coming of Christ subsequent to the tribulation is future. Historicists will differ from futurists in believing that major

Bible prophecies have been and are being fulfilled throughout the present church age. Simply stated, historicism results in "the progressive and continuous fulfillment of prophecy, in unbroken sequence, from Daniel's day and the time of John, on down to the second advent and the end of the age."[6]

The historicist interpretation of biblical prophecies certainly has found representation throughout the majority of church history. Adventist scholar LeRoy Edwin Froom traced the view through such prominent church figures as Hippolytus (ca. 170–236) in early church history, Joachim of Fiore (ca. 1135–1202) and John Wycliffe (ca. 1329–84) in the Middle Ages, Martin Luther (1483–1546) and John Knox (ca. 1817–1892) during the Reformation, and Isaac Newton (1642–1727) and John Wesley (1703–91) of prior centuries, and into contemporary Christianity.[7] From the time of the Reformation to the twentieth century (approximately), virtually all Protestants held the historicist view (or, at least, some variant of the doctrine). The majority of the nineteenth century cults, such as Jehovah's Witnesses (1884) and Mormonism (1829), and the *pseudo*-cult of Seventh-day Adventism (1860),[8] have also adopted the historicist interpretation.

Historicism equates the current church age with the period of the tribulation. Some historicists teach the tribulation began in AD 300 with the rise of the papacy as the antichrist. The Protestant reformers supplemented Augustine's amillennialism with the view that the papacy (as a system) was the antichrist. The seal, trumpet, and bowl judgments were regarded as fulfilled throughout various historical events in Europe. The seal judgments could include the rise of Islam, whereas the trumpet judgments could include Napoleon's campaign across Europe. Since the majority of the judg-

---

[6] Leroy Edwin Froom, *The Prophetic Faith of Our Fathers* (Washington, DC: Review and Herald, 1950), 1:22–23.

[7] Ibid., 1:2.

[8] The Adventist doctrine of the "investigative judgment" is antithetical to the biblical gospel. Christians have debated whether every Adventist denomination should be properly classified as a cult. Adventist denominations that affirm the "investigative judgment" are rightly classified as teaching cultic doctrine, but for the purpose of this chapter, the author is not engaging in the debate regarding the entire theological structure of Seventh-day Adventism.

ments are believed to have already occurred in church history, it is not un-common for historicists to anticipate the Battle of Armageddon. For in-stance, the Branch Davidian leader David Koresh was a premillennial his-toricist. He was anticipating the Battle of Armageddon since he regarded himself as the last of the seven angels of Revelation.[9]

The majority of historicists interpret the Olivet Discourse preteristi-cally (Matt 24–25; Mark 13; Luke 21:8–11, 25–27); however, they will nev-ertheless interpret the book of Revelation historicistically. William Hen-driksen[10] and Seventh-day Adventists[11] are exceptions to historicists who do not interpret the Olivet Discourse preteristically. The only *group* of histori-cists today is the Seventh-day Adventists. Charles Hodge[12] and Jonathan Edwards[13] were postmillennial historicists. Martin Luther was an amillen-nial historicist.[14] Whereas preterists generally only embrace postmillennial-ism or amillennialism in their eschatology, the historicist view of prophetic

---

[9] James D. Faubion, *The Shadows and Lights of Waco: Millennialism Today* (Prince-ton, NJ: Princeton University Press, 2001), 59.

[10] William Hendriksen, *Exposition of the Gospel According to Matthew* (Grand Rap-ids: Baker, 1973), 846–57. Hendriksen's approach is essentially idealist in nature, yet he does have some preterist and historicist aspects (i.e. synchronous historicism).

[11] William H. Shea, "The Prophecy of Daniel 9:24–27," in *The Seventy Weeks, Leviticus, and the Nature of Prophecy*, ed. Frank B. Holbrook (Washington, DC: Biblical Research Institute, 1986), 97–99.

[12] Charles Hodge, *Systematic Theology*, 3 vols. (1872; repr., Grand Rapids, MI: Eerdmans, 1993), 3:812–36. Hodge believed the reformers were mostly correct in iden-tifying the papacy as antichrist, yet affirmed antichrist as an institution (as opposed to an individual).

[13] Christopher B. Holdsworth, "The Eschatology of Jonathan Edwards," *Refor-mation and Revival* 5 (Summer 1996): 119–43.

[14] David A. deSilva, *Seeing Things John's Way: The Rhetoric of the Book of Revelation* (Louisville, KY: Westminster John Knox Press, 2009), 3; Wilfried E. Glabach, *Reclaim-ing the Book of Revelation* (New York: Peter Lang, 2007), 11–12; Jonathan Menn, *Biblical Eschatology* (Eugene, OR: Wipf and Stock, 2013), 65. John Calvin interpreted the Olivet Discourse historicistically, but whether he was clearly amillennial or postmillen-nial is still a matter of research. The influence of the reformer's eschatology is evident in the Westminster Standards—the official teaching of all Presbyterian churches—which is entirely historicist. The antichrist is said to be the beast of Revelation in contrast to

Historist view

timing fulfillment can accommodate all millennial views (pre-, post-, and a-). William Miller[15] and John Gill[16] were premillennial historicists. Every historicist predicts dates for the fulfillment of Bible prophecy since they believe current events fulfill the Olivet Discourse and prophetic books (such as Daniel and Revelation). John Gill, for example, believed that the Olivet Discourse was fulfilled preteristically but separated it from prophetic teaching in the Epistles and Revelation.

Historicism was dominant in the United States until the Civil War. Dispensational premillennialism became dominant after the American Civil War. One reason for the decline of historicism was the "Great Disappointment" of William Miller, who brought the doctrine into disrepute for centuries. The popularity of dispensationalism was due its teachers communicating accurately the rapture as a timeless event and the tribulation as eschatological (i.e. any "date setting" was unbiblical). Dispensationalism was entirely anti-date setting. Unfortunately, many dispensationalists today resort to historicist interpretations when they quote Matthew 24:4–8 (for example) as being fulfilled in the present time. The lack of interpretative consistency is unfortunate since historicist interpretation militates against a

---

the preterist notion of first century Rome or futurist teaching of an eschatological individual. One should note that covenant theology is not found among the Protestant reformers. Prior to the 1647 *Westminster Confession of Faith*, there were no references to covenant theology. *The Westminster Confession* is one of the first documents to mention a covenant of works and covenant of grace. Covenant theology was not fully systematized until Cocceius. Covenant theology was introduced in America through the Puritan influence of the writings of Francis Turretin and Herman Witsius; it was communicated extensively in America with the writings of John Cotton and others. Covenant theology, as a theological system today, is a combination of the theology of the reformers, the writings of Cocceius, and the *Westminster Confession* (i.e. certainly not an exegesis of Scripture in all areas of doctrine and theology, especially ecclesiology and eschatology).

[15] Sylvester Bliss, *Memoirs of William Miller* (Boston, MA: Joshua V. Himes, 1853), 71–77; Timothy P. Weber, "Millennialism," in *The Oxford Handbook of Eschatology*, ed. Jerry L. Walls (New York: Oxford University Press, 2008), 376.

[16] John Gill, *Gill's Commentary*, 6 vols. (1852–54; repr., Grand Rapids, MI: Baker Book House, 1980), 5:232, 6:1016.

pretribulational rapture. Although the intricacies of historicism allow its advocates to embrace any of the three millennial views, historicists cannot believe in pretribulationism because they believe the tribulation has already commenced. Therefore, "dispensationalist" teachers who quote events of the tribulation as being fulfilled today are practicing historicist principles that undermine the teaching of a pretribulation rapture and are thus not consistently dispensational.[17]

9.2.1 Jesuit Interpretation and the Protestant Reformers

Historicists generally attribute the rise of futurism and preterism, from an almost unanimous view among Protestants,[18] to the rise of Roman Catholic leaders during the Counter-Reformation (beginning 1534). For instance, historicists understand the prophecies of the "beast" in Revelation 13 as an ecclesiastical system best represented by the Roman Catholic Church. The reformers identified the Roman Catholic Church as the beast of Revelation; therefore, historicists claim that it was critical for the Roman Catholic Counter-Reformation to promulgate an eschatological system to alleviate the papacy of that ignominy. Regarding the Protestant interpretation of the antichrist, *The Catholic Encyclopedia* reads:

> To the "reformers" particularly the Apocalypse was an inexhaustible quarry where to dig for invectives that they might hurl then against the Roman hierarchy. The seven hills of Rome, the scarlet robes of the cardinals, and the unfortunate abuses of the papal court made the application easy and tempting. Owing to the patient and strenuous research of scholars, the interpretation of the Apocalypse has been transferred to a field free from the *odium theologicum* [theological hatred due to differences in religious belief]. But then the meaning of the Seer is determined by the rules of common exegesis. Apart from

---

[17] Ron J. Bigalke, "The Olivet Discourse: A Resolution of Time," *Chafer Theological Seminary Journal* 9, no. 1 (Spring 2003): 106–40.

[18] George E. Ladd commented, "This 'historical' type of interpretation with its application of the Antichrist to papal Rome so dominated Protestant study of prophetic truth for three centuries that it has frequently been called the 'Protestant' interpretation." George E. Ladd, *The Blessed Hope* (Grand Rapids, MI: Eerdmans, 1956), 32.

the resurrection, the millennium, and the plagues preceding the final consummation, they see in his visions references to the leading events of his time. Their method of interpretation may be called historic as compared with the theological and political application of former ages. The key to the mysteries of the book they find in 17:8–14. For thus says the Seer: "Let here the mind that hath understanding give heed."[19]

The alleged action of the Roman Catholic Church was a Jesuit effort to circulate an eschatological system of belief that would remove the stigma upon the Catholic Church. Francisco Ribera (1537–91) and Luis de Alcazar (1554–1613), sixteenth century Spanish Jesuits, would challenge the historicist view in an effort to confuse the Protestant prophetic interpretation.[20] Sometimes Roman Jesuit, Robert Bellarmine (1542–1621), is added beside Ribera as also contributing to the futurist view.[21]

Francisco Ribera of Salmanca, Spain, is generally credited with the origin of the futurist view as a Catholic response to the historicism of the reformers. Approximately 1590, he published a 500-page exposition of the book of Revelation. The historicists objected strongly to futurism since it does not address the history of the church in prophetic analysis, which historicists believe produces a historical and prophetical vacuum. Historicists remain critical that major Bible prophecy will not find fulfillment until the final seven years of Daniel's Seventieth Week occurs. The futurism of Ribera placed the antichrist in a distant future from the time of the Protestant Reformation. According to Ribera, the initial chapters of Revelation pertained to ancient Rome, while the reign of antichrist would not be until the last three and one-half years of Daniel's seventieth week.

The Protestant reformers never abandoned the amillennialism of the

---

[19] Christian van den Biesen, "Apocalypse," in *The Catholic Encyclopedia*, ed. Charles G. Herbermann (New York: Appleton, 1907), accessed May 24, 2017, http://www.newadvent.org/cathen/01594b.htm.

[20] Francis D. Nichol, ed., "History of the Interpretation of Daniel," in *The Seventh-day Adventist Bible Commentary* (Washington, DC: Review and Herald, 1953–80), 4:42; James Durham, *A Commentarie upon the Book of the Revelation* (Edinburgh: Christopher Higgins, 1658), 667.

[21] Froom, *Prophetic Faith*, 2:486.

Catholic Church. For instance, it was through his use of the Scriptures, which the reformers rightly claimed as their sole authority (*sola Scriptura*), that Ribera was able to use in order to demonstrate the truth of the futurist position. One accusation against futurism is that it was a Catholic effort. However, Martin Luther was also a Catholic when the Holy Spirit illumined his mind to embrace the biblical teaching of justification by faith alone (in contrast to Romanism). In like manner, Ribera may have been another individual whose mind the Holy Spirit illumined within great spiritual darkness so that he would understand the Word of God literally.

What should be brought to mind is the fact that Ribera contradicted official Catholic dogma. He did not present his interpretation in a pamphlet against the reformers; rather, he composed a major commentary on the book of Revelation. Indeed, it would be odd for Ribera to formulate a doctrine opposed to official Catholic doctrine. If it is said that Ribera wrote his commentary to convince the reformers of the futurist system, it is not possible to imagine any Protestant taking seriously the interpretation of a Jesuit bishop. If it were said that he wrote to convince Catholics that the Pope was not the antichrist, his literal interpretative method would have been completely opposed by the Catholic Church (which would be an argument in favor of the reformers). The more natural approach is to conclude that Ribera's futurism was the result of a literal interpretation of the Word of God, which, in turn, would lead to the conclusion that the antichrist was an individual who would appear during a seven-year period just prior to the return of Christ.

Furthermore, any who opposed the dogma of the Roman Catholic Church (especially in Spain) would be branded as the worst type of heretic, and would be murdered if the Spanish Inquisition captured them.[22] The Spanish Inquisition began in 1478 and continued well into the eighteenth century, which is during the time Ribera wrote his commentary. Ribera would have demonstrated great courage to publish his teachings, especially in Spain. Perhaps Ribera not only learned that the reformers were wrong in proclaiming the Catholic Church as the antichrist, but also the Roman Church was wrong in spiritualizing biblical prophecy. Consequently, it

---

[22] Philip Schaff, *History of the Christian Church*, vol. 6, *From Boniface VIII to Martin Luther, A.D. 1294-1517* (1858; repr., Peabody, MA: Hendrickson, 1996), 533.

would appear that Ribera adopted his conclusions through a literal interpretation of Scripture. The accusation that Ribera originated the futurist view does not accurately consider the development of eschatological systems. Crutchfield meticulously demonstrated the belief of the early church fathers in the return of the Lord and the establishment of his kingdom on earth.[23]

> The position of the early fathers on the tribulation and its relation to the saints and Christ's return, is impossible to completely decipher. Many of them, especially in the first century, did indeed make explicit statements which indicated a belief in the imminent return of Christ. The doctrine of imminency is especially prominent in the writings of the apostolic fathers. It is on the basis of Christ's impending return (e.g., Didache) and on the strength of the literal fulfillment of past prophecy (e.g., Barnabas), that they exhorted the Christian to live a life of purity and faithfulness.

> In addition to direct statements on imminency, in some fathers language decidedly associated with the rapture is also found. And still others maintained that the saints will escape the time of persecution under Antichrist in a manner reflective of Revelation 3:10. But due to the circumstances of that period of church history, there was no exact correlation between tribulationism as held by the early fathers and views commonly held today.[24]

---

[23] Larry V. Crutchfield, "The Early Church Fathers and the Foundations of Dispensationalism: Part I," *Conservative Theological Journal* 2, no. 4 (March 1998): 19–31; Larry V. Crutchfield, "The Early Church Fathers and the Foundations of Dispensationalism: Part II," *Conservative Theological Journal* 2, no. 5 (June 1998): 123–40; Larry V. Crutchfield, "The Early Church Fathers and the Foundations of Dispensationalism: Part III," *Conservative Theological Journal* 2, no. 6 (September 1998): 247–69; Larry V. Crutchfield, "The Early Church Fathers and the Foundations of Dispensationalism: Part IV," *Conservative Theological Journal* 2, no. 7 (December 1998): 375–403; Larry V. Crutchfield, "The Early Church Fathers and the Foundations of Dispensationalism: Part V," *Conservative Theological Journal* 3, no. 8 (April 1999): 26–52; and Larry V. Crutchfield, "The Early Church Fathers and the Foundations of Dispensationalism: Part VI," *Conservative Theological Journal* 3, no. 9 (August 1999): 182–97.

[24] Crutchfield, "The Early Church Fathers: Part VI," 194.

Crutchfield mentioned first century fathers, such as Clement of Rome, Ignatius, Hermas, Barnabas, and second century fathers, such as Tertuallian and Cyprian as a few examples of those early church fathers affirming an imminent return of the Lord. Therefore, the early church affirmed a futurist, premillennial interpretation of prophecy in a primitive and non-systematized form. Ladd was incorrect when he stated the "futurist, premillennial interpretation" was "not of the pretribulation type."[25] Erickson attempted to be more truthful: "To be sure, the premillennialism of the church's first centuries may have included belief in a pretribulational rapture of the church. . . . while there are in the writings of the early fathers seeds from which the doctrine of the pretribulational rapture could be developed . . . ."[26]

If the church of the Middle Ages had not abandoned the futurist premillennialism of the early church, one may only speculate what doctrinal developments may have "grown" from those "seeds" rather than allegoricism inhibiting germination. Posttribulationists will often refer to their view as "historic premillennialism." The term is not accurate though since the eschatological system of the early church is difficult to classify. The difficulty is the consequence of frequent contradictory perspectives of the early church, without any conscientious regard for consistency. The early church was largely premillennial.[27] Walvoord referred to the belief of the early church fathers being "that the coming of the Lord could occur any hour."[28]

The term "imminent intratribulationism" is more accurate to describe the beliefs of the early church, rather than asserting that they embraced a contemporary form of posttribulationism. (With the exception of Caius, there is no church father who opposed premillennialism until the advent of

---

[25] Ladd, *Blessed Hope*, 35.

[26] Millard J. Erickson, *Contemporary Options in Eschatology: A Study of the Millennium* (Grand Rapids, MI: Baker, 1977), 112, 131.

[27] Larry V. Crutchfield, "The Blessed Hope and the Tribulation in the Apostolic Fathers," in *When the Trumpet Sounds*, ed. Thomas Ice and Timothy Demy (Eugene, OR: Harvest House, 1995), 91–94, 101.

[28] John F. Walvoord, *The Return of the Lord* (Grand Rapids, MI: Dunham Publishing, 1955), 80.

Origen's allegorical method of interpretation, which then dominated eschatological thought through the spiritualized [gnostic] interpretation of Revelation 20 by Augustine, and as a consequence of the legalization of Christianity by Constantine.) In the midst of continual persecution, the early church believed the tribulation was presently upon them and anticipated the imminent return of Jesus Christ within this context. Although indeterminate, the climax of the tribulation would be the rapture of the church, and thus it was regarded as an imminent event. The belief in the imminent return of Jesus Christ by the early church fathers is a primary aspect of pretribulational thought.

The absence of any systematic eschatology by the early church fathers is the consequence of the lack of consistency by them regarding the exact chronology of the premillennial return of Jesus Christ. The early church did believe in an imminent return of the Lord; therefore, it would seem that any references to them by posttribulationists must explain how they could believe in a doctrine of imminence, yet also thought they were experiencing the tribulation. The reason why the early church did not give systematic thought to eschatological doctrines is understandable. Walvoord observed: "The church soon became involved in problems other than the study of prophecy, however, and church councils in the fourth century and in following centuries were concerned primarily with the doctrine of the Trinity, the doctrine of sin, and various controversies. Paganism and ritualism engulfed the church after the fourth century, and it was not until the Protestant Reformation in the sixteenth century that Biblical doctrines began to be restored."[29]

The systematic teaching of premillennial pretribulationism is a consequence of the Protestant Reformation. Amillennial and postmillennial theologies essentially deny the principle of *sola Scriptura* by not applying the Reformation hermeneutic consistently. (Due to their own historical context, the Protestant reformers themselves cannot be *directly* accused of this deficiency.) However, it is not apparent why the majority of modern posttribulationists deny imminency. Although posttribulationists make fre-

---

[29] Walvoord, *Return of the Lord*, 81.

quent appeals to the church fathers for defense of their view, it is unmistakable that there is a lack of continuity between the early church and posttribulationists today. Nevertheless, the early church simply did not articulate a systematized form of eschatological doctrine.

A major change to prophetic interpretation occurred in the second and third centuries with Origen (ca. 185–254). He absolutely ignored the literal, normal meaning of Scripture, and it was his method of spiritualizing and allegorizing that became unusually excessive throughout the church. Augustine of Hippo is best known as the father of amillennialism. Augustine dated the beginning of the millennium to the first coming of Christ and taught the kingdom of God was present on earth. He modified Origen's allegorical method by confining it solely to biblical prophecy. Following the teachings of Augustine, the church developed a sense of triumphalism (in the sense of an "unparalleled triumph of the church in the West" with Christianity as "the unchallenged, supreme religion of Europe")[30] that remained the dominant view of prophecy until Joachim of Fiore (ca. 1135–1202). Joachim developed the day-year theory, which understands the 1,260 days of Revelation as 1,260 years. He taught that Babylon was Rome, the Pope was the antichrist, and the Age of the Spirit would begin in AD 1260. Joachim's historicism thrived during the Middle Ages (among those who did not merely allegorize prophetic truths) and into the period of the Reformation.[31]

Ribera's futurism and Alcazar's preterism was a product of the counter-Reformation since the majority of the reformers still followed the historicist views of Joachim. Of course, Ribera and Alcazer interpreted differently, but they were united in their efforts to remove the stigma of Babylon upon Rome, and thus opposed any teaching from contemporary history that the antichrist was Pope. In removing such stigmas, they would free Rome from the accusations raised by the historicism of the Protestant reformers; it is wrong though to attribute futurism and preterism to a counter-Reformation movement since both views were in existence, in some form, prior to the

---

[30] John Hannah, *Our Legacy* (Colorado Springs, CO: NavPress, 2001), 315.

[31] David Larsen, "Joachim of Fiore: The Rebirth of Futurism," *Covenant Quarterly* 60, no. 1 (2002): 1–15.

writings of Ribera and Alcazer. The Jesuit theologian and shrewd controversialist, Cardinal Robert Bellarmine (1542-1621) of Italy, is said to have refined the futurism of Ribera. In the third book of his *Disputationes de Controversiis Christianae Fidei Adversus Huius Temporis Haereticos* (1586-93; "Lectures Concerning the Controversies of the Christian Faith against the Heretics of This Time"), Bellarmine argued that the prophecies of the antichrist in Daniel, Revelation, and throughout Pauline epistles bore no identification to the papacy. Bellarmine sought to demonstrate that the antichrist was not the papacy; rather, it was a single man who would be revealed at the end times.[32]

Luis de Alcazar (1554-1613) advanced the preterist view of the book of Revelation. He also taught that Nero was the antichrist and had already fulfilled the prophecies of Revelation 1–11 in the AD 70 destruction of Jerusalem. He taught Revelation 12–19 was fulfilled by the fall of pagan Rome in AD 410, and that Revelation 20 was interpreted as the final judgment of the antichrist and the Day of Judgment. Moreover, Revelation 21 was the current age wherein the New Jerusalem is the Roman Catholic Church.[33] Both Ribera and Alcazar placed the antichrist outside the Middle Ages and Protestant Reformation, which is the time that Protestant historicists identify the 1,260 year reign of antichrist.

With the exception of the kingdom of the cults, historicism has few advocates in contemporary times. Protestant historicists believe the reason for this is the outcome of Ribera's futurism and Alcazar's preterism. The result has been an easing of the pressure once felt by the papacy during the Reformation. However, the historicist claim that the idea of the antichrist as an individual is a recent development by Catholic scholars during the Reformation is not true. McGinn demonstrated that the only view of the

---

[32] Roberti Bellarmini, *Disputationes de Controversiis Christianae Fidei Adversus Huius Temporis Haereticos*, 3 vols. (Ingolstadt: David Sartorius, 1593-93). See also, James Broderick, *Robert Bellarmine, Saint and Scholar* (Westminster, MD: Newman Press, 1961); Giorgio de Santillana, *The Crime of Galileo* (Chicago, IL: University of Chicago Press, 1955), 74-109; and, William Whitaker, *A Disputation on Holy Scripture, Against the Papists, Especially Bellarmine and Stapleton*, trans. and ed. William Fitzgerald (1588; repr., Cambridge: University Press, 1849).

[33] Froom, *Prophetic Faith*, 2:507.

antichrist in the early church was that of an individual.[34]

Protestant historicists believe that Daniel's seventieth week and the 2,300 year-day prophecy have a common starting point. The rebuilding of the walls of Jerusalem (Neh 5:15) in 454 BC is the starting point for the 2,300 years and 490 years. Therefore, there are 1,810 year-days remaining subsequent to the end of the seventieth week. The entire prophecy of Daniel 9:24–27 is reinterpreted to fit the historicist scheme. According to Hebrews 9:26, the prophecy of Daniel 9:24, "to make an end of sin," is fulfilled. The forgiveness of the sins of the church is the fulfillment of "make atonement for iniquity." The prophecy "to bring in everlasting righteousness" means to accomplish everlasting justification. "To seal up vision and prophecy" is the vision of the 2,300 year-days and the seal placed upon Daniel the prophet (i.e. 490 years are cut-off from the vision of the 2,300 years, which means 1,810 years remain). The prophecy "to anoint the most holy" was fulfilled on Pentecost with the outpouring of the Holy Spirit upon the church. Historicists offer the same radical reinterpretation to Daniel 9:27. The confirming of the covenant "with the many for one week" was the seven years from AD 29 to 36. The covenant with Israel would be confirmed for the last of the week. During this time, no Gentiles could be accepted. The "middle of the week" was AD 33 when Jesus Christ "put a stop to sacrifice," and his sacrifice would end on the cross in the "middle of the week." The historicist view has to spiritualize Daniel's prophecies in order to find fulfillment with historical events.

Froom blamed the futurist Protestants (inspired by Jesuits, in his view) for abandonment of the historicist school:

> The inroad of the Futurist theory also served to divert attention and understanding from the relationship of the seventy weeks to the terminus of the 2300 years. If the seventieth week is separated from the sixty-nine weeks, then the inseparable relationship of the remaining 1810 years of the 2300 is hidden, and the divine harmony and understanding of the whole is ruptured. By fixing the eyes upon a transcendent future, one obscures the epochal events of the present. And when

---

[34] Bernard McGinn, *Visions of the End: Apocalyptic Traditions in the Middle Ages* (New York: Columbia University Press, 1979), 16–17.

the 2300 days are conceived of as but literal time, any consideration of a nineteenth-century terminus is obviously puerile. Confusion of the Historical School of interpretation, and its final breakdown, is now definitely under way.[35]

Tanner wrote similar to Froom:

Accordingly, towards the close of the century of the Reformation, two of her most learned doctors set themselves to the task, each endeavouring by different means to accomplish the same end, namely, that of diverting men's minds from perceiving the fulfilment of the prophecies of the Antichrist in the Papal system. The Jesuit Alcasar devoted himself to bring into prominence the *Preterist* method of interpretation . . . and thus endeavoured to show that the prophecies of Antichrist were fulfilled before the Popes ever ruled at Rome, and therefore could not apply to the Papacy. On the other hand the Jesuit Ribera tried to set aside the application of these prophecies to the Papal Power by bringing out the *Futurist system*, which asserts that these prophecies refer properly not to the career of the Papacy, but to that of some future supernatural individual, who is yet to appear, and to continue in power for three and a half years. Thus, as Alford says, the Jesuit Ribera, about A.D. 1580, may be regarded as the Founder of the Futurist system in modern times.[36]

Froom perceived the development of the futurist view as a counter Protestant position in the sixteenth century, which (he laments) is now the majority belief among Protestants in the modern church. He credited Samuel R. Maitland (1792–1866) as the first Protestant to accept Ribera's futurist interpretation of the antichrist.[37] Maitland, curate of Christ's Church in Gloucester, first published *An Enquiry into the Grounds on which the Prophetic Period of Daniel and St. John, Has Been Supposed to Consist of 1260 Years* (1826),

---

[35] Froom, *Prophetic Faith*, 3:658.

[36] Joseph Tanner, *Daniel and the Revelation* (London: Hodder and Stoughton, 1898), 16–17.

[37] Froom, *Prophetic Faith*, 3:541.

which was widely read and opposed the day-year theory. James Todd, professor of Hebrew at the University of Dublin, began teaching futurism and published several pamphlets and books. John Newman, a leading figure of the Oxford Tractarian Movement, published a pamphlet that endorsed futurism, and eventually converted to Roman Catholicism.[38]

Froom's conspiracy theory fails to understand that Ribera did not originate the futurist view. Ribera revived a view that was widely held by many of the early church fathers. Since premillennial dispensationalism is based upon a futurist interpretation of the books of Daniel and Revelation, Ribera's futurism is thought to have revived premillennial teaching; however, it needs to be noted that the view was not entirely systematized in his time. Nevertheless, Froom connected the development of futurism to another Jesuit priest, the Spaniard, Manuel de Lacunza (1731–1801).

Lacunza wrote *La Venida del Mesías en Gloria y Magestad* ("The Coming of the Messiah in Glory and Majesty") in approximately 1791, pseudonymously as Juan Josafa [Rabbi] Ben-Ezra. The work was entirely premillennial and opposed to Roman Catholicism. Although Lacunza argued for a literal and premillennial second coming, he was not a pretribulationist. He held a peculiar view of a 45-day partial rapture. His book was discussed at the Albury Conference (with Edward Irving in attendance) at the home of Henry Drummond.[39]

Contrary to belief among some dispensationalists, John Nelson Darby (1800–82) was not present at the Albury Conference.[40] During the nineteenth century, the French Revolution and the actions of Napoleon anguished Christians, which caused some to fear that the Emperor might be the antichrist, and thus developed a renewed interest in biblical prophecy. Lady (Theodosia) Powerscourt held one of many similar meetings that arose

---

[38] Froom, *Prophetic Faith*, 3:655–58.

[39] Harold H. Rowdon, *The Origins of the Brethren, 1825–1850* (London: Pickering & Inglis, 1967), 87.

[40] In fact, as Weremchuk has pointed out: "Some have tried to connect Irving's thoughts and Darby's thoughts regarding the Lord's coming. There is no connection possible, though Irving and Darby arose out of the same milieu, because their thoughts on this subject conflict just as their views on the church differ." Max S. Weremchuk, *John Nelson Darby: A Biography* (Neptune, NJ: Loizeaux, 1992), 112.

to address prophetic concerns. Darby was invited to the Powerscourt Conferences of 1831 to 1833, which had a lasting influence upon him. The transition from the present church age to the millennial kingdom in which Israel had prominence under Christ's rule was understood by interpreting the seventieth week of Daniel 9 as future. Based upon Darby's resolute belief in a literal interpretation of Scripture, he developed a precise design for eschatological events. Darby believed in a distinction between Israel and the church that extends into eternity. He also taught dispensations as economies of God, and that the church age is a parenthesis. Darby first began to articulate his views of a pretribulational rapture and to develop his dispensational thinking during a convalescence (Dec 1826–Jan 1827). By 1833, he developed a complete systematization of premillennial dispensationalism.

The problem with Froom's conspiracy theory is that he believes premillennial dispensationalism is unbiblical if it bears any connections or similarities to the writings of two Jesuit priests. No problems exist in crediting Ribera with reviving futurism during the Protestant Reformation. God can use both believers and nonbelievers to accomplish his purposes. Furthermore, the actual issue is not who developed the futurist view, but is it biblical?

9.3 The Eschatology of the Reformers

Martin Luther (and the other Protestant reformers of the sixteenth century) caused immeasurable transformation to the church by demanding reform. They declared the theology of the church in Western Europe was a deviation from biblical, apostolic teaching. The rallying call of the reformers was *sola Scriptura*, which meant the Bible alone was their ultimate authority, in contrast to the pope, church councils, or tradition. In calling the church to live with the Bible alone as her authority, the reformers did not attempt to transform their eschatology. The neglect to apply the principle of *sola Scriptura* to all God's Word has resulted in many Christians denying a literal, plenary interpretation of the Bible. For instance, the historical portions of the Bible are considered allegorical, and the prophetic sections of Scripture suffer an even worse destiny.

The Reformation (1500–1650) was a theological revolution, and biblical interpretation also witnessed a transformation because of it. Ramm wrote, "Although historians admit that the West was ripe for the Reformation due to several forces at work in European culture, nevertheless there was a *hermeneutical Reformation* which preceded the ecclesiastical Reformation."[41] Zuck explained the "forces at work" as "the literal approach of the Antiochene school and the Victorines."[42] The legacy of scholasticism was also a contributing factor to the Reformation since the biblical languages were revived during this time. Men such as Luther and Calvin returned to the biblical text and the natural attractiveness of the more scientific, literal interpretation of Scripture.

As a monk, Martin Luther (1483–1546) did interpret allegorically. One author has observed: "his lecture on Romans and on the Psalms plus his own independent study of Scripture made him discontented with the traditionalism and allegorizing in the church of Rome."[43] Luther's dissatisfaction with some of the traditionalism of the scholastics and his desire for a perceived apostolic Christianity also motivated him. Since the early church only had Scripture, he developed the radical and nontraditional view of *sola Scriptura.*[44] When Luther was studying Romans, he came to realize that Christ is not an allegory and he desired to know Christ. Luther denounced allegorizing as empty speculation and called it "dirt," "scum," and, "obsolete loose rags." However, as Ramm wrote, "He was not adverse to allegory if the content were Christ and not something of the papacy."[45]

---

[41] Bernard Ramm, *Protestant Biblical Interpretation: A Textbook of Hermeneutics*, 3rd rev. ed. (1970; repr., Grand Rapids, MI: Baker, 1997), 51–52.

[42] Roy B. Zuck, *Basic Bible Interpretation* (Colorado Springs, CO: Victor, 1991), 44.

[43] A. Berkeley Mickelsen, *Interpreting the Bible* (1963; repr., Grand Rapids, MI: Eerdmans, 1984), 38.

[44] "Luther's subsequent thought on 'Scripture alone' did not exclude all other sources of theological reflection such as church, canon, and ecclesial confessions. Instead, it held that Scripture was the lens through which other sources for theology would need to be viewed; it was primary, not exclusive." Marit Trelstad, "Scholasticism as Theological Method," in *Encyclopedia of Martin Luther and the Reformation*, ed. Mark A. Lamport (Lanham, MD: Rowman & Littlefield, 2017), 2:694.

[45] Ramm, *Protestant Biblical Interpretation*, 54.

The importance Luther gave to literal interpretation also meant an emphasis upon the original languages. Rejecting allegory, Luther emphasized the *sensus literalis (literal sense)*. He stated, "We shall not long preserve the Gospel without the languages. The languages are the sheath in which this sword of the Spirit is contained."[46] Nevertheless, one must be more than a philologist, historian, or even theologian; the Holy Spirit must illumine the mind of the interpreter. The observation has been made elsewhere that "Luther called for a 'simple' or 'literal' reading of Scripture that relied on neither philosophical distinctions nor complicated, formalized theological arguments of objections and replies."[47]

Luther's writings were filled with eschatology, but he was not a revolutionary (as were some of the sixteenth century Anabaptists, particularly those associated with Melchoir Hoffman, Hans Hut, Jan van Leiden, Jan Matthijs, and Thomas Müntzer). He interpreted events in his time as fulfilling prophecy and believed that current events of his day were the fulfillment of eschatological events. Current events, such as the so-called 1529 apparitions, the heat wave subsequent to the solar eclipse of 1540, the spread of syphilis, and the changing water level of one of the commercial waterways of central Europe were interpreted as signs of Christ's return.[48] The papacy was considered the antichrist, and the Turks were regarded as the antichrist's servants.[49] Luther's identification of the antichrist meant "the last day is at hand" and the end of history was near. Luther viewed his present time as that of great tribulation, which would be climaxed without

---

[46] Martin Luther, "To The Councilmen of All Cities in Germany That They Establish and Maintain Christian Schools," in *Works of Martin Luther, with Introductions and Notes*, ed. Adolph Spaeth, 6 vols. (Philadelphia, PA: A. J. Holman, 1915–1932), 4:114–115.

[47] Trelstad, "Scholasticism as Theological Method," 2:694.

[48] Martin Luther, *Luther's Works*, ed. Helmut T. Lehmann, vol. 54, *Table Talk*, ed. and trans. Theodore G. Tappert (Philadelphia, PA: Fortress Press, 1967), 134.

[49] Luther, *Table Talk*, 54:346; see also, Nabil Matar, *Islam in Britain, 1558–1685* (New York: Cambridge University Press, 1998) 153–83; and, Henry Worsley, *The Life of Martin Luther*, 2 vols. (London: Bell and Daldy, 1856) 2:183–85. Luther believed that the growth of the Ottoman Empire by the Turks was connected with the description of Gog in Ezekiel 38.

delay (i.e. imminently) by the return of Jesus Christ.[50] Sometimes he spiritualized the millennium, whereas other times Luther taught that the millennium had already past. Luther did set dates for the end of the age, and for the most part believed he was somewhere in between the millennium and the end of the age.[51] (John Calvin also believed the papacy was equivalent to the antichrist.)[52]

Luther did not develop his eschatological views systematically because the priority of his emphasis was upon soteriological issues, which is why he could maintain the amillennial (Augustinian) perspective of Roman Catholicism:

> The gift of the Protestant reformers to the Christian church thus consists not only in an open Bible but also in the literal method of interpreting that Bible. Unfortunately, however, the reformers refused to be involved in the issue of prophetic interpretation, and so the whole of Protestantism went the way of Roman Catholic amillennialism by default. This omission of the reformers is probably explainable by the fact that truths such as justification by faith and the problems of ecclesiology were claiming the immediate attention of the reformers as the latter sought to sift through the Roman debris.[53]

In regards to Luther's general understanding of history, "he identified a thousand years with one day in God's sight, and in the same year he divided the world's history into six ages whose governors were Adam, Noah, Abraham, David, Christ, and the Pope, respectively";[54] that meant the latter began approximately 5000 years after creation, which is when Hildebrand

---

[50] Luther, *Table Talk*, 54:134.

[51] Richard G. Kyle, *The Last Days Are Here Again* (Grand Rapids, MI: Baker, 1998) 61; Gordon H. Johnston, "Reformation Hermeneutics," in *Dictionary of Premillennial Theology*, ed. Mal Couch (Grand Rapids, MI: Kregel, 1996), 164.

[52] John Calvin, *Commentary on First John*, Christian Classics Ethereal Library, accessed 29 June 2017, http://www.ccel.org/c/calvin/comment3/comm_vol45/htm/v.iii.vi.htm.

[53] Paul Lee Tan, *The Interpretation of Prophecy* (Dallas, TX: Bible Communications, 1974), 54.

[54] John M. Headley, *Luther's View of Church History* (New Haven, CT: Yale Uni-

overtly disparaged priestly marriages in the time of Henry IV. Luther believed the Pope would not complete his millennium. Luther's division of history into six millennial periods is an ancient view known as the septamillennial theory, which teaches that Christ will return at the end of six thousand years of history, and then inaugurate a time of Sabbath, and ultimately eternal rest (thus corresponding with the six days of creation that were followed with a seventh day of rest, Gen 2:2; and, the belief that each day represents one thousand years, cf. Ps 90:4; Heb 4:9; 2 Pet 3:8).

Calvin did not speculate prophetically, yet he did believe the antichrist was the papacy. His interpretative views are interesting, and consequential among historicists. Calvin interpreted the 1,335 days of Daniel 12:12 as years, and regarded that time as corresponding to church history. He understood the Olivet Discourse as predicting both the destruction of the Jewish Temple in AD 70 and a time of lengthy affliction and persecution for the church, which would then climax in the return of Christ to rescue his people.[55] Theologians who adopted Calvin's hermeneutic divided into two entirely different persuasions. The first group, which dominated the interpretative approach of Calvinists for the next 250 years, was exemplified by the methodology of Johannes Cocceius, while the other group was characterized by the hermeneutic of Pierre Poiret, whose approach remained undeveloped until the nineteenth century.

With regard to eschatological events, the interpretative methodology of Augustine, and even antagonism towards a literal reign of Christ on the earth is evident among Luther and Calvin, yet both men are characterized by their resolute insistence upon the literal method of interpretation to formulate other biblical doctrines. Consequently, to be "reformed" is to accept the interpretative methodology upon which the reformer's theology was formulated. The reformers abandoned the allegorical method of interpretation (characteristic of Catholicism) in all areas but eschatology. Amillennialism

---

versity Press, 1963), 110; Martin Luther, *Conversations with Luther*, ed. and trans. Preserved Smith and Herbert Percival Gallinger (Boston: Pilgrim Press, 1915), 245.

[55] John Calvin, *Harmony of the Gospels*, trans. William Pringle, *Master Christian Library*, CD-ROM, version 6.02 (Albany, OR: AGES Software, 1998), 3:83–85, 98–101, 115.

is the prophetic viewpoint of the Catholic Church, and it was also the prophetic viewpoint of the great reformers. The reason that the reformers retained the amillennialism of Catholicism was due to the time in which they lived. They did embrace a grammatical-historical interpretation of the Scripture in regards to soteriology and ecclesiology. Since eschatology was not a major issue, the reformers did not have the opportunity to apply their hermeneutic consistently.

Fanatical apocalyptic ideas and speculation in the sixteenth century were often characterized by political extremism, which led to dismissal and rejection of a literal reign of Messiah. For instance, apocalyptic expectations were so pervasive that the Fifth Lateran Council (1516) issued a statement denouncing anyone who would propagate any catastrophic predictions:

> They are in no way to presume to preach or declare a fixed time for future evils, the coming of antichrist or the precise day of judgment . . . Let it be known that those who have hitherto dared to declare such things are liars, and that because of them not a little authority has been taken away from those who preach the truth.[56]

Roman Catholicism continues to be radically opposed to millennialism, as evident in the following condemnation:

> The Antichrist's deception already begins to take shape in the worldy every time the claim is made to realize within history that messianic hope which can only be realized beyond history through the eschatological judgment. The Church has rejected even modified forms of this falsification of the kingdom to come under the name of millenarianism, especially the "intrinsically perverse" political form of a secular messianism [§ 676].[57]

Another reason why chiliast (millennialism) beliefs were disregarded subsequent to the time of the patristic era was due to its supposed origins,

---

[56] Fifth Council of the Lateran, Session 11, "On How to Preach," quoted in William C. Nicholas, *I Saw the World End: An Introduction to the Bible's Apocalyptic Literature* (Mahwah, NJ: Paulist Press, 2007), 11–12.

[57] United States Catholic Conference, *Catechism of the Catholic Church* (New York: Doubleday, 1994), 194.

such as Jewish apocryphal writings, the writings of the gnostic teacher Cerinthus, and church father Papias (who was perceived as being "very limited in his comprehension").[58] Other reasons for rejecting a literal millennium were based upon opposition to the fact that people during that period would be eating, drinking, marrying, and propagating children, which was understood to contradict Jesus' teaching ("For in the resurrection they neither marry nor are given in marriage, but are like angels in heaven," Matt 22:30) and the following assertion: "the kingdom of God is not eating and drinking, but righteousness and peace and joy in the Holy Spirit" (Rom 14:17).[59] Another rationale against a literal millennium is the supposed con-

---

[58] In addition to expressing his opposition to a literal millennium, Eusebius further depicted Papias as follows: "The same historian also gives other accounts, which he says he adds as received by him from unwritten tradition, likewise certain strange parables of our Lord, and of his doctrine and some other matters rather too fabulous. In these he says there would be a certain millennium after the resurrection, and that there would be a corporeal reign of Christ on this very earth; which things he appears to have imagined, as if they were authorized by the apostolic narrations, not understanding correctly those matters which they propounded mystically in their representations." Eusebius Pamphilus, *Ecclesiastical History*, trans. Christian Frederick Cruse (Grand Rapids, MI: Baker, 1994), 126.

[59] One should not miss the fact that Papias had an intimate relationship with the apostles (and John in particular), and was convinced that the Lord's kingdom was earthy and eschatological. Irenaeus was not associated with John the Apostle as Papias was; yet he was discipled by Polycarp, who was John's disciple. Indeed, premillennialism was a primary argument against the unbiblical dualism between matter and spirit that the Gnostics taught. Irenaeus used premillennial doctrine to refute the gnostic belief that matter is evil, and the false notion that God did not purpose to redeem the earth; see Martin Erdmann, *The Millennial Controversy in the Early Church* (Eugene, OR: Wipf and Stock Publishers, 2005), 107–09. If premillennialism were the received doctrine of John the Apostle, it would only be natural for those also in close association with him to affirm premillennial teachings. Erdmann referenced the premillennialism of Asia Minor in the second century as "Asiatic millennialism," with "the decisive authority" being "John, from whom the elders claimed to have obtained their information." Ibid., xix, 107–10, 111. Assuming that John lived in Asia Minor, it would be probable that Christians near his sphere of influence would have similar views of his concerning the millennium. The testimony of church history provides resolute corroboration for premillennialism. Conversely, if amillennialism or postmillennialism were biblical, one

tradiction between a functioning eschatological Temple (with animal sacrifices) and the finality of Christ's offering.[60] Millennialism was also obscured
and rejected by the early church's opposition to Marcionism and Monta-
nism.[61]

Luther's perception of millennialism was based upon the teachings of
Thomas Müntzer, whose apocalypticism was coupled with violence, as he
perceived himself as a "biblical warrior-priest."[62] With apocalyptic expec-
tancy, Müntzer "called upon the princes [of Saxony] to kill godless rulers,
and cited Jesus' words in Matthew 10:34 about not bringing peace, but a
sword." Müntzer regarded the Peasants' Revolt as the conclusion of the fifth
kingdom prophesied in the books of Daniel and Revelation. He was eventually "captured, tortured, and beheaded" in 1525.[63] One historian has
noted:

> Initially, Luther saw the peasants' concerns as God's judgment on un-
> just rulers. With princes demanding his allegiance, Luther's views of
> the need to submit to civil authorities on civil matters led him to react
> vehemently against the Peasants' Revolt. With inflamed and very vio-
> lent language, Luther wrote *Against the Robbing and Murdering Hordes of
> Peasants* and urged the German princes to be "God's sword on earth"

---

would have to explain how those enjoying such intimate relationship with John could
be so erroneous with regard to their understanding of the millennium. Of course, the
validity of a particular doctrine is not determined exclusively from church history, yet
the historical facts do corroborate the assertion that premillennialism was the prevailing viewpoint of those in Asia Minor and the patristic era.

[60] For just two excellent answers to this alleged contradiction, see Jerry M. Hullinger, "Two Atonement Realms: Reconciling Sacrifices in Ezekiel and Hebrews," *Journal of Dispensational Theology* 11, no. 32 (March 2007): 33–63; and, John C. Whitcomb,
"Christ's Atonement and Animal Sacrifices in Israel," *Grace Theological Journal* 6, no. 2
(Fall 1985): 201–17.

[61] Hans Bietenhard, "The Millennial Hope in the Early Church," *Scottish Journal
of Theology* 6 (March 1953): 17.

[62] George Huntston Williams, *The Radical Reformation*, 3rd ed. (Kirksville, MO:
Truman State University Press, 1992), 163.

[63] W. Barnes Tatum, *Jesus: A Brief History* (Malden, MA: John Wiley & Sons,
2009), 117–18.

and put down the revolt.[64]

Another significant event occurred in Münster, where the self-proclaimed prophet, Jan Matthijs, taught that the city was the New Jerusalem. Matthijs led a small group of radicals whose apocalypticism was manifested in the type of behavior that influenced most people to reject any notion of a literal millennium.[65] Unfortunately, much falsification of biblical truth was prevalent among both advocates and detractors, and such extremes led to any belief or proclivity toward millennialism being quickly dismissed.

Seeking to identify any Reformation commentaries based upon prophetic books or writings that even address biblical prophecy is a rather desolate task. It has been well observed that "the strongest statements concerning imminency during this period actually come from Anabaptists, known as the Taufer, who drew their theology from the Scriptures more than other groups that bore the name Anabaptist."[66] Stitzinger also noted how Luther and Calvin made "similar statements concerning imminency," and concluded, "the Lord's return was one of the great undeveloped themes of the Reformation era."[67]

9.4 Prophetic Development Subsequent to the Reformation

By the late 1500s and early 1600s, premillennial interpreters began to flourish, as a consequence of biblical interpretation during the late Reformation period. The renewed concentration given to biblical studies revived interest in developing a scriptural perception concerning the future. Augustinian eschatology was fundamentally beginning to lose its pervasiveness. Perspectives remained unchanged concerning Christ's return in final judgment and the establishing of the eternal state (i.e. the new heavens and new

---

[64] Donald K. McKim, *Reformation Questions, Reformation Answers* (Louisville, KY: Westminster John Knox Press, 2017) 32–33.

[65] Walter Klaasen, *Living at the End of the Ages* (Lanham, MD: University Press of America, 1992), 48.

[66] James F. Stitzinger, "The Rapture in Twenty Centuries of Biblical Interpretation," *The Master's Seminary Journal* 13, no. 2 (Fall 2002): 159–60.

[67] Ibid., 160.

earth); however, the events culminating in those future realities were conveyed with a slightly different viewpoint. For instance, there was an increased optimism concerning the advancement of the gospel for some, whereas others were pessimistic regarding that progress. Nevertheless, the fundamental distinction with prior convictions was to understand that church history could fluctuate—either improving or worsening—as opposed to times remaining generally unchanged.[68]

The inclination to reconsider the progress of the gospel in relation to the church's experience in the world (which was tremendously important for the development of eschatology) was precipitated by several factors,[69] including the emergence of Hebrew studies in Protestant universities,[70] pessimism in Germany due to the breakdown of morals, destruction of property, and loss of life arising from the Thirty Years' War (1618–48), and yet

---

[68] Hannah, *Our Legacy*, 320–21. Hannah noted, "the things-are-about-the-same understanding of Augustine . . . is a bit unfair because amillennialists do see a progressive unfolding of the kingdom of God in time, yet not to the extent of postmillennialists" (321).

[69] Ibid., 321.

[70] In 1549, the German scholar Paul Fagius was appointed by Cambridge University to the chair of Hebrew, which (to a certain extent) distinguished him as the first competent specialist to hold such a position in England. By 1600, there was a small availability of capable scholars of the Hebrew language, and King James commissioned their expertise to produce the translation of the Old Testament for the Authorized Version of the Bible. See David Daiches, *The King James Version of the English Bible* (Chicago, IL: University of Chicago Press, 1941). Not only were these Hebrew scholars able to study the Old Testament in its original language (and Aramaic), but also they read the rabbinical commentaries that foretold a future restoration of the Jewish people. The study of the Hebrew Bible (in addition to the rabbinical literature) made it possible to understand Jewish exegesis and the Old Testament prophecies concerning a glorious future on earth for the Jewish people. Furthermore, the word "Israel" (cf. Rom 11:25–27) was demonstrated as referring to ethnic Jews, in contradiction to Luther and Calvin's interpretation that it was indicative of the church, both Christian Jews and Gentiles. The first edition of the *Geneva Bible* (London: Samuel Bagster and Sons, 1557) reflected the understanding that "Israel" meant "the whole nation of the Jews" as evident in the marginal note for Romans 11:26, "He sheweth that the tyme shal come that the whole natiō of the Iewes, not every one particularly, shal be ioyned to the Churche of Christe" (258).

optimism among the church (especially in England) that the Romish anti-christ had been defeated and, thus, a new unparalleled era of triumph was imminent. Particularly, in regards to optimistic viewpoints, Thomas Bright-man (1562–1607) introduced a new phase in English millenarian thought.[71] Brightman's eschatology "was largely transitional in that it departed from the amillennialism of the reformers while anticipating the postmillen-nialism of the English Unitarian, Daniel Whitby (1638–1726)."[72] (Despite the fact that Whitby "is commonly given the credit for the rise of postmil-lennialism," there are many biblical varieties of the doctrine, which find basis for interpretation "in the Scriptures and its power in God").[73] Bright-man perceived the millennial age as progressing already, interpreting "the first resurrection" (cf. Rev 20:1–3) as the revival of biblical preaching and theology in the time of the Reformation, which he equated with the con-version of Christians only. Brightman's perspective was in contrast to Au-gustine, who understood the millennium as equivalent to the entire age in which the gospel is proclaimed, yet (in this sense) Brightman reflected the historicism of the time,[74] which views major Bible prophecies as reflecting the history of the church. Brightman's eschatology also varied from Augus-tine in its optimism. Augustine believed the present church age would con-clude with a brief tribulation, while Brightman argued that the tribulation occurred at the time of the defeat of the Papacy and the Turks, and thus preceded the future glory of the second millennium (i.e. "the second resur-rection"), which he identified with the conversion of the Jews. In contrast to the prevailing Augustinian view of history remaining generally the same,

---

[71] The assertion herein is not denying that a nascent postmillennial preterism is evident among some of the church fathers, such as Origen, Eusebius, Athanasius, and Augustine.

[72] Paul Richard Wilkinson, *For Zion's Sake: Christian Zionism and the Role of John Nelson Darby* (Eugene, OR: Wipf & Stock, 2008), 142.

[73] Walvoord, *Millennial Kingdom*, 19, 23.

[74] Thomas Brightman's eschatology does reflect elements of historicism, yet he was opposed to a broadly historicist understanding of major Bible prophecies. See, for instance, his *Revelation of Saint John: Illustrated with Analysis and Scholions* (London: Staf-ford, 1644), 205–6.

Brightman "encouraged a confident, militant Protestantism that deeply affected English society and culture."[75]

In addition to many preachers of seventeenth century Europe, the
German Calvinist minister, Johann Heinrich Alsted (1588-1638), also
taught a victorious progress of the gospel in the experience of the church.
Alsted, in particular, began rethinking the amillennial doctrine concerning
end-time events "because of the tragedies and devastations connected with
the Thirty Years War that ravaged Germany. He identified the horrors of
the war with judgmental descriptions in various prophetic passages."[76] Obviously, someone's perspective regarding present circumstances, in addition
to the anxieties and pressures therein, "influences one's perspectives on the
Scriptures."[77]

Brightman's influence is readily apparent upon his contemporaries,
such as Henry Finch (ca. 1558-1625),[78] and later with John Cotton (1585-
1652) and Jonathan Edwards (1703-58).[79]

> Previous to the seventeenth century, Protestant theologians...followed
> the Augustinian interpretation of Romans 11, which held that Jews
> would only be converted and saved as *individuals*—but never as a na-
> tion....However, by the turn of the seventeenth century, some exegetes
> began to accept first the eventual conversion of the Jewish people to
> Christianity and then even their Restoration to the land of Israel. Em-
> blematic of this new hermeneutic is Sir Henry Finch's 1621 work *The
> worlds* [sic] *great restauration or calling of the Jews*, in which he argued
> against allegorical interpretations of Israel and linked the return and
> calling of the Jews with the salvation of the Gentiles.[80]

---

[75] Robin Barnes, "Images of Hope and Despair: Western Apocalypticism: ca.
1500-1800," in *The Encyclopedia of Apocalypticism*, ed. John J. Collins, Bernard
McGinn, and Stephen J. Stein (New York: Continuum, 1998), 2:162.

[76] Hannah, *Our Legacy*, 324

[77] Ibid.

[78] Wilkinson, *For Zion's Sake*, 144-45.

[79] Hannah, *Our Legacy*, 322.

[80] Stephen D. Snobelen, "'The Mystery of This Restitution of All Things': Isaac
Newton on the Return of the Jews," in *Millenarianism and Messianism in Early Modern
European Culture*, vol. 3, *The Millenarian Turn: Millenarian Contexts of Science, Politics and*

John Cotton was the colleague of English scholar Joseph Mede (1586–1638). Mede's most notable work (and maybe even more prominent than Brightman's writings) was his 1627 *Clavis Apocalyptica*, "a commentary on the Revelation that described St. John's visions as coterminous prophecies about the development of church and state."[81] Mede was similar to Alsted in that he believed the millennium to be future with the fall of antichrist "and made Satan's binding for a thousand years coterminous with the corporeal resurrection of the raised saints (first resurrection)."[82] While "Mede's scheme, based like many others on years of intensive study, was less gradualist than Brightman's; it saw all fulfillment as still in the future," as both writers stimulated a Protestant triumphalism.[83] As Smolinski explains: "Cotton adapted Thomas Brightman's Augustinian First Resurrection (Rev. 20:4-6) as a *spiritual rebirth* of individuals and of reformed churches that excluded the unregenerate by making conversion the litmus test for church membership," an emphasis that was "galvanized by his millennialist endeavor to set up the New Jerusalem in the American wilderness."[84] Earnest Sandeen notes the impact this had American fundamentalism:

> The eschatology of United States Protestants, reflecting their brimming optimism and hope, was expressed most frequently as a blending of millennialism and American nationalism. Stemming from the Puritan conviction that the colonists were a chosen people and their commonwealth a 'citty set vpon a hill,' reinforced by the War for Independence and the potentialities of the West, Americans vied with each other in producing grander and more glorious prospects for the

---

Everyday Anglo-American Life in the Seventeenth and Eighteenth Centuries, ed. James E Force and Richard H. Popkin, Archives Internationales d'Histoire des Idées 175 (Dordrecht, The Netherlands: Kluwer, 2001), 96.

[81] Ibid., 157.

[82] Reiner Smolinski, "General Introduction," in *The Kingdom, the Power, and the Glory*, ed. Smolinski (Dubuque, IA: Kendall Hunt, 1998), xvi.

[83] Barnes, "Images of Hope and Despair," 2:162.

[84] Smolinski, "General Introduction," xvi. See also, Andrew Crome, *The Restoration of the Jews: Early Modern Hermeneutics, Eschatology, and National Identity in the Works of Thomas Brightman* (Dordrecht, The Netherlands: Springer, 2014), 179.

United States.[85]

The most eloquent spokesman for the concept of American destiny was unquestionably Jonathan Edwards.[86] Edwards developed his eschatology from years of studying English Protestant commentators on the book of Revelation. He was convinced "that the lowest days of the church had passed and that the future of the church would involve an advancement into 'glorious times.' Edwards expected "a progressive, gradual transition in the world, during which all the world would be renewed."[87] He was convinced "that the progress of humanity was largely consistent and continuous: all 'will not be accomplished at once, as by some miracle,' such as a spectacular raising of the dead, but will be *gradually* brought to pass.'"[88]

By the early seventeenth century, according to Hannah, a significant number of English Puritans were compelled by their biblical exegesis and events of their time to interpret the χίλια ἔτη (*chilia etē*, thousand years) of Revelation 20 literally: "However, they hesitated to take the final step, to advocate the doctrine of a future reign of Christ on earth, because of the onus placed upon the teaching of Augustine, Luther, and Calvin"[89] The early American Puritans held aspects of various millennial views, and such lack of systematization "makes them difficult to categorize strictly." Moreover, "such a difference of views was not a ground of division among Christians as it would become later."[90]

9.4. The Systematization of Biblical Eschatology

From the time of the Reformation until the 1820s, historicism was the dominant view among Protestants within premillennial circles. Apart from the Seventh-day Adventists (or the cults), there is little inducement to

---

[85] Ernest R. Sandeen, *The Roots of Fundamentalism* (1970; repr., Grand Rapids, MI: Baker, 1978), 43.

[86] Ibid.; Wilkinson, *For Zion's Sake*, 232.

[87] Michael James McClymond and Gerald R. McDermott, *The Theology of Jonathan Edwards* (New York: Oxford University Press, 2012), 572.

[88] Alan Heimert, *Religion and the American Mind* (1966; repr., Eugene, OR: Wipf & Stock, 2006), 65.

[89] Hannah, *Our Legacy*, 323.

[90] Ibid., 323–25.

historicism as a system of prophetic interpretation today. Among premillennialists, futurism began to replace historicism in the 1820s. Dispensational premillennialism was proliferated throughout the United States through the Plymouth Brethren, with which John Nelson Darby was associated. As a young parish priest, Darby became disillusioned by a decree from his bishop requiring all Anglicans to swear allegiance to the King of England. Darby's parish ministry was resulting in hundreds of Roman Catholics converting to Protestantism, and he regarded the ruling as a hindrance to his ministry with Catholics, in addition to perceiving it as a compromise with the Lordship of Christ. Subsequent to his reform attempts for several years, Darby resigned his parish in 1829, and joined believers in Plymouth, England, with whom he had already been meeting. During this time, until 1833, he sought to reconcile his understanding of ecclesiology with the description in the book of Acts.

Dispensationalists believe the Old Testament promises to Israel will be literally fulfilled by a future national Israel. Premillennialism views history as generally declining toward a culmination in the tribulation period. Unique to premillennial chronology is the timing of the Lord's second coming as either pretribulational, midtribulational, or posttribulational. Amillennial views, for instance, are far more simplistic regarding end-time events since those occurrences are located in the brief period that concludes the present age.

By 1614 (just shy of the centennial birth of the Reformation), the preterist view of biblical prophecy was roused. The preterist view denied the apparent meaning of biblical prophecy by relegating the majority of prophetic statements to a first century fulfillment. Since most of biblical eschatology was already fulfilled, this meant God had completed any plans for national Israel and now the church inherited all the promises to Israel. The view relegates most of biblical eschatology to allegorical interpretation, which actually weakens the very foundation of the New Testament. The postmillennial form of preterism is mostly responsible for keeping preterism alive in the present time.

In his book *Every Prophecy of the Bible* (formerly titled, *The Prophecy Knowledge Handbook*), Walvoord completed the enormous task of compiling a list of every significant Bible prophecy and included an exposition of each.[91] He expounded over a thousand individual verses and demonstrated the literal fulfillment for half of those prophecies having occurred already. His work is unavoidable evidence that prophecy should be understood literally, since God always fulfills his Word exactly as He said. When the history of humanity is completed, every prophecy will be literally fulfilled. Since half of the biblical prophecies have been fulfilled literally, it would make sense to expect that God will fulfill those remaining prophecies in the same accurate and historical manner.

In contrast to Walvoord's work, the majority of non-literal approaches to biblical eschatology teach that prophetic texts are not actually relevant to specific events or historical fulfillment; rather, they merely provide comfort that the church will be victorious in Christ. As opposed to stimulating the church to confidence in God's sovereignty over world affairs, the non-literal approach to biblical prophecy mollifies the church into a narcissistic view of a world in troubled times. Whereas preterism and historicism do find historical meaning in prophetic texts, as does the futurist, who anticipates a historical fulfillment in the final events of God's divine plans for history, idealism offers little hope that the kingdom of God will be truly consummated when Christ returns to earth in power and glory (and will then be extended into the new heaven and new heaven, or eternity itself).

Much of the church today is opting for non-literal interpretations of the Genesis record believing God used the process of evolution to bring creation into existence. The church is not only applying the approach that the Bible does not mean what it says to the creation account, but also to biblical eschatology. The mentality is that prophecy cannot be understood or mean what it says, but such thinking is contrary to the Old Testament (or even the book of Revelation), which explains the symbolism of the prophetic books. Kromminga noted accurately: "the preterist and the futurist methods, or approaches, stand at opposite extremes."[92] The "opposite extremes" may help explain the later ascendancy of historicism and idealism, while the futurist and preterist views are in the forefront. From the 1820s

---

[91] John F. Walvoord, *Every Prophecy of the Bible* (Colorado Springs, CO: Chariot Victor Publishing, 1999).

[92] Diedrich H. Kromminga, *The Millennium and the Church: Studies in the History of Christian Chiliasm* (Grand Rapids, MI: Eerdmans, 1945), 295.

until fairly recently, futurism generally remained unchallenged. Preterism has emerged, as the opposite extreme of futurism, to challenge the ascendancy of futurism within evangelicalism.

Although dispensationalism was largely systematized by John Nelson Darby in the mid-1800s, there were individuals throughout the history of the church who affirmed a dispensational system of some variety. [93] Two early proponents of dispensational thought in the U.S. include Baptist James R. Graves (1820–93) and Presbyterian James H. Brookes (1830–97). Dispensationalism was communicated to North America widely by means of annual Bible conferences, such as the Niagara Bible Conference (1878–1909), and numerous publications. A Bible institute/college or seminary, which articulated dispensational teachings, was founded in almost every principal metropolitan region in the United States.[94] Initially, dispensationalism was taught among Baptists, Bible and independent churches, and a significant number of Presbyterian congregations. Many of the Pentecostal denominations, such as the Assemblies of God and The Foursquare Church, adopted dispensationalism, and it was also dominant within the charismatic movement throughout the 1960–70s. While dispensationalism is still widely taught among evangelicals and fundamentalists, its influence began first to dissipate within academia in the 1950–60s. Dispensational teaching also declined in the 1980s, as more charismatics, evangelicals, and Pentecostals became concerned with social issues.

Undeveloped aspects of dispensational theology can be identified prior to the nineteenth century, especially among the early church and even centuries prior to Darby. In the midst of continual persecution, the early church believed tribulation was presently upon them and anticipated the imminent return of Jesus Christ within this context, hence the term "imminent intratribulationism" may be a better term to describe the views of the early church; nevertheless, aspects of imminency, which is a primary aspect

---

[93] A recent book that addresses this topic is William C. Watson, *Dispensationalism Before Darby: Seventeenth-Century and Eighteenth Century English Apocalypticism* (Silverton, OR: Lampion Press, 2015).

[94] For a list of some of the Bible colleges and seminaries influenced by dispensational thought, see Cory M. Marsh's chapter "Luther Meets Darby" in the current volume.

of pretribulational thought, is evident among the early church fathers. During the medieval period, evidence of pretribulational notions can be identified in a sermon attributed to Ephraem the Syrian, entitled "Sermon on the Last Times, the Antichrist, and the End of the World," and in a text entitled *The History of Brother Dolcino*, from the fourteenth century.

During the Protestant Reformation, evidence of individuals who distinguished the rapture from the coming of Christ to earth is found in the writings of Peter Jurieu, Increase Mather, Joseph Mede, (et al.), and later within a eighteenth century treatise by Baptist minister Morgan Edwards. Centuries before Darby, the French philosopher Pierre Poiret (1646–1719) published a multi-volume work in which he articulated a complete system of theology that was both premillennial and dispensational. Around that same time, John Edwards (1637–1716) wrote his two-volume work: *A Compleat History of all Dispensations and Methods of Reliion* and Issac Watts (1674–1748) gave an extensive outline of dispensations in works. C. I. Scofield's dispensational structure is more similar to the teaching of Watts than Darby, thus the obvious conclusion is that individuals prior to Darby taught dispensational concepts.

Classical dispensationalism (ca. 1878–1940s) is a term denoting the theology of dispensationalists—both in the United States and United Kingdom—between the writings of Darby and Lewis Sperry Chafer (especially the latter's multi-volume *Systematic Theology*). The interpretative notes within the *Scofield Reference Bible* are representative of classical dispensationalism. One significant aspect of classical dispensationalism was the dualistic notion of redemption, with regard to heavenly and earthly purposes. Revised (modified) dispensationalism (ca. 1950–70s) is a designation adopted from the 1967 revision of the *Scofield Reference Bible*. Revised dispensationalists rejected the eternal, dualistic distinction between earthly and heavenly peoples, with emphasis instead upon the two peoples of God (Israel and the church), each with different responsibilities dispensationally, yet both eternally saved in the same manner.

Another important emphasis was the rejection of two new covenants, one for national Israel (Jer 31:31–34; Heb 8:7–12) and one for the church (Luke 22:20). Progressive dispensationalism (1980s–present) denotes a recent development that is regarded as abnormal from normative (traditional) dispensationalism, particularly as these dispensationalists perceive more continuity between Israel and the church. Progressive dispensationalists also affirm an "already, not yet" aspect to the Davidic reign of Jesus Christ, which means the Lord's reign is "already" inaugurated (as He reigns upon the throne of David in heaven), albeit complete fulfillment of the David reign is "not yet" as it awaits the future millennial kingdom; therefore, the Father's throne and the Davidic throne are synonymous.

Throughout the history of dispensationalism, there has been systematic development since the time of Darby. Modern dispensationalists continue to develop and refine dispensationalism; however, progressive dispensationalism remains controversial for introducing fundamental changes to dispensationalism, as progressive dispensationalists are perceived as departing from refinement of the views of former dispensationalists and introducing drastic revision. Even among progressive dispensationalists, there is disagreement regarding particular issues since some theologians have been more prolific than others in advancing the notion. Wherever dispensationalism is taught, one will find an emphasis upon literal historical-grammatical interpretation, a distinction between Israel and the church, and the overall purpose of God as being doxological (as evident in dispensations, which are successive revelations of God's plans for each age). By the early twentieth century, dispensationalism became the most popular evangelical system of theology.

9.5 Conclusion

Often historicism has thrived during momentous eras of the church (e.g. during persecution or revival). What is evident regarding classic historicism is the vigorous promotion of the teaching that the antichrist is an ecclesiastical system (viz. the Roman Catholic Church), and the vehement denial of the biblical teaching that the antichrist will be an individual. The reformers endured such incredible persecution under the Catholic Church that it was only natural to spiritualize Scripture and understand the pope to be the antichrist (*it is, therefore, understandable why the reformers developed their conclusions!*). The reformers abandoned the allegorical method of interpretation (characteristic of Roman Catholicism) in all areas but eschatology. Amillennialism is the prophetic viewpoint of the Catholic Church, and a non-literal millennium was also the prophetic viewpoint of the Protestant reformers. The reason that many of the reformers retained the amillennialism of Catholicism was due to the time in which they lived. They did embrace a grammatical-historical interpretation of the Scripture in regards to soteriology and ecclesiology. Since eschatology was not a major issue during the Reformation, the reformers did not have the opportunity to apply their hermeneutic consistently. Although human personalities do not endure, thankfully, the Word of God does abide forever.

Bibliography

Bellarmini, Roberti. *Disputationes de Controversiis Christianae Fidei Adversus Huius Temporis Haereticos.* 3 vols. Ingolstadt: David Sartorius, 1593–93.

Bliss, Sylvester. *Memoirs of William Miller.* Boston, MA: Joshua V. Himes, 1853.

Bietenhard, Hans. "The Millennial Hope in the Early Church." *Scottish Journal of Theology* 6 (March 1953): 12–30.

Bigalke, Ron J. "Historical Survey of Biblical Interpretation." *Journal of Dispensational Theology* 14, no. 42 (August 2010): 35–50.

———. "The Olivet Discourse: A Resolution of Time." *Chafer Theological Seminary Journal* 9, no. 1 (Spring 2003): 106–40.

Brightman, Thomas. *Revelation of Saint John: Illustrated with Analysis and Scholions.* London: Stafford, 1644.

Broderick, James. *Robert Bellarmine, Saint and Scholar.* Westminster, MD: Newman Press, 1961.

Calvin, John. *Commentary on First John.* Christian Classics Ethereal Library. Accessed 29 June 2017. http://www.ccel.org/c/calvin/comment3/comm_vol45/htm/v.iii.vi.htm.

———. *Harmony of the Gospels.* Translated by William Pringle. *Master Christian Library.* CD-ROM. Version 6.02. Albany, OR: AGES Software, 1998.

Catholic Conference, United States. *Catechism of the Catholic Church.* New York: Doubleday, 1994.

Collins, John J., Bernard McGinn, and Stephen J. Stein, eds. *The Encyclopedia of Apocalypticism.* 3 vols. New York: Continuum, 1998.

Couch, Mal, ed. *Dictionary of Premillennial Theology.* Grand Rapids, MI: Kregel, 1996.

Crome, Andrew. *The Restoration of the Jews: Early Modern Hermeneutics, Eschatology, and National Identity in the Works of Thomas Brightman.* Dordrecht, The Netherlands: Springer, 2014.

Crutchfield, Larry V. "The Early Church Fathers and the Foundations of Dispensationalism: Part I." *Conservative Theological Journal* 2, no. 4 (March 1998): 19–31.

———. "The Early Church Fathers and the Foundations of Dispensationalism: Part II." *Conservative Theological Journal* 2, no. 5 (June 1998): 123–40.

———. "The Early Church Fathers and the Foundations of Dispensationalism: Part III." *Conservative Theological Journal* 2, no. 6 (September 1998): 247–69.

———. "The Early Church Fathers and the Foundations of Dispensationalism: Part IV." *Conservative Theological Journal* 2, no. 7 (December 1998): 375–403.

———. "The Early Church Fathers and the Foundations of Dispensationalism: Part V." *Conservative Theological Journal* 3, no. 8 (April 1999): 26–52.

———. "The Early Church Fathers and the Foundations of Dispensationalism: Part VI." *Conservative Theological Journal* 3, no. 9 (August 1999): 182–97.

Daiches, David. *The King James Version of the English Bible.* Chicago, IL: University of Chicago Press, 1941.

de Santillana, Giorgio. *The Crime of Galileo.* Chicago, IL: University of Chicago Press, 1955.

deSilva, David A. *Seeing Things John's Way: The Rhetoric of the Book of Revelation.* Louisville, KY: Westminster John Knox Press, 2009.

Durham, James. *A Commentarie upon the Book of the Revelation.* Edinburgh: Christopher Higgins, 1658.

Erdmann, Martin. *The Millennial Controversy in the Early Church*. Eugene, OR: Wipf and Stock Publishers, 2005.

Erickson, Millard J. *Contemporary Options in Eschatology: A Study of the Millennium*. Grand Rapids, MI: Baker, 1977.

Faubion, James D. *The Shadows and Lights of Waco: Millennialism Today*. Princeton, NJ: Princeton University Press, 2001.

Force, James E., and Richard H. Popkin, eds. *Millenarianism and Messianism in Early Modern European Culture*. Vol. 3, *The Millenarian Turn: Millenarian Contexts of Science, Politics and Everyday Anglo-American Life in the Seventeenth and Eighteenth Centuries*. Archives Internationales d'Histoire des Idées 175. Dordrecht, The Netherlands: Kluwer, 2001.

Froom, Leroy Edwin. *The Prophetic Faith of Our Fathers*. 4 vols. Washington, DC: Review and Herald, 1950.

Gill, John. *Gill's Commentary*, 6 vols. 1852–54. Reprint, Grand Rapids, MI: Baker Book House, 1980.

Glabach, Wilfried E. *Reclaiming the Book of Revelation*. New York: Peter Lang, 2007.

Hannah, John. *Our Legacy*. Colorado Springs, CO: NavPress, 2001.

Headley, John M. *Luther's View of Church History*. New Haven, CT: Yale University Press, 1963.

Heimert, Alan. *Religion and the American Mind*. 1966. Reprint, Eugene, OR: Wipf & Stock, 2006.

Hendriksen, William. *Exposition of the Gospel According to Matthew*. Grand Rapids, MI: Baker, 1973.

Hodge, Charles. *Systematic Theology*. 3 vols. 1872. Reprint, Grand Rapids, MI: Eerdmans, 1993.

Holdsworth, Christopher B. "The Eschatology of Jonathan Edwards." *Reformation and Revival* 5 (Summer 1996): 119–43.

Hullinger, Jerry M. "Two Atonement Realms: Reconciling Sacrifices in Ezekiel and Hebrews." *Journal of Dispensational Theology* 11, no. 32 (March 2007): 33–63.

Ice, Thomas, and Timothy Demy, eds. *When the Trumpet Sounds*. Eugene, OR: Harvest House, 1995.

Klaasen, Walter. *Living at the End of the Ages*. Lanham, MD: University Press of America, 1992.

Kromminga, Diedrich H. *The Millennium and the Church: Studies in the History of Christian Chiliasm*. Grand Rapids, MI: Eerdmans, 1945.

Kyle, Richard G. *The Last Days Are Here Again*. Grand Rapids, MI: Baker, 1998.

Ladd, George E. *The Blessed Hope*. Grand Rapids, MI: Eerdmans, 1956.

Lamport, Mark A., ed. *Encyclopedia of Martin Luther and the Reformation*. 2 vols. Lanham, MD: Rowman & Littlefield, 2017.

Larsen, David. "Joachim of Fiore: The Rebirth of Futurism." *Covenant Quarterly* 60, no. 1 (2002): 1–15.

Luther, Martin. *Conversations with Luther*. Edited and translated by Preserved Smith and Herbert Percival Gallinger. Boston: Pilgrim Press, 1915.

———. *Luther's Works*. Edited by Helmut T. Lehmann. Vol. 54, *Table Talk*, edited and translated by Theodore G. Tappert. Philadelphia, PA: Fortress Press, 1967.

———. *Works of Martin Luther, with Introductions and Notes*. Edited by Adolph Spaeth. 6 vols. Philadelphia, PA: A. J. Holman, 1915–1932.

Matar, Nabil. *Islam in Britain, 1558–1685*. New York: Cambridge University Press, 1998.

McClymond, Michael James, and Gerald R. McDermott. *The Theology of Jonathan Edwards*. New York: Oxford University Press, 2012.

McGinn, Bernard. *Visions of the End: Apocalyptic Traditions in the Middle Ages.* New York: Columbia University Press, 1979.

McKim, Donald K. *Reformation Questions, Reformation Answers.* Louisville, KY: Westminster John Knox Press, 2017.

Menn, Jonathan. *Biblical Eschatology.* Eugene, OR: Wipf and Stock, 2013.

Mickelsen, A. Berkeley. *Interpreting the Bible.* 1963. Reprint, Grand Rapids, MI: Eerdmans, 1984.

Nichol, Francis D., ed. *The Seventh-day Adventist Bible Commentary.* 7 vols. Washington, DC: Review and Herald, 1953-80.

Nicholas, William C. *I Saw the World End: An Introduction to the Bible's Apocalyptic Literature.* Mahwah, NJ: Paulist Press, 2007.

Pamphilus, Eusebius. *Ecclesiastical History.* Translated by Christian Frederick Cruse. Grand Rapids, MI: Baker, 1994.

Ramm, Bernard. *Protestant Biblical Interpretation: A Textbook of Hermeneutics.* 3rd rev. ed. 1970. Reprint, Grand Rapids, MI: Baker, 1997.

Rowdon, Harold H. *The Origins of the Brethren, 1825-1850.* London: Pickering & Inglis, 1967.

Sandeen, Ernest R. *The Roots of Fundamentalism.* 1970. Reprint, Grand Rapids, MI: Baker, 1978.

Schaff, Philip. *History of the Christian Church.* 8 vols. 1858. Reprint, Peabody, MA: Hendrickson, 1996.

Shea, William H. "The Prophecy of Daniel 9:24-27." In *The Seventy Weeks, Leviticus, and the Nature of Prophecy*, edited by Frank B. Holbrook, 75-118. Washington, DC: Biblical Research Institute, 1986.

Smolinski, Reiner, ed. *The Kingdom, the Power, and the Glory.* Dubuque, IA: Kendall Hunt, 1998.

Stitzinger, James F. "The Rapture in Twenty Centuries of Biblical Interpretation." *The Master's Seminary Journal* 13, no. 2 (Fall 2002): 149–71.

Tan, Paul Lee. *The Interpretation of Prophecy.* Dallas, TX: Bible Communications, 1974.

Tanner, Joseph. *Daniel and the Revelation.* London: Hodder and Stoughton, 1898.

Tatum, W. Barnes. *Jesus: A Brief History.* Malden, MA: John Wiley & Sons, 2009.

van den Biesen, Christian. "Apocalypse." In *The Catholic Encyclopedia,* edited by Charles G. Herbermann. Vol. 1. New York: Appleton, 1907. Accessed May 24, 2017. http://www.newadvent.org/cathen/01594b .htm.

Walvoord, John F. *Every Prophecy of the Bible.* Colorado Springs, CO: Chariot Victor Publishing, 1999.

———. *The Millennial Kingdom.* 1959. Reprint, Grand Rapids, MI: Zondervan, 1976.

———. *The Return of the Lord.* Grand Rapids, MI: Dunham Publishing, 1955.

Watson, William C. *Dispensationalism Before Darby: Seventeenth-Century and Eighteenth Century English Apocalypticism.* Silverton, OR: Lampion Press, 2015.

Weber, Timothy P. "Millennialism." In *The Oxford Handbook of Eschatology,* edited by Jerry L. Walls, 365–383. New York: Oxford University Press, 2008.

Weremchuk, Max S. *John Nelson Darby: A Biography.* Neptune, NJ: Loizeaux Brothers, 1992.

Whitaker, William. *A Disputation on Holy Scripture, Against the Papists, Especially Bellarmine and Stapleton.* Translated and edited by William Fitzgerald. 1588. Reprint, Cambridge: University Press, 1849.

Whitcomb, John C. "Christ's Atonement and Animal Sacrifices in Israel." *Grace Theological Journal* 6, no. 2 (Fall 1985): 201–17.

Wilkinson, Paul Richard. *For Zion's Sake: Christian Zionism and the Role of John Nelson Darby.* Eugene, OR: Wipf & Stock, 2008.

Williams, George Huntston. *The Radical Reformation.* 3rd ed. Kirksville, MO: Truman State University Press, 1992.

Worsley, Henry. *The Life of Martin Luther.* 2 vols. London: Bell and Daldy, 1856.

Zuck, Roy B. *Basic Bible Interpretation.* Colorado Springs, CO: Victor, 1991.

10

SOLA SCRIPTURA:
Return to Literal Grammatical-Historical Hermeneutics

Thomas S. Baurain
Calvary University

10.0 Introduction

Throughout the history of the Christian church there has been regular disagreement over how to understand and interpret Scripture. The extremes have been a very literal approach on the one hand and full-blown allegorizing on the other. For approximately one thousand years prior to the Protestant Reformation, the Roman Catholic Church used a three-tiered approach supposedly centered on the authority of the Bible, but relying on the traditional interpretations of the Church, as well as magisterial pronouncements of Church hierarchy. The Bible, viewed as obscure in meaning, needed the careful interpretation of the Church to understand the correct meaning for the laity. Even then, however, many church leaders articulated better hermeneutical principles than they practiced.

10.1 The Reformed Legacy: A Return to Normal Hermeneutics

With the coming of the Protestant Reformation,[1] the 1500s witnessed a return to careful exegesis of the Scriptures utilizing the original languages,

---

[1] For an excellent treatment of the history of the Reformation see G. R. Evans, *The Roots of the Reformation* (Downers Grove, IL: InterVarsity Press, 2012).

311

concurrent with the Renaissance study of languages and the classics. Knowledge of Greek and Hebrew aided the understanding of the author's intended meaning. The multiple sense of Scripture characteristic of the Medieval church was abandoned in favor of the presupposition that a single meaning which could be determined from the written text itself—not needing to search for the "deeper meaning."

Martin Luther (1483–1546) rejected the Roman Catholic practice of allegorical interpretation in favor of a literal understanding of the Bible. A literal understanding was demonstrably clearer from the text, not obscure as the church had said. His focus was on the historical and grammatical context of the Bible, utilizing a Christocentric unity. Melanchthon and others carried forward Luther's work.

John Calvin (1509–1564) also rejected allegorical interpretation for the literal approach and is credited with the "Scripture interprets Scripture" paradigm, which focuses on the historical background, grammar, words, context, and parallel passages. Many would argue that these are still guiding principles for modern orthodox Protestants today. Even so, many Christians continue to articulate better hermeneutical principles than they practice.

Even a cursory reading of church history confirms that Post-Reformation (1550–1800) hermeneutics saw a return to confessionalism and dogmatics by Roman Catholics (Council of Trent), as well as hermeneutical deviations into Pietism (1600s) with no apparent concern for the author's intended meaning of a text (read that as subjectivism), and, later, an elevation of rationalism, or the authority of human reason over divine revelation.

Modern hermeneutics (1800–present) has seen liberalism (based entirely on rationalism) and neo-orthodoxy, neither of which take the truth of the Bible seriously. Add to that, empiricism and naturalism applied to Scripture and the result is the twenty-first century "science has all the answers" approach to hermeneutics.[2]

---

[2] For general discussion of the history of interpretation, see Bernard Ramm, *Protestant Biblical Interpretation: A Textbook of Hermeneutics*, 3rd rev. ed. (Grand Rapids, MI: Baker, 1970); Henry A. Virkler, *Hermeneutics: Principles and Processes of Biblical Interpretation*, 2nd ed. (Grand Rapids, MI: Baker, 2007); Roy B. Zuck, *Basic Bible Interpretation: A Practical Guide to Discovering Biblical Truth* (Colorado Springs, CO: Victor, 1991);

10.2 The Issues That Precipitated the Reformation

The Reformation is usually summarized by the five *solas*; *sola Scriptura* (Scripture alone), *sola gratia* (grace alone), *sola fide* (faith alone), *solus Christus* (by Christ alone), *and soli Deo gloria* (to the glory of God alone)—a return to Scripture alone as the only authority for a Christian—salvation is by grace alone, through faith alone, in Christ alone, for the glory of God alone. Obviously, this is a repudiation of the Roman Catholic doctrine of salvation being found only in the Church and correct biblical interpretation only by the Church hierarchy.

Doctrinally, the primary areas of systematics addressed by the Reformation were Bibliology, soteriology, ecclesiology, and to some extent Christology. Other areas of systematics not directly addressed were anthropology, angelology, pneumatology, and eschatology. Of the four main streams of Protestantism issuing from the Reformation: Lutheran, Reformed/Presbyterian, Anglican, and Anabaptist, only the Anabaptists did not carry over infant baptism or amillennialism. The reason Anabaptists did not adopt these doctrines and practices was a scriptural one. Literal interpretation of the biblical text did not yield support for infant baptism or amillennialism. This, of course, caused Anabaptists further persecution by the other Protestant groups as well as the Roman Catholics.

Further consideration of *sola Scriptura*, the authority of Scripture, and Scripture *alone*, implies the need for a consistent set of hermeneutic principles. If Scripture is to be the authority, then Christians must be able to discover the correct meaning of all of Scripture and not be dependent on the church hierarchy to determine the meaning for them. Thus, another repudiation of Roman Catholic tradition. For a Christian to rely on the authority of Scripture, he/she must be able to understand the Bible and its teachings and be able to draw correct application from it for theology and Christian living. For conservative evangelical Christians that consistent hermeneutic is the literal, plain, normal, grammatical, historical, and contextual approach to which the reformers all returned (at least in the beginning). If this approach is consistently applied to the Bible, from cover-to-cover,

---

and other sources on basic hermeneutics.

Genesis through Revelation, the meaning of the biblical authors will be discovered, and the theological system emerging from the meaning will be normative dispensationalism. To the extent that dispensationalists continue the consistent use of literal grammatical-historical hermeneutics to all of Scripture, it may be judged that dispensationalism best carries on the legacy of the Reformation.

10.3 Literal Interpretation

While all dispensationalists have an understanding of what literal interpretation is when asked to define it, sometimes one definition does not match another. This is true even when two Bible students/scholars both agree that literal interpretation is the correct method. It is painfully true when someone is criticizing the "literal interpretation" methodology. Several questions need to be answered:

1. What is "literal" interpretation?
2. Exactly what is "literal"?
3. Does everyone agree on what is "literal"?
4. How "literal" should "literal" interpretation be?
5. What is the effect on biblical interpretation, not only on prophecy, but also on ancient biblical history, including the issue of origins?

10.3.1 Presuppositions

In order to proceed it is necessary to delineate several presuppositions which are *very basic* and hardly revolutionary. They are as follows:

- The Bible is God's revelation to humanity.
- The Bible is inspired by God.
- God's character does not allow Him to lie.
- What God has revealed to mankind must be true.
- Accumulated manuscript evidence and translation fidelity yields confidence in the trustworthiness of the Bible.
- God's revelation to humanity is meant to be understood.
- Man's responsibility is to understand what God has revealed in the Bible and to be 'doers of the Word' and not hearers only.

- Therefore, the goal is to determine the Author's intended meaning as delivered through the human author's words in the text of the Bible.

Because God does a perfect job of inspiration, there are no hidden meanings.

10.3.2 Definitions

What are some typical definitions of "literal interpretation" of the Bible? Paul Lee Tan says, "Literal interpretation of the Bible simply means explaining the original sense of the Bible according to the normal and customary usages of its language."[3] He goes on to say that in the process of interpreting literally we must consider the accepted rules of grammar and the historical and cultural data of biblical times. This is often referred to as the grammatical-historical method of interpretation.[4]

When dealing with the proper interpretation of Scripture, Roy Zuck establishes the method of literal interpretation. What is the literal meaning of a biblical text? The opposite of literal is assumed to be "allegorical" (which presupposes many possible hidden meanings). By contrast literal interpretation may be termed the *correct method* of biblical interpretation, as Zuck writes: "We believe that to be the literal method which approaches the Scripture in the normal, customary way in which we talk, write, and think. It means taking the Scriptures at face value in an attempt to know what God meant by what He said."[5] In establishing a literal hermeneutic, Zuck advocates for this method: "The Bible itself follows the normal or literal method of interpretation."[6] He then cites Old Testament prophecy which was literally fulfilled.

Clearly, the literal method of interpretation is not universally endorsed by Christendom. The method is not even endorsed by all of evangelicalism. It is often ridiculed as ignorant and "fundamentalistic" as well as unsophisticated and "flat earthy." Mostly it is criticized for not recognizing

---

[3] Paul Lee Tan, *Literal Interpretation of the Bible* (Rockville, MD: Assurance Publishers, 1978), 15.

[4] Ibid.

[5] Zuck, *Basic Bible Interpretation*, 7.

[6] Ibid., 63.

figures of speech, not recognizing different genres, and generally for being "woodenly literal." All of these assaults are straw men constructed by non-dispensationalists who do not really do their homework, and are easily blown over.

10.4 The Importance of Hermeneutics to Dispensational Theology

Once again, what are the distinguishing features of dispensationalism? Ryrie asked and answered this question by suggesting the *sine qua non* (without which not) of the system in his definitive book.[7] The answer included three critical elements. The first is the distinction between Israel and the church. The second is the matter of plain hermeneutics or literal interpretation. The third aspect concerns the ultimate purpose of God in the world to be bringing glory to Himself.[8] While the essence of dispensationalism is the distinction between Israel and the church, Ryrie emphasized that "this grows out of the dispensationalist's consistent employment of normal or plain or historical-grammatical interpretation."[9]

In Ryrie's chapter, "Update on Dispensationalism" in Willis and Master's book examining issues in dispensational theology,[10] he notes that John Nelson Darby (1800–1882) and other contemporaries, who, in the early formulation of the dispensational system, did not necessarily agree on all details of dispensationalism, did insist on the literal interpretation of all of Scripture. Ryrie states: "This literal hermeneutic was deemed especially important to the correct understanding of Revelation, Daniel, and other Old Testament prophecies....The hermeneutic of early dispensationalism was literalistic."[11] As dispensationalism developed in America through the several Bible conferences of the late 19th and early 20th centuries, the various speakers utilized what they themselves called a grammatical-historical

---

[7] Charles C. Ryrie, *Dispensationalism Today* (Chicago, IL: Moody Press, 1965).

[8] Charles C. Ryrie, *Dispensationalism*, rev. and exp. ed. (Chicago, IL: Moody Press, 1995), 38–41.

[9] Ibid., 41.

[10] Charles C. Ryrie, "Update on Dispensationalism," in *Issues in Dispensationalism*, ed. Wesley R. Willis and John R. Master (Chicago, IL: Moody Press, 1994), 15–27.

[11] Ibid., 17.

method of interpretation. In a comment about the very popular and influential *Scofield Reference Bible* (1909), Ryrie acknowledges that this work popularized dispensationalism perhaps more than any other entity: "Literal interpretation and the distinction between Israel and the church (and other distinctions) are preeminent in its notes."[12] The emphasis on the *consistent* use of a literal hermeneutic which leads the interpreter to maintain the clear distinction between Israel and the church continues to be a key element in *normative* dispensationalism.

10.4.1 A Literal Hermeneutic Explained

Critics of literal interpretation often refer to it as "wooden literalism." They accuse literal interpreters of not recognizing figures of speech, symbolism, or apocalyptic imagery.[13] For instance, when the Bible uses the phrase "the four corners of the earth," critics say that a literal interpretation demands that the Bible teaches that the world is flat, or even square! Conversely, they insist that the number 1,000 (as in 1,000 years) does not always mean 1,000. By taking a symbolic meaning for the number from a different context and reading that meaning into Revelation 20:2-7, a literal millennial kingdom is negated.[14]

A typical example of this kind of criticism is frequently found in *Christianity Today* magazine. In an article ironically titled, "Defending Scripture. Literally." the author begins by stating, "Not everything the Bible has to say should be literally interpreted. But that doesn't make it less powerful."[15] She recalls attending a Christian university decades ago when zealous students

---

[12] Ryrie, "Update on Dispensationalism," 18.

[13] An example of such criticism is dealt with in Thomas Ice, "Literal vs. Allegorical Interpretation," Pre-Trib Research Center Article Archives, Paper 62 (May 2009), accessed August 29, 2017, http://digitalcommons.liberty.edu/pretrib_arch/62/.

[14] Hank Hanegraaff, the Bible Answer Man, is guilty of this. See Thomas Ice, "One Thousand Years: Literal or Figurative?" Pre-Trib Research Center Article Archives, Paper 25 (May 2009), accessed August 29, 2017, http://digitalcommons.liberty.edu/pretrib_arch/25/.

[15] Carolyn Arends, "Defending Scripture. Literally," *Christianity Today*, May 2, 2012.

wanted to defend the authority of Scripture to prove they were sincere evangelicals. She goes on to state, "One of the unintended side effects of our fervor was that we took almost everything literally, at least in spiritual matters. Generally, we weren't very good with oblique metaphors and analogies."[16] She only learned later that it was more difficult to understand the Bible than she and others had imagined: "We'd been blithely unaware that there is more than one genre in the Bible, or that literary context profoundly matters to meaning. We didn't understand that when we read ancient Hebrew prose poems (like Genesis 1)...as if they were science textbooks, we were actually obscuring their meaning."[17]

A better term than literal would be "normal." According to Ramm,

> The literal method of interpretation is the usual practice in the interpretation of literature. Whenever we read a book, an essay, or a poem we presume the literal sense in the document until the nature of the literature may force us to another level. This is the only conceivable method of beginning or commencing to understand literature of all kinds. The non-literal is always a secondary meaning which presumes an already existing literal understanding of literature.[18]

When one reads the newspaper, for example, one has little trouble understanding what is being communicated. The reporter uses words, putting them together in sentences, in order to communicate ideas, historical facts or even his own opinions. The same is true for magazines, novels, fiction and nonfiction books, and technical articles. The reader understands that

---

[16] Arends, "Defending Scripture. Literally."

[17] Ibid. Frankly, I know of no actual person who reads Genesis as a science textbook. Nor do I know of anyone today who is unaware of figures of speech, such as similes and metaphors. The book *Figures of Speech Used in the Bible* lists over 8,000 examples/illustrations of some 200 such figures covering over 1100 pages. Incidentally, this is the most definitive work on the figures of speech used in the Bible and it was produced by an ultadispensationalist. E. W. Bullinger, *Figures of Speech Used in the Bible* (1898; repr., Grand Rapids, MI: Baker, 1968). Mercifully, this book is now digitized and is part of many electronic Bible study software programs and also available online; see: https://archive.org/details/cu31924029277047

[18] Bernard Ramm, *Protestant Biblical Interpretation: A Textbook of Hermeneutics*, 3rd rev. ed. (1970; repr., Grand Rapids, MI: Baker, 1997), 123.

words have meaning as they are used in sentences (the literary context) expecting facts from a newspaper, entertainment from a novel, and analysis of historical events from a book on the Second World War. If one is simply trying to understand what the author wrote, regardless of the type or style of writing, and shares the language of the writer, the task is really not that formidable.

The same should be true when interpreting the Bible. The interpreter's task is really straightforward. He must come to an understanding of what the author of the biblical passage was communicating—*the author's intended meaning*.[19] How is this done? The Bible was originally written in three languages (Hebrew, Aramaic, and Greek) over a period of at least 1500 years by about 40 different human authors covering a very long time, historically speaking. The challenge is that twenty-first century American Christians most often have an English translation of the Bible with some notes and cross references to help them understand what they are reading. Without the knowledge or skill of Hebrew or Greek exegesis, the only way to come to an understanding of the author's intended meaning is by an inductive method of the study of the English translation. First, one must observe what the passage says. Then, using a normal hermeneutic, one interprets the passage understanding the meaning of the words by the way they are used in the context of the passage, taking into account the grammar and syntax of the passage, as well as the historical situation surrounding the passage being studied. This is the time honored method known as the grammatical-historical method of interpretation.[20] The consistent application of this method will yield the author's intended meaning of each book of the Bible.

Why is it necessary to determine the *author's* intended meaning? What if the interpreter thinks the passage means something else? The answer is

---

[19] See Elliott E. Johnson, *Expository Hermeneutics: An Introduction* (Grand Rapids, MI: Zondervan, 1990); Robert L. Thomas, *Evangelical Hermeneutics: The New Versus the Old* (Grand Rapids, MI: Kregel Publications, 2002); and other works advocating a normal hermeneutic.

[20] For classical works describing this system of hermeneutics see Milton S. Terry, *Biblical Hermeneutics* (1890; repr., Eugene, OR: Wipf and Stock, 1999); and Bernard Ramm, *Protestant Biblical Interpretation: A Textbook of Hermeneutics*, 3rd rev. ed. (Grand Rapids, MI: Baker, 1970).

obvious. The meaning of any biblical passage or book, indeed, the meaning of anything written, resides in the text being examined and is determined by the author of the text *when it was written*—not by the interpreter. The biblical interpreter's function is to uncover/discover by careful and diligent examination the meaning that the author intended to communicate to his original readers. The interpreter is never to impose his meaning or any other foreign meaning onto the text of Scripture. That would not be exegesis but eisegesis. The contention is that a careful and consistent application of a normal hermeneutic—a normal system of interpretation—to the entirety of Scripture results in a dispensational theology, nothing else.[21]

By this time, it should be clear that consistently using a normal hermeneutic—not to be confused with a woodenly literal methodology—recognizes the author's use of figurative language, symbols, figures of speech, parables, and allegories. However, the use of the normal hermeneutic is determined from the context, the way the author uses language, analysis of the grammar of the passage, and a recognition of the historical circumstances surrounding the passage. The interpreter should not determine the hermeneutic after deciding that all remaining unfulfilled prophecies must be fulfilled spiritually, as is done by covenant theologians and/or amillennial commentators.

10.5 Covenant Theology

As a system of theology, Covenant theology antedates dispensationalism, being associated with the *Westminster Confession of Faith* of 1648. In this system the whole of Scripture is viewed as being covered by the covenant of works, the covenant of grace, and the covenant of redemption (although not all covenant theologians include the latter covenant). The entire Bible is understood in terms of these covenants. The problem, however, is that these covenants are not biblically stated covenants, as is the Abrahamic, Palestinian, Davidic, and New Covenants. They are theological covenants inferred from Scripture, but not explicitly found therein.

The covenant of works is understood to be between God and Adam

---

[21] It also results in other conclusions, of course, but the present subject at hand is dispensationalism.

before the Fall in Genesis 3. In this covenant God offers life for obedience and death for disobedience. Man fell. Therefore, God instituted the covenant of grace between Himself and the elect sinner in which He offers salvation by faith in Christ. This creates the need for the covenant of redemption between the Father and the Son in which the Son agrees to redeem the elect as a basis for the covenant of grace. This third covenant is more recent in development and is not found in the *Westminster Confession*.

The biblical basis for these three covenants is scant. Rather than resulting from an inductive examination of Scripture, it results as a deduction from certain assumptions. There is no scriptural reference to these specific covenants. Consequently, these covenant ideas—the hermeneutic of Covenant theology—result in an *inconsistent* literalism. The Old Testament is interpreted in light of the New Testament which produces forced interpretations, faulty exegesis, bad typology, and allegorizing and spiritualizing of Scripture. The New Testament must be read back into the Old, and so the church becomes the "true Israel" and the promises to Israel must be realized by the church—hence, according to replacement theology, the church takes the place of Israel inheriting all the promises (but none of the curses).

10.5. Inconsistent Literalism

The basic rules of interpretation accepted by covenant theologians[22] include: (1) words must be understood in their plain historical sense (the grammatical-historical sense); (2) Scripture is of divine origin and contains no contradictions; (3) Scripture should explain Scripture (the so-called "analogy of Scripture"); and (4) the Holy Spirit must illuminate the meaning of the text. However, covenant theologians modify these basic rules in actual application as follows:

- Literal interpretation of prophecy not yet fulfilled is entirely untenable.[23]

---

[22] Refer to the following sources: Louis Berkhof, *Systematic Theology* (Grand Rapids, MI: Eerdmans, 1941), 712; Charles Hodge, *Systematic Theology* (1873; repr., Grand Rapids, MI: Eerdmans, 1973), 1:187-188; Lewis Sperry Chafer, *Systematic Theology*, (Dallas, TX: Dallas Seminary Press, 1947), 2:114-119; Charles C. Ryrie, *Dispensationalism Today*, 86-109, 187-189.

[23] Berkhof, *Systematic Theology*, 712.

- Prophecy must be interpreted in a spiritual or allegorical sense (that is, prophecy not yet fulfilled).
- A "theological interpretation" must be added to the grammatical-historical method (especially to unfulfilled prophecy).[24]
- The Old Testament must be interpreted by the New Testament (resulting at times in a new meaning of the Old Testament passage).

With such modifications, of course, the result is an artificial exegesis. As stated previously, it is frequently found, however, that some Christians articulate a better system of hermeneutics than they actually practice.

The imposition of the Covenant theology system upon the Bible forces a re-interpretation of prophecy not yet clearly fulfilled—after all, it is difficult to reinterpret a prophecy already literally fulfilled, such as the birth place of Jesus (Mic 5:2). The extent of this imposition controls the interpretive outcome. The outstanding characteristic of nondispensational hermeneutics is the inconsistent use of the basic rules, which if applied would yield normal, literal interpretation—especially in the area of prophecy. Thus, a normal hermeneutic using the principles of grammatical-historical interpretation *applied consistently* throughout Scripture, will lead the interpreter to dispensational theology. If the rules are modified and a theological interpretation is added to the grammatical-historical method (i.e. an inconsistent literalism), the result is Covenant theology. The spiritualizing of all unfulfilled prophecy and the identification of true Israel with the church results in full-blown amillennialism and replacement theology, while less spiritualizing of prophecy and the allowance of a future of some kind for Israel leads to covenant premillennialism.

10.5.2 Examples of Abnormal Hermeneutics

If the grammatical-historical method of interpretation is rightly labeled as the "normal" method, then any other hermeneutic that deviates from these principles could rightly be referred to as "abnormal." The inconsistent literalism discussed above falls into this abnormal category as does a

---

[24] Daniel P. Fuller, "The Hermeneutics of Dispensationalism" (ThD diss., Northern Baptist Theological Seminary, 1957), 147.

full-blown allegorical method of interpretation.

Allegorical interpretation may have originated with the ancient Greeks to cover up embarrassing episodes in Greek mythology, but then it was passed on to the Jews who in turn handed the method on to the church Fathers and it became the dominant mode of biblical interpretation throughout the Middle Ages up to the Protestant Reformation. Allegorical interpretation creates a level of meaning completely foreign to the author's intentions by the use of figurative language. However, unlike legitimate uses of figurative language, allegorizing is often far-fetched, absurd, or unreal—meanings are imported into the text by the interpreter. Rather than attempting to determine the author's intended meaning, allegorical interpretations are highly subjective and liable to change with the moods and feelings of the interpreter.

An example of allegorical interpretation from early church history is seen in one of Augustine's sermons on the gospel of John. John 2 describes Jesus' first public miracle of turning water into wine at the wedding feast in Cana of Galilee. Water was placed into six large stone water pots, each holding twenty to thirty gallons. The water was turned into wine by the Son of God. Augustine interprets the six water pots to signify the six ages or six periods, each probably referring to a thousand years—hence, six thousand years.[25]

An example of allegorizing from the medieval period is taken from a commentary of the gospel of John by Rupert of Deutz (about the 12th century). Commenting on the 153 fish caught by the disciples (see John 21:11), Westcott summarizes Rupert's interpretation: "Rupert of Deutz . . . regards the three numbers [100, 50, and 3] as the proportions of three different classes united in one faith. The 'hundred' are the married, who are the most numerous, the 'fifty' the widowed or continent who are less numerous, the 'three,' the least in number, are the virgins."[26] Examples could be multiplied, but the point is made. The interpretation obviously did not come

---

[25] Augustine, "Lectures or Tractates on the Gospel According to St. John," in *A Select Library of the Nicene and Post-Nicene Fathers*, ed. Phillip Schaff, ser. 1, vol. 7, *St. Augustin: Homilies on the Gospel of John, Homilies on the First Epistle of John, Soliloquies* (Grand Rapids, MI: Eerdmans, 1983), 65.

[26] B. F. Westcott, *The Gospel According to St. John* (Grand Rapids, MI: Eerdmans,

from the text; rather it was read into the text. It did not result from carefully applied normal hermeneutics, but from inconsistent hermeneutics, which would be "abnormal."

To illustrate what is done with prophecy using abnormal hermeneutics, consider the following: Revelation 7:4–8 describes the 144,000, stated in the passage to be 12,000 from each of the twelve tribes of Israel. They are identified by Ladd to be the "true Israel" (the true people of God) in the tribulation.[27] In his view they are not the literal twelve tribes and not literal Jews. Rather, there is a spiritual significance to this group of people. The true people of God will be preserved complete during this time. Not one "true one" will be lost during the time of God's wrath. However, Ladd apparently is not so certain about his interpretation to be dogmatic about it; for example, he says " whoever they are." Fairbairn also sees the 144,000 as "the Lord's people generally" who are kept safe from the desolations sweeping the earth during the tribulation. [28] The twelve tribes historically composed the professing church in the first century. The problem with interpretations such as these is that the biblical text plainly states that the 144,000 are composed of 12,000 from each of the twelve tribes of Israel and then goes on to name each of the individual tribes: Judah, Reuben, Gad, Asher, Naphtali, Manasseh, Simeon, Levi, Issachar, Zebulun, Joseph, and Benjamin. This would seem to be wasted information if all the author intended to communicate was that the true people of God—whoever they might be—will be preserved through the tribulation period.

Another curious interpretation is given by Fairbairn of Ezekiel 38–39—the attack by Gog against the people of Israel. Fairbairn regards this as an ideal delineation of certain dangers and assaults against the people of God in the distant future.[29] At this "future" time the condition will be peace, the enemies of the people of God will be hostile powers from remote regions under the command of an enterprising leader named Gog, and the

---

1950), 307.

[27] George Eldon Ladd, *The Blessed Hope* (Grand Rapids, MI: Eerdmans, 1956), 126.

[28] Patrick Fairbairn, *Prophecy Viewed in Its Distinctive Nature, Its Special Function, and Proper Interpretation* (New York: Carlton & Porter, 1866), 251.

[29] Ibid., 485–487.

distance really means a moral distance from God, not a literal physical distance.

Mickelsen proposes a slight variation of method interpreting prophecy in terms of equivalents, analogy, or correspondence.[30] He notes that since prophecy is fulfilled in the future, therefore, all language would be symbolic of something future at the time of fulfillment. Some examples of the equivalents or correspondence would be: cars instead of chariots, guns instead of swords, and church instead of temple. On the surface this sounds very appealing. The problem is that we must know the time of fulfillment in order to identify the exact equivalent. When Mickelsen applies this technique to Ezekiel 40–48, the twelve tribes of Israel are equivalent to the unity of the people of God. The 144,000 of Revelation 7 are equivalent to the entire church of the end time. This use of equivalents is not used exclusively by nondispensationalists. Hal Lindsey of *The Late Great Planet Earth* fame used these same principles to equate the weapons of war of Ezekiel 39 to atomic bombs, missiles, tanks, helicopters, and the like.[31] This, however, assumes that he knows the time of fulfillment, which, of course, no one knows except God alone.

10.6 Is Consistent Literalism Biblical?

Up to this point, the argument has been that normal hermeneutics—consistent literalism—applied to the entire Bible leads the interpreter to normative dispensational theology. It also leads the interpreter to other conclusions: such as a supernatural (miraculous) creation of all things from nothing by God in six normal days (as we would define them), in thousands of years, not billions of years. Mark Noll has observed that "a biblical literalism, gaining strength since the 1870s, has fueled both the intense concern for human origins and the end times. Literal readings of Genesis 1–3 find their counterpart in literal readings of Revelation 20 (with its description of the thousand-year reign of Christ)."[32] Noll also speculates that the earlier

[30] A. Berkeley Mickelsen, *Interpreting the Bible* (Grand Rapids, MI: Eerdmans, 1963), 296–305.

[31] Hal Lindsey, *The Late Great Planet Earth* (Grand Rapids, MI: Zondervan, 1970).

[32] Mark A. Noll, *The Scandal of the Evangelical Mind* (Grand Rapids, MI: Eerdmans, 1994), 194.

spread of dispensationalism connects with the later popularity of Creation Science through the common thread of literal (normal) interpretation and the observation of major discontinuities in biblical history, both past and future.[33]

In a collection of essays arrayed against Creationism, historian George M. Marsden makes the astounding claim that literalism or normal interpretation of Scripture is "not derived from the Bible itself, but from philosophical assumptions that appear to be closely related to the Enlightenment Baconianism of their tradition – which lends itself toward a strong preference for definite and precise statements of fact."[34] Marsden further suggests that fundamentalists can abandon the "literal where possible" approach while still believing that "the Bible is true." He concludes his analysis by saying that "the point of Genesis . . . is not to tell us the details of *how* God created, but to assure us *that* God created the universe and the human race."[35] If this is actually the case, then why are there details in the text at all? Using this line of thinking, we might then suggest that the point of the Bible is not to tell us the details of *what* God revealed, but to assure us *that* God revealed His Word to the human race. Or, the point of the Bible is not to tell us the details of *how* we can be saved, but to assure us *that* we can be saved. And again, the point of the Bible is not to tell us the details of *what* will occur at the second coming, but to assure us *that* there will be a second coming. The absurdity of such reasoning is self-evident.

Clearly, if God communicated His Word through the special revelation of the Bible, it seems obvious that He expects readers to understand what He has communicated. It seems apparent that God "hard-wired" humans to communicate plainly, normally, and literally. Just as He originated communication, He also originated the ability to understand communication. From the perspective of philosophy, it seems that the purpose of language requires normal interpretation. How would we even be able to understand the criticism of a normal hermeneutic from Noll and Marsden, for

---

[33] Noll, *Scandal of the Evangelical Mind*, 195.

[34] George M. Marsden, "Understanding Fundamentalist Views of Science," in *Science and Creationism*, ed. Ashley Montagu (New York: Oxford University Press, 1984), 111.

[35] Ibid.

example, except by understanding what they wrote in a normal, literal manner? Contrary to Marsden's claim that literalism is not derived from the Bible, we simply point out that the prophecies in the Old Testament of the first coming of Christ, including His birth, childhood, ministry, death, and resurrection, were all fulfilled literally! There simply are no nonliteral fulfillments of these prophecies in the New Testament. If this does not argue for a biblical basis for the literal method, what does?[36]

Likewise, examine the beginning of the Bible. In a paper presented by Christopher Cone, he argues quite convincingly that a literal hermeneutic is actually imbedded in the text of Genesis itself.[37] After examining ninety-four passages in Genesis and Job, he concludes that the evidence is overwhelming that "God intended for His words to be taken at face value, using a plain-sense interpretive approach. The hermeneutic method that reflects this straightforward methodology has become known as the *literal grammatical historical hermeneutic.*"[38] Cone concluded: "This method recognizes that verbal expression has meaning rooted in and inseparable from the grammatical and historical context of the language used, and that these components require that readers be consistent in applying the interpretive method in their study of the Scriptures."[39] Therefore, literal interpretation is not linked to the adoption of Enlightenment Baconianism, as suggested by Mark Noll and George Marsden, but rather to the Scriptures themselves.

10.7 Conclusion

The key to a person's theological convictions resides with his hermeneutic. Without the normal interpretation of Scripture, any objectivity toward determining the author's intended meaning is lost. A consistent application of a normal hermeneutic to the entirety of the Bible will lead the interpreter to dispensational theology, among other critical conclusions.

---

[36] For a fuller discussion of this issue, see the chapter on "The Hermeneutics of Dispensationalism" in Charles C. Ryrie, *Dispensationalism Today*, 86–89.

[37] Christopher Cone, "The Genesis Account as Early Model for Scriptural Hermeneutics" (paper presented at the *Symposium on Scripture, Hermeneutics and Language*, San Diego State University, April 13, 2015).

[38] Ibid.

[39] Ibid.

With the extent to which a literal grammatical-historical hermeneutic is consistently applied to all of Scripture, the conclusion is that dispensationalism best preserves the legacy of the Reformation. But Christians must not only articulate a good system of hermeneutics, they must also practice that which they profess.

In some sense, evangelicalism faces the same challenges that the Reformation and the Roman Catholic Church did 500 years ago. The concerns of the Reformation, expressed in the five *solas*, dealt with justification by faith alone, eliminating the burden of works; the content of faith defined in the Scriptures, not by the church; the literal meaning of the biblical text, accessible to the common man, not policed by the church hierarchy; and the power and nature of the institutional church.

As evangelicalism moves into the twenty-first century, 500 years away from the Reformation, the problems and struggles seem very familiar. Instead of a monolithic church dictating the terms of salvation, there are many evangelical voices arguing the same issues; lordship salvation vs. free grace salvation; premillennialism vs. amillennialism; supernatural creation vs. theistic evolution; the authority of Scripture vs. imposed ideas of science or psychology or feminism or liberation theology; the list goes on. The greatest challenge today still seems to be the authority of Scripture, correctly interpreted using a normal hermeneutic; literal, grammatical, historical, plain, contextual, and objective; not by a "Protestant pope," but by every Christian following Christ.

> Sola Scriptura
> Sola gratia
> Sola fide
> Solus Christus
> Soli Deo gloria

Bibliography

Arends, Carolyn. "Defending Scripture. Literally." *Christianity Today*, May 2, 2012.

Augustine. "Lectures or Tractates on the Gospel According to St. John." In *A Select Library of the Nicene and Post-Nicene Fathers*, edited by Phillip Schaff. Ser. 1. Vol. 7, *St. Augustin: Homilies on the Gospel of John, Homilies on the First Epistle of John, Soliloquies*, 7–452. Grand Rapids, MI: Eerdmans, 1983.

Berkhof, Louis. *Systematic Theology*. Grand Rapids, MI: Eerdmans, 1941.

Bullinger, E. W. *Figures of Speech Used in the Bible*. 1898. Reprint, Grand Rapids, MI: Baker, 1968.

Chafer, Lewis Sperry. *Systematic Theology*. 8 vols. Dallas, TX: Dallas Seminary Press, 1947.

Cone, Christopher. "The Genesis Account as Early Model for Scriptural Hermeneutics." Paper presented at the *Symposium on Scripture, Hermeneutics and Language*, San Diego State University, April 13, 2015.

Evans, G. R. *The Roots of the Reformation*, Downers Grove, IL: InterVarsity Press, 2012.

Fairbairn, Patrick. *Prophecy Viewed in Its Distinctive Nature, Its Special Function, and Proper Interpretation*. New York: Carlton & Porter, 1866.

Hodge, Charles. *Systematic Theology*. 3 vols. 1873. Reprint, Grand Rapids: Eerdmans, 1973.

Ice, Thomas. "Literal vs. Allegorical Interpretation." Pre-Trib Research Center Article Archives, Paper 62 (May 2009). Accessed August 29, 2017. http://digitalcommons.liberty.edu/pretrib_arch/62/.

———. "One Thousand Years: Literal or Figurative?" Pre-Trib Research Center Article Archives, Paper 25 (May 2009). Accessed August 29, 2017. http://digitalcommons.liberty.edu/pretrib_arch/25/.

Johnson, Elliott E. *Expository Hermeneutics: An Introduction*. Grand Rapids, MI: Zondervan, 1990.

Ladd, George Eldon. *The Blessed Hope*. Grand Rapids: Eerdmans, 1956.

Lindsey, Hal. *The Late Great Planet Earth*. Grand Rapids, MI: Zondervan, 1970.

Marsden, George M. "Understanding Fundamentalist Views of Science." In *Science and Creationism*, edited by Ashley Montagu, 95–116. New York: Oxford University Press, 1984.

Mickelsen, A. Berkeley. *Interpreting the Bible*. Grand Rapids, MI: Eerdmans, 1963.

Noll, Mark A. *The Scandal of the Evangelical Mind*. Grand Rapids, MI: Eerdmans, 1994.

Ramm, Bernard. *Protestant Biblical Interpretation: A Textbook of Hermeneutics*. 3rd rev. ed. Grand Rapids, MI: Baker, 1970.

Ryrie, Charles C. *Dispensationalism*. Rev. and exp. ed. Chicago, IL: Moody Press, 1995.

———. *Dispensationalism Today*. Chicago, IL: Moody Press, 1965.

———. "Update on Dispensationalism." In *Issues in Dispensationalism*, edited by Wesley R. Willis and John R. Master, 15–27. Chicago, IL: Moody Press, 1994.

Tan, Paul Lee. *Literal Interpretation of the Bible*. Rockville, MD: Assurance Publishers, 1978.

Terry, Milton S. *Biblical Hermeneutics*. 1890. Reprint, Eugene, OR: Wipf and Stock, 1999.

Thomas, Robert L. *Evangelical Hermeneutics: The New Versus the Old*. Grand Rapids, MI: Kregel Publications, 2002.

Virkler, Henry A. *Hermeneutics: Principles and Processes of Biblical Interpretation*. 2nd ed. Grand Rapids, MI: Baker, 2007.

Westcott, B. F. *The Gospel According to St. John*. Grand Rapids, MI: Eerdmans, 1950.

Zuck, Roy B. *Basic Bible Interpretation: A Practical Guide to Discovering Biblical Truth.* Colorado Springs, CO: Victor, 1991.

11

THE HERMENEUTICAL FOUNDATIONS OF *SOLA SCRIPTURA*:
A Critical Examination of Luther's Christocentric Method of Interpretation

James I. Fazio
Southern California Seminary

11.0 Introduction

The Reformation principle of *sola Scriptura* rests squarely upon a hermeneutical foundation of protestant Bible interpretation. In an article written in commemoration of the 500th anniversary of Luther's birthday, David S. Dockery wrote: "Luther initiated and fostered a hermeneutical revolution which changed the course of history. The Protestant Reformation would have been impossible apart from this change in hermeneutics which was employed to interpret both the OT and the NT. In a very real sense, Luther is the father of Protestant interpretation and his influence is profound."[1] This chapter is intended to provide a critical evaluation of those principles which defined Martin Luther's hermeneutical method. Emphasis will be given to the internal consistency of Luther's literal historical-grammatical hermeneutic with his Christocentric method.

The first part of the chapter will include a summary of those Protestant principles of biblical interpretation upon which the cries of 'Sola Scriptura'

---

[1] David S. Dockery, "Martin Luther's Christological Hermeneutics," *Grace Theological Journal* 4, no. 2 (1983): 189–190.

rest, including: (1) the authority of Scripture; (2) the sufficiency of Scripture; (3) the perspicuity of Scripture; (4) the requirement of faith and spiritual illumination; (5) an affirmation of the literal or grammatical-historical interpretive method; (6) the rejection of allegory as a valid interpretive method; and finally (7) the Christocentric principle which perceived the centrality of Christ in all of Scripture.[2] The latter part of the chapter will contain a critique of the compatibility of the seventh point listed above with the six which precedes it. In other words, it will assess the consistency of Luther's appeal to a normal historical-grammatical hermeneutical method with his Christocentric principle of biblical interpretation.

11.0.1 The Reformation Principle of 'Sola Scriptura'

In his comprehensive work on the history of biblical interpretation, Professor of Anglican studies, Gerald Bray, has offered the following observation: "the Reformers developed methods of textual analysis which are still in use, and conservative Protestants continue to look at them as a source of inspiration."[3] He afterward goes on to state: "To understand the biblical interpretation of this period, it is necessary to grasp the implications of the Reformed doctrine of *sola Scriptura*. Only then can we proceed to particular types of exegesis."[4] Therefore, given this recommendation—and in light of the quincentennial anniversary of Luther's nailing of the *95 Theses* on that door in Wittenberg on the eve of All Saint's Day, October 31, 1517—a brief consideration of the reformation principle of *sola Scriptura* is an appropriate place to begin an examination of Luther's hermeneutical method which fueled the Protestant Reformation and has continued to define the protestant and evangelical view of Scripture for the past 500 years.

In Phillip Schaff's defining work, *History of the Christian Church*, he points to "three fundamental principles of the Reformation,"[5] the first of

---

[2] This list is adapted from Frederic W. Farrar, *History of Interpretation* (1886; repr., Grand Rapids, MI: Baker Book House, 1961), 332; c.f. A. Skevington Wood, *Luther's Principles of Biblical Interpretation* (London: The Tyndale Press, 1960).

[3] Gerald Bray, *Biblical Interpretation: Past and Present* (Downers Grove, IL: IVP Academics, 1996), 190.

[4] Ibid., 191.

[5] Phillip Schaff, *History of the Christian Church*, vol. 7, *History of the Reformation*,

which he identifies as "the supremacy of the *Scriptures* over tradition."[6] To this, he adds: "the supremacy of *faith* over works,"[7] commonly expressed by the maxim *sola fide* or "by faith alone," and third, he points to "the supremacy of the Christian *people* over an exclusive priesthood,"[8] commonly expressed by the maxim: "the common priesthood of every believer."

Concerning this observation by Schaff, it is important to point out that the latter two principles are derived from the first, inasmuch as the Scriptures, alone, served as the authority to which the reformers were able to make appeals against the magisterium. Whereas Rome appealed to the authority of the church as the arbiter of the words of Scripture, Luther appealed to Scripture alone as it was understood through the individual reader's God-given faculty of reason.

Phillip Schaff reinforces this point by clarifying: "The objective principle of Protestantism maintains that the Bible, as the inspired record of revelation, is the only infallible rule of faith and practice; in opposition to the Roman Catholic coordinating of Scripture and ecclesiastical *tradition*, as the joint rules of faith."[9] Schaff does well to point out that the claim of *sola Scripture* is one which speaks to authority. It says, in effect, Scripture serves as the chief authority to which Christians must appeal for faith and practice. No higher authority exists than Scripture alone; neither on earth is there found its equal.

11.1 The Authority of Scripture

In the *Historical Handbook of Major Biblical Interpreters*, Luther's view on the authority of Scripture is summed up in the following words: "Scripture is its own authority because it is clear. No other authority is needed to see through its meaning."[10] Whereas the papacy did not, in word, deny Luther's appeal to the authority of Scripture, instead, they skirted the issue of

---

1517-1648 (1888; repr., Peabody, MA: Hendrickson Publishers, 1996), 16.

[6] Schaff, *History of the Christian Church*, 16.

[7] Ibid.

[8] Ibid.

[9] Ibid.

[10] Kenneth Hagen, "Martin Luther," in *Historical Handbook of Major Biblical Interpreters*, ed. Donald K. McKim (Downers Grove, IL: InterVarsity Press, 1998), 215.

Scripture's authority in practice by erecting a magisterium, which alone could serve as the arbiter of the meaning of Scripture.

Luther was appalled that, at times, the meaning of Scripture could be explained by the magisterium in a way that defied the plain message apparent in the text. Thus, the German reformer became acutely aware that the issue of the authority of Scripture was subject to the interpreter. In light of recent abuses by Pope Leo X, who had promulgated the most famous of all indulgences on March 15, 1517,[11] and Tetzel, of whom it was reported that "He gave sealed letters stating that even the sins which a man was intending to commit would be forgiven. The pope, he said, had more power than all the Apostles, all the angels and saints, more even than the Virgin Mary herself; for these were all subject to Christ, but the pope was equal to Christ."[12]

For Luther, if the magisterium's interpretation of Scripture could differ so radically from his own, then the conflict must reside with the subjectivity of the interpreter. Luther's conclusion, as testified by the confession of his own mouth at the Diet of Worms was: "I will never permit any man to set himself above the Word of God."[13] Upon being flatly asked by the Elector of Brandenburg, "If I rightly understand you doctor, you will acknowledge no other judge than the Holy Scriptures?"[14] Luther replied: "Precisely so, my Lord, and on them I take my stand."[15]

This was Luther's response after so many attempts were afforded him to retract his statements, when, at last, he dug in his heels with the following declaration:

Since your most serene majesty and your high mightinesses require from me a clear, simple, and precise answer, I will give you one, and it is this: I cannot submit my faith either to the pope or to the councils,

---

[11] Will Durant, *The Story of Civilization*, vol. 4, *The Reformation: A History of European Civilization from Wyclif to Calvin 1300–1564* (New York: Simon and Schuster, 1957), 337.

[12] Ibid., 339.

[13] J. H. Merle d'Aubigné, *History of the Reformation of the Sixteenth Century*, trans. Henry White (1846; repr., Rapidan, VA: Hartland Publications, n.d.), 251.

[14] Ibid., 250.

[15] Ibid.

because it is clear as the day that they have frequently erred and contradicted each other. Unless therefore I am convinced by the testimony of Scripture, or by the clearest reasoning—unless I am persuaded
by means of the passages I have quoted, and unless they thus render
my conscience bound by the Word of God, *I cannot and I will not retract.*[16]

The accompanying statement: "Here I stand. I cannot do otherwise"
so often associated with Luther's protest may not have been included. It
would seem that the earliest printed version may have included these words,
though they were not recorded at the time of delivery.[17] Nevertheless, the
sentiment is fully present in the words of Luther: "on [Scripture] I take my
stand"[18] and "I cannot and I will not retract."[19] Thus, Luther stood solely
upon the authority of Scripture being rightly interpreted through the God-
given faculty of human reason that is common to all men.

The keen observer could contend from Luther's words that he did not
appeal to Scripture alone. Rather, he included an appeal to the faculty of
human reason, saying: "Unless therefore I am convinced by the testimony
of Scripture, or by the clearest reasoning... *I cannot and I will not retract.*"[20]
Nevertheless, the Reformation principle is one of *sola Scriptura*, not *Scriptura*-plus-reason...or is it?

11.1.1 The Sufficiency of Scripture

Akin to the Reformation appeal to the authority of Scripture is the
appeal to the sufficiency of Scripture. These two ideals are intrinsically
bound up in the reformers' cry of '*Sola Scriptura.*' What role then does reason serve, if Scripture is sufficient in and of itself to direct the believer in
all matters of faith and practice? The contention of the reformers was that
reason played a major role. After all, one must judge—by means of Scripture,

---

[16] d'Aubigné, *History of the Reformation*, 245.
[17] See d'Aubigné, *History of the Reformation*, 145 c.f. Roland Bainton, *Here I Stand:
A Life of Martin Luther* (1950; repr., Nashville, TN: Abingdon Press, 2013), 140-144.
[18] d'Aubigné, *History of the Reformation*, 251.
[19] Ibid., 245.
[20] Ibid.

of course—whether certain teachings were from men or whether they were from God. Such judgment demanded an exercise of human reason that was unforgiving. On one hand, a wrong determination could result in physical death. On the other hand, there existed an even graver perceived threat, where doctrinal error could result in eternal damnation.

In Luther's own words, he offered the following appeal to the court:

> Yet I am but a mere man, and not God; I shall therefore defend myself as Christ did. *If I have spoken evil, bear witness of the evil* (John xviii, 23), said he. How much more should I, who am but dust and ashes, and who may so easily go astray, desire every man to state his objections to my doctrine!
>
> For this reason, most serene emperor, and you, most illustrious princes, and all men of every degree, I conjure you, by the mercy of God, to prove from the writings of the prophets and apostles that I have erred. As soon as I am convinced of this, I will retract every error, and be the first to lay hold of my books and throw them in the fire.
>
> What I have just said plainly shows, I hope, that I have carefully weighed and considered the dangers to which I expose myself.[21]

Luther took his stand upon Scripture alone, though his was no less a carefully weighed and measured position. He relied upon his basic faculty of human reason, being keenly aware of the doctrine of man's depravity. Nevertheless, he trusted that Scripture was wholly sufficient to illuminate man's reason and to serve as an adequate guide into matters of doctrinal truth. The Word of God and the mind of man were designed for one another. Luther was convinced that it was incumbent upon the man of God to fully employ his faculty of mind and reason in the interpretation and application of Holy Scripture. Reason's job was not to perform mental gymnastics in search of strained interpretations that were not plainly discernable from the text. Rather, the reader's job was to look for the plain and straightforward meaning of Scripture.

---

[21] d'Aubigné, *History of the Reformation*, 244.

11.1.2 *The Perspicuity of Scripture*

In speaking to the matter of interpretation as it concerns the Reformation principle of *sola Scriptura*, Bray notes: "The key issue which distinguished Protestants from Catholics was whether Scripture was self-interpreting, or whether it required the teaching authority of the church to make it plain."[22] This issue is summed up by the term the perspicuity of Scripture. This tenet was so central to the reformers' view of *sola Scriptura* that Bernard Ramm lists it first in his list of theological assumptions underlying the Protestant method of hermeneutics.[23]

In his book *Protestant Biblical Interpretation*, Ramm expresses the idea as follows:

> The Roman Catholic Church had its view of the clarity of Scripture. In that both Christ and the Spirit mystically indwell the Roman Church, the Church shares in the mind of Christ and the Spirit. It is therefore its gift to know the meaning of Scripture and in the exercise of this gift the Roman Catholic Church solves the problem of the clarity of Scripture.
>
> The Reformers rejected this view of the solution to the problem of the clarity of Scripture.[24]

Luther famously described his position concerning the perspicuity of Scripture in *The Bondage of the Will*, where he affirmed "The clearness of the Scripture is twofold,"[25] perceiving both an internal as well as an external clarity of Scripture. In Luther's estimation, the internal clarity involved the work of the Spirit in shaping the understanding of the human heart and mind of the reader, while the external clearness involved the use of normal

---

[22] Bray, *Biblical Interpretation*, 192.

[23] Bernard Ramm, *Protestant Biblical Interpretation: A Textbook of Hermeneutics*. 3rd rev. ed. (1950; repr., Grand Rapids, MI: Baker Book House, 1970), 97.

[24] Ibid., 98.

[25] Martin Luther, *De Servo Arbitrio: The Bondage of the Will*, trans. Henry Cole (1525; repr., The Sovereign Grace Union, 1931), sect. 4, accessed on April 13, 2017, https://www.monergism.com/thethreshold/sdg/pdf/luther_arbitrio.pdf.

human language which was intended to convey the Divine mind grammatically.[26] For Luther, both of these were requisite in order for Scripture to be
rightly understood. Therefore, both of these will now be considered in turn,
beginning with the need for internal clarity, or the requirement of faith and
spiritual illumination.

11.2 The Requirement of Faith and Spiritual Illumination

In his classic work on hermeneutics, Henry A. Virkler made the following observation about Luther's emphasis on the need for internal clarity
in biblical interpretation: "Luther believed that faith and the Spirit's illumination were prerequisites for an interpreter of the Bible. He asserted that
the Bible should be viewed with wholly different eyes from those with which
we view other literary productions."[27] In his own words, Luther described
the need for the Holy Spirit's illumination in this way: "If you speak of the
internal clearness, no man sees one iota in the Scriptures, but he that hath
the Spirit of God."[28] By this, Luther does not mean that the plain language
of Scripture is incapable of expressing itself clearly to the unregenerate man.
Rather, he clarifies that without the Spirit's illumination, the heart and
mind of the unregenerate reader is darkened and thus he is unable to rightly
and fully perceive its meaning.

The German doctor goes on to say: "All have a darkened heart, so
that, even if they know how to speak of, and set forth, all things in the
Scripture, yet they cannot feel them nor know them...For the Spirit is required to understand the whole of the Scripture and every part of it."[29]
Thus, Luther regarded the Holy Spirit's role of divine illumination as a critical component in yielding the full understanding of a biblical text. In his
notable work titled *Luther's Principles of Biblical Interpretation*, Skevington
Wood remarks: "The way in which the Spirit conveys His interpretation of
the Word is through the mind and soul of the man who submits himself to

---

[26] Luther, *Bondage of the Will*, c.f. Ramm, *Protestant Biblical Interpretation*, 98.

[27] Henry A. Virkler, *Hermeneutics: Principles and Processes of Biblical Interpretation*
(Grand Rapids, MI: Baker Book House, 1981), 65.

[28] Luther, *Bondage of the Will*, sect. 4.

[29] Ibid.

the discipline of instruction…Hence his maxim: *Sola experiential fecit theologum.* 'Experience is necessary for the understanding of the Word. It is not merely to be repeated and known, but to be lived and felt.'"[30]

Bernard Ramm offers the following remarks about the reformer's view: "The internal clarity of Scripture is the work of the Holy Spirit in the heart or mind of the believer, illuminating his mind to see the truth of Scripture as the truth of God. By the use of scientific philology and the illumination of the Spirit we arrive at the clarity of Scripture."[31] By scientific philology, Ramm refers to the science of interpretation, or hermeneutics, which is an essential component to all forms of human communication, and serves as the crux for Luther's view concerning the external clarity of Scripture.

11.3 The Literal Grammatical-Historical Hermeneutic

The Protestant understanding of the perspicuity of Scripture speaks to that quality of the written Word of God whereby it communicates clearly through the use of plain language. Nevertheless, communication does not occur without an agent or interpreter to receive the meaning that God has endeavored to transmit to man through the Sacred Text. This forms the basis for the need of a Protestant hermeneutic or method of interpretation which informs the reader's understanding of a text.

Luther's governing principle of biblical interpretation was to look for what he called the "literal sense" of the biblical text. Wood has regarded the reformer's insistence on the primacy of the literal sense as "One of the most valuable of Luther's hermeneutical principles,"[32] noting:

> He resolutely sets aside the verbal jugglery involved in multiple exegesis and firmly takes his stand upon the plain and obvious significance of the Word. 'The literal sense of Scripture alone', he asserts, 'is the whole essence of faith and Christian theology.' And again: 'If we wish to handle Scripture aright, our sole effort will be to obtain the one,

---

[30] Wood, *Luther's Principles*, 15.
[31] Ramm, *Protestant Biblical Interpretation*, 98.
[32] Wood, *Luther's Principles*, 24.

simple, seminal and certain literal sense.'[33]

This principle has been summed up in a few words by a twentieth century Protestant interpreter: "When the plain sense of Scripture makes common sense, seek no other sense."[34] Ramm seems to regard this interpretive method as a logical extension of Luther's second principle of the perspicuity of Scripture when he writes the following: "Luther said that the external clarity of Holy Scripture was its grammatical clarity. If an interpreter properly follows what has been called 'the laws of language,' or 'the rights of language,' he can know what the Scriptures specifically mean."[35]

Similarly, another classical work which describes this Protestant method of interpretation is Milton Spenser Terry's *Biblical Hermeneutics*. In it, he describes the grammatical-historical hermeneutic using the following language:

> The grammatico-historical sense of a writer is such an interpretation of his language as is required by the laws of grammar and the facts of history. Sometimes we speak of the literal sense, by which we mean the most simple, direct, and ordinary meaning of phrases and sentences. By this we usually denote a meaning opposed to the figurative or metaphorical. The grammatical sense is essentially the same as the literal.[36]

The grammatical-historical interpretive method then serves as the necessary counterpart to Luther's understanding of "the external clearness of the Holy Scripture."[37] In other words, it is not enough for Scripture to merely speak using plain language, but it must also be read and understood according to that very same manner in which it was given in order for Protestant interpretation to occur. In affirmation of this hermeneutical

---

[33] Wood, *Luther's Principles*, 24.

[34] David L. Cooper, *What Men Must Believe* (Los Angeles, CA: Biblical Research Society, 1943), 63.

[35] Ramm, *Protestant Biblical Interpretation*, 98.

[36] Milton Spenser Terry, *Biblical Hermeneutics: A Treatise on the Interpretation of the Old and New Testaments* (1883; repr., New York: Eaton and Mains, 1890), 101.

[37] Luther, *Bondage of the Will*, sect. 34.

method, Luther once more appeals to reason when he writes: "If the Scripture be obscure or ambiguous, what need was there for its being sent down from heaven? Are we not obscure and ambiguous enough in ourselves, without an increase of obscurity, ambiguity, and darkness being sent down unto us from heaven?"[38]

Luther, along with John Calvin and as many others as walked in the tradition of the reformers, accepted this principle of interpretive methodology which assigned to the text that plain and ordinary sense that the grammar, as used in its historical context, would convey in normal-everyday usage regardless of whether the source were mundane or divine. The German doctor felt so strongly about this that he wrote: "they who deny the all-clearness and all-plainness of the Scriptures, leave us nothing else but darkness."[39]

At this point a brief sample may serve well to reveal Luther's interpretive methodology applied to the Epistle of Paul to the Romans:

What conclusion then remains to be drawn...The words are plain—the division is certain—nothing can be said against it.

Sect. 139.—BUT let us hear Paul, who is his own interpreter. In the third chapter, drawing up, as it were, a conclusion . . . What would the 'invented interpretations' of the whole world do against this all-clear sentence? . . . Here let him that can produce his 'convenient interpretation,' invent 'tropes,' and pretend that the words 'are ambiguous and obscure!'[40]

It can be seen from the strong language that Luther employs here that for every bit as much as he affirms the normal-grammatical method of interpretation, he just as strongly denounces what he sees as its alternative, namely, the allegorical method of interpretation.

11.3.1 The Rejection of Allegory as a Valid Interpretive Method

Luther's vehemence toward the allegorical method of interpretation was not one that resulted from unfamiliarity with the despised hermeneutic.

---

[38] Luther, *Bondage of the Will*, sect. 36.
[39] Ibid., sect. 36.
[40] Ibid., sect. 138–140.

To the contrary, he had witnessed it from the papal edicts of Leo X to Johann Tetzel's merchandizing of indulgences. Wood notes that "For a thousand years the Church had buttressed its theological edifice by means of an authoritative exegesis which depended upon allegory as its chief medium of interpretation."[41] Moreover, he had personally been trained to utilize it in his monastic training prior to his conversion to Christ. Concerning this, Wood writes:

> From his own experience he knew the futility of allegorization: 'mere jugglery', 'a merry game', 'monkey tricks'—that is how he stigmatizes it. He had suffered much from that sort of pseudo-exposition of which Dr. John Lowe speaks so trenchantly, where 'anything can mean anything'. 'When I was a monk', Luther frankly acknowledges, 'I was adept in allegory. I allegorized everything. But after lecturing on the Epistle to the Romans, I came to have some knowledge of Christ. For therein I saw that Christ is no allegory, and learned to know what Christ was.'[42]

Nevertheless, despite all of the lucidity that the reformer demonstrated in his affirmation of the necessity for adherence to the normal grammatical-historical method and his repudiation of the allegorical method of interpretation, Dockery rightly observed: "his theoretical rules were better than the outworking of them."[43] Moreover, Roy Zuck affirmed the same, noting: "Though Luther vehemently opposed the allegorizing of Scripture, he too occasionally allegorized. For instance, he stated that Noah's ark is an allegory of the church."[44]

11.4 The Christocentric Hermeneutic

These critiques offered by Dockery and Zuck serve well to introduce the seventh and final principle of Luther's biblical interpretation: the Chris-

---

[41] Wood, *Luther's Principles*, 25.

[42] Ibid.

[43] Dockery, "Martin Luther's Christological Hermeneutics," 193.

[44] Roy B. Zuck, *Basic Bible Interpretation: A Practical Guide to Discovering Biblical Truth* (Colorado Springs, CO: David C. Cook, 1991), 45.

tocentric hermeneutic or the perceived centrality of Christ in all of Scripture. Robert Preus offers a favorable view of the reformer's use of this principle; therefore, his perspective serves as a good place to start:

> Like the church fathers, Luther saw the Scriptures as Christocentric in their entire sweep and soteriological in their purpose...To Luther, "Christ is the sum and truth of Scripture." "The Scriptures from beginning to end do not reveal anyone besides the Messiah, the Son of God, who should come and through His sacrifice carry and take away the sins of the world." "The entire Scripture points only to Christ."[45]

For Luther, both the Old and New Testaments, as well as everything in them, center on Christ. Wood observes that "[for Luther] this Christocentric orientation of Scripture is raised to a major hermeneutical principle. 'If, then, you would interpret well and truly, set Christ before you,' Luther advises, 'for He is the man to Whom it all applies.'"[46]

For the past 500 years, Protestants have largely embraced this seventh principle of Luther's Christocentric hermeneutic, along with all of the others which preceded it. The uncritical acceptance of this principle is evidenced in Preus' quote, above, which claims that Luther's perspective is shared by "the church fathers." Moreover, Preus goes on to claim: "The principle of the Christocentricity of Scripture was not something Luther inherited from the early church and then superimposed on the Scriptures. He derived the principle from Scripture itself; He found Christ there inductively through sound and serious exegesis."[47]

Not all Reformed interpreters have so unreservedly lauded Luther's exegetical method, however. Louis Berkhof, in his *Principles of Biblical Interpretation* observed that Luther's "hermeneutical rules were far better than his exegesis. Though he was not willing to recognize any but the literal sense, and scornfully spoke of the allegorical interpretation as *Affenspiel*, he did

---

[45] Robert D. Preus, "The View of the Bible Held by the Church: The Early Church through Luther," in *Inerrancy*, ed. Normal L. Geisler (Grand Rapids, MI: Zondervan, 1980), 374.

[46] Wood, *Luther's Principles*, 33–34.

[47] Preus, "The View of the Bible Held by the Church," 375.

not entirely steer clear of the despised method." [48] That is to say, despite Luther's appeal to a plain-sense interpretation of Scripture, and his adamant rejection of fanciful allegory and mystical meanings behind a text, Luther may have inadvertently shut-and-barred the front door while leaving the rear-entry ajar. It therefore seems necessary at this point to carry on in that very same spirit of the reformers, and to offer a critical evaluation of this seventh principle, to determine whether it is possible to be "convinced by the testimony of Scripture, or by the clearest reasoning,"[49] and to assess whether these things be of men or of God.

11.4.1 Critique of the Christocentric Hermeneutic

It should be noted at this point that it is not necessary for a Christ-honoring reading of Scripture to be one which seeks to find Christ in every verse, or even every chapter of the Bible in order for Him to have the place of preeminence throughout the whole thing. It is one thing to say: "All of Scripture testifies to Christ," and yet it is quite another to say: "All Scriptures testify to Christ." The first claim communicates that the Scriptures as a whole speak to Christ, while the second claim implies that the Scriptures in each individual part speak of Christ.[50] Luther assumed a position that more closely reflects the latter idea: "All Scriptures testify to Christ."

In his evaluation of Luther's Christological hermeneutics, David Dockery risks being too charitable when he remarks: "Practically, it may be concluded that Luther's rule is true; exegetically, it leads to difficulties."[51] Farrar's assessment strikes truer: "It is exegetical fraud to read developed Christian dogmas between the lines of Jewish narratives. It may be morally edifying but it is historically false...We cannot find the New Testament in

---

[48] Louis Berkhof, *Principles of Biblical Interpretation* (1950; repr., Grand Rapids, MI: Baker Book House, 1973), 26; c.f. Dockery, "Martin Luther's Christological Hermeneutics," 194.

[49] d'Aubigné, *History of the Reformation*, 245.

[50] This is commonly referred to as the fallacy of division, which ascribes to the individual parts that which is true of the whole. J. L. Mackie, "Fallacies," in *Encyclopedia of Philosophy*, ed. Donald M. Borchert, 2nd ed. (Detroit, MI: Macmillan Reference, 2006), 3:537–550.

[51] Dockery, "Martin Luther's Christological Hermeneutics," 193.

the ordinary historic narratives of the Old without large recourse to some form or other of the figurative interpretation which Luther had so decisively rejected."[52]

Despite the approval of Preus concerning Luther's Christocentric hermeneutic, he cannot help but admit that: "It was just his failure to find Christ and justification by faith in certain books of the Old and New Testaments (all *antilegomena*) that prompted Luther to depreciate the value of these books and question their canonicity."[53] In other words, when Luther's hermeneutical principle did not yield the kind of results he had expected, he displayed a tendency to call into question Scripture, itself, rather than his own interpretive method.

On account of this strained hermeneutical principle, the reformer came to regard some parts of Scripture to be less inspired than others. Those biblical books which fit Luther's criteria were elevated to a level of super-Scripture while others were regarded as mere straw.[54] It must be observed

---

[52] Farrar, *History of Interpretation*, 334–335.

[53] Preus, "The View of the Bible Held by the Church," 375.

[54] Farrar notes: "There were books of Scripture which failed to come up to his test of canonicity, and when this was the case, he unhesitatingly placed them in a lower position. Had he accepted an infallible canon it could only have been on a human tradition which he fundamentally refused to recognize as authoritative. 'That which does not teach Christ is not apostolic,' he said, 'even if a Peter or a Paul taught it.' Hence he put some books far above others in value. He declared that St. Paul's Epistles were more a gospel than Matthew, Mark, and Luke, and that St. John's Gospel, the Epistle to the Romans, and the First Epistle of Peter were 'the right kernel and marrow of all books.' He has little to say of the Book of Esther. He saw the complete historic inferiority of the Book of Chronicles as compared with the Book of Kings. He saw that some of the Old Testament books had passed through revising hands. He refused to believe that Solomon could have written Canticles. He points out the unchronological order of the present arrangement of the Book of Jeremiah. Believing that all the prophets had built on the one foundation, he thought that there was hay and stubble as well as gold and precious stones in the superstructure. He was evidently startled and perplexed by the story of Jonah. He regarded the Book of Job as a drama in glorification of resignation. He believed that the Book of Ecclesiastes belonged to the time of the Maccabees. He considered one of St. Paul's proofs in the Galatians too weak to hold. Of the Epistle to the Hebrews, he said, 'Who wrote it is unknown, but also it does not matter.' He believed the Epistle of St. Jude to be unnecessary, second-hand, and non-

that these conclusions were reached no less out of a devotion to honor Christ in the reading of Scripture. Yet the end result was one which marginalized the Word of God—placing the reader as not merely Scripture's interpreter, but as its arbiter.

11.5 Conclusion

What then may be concluded from a review of the hermeneutical foundation of *sola Scriptura* as it was modeled by Martin Luther 500 years ago? First, it should be noted that the Reformation principle of *sola Scripture* was intrinsically linked to the hermeneutical methodology which the reformers themselves employed. These principles which have been enumerated above include: (1) the authority of Scripture; (2) the sufficiency of Scripture; (3) the perspicuity of Scripture; (4) the requirement of faith and spiritual illumination; (5) an affirmation of the literal or grammatical-historical interpretive method; (6) the rejection of allegory as a valid interpretive method; and finally (7) the Christocentric principle which perceived the centrality of Christ in all of Scripture.

The critical evaluation offered above serves to reveal an inconsistency of Luther's hermeneutical method which many Protestant and Reformed interpreters are sometimes reluctant to acknowledge. Specifically, Luther's Christocentric hermeneutic risks undermining all of those essential principles which precede it. It is, therefore, the conclusion of this paper that Protestant interpreters today who seek to follow in the footsteps of the reformers would do well to follow the six points enumerated above while steering clear of a forced Christocentric hermeneutic which threatens to undermine the perspicuity of Scripture, the adherence to a literal or grammatical-historical interpretive method, and finally the rejection of allegory

---

apostolic. He called the Epistle of St. James a right strawy epistle and one which flatly (*stracks*) contradicted St. Paul, and he did not believe it to be written by an Apostle at all. Of the Apocalypse he said that 'his spirit could not accommodate itself to the book, and that it was insufficient reason for the small esteem in which he held it, that Christ was neither taught in it nor recognized.' He classed it with Esdras, and did not believe it to be inspired. He thought it a matter of no consequence whether Moses had written the Pentateuch or not. Thus without the least hesitation he sought for the canon within the canon." Farrar, *History of Interpretation*, 335–336.

as a valid method of interpretation.

Bibliography

Bainton, Roland. *Here I Stand: A Life of Martin Luther*. 1950. Reprint, Nashville, TN: Abingdon Press, 2013.

Berkhof, Louis. *Principles of Biblical Interpretation*. 1950. Reprint, Grand Rapids, MI: Baker Book House, 1973.

Bray, Gerald. *Biblical Interpretation: Past and Present*. Downers Grove, IL: IVP Academics, 1996.

Cooper, David L. *What Men Must Believe*. Los Angeles, CA: Biblical Research Society, 1943.

d'Aubigné, J. H. Merle. *History of the Reformation of the Sixteenth Century*. Translated by Henry White. 1846. Reprint, Rapidan, VA: Hartland Publications, n.d.

Dockery, David S. "Martin Luther's Christological Hermeneutics." *Grace Theological Journal* 4, no. 2 (Fall 1983): 209–225.

Durant, Will. *The Story of Civilization*. Vol. 4, *The Reformation: A History of European Civilization from Wyclif to Calvin 1300–1564*. New York: Simon and Schuster, 1957.

Farrar, Frederic W. *History of Interpretation*. 1886. Reprint, Grand Rapids, MI: Baker Book House, 1961.

Hagen, Kenneth. "Martin Luther." In *Historical Handbook of Major Biblical Interpreters*, edited by Donald K. McKim, 212–220. Downers Grove, IL: InterVaristy Press, 1998.

Luther, Martin. *De Servo Arbitrio: The Bondage of the Will*. Translated by Henry Cole. 1525. Reprint, The Sovereign Grace Union, 1931. Accessed April 13, 2017. https://www.monergism.com/thethreshold/sdg/pdf/luther_arbitrio.pdf.

Mackie, J. L. "Fallacies." In *Encyclopedia of Philosophy*, edited by Donald M. Borchert, 3:537–550. 2nd ed. Detroit, MI: Macmillan Reference, 2006.

Preus, Robert D. "The View of the Bible Held by the Church: The Early Church through Luther." In *Inerrancy*, edited by Normal L. Geisler, 355–382. Grand Rapids, MI: Zondervan, 1980.

Ramm, Bernard. *Protestant Biblical Interpretation: A Textbook of Hermeneutics.* 3rd rev. ed. 1950. Reprint, Grand Rapids, MI: Baker Book House, 1970.

Schaff, Phillip. *History of the Christian Church.* Vol. 7. 1888. Reprint, Peabody, MA: Hendrickson Publishers, 1996.

Terry, Milton Spenser. *Biblical Hermeneutics: A Treatise on the Interpretation of the Old and New Testaments.* 1883. Reprint, New York: Eaton and Mains, 1890.

Virkler, Henry A. *Hermeneutics: Principles and Processes of Biblical Interpretation.* Grand Rapids, MI: Baker Book House, 1981.

Wood, A. Skevington. *Luther's Principles of Biblical Interpretation.* London: The Tyndale Press, 1960.

Zuck, Roy B. *Basic Bible Interpretation: A Practical Guide to Discovering Biblical Truth.* Colorado Springs, CO: David C. Cook, 1991.

12

NEITHER WOODENLY-LITERAL NOR ALLEGORICAL:
The Dispensationalist Legacy of the Reformers' Doctrine of *Sola Scriptura*

Jeremiah Mutie
Southern California Seminary

12.0 Introduction

The fundamental assertion of nearly all Protestant biblical hermeneutics is that it owes its impetus to the Reformation cry of the first of the five *solas*: *sola Scriptura,* and its accompanying doctrine of the perspicuity of Scripture. What is not so clear, however, is how the principle of *sola Scriptura* has been adopted into in the hermeneutics of the Reformation posterity. That is, while extreme literalists have adopted it in such a way that their hermeneutics led to various failed predictions of the second advent, others also claiming to be the proper descendants of the tradition of the reformers have been unable to completely break away from the allegorical shackles of the medieval times.

After re-orienting the reader on some of the basic tenets of the principle of *sola Scriptura*, this chapter will briefly trace the adoption of this principle together with its attendant doctrine of the perspicuity of Scripture in these main Protestant traditions: Reformed tradition (Calvinism), Lutheranism, the Millerite tradition and dispensationalism. In so doing, the argument will be made that, in all these traditions, it is dispensationalism that has remained true to the spirit of this grand Reformation principle in its hermeneutics by neither reverting to the pre-Reformation allegorism nor swerving to the woodenly-literal hermeneutics of the Millerite traditions.[1]

12.0.1 Some Brief Definitions

In his contribution to The Five Solas Series entitled *God's Word Alone: The Authority of Scripture*, Matthew Barrett reminds his reader of some of the key tenets of the reformers' principle of *sola Scriptura*. First, as he notes, the principle "means that Scripture alone is our *final* authority."[2] For the reformers, the principle was not *nuda Scriptura*, that is, "only Authority," but that Scripture is the *final* authority. Second, Barrett notes that, for the reformers, *sola Scriptura* means that "Scripture alone is our *sufficient* authority."[4] Thus, according to the reformers, "Not only is the Bible our final authority, but it is the authority that provides believers with all the truth they need for salvation and following after Christ."[5] Finally, *sola Scriptura* also "means that only Scripture, because it is God's inspired Word, is our inerrant authority."[6]

In all fairness to Martin Luther, one should remember that, as Lotz notes, he "never offered a comprehensive, systematic formulation of the concept of biblical authority,"[7] a task left for John Calvin to complete in his

---

[1] The Millerite traditions refer to the followers of William Miller (February 15, 1782–December 20, 1849), who, after what is known as the Great Disappointment of October 22, 1844 (when, according to the Millerites, Christ was supposed to come again but did not), branched into several ecclesial groups. Key among them are the Freewill Baptists, the Advent Christian Church and the Seventh-day Adventists. The chapter concerns itself with the earliest stages of the movement (1800s).

[2] Mathew Barret, *God's Word Alone: The Authority of Scripture: What the Reformers Taught...and Why It Still Matters*, The Five Solas Series (Grand Rapids, MI: Zondervan, 2016), 23.

[3] Ibid.

[4] Ibid. While the reformers recognized the existence of other sources, they accorded them their proper place in doing theology: a secondary status compared to the Word of God.

[5] Ibid.

[6] Ibid., 24.

[7] David W. Lotz, "Sola Scriptura: Luther on Biblical Authority," *Interpretation* 35, no. 3 (1981): 259.

Institutes.[8] However, by the time the various key Reformation creeds were

---

[8] For Luther, the principle of *sola Scriptura* was more or less like a rallying call for the return to the Word of God. This is how Theo Engelder described this battle cry in a volume celebrating four hundred years of the Reformation in 1916: "The divine truths which, voiced by Luther, awakened men from death (for only a Romanist will speak of a mere lethargy in this connection) were, first, *Sola Scriptura*. This was the reassuring answer given to the insistent cry of men: Who shall tell us the truth, God's truth, in the matter concerning our soul's salvation? The very first words of Luther spoken before the world at large proclaimed this principle. It found utterance in the opening words of the *95 Theses*, 'When our Lord and Master Jesus said—,' and in their conclusion, 'I am not so senseless as to be willing that the Word of God should be made to give place to fables, devised by human reason.' Those were strange words for that day and generation." Theo Engelder, "The Three Principles of the Reformation: Sola Scriptura, Sola Gratia, Sola Fides," in *Four Hundred Years: Commemorative Essays on the Reformation of Dr. Martin Luther and Its Blessed Results*, ed. W. H. T. Dau (St. Louis, MO: Concordia, 1916), 98. For an elaborate exposition of the principle of *sola Scriptura* by Calvin, see John Calvin, *Institutes of the Christian Religion*, ed. John T. McNeil (Philadelphia, PA: Westminster Press, 1960), 1:69–96. On this last point, Calvin wrote: "But a most pernicious error widely prevails that Scripture has only so much weight as if conceded to it by the consent of the church. As if the eternal and inviolable truth of God depended upon the decision of men! For they mock the Holy Spirit when they ask: Who can convince us that these writings came from God? Who can assure us that Scripture has come down whole and intact even to our very day? Who can persuade us to receive one book in reverence but to exclude another, unless the church prescribe a sure rule for all these matters? What reverence is due Scripture and what books ought to be reckoned within its canon depend, they say, upon the determination of the church. Thus these sacrilegious men, wishing to impose an unbridled tyranny under the cover of the church, do not care with what absurdities they ensnare themselves and others, provided they can force this one idea upon the simple-minded." Ibid., 75. He concludes by insisting that the doctrine of scriptural perspicuity is enshrined in the illumination of the Holy Spirit who speaks through the Word. He writes: "In this manner Christ opened the minds of two of his disciples [Luke 24:27, 45], not that they should cast away the Scriptures and become wise of themselves, but that they should know the Scriptures. Similarly Paul, while he urges the Thessalonians not to 'quench the Spirit' [1 Thess 5:19–20], does not loftily catch them up to empty speculations without the Word, but immediately adds that prophets are not to be despised. By this, no doubt, he intimates that the light of the Spirit is put out as soon as prophecies fall into contempt. What say these fanatics, swollen with pride, who consider this the one excellent illumination when, carelessly forsaking and bidding farewell to God's Word,

composed, the principle of *sola Scriptura* had been firmly fleshed out. *The Westminster Confession of Faith* (1646), for example, states in chapter 1.10:

> The supreme judge by which all controversies of religion are to be determined, and all decrees of councils, opinions of ancient writers, doctrines of men, and private spirits, are to be examined, and in whose sentence we are to rest, can be no other but the Holy Spirit speaking in the Scripture.[9]

Similarly, *The Gallican (French) Confession of Faith* (1559), Article V states:

> Whence it follows that no authority, whether of antiquity, or custom, or numbers, or human wisdom, or judgments, or proclamations, or edicts, or decrees, or councils, or visions, or miracles, should be opposed to these Holy Scriptures, but, on the contrary, all things should be examined, regulated, and reformed according to them.[10]

This understanding of the Scriptures, clearly a reflection of the Reformation principle of *sola Scriptura*, is evident in all the major confessions of faith within the Protestant tradition. "For the Reformers," therefore, as Hannah writes, "the quest for personal faith led to the rejection of 'false' tradition and the embrace of the Bible"[11] as the final authority.

---

they, no less confidently than boldly, seize upon whatever they may have conceived while snoring? Certainly, a far different sobriety befits the children of God, bereft of the whole light of truth, so are not unaware that the Word is the instrument by which the Lord dispenses the illumination of his Spirit to believers. For they know no other Spirit than him who dwelt and spoke in the apostles, and by whose oracles they are continually recalled to the hearing of the Word." Ibid., 96. For Calvin, therefore, a proper appropriation of the perspicuity of Scripture precludes both unscriptural declarations of church councils and popes and the fanatical prophecies of religious enthusiasts outside the Word of God.

[9] John H. Leith, ed. *Creeds of the Churches: A Reader in Christian Doctrine from the Bible to the Present* (Louisville, KY: Westminster John Knox, 1982), 196.

[10] Philip Schaff, *The Evangelical Protestant Creeds, with Translations*, vol. 3, *The Creeds of Christendom: With a History and Critical Notes* (Grand Rapids, MI: Baker Books, 1983), 362.

[11] John Hannah, *Our Legacy: The History of Christian Doctrine* (Colorado Springs, CO: NavPress, 2001), 57.

As noted above, for the reformers the doctrine of scriptural perspicuity was the foundation upon which the principle of *sola Scriptura* was based. While the doctrine of the perspicuity of Scripture simply means, "the Bible is a plain book,"[12] the phrase needs further elaboration since, as some have joked, with time, "the term is not very perspicuous anymore."[13] Hodge provided this elaboration when he wrote, "Protestants hold that the Bible, being addressed to the people, is sufficiently perspicuous to be understood by them, under the guidance of the Holy Spirit; and that they are entitled and bound to search the Scripture, and to judge for themselves what is its true meaning."[14] Callahan notes that there are a number of key assumptions or themes embedded in the doctrine of the perspicuity of Scripture. He writes:

> The significant themes attached to the advocacy of perspicuity include the belief that (1) Scripture is a clear and certain rule of faith since no necessary doctrine is obscure, (2) clarity is a necessity since Scripture alone is the means of saving faith, (3) Scripture functions as its own interpreter with the unclear being explained by the clear, (4) perspicuity is only limited by human sin and ignorance, and (5) Scripture must be clear because God, its author, can only speak clearly and understandably. Each assertion is predicated upon a consensual perception of Scripture's authority within Protestant hermeneutics: Scripture is clear because it is read as (if it is) clear.[15]

Understood this way, the doctrine of the perspicuity of Scripture may actually imply that there is no need for hermeneutics. However, from the very start, "Protestants conceded that perspicuity was never intended to supplant the necessity of interpretation."[16] Rather, as a guardrail against Rome's insistence on Scriptural obscurity, this doctrine actually lends itself naturally

---

[12] Larry D. Pettegrew, "The Perspicuity of Scripture," *The Master's Seminary Journal* 15, no. 2 (2004): 209.

[13] Ibid., 209.

[14] Charles Hodge, *Systematic Theology* (Grand Rapids, MI: Eerdmans, n.d.) 1:183.

[15] James Patrick Callahan, "*Claritas Scripturae*: The Role of Perspicuity in Protestant Hermeneutics," *Journal of the Evangelical Theological Society* 29, no. 3 (1996): 356.

[16] Ibid.

to a literal-grammatical interpretation of Scripture. Callahan continues, "The Protestant assertion of Scripture's clarity both assumes and transcends literary and grammatical analysis of the text."[17] In Luther's mind, for example, "the message of Scripture is presented in its literal or historical sense, and it is accessible according to the confession of its clarity."[18] Thus, these hermeneutical assertions "buttressed the Reformer's rejection of ecclesiastical tradition and authority and codified the fundamental theological relationship of Scripture's character as revelation from God, its grammatical form, and its accessibility and clarity within Protestant hermeneutics."[19]

Right from its start, Protestant hermeneutics (at least in theory), was a literal-grammatical hermeneutic. The Protestant principle of *sola Scriptura* and its attendant doctrine of the perspicuity of Scripture, would lead nowhere else. The contention of this chapter, however, is that only dispensationalism and its hermeneutics have continued to adhere to the letter and spirit of the Reformation principle of *sola Scriptura* and the doctrine of the perspicuity of Scripture. Although this cannot be said of all forms of dispensationalists today, it is certainly true of a significant group of believers within dispensationalism. To sustain this claim, a brief presentation of the status of Lutheran, Reformed and Millerite hermeneutics will be made. These will be contrasted with the literal-grammatical hermeneutics of dispensationalism. In so doing, the chapter will be correcting the problem that Lotz succinctly captures when, referring to the appropriation of the principle of *sola Scriptura*, makes this observation, "Scholarship in this area has been plagued by anachronistic attempts to link Luther's position with latter-day biblicistic fundamentalism or with modern biblical criticism."[20] He adds, "No other topic in Luther's theology has been so liable to misinterpretation through incautious assertion and tendentious argument."[21]

---

[17] Callahan, "*Claritas Scripturae*," 362.

[18] Ibid. We must admit, however, that for Luther, because of his Christological hermeneutics, ultimately Christ was the *sensus plenior* of every Scripture.

[19] Ibid.

[20] Lotz, "Sola Scriptura," 259–60.

[21] Ibid., 260.

12.1 *Sola Scriptura* in Reformed and Lutheran Traditions

While, on the one hand, all confessional creeds on the doctrine of Scripture continued to imply adherence to the principle of *sola Scriptura* and the perspicuity of Scripture, on the other hand, a gradual hermeneutical shift within many of these traditions emerged. That is, with time, in these traditions, gradually, dogmatics overtook hermeneutics. Ernst F. Kevan captured this subtle shift noting in 1958 the following:

> Those who immediately followed the Reformation retained the sound principle of the interpretation of Scripture by Scripture. While they refused, however, to submit exegesis to the domination of ecclesiastical tradition as formulated by councils and popes, they, nonetheless "were in danger of leading it into bondage to the confessional standards of the Church. ... Exegesis became the hand-maid of dogmatics and degenerated into a mere search for proof-texts."[22]

With this gradual shift, most confessional faiths have moved further from the reformers' principle of *sola Scriptura*.

Concerning the differences between these two traditions born out of the Protestant Reformation—Lutheranism and the Reformed traditions—Leith writes:

> The designation "Reformed" refers to those Reformation churches that have their source in the work of Zwingli and Calvin. In one sense all Reformation churches are reformed, but the term is applied more strictly to the churches that are related to Zwingli and Calvin because they were more radical in the reform of the Church according to the Word of God than were Lutherans.[23]

Because of this emphasis on the Word of God, Leith notes that the early Reformed churches produced a significant amount of creeds and confessions of faith.[24]

---

[22] Ernest F. Kevan, "The Principles of Interpretation," in *Revelation and the Bible*, ed. Carl F. H. Henry, Contemporary Evangelical Thought (Grand Rapids, MI: Baker Book House, 1958), 291.

[23] Leith, *Creeds of the Churches*, 127.

[24] Ibid., 127.

12.1.1 Reformed Tradition and Sola Scriptura

In an article discussing if there is "something unique...that warrants the label 'Reformed'"[25] for Reformed theology, Fred Klooster notes there are difficulties in identifying its uniqueness. After surveying such Reformed characteristics as its being "authentic biblical Christianity," he observes that such kinds of tenets are not unique to Reformed theology: they are common to the Protestant Christian movement within Christianity.[26] He wonders if this "something unique" can found by listing the main representatives of Reformed theology, such as: H. Bavinck, A. Kuyper, L. Berkhof, C. Van Til, G. C. Berkouwer, C. Hodge, B. B. Warfield and W. Shedd, among others; or even through "the key doctrines or major theological themes which Reformed theologians have generally emphasized in distinction from other theologians."[27] Rejecting all of these approaches, he declares "the Scriptural principle" to be the "unique touchstone by which a theology may be properly classified as 'Reformed' in the historic sense of that term."[28]

So, what does Klooster mean by the term "Scriptural principle?" Elucidating further, he writes:

> The Scriptural principle involves both *sola Scriptura* and *tota Scriptura*, and the complex question of hermeneutics is raised. The difference between Reformed and Lutheran interpretation of Scripture on the presence of Christ in the sacraments was fundamentally a question of hermeneutics. Indeed, the full meaning of "the Scriptural principle" has become problematical in our day.[29]

While it is not very clear here how Reformed hermeneutics really differs from Lutheran hermeneutics, what Klooster is hinting at is a difference that became observable earlier on in these traditions. This is observable in the works of Calvin himself. "If one searches Calvin's writings for a recurrent emphasis," writes Klooster, "this is what one finds: Speak where the

---

[25] Fred D. Klooster, "The Uniqueness of Reformed Theology: A Preliminary Attempt at Description," *Calvin Theological Journal* 14, no. 1 (April 1979): 32.

[26] Ibid., 32–33.

[27] Ibid., 34.

[28] Ibid., 38.

[29] Ibid., 39.

Scriptures speak; be silent where they are silent."[30] In other words, *sola Scriptura* appears to be itself taken as the hermeneutical principle in need of no further elaboration. This is akin to how the Lutheran theologian, Gerhard Ebeling, described *sola Scriptura* as the hermeneutic basis for the Reformation, when he wrote, "The Reformers' principle of Scripture does not therefore need to be supplemented by a hermeneutic principle in the sense of a material principle guiding the interpretation of Scripture, but the Scripture principle itself, as such, is a hermeneutic principle."[31]

However, over time, Klooster argues the Reformed tradition abandoned the "Scriptural principle." Although it may not be possible to pinpoint exactly when this took place, it seems clear that when Karl Barth addressed the Emden audience in 1923 the "Scriptural principle" had largely been abandoned.[32] In this lecture to the General Assembly of the German Reformed Church, Barth expressed the idea that "Authentic Reformed perspectives were abandoned through the influences of Orthodoxy, Pietism, the Enlightenment and Liberalism."[33] Indeed, Klooster does not see the situation as having changed much in the many years since that famous address by Barth. "How contemporary these words Barth wrote in 1923 sound today!"[34] Klooster adds, "If anything, our situation has only expanded the dimensions of the prison. The roof has now more than four cornerstones, but it is still the roof of a prison. The challenge facing Reformed churches and Reformed theologians today is staggering in its dimensions."[35]

The question is this: where does Reformed theology stand today as far as *sola Scriptura* and the doctrine of the perspicuity of Scripture is concerned? It seems that the continued insistence on covenantalism as the organizing principle of Scripture has obscured the embedded principle of a literal-grammatical interpretation of the Bible. For example, in a recent book on Reformed hermeneutics by members of the faculty of Westminster

---

[30] Klooster, "Uniqueness of Reformed Theology," 39.

[31] Gerhard Ebeling, *The Word of God and Tradition: Historical Studies Interpreting the Divisions of Christianity*, trans. S. H. Hooke (Philadelphia, PA: Fortress, 1964), 127.

[32] Klooster, "Uniqueness of Reformed Theology," 46.

[33] Ibid.

[34] Ibid.

[35] Ibid., 46–47.

Theological Seminary, Peter Lillback writes, "These classic Reformed emphases on the covenantal unity of the Bible highlight the necessity of an
organic Christ-centered interpretation of Scripture."[36] In a stunning paragraph in the same work which attempts to define the reformers' doctrine of
the perspicuity of Scripture, G. K. Beale locates its meaning in the "intentions" of God in giving His Word to man. He writes:

> The divine authorial intentions communicated through the human
> authors of Scripture are accessible to contemporary readers. Though
> no one can comprehend these intentions exhaustively, we can under-
> stand them sufficiently, especially for the purposes of salvation, sanc-
> tification (growth in faith, love, and hope), and the glorification of
> God. The Reformers argued for this understanding of the perspicuity
> or clarity of Scripture, rejecting medieval Catholicism's method of in-
> terpretation, which allowed interpreters to read their own meanings
> into Scripture.[37]

The reader cannot help but notice that the entire concept of the Bible as a
"plain book" is missing in this definition of Scriptural perspicuity. Neither
is the concept of the literal grammatical-historical method of biblical interpretation—which was a corollary of the reformers' concept of the perspicuity
of Scripture—mentioned anywhere (nowhere does the book even use the
words "literal" or "grammatical"). All aspects of the perspicuity of Scripture
seem to have been subsumed under the concept of the sufficiency of Scripture.

Reformed theology has abandoned the concept of the literal grammatical-historical method of biblical interpretation, though this method was
clearly embedded into the Reformation doctrine of the perspicuity of Scripture. In its creeds and other writings, Reformed theology continues to talk
about *sola Scriptura* and the perspicuity of Scripture, but in practice this is

---

[36] Peter A. Lillback, "Introduction," in *Seeing Christ in all of Scripture: Hermeneutics
at Westminster Theological Seminary*, ed. Peter A. Lillback (Philadelphia, PA: Westminster
Seminary Press, 2016), 6.

[37] G. K. Beale, "New Testament Hermeneutics," in *Seeing Christ in all of Scripture:
Hermeneutics at Westminster Theological Seminary*, ed. Peter A. Lillback (Philadelphia, PA:
Westminster Seminary Press, 2016), 30–31.

not the case.

12.1.2 Lutheran Tradition and Sola Scriptura

Without repeating many of the observations already made about the early Lutheran reformers and *sola Scriptura*, the question here is simply this: have Lutherans continued to hold onto this principle in their hermeneutics? Two recent articles, written by leading Lutheran scholars, answer this question with somewhat similar ideas.

In his article entitled, "How Lutherans Read the Bible," Dennis Olson argues that Lutherans—although still claiming to hold to the distinctives of "Scripture alone (*sola Scriptura*), the clarity and straightforward meaning of Scripture (*claritas scripturae*), [and] the capacity of Scripture to interpret itself (*sui ipsius interpres*),"[38] focus more on the function of Scripture instead of its meaning. He writes:

> Lutherans often emphasize less what the Bible means and emphasize more what the Bible does. More pointedly, what does God do with the Bible in, with and through God's people and God's church? Lutherans often tend to think of the Bible as primarily an instrument of the Holy Spirit who works through the power of the gospel (Rom 1:16) to shape and reshape people and communities, to wound and to heal, to kill and to make alive (Deut 32:39).[39]

According to him, the focus has shifted from the meaning of the Bible to its usage: "The performative use of human language," he writes, "the centrality of communication, the stretching of metaphors, and the use of paradox and dialectic, all play some role in what Lutherans think about when they think about the Bible and its role in shaping life, faith and theology."[40] For modern Lutheranism, the emphasis is more on what the Bible does (i.e., its functions) than on what it means (i.e., its interpretation).

---

[38] Dennis T. Olson, "How Lutherans Read the Bible: A North American and Global Conversation," *Dialog: A Journal of Theology* 45, no. 1 (Spring 2006): 4. Olson, an ordained Lutheran minister, is the Charles T. Haley Professor of Old Testament Theology at Princeton Theological Seminary, New Jersey.

[39] Ibid., 4.

[40] Ibid., 5.

In the same volume, H. Frederick Reisz, Jr., also argues that Lutherans today are more focused on how Bible reading shapes "communities of interpretation"[41] throughout Lutheran communities. There are varying opinions when it comes to Lutheran hermeneutics today; Reisz writes:

> Lutherans assert the crucial importance of the Bible. However, through the ages, competing and often violently disagreeing Lutheran theologies all have claimed a "Lutheran" hermeneutic. The assertion of the authority of the Bible in Lutheranism precedes actual biblical interpretation. However, in the practical life of the Church and much writing and discourse the two go together, even if distinguishable. In some instances, one suspects that the interpretation either denies the range of the Bible's authority either for the interpreter or her opponents.[42]

This language of a possible dichotomy between biblical authority and interpretation is a long stretch from the principle of the perspicuity of Scripture and the embedded principle of a literal grammatical-historical interpretation perceived by the reformers. For Luther the principle of *sui ipsius interpres* (Scripture interprets itself) meant that Scripture "is itself the source of understanding, illumination and certainty in the very measure in which it brings everything into light."[43] Luther did not talk about what comes first— biblical authority or interpretation: "Since the Word of God is the subject-matter of Holy Scripture, Scripture in the last resort does not require illumination, but is itself the source of enlightenment."[44] The nature of the Holy Scripture rules out such a conversation.

In an astonishing conclusion concerning the status of Lutheran hermeneutics today, Reisz throws up his hands:

> Characteristically, in the end, Lutheran hermeneutics throws itself upon God! We must trust and hope in the Word of God. We pray to

---

[41] H. Frederick Reisz Jr., "Reading the Bible in the Lutheran Tradition," *Dialog: A Journal of Theology* 45, no. 1 (Spring 2006): 21. Reisz is former President of Lutheran Theological Southern Seminary, Columbia, SC.

[42] Ibid.

[43] Ebeling, *Word of God*, 130–31.

[44] Ibid., 131.

the Holy Spirit to engraft us in Christ. We live in Christ as faithful servants of the Word of God for the mission of God in the world. We do our hermeneutical work anticipating that God will speak to us and at the same time, praying "Lord have mercy!" The authority of the Bible is the self-authenticating authority of the Word of God as it proclaims the Word in, and under the biblical texts, and as it also judges the human appropriation and specifications of those texts as it is the Word of God with those texts.[45]

While one certainly admires this humble approach to the Word of God by present-day Lutherans, humility in and of itself does not substitute for sound biblical principles of interpretation. Furthermore, this is very different from the reformers' concept of the clarity of Scripture.[46]

One observes that just as with Reformed theology, Lutheranism has not faired any better in appropriating the reformers' principle of *sola Scriptura* and the attendant doctrine of the perspicuity of Scripture. At this point, one asks, how have other adherents of Protestant Reformation, especially those that have insisted on the literal-grammatical method of interpretation, faired in appropriating this key principle in their hermeneutics? For the answer to this question, the two final groups will be considered: the Millerites

---

[45] Reisz, "Reading the Bible," 26.

[46] To be fair to Lutherans, this denomination has produced an unfair share of liberal theologians. One thinks of Adolf Harnack and Albrecht Ritschl here. Schleiermacher was a Moravian. Even, most significant is the fact that Luther's allowance for a double meaning of Scripture, possibly opened the way for this kind of hermeneutics that focuses not on the meaning of Scripture, but its use in "communities of interpretation." Ebeling summarized this Lutheran tenet thusly: "Luther further developed the hermeneutic significance of *sola scriptura* in his treatise *De Servo Arbitrio*, as an exposition of the double clarity of Scripture. Erasmus, making the use of the scholastic idea that some parts of Scripture were obscure, taught that in the last resort the doctrinal decisions of the Church, even if not understood, must be accepted; against this Luther set, as his '*primum principium*' [first principle], the clarity of Scripture which, in spite of individual obscurities, was the clarity of the content of Scripture, and in a double sense: namely, 'external clarity' of the *verbum externum* of public proclamation, and the 'inward clarity' of the illumination of the heart through the Holy Spirit." Ebeling, *Word of God*, 132. It seems clear that this latter understanding of Luther's *sola Scriptura* has taken dominance in current Lutheran hermeneutics.

and the dispensationalists.

12.2 The Millerite Tradition and *Sola Scriptura*

While both Reformed and Lutheran theological traditions have veered towards a non-literal appropriation of the reformers' principle of *sola Scriptura*, on the other end of the spectrum the Millerites pushed the principle to what may be referred to a "woodenly-literal" hermeneutics.[47] The meaning of the phrase will become clear in the succeeding discussion of the Millerite movement within Protestantism.

12.2.1 The Origins of the Millerites

The term "Millerite" is used to refer to a group of adherents of a Protestant Reformation movement that emerged, especially in 1800s America, based on the teachings of William Miller of Low Hampton, New York (1782–1849).[48] According to Earnest Sandeen, the development of this group in America coincided with the emergence of British millenarian movements (the age of John Nelson Darby).[49] Sandeen wonders about the striking similarities between the British millenarian movement and that of William Miller. "What is most striking about William Miller in this context," he writes, "is the degree of similarity—in content, style, and timing—between his witness and that of the British millenarians."[50] He continues by asking: "Is it only a coincidence that the excitement over the imminent second advent and the dawning millennium broke out in both Britain and America during 1828–32?"[51] He concludes his series of questions by asking: "Is it only a coincidence that a return to apostolic simplicity and power was being sought in both countries just at this time or that speaking in tongues

---

[47] I give credit to Dr. Glenn Kreider for the phrase "woodenly-literal." He briefly referred to it in our eschatology class in Dallas Seminary in 2004.

[48] C. Mervyn Maxwell, "A Brief History of Adventists Hermeneutics," *Journal of the Adventist Theological Society* 4, no. 2 (Autumn 1993): 209.

[49] Ernest R. Sandeen, *The Roots of Fundamentalism: British and American Millenarianism 1800–1930* (Chicago, IL: University of Chicago Press, 1970), 57.

[50] Ibid.

[51] Ibid.

and healing should become local sensations for a few months?"[52]

It is clear from these hypothetical questions that Sandeen seeks to tie the Millerites squarely to British millenarianism (specifically, Darbyism) in terms of content and style because of their literal hermeneutics. Is this connection accurate? The answer lies in a proper investigation of Millerite hermeneutics as a prelude to a discussion of Darbyism and subsequent dispensational hermeneutics.

12.2.2 Millerite Hermeneutics

William Miller laid down the foundation for later Millerite movements, including what became Adventism. Insisting that he was following the principles established during the Reformation which were not held by the liberal Protestant movement, Miller laid out a set of fourteen principles for the literal interpretation of the Bible. These principles resulted in the essential characteristics of Seventh-Day Adventism. "The essential characteristic doctrines [of Adventism]," writes Maxwell, "include the imminence and literalness of the premillennial second coming, the holiness of the seventh-day as the Sabbath, the unconscious sleep of the dead, the presence of spiritual gifts in the end-time (specifically in the ministry of Ellen G. White), and the datability of the pre-advent judgment to 1944."[53] With the exception of the first two tenets, one wonders how, through a literal-grammatical method of interpretation, the Millerites have arrived at the rest. The answer is found in their extreme literalism in the application of the reformers' literal interpretation. This insight is missing in Sandeen's treatment of both movements (Millerites and British millenarianism), leading him to make the remark that "Although the non-Millerite millenarians seldom became committed to a specific month and day [of the second advent], there was scarcely a year that passed without one or another millenarian expectation being disappointed."[54] The question that Sandeen seems to leave at the table is this: why did the non-Millerite millenarians not come up with a month or a day for the second advent, just as the Millerites were fond of

[52] Sandeen, *Roots of Fundamentalism*, 57.
[53] Maxwell, "A Brief History," 209.
[54] Sandeen, *Roots of Fundamentalism*, 59.

doing? One need not look beyond the Millerite's woodenly-literal hermeneutics to find an answer to this question.

It is not possible to explore in detail Miller's fourteen "Rules for Interpretation." In one way or the other, these have been explained further in
subsequent Adventism.[55] It seems that it was in the area of biblical typology
and the concept of the fulfillment of prophecy as a hermeneutical tool,
where Adventism became extremely literal in its hermeneutics. As Maxwell
notes, although Luther and some reformers "honored the historicist interpretation of prophecy, including the year-day principle,"[56] it was the Seventh-Day pioneers who "used that fulfillment principle as a hermeneutic
principle to further the development of their message."[57] Having now established it as their primary method of hermeneutics, Adventists now applied
the "fulfilment principle" to all areas of doctrine. Maxwell further observes,
"Once established as scriptural, the fulfillment of prophecy in the second
advent movement now became a hermeneutical tool for helping establish
the Sabbath, sanctuary, spiritual gifts, true church, second advent doctrines,
etc."[58]

It was because of this extreme application of fulfilled prophecy as a
tool of interpretation that, following the conclusion of John Aquila Brown
that the 2,300 years of Daniel 8 ended in 1844, William Miller set October
22, 1844 as the day for the second advent of Christ. This date has come to
be is referred to as the day of Great Disappointment. The results were dis-
astrous for the Millerite movement. David Bebbington comments:

> Thousands of humble followers prepared for the event, only to be dis-
> appointed on successive days during the two years [1843–1844, the
> window originally given by Miller for the second advent], A section of

---

[55] The reader will do well to consult Gordon M. Hyde, ed., *A Symposium on Biblical Hermeneutics* (Washington, DC: The Review and Publishing Association, 1974).
This document, prepared by the Biblical Research Committee of the General Conven-
tion of Seventh-Day Adventists, presents the general principles of interpretation that
undergird biblical interpretation within this group, "following largely in the Reformation tradition."

[56] Maxwell, "A Brief History," 214.

[57] Ibid.

[58] Ibid., 214–15.

them, however, retained the belief that the second coming could not be long delayed, evolving into two new denominations, the Seventh-Day Adventists and the Adventist Christians.[59]

Sandeen remarks, "After 1844 the historicist's position began to lose the almost undisputed position that it had held the first generation of the millenarian revival."[60]

Maxwell, noting that the Millerites were true to the hermeneutical principles of the reformers, wonders why they came to "some conclusions that differed markedly from those of the Reformers."[61] He argues that even the reformers themselves did not arrive at the same conclusions.[62] However, it seems that the problem was a woodenly-literal hermeneutic employed by the early Adventists. If this were not the case, a significant amount of William Miller's conclusions about certain key tenets of the Bible would not have needed correction. Among the Millerite doctrines rejected by Seventh-Day Adventism, Maxwell includes: the day to observe the Sabbath, the immortality of the soul, as well as the location of the sanctuary of Daniel 8:14.[63] A better question is, while Darby and other dispensationalists were part of this millenarian movement in both Britain and America at the same time, why did they not turn to date setting as far as the second advent of Christ was concerned? This was only possible because of dispensationalism's unequivocal adherence to the reformers' principle of *sola Scriptura* and its attendant doctrine of the perspicuity of Scripture with its embedded

---

[59] David W. Bebbington, *The Dominance of Evangelicalism: The Age of Spurgeon and Moody*. A History of Evangelicalism: People, Movements and Ideas in the English-Speaking World 3, ed. David W. Bebbington and Mark Noll (Downers Grove, IL: InterVarsity Press, 2005), 192.

[60] Sandeen, *Roots of Fundamentalism*, 60. Sandeen writes in an almost satirical style. For example, commenting on the millenarian idea of utilizing fulfilled prophecy as a hermeneutical tool, he wryly comments: "By adopting the year-day theory of interpretation for the 1,260 days of the book of Daniel and Revelation and identifying the tableaux of Revelation with contemporary events, these commentators found their credibility mortgaged to the future." Ibid., 60.

[61] Maxwell, "A Brief History," 212.

[62] Ibid., 212–13.

[63] Ibid., 220.

method of literal-grammatical-historical interpretation of Scripture.[64]

12.3 Darby, Dispensationalism and *Sola Scriptura*

In this final section, the topic will concern the adoption of *sola Scriptura* in dispensationalism. Perhaps the question should first be asked: what is dispensationalism and who are dispensationalists? Introducing their book, *Progressive Dispensationalism*, Craig A. Blaising and Darrell L. Bock note the widespread, albeit uncelebrated, dispensationalism among Protestant evangelical Christianity.[65] "If you are an evangelical Christian," they write, "it is most likely that you know some who call themselves dispensationalists. And it is just as likely that you have certain beliefs and interpretations of Scripture that have been shaped in some way by dispensationalism."[66] As Glenn Kreider observes, "Dispensationalism is a popular, and populist, movement,"[67] adding, "It has a huge influence in the evangelical culture due to pastors and churches, pamphlets and books, seminars

---

[64] It is important to note that this review of these theological systems is neither exhaustive nor monolithic. However, it is representative of the main tenets in these traditions. Indeed, even a cross-check of other main Reformation traditions that are not discussed here, yields the same results. Mention should be made here of Anglicanism as an example. Recent studies in the use of the Bible in Anglicanism worldwide have focused primarily in its application. For this observation, see Clare Amos, ed. *The Bible in the Life of the Church*, Canterbury Studies in Anglicanism, ed. Martyn Percy and Ian Markham (Norwich, England: Canterbury Press, 2013); Alexander Ross, "Gaping Gaps? Implications of the 'Bible in the Life of the Church' Project for Bridging the Anglican Hermeneutic Divide," *Journal of Anglican Studies* 12, no. 2 (November 2014): 143–64; Darren C. Marks, "The Windsor Report: A Theological Commentary," *Journal of Anglican Studies* 4, no. 2 (December 2006): 157–76.

[65] Craig A. Blaising and Darell L. Bock, *Progressive Dispensationalism* (Grand Rapids, MI: Baker Books, 2000), 9.

[66] Ibid. "The term *dispensationalism*," writes Blaising and Bock, "comes from the word *dispensation* which refers to a distinctive way in which God manages or arranges the relationship of human beings to Himself. Recognizing different dispensations in Scripture, such as the dispensation of Israel with its distinctive regulations and ceremonies and the dispensation of the church today, has been quite common in the history of biblical interpretation." Ibid., 11.

[67] Glenn R. Kreider, "What Is Dispensationalism? A Proposal," in *Dispensationalism and the History of Redemption: A Developing and Diverse Tradition*, ed. D. Jeffrey

and conferences, radio and television programming, and mission agencies and parachurch ministries."[68]

12.3.1 A Brief History of Dispensationalism

Historians agree that modern-day dispensationalism owes its origin to the Brethren Movement. This movement, which was active in Britain in early nineteenth century, "emphasized the unity of all believers in Christ and the freedom of Christians to gather in His name without regard for sectarian or denominational divisions."[69] Without doubt one of the movement's greatest leaders was John Nelson Darby (November 18, 1800–April 29, 1882). By all estimations, Darby was an enigma—something clearly recognized even by some of the fiercest critics of dispensationalism (the theological system that is forever associated with him). For example, Clarence B. Bass, himself not a friend of dispensationalism, writes concerning Darby:

> The single motivation of Darby's entire life was his love for Christ. If any principle is sufficient to explain the multiple facets of his personality, most probably it is this love. Because of it he has been called "a saint of the highest and purest stamp." At the same time, this love for Christ caused him to strike relentlessly against any, even close friends, whom he thought to be subverting the truth of Christ's gospel.[70]

On his part, Sandeen argues that Darby's "doctrine of the church seems to have acted as the catalytic agent for the rest of his beliefs."[71]

Bingham and Glenn R. Kreider (Chicago, IL: Moody 2015), 16.

[68] Ibid.

[69] Blaising and Bock, *Progressive Dispensationalism*, 10.

[70] Clarence B. Bass, *Backgrounds to Dispensationalism: Its Historical Genesis and Ecclesiastical Implications* (Eugene, OR: Wipf and Stock, 2005), 52. Summarizing the nature of the man that Darby was, Bass writes, "Any estimate of Darby—as a man, author-scholar, and religious leader—must inevitably involve contradictions and contrasts, since many of his personality traits were diametrically opposed to each other. Simple in taste, benevolent in disposition, kind in temperament, considerate in his awareness of others, humble in spirit, sympathetic in nature, he was at the same time ruthless in controversy, belligerent to those who opposed him, jealous of his position of authority, and exacting in his demands." Ibid., 51.

[71] Sandeen, *Roots of Fundamentalism*, 66–67.

Through his study and teaching of the Bible, Darby played a major role in the inception of modern-day dispensationalism, with its emphasis on the imminent return of Christ. As Sandeen notes, "This expectation of the imminent advent, with no obstacle in the way of Christ's return, proved to be one of the greatest attractions of dispensational theology."[72] Through his labors in both Britain and America, Darby slowly won converts to dispensationalism. "The truth is spreading; that truth of the Holy Spirit's presence consequent upon the Lord being glorified," Darby wrote at the age of 77 in his last letter to America as he crossed the Atlantic in 1877, "for that He as Son of man glorified on the cross; and the coming Lord."[73]

Hannah notes that there have been three discernible emphases within dispensationalism. These are: first, classical dispensationalism as evidenced in the *Scofield Reference Bible* and Lewis Sperry Chafer; second, revised dispensationalism such as reflected in *The New Scofield Reference Bible* (1967) as well as in the works of such dispensationalists as Charles Ryrie, John F. Walvoord and J. Dwight Pentecost; and finally, progressive dispensationalism of Blaising and Bock, among others.[74] While classical dispensationalism reflects the thought of Darby, revised dispensationalism "sought to answer certain criticisms leveled by covenantalists, such as the charge that their systems advocated two ways of salvation (law keeping in the Old Testament and grace in the New Testament),"[75] as well as other matters needing clarification. Progressive dispensationalists, as Hannah describes them, "maintain the seminal distinctive of the two peoples of God but have ameliorated the sharpness of the separation by suggesting the Christ is now on the throne of David and the promises made to Israel are now being fulfilled in the church, though the fullness manifestation of them awaits the millennial kingdom."[76] However, it has been demonstrated by some leading traditional dispensationalists that this most recent movement within dispensationalism

---

[72] Sandeen, *Roots of Fundamentalism*, 64.
[73] *Letters of J. N. D.*, 2:395, quoted in Sandeen, *Roots of Fundamentalism*, 79.
[74] Hannah, *Our Legacy*, 335–36.
[75] Ibid., 336.
[76] Ibid.

is a serious departure from the literal-grammatical hermeneutics—the hallmark of dispensationalism.[77]

12.3.2 *Dispensational Hermeneutics and Sola Scriptura*

From its beginning, dispensationalism has insisted on literal grammatical-historical hermeneutics as the proper method of interpreting Scripture. While dispensational practitioners rarely affirm that their employment of literal hermeneutics is in accordance with the reformers' principle of *sola Scriptura* and the perspicuity of Scripture, this is indeed the case.[78] As Bass observes, "The basic implications of dispensationalism arise, not out of its chronology of eschatological events, but out of its principle of literal interpretation."[79] This was the method of biblical interpretation embedded in *sola Scriptura*. Nevertheless, some nineteenth century critics considered dispensationalism to be almost novel. Sandeen quotes James Grant, a nineteenth century British critic of millennialism, as complaining,

> Nor do Millenarians hesitate to make an admission of the fact. On the contrary, they are forward to confess that, if they cannot prove that we are bound in connection with the question of Christ's second coming to the earth, to accept a literal rendering of the Word of God, they are not in a position to make a case for their faith in the personal reign of the Lord.[80]

Even more telling are those critics who have often wondered why dispensational hermeneutics claims to be strictly literal, yet it has not swerved into the pitfalls of date setting for the second advent. What these critics fail

---

[77] Robert L. Thomas, "The Hermeneutics of Progressive Dispensationalism," in *Evangelical Hermeneutics: The New Versus the Old* (Grand Rapids, MI: Kregel, 2002), 351–372.

[78] Dispensationalists rarely mention *sola Scriptura* in their hermeneutics. Even when they do, it is mentioned together with the other Reformation *solas* mainly to make the case that they are within the larger Protestant tradition and not outside of Protestantism.

[79] Bass, *Backgrounds to Dispensationalism*, 149.

[80] James Grant, *The End of All Things or, the Coming and Kingdom of Christ*, 2nd ed. (London: Darton, 1866), 1:199, quoted in Sandeen, *Roots of Fundamentalism*, 107–108.

to recognize is that, in adherence to the reformer's principle of *sola Scriptura* and the perspicuity of Scripture, dispensationalists have been careful to qualify the literal grammatical-historical method (but not according to requirements external to dispensationalism). This elucidation was made especially during the time of dispensational revisionism (c. 1960's). Defending the literal hermeneutics, for example, Pentecost made a few clarifications; the most relevant is this: "That the literalistic approach does not blindly rule out figures of speech, allegories, and types; but if the nature of the sentence so demands, it readily yields to the second sense."[81]

Significantly, Pentecost connects this method of biblical interpretation to the reformers' methods of interpretation. After restating Luther's principles of interpretation and those of Calvin (both emphasizing literal interpretation), Pentecost aptly concludes, "If one is to return to the Reformers for his theology, he must accept the method of interpretation on which their theology rests."[82] Essentially, if one wants to claim to stand in

---

[81] J. Dwight Pentecost, *Things to Come: A Study in Biblical Prophecy* (Grand Rapids, MI: Zondervan, 1958), 10.

[82] Ibid., 30. Farrar summarized Luther's methods of biblical interpretation by writing, "i. First, among them was the supreme and final authority of Scripture itself apart from all ecclesiastical authority or interference. ... ii. Secondly, he asserted not only the supreme authority but the sufficiency of Scripture. ... iii. Like all the other Reformers he set aside the dreary fiction of the fourfold sense. ... 'The literal sense of Scripture alone,' said Luther, 'is the whole essence of faith and theology.' 'I have observed this, that all the heresies and errors have originated, not from the simple words of Scripture, as is so universally asserted, but from neglecting the simple words of Scripture, and from the affectation of purely subjective ... tropes and inferences.' 'In the schools of theologians it is a well-known rule that Scripture is to be understood in four ways, literal, allegoric, moral, anagogic. But if we wish to handle Scripture aright, our one effort will be to obtain *unum, simplicem, germanum, et certum sensum* literalem.' 'Each passage has one clear, definite, and true sense of its own. All others are but doubtful and uncertain opinions.' iv. It need hardly be said, therefore, that Luther like most of the Reformers, rejected the validity of allegory. He totally denied its claim to be regarded as a *spiritual* interpretation. v. Luther also maintained the *perspicuity* of Scripture. ... He sometimes came near to the modern remark, that 'the Bible is to be interpreted like any other book.' vi. Luther maintained with all his force, and almost for the first time in history, the absolute indefensible *right of private judgement*, which, with the doc-

the legacy of the reformers, he has to adopt the literal grammatical-historical method of biblical interpretation.

While dispensationalists have continued (albeit with revisions here and there) to employ reformers' principle of *sola Scriptura* and the imbedded method of the literal-grammatical interpretation of Scripture, they rarely make the connection between their method and that of the reformers. Both Nathan D. Holsteen and Michael Svigel come closest to making this connection between *sola Scriptura* and dispensational hermeneutics explicit. For example, while arguing for the ancient origins for authorial intent in hermeneutics (literal hermeneutics) in early Christianity, Holsteen notes that this kind of hermeneutics reappeared after the Reformation. He writes, "While the seeds of this hermeneutic—like the seeds of the covenant hermeneutic—may be traced, at least in snippets, to the earlier stages in Christian history, its developed form—again like the covenant hermeneutic—appeared after the Reformation."[83] He concludes, "This approach to the reading of Scripture we might call the dispensational hermeneutic."[84] Although the chronological connection is made (that is, this kind of hermeneutics re-appeared after the Reformation), the logical connection needs to be made. Dispensationalists employed the principle of *sola Scriptura* and the doctrine of the perspicuity of Scripture, both of which naturally lead to a literal grammatical-historical hermeneutic. It is only dispensational hermeneutics that has been able to capture the essence of the reformers' hermeneutics. As this chapter has argued, this is an observation that can be made without resorting to subtlety or imprecision.[85]

---

trine of spiritual priesthood of all Christians, lies at the base of all Protestantism." Frederick W. Farrar, *History of Interpretation* (New York: E. P. Dutton, 1888), 325–30, quoted in Pentecost, *Things to Come*, 28.

[83] Nathan D. Holsteen, "The Hermeneutic of Dispensationalism," in *Dispensationalism and the History of Redemption: A Developing and Diverse Tradition*, ed. D. Jeffrey Bingham and Glenn R. Kreider (Chicago, IL: Moody, 2015), 109.

[84] Ibid.

[85] See Michael J. Svigel, "The History of Dispensationalism in Seven Eras," in *Dispensationalism and the History of Redemption: A Developing and Diverse Tradition*, ed. D. Jeffrey Bingham and Glenn R. Kreider (Chicago, IL: Moody, 2015). Svigel observes: "Dispensationalism shares common ground with other orthodox, Protestant evangeli-

12.4 Conclusion

The reformer's doctrine of *sola Scriptura* has been adopted by various traditions since the time of the Reformation. Throughout the chapter, it has been argued that dispensationalism (particularly classical and revised dispensationalism), has been the most faithful in carrying forward this doctrine together with its attendant principle of the perspicuity of Scripture. The main basis for this argument is the fact that, out of all the leading traditions surveyed (that is, Reformed, Lutheranism, Millerite and dispensationalism), it is only dispensationalism that has tenaciously held to a literal grammatical-historical method of interpretation—a method itself embedded in the doctrine of *sola Scriptura* and the principle of scriptural perspicuity. Only dispensationalism's hermeneutics have continued to adhere to the letter and spirit of the Reformation principle of *sola Scriptura* and the doctrine of the perspicuity of Scripture.

cal traditions. ... The vast majority of its adherents have held to classic orthodox theology (the Christocentric Trinitarian creation-redemption narrative summarized in the Nicene-Constantinopolitan Creed and the Definition of Chalcedon). They have generally embraced Protestant principles of *sola Scriptura, sola gratia, sola fide, solus Christus* and *soli Deo gloria.* They have vigorously defended the inspiration and accuracy of conservative evangelicalism. They also occupy a tract of land within the territory of 'premillennialism,' though not all premillennialists have been dispensationalists." Svigel, "History of Dispensationalism in Seven Eras," 94n12.

Bibliography

Amos, Clare, ed. *The Bible in the Life of the Church*. Canterbury Studies in Anglicanism, edited by Martyn Percy and Ian Markham. Norwich, England: Canterbury Press, 2013.

Barrett, Matthew. *God's Word: The Authority of Scripture: What the Reformers Taught...and Why It Still Matters*. The Five Solas Series. Grand Rapids, MI: Zondervan, 2016.

Bass, Clarence B. *Backgrounds to Dispensationalism: Its Historical Genesis and Ecclesiastical Implications*. Eugene, OR: Wipf and Stock, 2005.

Beale, G. K. "New Testament Hermeneutics." In *Seeing Christ in All of Scripture: Hermeneutics at Westminster Theological Seminary*, edited by Peter A. Lillback. Philadelphia, PA: Westminster Seminary Press, 2016.

Bebbington, David W. *The Dominance of Evangelicalism: The Age of Spurgeon and Moody*. A History of Evangelicalism: People, Movements and Ideas in the English-Speaking World 3, edited by David W. Bebbington and Mark Noll. Downers Grove, IL: Intervarsity Press, 2005.

Blaising, Craig A., and Darrell L. Bock. *Progressive Dispensationalism*. Grand Rapids, MI: Baker Books, 2000.

Callahan, James Patrick. "*Claritas Scripturae*: The Role of Perspicuity in Protestant Hermeneutics." *Journal of the Evangelical Theological Society* 29, no. 3 (1996): 353–72.

Calvin, John. *Institutes of the Christian Religion*. Edited by John T. McNeill. 2 vols. Philadelphia, PA: Westminster Press, 1960.

Ebeling, Gerhard. *The Word of God and Tradition: Historical Studies Interpreting the Divisions of Christianity*. Translated by S. H. Hooke. Philadelphia, PA: Fortress, 1964.

Engelder, Theo. "The Three Principles of the Reformation: Sola Scriptura, Sola Gratia, Sola Fides." In *Four Hundred Years: Commemorative Essays on the Reformation of Dr. Martin Luther and Its Blessed Results*, edited by W. H. T. Dau. St. Louis, MO: Concordia, 1916.

Farrar, Frederick W. *History of Interpretation*. New York: E. P. Dutton, 1888.

Grant, James. *The End of All Things or, the Coming and Kingdom of Christ*. 2nd ed. Vol. 1. London: Darton, 1866.

Hannah, John. *Our Legacy: The History of Christian Doctrine*. Colorado Springs, CO: NavPress, 2001.

Hodge, Charles. *Systematic Theology*. 3 vols. Grand Rapids, MI: Eerdmans, n.d.

Holsteen, Nathan D. "The Hermeneutic of Dispensationalism." In *Dispensationalism and the History of Redemption: A Developing and Diverse Tradition*, edited by D. Jeffrey Bingham and Glenn R. Kreider. Chicago, IL: Moody, 2015.

Hyde, Gordon M., ed. *A Symposium on Biblical Hermeneutics*. Washington, DC: The Review and Publishing Association, 1974.

Kevan, Ernest F. "The Principles of Interpretation." In *Revelation and the Bible*, edited by Carl F. H. Henry. Contemporary Evangelical Thought. Grand Rapids, MI: Baker Book House, 1958.

Klooster, Fred D. "The Uniqueness of Reformed Theology: A Preliminary Attempt at Description." *Calvin Theological Journal* 14, no. 1 (April 1979): 32–54.

Kreider, Glenn R. "What Is Dispensationalism? A Proposal." In *Dispensationalism and the History of Redemption: A Developing and Diverse Tradition*, edited by D. Jeffrey Bingham and Glenn R. Kreider. Chicago, IL: Moody, 2015.

Leith, John H., ed. *Creeds of the Churches: A Reader in Christian Doctrine from the Bible to the Present*. Louisville, KY: Westminster John Knox, 1982.

Lillback, Peter A. "Introduction." In *Seeing Christ in All of Scripture: Hermeneutics at Westminster Theological Seminary*, edited by Peter A. Lillback. Philadelphia, PA: Westminster Seminary Press, 2016.

Lotz, David W. "Sola Scriptura: Luther on Biblical Authority." *Interpretation* 35, no. 3 (1981): 258–273.

Marks, Darren C. "The Windsor Report: A Theological Commentary." *Journal of Anglican Studies* 4, no. 2 (December 2006): 157–76.

Maxwell, C. Mervyn. "A Brief History of Adventists Hermeneutics." *Journal of the Adventist Theological Society* 4, no. 2 (Autumn 1993): 209–26.

Olson, Dennis T. "How Lutherans Read the Bible: A North American and Global Conversation." *Dialog: A Journal of Theology* 45, no. 1 (Spring 2006): 4–8.

Pentecost, J. Dwight. *Things to Come: A Study in Biblical Prophecy.* Grand Rapids, MI: Zondervan, 1958.

Pettegrew, Larry D. "The Perspicuity of Scripture." *The Master's Seminary Journal* 15, no. 2 (2004): 209–25.

Reisz, H. Frederick, Jr. "Reading the Bible in the Lutheran Tradition." *Dialog: A Journal of Theology* 45, no. 1 (Spring 2006): 21–28.

Ross, Alexander. "Gaping Gaps? Implications of the 'Bible in the Life of the Church' Project for Bridging the Anglican Hermeneutic Divide." *Journal of Anglican Studies* 12, no. 2 (November 2014): 143–64.

Sandeen, Ernest R. *The Roots of Fundamentalism: British and American Millenarianism 1800–1930.* Chicago, IL: University of Chicago Press, 1970.

Schaff, Philip. *The Evangelical Protestant Creeds, with Translations.* Vol. 3, *The Creeds of Christendom: With a History and Critical Notes.* 3 vols. Grand Rapids, MI: Baker Books, 1983.

Svigel, Michael J. "The History of Dispensationalism in Seven Eras." In *Dispensationalism and the History of Redemption: A Developing and Diverse Tradition*, edited by D. Jeffrey Bingham and Glenn R. Kreider. Chicago, IL: Moody, 2015.

Thomas, Robert L. "The Hermeneutics of Progressive Dispensationalism." In *Evangelical Hermeneutics: The New Versus the Old*. Grand Rapids, MI: Kregel, 2002.

Sola Gratia
[Grace Alone]

13

HOW DISPENSATIONALISM ADVANCES *SOLA GRATIA*

Grant Hawley
Bold Grace Publishing

13.0 Introduction

Christians owe a lot to the Reformation. While the Bible is full of truth and liberty, the medieval period was filled with superstition and bondage. In the darkness of 1517, Martin Luther lit a candle, and many others saw the light and lit their own tapers. In the light of Scripture, the reformers began to recover many important doctrines.

One of these lights is represented in the Reformation's cry *sola gratia*, by grace alone. This light directed all to give honor to God in humility, as thankful beneficiaries of God's unmerited favor. Where the Reformation first shined its candle light of *sola gratia*, dispensationalism lit a flood light; however, that work would have been impossible to do in the darkness. Thanks be to God that five-hundred years ago certain men stood up to the captors who had usurped the authority of Scripture and, by God's grace, set the captives free.

The biblical idea of grace should first be considered before the significance of *sola gratia* and the advancements to that doctrine which were made through the Reformation as well as in the rise of dispensationalism, can be appreciated.

13.1 Grace in the Old Testament

In the Old Testament, the number of occurrences of the English term "grace" varies widely from translation to translation.[1] The noun "grace" in the Old Testament is most often translated from חֵן (*chên*), which usually carries the idea of "favor" from someone of higher station (kings, the LORD, etc.).[2] חֵן is used eighteen times of God granting favor to men (see Gen 6:8; Ex 3:21, 11:3, 12:36, 33:12–13, 33:16–17, 34:9; Num 11:11, 15; Judg 6:17; 2 Sam 15:25; Ps 84:11; Prov 3:4, 34; Jer 31:2; Zech 12:10). As is often the case, the first occurrence of חֵן is significant. It is found in Genesis 6:8, "But Noah found favor [חֵן, grace] in the eyes of the Lord." Contextually, Noah is being granted salvation for him and his family from the coming flood. This is significant for two reasons. The first is that it carries the idea of "favor," as the NASB has captured in the translation. The second is that it refers to a person being delivered from a helpless state. These two concepts become the foundation for the biblical idea of grace as it stretches across both Testaments. In God's grace, He shows favor in man's helplessness.

In comparison with the New Testament, there are few uses of the term "grace" referring God's grace in the Old Testament. However, God's graciousness is highlighted in the terms חָנַן (*chenen*) and the related word, חָנוּן (*chenun*), which are often translated with a being verb plus "gracious" (Ex 22:27, 34:6; 2 Chron 30:9; Neh 9:17, 31; Ps 86:15, 103:8, 111:4, 112:4, 116:5, 145:8; Joel 2:13; Jonah 4:2), or simply, "gracious" (Gen 33:5, 33:11, 43:29; Ex 33:19; Num 6:25; 2 Sa 12:22; 2 Kings 13:23; Job 33:24; Ps 4:1, 6:2, 9:13; Isa 30:18–19, 33:2; Amos 5:15; Mal 1:9), respectively, and חֶסֶד

---

[1] For example, the KJV uses the term "grace" 39 times in the Old Testament (Gen 6:8, 19:19, 32:5, 33:8, 33:10, 33:15, 34:11, 39:4, 47:25, 47:29, 50:4; Ex 33:12, 33:13 [2x] , 33:16, 33:17, 34:9; Num 32:5; Judg 6:17; Ruth 2:2, 2:10; 1 Sam 1:18, 20:3, 27:5; 2 Sam 14:22, 16:4; Ezra 9:8; Est 2:17; Ps 45:2, 84:11; Prov 1:9, 3:22, 3:34, 4:9, 22:11; Jer 31:2; Zech 4:7 [2x] , 12:10), mostly from חֵן, while the NASB only uses the term nine times (Ezra 9:8; Ps 45:2, 84:11; Prov 3:34, 4:9; Jer 31:2; Ezek 16:1; Zech 4:7 [2x], 12:10). Instead, the NASB tends to use "favor" when translating חֵן and its derivatives.

[2] Walther Zimmerli, "χάρις," in *Theological Dictionary of the New Testament*, ed. Gerhard Kittel (Grand Rapids, MI: Eerdmans, 1974), 9:376–87. This was confirmed in the author's own word studies.

(*chesed*), often translated, "lovingkindess"[3] or, in some translations, "loyal love."[4]

חסד (*chesed*) first occurs in Genesis 19:19, in which it appears with and is closely associated with חן. Here Lot thanks Abraham and his angel companions for saving his life from the destruction coming upon Sodom: "Now behold, your servant has found favor in your sight, and you have magnified your lovingkindness, which you have shown me by saving my life" (Gen 19:19a).

חַנּוּן (*chenun*) in combination with חסד (*chesed*) in Psalm 145:8–9 reads, "The LORD is gracious and merciful; Slow to anger and great in lovingkindness. The LORD is good to all, And His mercies are over all His works." Here "merciful," which is perhaps better translated "compassionate" (NET), is translated from רחום (*rihum*) which is paired with חסד (*chesed*) eleven times (Ex 34:6; 2 Chron 30:9; Neh 9:17, 31; Ps 86:15, 103:8, 111:4, 112:4, 145:8; Joel 2:13; Jonah 4:2), each occurrence looking at the character of God. The scope of His goodness and mercy, that is, His gracious and compassionate disposition, is to "all." Thus, grace and mercy/compassion are related and are defining aspects of the character of God.

The LORD proves His character through His actions.[5] He demonstrated His grace, compassion, and lovingkindness in His deliverance of Noah from the flood (Gen 6–9), in His justifying Abraham by faith (establishing the doctrine of justification by grace through faith), in His saving Israel from slavery and from Pharaoh's army (Ex 3–14), in His sparing Nineveh at their reception of Jonah's message, in His delivering Jonah from the disobedience he determined to do, patiently teaching him about His

---

[3] 182 times in the NASB.

[4] For example, 121 times in the NET Bible.

[5] "He is the God who 'is,' היה, in the fullest meaning of the word . . . . But this 'being' is not the abstract Greek εἰμι the mere existence per se. To the Hebrew 'to be' does not just mean to exist—as all other beings and things do as well—but to be active, to express oneself in active being, 'The God who acts.' 'I am what in creative activity I always and everywhere turn out to be,' or 'I am (the God) that really acts.'" Sigmund Mowinckel, "The Name of the God of Moses," *Hebrew Union College Annual* 32 (1961): 127.

compassion, and in many other wonderful works. But God's grace, compassion, and lovingkindness are perhaps most clearly seen in His gracious commitment, restated often, to ultimately deliver and restore Israel, even when she had been an unfaithful wife to Him (Hos 2:14–23, see also the context of Hos 1:1–2:13). This shows that His grace toward His people is endless, "where sin increased, grace abounded all the more" (Rom 5:20b).

13.2 Grace in the New Testament

Grace is prevalent in the Old Testament, but it is expounded in the New Testament, especially in the epistles of Paul. In the New Testament, "grace" is translated from χάρις (*charis*), "The linguistic starting-point is the sense of 'making glad by gifts,' of showing free unmerited grace."[6] The word does have some flexibility, however, as it is also used for giving thanks (Luke 17:9; Rom 6:17, 7:25; 1 Cor 1:4, 10:30, 15:57; 2 Cor 2:14, 4:15, 8:16, 9:15, 1 Tim 1:12; 2 Tim 1:3; Heb 12:28, unlikely), for the favor of men (Luke 2:52; Acts 2:47, 7:10, 24:27, 25:9; 2 Cor 8:4), gracious work (2 Cor 8:6, 7, 19), and even credit (Luke 6:32, 33, 34). Often, it refers to receiving a ministry (frequently related to spiritual gifts; Rom 12:3, 12:6, 15:15; 1 Cor 3:10, 15:10; Eph 3:2, 7–8, 4:7; Phil 1:7 [probably]; 1 Tim 1:14; 2 Tim 1:9). But there are several key passages in which the biblical authors (mostly Paul) give amazing insight into the meaning of God's grace by contrasting it with either works or the law (John 1:16–17; Rom 3:21–4:5, 4:16, 5:2, 6:14, 11:6; Gal 1:6, 2:21, 5:4; Eph 2:1–10; Titus 3:4–7; Heb 13:9; this list is not intended to be exhaustive). Because of the limitations of this chapter, only two of these incredible passages can be expounded here.

13.2.1 Romans 3:21–4:5

The first passage is the foundational pericope for the Pauline doctrine of justification by faith apart from works found in Romans 3:21–4:5. Romans 3:21–31 forms a chiasm:

A. But now apart from the Law *the* righteousness of God has been manifested, being witnessed by the Law and the Prophets,

B. even *the* righteousness of God through faith in Jesus Christ for all

---

[6] Hans Conzelmann, "χάρις," in *TDNT*, 9:394.

those who believe; for there is no distinction;

 C. for all have sinned and fall short of the glory of God,

  D. being justified as a gift by His grace through the redemption which is in Christ Jesus;

   E. whom God displayed publicly as a propitiation in His blood through faith.

    F. *This was* to demonstrate His righteousness, because in the forbearance of God He passed over the sins previously committed;

    F. for the demonstration, *I say,* of His righteousness at the present time,

   E'. so that He would be just and the justifier of the one who has faith in Jesus.

  D'. Where then is boasting? It is excluded. By what kind of law? Of works? No, but by a law of faith.

 C'. For we maintain that a man is justified by faith apart from works of the Law.

 B'. Or is God *the God* of Jews only? Is He not *the God* of Gentiles also? Yes, of Gentiles also, since indeed God who will justify the circumcised by faith and the uncircumcised through faith is one.

A'. Do we then nullify the Law through faith? May it never be! On the contrary, we establish the Law.

Overall, this passage is translated fairly accurately, but Lenski is correct to note regarding προεθετο (*proetheto*, design beforehand) in verse 25 that, "While this verb is very common, in the present sacred connection it is undoubtedly a cultus term and is used with reference to things relating to the Jewish Tabernacle and its worship."[7] So, "displayed publicly" does not catch the meaning of the term. Related is that ἱλαστήριον (*hilasterion*) is better translated "mercy seat" than "propitiation" (which would be ἱλασμόςι [*hilasmos*], see 1 John 2:2).[8] Lost in the NASB translation is the connection Paul is

---

[7] R. C. H. Lenski, *The Interpretation of St. Paul's Espistle to the Romans* (1945; repr., Minneapolis, MN: Augsburg Publishing House, 1961), 254.

[8] Ibid., 254–59. Lenski here translates ἱλαστήριον as "cover of the mercy seat," however, the mercy seat is actually the cover of the ark of the covenant, so it is better

making with the Tabernacle and the Day of Atonement. What the Day of Atonement was in type and shadow, Jesus Christ is in antitype and reality.

When Paul's Tabernacle illustration is seen, it also brings light to Romans 5:1–2, which reads, "Therefore, having been justified by faith, we have peace with God through our Lord Jesus Christ, through whom also we have obtained our introduction [lit. access] by faith into this grace in which we stand; and we exult in hope of the glory of God." Access to God's grace is by faith apart from works, and, just as the High Priest on the Day of Atonement could not enter the Holy of Holies and see the glory of God without blood (cf. Heb 9:7), access to God by faith is only possible through Christ's blood (compare Rom 3:24–25), which was shed once for all (cf. Heb 9:11–14).

There are two connections demonstrated in the chiasm which should be noted here. The first is found in the following:

D. being justified as a gift by His grace through the redemption which is in Christ Jesus;

D'. Where then is boasting? It is excluded. By what kind of law? Of works? No, but by a law of faith.

By this is seen that "being justified as a gift by His grace through the redemption which is in Christ Jesus" is compared with the exclusion of boasting "by a law of faith." Justification by faith excludes boasting because it is not of works.

The second connection is found in:

A. But now apart from the Law *the* righteousness of God has been manifested, being witnessed by the Law and the Prophets,

A'. Do we then nullify the Law through faith? May it never be! On the contrary, we establish the Law.

This connection clears up the mystery of what is meant by "we establish the Law." It is not that the Law of Moses is made binding on the church. In verse 21 (A.), Paul is referring to the fact that the Law (here referring to the Old Testament) witnesses that the righteousness of God comes through

---

to translate it simply, "mercy seat." See also Zane Hodges, *Romans: Deliverance from Wrath* (Corinth, TX: Grace Evangelical Society, 2013), 99–102.

faith apart from the Law of Moses. Paul goes through several examples from the Old Testament of righteousness being by faith apart from the Law. The Old Testament establishes Paul's doctrine that he is expounding here. In this way "we establish the Law" (i.e. we ascribe validation to the Old Testament) by preaching salvation by grace through faith apart from works.

Paul's first choice for an Old Testament example of justification by grace through faith is Abraham's justification. Romans 4:1-5 reads:

> What then shall we say that Abraham, our forefather according to the flesh, has found? For if Abraham was justified by works, he has something to boast about, but not before God. For what does the Scripture say? "ABRAHAM BELIEVED GOD, AND IT WAS CREDITED TO HIM AS RIGHTEOUSNESS." Now to the one who works, his wage is not credited as a favor, but as what is due. But to the one who does not work, but believes in Him who justifies the ungodly, his faith is credited as righteousness.

This pericope contains a parallel structure:

A. For if Abraham was justified by works, he has something to boast about, but not before God.

B. For what does the Scripture say? "ABRAHAM BELIEVED GOD, AND IT WAS CREDITED TO HIM AS RIGHTEOUSNESS."

A'. Now to the one who works, his wage is not credited as a favor, but as what is due.

B'. But to the one who does not work, but believes in Him who justifies the ungodly, his faith is credited as righteousness.

The translation here is accurate, though it is unfortunate that the NASB chooses "a favor" instead of "grace" for χαριν (*charin*), since this is a foundational passage on the definition of grace. An English-only reader could miss this. Additionally in most people's eyes, "a favor" is what you are doing when you mow your neighbor's lawn, so such a translation fails to do justice to the majesty of justification.

Paul makes the point here that justification by works by necessity gives ground for boasting before God. But justification before God by works is impossible, as Paul proved in Romans 2:1-3:20. Also, the Old Testament testifies that justification is by faith, not by works. Righteousness in God's eyes is not earned, it is credited as a gift of free grace to the one who believes. Boasting is excluded (cf. 3:27).

Paul ends his illustration with a clear declaration that man cannot work for his justification, but that it is through faith alone in Christ alone. God justifies the one who simply believes the gospel (cf. Rom 1:16-17), not the one who depends on his works. The contrast between grace and works as a means of obtaining justification before God cannot be clearer: grace and works religion are mutually exclusive. Likewise, it is clear from "But to the one who does not work, but believes..." that belief cannot be a work. It is contrasted with works in the strongest possible terms here.

13.2.2 Ephesians 2:1-10

The second passage is Ephesians 2:1-10, which is also a chiasm:

A. And you were dead in your trespasses and sins, in which you formerly walked according to the course of this world, according to the prince of the power of the air, of the spirit that is now working in the sons of disobedience. Among them we too all formerly lived in the lusts of our flesh, indulging the desires of the flesh and of the mind, and were by nature children of wrath, even as the rest.

 B. But God, being rich in mercy, because of His great love with which He loved us, even when we were dead in our transgressions, made us alive together with Christ (by grace you have been saved), and raised us up with Him, and seated us with Him in the heavenly *places* in Christ Jesus,

  C. so that in the ages to come He might show the surpassing riches of His grace in kindness toward us in Christ Jesus.

 B'. For by grace you have been saved through faith; and that not of yourselves, *it is* the gift of God; not as a result of works, so that no one may boast.

A'. For we are His workmanship, created in Christ Jesus for good works, which God prepared beforehand so that we would walk in them.

Again, this translation is good with just a few exceptions. Verse 1a, "And you were dead in your trespasses and sins" makes little sense here. If "And" is meant to be a soft conjunction with little force, as it seems to in this translation, Paul would have likely used δέ (*de*). But instead, Paul uses καί (*kai*), which is a much stronger connective than δέ (*de*). Here it should be translated "even"[9] as a continuation from chapter 1. The chapter break obscures this. To catch the flow it is helpful to quote the adjusted 2:1a together with 1:22–23:

> And He put all things in subjection under His feet, and gave Him as head over all things to the church, which is His body, the fullness of Him who fills all in all, even you [who] were dead in trespasses and sins...[10]

Thus, Paul is setting up his exposition on the gracious work of God in creating the Body of Christ ("one new man" [2:15]) by pointing out the absurd (according to natural means) thought that we who were dead in trespasses and sins could make up the very Body of Christ, that we could become the fullness of Christ Himself. But God's grace is sufficient even in this.

Additionally, the translation "workmanship" for ποίημα (*poiēma*) in this context could be improved. The biggest issue being that in English it is not clearly singular, as it is in the Greek. We—together, as the body of Christ—are His single work in this context. Likewise, Paul is clearly pointing to the master craftsmanship of this particular work (cf. 1:15–23 and 2:11–22), so the term "masterpiece," (which is clearly singular) is more appropriate. We are His masterpiece. And how appropriate is this? If God has taken this dead and wicked group of human beings and created something so incredible as the Body of Christ, we are His masterpiece indeed!

Finally, "would" in verse 10 does not capture the force of the subjunctive Paul uses. We *should* (ESV, NKJV, KJV, and others) walk in the good works God has prepared beforehand because that is our purpose, "For we are...created in Christ Jesus *for good works*..." (2:10, emphasis added). Verse 10 plays an important role here, not in defining grace, but in demonstrating

---

[9] Καί is an ascensive conjunction here, building upon the end of chapter 1. See Daniel B. Wallace, *Greek Grammar beyond the Basics: An Exegetical Syntax of the New Testament* (Grand Rapids, MI: Zondervan, 1996), 670.

[10] "Your" was dropped from the modified translation because it is not in the Greek, though the change is not theologically significant.

that, even though salvation is completely apart from works, good works are still *good*. The order is significant. Christians do not do good works because they hope to be saved or hope they are saved, Christians do them because they have already been saved, and God empowers them to do good works.

Verses 1–4 and 10 set important context, but the part of this passage that defines grace is verses 5–9, which reads:

> B. But God, being rich in mercy, because of His great love with which He loved us, even when we were dead in our transgressions, made us alive together with Christ (by grace you have been saved), and raised us up with Him, and seated us with Him in the heavenly *places* in Christ Jesus,
>
> C. so that in the ages to come He might show the surpassing riches of His grace in kindness toward us in Christ Jesus.
>
> B'. For by grace you have been saved through faith; and that not of yourselves, *it is* the gift of God; not as a result of works, so that no one may boast.

The parallelism in this chiasm is helpful in defining what it means to be saved by grace in verse 8. Verse 5 defines it as nothing less than believers being made alive together with Christ, or, in theological terms, regeneration. It is clear from verses 8–9, then, that regeneration is by grace, through faith, and that it is not as a result of works.

Some have seen "the gift of God" to be faith, taking "that," τοῦτο (*touto*), to refer to πιστεως (*pisteōs*), "faith," but the Greek forbids it. "Faith," πιστεως (*pisteōs*), is feminine, and "that," τοῦτο (*touto*), is a neuter pronoun. "Grace" is not the gift either, for the same reason. Neuter pronouns do not refer to feminine nouns. Neuter pronouns do, however, refer to implied nouns or to concepts that are not expressed with nouns,[11] and the former is the case here. The implied noun is the *salvation* in view in the verb σεσωσμενοι (*sesosmenoi*), "you have been saved." Salvation is the gift of God.[12]

It is important to note that Paul does address the *ordo salutis* (order of

---

[11] See 1 Corinthians 6:6 for a clear example with similar syntax.

[12] See Wallace, *Greek Grammar beyond the Basics*, 334–35. Wallace leaves room for regeneration preceding faith theologically, but concedes that this passage does not support it. In the following paragraph, the *ordo salutis* with the present passage will be addressed.

salvation) here. When he says, "you have been saved through faith," he means "you have been made alive together with Christ through faith" (comparing v. 5). Faith is the channel to the Cause of regeneration, namely God. It is God who effects regeneration, and He does it alone, not with the help of man's works. But He does it "through faith." Paul asserts in this very passage that faith is not a work, just as he did in Romans 4:5. Grace and works religion are polar opposites.

And why did God do this? The peak of the chiasm (2:7) reveals that God did so in order that He could spend eternity showing believers just how much He loves them. The full power of the Almighty will be summoned to pour out His exceeding riches of grace upon believers forever.

Because of the space limitations of this chapter, only these two passages will be briefly covered. It is the hope of this author that the reader will continue his study of the grace of God in the New Testament, not just as it relates to salvation, but as it relates to Christian liberty as well (cf. Rom 6:14; Gal 2:11–3:14). Thus, in the defining passages, the New Testament authors define the essence of grace as related to faith and, when dealing with salvation, is presented primarily as a contrast to works as a means of obtaining justification before God. Thus, Paul's statement truly gets to the heart of the issue: "But if it is by grace, it is no longer on the basis of works, otherwise grace is no longer grace" (Rom 11:6). There is no such thing as salvation by grace and works.

13.3 Sola Gratia in the Reformation

While the New Testament doctrine of grace is related to faith and is presented as a contrast to works religion, perhaps the major focus of the Reformation's teaching on grace was as a contrast with human freedom.

More than a thousand years before Martin Luther posted his *95 Theses*, the Reformation's theology of grace had already undergone a great deal of development through the writings of Augustine, especially in his dispute with Pelagius over the depravity of man. Pelagius argued that man was not sinful by nature but instead could, by free choice, be glorious and virtuous.[13]

---

[13] For example: "Whenever I have to speak on the subject of moral instruction and the conduct of a holy life, it is my practice first to demonstrate the power and

Augustine argued that man is wholly depraved and cannot even turn to God unless God first gives him a will to do so.[14] This distinction becomes the basis for all disputes about grace in the Reformation and even long afterward. church historian Carl Trueman writes:

> the Pelagian controversy...is fundamental to all future discussions of grace. This conflict forced Augustine to offer deeper exegetical and systematic foundations for the intuitive understandings of grace he had put forth in the *Confessions*. In doing so, he clarified what was really at stake, laying down the basic framework for later medieval, Reformation, and post-Reformation arguments on this issue.[15]

This may seem like an overstatement, but it is largely accurate. The one exception, which will be explained in this chapter, is that many dispensationalists have discussed grace as a contrast to works religion, rather than as a contrast to human freedom. This dispensational perspective is neither Augustinian nor Pelagian.

For the reformers, the sticking point of the doctrine of grace is whether faith *results in* regeneration or is the *result of* regeneration. As Calvin, commenting on John 1:13, notes:

---

quality of human nature and to show what it is capable of achieving, and then to go on to encourage the mind of my listener to consider the idea of different kinds of virtues, in case it may be of little or no profit to him to be summoned to pursue ends which he has perhaps assumed hitherto to be beyond his reach; for we can never enter upon the path of virtue unless we have hope as our guide and companion and if every effort expended in seeking something is nullified in effect by despair of ever finding it." Pelagius, "A Letter from Pelagius (to Demetrius)," in *The Letters of Pelagius and His Followers*, trans. B. R. Rees (Woodbridge, Suffolk: Boydell, 1991), 2.1, accessed June 20, 2017, https://epistolae.ccnmtl.columbia.edu/letter/1296.html.

[14] "Forasmuch then as our turning away from God is our own act, and this is evil will; but our turning to God is not possible, except He rouses and helps us, and this is good will,—what have we that we have not received? (...) it comes from His mercy, not their merit, that God wills to impart this to some, but from His truth that He wills not to impart it to others." Augustine, "On Forgiveness of Sins, and Baptism," in *A Select Library of the Nicene and Post-Nicene Fathers of the Christian Church*, ed. Philip Schaff, ser. 1, vol. 5, *Writings Against the Pelagians* (Grand Rapids, MI: Eerdmans, 1980), 56.

[15] Carl R. Trueman, *Grace Alone: Salvation as a Gift of God*. The 5 *Solas* Series. (Grand Rapids, MI: Zondervan, 2017), 73.

the glorifying of faith claims nothing at all for fleshly begetting but declares that it has received all that is good from the grace of God alone. (...) we are reckoned sons of God, not on account of our own nature, nor from our initiative, but because the Lord begat us voluntarily, that is, from spontaneous love. Hence it follows, first, that faith is not our production, but is the fruit of spiritual regeneration. For the Evangelist says that none can believe save he who is begotten of God.[16]

Thus, to Calvin, salvation is by grace because faith is a gift of God.

One of Martin Luther's most significant works was his *The Bondage of the Will*, in which, in opposition to Erasmus, he too spoke of God's grace with the same focus as Augustine. The apogee of his conclusion is found in the following paragraphs:

Again:—If we believe that original sin has so destroyed us, that even in the godly who are led by the Spirit, it causes the utmost molestation by striving against that which is good ; it is manifest, that there can be nothing left in a man devoid of the Spirit, which can turn itself towards good, but which must again turn towards evil!

Again:—If the Jews, who followed after righteousness with all their powers, ran rather into unrighteousness, while the Gentiles who followed after unrighteousness attained unto a free righteousness which they never hoped for ; it is equally manifest, from their very works, and from experience, that man, without grace, can do nothing but will evil![17]

---

[16] John Calvin, *The Gospel According to St John 1-10*, Calvin's Commentaries 4, trans. T. H. L. Parker (Grand Rapids, MI: Eerdmans, 1961), 18-19. It should be noted here that the Evangelist does not say, "none can believe save he who is begotten of God," but is rather demonstrating that regeneration is not of man's will but God's. John is saying that *regeneration* is by the will of God, not that *faith* is. The time of participles is relative to the main verb. Thus, the present participle τοῖς πιστεύουσιν, "those who believe" is concurrent with ἔλαβον "received" and ἐγεννήθησαν "were born," both aorists. Faith and regeneration are seen as concurrent in this passage. It does not comment on the *ordo salutis*.

[17] Martin Luther, *The Bondage of the Will*, trans. Henry Cole (Grand Rapids, MI:

Thus, like Augustine, Luther argues that the will of man is so corrupted that it is only by God's work of grace to turn him that he can turn to God in faith.

It may seem odd to some that the reformers (and Augustine before them) presented grace as a contrast to faith preceding regeneration rather than a contrast to works religion. However, this is clear when it is understood in light of the Reformation doctrine of the perseverance of the saints. After his departure from premillennialism, Augustine taught that there could be no ultimate salvation apart from perseverance in good works, and the reformers carried on this teaching (though inconsistently).[18] Calvin explains this doctrine in his comments on 1 John 3:9:

> John...not only shews that we cannot sin, but also that the power of the Spirit is so effectual, that it necessarily retains us in continual obedience to righteousness. Nor is this the only passage of Scripture which teaches us that the will is so formed that it cannot be otherwise than right. For God testifies that he gives a new heart to his children, and promises to do this, that they may walk in his commandments. Besides, John not only shews how efficaciously God works once in man, but plainly declares that the Spirit continues his grace in us to the last, so that inflexible perseverance is added to newness of life.[19]

How can the saved man's boasting be excluded if only those who persevere until death in good works obtain ultimate salvation? Calvin's answer, echoing Augustine, was that his turning to God and his perseverance in good works were both gifts of God's grace. One cannot rightly boast in what he receives as a gift from God. This does come short of the biblical doctrine of grace (cf. Rom 11:6), but it nevertheless gives the credit fully to God. God

---

Baker, 1976), 390–91.

[18] See David R. Anderson, "The Soteriological Impact of Augustine's Change from Premillennialism to Amillennialism, Part 1," *Journal of the Grace Evangelical Society* 15, no. 1 (Spring 2002): 25–36; and David R. Anderson, "The Soteriological Impact of Augustine's Change from Premillennialism to Amillennialism, Part 2," *Journal of the Grace Evangelical Society* 15, no. 2 (Autumn 2002): 23–39.

[19] John Calvin, *Commentaries on the Catholic Epistles*, trans. John Owen (Edinburgh: Calvin Translation Society, 1855), 213.

getting the credit for salvation is a constant focus of the Augustinian reformers, and this is a major stride forward from medieval Catholic doctrine.

While it was Augustine who solidified the Catholic Church's claim on authority so that he became the father of the Roman Catholic Church,[20] it was his doctrine of grace that ignited the Reformation, of which he became perhaps the central figure. As Warfield notes:

> The problem which Augustine bequeathed to the Church [i.e. the authority of the Catholic Church] for solution, the Church required a thousand years to solve. But even so, it is Augustine who gave us the Reformation. For the Reformation, inwardly considered, was just the ultimate triumph of Augustine's doctrine of grace over Augustine's doctrine of the Church.[21]

13.3.1 The Reformation Brought Augustine's Doctrine of Grace Back to the Forefront

The reformers were not the first to teach Augustine's doctrine of grace after the turn of the millennium. For example, Thomas Aquinas writes:

> since man, by assenting to matters of faith, is raised above his nature, this must needs accrue to him from some supernatural principle moving him inwardly ; and this is God. Therefore faith, as regards the assent which is the chief act of faith, is from God moving man inwardly by grace.[22]

So, the teaching of Augustine's doctrine of grace was not lost entirely. But it was obscured by contradictory practices. For example, the Catholic Church's doctrine of purgatory (especially at that time, with the practice of selling indulgences) flies in the face of Augustine's doctrine, as MacCulloch

---

[20] B. B. Warfield, *Calvin and Augustine* (Philadelphia, PA: Presbyterian and Reformed, 1956), 307–22. Augustine did not originate the doctrine, but his immense popularity among the people and the Roman Church's recognition of him as an authoritative doctor of the Church made his exposition on the authority of the Church effective in granting that same authority to all who are similarly recognized.

[21] Ibid., 322.

[22] Thomas Aquinas, *Summa Theologica*, trans. Fathers of the English Dominican Province (1911; repr., Westminster, MD: Christian Classics, 1948), 3:1195.

notes: "elaborations of the theology of purgatory, God's merciful provision for humanity to do its best for its salvation, sat rather uneasily with what Augustine had said about human worthlessness."[23] Clearly, any teaching that man can earn his salvation by doing his best cannot be reconciled with salvation by grace alone.

4.   Though Augustine's doctrine of grace was present before Luther, it was Augustine's doctrine of the church that dominated prior to the Reformation. Because of the authority claimed by the Catholic Church, their teaching on the sacraments was incompatible with the Reformation doctrine of grace. Like the doctrine of purgatory and the selling of indulgences, the sacraments, instead of being an act of worship, were simply a means for controlling the people. They saw the sacraments as the means to obtaining justification, so the Catholic Church could withhold sacraments, and thus withhold salvation from anyone who was unruly. In 1520, Luther took issue with it in *The Babylonian Captivity of the Church*,[24] in which he addressed one by one the problems with the Catholic Church's seven sacraments. In his exposition on baptism, he writes:

> For if a sacrament confers grace on me, merely because I receive it, then it is certainly by my own work and not by faith that I obtain grace; nor do I apprehend any promise in the sacrament, but only a sign instituted and commanded by God. It is evident from this how utterly the sacraments are misunderstood by these theologians of the Sentences, inasmuch as they make no account either of faith or of the promise in the sacraments, but cleave only to the sign and the use of the sign, and carry us away from faith to works, from the word to the sign. Concerning the Sacrament of Baptism. Thus, as I have said, they have not only brought the sacraments into bondage, but, as far as in them lay, have entirely done away with them.[25]

In the Catholic system, the church sought a share in the glory of salvation,

---

[23] Diarmaid MacCulloch, *The Reformation: A History* (New York: Penguin Group, 2003), 107.

[24] Martin Luther, *The Babylonian Captivity of the Church*, ed. Henry Wace and C. A. Buchheim (London: John Murray, 1883), Christian Classics Ethereal Library, accessed June 21, 2017, http://www.ccel.org/ccel/luther/first_prin.pdf.

[25] Luther, *Babylonian Captivity of the Church*, 209–210.

because they were the only ones who could administer the sacraments, which were essential to justification. The reformers maintained some Catholic teaching on sacraments (for example, they taught infant baptism,[26] and that baptism makes one part of the body, even if one is not yet capable of belief),[27] but they rejected using the sacraments to usurp God's glory in salvation. In fact, defending God's sole right to glory in salvation was the core element of their doctrine.

As noted above, Calvin taught that all of the elect would persevere in faith and good works until the end of life, which makes complete assurance impossible, since no one can know if he will persevere. However, the *emphasis* of his teaching on faith was assurance. For example:

> Here, indeed, is the chief hinge on which faith turns: that we do not regard the promises of mercy that God offers as true only outside ourselves, but not at all in us; rather that we make them ours by inwardly embracing them. Hence, at last is born that confidence which Paul elsewhere calls "peace" [Rom. 5:1], unless someone may prefer to derive peace from it. Now it is an assurance that renders the conscience calm and peaceful before God's judgment.[28]

Kendall is correct to note that: "What stands out in these descriptions [i.e. Calvin's descriptions of faith] is the given, intellectual, passive, and assuring nature of faith."[29]

Though written in 1776, John Stocker's hymn, "Thy Mercy My God" captures the Reformation doctrine of grace:

Thy mercy my God is the theme of my song,
The joy of my heart, and the boast of my tongue.
Thy free grace alone, from the first to the last,
Hath won my affection and bound my soul fast.

---

[26] For example, Calvin, *Institutes of the Christian Religion*, ed. John T. McNeill, trans. Ford Lewis Battles (Philadelphia, PA: Westminster, 1960), 4.16.1–32.

[27] Ibid., 4.16.9.

[28] Ibid., 3.2.16.

[29] R. T. Kendall, *Calvin and English Calvinism to 1649* (1979; repr., Waynesboro, GA: Paternoster Press, 1997), 19.

Without Thy sweet mercy, I could not live here.
Sin would reduce me to utter despair,
But through Thy free goodness, my spirits revive
And He that first made me still keeps me alive.

Thy mercy is more than a match for my heart,
Which wonders to feel its own hardness depart.
Dissolved by Thy goodness, I fall to the ground
And weep for the praise of the mercy I've found.[30]

13.3.2 *Sola Gratia after Luther and Calvin*

After Luther and Calvin, however, the emphasis of many Protestant teachers drifted away from God's work in salvation and toward human works. R. T. Kendall's groundbreaking work, *Calvin and English Calvinism to 1649*, catalogues this shift.

Because Calvin taught that all the elect will persevere in good works, there was an opening for those who came after him to focus on works in salvation by simply changing emphasis. Church history has shown repeatedly that when there is room for legalism, man will hastily move into it. Instead of focusing on the comforting, assuring aspects of faith, the focus shifted to testing one's own experience for evidence of salvation. Calvin soundly rejected looking to works for assurance,[31] but those who came after him did not.[32]

---

[30] Original publication information is unavailable. However, Sandra Mc-Cracken, who wrote a new melody for the hymn, writes: "John Stocker wrote a hymn, 'Thy Mercy My God, Is The Theme Of My Song,' in 1776 that I discovered on the pages of a Gadsby's Hymnal about ten years ago. I wrote a new melody to his four stanzas that afternoon, and these words have been an arresting companion for me in many changing seasons since that day." The full story along with the lyrics of the hymn can be found online: "Thy Mercy My God," Indelible Grace Hymn Book, accessed June 28, 2017, http://hymnbook.igracemusic.com/hymns/thy-mercy-my-god. John Stocker wrote several hymns for the Calvinist publication *Gospel Magazine* in 1776 and 1777, though "Thy Mercy My God" was not among them.

[31] See Calvin, *Institutes*, 3.2.24 and 3.16.19.

[32] For a fuller treatment, the reader is encouraged to read Kendall's excellent work cited above, along with Charles Bell's similarly excellent, *Calvin and Scottish Theology: The Doctrine of Assurance* (Haddington, UK: Handsel Press, 1986).

Theodore Beza, the son-in-law of John Calvin, made the practical out-working of salvation a necessary test of election:

Beware thou begin not at that most high degree: for so thou shouldest not be able to sustain the most shining light of God's majesty. Begin therefore beneath at the lowest order, and when thou shalt hear the voice of God (10) sound in thine ears, & in thy heart, which calleth thee to Christ the only mediator, consider by little and little, & try diligently (11), if thou be justified & sanctified in Christ through faith: for these two be the effects or fruits, whereby the faith is known, which is their cause. As for this thou shalt partly know by the spirit of adoption, which crieth within thee, Abba, father (12): & partly by the virtue & effect of the same spirit, which is wrought in thee. As if thou fall, & so declare indeed that although sin dwell in thee, yet it doth no more reign in thee (13): for is not the holy ghost he that causeth us not to let slip the bridle, & give liberty willingly to our naughty & vile concupiscences (14), as they are accustomed, whose eyes the prince of this world blindeth (15), or else who moveth us to pray when we are cold, and slothful? who stirreth up in us those unspeakable groanings (16)? who is he that when we have sinned (yea & sometimes willingly and wittingly) engendereth in us an hate of the sin committed, and not for the fear of punishment which we have therefore deserved, but because we have offended our most merciful father (17)? Who is he, I say, that testifieth unto us that our sighings are heard, and also moveth us to call daily God, our God, and our Father, even at that time when we have trespassed against him (18)? Is it not that spirit, which is freely given to us as a gift, for a sure and certain pledge of our adoption (19)? Wherefore if we can gather by these effects, that we have faith, it followeth that we are called and drawn effectually. And again, by this vocation, which we have declared properly to belong to the children of God; that is evidently proved which we took in hand to shew, that is, forasmuch as we were Predestinate by the Eternal counsel and decree of God, (the which he had determined in himself) to be adopted in his son, therefore we were given to him, whereof the conclusion followeth, that since by the most constant will of God (20), which only is grounded on itself, and dependeth on none other thing, we are predestinate, and no man can take us out of the hands of the son: also seeing that to continue and persevere in the faith is necessary.[33]

This passage occurs in the chapter entitled, "HOVV EUERIE MAN MAIE VVITH PROFIT APPLIE THIS VNIUERSALL DOCTRINE [i.e. predestination] TO HIMSELFE," in which Beza seeks to answer the question of how one can know that he is elect instead of reprobate. Calvin taught that all of the elect persevere in faith and good works, but he did not direct the believer to look to those works for assurance. For assurance, the believer was to look to Christ alone. Beza instead directs the believer to his sanctification for assurance.

Zacharius Ursinus, who with the other Heidelberg theologians systematized Covenant theology,[34] defines salvation in terms of an exchange of responsibilities:

> It is easy to perceive what we are to understand by the Covenant here spoken of, which we may define as a mutual promise and agreement between God and men, in which God gives assurance to men that he will be merciful to them, remit their sins, grant unto them a new righteousness, the Holy Spirit, and eternal life by and for the sake of his Son, our Mediator. And on the other side, men bind themselves to God in this covenant that they will exercise repentance and faith, or that they will receive with a true faith this great benefit which God offers, and render such obedience as will be acceptable to him. This mutual engagement between God and man is confirmed by those outward signs which we call sacraments, which are holy signs, declaring and sealing unto us God's good will, and our thankfulness and obedience.[35]

---

[33] Theodore Beza, "A Briefe Declaration of the Cheife Poyntes of Christian Religion, Set Forth in a Table," Reformed Presbyterian Church (Covenanted), accessed June 27, 2017, http://www.covenanter.org/reformed/2015/8/17/theodore-bezas-a-briefe-declaration-of-the-table-of-predestination-1?rq=beza.

[34] Zacharias Ursinus, *The Commentary of Dr. Zacharias Ursinus, on the Heidelberg Catechism*, trans. G. W. Williard (Columbus, OH: Scott and Bascom, 1852), 96–100.

[35] Ursinus, *Commentary of Dr. Zacharias Ursinus*, 97. This language of an exchange between man and the God of salvation for obedience was also novel among Protestants.

William Perkins, synthesizing the doctrines of Theodore Beza and the Heidelberg Theologians, made 2 Peter 1:10 central to his theology of assurance. He writes:

> This is the charge of the holy Ghost upon every childe of God, 2 Pet. 1. 10. *Give all diligence to make your calling and election sure:* this is, get the assurance thereof sealed up in your hearts, by the saving graces of God's spirit, *joyning vertue with your faith, and with your vertue knowledge, and with your knowledge temperance, and with temperance patience, and with patience godlinesse, and with godliness brotherly kindnesse, and with brotherly kindnesse love, v. 5,6,7.* and indeed if we would have true peace and comfort in every estate, whether adversity or prosperitie, let us labour for the knowledge of our Adoption.[36]

In this way, Perkins challenges the reader to obtain assurance by the saving graces of God's spirit, that is, in sanctification. Perkins' theology was codified in the *Westminster Confession of Faith*, which reads:

> The doctrine of this high mystery of predestination is to be handled with special prudence and care, that men, attending the will of God revealed in His Word, and yielding obedience thereunto, may, from the certainty of their effectual vocation, be assured of their eternal election.[37]

By this, the duty of Christians to seek assurance by good works was made official. And so, while many in the Reformed tradition view the *Westminster Confession* to be an expression of Calvin's theology, it is actually an expression of the theology of Beza, the Heidelberg theologians, and especially Perkins, who synthesized the two.

Over time the focus shifted further and further away from God's work in salvation toward the work of man. For example, the well-known Puritan,

---

[36] William Perkins, *The Workes of that Famovs and Worthy Minister of Christ In the Universitie of Cambridge, M. W. Perkins* (1608; repr., London: Iohn Haviland, 1631), 3:382; emphasis in original. See also Kendall, *Calvin and English Calvinism*, 55–76.

[37] Westminster Assembly, *The Humble Advice of the Assembly of Divines, Now by Authority of Parliament Sitting at Westminster, Concerning a Confession of Faith, with the Quotations and Texts of Scripture Annexed* (1647), 3.8.

Thomas Watson (c 1620–1686) writes:

> It is a long race from earth to heaven; lay aside all weights of sin which
> will hinder you in the race, and reach forward with a winged swiftness
> to lay hold upon the mark. Fourthly, Sometimes [sic] it is called offer-
> ing violence to heaven, Matt. xi. 12. 'The kingdom of heaven suffers
> violence.' There must not only be diligence, but violence ; we must
> not only pray, but pray fervently, James v. 16. 'be zealous and repent,'
> Rev. iii. 19. not only love, but 'be sick of love,' Cant. ii. 5. This is
> offering violence ; it is a metaphor taken from a castle that holds out
> in siege, and will not be taken but by storm.
>
> I proceed now to the reasons enforcing this holy sweat and in-
> dustry about salvation ; and they are three ; we must work out our
> salvation, because of,
>
> 1. The difficulty of this work. 2. The rareness of it. 3. The possi-
> bility of it.
>
> 1. The difficulty of this work; it is a work that may make us la-
> bour to the going down of the sun of our life, Dan. vi. 14.[38]

Heaven is not presented here as a gift, but as a castle that "will not be taken
but by storm" of violence. If someone wants to reach heaven, Watson calls
him to produce "holy sweat and industry," in contrast to the apostles' call,
"Believe in the Lord Jesus, and you will be saved" (from Acts 16:31). Watson
here presents salvation as monergistic, but the one worker is man, not God.
God is actually presented as an enemy fighting to keep grace from us.

Jonathan Edwards, considered by many to be the greatest American

---

[38] Thomas Watson, "The One Thing Necessary (Philippians 2:12)," in *Discourses
on Important and Interesting Subjects* (1829; repr., Ligonier, PA: Soli Deo Gloria Publications, 1990), 352; paragraph breaks in original. Watson was controversial, though not
for his doctrine of salvation. The controversy was because "he was one of the Presbyterian ministers who went to Oliver Cromwell to protest the execution of Charles I.
along with Christopher Love, William Jenkyn, and others, he was imprisoned in 1651
for his part in a plot to restore the monarchy." Joel R. Beeke and Randall J. Pederson,
Meet the Puritans: With a Guide to Modern Reprints (Grand Rapids, MI: Reformation
Heritage Books, 2006), 605.

theologian,[39] does not present salvation as entirely the work of man. But when discussing "Why natural men are not willing to come to Christ, and their dreadful condition," he makes giving up all sins a condition for salvation:

> There are some things in him [Jesus] that they like, and others that they greatly dislike ; but consider him as he is, and as he is offered to them in the gospel, and they are not willing to accept of Christ ; for in doing so, they must of necessity part with all their sins ; they must sell the world...[40]

Since mature Christians still commit sins (and are even more aware of them than the baby Christian), how could a believer ever be assured of salvation? Those in the theological tradition of Perkins and the Puritans have noted that lack of assurance is a major pastoral problem.[41] When the source of assurance shifted from the objective work of Christ to the subjective work of the Holy Spirit, grace faded from view.

13.3.3 More Clarification Needed

It is said that a mist in the pulpit is a cloud in the pew. Likewise, a mist in history becomes a cloud as time passes. In Puritan theology, the reformers' mist had become a very dark cloud indeed. Because of this, more clarity regarding grace was needed, which was later advanced by dispensational thought.

---

[39] For example, Mark Galli and Ted Olsen, "Jonathan Edwards: America's Greatest Theologian," in *131 Christians Everyone Should Know* (Nashville, TN: Broadman & Holman, 2000), 43–45, accessed June 28, 2017, http://www.christianitytoday.com /history/people/theologians/jonathan-edwards.html.

[40] Jonathan Edwards, *The Works of Jonathan Edwards* (1834; repr., Edinburgh, UK: Banner of Truth Trust, 1974), 2:138.

[41] For example, John Piper, "The Agonizing Problem of the Assurance of Salvation," DesiringGod, April 28, 1998, accessed June 28, 2017, http://www.desiringgod .org/articles/the-agonizing-problem-of-the-assurance-of-salvation. For those who rest on the biblical teaching on grace and assurance, assurance of salvation is not an agonizing problem, but a source of great joy (Rom 8:33–39).

13.4 Dispensationalism Clarifies *Sola Gratia*

With the rise of dispensationalism, however, came a return to the biblical doctrine of grace. [42] In sharp contrast to the non-dispensationalists, the belief that assurance should be found in looking to Christ and His promises alone, rather than to works, was almost universally held among the early dispensationalists. And some of them argued vigorously for it. Some extended quotes are necessary to demonstrate how forcefully these dispensationalists expounded this belief.

J. N. Darby presented faith and the peace (assurance) which it brings as properly resting on God's Word, not on experience:

> In real communion the conscience must be purged; there can be no communion if the soul be not at peace. We read here, "By one offering he hath perfected forever them that are sanctified." There is very frequently the confounding of what faith produces with what faith rests upon. Faith always rests upon God's estimate of the blood of Jesus as He has revealed it in His word: faith rests on no experience. [43]

C. H. Mackintosh expressly contradicts the works of the Beza, Perkins, the Westminster divines, and others who taught that the believer should look to the subjective work of the Holy Spirit for assurance:

> The Spirit of God never leads any one to build upon His work as the ground of peace, but only upon the finished work of Christ, and the unchangeable word of God; and we may rest assured that the more simply we rest on these the more settled our peace will be, and the clearer our evidences, the brighter our frames, the happier our feelings, the richer our experiences.

---

[42] This section is adapted from Grant Hawley, *Dispensationalism and Free Grace: Intimately Linked* (Taos, NM: Dispensational Publishing House, forthcoming), chap. 3, "Assurance without Introspection."

[43] J. N. Darby, "No More Conscience of Sins," in *The Collected Writings of J. N. Darby*, ed. William Kelly, vol. 12, *Evangelic No. 1* (Winschoten, Netherlands: H. L. Heijkoop, 1971-1972), accessed March 1, 2012, http://www.stempublishing.com/authors /darby/EVANGEL/12018E.html. See also J. N. Darby, "A Voice from the Past: The True Grace of God in Which You Stand," *Journal of the Grace Evangelical Society* 8, no. 2 (Autumn 1995): 69-73.

In short, the more we look away from self and all its belongings, and rest in Christ, on the clear authority of scripture, the more spiritually minded we shall be; and the inspired apostle tells us that "to be spiritually minded (or, the minding of the Spirit) is life and peace." The best evidence of a spiritual mind is child-like repose in Christ and His word. The clearest proof of an unspiritual mind is self-occupation. It is a poor affair to be trafficking in *our* evidences, or *our* anything. It looks like piety, but it leads away from Christ—away from scripture—away from God; and this is not piety, or faith, or Christianity.[44]

Thus, from the earliest days of systematized dispensationalism, the biblical doctrine of grace and assurance was already strongly represented and had near universal acceptance.

James Hall Brookes, who has been called the "father of American dispensationalism,"[45] makes perhaps an even more robust defense of the freeness of grace and assurance through Christ alone. His work, *Salvation: The Way Made Plain*, devotes 362 pages to the topic[46] (the rest of the book expresses the impossibility of man earning salvation through works) and argues from many different angles for the believer's right to absolute assurance apart from works. For example:

---

[44] C. H. Mackintosh, *The Mackintosh Treasury: Miscellaneous Writings* (1976; repr., Sunbury, PA: Believers Bookshelf, 1999), 670.

[45] "Perhaps the father of American dispensationalism was James Brookes... Brookes wrote the book *Maranatha*, which achieved wide distribution as it popularized a dispensational view of prophecy...Perhaps Brookes will best be remembered as the one who introduced C.I. Scofield to Dispensationalism shortly after his conversion." Thomas Ice, "A Short History of Dispensationalism," Pre-Trib Research Center Article Archives, Paper 37 (May 2009), accessed August 8, 2017, http://digitalcommons.liberty.edu/pretrib_arch/37. Scofield said of Brookes, "During the last twenty years of his life Dr. Brookes was perhaps my most intimate friend, and *to him I am indebted more than to all other men in the world for the establishment of my faith.*" Ernest Sandeen, *The Origins of Fundamentalism*, Historical Series no. 10 (Philadelphia, PA: Fortress Press, 1968), 223, quoted in Larry Crutchfield, *The Origins of Dispensationalism: The Darby Factor* (Lanham, MD: University Press of America, 1992), 17.

[46] James Hall Brookes, *Salvation: The Way Made Plain* (Philadelphia, PA: American Sunday-School Union, 1871), 123–484.

It is my earnest desire and effort to turn your thoughts entirely away from yourself to the Saviour, for it is the most melancholy business that can engage even a redeemed sinner to be probing into his own soul to find some assurance that he is saved. You can never find it there, but only in the word; and, thank God! having once seen it in the word, you can see it every day and every hour, and as often as you read and believe what Jesus says. Nor is this assurance the privilege exclusively of ministers or of a favoured few who have made higher attainments in holiness than the common crowd can ever hope to reach, but it is the privilege of every one without exception who believes the testimony of God's word addressed alike to all.[47]

Illustrating the distinctiveness of the dispensational position on this issue, Brookes commented on the profound difference between the lack of assurance that was prevalent in his day and what he saw in the New Testament:

[T]here is abundant proof that [the believers to whom the NT epistles were written] were strangers to the fear and uncertainty that make up the gloomy experience of at least nine-tenths of the people of God in modern times. Whoever they were, whatever they had been, wherever they lived, they had an assurance of salvation which must have formed at once an unfailing fountain of joy to their hearts and an effective instrument for achieving an easy victory over the world.[48]

Examples such as these could be multiplied in this work. Likewise, other early dispensationalists, Robert Govett,[49] C. I. Scofield,[50] D. M. Panton[51]

---

[47] Ibid., 445.

[48] Ibid., 283.

[49] See Robert Govett, "The Gift and the Prize," in *Kingdom Studies* (Miami Springs, FL: Schoettle, 1989), 1–6.

[50] Space does not permit a proper treatment of the significance of the *Scofield Reference Bible* (Oxford: Oxford University Press, 1909), but it should be noted that it was instrumental in the grassroots rise of dispensationalism and was for many the first exposure to the sharp distinction between law and grace (see note on John 1:17), the idea that James 2:14–26 was discussing justification before men (see note on James 2:24), and the idea that the Sermon on the Mount was a manifesto for the Messianic kingdom intended in primary application to the Jews (see note on Matt 5:2).

[51] D. M. Panton, *The Judgment Seat of Christ* (Hayesville, NC: Schoettle, 1984), 3–

and, to a lesser extent, William Kelly[52] shared this view.

13.4.1 A Better Theological Foundation for Grace

It is no accident that dispensationalists taught a biblical view of grace. Dispensationalism provides a better foundation than Covenant theology for discussing grace as a contrast to works. Many aspects of the theology of dispensationalism lead to grace. The following three dispensational distinctives are especially key to establishing the biblical doctrine of grace: (1) doxological priority, (2) God's faithfulness in keeping His promises despite Israel's disobedience, and (3) the Judgment Seat of Christ.

13.4.1.1 Doxological Priority

The first distinctive is what is often called doxological priority. In doxological priority, it is recognized that the chief unifying theme of Scripture is the glory of God as it is worked out in many different ways. By contrast, Covenant theology views the outworking of predestination and sometimes reprobation as the unifying theme of Scripture.[53] In other words, soteriology unites Scripture for the covenant theologian and the totality of it is read through that lens. The dispensationalist, however, sees the glory of God as the unifying theme of Scripture. When freed to look at doctrines other than soteriology as central, it became apparent to the dispensationalist that most of Scripture was written to those who were already justified by grace through faith. So it follows that the Bible addresses many other important doctrines.

Mackintosh expresses the novel dispensational point that soteriology is just one of many key doctrines in Scripture:

4.

[52] William Kelly, "The Well of Water Springing up into Everlasting Life," in *Lectures on the New Testament Doctrine of the Holy Spirit* (London: A. S. Rouse, 1906), accessed June 11, 2017, http://www.stempublishing.com/authors/kelly/6h_s/hs2 _well .html.

[53] William Perkins, *A Golden Chaine: Or, the Description of Theologie Containing the Order of the Causes of Saluation and Damnation, According to God's Word* (Cambridge, Iohn Legat, 1600).

We believe these five points, so far as they go;[54] but they are very far indeed from containing the faith of God's elect. There are wide fields of divine revelation which this stunted and one-sided system does not touch upon, or even hint at, in the most remote manner. Where do we find the heavenly calling? Where, the precious sanctifying hope of the coming of Christ to receive His people to Himself? Where have we the grand scope of prophecy opened to the vision of our souls, in that which is so pompously styled "the faith of God's elect"?[55]

With dispensationalism came the recovery of so many doctrines, including "the grand scope of prophecy." Because of this, passages which are not about how to be saved can be taken for what they are. In Anderson's articles on Augustine cited above, he notes that Matthew 24:13, "But the one who endures to the end, he will be saved," forms the basis of Augustine's soteriology, especially the doctrine of the Perseverance of the Saints.[56] He did this even though the context is not dealing with salvation from the penalty of sins, but salvation from the persecution of the saints in the tribulation. Non-dispensational systems greatly confused soteriology by importing into it passages that have nothing to do with it. By decentralizing soteriology, dispensationalism clarified the same.

---

[54] Later in the same article, Mackintosh seems to repudiate limited atonement. In addition, in an essay entitled, "God For Us," he wrote, "When we have from the lips of our blessed Lord Himself, the eternal Son of God, such words as these, 'God so loved *the world*,' we have no ground whatever for questioning their application to each and all who come under the comprehensive word 'world.' Before any one can prove that the free love of God does not apply to him, he must first prove that he does not form a part of the world, but that he belongs to some other sphere of being. If indeed our Lord had said, 'God so loved a certain portion of the world,' call it what you please, then verily it would be absolutely necessary to prove that we belong to that particular portion or class, ere we could attempt to apply His words to ourselves. If He had said that God so loved the predestinated, the elect, or the called, then we must seek to know our place amongst the number of such, before we can take home to ourselves the precious assurance of the love of God, as proved by the gift of His Son. But our Lord used no such qualifying clause." Mackintosh, *Mackintosh Treasury*, 607. Clearly, Mackintosh rejected limited atonement.

[55] Mackintosh, *Mackintosh Treasury*, 605.

[56] Anderson, "The Soteriological Impact of Augustine's Change," part one and two.

13.4.1.2 *God's Faithfulness in Israel's Unfaithfulness*

God keeps His promises. If Christians insist that God abandoned His promises to Israel because of their disobedience, how do they know He will be faithful to keep His promises to them if at some time in the future they are faithless? Paul had no doubts about this: "If we are faithless, He remains faithful, for He cannot deny Himself" (2 Tim 2:13). Recognizing that God is always faithful to keep His promises gives believers this same confidence. God asserts His faithfulness to keep His promises:

> My lovingkindness I will keep for him [David] forever, And My covenant shall be confirmed to him. So I will establish his descendants forever And his throne as the days of heaven. If his sons forsake My law And do not walk in My judgments, If they violate My statutes And do not keep My commandments, Then I will punish their transgression with the rod And their iniquity with stripes. But I will not break off My lovingkindness from him, Nor deal falsely in My faithfulness. My covenant I will not violate, Nor will I alter the utterance of My lips. Once I have sworn by My holiness; I will not lie to David. His descendants shall endure forever And his throne as the sun before Me. It shall be established forever like the moon, And the witness in the sky is faithful. Selah. (Ps 89:28–37)

There is punishment for iniquity and transgression, but that punishment is temporary and His promise is eternal. This is why Paul can say, without qualification, "for the gifts and the calling of God are irrevocable" (Rom 11:29, cf. 11:26a). They are irrevocable because God cannot lie (Titus 1:2; Heb 6:18).

This is why Chafer, in his great exposition on grace, writes:

> Every dispensation represents a new divine purpose in the testing of man. In every case man is seen to fail, and to be guilty before God ; yet we behold God patiently and faithfully bringing man face to face with the issues involved. After a brief experience in the wilderness, He took Israel to Kadesh Barnea where He provided and offered an immediate entrance into their own land. The choice was theirs ; they refused to enter. They were guilty. God knew they would refuse to

enter the land ; yet His offer was genuine, and His purposes were realized. In chastisement, God sent them back into the wilderness for
forty years of added discomfort. In His own time, and by His own
power, they finally entered the land. This portion of Israel's history
may be taken to be typical. When Christ came, the nation had then
experienced over five hundred years of trial in dispossession of their
land and the vacancy of David's throne. When their Messiah came,
they refused the divine provisions centered in the King, and, as typi-
fied at Kadesh, they returned to what has now proven to be two thousand years of added affliction. The day is coming, however, when, according to the faithfulness of God, they will receive their King and
abide under His undimmed glory.[57]

Dispensationalism clarifies *sola gratia* (grace alone) by defending the faithfulness of God relative to Israel.

13.4.1.3 The Judgment Seat of Christic

There is clearly a judgment for believers based upon works (Luke
19:11-27; Rom 14:10-12; 1 Cor 3:9-15, 9:24-27; 2 Cor 5:10, et al.).[58] Dispensationalism recognizes that this is a separate judgment from the great
white throne judgment. As Anderson writes:

> Which judgment seat [the Bema or the Great White Throne] a person
> appears before is determined not by their works, but by their faith in
> Christ or lack thereof. At each judgment seat a person is judged for
> his works, but not to determine his destiny in eternity. That has al-
> ready been determined by his faith (with God forever) or lack of faith
> (apart from God forever). The judgment seat for his works is to deter-
> mine his rewards, not his destiny. When the thousand year reign of
> Christ on earth is removed (which all amillennialists do), then the two

---

[57] Lewis Sperry Chafer, *Grace: The Glorious Theme* (1922; repr., Grand Rapids,
MI: Academie Books, 1950), 135–36.

[58] For a fuller exposition of the judgment seat of Christ, see Grant Hawley,
"What Is the Judgment Seat of Christ?" in *21 Tough Questions about Grace*, ed. Grant
Hawley (Allen, TX: Bold Grace, 2015), 91–98.

judgment seats collapse into one judgment for believers and unbelievers simultaneously. Since these people (believers and unbelievers) are judged for their works at this single judgment seat, the basis for salvation can become muddled very quickly.[59]

Because the literal thousand-year reign of Christ on earth is maintained in dispensationalism, the judgments can be kept separate. The judgment seat of Christ occurs at the return of Christ (Matt 16:27; Rev 22:12) and is related to rewards which will be enjoyed during the millennium (Rev 3:21), so it must occur before the millennium. The great white throne, however, occurs after the millennium is over (Rev 20:11–15), when believers will have already been living for a thousand years in glory. Believers are not among "the dead" (Rev 20:11) who are judged at the great white throne.

Dispensationalists have served a critical role in emphasizing the biblical doctrine of rewards according to works as separate from salvation by grace through faith. For example, commenting on 2 Corinthians 5:10, Scofield writes:

> The judgment of the believer's works, not sins, is in question here. These have been atoned for, and are "remembered no more forever" (Heb. x.17); but every *work* must come into judgment (Mt. xii.36; Rom. xiv.10; Gal. vi.7; Eph. vi.8; Col. iii.24, 25). The result is "reward" or "loss" (of the reward), "but he himself shall be saved" (1 Cor. iii.11–15). This judgment occurs at the return of Christ (Mt. xvi.27; Lk. xiv.14; 1 Cor. iv.5; 2 Tim. iv.8; Rev. xxii.12).[60]

Judgment by works for rewards does not confuse grace and works, but this doctrine was hidden by the fact that the various amillennial systems

---

[59] David R. Anderson, *Free Grace Soteriology*, rev. ed. (Conroe, TX: Grace Theology Press, 2012), x–xi.

[60] C. I. Scofield, ed., *Scofield Reference Bible* (New York: Oxford University Press, 1909), 1233n, accessed August 8, 2017, https://archive.org/details/TheScofield ReferenceBible; referenced also by Lewis Sperry Chafer, *Systematic Theology* (Dallas, TX: Dallas Seminary Press, 1948), 4:377. See also Chafer, *Systematic Theology*, 4:404–406. See also Panton, *The Judgment Seat of Christ*, and Arthur W. Pink, *The Redeemer's Return* (1918; repr., Asheville, NC: Revival Literature, 2002), 189. Pink later taught amillennialism, but was a premillennial dispensationalist when he wrote this.

lump this judgment in with the great white throne. This key biblical doctrine was recovered by dispensationalists. Dispensationalism clarifies and advances grace by maintaining the separation of the two judgments by one-thousand years, and allowing each to be kept in its proper place—salvation by grace and reward according to works. Doxological priority also helps to rightly divide this judgment from the great white throne.

13.5 Conclusion

The biblical doctrine of grace brings awe and wonder to anyone who takes it seriously. God has shown His gracious character by his dealings with the Old Testament saints. Additionally, His faithfulness in covenant-keeping love for His people, Israel, illustrates the depths of His unmerited favor for His beloved. In the New Testament, God's grace is even more clearly seen, since "grace and truth were realized through Jesus Christ." The apostle Paul especially expounds upon grace by contrasting it with works religion, either in justification or in Christian living. Grace and works religion can never be mixed, or grace is negated (Rom 11:6).

Prior to the Reformation, grace was almost completely obscured, but the reformers made great strides toward recovering that doctrine. Their doctrine of grace was developed from Augustine, whom the reformers held in high esteem. The emphasis of their doctrine of grace was not the separation of grace from works religion, but the separation of grace from human ability to believe without first being regenerated. This nevertheless returned the glory to God alone for salvation.

But because the early reformers opened up the door to looking to works for assurance in their doctrine of the perseverance of the saints (as distinct from eternal security), later reformers drifted away from grace and toward works religion. This continued on through gradual steps in that direction, and by the time Puritanism was in full swing, grace was barely discernable.

Dispensationalism gives a firm foundation for discerning the biblical doctrine of grace by recovering the doxological priority of Scripture, allowing for accurate interpretation of non-soteriological passages which had previously confused the church due to the soteriological priority in interpretation. Additionally, God's faithfulness to Israel despite her repeated unfaithfulness illustrates and proves the depths of God's grace. Only dispensation-alism affirms God's unwavering faithfulness to national Israel. Finally, the doctrine of the judgment seat of Christ as a separate judgment from the great white throne judgment allows passages about judgment of believers based on works to take their proper place in a doctrine of rewards, rather than confusing the issue of salvation. These doctrinal foundations allowed dispensationalists to clarify and champion the biblical doctrine of grace, so that the early dispensationalists' writings on grace can be seen in stark contrast to the gloomy religion of their time. In all of these ways, dispensation-alism both clarifies and advances the biblical doctrine of *sola gratia*.

Bibliography

Anderson, David R. *Free Grace Soteriology*. Rev. ed. Conroe, TX: Grace Theology Press, 2012.

———. "The Soteriological Impact of Augustine's Change from Premillennialism to Amillennialism, Part 1." *Journal of the Grace Evangelical Society* 15, no.1 (Spring 2002): 25–36.

———. "The Soteriological Impact of Augustine's Change from Premillennialism to Amillennialism, Part 2." *Journal of the Grace Evangelical Society* 15, no. 2 (Autumn 2002): 23–39.

Aquinas, Thomas. *Summa Theologica*. Translated by the Fathers of the English Dominican Province. 5 vols. 1911. Reprint, Westminster, MD: Christian Classics, 1948.

Augustine. "On Forgiveness of Sins, and Baptism." In *A Select Library of the Nicene and Post-Nicene Fathers of the Christian Church*, edited by Philip Schaff, *Writings Against the Pelagians*. Ser. 1. Vol. 5. Grand Rapids, MI: Eerdmans, 1980.

Beeke, Joel R., and Randall J. Pederson. *Meet the Puritans: With a Guide to Modern Reprints*. Grand Rapids, MI: Reformation Heritage Books, 2006.

Bell, Charles. *Calvin and Scottish Theology: The Doctrine of Assurance*. Haddington, UK: Handsel Press, 1986.

Beza, Theodore. "A Briefe Declaration of the Cheife Poyntes of Christian Religion, Set Forth in a Table." Reformed Presbyterian Church (Covenanted). Accessed June 27, 2017. http://www.covenanter.org/reformed/2015/8/17/theodore-bezas-a-briefe-declaration-of-the-table-of-predestination-1?rq=beza.

Brookes, James Hall. *Salvation: The Way Made Plain*. Philadelphia, PA: American Sunday-School Union, 1871.

Calvin, John. *Commentaries on the Catholic Epistles*. Translated by John Owen. Edinburgh: Calvin Translation Society, 1855.

Calvin, John. *The Gospel According to St John 1–10*. Calvin's Commentaries

4. Translated by T. H. L. Parker. Grand Rapids, MI: Eerdmans, 1961.

———. *Institutes of the Christian Religion.* Edited by John T. McNeill. Translated by Ford Lewis Battles. 2 vols. Philadelphia: Westminster, 1960.

Chafer, Lewis Sperry. *Grace: The Glorious Theme.* 1922. Reprint, Grand Rapids, MI: Academie Books, 1950.

———. *Systematic Theology.* 8 vols. Dallas, TX: Dallas Seminary Press, 1948.

Crutchfield, Larry. *The Origins of Dispensationalism: The Darby Factor.* Lanham, MD: University Press of America, 1992.

Darby, J. N. "No More Conscience of Sins." In *The Collected Writings of J.N. Darby.* Edited by William Kelly. Vol. 12, *Evangelic No. 1.* Winschoten, Netherlands: H.L. Heijkoop, 1971-1972. Accessed March 1, 2012. http://www.stempublishing.com/authors/darby/EVANGEL/12018 E.html.

———. "A Voice from the Past: The True Grace of God in Which You Stand." *Journal of the Grace Evangelical Society* 8, no. 2 (Autumn 1995): 69-73.

Edwards, Jonathan. *The Works of Jonathan Edwards.* 2 vols. 1834. Reprint, Edinburgh, UK: Banner of Truth Trust, 1974.

Govett, Robert. "The Gift and the Prize." In *Kingdom Studies*, 1-6. Miami Springs, FL: Schoettle, 1989.

Hawley, Grant. *Dispensationalism and Free Grace: Intimately Linked.* Taos, NM: Dispensational Publishing House, forthcoming.

———. "What Is the Judgment Seat of Christ?" In *21 Tough Questions about Grace*, edited by Grant Hawley, 91-98. Allen, TX: Bold Grace, 2015.

Hodges, Zane. *Romans: Deliverance from Wrath.* Corinth, TX: Grace Evangelical Society, 2013.

Ice, Thomas. "A Short History of Dispensationalism." Pre-Trib Research Center Article Archives, Paper 37 (May 2009). Accessed August 8, 2017. http://digitalcommons.liberty.edu/pretrib_arch/37.

Kelly, William. "The Well of Water Springing up into Everlasting Life." In *Lectures on the New Testament Doctrine of the Holy Spirit*. London: A. S. Rouse, 1906. Accessed June 11, 2017. http://www.stempublishing.com/authors/kelly/6h_s/hs2_well.html.

Kendall, R. T. *Calvin and English Calvinism to 1649*. 1979. Reprint, Waynesboro, GA: Paternoster Press, 1997.

Kittel, Gerhard, ed. *Theological Dictionary of the New Testament*. 10 vols. Grand Rapids, MI: Eerdmans, 1974.

Lenski, R. C. H. *The Interpretation of St. Paul's Espistle to the Romans*. 1945. Reprint, Minneapolis, MN: Augsburg Publishing House, 1961.

Luther, Martin. *The Babylonian Captivity of the Church*. Edited by Henry Wace and C. A. Buchheim. London: John Murray, 1883. Christian Classics Ethereal Library. Accessed June 21, 2017. http://www.ccel.org/ccel/luther/first_prin.pdf.

———. *The Bondage of the Will*. Translated by Henry Cole. Grand Rapids, MI: Baker, 1976.

MacCulloch, Diarmaid. *The Reformation: A History*. New York: Penguin Group, 2003.

Mackintosh, C. H. *The Mackintosh Treasury: Miscellaneous Writings*. 1976. Reprint, Sunbury, PA: Believers Bookshelf, 1999.

Mowinckel, Sigmund. "The Name of the God of Moses." *Hebrew Union College Annual* 32 (1961): 121–133.

Panton, D. M. *The Judgment Seat of Christ*. Hayesville, NC: Schoettle, 1984.

Pelagius, "A Letter from Pelagius (to Demetrius)." In *The Letters of Pelagius and His Followers*, translated by B. R. Rees. Woodbridge, Suffolk: Boydell, 1991. Accessed June 20, 2017. https://epistolae.ccnmtl.columbia.edu/letter/1296.html.

Perkins, William. *A Golden Chaine: Or, the Description of Theologie Containing the Order of the Causes of Saluation and Damnation, According to God's Word.* Cambridge, Iohn Legat, 1600.

———. *The Workes of that Famovs and Worthy Minister of Christ In the Universitie of Cambridge, M. W. Perkins.* 1608. Reprint, London: Iohn Haviland, 1631.

Pink, Arthur W. *The Redeemer's Return.* 1918. Reprint, Asheville, NC: Revival Literature, 2002.

Piper, John. "The Agonizing Problem of the Assurance of Salvation." DesiringGod. April 28, 1998. Accessed June 28, 2017. http://www .desiringgod.org/articles/the-agonizing-problem-of-the-assurance-of-salvation.

Scofield, C. I., ed. *Scofield Reference Bible.* Oxford: Oxford University Press, 1909. Accessed August 8, 2017. https://archive.org/details/The ScofieldReferenceBible.

Trueman, Carl R. *Grace Alone: Salvation as a Gift of God.* The 5 Solas Series. Grand Rapids, MI: Zondervan, 2017.

Ursinus, Zacharias. *The Commentary of Dr. Zacharias Ursinus, on the Heidelberg Catechism.* Translated by G. W. Williard. Columbus, OH: Scott and Bascom, 1852.

Wallace, Daniel. *Greek Grammar beyond the Basics: An Exegetical Syntax of the New Testament.* Grand Rapids, MI: Zondervan, 1996.

Warfield, B. B. *Calvin and Augustine.* Philadelphia, PA: Presbyterian and Reformed, 1956.

Watson, Thomas. "The One Thing Necessary (Philippians 2:12)." In *Discourses on Important and Interesting Subjects,* 349–383. 1829. Reprint, Ligonier, PA: Soli Deo Gloria Publications, 1990.

Sola Fide
[Faith Alone]

14

SOLA FIDE:
Salvation is by Grace Through Faith Alone in Every Dispensation

Glenn R. Kreider
Dallas Theological Seminary

For by grace you have been saved through faith. And this is not your own doing; it is the gift of God, not a result of works, so that no one may boast. For we are his workmanship, created in Christ Jesus for good works, which God prepared beforehand, that we should walk in them. (Eph 2:8–10, NIV)

14.0 Introduction

While reflecting on dispensationalism's emphasis on faith, John Walvoord offered the following: "In every dispensation salvation is by grace through faith, made possible by the death of Christ. On the one hand the dispensations have diversity of requirements for human conduct, but on the other hand salvation is always by God's grace. Salvation is the unifying factor in Scripture."[1] Salvation is by grace alone through faith alone in Christ alone.[2]

---

[1] John F. Walvoord, "Reflections on Dispensationalism," *Bibliotheca Sacra* 158, no. 630 (April 2001): 137.

[2] See Thabiti Anyabwile, "God Does Not Justify Sinners by Grace Alone through Faith Alone in Christ Alone to Make Salvation Easy for Us," Gospel Coalition, August 31, 2010, accessed July 23, 2017, https://blogs.thegospelcoalition.org/thabitiayabwile /2010/08/31/god-does-not-justify-sinners-by-grace-alone-through-faith-alone-in-christ-

The teaching of the New Testament, perhaps most clearly stated in Ephesians 2:8-9, is that righteousness comes to the unrighteous only as a gift from God—this is consistent throughout Scripture.[3] This conviction became the rallying cry of the Reformation, not because the reformers discovered something new, but because the Roman Catholic Church of the time had departed from the original and essential teachings of Christianity.[4] Ragusa summarizes the reformers well:

> *Sola fide* ("by faith alone") is the Reformation's most notorious doctrine and resides at the core of all Protestant identity. Of course, it would be a reductionism to say the Reformers were *only* concerned with justification by faith alone; nonetheless, it was, in the words of Luther, *articulus stantis et cadentis ecclesiae* ("the article by which the church stands and falls"). It was here the true church fought the good fight of faith, many even unto martyrdom.[5]

Sola fide, sometimes called "divine monergism," asserts that salvation is solely God's work. Humans contribute nothing to their salvation except need:

> Implicit in solafidianism is the doctrine of divine monergism, which declares that man's salvation is totally dependent upon God's activity and is in no way conditioned by the action of man. Man's choice of

alone-to-make-salvation-easy-for-us/.

[3] This is the claim Paul makes in Romans 3:21.

[4] Justin Holcomb, "The Five Solas: Points from the Past that Should Matter to You," Christianity Today, accessed July 23, 2017, http://www.christianity.com /church/church-history/the-five-solas-of-the-protestant-reformation.html. See also Kevin J. Vanhoozer, *Biblical Authority after Babel: Retrieving the Solas in the Spirit of Mere Protestant Christianity* (Grand Rapids, MI: Brazos Press, 2016).

[5] Daniel Ragusa, "The Five Solas: Sola Fide," Reformed Forum, October 25, 2016, accessed May 31, 2017, https://reformedforum.org/five-solas-sola-fide/. On Lutheranism and Catholicism see Larry Rinehart, "*Sola Fide*: The Mystery of Salvation by Faith," *Journal of Ecumenical Studies* 49 (Fall 2014): 577–600. See Glenn R. Kreider, Nathan D. Holsteen and Michael J. Svigel, "Wise unto Salvation: Gospel, Atonement, and Saving Grace," in *Exploring Christian Theology*, ed. Nathan D. Holsteen and Michael J. Svigel, vol. 2, *Creation, Fall, and Salvation* (Grand Rapids, MI: Bethany House, 2015), 187–88.

sin has rendered him incapable of spiritual action; he is spiritually dead. Unless rescued by a source outside himself, he would eternally perish in this state. God has taken the initiative by restoring mankind to himself through the death of Christ (Christ's passive obedience to the law), which removes man's guilt, and by imputing Christ's righteousness (which he achieved while on earth through his active obedience to the law) to those who believe. Saving faith is not an innate quality of fallen man but a gift of God (Eph. 2:8; Phil. 1:29) communicated through hearing the gospel (Rom. 10:17).[6]

The theological tradition known as dispensationalism emerged in the nineteenth century, "growing steadily from a fertile ground of eschatological exploration, innovation, and rediscovery that had been under way for several centuries since the Reformation."[7] Dispensationalism's innovation is not soteriological but hermeneutical. As a tradition rooted in the Scriptures and in the Protestant Reformation, dispensationalists agree that salvation is God's work on the believer's behalf, by grace through faith and not by or through works. In short, dispensationalism is a hermeneutical approach that interprets the biblical story as the progressive revelation of God's work of redemption. Although dispensationalists recognize continuity in the plan of God, they believe that the Scriptures reveal distinguishable periods of time in the administration of God's relationship with His creation. The elements of discontinuity in these eras do not indicate different means or ways of salvation, since salvation is always by grace through faith and based in the person and work of Christ.[8]

---

[6] F. R. Harm, "Solafidianism," in *Evangelical Dictionary of Theology*, ed. Walter A. Elwell (Grand Rapids, MI: Baker, 1984), 1032. See also Carl S. Meyer, "Solafidianism," in *The New International Dictionary of the Christian Church*, ed. J. D. Douglas (Grand Rapids, MI: Zondervan, 1978), 914; solafidianism is "the doctrine that eternal salvation is had only through faith by grace in the work of Jesus Christ." Although Meyer's word order is non-standard, he does have the prepositions correct.

[7] Michael J. Svigel, "The History of Dispensationalism in Seven Eras," in *Dispensationalism and the History of Redemption: A Developing and Diverse Tradition*, ed. D. Jeffrey Bingham and Glenn R. Kreider (Chicago, IL: Moody Publishers, 2015), 70.

[8] Glenn R. Kreider, "What Is Dispensationalism?" in *Dispensationalism and the History of Redemption: A Developing and Diverse Tradition*, ed. D. Jeffrey Bingham and

According to Lewis Sperry Chafer, the founder and first president of Dallas Theological Seminary, "Salvation is a work of God for man, rather than a work of man for God. No aspect of salvation, according to the Bible, is made to depend, even in the slightest degree, on human merit or works."[9] John Walvoord, the long tenured second president of the seminary, puts it this way: "The dispensational view of Scripture . . . magnifies the death of Christ as providing not only the ground of salvation of all saints of all ages—essentially one way of salvation for all—but also the ground for the peculiar and unique features of grace revealed to the church, the body of Christ, the saints of this present dispensation."[10]

14.1 Does Dispensationalism Teach Multiple Ways of Salvation?

In his classic *Dispensationalism Today*, Charles Ryrie lamented,

> Without doubt the most frequently heard objection against dispensationalism is that it is supposed to teach several ways of salvation. In particular, dispensationalists are said to teach salvation by works in some dispensations and salvation by grace in others. This is a very serious charge and therefore must be examined with extreme care.[11]

Ryrie identifies several reasons for this charge. First, "labeling the present dispensation as that of Grace has been taken to mean dispensationalism teaches there was no grace in any other age."[12] Second, the critics sometimes "misunderstand the entire concept of dispensations and often make them

---

Glenn R. Kreider (Chicago, IL: Moody Publishers, 2015), 21.

[9] Lewis Sperry Chafer, *Salvation* (Wheaton, IL: Van Kampen Press, 1917), 42.

[10] John F. Walvoord, "Millennial Series: Part 7: Amillennial Soteriology," *Bibliotheca Sacra* 107, no. 427 (July 1950): 289.

[11] Charles Ryrie, *Dispensationalism Today* (Chicago, IL: Moody Press, 1965), 110. John F. Walvoord, "Reflections on Dispensationalism," *Bibliotheca Sacra* 158, no. 630 (April 2001): 134–35, wrote of *Dispensationalism Today*, Ryrie "presented the subject in such a proper biblical and historical light that for some years afterwards the attacks on dispensationalism were muted. After several years, however, those who objected to dispensationalism thought it possible to ignore this work. But in 1995 he issued a revised and expanded work entitled *Dispensationalism*. This work will undoubtedly be unsurpassed by any work on the subject for years to come."

[12] Ryrie, *Dispensationalism Today*, 111.

equivalent to ways of salvation."[13] Finally, "without question, the primary reason for the persistence of the charge has been the fact that dispensationalists have made unguarded statements which, if they were being made in the light of today's debate, would have been more carefully worded."[14] Ryrie's response to this charge begins with the admission that "Scofield did write, 'The point of testing is no longer legal obedience as the condition of salvation, but acceptance or rejection of Christ.' But Scofield also wrote some other things, and what he would write today if he were alive and answering Bass or Fuller might be phrased differently."[15] Then Ryrie points out "a few unguarded statements" from nondispensationalists.[16] His point is clear:

---

[13] C. I. Scofield, ed. *The Scofield Reference Bible* (New York: Oxford University Press, 1917), 1115n2, quoted in Ryrie, *Dispensationalism Today*, 112.

[14] Ryrie, *Dispensationalism Today*, 112. See also Charles Caldwell Ryrie, "The Necessity of Dispensationalism," *Bibliotheca Sacra* 114, no. 455 (July 1957): 244: "This article is not an answer to anybody. Neither is it a redefining of the dispensational position, for the author does not feel that it needs redefining—the able exponents of this and past generations have ably defined it." A short while later he apparently changed his mind: "Like all doctrines, dispensational teaching has undergone systematization and development." Ryrie, *Dispensationalism Today*, 9.

[15] Ryrie, *Dispensationalism Today*, 112. Here is the extended Scofield statement: "As a dispensation, grace begins with the death and resurrection of Christ (Romans 3:24–26; Romans 4:24; Romans 4:25). The point of testing is no longer legal obedience as the condition of salvation, but acceptance or rejection of Christ, with good works as a fruit of salvation." Scofield, ed. *The Scofield Reference Bible*, 1115 (note on John 1:17). Mal Couch et al., "The New Dispensation, the Church," in *Biblical Theology of the Church*, ed. Mal Couch (Grand Rapids, MI: Kregel, 1999), 34, argues similarly, "Anyone who is intellectually honest will go beyond their few misstatements and look at the overall belief of these dispensational theologians. . . . [C. I. Scofield, Lewis Sperry Chafer, Charles Ryrie and other dispensational theologians] never believed that one is saved by keeping the Law. They have always taught that the basis of salvation was the death of Christ."

[16] Ryrie, *Dispensationalism Today*, 112. This response is an example of a logical fallacy which has been designated "so's your old man." William Briggs succinctly observes, "The "So's-Your-Old-Man fallacy belongs on the playground, where it originated." William Briggs, "The So's-Your-Old-Man Fallacy," July 11, 2016, accessed July 27, 2017, http://wmbriggs.com/post/12648/.

Though these unguarded statements of covenant writers indicate two ways of salvation, we know full well that covenant theology insists on a single way of salvation, and it would not be fair to insist or imply otherwise. Similarly, antidispensationalists who seize on one unguarded statement of Scofield ought to have the same consideration and not leave the wrong impression.[17]

One should not speculate how Scofield would respond to this critique, but the unguarded statements he made are indefensible; they are at a minimum, unclear and confusing. That other people commit the same error does not excuse any offender.[18] Feinberg admits this and, like Ryrie, calls critics to consider the "full thinking" of these men:

> As a matter of fact, dispensationalists (older and contemporary) do hold that Scripture teaches only one way of salvation. In all honesty, however, it must be admitted that statements made by certain dispensationalists in the past appeared to teach multiple ways of salvation. That such careless statements did not reflect the full thinking of those theologians (as can be seen from other statements they made) seems to have escaped many critics of dispensationalism.[19]

---

[17] Ryrie, *Dispensationalism Today*, 113.

[18] Charles C. Ryrie, *Dispensationalism*, rev. and exp. ed. (Chicago, IL: Moody Press, 1995), 107, modifies this statement: "But Scofield also wrote some other things, and what would he write today if he were alive and answering present-day critics of dispensationalism?" He also explains that the editors of the revised *New Scofield Bible* removed that note and added: "Under the former dispensation, law was shown to be powerless to secure righteousness and life for a sinful race (Gal. 3:21–22). Prior to the cross man's salvation was through faith (Gen. 15:6; Rom. 4:3), being grounded on Christ's atoning sacrifice, anticipatively by God . . . ; now it is clearly revealed that salvation and righteousness are received by faith in the crucified and resurrected Savior." Scofield, C. I. et al., eds., *The New Scofield Reference Bible* (New York: Oxford University Press, 1967), 1124n2. On the history and impact of the *Scofield Reference Bible*, see R. Todd Mangum and Mark S. Sweetnam, *The Scofield Bible: Its History and Impact on the Evangelical Church* (Colorado Springs, CO: Paternoster, 2009).

[19] John S. Feinberg, "Salvation in the Old Testament," in *Tradition and Testament: Essays in Honor of Charles Lee Feinberg*, ed. John S. Feinberg and Paul D. Feinberg (Chicago, IL: Moody Press, 1981), 42. Admitting the errors of our forefathers does not

The charge of multiple ways of salvation continues to be leveled against dispensationalism. Seldom do those who bring the charge provide evidence for it.[20]

Although Scofield's statement on John 1:17 is perhaps the most well-known, as Ryrie explains, other "dispensationalists have made unguarded statements" which seem at odds with other clear statements of salvation by grace through faith alone.[21] Among the early Brethren dispensationalists, John Nelson Darby quickly became the most prominent and dominant leader.[22] Darby observes on John 1:17: "Grace and truth came by Jesus Christ, not by Moses. Nothing can be more essentially important than this statement. Law requires from man what he ought to be before God, and, if he fulfils it, it is his righteousness. Truth in Christ shews what man is (not ought to be), and what God is, and, as inseparable from grace, does not require but brings to man what he needs."[23] In this statement, Darby seems

---

disrespect them. Rather, it is a reminder of human fallibility and the need to be open to correction.

[20] For example, "Probably the greatest problem then, between Dispensationalism and Covenant Theology concerns God's saving purposes in the Old Testament. Some of the older Dispensationalists used to actually even argue that salvation was by works in the Old Testament and by faith in the New Testament." J. Ligon Duncan, "Dispensationalism," First Presbyterian Church, Jackson MS, October 29, 1998, accessed July 25, 2017, http://www.fpcjackson.org/resource-library/classes-and-training/dispensationalism. See also Michael Horton, *Introducing Covenant Theology* (Grand Rapids, MI: Baker, 2006), 129, "While many of [Dispensational Premillennialism's] representatives have moved away from an extreme position that commits old covenant Israelites to salvation by works in contrast to salvation by grace in the new covenant, this strong discontinuity between two distinctive covenants and peoples in God's plan remains firmly in place." Neither author cites evidence for the claim.

[21] Ryrie, *Dispensationalism Today*, 112.

[22] J. D. Hannah, "John Nelson Darby," in *Dictionary of Christianity in America*, ed. David G. Reid et al. (Downers Grove, IL: InterVarsity Press, 1990), 339–40. See also N. Dickson, "John Nelson Darby," in *Biographical Dictionary of Evangelicals*, ed. Timothy Larsen (Downers Grove, IL: InterVarsity Press, 2003), 178–81.

[23] John Nelson Darby, *Synopsis of the Books of the Bible*, 2nd ed. (New York: Loizeaux Bros., 1950); John 1, accessed August 10, 2017, http://stempublishing.com/authors/darby/synopsis/john/john1.html.

to imply the possibility of achieving righteousness through the law. In "Connection of the Cross with the Entire Development of God's Ways with Man," Darby writes:

> The law raised the question of righteousness—it claimed it on the part of God. The promise was addressed to those under it on condition of obedience. "If you will obey my voice indeed, and keep my covenant, then ye shall be a peculiar treasure unto me above all people, for all the earth is mine, and ye shall be unto me a kingdom of priests and an holy nation. . . . And all the people answered together, and said, All that Jehovah hath spoken we will do."
>
> Here then the blessing was made dependent on the obedience of man. The mediator was not of one, but between two parties; and the covenant rested not simply on the infallibility of one who promised, but upon the obedience of another party also. For God is one: a mediator implies two parties; and here the accomplishment of the blessing rests on the condition of the obedience of the human party. The law then raised the question of righteousness which the promise had not at all. But on man's part there was utter failure as to it, and the law worked wrath and brought men under a curse.[24]

Although he does assert that blessings can be earned, Darby here acknowledges that failure to keep the law brings a curse. And, of course, Israel did not obey the law completely and consistently, and yet God continued to bless them, as will be argued in a later section of this article.

Lewis Sperry Chafer clearly articulates that salvation is by grace alone:

> Salvation is a work of God for man, rather than a work of man for God. No aspect of salvation, according to the Bible, is made to depend, even in the slightest degree, on human merit or works. Great stress is laid on the value of good works which grow out of a saved life,

---

[24] John Nelson Darby, "Connection of the Cross with the Entire Development of God's Ways with Man," in *The Collected Writings of J. N. Darby*, ed. William Kelly, vol. 22, *Doctrinal No. 6* (London: G. Morrish, 1867), 369, accessed August 10, 2017, http://stempublishing.com/authors/darby/DOCTRINE/22006E.html.

but they do not precede salvation or form any part of a basis for it.[25]

Elsewhere he notes, "Salvation must be of God alone, for every aspect of it is beyond human power and strength."[26] Yet, in his early work on salvation, he drew an apparent contrast between salvation in the previous and current dispensations by the use of "now":

> The word salvation is used in the Bible to indicate a work of God in behalf of man. In the present dispensation its use is limited to His work for individuals only, and is vouchsafed to them upon one definite condition. Too much emphasis cannot be placed on the fact that now, according to the Bible, salvation is the result of the work of God for the individual, rather than the work of the individual for God, or even the work of the individual for himself."[27]

The emphasis on "now" seems to emphasize a temporal contrast connected to a change in dispensations.

In his *Systematic Theology* Chafer contrasts law and grace in a way which seems to minimize the need for grace to receive blessings from God:

> When the human obligation is presented first, and the divine blessing is made to depend on the faithful discharge of that obligation, it is of and in conformity with pure law. When the divine blessing is presented first, and the human obligation follows, it is of and in conformity with pure grace. The varying orders under law and grace may be stated in the words "do and live" or "live and do." In the case of the law, it is *do* something with a view to being something; in the case of grace, it is to be *made* something with a view to doing something. Is the Christian who is under grace saved and kept *by* good works, or is he saved and kept *unto* good works? The law said "If you will do good I will bless you": grace says "I have blessed you, now do good." Under the law, man lives well to *become* accepted of God; under grace man

---

[25] Lewis Sperry Chafer, *Grace* (Philadelphia, PA: Sunday School Times, 1922), 42.

[26] Lewis Sperry Chafer, *Systematic Theology* (Dallas, TX: Dallas Seminary Press, 1948), 6:291.

[27] Chafer, *Salvation*, 1.

lives well since it *becomes* one to live well who is already accepted. The law presents first a human work to be *done*; grace presents first a divine work to be *believed*. Law begins with what man ought to *do*; grace begins with the question of what God has *done*. Every word of the law revelation is thus made to be a conditional covenant of *human* works, while every word of the grace revelation is thus made to be an unconditional covenant of *divine* works.[28]

According to Chafer, the law was a temporary intrusion into God's covenant of grace:

Since the covenant of grace which is based on human faith was established in the promises made to Abraham, the covenant of the law, made four hundred years later, and added only for a temporary purpose, cannot disannul it. The reign of law, with its covenant of works, ceased with the death of Christ. Its purpose had been accomplished, and its appointed time had expired. Thus the by-faith principle which was announced in the Abrahamic covenant is brought again into force, through the death of Christ.[29]

Chafer later makes the point about intrusion explicit:

This word [grace], which in salvation truth has but the one meaning of unmerited favor, represents a divine method of dealing with men which has obtained from Adam until the present time, except for the intrusion of the law system which was in force in the time between Moses and Christ. Under grace, God does not treat men as they deserve, but He treats them in infinite grace, without reference to their deserts.[30]

Thus, Chafer appears to overstate the contrast between law and grace. He continues:

---

[28] Chafer, *Systematic Theology*, 4:226.
[29] Ibid., 4:229.
[30] Lewis Sperry Chafer, *Major Bible Themes* (Findlay, OH: Dunham, 1926), 150. This section was significantly revised by John Walvoord in the revised edition: Lewis Sperry Chafer, *Major Bible Themes: 52 Vital Doctrines of the Scripture Simplified and Explained*, rev. John F. Walvoord (Grand Rapids: Zondervan, 1974), 192–93.

In Exodus 19:3–25 a record is given of Israel's choice by which they passed from a grace relationship to God into a law relationship. . . . God proposed the law to them, but did not impose it upon them (19:5–7), which law the people accepted (19:8). Thus they deliberately forsook their priceless position under grace, which was according to the covenant made with Abraham, and assumed the impossible responsibility of law by which they must stand or fall before God on the basis of their own merit. Immediately upon this choice God became unapproachable (19:9–24), though before, He had brought them to himself on eagles' wings. The nation thus fell from grace by choosing a covenant of works in place of the gracious mercy of God. The experience of that nation is the experience of every individual who trusts in his own good works or merit, and does not depend on the boundless grace of God, which in Christ Jesus is provided for and offered to all.[31]

When critics pointed out an apparent contradiction to the doctrine of salvation through faith in his writings, Chafer responded in an editorial in *Bibliotheca Sacra*:

Are there two ways by which one may be saved? In reply to this question it may be stated that salvation of whatever specific character is always the work of God in behalf of man and never a work of man in behalf of God. This is to assert that God never saved any one person or group of persons on any other ground than that righteous freedom to do so which the Cross of Christ secured. There is, therefore, but one way to be saved and that is by the power of God made possible through the sacrifice of Christ.

The far lesser question as to the precise human terms upon which men may be saved is quite a different issue. This feature is of less import for the reason that man never contributes anything to his salvation whether he be one who keeps the Law or one who trusts Christ alone apart from human works. The colossal error which sup-

---

[31] Chafer, *Major Bible Themes*, 150–51.

plies any point to the contention of those who accuse others of believing that there are two ways by which the lost may be saved is just this,
that neither works nor faith of themselves can ever save anyone. It is
God's undertaking and always on the ground, not of works or faith,
but on the blood of Christ.[32]

Of this editorial, Ryrie says,

It must be remembered that this statement was made in direct answer
to the charge that Chafer taught two ways of salvation, and Chafer
himself said that the other statements so often quoted to show he
taught two ways of salvation had no bearing on the subject. May we
not take him at his word as being his own best interpreter, especially
when he is speaking to the specific point on which he was being attacked?[33]

Since most people have been guilty of misstatements and unclear comments—and would like to be given the opportunity to clarify or correct those
errors—it would be good for critics of dispensationalism to grant the same
charity to Darby, Scofield, and Chafer.[34]

What do dispensationalists believe about salvation? Ryrie summarizes
the dispensational position thusly: "The *basis* of salvation in every age is the
death of Christ; the *requirement* for salvation in every age is faith; the *object*
of faith in every age is God; the *content* of faith changes in the various dispensations."[35] Salvation is by grace through faith, what changes in the dis-

---

[32] Lewis Sperry Chafer, "Editorial: Inventing Heretics through Misunderstanding," *Bibliotheca Sacra* 102, no. 405 (January 1945): 1–2.

[33] Ryrie, *Dispensationalism Today*, 114.

[34] At the same time, it behooves dispensationalists to recognize the "unguarded"
statements, and not to deny their existence.

[35] Ryrie, *Dispensationalism Today*, 123. Even this statement has been criticized by
non-dispensationalists. For example, see Walter C. Kaiser, Jr, "Is It the Case that Christ
Is the Same Object of Faith in the Old Testament? (Genesis 15:1–6)," *Journal of the
Evangelical Theological Society* 55 (2012): 291–98. Ramesh P. Richard, "Soteriological
Inclusivism and Dispensationalism," *Bibliotheca Sacra* 151, no. 601 (January 1994): 88,
emphasizes, "Every dispensation has an explicit and exclusive content to faith." Later,

pensations is the content of that faith. Like most Christian traditions, dispensationalism recognizes progressive revelation in the unfolding of the work of redemption.[36] The doctrinal statement of Dallas Theological Seminary puts it this way:

> We believe that it has always been true that "without faith it is impossible to please" God (Heb. 11:6), and that the principle of faith was prevalent in the lives of all the Old Testament saints. However, we believe that it was historically impossible that they should have had as the conscious object of their faith the incarnate, crucified Son, the Lamb of God (John 1:29), and that it is evident that they did not comprehend as we do that the sacrifices depicted the person and work of Christ. We believe also that they did not understand the redemptive significance of the prophecies or types concerning the sufferings of Christ (1 Pet. 1:10–12).[37]

---

he goes even further, "One of the distinctives of dispensationalism may well focus on this point that the specific content of saving faith distinguishes a dispensation" (94). On the necessity of faith in Christ for salvation, see Michael A. Rydelnick, "The Jewish People and Salvation," *Bibliotheca Sacra* 165, no. 660 (October 2008): 447–62.

[36] "If we grant that revelation was progressive, then the content of faith would have been cumulative throughout biblical history. Ultimately the content of saving faith in any age must be God and his revelation concerning participation in his covenant (what we call salvation). Believers were ultimately taking God at his word when they responded to the truth in their situations. But as revelation continued, the content of faith grew." Allen P. Ross, "The Biblical Method of Salvation: A Case for Discontinuity," in *Continuity and Discontinuity: Perspectives on the Relationship between the Old and New Testaments: Essays in Honor of S. Lewis Johnson, Jr.*, ed. John S. Feinberg (Westchester, IL: Crossway Books, 1988), 172.

[37] "DTS Doctrinal Statement: Article V: The Dispensations," Dallas Theological Seminary, accessed July 27, 2017, https://www.dts.edu/about /doctrinalstatement/. "The sacrificial system was given to Israel as the means whereby she could maintain her covenant relationship with her holy God and his salvation. The sacrifices enabled people to renew this relationship when it was broken by sin; in so doing, the sacrifices focused the worshipers' attention on the past events and present realities of salvation. Therefore, the sacrificial system is more closely related to the NT doctrine of sanctification than any other soteriological category. But even so the sacrifices did deal with atonement and forgiveness, and their features were typological of the atonement and

This statement emphasizes that salvation has always been through faith, but as Ryrie stated, the content of faith is progressively revealed. No one could be responsible to believe what had not yet been revealed.

Feinberg summarizes the dispensational view: "Neither the approach of Scripture nor that of dispensationalism *necessitates* holding to multiple ways of salvation. . . . To say that Scripture teaches only one way of salvation is not to specify what it is or how it has been implemented at various times in history, especially during the Old Testament times."[38] Similarly, Allen Ross explains, "There is no discontinuity between the Testaments in the method of salvation; that is, salvation has always been by grace through faith. Any discontinuity that exists comes in various aspects of salvation— notably the content of faith, the expression of faith, the work of the Holy Spirit, and the prospect of the saved."[39]

14.2 Is Faith a Gift of God?

Despite some inconsistencies or lack of clarity in several statements, dispensationalists have insisted that salvation is by grace through faith. Roy Aldrich wrote, "Salvation is by faith and by faith alone."[40] He states again, "Our thesis is that faith is the one and only condition of salvation."[41] Wil-

---

forgiveness of sins through the shed blood of Jesus Christ." Ross, "Biblical Method of Salvation," 175.

[38] Feinberg, "Salvation in the Old Testament," 40.

[39] Ross, "Biblical Method of Salvation," 161.

[40] Roy L. Aldrich, "Some Simple Difficulties of Salvation," *Bibliotheca Sacra* 111, no. 442 (April 1954): 158.

[41] Aldrich, "Some Simple Difficulties," 166. He distinguishes between "faith and FAITH. There is nominal faith and real faith. There is intellectual faith and heart faith. There is sensual faith and there is spiritual faith. There is dead faith and there is vital faith. There is traditional faith which may fall short of transforming personal faith. There is a faith that may be commended as orthodox yet have no more saving value than the faith of demons. What is saving faith? It must go beyond intellectual assent and include an act of the will. It means trust and committal. It means resting and depending entirely on Christ for salvation." In contrast, Zane C. Hodges, *Absolutely Free: A Biblical Reply to Lordship Salvation* (Grand Rapids, MI: Zondervan, 1989), 39, argues that saving faith is believing in "*saving* facts. That is, they are *divinely revealed facts which*

liam Walden Howard agrees: "There is but one divine condition for salvation; it is by faith and faith alone."[42] Later he asserts: "Salvation is distinctly and entirely an undertaking of God."[43] J. Dwight Pentecost concludes:

> Hebrews 11:1–40 makes clear that the only individual who was ever accepted by God was the individual who believed God. The principle of verse six, 'without faith it is impossible to please him,' is not a principle limited to this age, but is true in every age. The faith of Abraham is made the example of the method of approach to God (Rom. 4:2).[44]

Earl D. Radmacher also defends monergism: "Salvation is exclusively a work of God. . . . From beginning to end, therefore, 'Salvation is of the Lord' (Jon. 2:9). It is a work of God, by God, for God, to God. It is not our work for God; it is God's work for us. Nothing we can do in mind, attitude, or action can add anything to God's provision of salvation."[45] Finally, Charles

---

are to be believed for salvation." Later he argues that one might stop believing and would still be saved, "The Bible predicates salvation on an *act* of faith, not on the *continuity* of faith. Just as surely as regeneration occurs at a point in time for each individual, so surely does saving faith" (63). Zane Hodges, *Grace in Eclipse: A Study on Eternal Rewards* (Grand Rapids, MI: Zondervan, 1985), 8, writes, "to 'believe in' Jesus is to believe something about Him—namely, that He is the Christ." See also Zane Hodges, *The Gospel Under Siege: A Study on Faith and Works* (Dallas: Redencion Viva, 1981). For an evaluation of understandings of faith in church history, see Thomas G. Lewellen, "Has Lordship Salvation Been Taught Throughout Church History," *Bibliotheca Sacra* 147, no. 585 (January 1990): 54–68.

[42] William Walden Howard, "Is Faith Enough to Save? Part 1" *Bibliotheca Sacra* 98, no. 391 (July 1941): 361. He also asserts: "Faith is the mere human response to God's salvation, and consequently our appreciation of the nature and adequacy of faith is dependent largely on our appreciation of what God has wrought for the sinner" (364–65). In the third part of this series, "Is Faith Enough to Save? Part 3," *Bibliotheca Sacra* 99 (January 1942): 106–7, Howard lists "prominent Texts which set forth Faith as the Only Condition of Salvation."

[43] Howard, "Is Faith Enough to Save? Part 1," 365.

[44] J. Dwight Pentecost, "Salvation in the Tribulation," *Bibliotheca Sacra* 115, no. 457 (January 1958): 56.

[45] Earl D. Radmacher, "Salvation: A Necessary Work of God," in *Understanding Christian Theology*, ed. Charles R. Swindoll and Roy B. Zuck (Nashville, TN: Thomas Nelson, 2003), 808–9.

Ryrie explains,

> Salvation is a free gift; therefore, any statement of the terms must carefully avoid implying that we give God something. He gives it all; we receive that gift through faith (Jn 1:12). The preaching of any different gospel than that of salvation by grace through faith comes under the anathema of Galatians 1:8–9. This means an utter detesting because of the worthlessness of such a false gospel (later the word denoted excommunication). This is the strongest kind of warning that could be given, and yet through the centuries and in our own day there have been and are preached a number of false gospels.[46]

Faith is the means by which salvation is received. Ryrie explains, "Faith means 'confidence, trust, holding something as true.' . . . It is obvious that faith involves more than the knowledge of facts."[47] He concludes: "The New Testament always says that salvation is through faith, not because of faith (Ephesians 2:8). Faith is the channel through which we receive God's gift of forgiveness and eternal life. God has arranged it so that no one can boast, not even about his faith."[48]

Lewis Sperry Chafer, commenting on Ephesians 2:8–10 writes: "Most emphatic is the truth thus declared, that salvation is a divine undertaking on the basis of pure grace in which no human works or merit may enter."[49] Chafer argues that faith is the means by which salvation is received. Faith is not a work: "Faith can serve no greater purpose than to be the means by which that which God has determined may be realized. . . . It might be added that acceptable works and qualities are not resident in any fallen human being, except these characteristics are wrought in the human heart by divine energy. It would therefore be folly to expect that God would foresee in men what could never exist."[50] Later, Chafer asserts, "Though much

---

[46] Charles Caldwell Ryrie, *A Survey of Bible Doctrine* (Chicago, IL: Moody Press, 1972), 134.

[47] Charles Caldwell Ryrie, *So Great Salvation* (Wheaton, IL: Victor Books, 1989), 118–21.

[48] Ibid., 122.

[49] Chafer, *Systematic Theology*, 3:7.

[50] Ibid., 3:174.

Scripture of an indirect nature might be cited, enough has been presented
to establish the doctrine of man's natural inability to exercise saving faith.
Were men able to move themselves toward God, there would be no provision from God for this need. The fact that such enablement is provided
argues in favor of man's inability."[51]

There has not been, however, similar unanimity among dispensationalists on whether faith is a divine gift. Chafer's position is clear. Writing on
Ephesians 2:8-9, he asserts:

> So conclusive is this passage relative to man's inability in the field of
> saving faith that much has been attempted in the way of exegesis
> which proposes to make the salvation the gift of God, rather than the
> faith which receives it. When thus interpreted, the phrase "through
> faith" is practically eliminated. The contrast which the passage sets up
> between faith and works becomes a contrast between salvation and
> works, for which there is no ground either in Scripture or reason. If
> the passage stood alone in the Word of God, declaring a truth not
> elsewhere propounded, some reason might be assigned to such exeget-
> ical attempts which divest the context of its assured meaning; but,
> when rightly interpreted, it stands out as many of the same general
> character.[52]

Elsewhere he concludes,

> Faith accordingly is declared, in one aspect of it, to be 'the gift of God'
> (Eph. 2:8). Utter want of faith is the condition of unregenerate men
> (1 Cor. 2:14) until God be revealed to them by the Son through the

---

[51] Chafer, *Systematic Theology*, 3:217.

[52] Ibid., 3:216-17. The non-dispensationalist, J. I. Packer, argued similarly in,
"The Way of Salvation. Part II: What is Faith?" *Bibliotheca Sacra* 129, no. 515 (July
1972): 296, writes: Faith, "theologically, is a means, a means of entering a new relationship, a means of receiving a new life. It is itself, the Scriptures tell us, God's gift. 'By
grace are we saved through faith and it is not of ourselves'—neither the salvation nor
the faith. That I am sure is the true exegesis. It is all the gift of God. This faith which
God gives becomes the source of all good works." Packer later asserts, "it is the Lord
Jesus Himself, the living risen person, the person who is identical with the man of
Galilee—who is the central object of faith" (297).

Spirit. . . . While faith, basically considered, must be divinely in-wrought, it is ever increasing as the knowledge of God and experience in His fellowship increases.[53]

John Nelson Darby argued similarly in his comments on Ephesians 2:8-9:

> All is the gift of God. It was not even through works that we had part in this glorious salvation, but by faith, and this again the gift of God, that no man might boast. The glory of such a grace must all turn back again to God. He will make us understand that we are, indeed, blessed with all spiritual blessings in the heavenly places. What could we have more than to partake in the glory and the inheritance of Christ Himself, according to the power which has set Him there?[54]

Allen Ross summarizes what these dispensationalists affirm: "The Scriptures also affirm that the only requirement for salvation is faith; and faith itself, far from being a meritorious work, is a gift from God (Eph 2:8)."[55] He continues,

> Thus, we may affirm that according to the eternal purpose of God salvation in the divine reckoning is always by grace, through faith, and rests upon the shed blood of Christ; but we must acknowledge that it was historically impossible that OT saints should have had as the conscious object of their faith the incarnate, crucified Son, the Lamb of

---

[53] Chafer, *Systematic Theology*, 7:148. William Howard concludes from a survey of the biblical teaching of the Trinitarian work of salvation, "Upon these truths John Calvin has constructed the obvious truth that faith itself is a gift of the Holy Spirit, divinely imparted in order that men may respond to a Gospel that without His enlightening work must forever remain incomprehensible (1 Cor. 1:18)." "Is Faith Enough to Save? Part 1," 369. He notes, "The distinctive word of Christianity is grace." See "Is Faith Enough to Save? Part 2," *Bibliotheca Sacra* 98, no. 392 (October 1941): 489-501, for a discussion of the nature of faith.

[54] John Nelson Darby, "Notes on the Epistle to the Ephesians," in *The Collected Writings of J. N. Darby*, ed. William Kelly, vol. 27, *Expository No. 6* (London: G. Morrish, 1867), 17, accessed June 1, 2017, http://stempublishing.com/authors/darby/EXPOSIT/27002E.html#a2.

[55] Ross, "Biblical Method of Salvation," 167.

God, and that it is evident that they did not comprehend as we do that the sacrifices depicted the person and work of Christ.[56]

Rene Lopez argues for an alternative view. While he notes, "Some writers reason that God bestows faith as a gift that enables a person to believe in Jesus Christ for salvation,"[57] he then concludes, "The assumption that people are spiritually unresponsive and thus unable to exercise faith for salvation does not stand up to biblical scrutiny. . . . The Bible presents faith for salvation as a human response much like that of a beggar holding his hand for food."[58] Surprisingly, in this article published in the journal *Bibliotheca Sacra*, Lopez does not engage the arguments of Lewis Sperry Chafer, founder of Dallas Theological Seminary and long-time editor of the journal.

Roy Aldrich asserts that the interpretation of Ephesians 2:8 that faith is the gift of God "leads some to a hyper-Calvinistic doctrine of faith, which in turn leads to an unscriptural plan of salvation."[59] He argues,

---

[56] Ross, "Biblical Method of Salvation," 171.

[57] Rene A. Lopez, "Is Faith a Gift from God or a Human Exercise?" *Bibliotheca Sacra* 164, no. 655 (July 2007): 260. He cites James Bridges in support of this claim, but Bridges does not say that faith is a gift that enables a person to believe but "Faith for salvation is a gift from the Saviour. . . . The entirety of our salvation depends on God's gift of faith." James K. Bridges, "The Gift of Faith," in *Conference on the Holy Spirit*, ed. Gwen Jones (Springfield, MO: Gospel, 1983), 225, quoted in Lopez, 260n5. In short, faith does not enable belief, faith IS belief. Roy L. Aldrich, "The Gift of God," *Bibliotheca Sacra* 122, no. 487 (July 1965): 252, argues similarly, "It can be agreed that saving faith is the gift of God in the broad sense in which all things come from God (I Cor. 4:7; Rom. 11:35, 36). However, this is entirely different from the position that an unsaved person cannot believe until he first receives a special gift from God." But, see Aldrich, "Some Simple Difficulties of Salvation," 159, where he correctly notes that the words "faith" and "belief" are synonyms.

[58] Lopez, "Is Faith a Gift from God," 276.

[59] Aldrich, "Gift of God," 248. There is no hint in the article that Aldrich is aware that Chafer held the view he rejects. Aldrich also asserts "an unscriptural doctrine of total depravity leads to an unscriptural and inconsistent plan of salvation" (248). Later, he claims, "In the Bible there is no clear and dogmatic statement that saving faith is a gift of God" (252). Chafer thought there is. Aldrich concludes that those who believe faith is a gift teach salvation by works: "It is the hyper-Calvinist who is open to the charge of teaching salvation by works. Prayer *is doing something*, and the man who prays hard and gets saved could justly believe that he made his contribution

It can be agreed that saving faith is the gift of God in the broad sense in which all things come from God (I Cor. 4:7; Rom. 11:35, 36). However, this is entirely different from the position that an unsaved person cannot believe until he first receives a special gift of faith from God. Such a doctrine is opposed by the 'whosover' passages of the Bible, and by passages which beseech the sinner to be saved (i.e., John 3:16; II Cor. 5:20).[60]

His conclusion asserts: "Many passages, and whole books of the New Testament, are written to prove salvation is a gift of God and not the reward of good works. But where are the passages to prove saving faith is the gift of God? Is not this theory a deduction from the doctrine of election rather than an induction from the teaching of the Word?"[61]

Earl Radmacher approaches the question of whether or not faith is a gift of God by an evaluation of the grammar of Ephesians 2:8-9:

This word "gift" (*doron*) is used nineteen times in the New Testament, but this is the only time God is referred to as the Giver. Salvation is a grace gift and it is received only by faith. Some say the gift is faith. However, the word "that," which "gift" refers back to, is a neuter pronoun in Greek, whereas the Greek word for "faith" is a feminine noun. The word "that" therefore more likely refers to the whole preceding clause, meaning that salvation is the gift of God. . . . A gift, by definition, is free, with no cost whatsoever.[62]

---

to the plan of salvation. Those who deny the sinner the ability to believe end by imputing to him the impossible and unscriptural ability to find God through pious works" (253).

[60] Aldrich, "Gift of God," 252. He does discuss Ephesuabs 2:8-9 briefly, and dismisses the interpretation that faith is a divine gift.

[61] Ibid., 253.

[62] Radmacher, "Salvation," 869. For the argument that "this" in Ephesians 2:8 refers to salvation not faith as the gift, see Harold W. Hoehner, *Ephesians: An Exegetical Commentary* (Grand Rapids, MI: Baker Academic, 2002), 341-42. See also Daniel B. Wallace, *Greek Grammar beyond the Basics: An Exegetical Syntax of the New Testament* (Grand Rapids: Zondervan, 1996), 334-35. Wallace discusses several possible readings of this text. He concludes, "On a grammatical level, then, it is doubtful that either 'faith' or 'grace' is the antecedent of touto." Yet he also notes, "Whether faith is seen

There likely will never be consensus among dispensationalists on this question. There is, however, agreement that salvation is not by human works. John Feinberg puts it well: "Dispensationalists and nondispensationalists agree that [salvation] is by faith."[63] He concludes,

> According to Scripture, the sole requirement for salvation is that man exercise faith in the provision that God has revealed. Faith is not to be considered a meritorious work on man's part, for Scripture affirms everywhere that faith, as all of salvation, is God's gift to man (Eph 2:8; Rom 6:23; 2 Tim 1:9). There is no question that faith is clearly taught as the only prerequisite for salvation in the New Testament. Equally clear is the message that faith was the only prerequisite during Old Testament times."[64]

14.3 Was Salvation by Grace through Faith under the Old Covenant?

In Romans 3:21–24, the Apostle Paul concludes:

> But now apart from the law the righteousness of God has been made known, to which the Law and the Prophets testify. This righteousness is given through faith in Jesus Christ to all who believe. There is no difference between Jew and Gentile, for all have sinned and fall short of the glory of God, and all are justified freely by his grace through the redemption that came by Christ Jesus." (NIV)

Thus, as Ross writes,

> The dictum of the apostle that salvation is by God's grace—it is the gift of God and not of works, lest any man should boast (Eph 2:8–9)—applies equally to salvation in the OT. That this is the case may be argued theologically in light of the fact that no human being apart from Jesus Christ has ever been able to live a perfectly righteous life and thereby merit salvation.[65]

---

as a gift here or anywhere else in the NT is not addressed by this."

[63] Feinberg, "Salvation in Old Testament," 49.

[64] Ibid., 56.

[65] Ross, "Biblical Method of Salvation," 164.

The blessings of God can never be earned, they are gracious gifts.[66] So, salvation is by grace alone. Since these blessings are mediated through faith, and not works, they are gracious gifts. Whether or not faith is a gift of God, the blessings of salvation unquestionably are. Ross continues,

> That there is one method of salvation for every age is clear, for salvation by the grace of God through faith is necessitated by the universal problem of sin and is consonant with the unchanging nature of God. But a clear analysis of Scripture indicates to us that the content of faith was progressively revealed, so that OT believers would not have had the specific revelation about Jesus Christ.[67]

The biblical story provides compelling evidence of God's gracious provision of salvation, not only through explicit teaching, but also by narrating the stories of the people of faith. Rather than an unbroken narrative of consistent faithfulness, or even an overwhelming majority of stories of faithfulness with rare accounts of sinfulness and rebellion, the biblical story consistently presents God's people struggling to live out their faith. And God's consistent response is unmerited favor. In short, if salvation under the Old Covenant was through works, *then no one has ever been saved.*

Salvation has always been through faith, but as many of us know from experience, people of faith often struggle to live out that faith. Thus, that salvation is not dependent upon us but upon the amazingly consistent gracious God is a source of indescribable comfort. Were it dependent upon human effort, we would have no hope.

In 1965, Ryrie issued a challenge: "Dispensationalism does need to show in a systematic way how grace was displayed in the Mosaic Law. We need not more brief statements that we believe in only one way of salvation (though these should not be ignored), but we need to expound the doctrine

---

[66] "In a general sense, the terms for blessing in the New Testament are used to designate that one is favored by God." William B. Brown, "Blessing," in *Evangelical Dictionary of Biblical Theology*, ed. Walter A. Elwell (Grand Rapids, MI: Baker, 1996), 70. Divine favor could never be earned; otherwise, it would be wages and not a gift. See Romans 4:4–5.

[67] Ross, "Biblical Method of Salvation," 178.

of salvation under the law."[68] What follows is an attempt at sketching out such a defense.[69]

From the beginning of the biblical story, God has been demonstrating his amazing grace. He created a good world when he created the heavens and the earth.[70] He created humans, named Adam (Gen 1:26-28; cf. 5:1-2), and gave them the simple command to be fruitful, multiply, and fill the earth and a simple prohibition, do not eat from one of the trees in the garden (Gen 2:16-17).[71] Of course, they did not do what God commanded and they did do what God forbade. Since the penalty for eating from that tree was death, they deserved to die (Gen 2:17). But God was gracious. The Lord clothed them with animal skins (Gen 3:21) and removed them from the Garden (Gen 3:22-24), but they did not physically die on the day they ate the fruit of the tree.[72] In fact, Adam lived until he was 930 years old

---

[68] Ryrie, *Dispensationalism Today*, 116. In the revised version (1995), Ryrie puts it this way: "Dispensationalists (and nondispensationalists) would do well to show in a systematic way how grace was displayed under the Mosaic Law, something that is not easy to do" (109). I intend to show, in what follows, that it is relatively easy to show how grace was displayed under the Mosaic Law. This section is unchanged in the most recent edition. Ryrie, *Dispensationalism*, 126.

[69] It would not be possible, in the short amount of space in this article, to provide a comprehensive response to Ryrie's challenge. But, he did not ask for a comprehensive one but a systematic one. For more on this see Glenn R. Kreider, *God with Us: Exploring God's Personal Interactions with His People throughout the Bible* (Phillipsburg, NJ: P&R Publishing), 2014.

[70] Multiple times in Genesis 1 the world is declared to be good (1:4, 10, 18, 21, 25). In Genesis 1:31, the narrator summarily declares: "God saw all that he had made, and it was very good."

[71] This simple prohibition follows a gracious provision: "You may surely eat of every tree of the garden, but of the tree of the knowledge of good and evil you shall not eat, for in the day that you eat of it you shall surely die" (Gen 2:16-17). That Adam was male and female does not deny that there was a man and a woman. In fact, Genesis 2:18-25 makes that explicit. Genesis 5:1-2 clearly states that both male and female were named "Adam."

[72] The first death in all creation was the death of an animal whose blood was shed instead of theirs and whose skin was used to make garments to cover their nakedness. Substitutionary atonement, the death of an innocent animal instead of the guilty humans, is thereby introduced into the created order. God's plan of redemption in every succeeding dispensation is through substitution. Their removal from the Garden

(Gen 5:5).[73]

When Cain killed his brother Abel, God again was gracious. Cain was guilty of pre-meditated murder. To make his decision even more insidious, God appeared to Cain prior to the act and warned him not to do it (Gen 4:6–7). Cain's anger culminated in an invitation to his brother to meet him out in the field. There Cain killed him (Gen 4:8). Rather than execute the murderer, God preserved his life (Gen 4:15) and blessed Cain's descendants and all humanity through technology and culture (Gen 4:20–22).[74]

God's judgment of human rebellion at the flood is also marked by grace. God declared to Noah, "I am going to put an end to all people, for the earth is filled with violence because of them. I am surely going to destroy both them and the earth" (Gen 6:13, NIV). But the earth was not utterly destroyed (Gen 8:15–17), which is only an act of grace. God also preserved the lives of eight humans (Gen 6:10, 18) as well as two of every clean and seven pairs of every unclean animal (Gen 6:19–20; 7:2–3). When the flood waters receded, and these creatures returned to the earth, God made a covenant with them and with the earth itself in which he promised never again to destroy all life on the earth (Gen 9:8–17), "even though every inclination of the human heart is evil from childhood" (Gen 8:21, NIV).[75]

The human rebellion at the Tower of Babel also brought judgment;

---

was also an act of grace; otherwise, they could have eaten from the tree of life and lived forever in a fallen state.

[73] Of course, there were immediate effects of the Fall on the humans and on all creation. But their death was not immediately experienced, as the genealogy in Genesis 5 makes clear.

[74] John Dyer, *From the Garden to City: The Redeeming and Corrupting Power of Technology* (Grand Rapids, MI: Kregel, 2011), 79, writes, "Cain's offspring—those born in the anti-garden at the center of humankind's rejection of God—developed (1) animal husbandry, (2) art and music, and (3) metal tools. Incredibly, these three areas—agriculture, art, and technology—broadly summarize human culture."

[75] This phrase forms an *inclusio* with the declaration of the Creator at the beginning of the flood narrative: "The Lord saw how great the wickedness of the human race had become on the earth, and that every inclination of the thoughts of the human heart was only evil all the time" (Gen 6:5). The judgment at the flood did not solve the human condition. On the promise that God would never destroy the earth, see Glenn R. Kreider, "The Flood Is as Bad as It Gets: Never Again Will God Destroy the Earth." *Bibliotheca Sacra* 171, no. 684 (October 2014): 162–77.

God confused their language (Gen 11:7). But out of the confusion of language came a variety of cultural expressions, more gifts to rebellious creatures. The multiplicity of languages brought with it multiplicity of cultural expressions, including music and other arts as well as culinary delights.

When God chose one man through whom he would bless all peoples on earth, he chose Abram, in Ur of the Chaldees (Gen 11:27–32). God promised Abram a series of blessings, "I will make you into a great nation, and I will bless you; I will make your name great, and you will be a blessing. I will bless those who bless you, and whoever curses you I will curse and all peoples on earth will be blessed through you" (Gen 12:2–3, NIV).[76] These blessings were, thankfully, not dependent upon Abram's faithfulness to God, but upon God's graciousness. The change of name from Abram to Abraham is particularly significant to illustrate this (Gen 17).[77]

Dispensationalists observe several distinguishable periods of time during which God administers His plan of redemption from creation to the Mosaic Covenant (Ex 19). Ryrie summarizes, "Most dispensationalists see seven dispensations in God's plan (although throughout the history of dispensationalism, they have not always been the same seven). Occasionally a dispensationalist may hold as few as four and some hold as many as eight. The doctrinal statement of Dallas Theological Seminary mentions only three by name."[78] The first transition occurs when Adam and Eve were exiled from the Garden of Eden. Dispensationalists differ on how to divide the period from the Fall to the Law. Ryrie argues for a dispensational change at the Fall, flood, Tower of Babel, and the call of Abraham.[79] Every dispensationalist recognizes the three named in the Dallas Theological Seminary statement: "We believe that three of these dispensations or rules of life are the subject of extended revelation in the Scriptures, viz., the dispensation

---

[76] "Understand, then, that those who have faith are children of Abraham. Scripture foresaw that God would justify the Gentiles by faith, and announced the gospel in advance to Abraham: 'All nations will be blessed through you.' So those who rely on faith are blessed along with Abraham, the man of faith" (Gal 3:7-9).

[77] The name change seems to be the Lord's response to Abram falling on his face (Gen 17:3), an apparent lack of faith (cf. Gen 17:17). See also Genesis 15:8, where Abram asks God for evidence or proof that he is trustworthy.

[78] Ryrie, *Dispensationalism*, 53.

[79] Ibid., 53-65. See his chart on page 62.

of the Mosaic Law, the present dispensation of grace, and the future dispensation of the millennial kingdom. We believe that these are distinct and are not to be intermingled or confused, as they are chronologically successive."[80]

When God delivered his people out of slavery in Egypt and met them at Mt. Sinai, he made a covenant with them. There were explicit instructions about how Israel was to prepare for the Lord's appearance (Ex 19:10–13). God then appeared in fire and smoke (Ex 19:16) and spoke the "ten words" (Ex 20:1–17). The God who brought Israel out of slavery continued to speak (Ex 20:22–23:33), and a covenant was cut. This covenant did not replace the eternal Abrahamic Covenant (Gen 15, 17); it was added alongside it (Gal 3:15–20). The Mosaic Covenant did, however, introduce a dispensational change.

The cutting of the covenant is described in some detail in Exodus 24:4–18. The Book of the Covenant was read to the people (Ex 24:7a) and their appropriate response was, "We will do everything the Lord has said; we will obey" (Ex 24:7b, NIV). Some early dispensationalists criticized Israel's response.[81]

Barely a month after God's appearance on Mt. Sinai, the people rebelled against him. They asked Moses' brother Aaron to make them a god. He shaped a golden calf which they worshiped as the god "who brought you up out of Egypt" (Ex 32:4, NIV). God's anger burned against the people. He threatened to destroy them, but Moses intervened, and God relented from his anger (Ex 32:14). Moses again interceded with God, and God

---

[80] "DTS Doctrinal Statement: Article V: The Dispensations." Many dispensationalists would observe that the millennium is not the end of God's plan for creation, so this final dispensation extends into the eternal state. Stanley D. Toussaint, "God's Plan for History: From the Ascension to the Second Coming of Christ," in *Dispensationalism and the History of Redemption: A Developing and Diverse Tradition*, ed. D. Jeffrey Bingham and Glenn R. Kreider (Chicago, IL: Moody, 2015), 192, calls the millennium "the front porch to eternity."

[81] It is beyond the scope of this article to evaluate this position. See Daniel M. Blosser, "An Examination of Dispensational Views of the Mosaic Law and Grace" (ThM thesis, Dallas Theological Seminary, 2007). See earlier comments by Darby and Chafer.

agreed to accompany the people of Israel to the land of promise. Then, surprising, Moses asked God to show him His glory—to allow Moses to see Him and to grant Moses the rare privilege of entering into God's presence. This is a shocking request, since Moses previously had eaten lunch in God's presence (Ex 24:9–11). In that earlier encounter, Moses "saw the God of Israel" (Ex 24:10). Moses had spent forty days on the mountain with God (Ex 24:18). Moses had regularly been in God's presence and even described his interaction with God: "The Lord would speak to Moses face to face, as one speaks to a friend" (Ex 33:11, NIV), the result of which was that Moses' face glowed (Ex 34:29). Thus, it seems like Moses was asking for more. Perhaps his desire was similar to the request of the people for a God who would be physically present.

God's gracious response to Moses both saved his life and gave him something better. The God of Abraham, Isaac, and Jacob came down to Moses and declared, "The Lord, the Lord, the compassionate and gracious God, slow to anger, abounding in love and faithfulness, maintaining love to thousands, and forgiving wickedness, rebellion and sin. Yet he does not leave the guilty unpunished; he punishes the children and their children for the sin of the parents to the third and fourth generation" (Ex 34:6–7, NIV). This God truly is compassionate and gracious and does not always punish sin, at least not immediately.[82]

This was not new information for Moses. He had watched God respond in mercy and compassion, he had seen God angry but not quick-tempered, he had seen God's abounding love poured out on him and the people, and he had experienced God's forgiveness. At the burning bush, God patiently endured a series of excuses and rationalizations from Moses, responding to him with grace and compassion (Ex 3–4). But when Moses requested that God send someone else (Ex 4:13), "the Lord's anger burned against Moses" (Ex 4:14, NIV). Yet even there, God was merciful to Moses. God did not reject or destroy Moses; he used him to deliver the Israelites out of slavery in Egypt. In a series of plagues, God demonstrated his power and his protection of his people.

---

[82] It must also be noted that the good news of the atoning work of Jesus is that the innocent one takes on himself what is due the guilty, and the guilty walk away forgiven, unpunished, because of his substitutionary work.

Were one not familiar with how depravity has impacted all humanity, one might expect these recipients of divine mercy and compassion to be grateful and faithful followers of their God. After all, to be delivered out of the hands of the Egyptian Pharaoh, multiple times, should have earned their loyalty and respect. But it did not. Rather, the history of the Israelites is marked by inconsistent obedience to a gracious God.

After the exodus, when the Pharaoh pursued them to the Red Sea, the Israelites complained to Moses, "Was it because there were no graves in Egypt that you brought us to the desert to die? What have you done to us by bringing us to the desert to die? Didn't we say to you in Egypt, 'Leave us alone; let us serve the Egyptians?' It would have been better for us to serve the Egyptians than to die in the desert!" (Ex 14:12, NIV). God delivered them (Ex 14:15-31). When the Israelites traveled into the desert where there was no water, the people grumbled against Moses (Ex 15:24). The Lord provided water (Ex 15:25). Then the Lord gave them a test: "If you listen carefully to the LORD your God and do what is right in his eyes, if you pay attention to his commands and keep all his decrees, I will not bring on you any of the diseases I brought on the Egyptians, for I am the LORD who heals you" (Ex 15:26, NIV). The Israelites failed this test every time it was given, and their gracious God responded in grace.

The next story Moses tells is of the community grumbling against Moses and Aaron and their God, when they were hungry: "If only we had died by the LORD'S hand in Egypt! There we sat around pots of meat and ate all the food we wanted, but you have brought us out into this desert to starve this entire assembly to death" (Ex 16:3, NIV). The Lord provided them "bread from heaven" (Ex 16:4). The manna came with another test: "The people are to go out each day and gather enough for that day. In this way I will test them and see whether they will follow my instructions. On the sixth day they are to prepare what they bring in, and that is to be twice as much as they gather on the other days" (Ex 16:5, NIV). And then the gracious God gave one more gift, meat in the evening even though, Moses explains, "You are not grumbling against us, but against the LORD" (Ex 16:8, NIV). That evening God sent quail and in the morning manna (Ex 16:13-15). The people failed the test: "Some of them paid no attention to Moses; they kept part of it until morning, but it was full of maggots and began to smell.

So Moses was angry with them" (Ex 16:20, NIV). They failed the test again less than a week later: "Some of the people went out on the seventh day to gather it, but they found none" (Ex 16:27, NIV). The Lord's response? He continued to provide manna for forty years (Ex 16:35).

When the people set out again, they did not find water. They "quarreled with Moses . . . [and] put God to the test" (Ex 17:2, NIV). The Lord responded by providing water (Ex 17:5-7). They arrived a Sinai (Ex 19) having experienced multiple gracious and compassionate acts of God. Even when they grumbled and complained, God was gracious to them.

After the golden calf incident, God reiterated the instructions for building the tabernacle. This time, they obeyed God: "The Israelite had done all the work just as the LORD had commanded Moses. Moses inspected the work and saw that they had done it just as the Lord had commanded. So Moses blessed them" (Ex 39:42-43, NIV).

The Israelites set up camp at Kadesh in the Desert of Paran, and the twelve spies Moses had sent into the land of Canaan returned with their report (Num 13:26). The majority testified that the land is fruitful, "it does flow with milk and honey! . . . But the people who live there are powerful, and the cities are fortified and very large" (Num 13:27-28, NIV). Caleb expressed his faith that they should obey God and go into the land (Num 13:30). But the majority was able to sway the people: "They spread among the Israelites a bad report about the land they had explored. They said, 'The land we explored devours those living in it. All the people we saw there are of great size. . . . We seemed like grasshoppers in our own eyes, and we looked the same to them'" (Num 13:32-33, NIV). The people grumbled and complained, and the Lord was angry: "How long will these people treat me with contempt? How long will they refuse to believe in me, in spite of all the signs I have performed among them. I will strike them down with a plague and destroy them, but I will make you into a nation greater and stronger than they" (Num 14:11-12, NIV).[83]

As he had in the aftermath of the golden calf incident (Ex 32:11-13), Moses pleaded with God to be merciful to the people, including an appeal to the Lord's reputation among the nations (Num 14:13-16). But then he

---

[83] The Lord's response here is almost word for word the same as back at the incident with the golden calf (Ex 32:9-10).

added an argument based upon God's character, and quoted God's own words:

> Now may the Lord's strength be displayed, just as you have declared: 'The LORD is slow to anger, abounding in love and forgiving sin and rebellion. Yet he does not leave the guilty unpunished; he punishes the children for the sin of the parents to the third and fourth generation.' In accordance with your great love, forgive the sin of these people, just as you have pardoned them from the time they left Egypt until now. (Num 14:17–19, NIV)

Thus, Moses seemed to have recognized that God had consistently treated Israel with grace, not according to what they deserve.

Again, as he had in Exodus 32:14, the Lord relented: "I have forgiven them as you asked" (Num 14:20, NIV). Yet, the Lord continued,

> Nevertheless, as surely as I live and as surely as the glory of the LORD fills the whole earth, not one of those who saw my glory and the signs I performed in Egypt and the wilderness but who disobeyed me and test me ten times—not one of them will ever see the land I promised on oath to their ancestors. No one who treated me with contempt will ever see it." (Num 14:21–23, NIV)

Only Caleb, who "has a different spirit and follows me wholeheartedly," would enter the land (Num 14:24, NIV). The Lord repeated the promise of judgment:

> In this wilderness your bodies will fall—every one of you twenty years old or more who was counted in the census and grumbled against me. Not one of you will enter the land . . . As for your children that you said would be taken as plunder, I will bring them in to enjoy the land you have rejected. But as for you, your bodies will fall in this wilderness. . . . For forty years—one year for each of the forty days you explored the land—you will suffer for your sins and know what it is like to have me against you." (Num 14:29–35, NIV)[84]

---

[84] Judgment on the spies was immediate; a plague struck all but Joshua and Caleb (Num 14:37–38). When the people heard this message of judgment from the Lord,

Yet, in the final book of Torah, Deuteronomy, Moses rehearsed the works of God to the generation who will enter the land of Canaan. It had been forty years since the events in Numbers 14 (Deut 1:3). In his summary statement of those years, Moses declared: "The LORD your God has blessed you in all the work of your hands. He has watched over your journey through this vast wilderness. These forty years the LORD your God has been with you, and you have not lacked anything" (Deut 2:7, NIV). During the forty years of judgment, the Lord was with his people.[85] A few chapters later, he wrote:

> Be careful to follow every command I am giving you today, so that you may live and increase and may enter and possess the land the Lord promised on oath to your ancestors. Remember how the LORD your God led you all the way in the wilderness these forty years, to humble and test you in order to know what was in your heart, whether or not you would keep his commands. He humbled you, causing you to hunger and then feeding you with manna, which neither you nor your ancestors had known, to teach you that man does not live on bread alone but on every word that comes from the mouth of the LORD. Your clothes did not wear out and your feet did not swell during these forty years. Know then in your heart that as a man disciplines his son, so the LORD your God disciplines you." (Deut 8:1-5, NIV)

During the forty years of judgment, the Lord not only continued to provide food generously for his people, he preserved their clothes and kept them healthy. Perhaps most striking, in Deuteronomy 29 when Moses lead the people in a covenant-making ceremony (Deut 29:9-15), Moses announced:

> Your eyes have seen all that the LORD did in Egypt to Pharaoh, to all his officials and to all his land. With your own eyes you saw those great trials, those signs and great wonders. But to this day the LORD has not given you a mind that understands or eyes that see or ears that hear.

---

they repented and tried to take the land but suffered defeat at the hands of the Amalekites and Canaanites (Num 14:41-45).

[85] Moses had reminded God that what made Israel unlike all the other nations is that the God of Abraham, Isaac, and Jacob actually exists, and is present with His people (Ex 33:15-16). Even during judgment, God is present, not absent.

Yet the LORD says, 'During the forty years that I led you through the wilderness, your clothes did not wear out, nor did the sandals on your feet. You ate no bread and drank no wine or other fermented drink. I did this so that you might know that I am the LORD your God.' (Deut 29:2-6, NIV)[86]

The Lord preserved the health of his people during these years of wandering in the wilderness, and even extended the life of their clothes and sandals. It would have been impossible to grow grain for bread and grapes for wine, not to mention building bakeries and distilleries and breweries, while in the wilderness. God fed them and gave them water during these wanderings.

The God of Abraham, Isaac, and Jacob is a gracious God. According to Hebrews 11:1-2 (NIV), "Now faith is confidence in what we hope for and assurance about what we do not see. This is what the ancients were commended for." The author then attributes faith to long list of these ancients. Thus, it can be concluded that these were people of faith, since "without faith it is impossible to please God, because anyone who comes to him must believe that he exists and that he rewards those who earnestly seek him" (Heb 11:6, NIV). Yet, even a cursory reading of the Penteteuch demonstrates that the Israelites were not faithful in their obedience to God. They were, rather, almost completely consistent in their rebellion against him. If their salvation, if the reception of divine blessings, was dependent upon works, they would never have received either one. If God treated them as they deserved, they would have been wiped from the face of the earth. But salvation is never dependent upon anything in the sinner; it is by grace alone through faith alone in Christ alone.

14.4 Conclusion

Dispensationalism is a Christian tradition rooted in the Protestant

---

[86] Most of the people gathered in this assembly had not seen what the Lord did in Egypt since they had not been born or were quite young. They did not actually see with their own eyes. Rather, being part of this people meant that the stories of the Israelites were the means by which this people's identity was formed and passed down through the generations. In a similar way, although Christians were not at the Exodus or at the Cross, the stories of redemption are their stories. Christians have seen them, as if were, through the eyes of faith.

Reformation, and nourished within British and North American Evangelicalism. Thus, it holds to salvation by grace alone through faith alone in Christ alone. Although some early dispensationalists spoke of the outworking of the divine plan of redemption in confusing ways, when confronted, all insisted that salvation is a gracious gift of God. In recent years, dispensationalists have been more careful and clearer in affirming this conviction.

Faith, and faith alone, is the means by which grace is received—not by works. In light of his impact upon dispensationalism, it is appropriate for Charles Ryrie to have the final word: "It is not easy to believe that Someone whom you and every living person has never seen did something nearly 2,000 years ago that can take away sin and make you acceptable before a holy God. But it is believing that brings eternal life."[87]

---

[87] Ryrie, *So Great Salvation*, 123.

Bibliography

Aldrich, Roy L. "The Gift of God." *Bibliotheca Sacra* 122, no. 487 (July 1965): 248–253.

———. "Some Simple Difficulties of Salvation." *Bibliotheca Sacra* 111, no. 442 (April 1954): 158–168.

Anyabwile, Thabiti. "God Does Not Justify Sinners by Grace Alone through Faith Alone in Christ Alone to Make Salvation Easy for Us." Gospel Coalition. August 31, 2010. Accessed July 23, 2017. https://blogs .thegospelcoalition.org/thabitianyabwile/2010/08/31/god-does-not-justify-sinners-by-grace-alone-through-faith-alone-in-christ-alone-to-make-salvation-easy-for-us/.

Blosser, Daniel M. "An Examination of Dispensational Views of the Mosaic Law and Grace." ThM thesis, Dallas Theological Seminary, 2007.

Brown, William B. "Blessing." In *Evangelical Dictionary of Biblical Theology*, edited by Walter A. Elwell, 70. Grand Rapids, MI: Baker, 1996.

Chafer, Lewis Sperry. "Editorial: Inventing Heretics through Misunderstanding." *Bibliotheca Sacra* 102, no. 405 (January 1945): 1–5.

———. *Grace*. Philadelphia, PA: Sunday School Times, 1922.

———. *Major Bible Themes*. Findlay, OH: Dunham, 1926.

———. *Major Bible Themes: 52 Vital Doctrines of the Scripture Simplified and Explained*. Revised by John F. Walvoord. Grand Rapids, MI: Zondervan, 1974.

———. *Salvation*. Wheaton, IL: Van Kampen Press, 1917.

———. *Systematic Theology*. 8 vols. Dallas, TX: Dallas Seminary Press, 1948.

Couch, Mal, Thomas Figart, Arnold Fruchtenbaum, Thomas Ice, and Russell L. Penney. "The New Dispensation, the Church." In *Biblical Theology of the Church*, edited by Mal Couch, 29–48. Grand Rapids, MI: Kregel, 1999.

Dallas Theological Seminary. "DTS Doctrinal Statement." Dallas Theological Seminary. Accessed July 27, 2017. https://www.dts.edu/about/doctrinalstatement/.

Darby, J. N. "Connection of the Cross with the Entire Development of God's Ways with Man." In *The Collected Writings of J. N. Darby*, edited by William Kelly. Vol. 22, *Doctrinal No. 6*. London: G. Morrish, 1867. Accessed August 10, 2017. http://stempublishing.com/authors/darby/DOCTRINE/22006E.html.

————. "Notes on the Epistle to the Ephesians." In *The Collected Writings of J. N. Darby*, edited by William Kelly. Vol. 27, *Expository No. 6*. London: G. Morrish, 1867. Accessed June 1, 2017. http://stempublishing.com/authors/darby/EXPOSIT/27002E.html.

————. *Synopsis of the Books of the Bible*. 2nd ed. New York: Loizeaux Bros., 1950. Accessed August 10, 2017, http://stempublishing.com/authors/darby/synopsis/index.html.

Dickson, N. "John Nelson Darby." In *Biographical Dictionary of Evangelicals*, edited by Timothy Larsen, 178–81. Downers Grove, IL: InterVarsity Press, 2003.

Dyer, John. *From the Garden to City: The Redeeming and Corrupting Power of Technology*. Grand Rapids, MI: Kregel, 2011.

Feinberg, John S. "Salvation in the Old Testament." In *Tradition and Testament: Essays in Honor of Charles Lee Feinberg*, edited by John S. Feinberg and Paul D. Feinberg, 39–77. Chicago, IL: Moody Press, 1981.

Hannah, J. D. "John Nelson Darby." In *Dictionary of Christianity in America*, edited by David G. Reid et al., 339–340. Downers Grove, IL: InterVaristy Press, 1990.

Harm, F. R. "Solafidianism." In *Evangelical Dictionary of Theology*, edited by Walter A. Elwell, 1031–1032. Grand Rapids, MI: Baker, 1984.

458   Forged from Reformation

Hodges, Zane C. *Absolutely Free: A Biblical Reply to Lordship Salvation*. Grand Rapids, MI: Zondervan, 1989.

———. *The Gospel Under Siege: A Study on Faith and Works*. Dallas: Redencion Viva, 1981.

———. *Grace in Eclipse: A Study on Eternal Rewards*. Grand Rapids, MI: Zondervan, 1985.

Hoehner, Harold W. *Ephesians: An Exegetical Commentary*. Grand Rapids, MI: Baker Academic, 2002.

Holcomb, Justin. "The Five Solas: Points from the Past that Should Matter to You." Christianity Today. Accessed July 23, 2017. http://www.christianity.com/church/church-history/the-five-solas-of-the-protestant-reformation.html.

Horton, Michael. *Introducing Covenant Theology*. Grand Rapids, MI: Baker, 2006.

Howard, William Walden. "Is Faith Enough to Save? Part 1." *Bibliotheca Sacra* 98, no. 391 (July 1941): 360–371.

———. "Is Faith Enough to Save? Part 2." *Bibliotheca Sacra* 98, no. 392 (October 1941): 489–501.

———. "Is Faith Enough to Save? Part 3." *Bibliotheca Sacra* 99, no. 393 (January 1942): 88–107.

Kaiser, Walter C., Jr., "Is It the Case that Christ Is the Same Object of Faith in the Old Testament? (Genesis 15:1–6)." *Journal of the Evangelical Theological Society* 55 (2012): 291–98.

Kreider, Glenn R. "The Flood Is as Bad as It Gets: Never Again Will God Destroy the Earth." *Bibliotheca Sacra* 171, no. 684 (October 2014): 162–77.

———. *God with Us: Exploring God's Personal Interactions with His People throughout the Bible*. Phillipsburg, NJ: P&R Publishing, 2014.

Kreider, Glenn R. "What Is Dispensationalism?" In *Dispensationalism and the History of Redemption: A Developing and Diverse Tradition*, edited by D. Jeffrey Bingham and Glenn R. Kreider, 15–46. Chicago, IL: Moody Publishers, 2015.

Kreider, Glenn R., Nathan D. Holsteen and Michael J. Svigel, "Wise unto Salvation: Gospel, Atonement, and Saving Grace." In *Exploring Christian Theology*, edited by Nathan D. Holsteen and Michael J. Svigel. Vol. 2, *Creation, Fall, and Salvation*, 131–248. Grand Rapids, MI: Bethany House, 2015.

Lewellen, Thomas G. "Has Lordship Salvation Been Taught Throughout Church History." *Bibliotheca Sacra* 147, no. 585 (January 1990): 54–68.

Lopez, Rene A. "Is Faith a Gift from God or a Human Exercise?" *Bibliotheca Sacra* 164, no. 655 (July 2007): 259–276.

MacArthur, John, and Richard Mayhue. *Biblical Doctrine: A Systematic Summary of Bible Truth*. Wheaton, IL: Crossway, 2017.

Mangum, R. Todd, and Mark S. Sweetnam. *The Scofield Bible: Its History and Impact on the Evangelical Church*. Colorado Springs, CO: Paternoster, 2009.

Meyer, Carl S. "Solafidianism." In *The New International Dictionary of the Christian Church*, edited by J. D. Douglas, 914. Grand Rapids, MI: Zondervan, 1978.

Packer, James I. "The Way of Salvation. Part II: What is Faith?" *Bibliotheca Sacra* 129, no. 515 (July 1972): 195–205.

Pentecost, J. Dwight. "Salvation in the Tribulation." *Bibliotheca Sacra* 115, no. 457 (January 1958): 50–61.

Radmacher, Earl D. "Salvation: A Necessary Work of God." In *Understanding Christian Theology*, edited by Charles R. Swindoll and Roy B. Zuck, 801–944. Nashville, TN: Thomas Nelson, 2003.

Ragusa, Daniel. "The Five Solas: Sola Fide." Reformed Forum. October 25, 2016. Accessed May 31, 2017. https://reformedforum.org/five-solas-sola-fide/.

Richard, Ramesh P. "Soteriological Inclusivism and Dispensationalism." *Bibliotheca Sacra* 151, no. 601 (January 1994): 85–108.

Rinehart, Larry. "*Sola Fide*: The Mystery of Salvation by Faith." *Journal of Ecumenical Studies* 49 (Fall 2014): 577–600.

Ross, Allen P. "The Biblical Method of Salvation: A Case for Discontinuity." In *Continuity and Discontinuity: Perspectives on the Relationship between the Old and New Testaments: Essays in Honor of S. Lewis Johnson, Jr.*, edited by John S. Feinberg, 161–178. Westchester, IL: Crossway Books, 1988.

Rydelnick, Michael A. "The Jewish People and Salvation." *Bibliotheca Sacra* 165, no. 660 (October 2008): 447–62.

Ryrie, Charles Caldwell. *Dispensationalism*. Rev. and exp. ed. Chicago, IL: Moody Press, 1995.

———. *Dispensationalism Today*. Chicago, IL: Moody Press, 1965.

———. "The Necessity of Dispensationalism." *Bibliotheca Sacra* 114, no. 455 (July 1957): 243–254.

———. *So Great Salvation*. Wheaton, IL: Victor Books, 1989.

———. *A Survey of Bible Doctrine*. Chicago, IL: Moody Press, 1972.

Scofield, C. I., ed. *The Scofield Reference Bible*. New York: Oxford University Press, 1917.

Scofield, C. I. et al., ed., *The New Scofield Reference Bible*. New York: Oxford University Press, 1967.

Svigel, Michael J. "The History of Dispensationalism in Seven Eras." In *Dispensationalism and the History of Redemption: A Developing and Diverse Tradition*, edited by D. Jeffrey Bingham and Glenn R. Kreider, 69–100. Chicago, IL: Moody Publishers, 2015.

Toussaint, Stanley D. "God's Plan for History: From the Ascension to the Second Coming of Christ." In *Dispensationalism and the History of Redemption: A Developing and Diverse Tradition*, edited by D. Jeffrey Bingham and Glenn R. Kreider, 169–194. Chicago, IL: Moody, 2015.

Vanhoozer, Kevin J. *Biblical Authority after Babel: Retrieving the Solas in the Spirit of Mere Protestant Christianity*. Grand Rapids, MI: Brazos Press, 2016.

Wallace, Daniel B. *Greek Grammar beyond the Basics: An Exegetical Syntax of the New Testament*. Grand Rapids, MI: Zondervan, 1996.

Walvoord, John F. "Millennial Series: Part 7: Amillennial Soteriology." *Bibliotheca Sacra* 107, no. 427 (July 1950): 281–290.

———. "Reflections on Dispensationalism." *Bibliotheca Sacra* 158, no. 630 (April 2001): 131–137.

Solus Christus
[Christ Alone]

15

SOLUS CHRISTUS

Paul J. Scharf
Dispensational Publishing House

15.0 Introduction

The subject of this chapter—*Christ alone*, which speaks of the supreme and superior sufficiency of the Son of God—is so vast and so profound that no one could ever pretend to exhaust it, to say nothing of doing so in one short chapter. Scripture offers the following prelude to set in context a proper understanding of His incarnation and earthly ministry:

> God, after He spoke long ago to the fathers in the prophets in many portions and in many ways, in these last days has spoken to us in His Son, whom He appointed heir of all things, through whom also He made the world. And He is the radiance of His glory and the exact representation of His nature, and upholds all things by the word of His power. When He had made purification of sins, He sat down at the right hand of the Majesty on high, having become as much better than the angels, as He has inherited a more excellent name than they. (Heb 1:1-4)

One great danger in any attempt to address such a topic as this would be to miss something that must be said, or to misstate some essential truth and thus lead anyone "astray from the simplicity and purity *of devotion* to Christ" (2 Cor 11:3, emphasis added). This chapter, therefore, makes no pretense, then, of giving a full or final treatment of all that Christ is, or of

all that the reformers understood Him to be—or even of all that dispensationalists must believe Him to be in light of the Reformed legacy that has
been passed down.[1]

Dr. John Walvoord wrote in a similar spirit when he made this insightful comment about the study of the one who, being God, became also
man: "Much necessarily remains inscrutable in the person of Christ. The
problem of the theologian is not to understand completely, but to state the
facts revealed in Scripture in such a way as to do full honor to the person
of Christ."[2] Therefore, before delving into Reformation history to learn
what the reformers said about Christ—and certainly before seeking to make
any pronouncements which offer any new insights regarding His person or
the believer's relationship to Him—it is imperative first to "sanctify Christ
as Lord in [our] hearts" (1 Pet 3:15).

In that light, the chapter will proceed from knowledge gained about
our Savior from the reformers, which will allow readers more fully to appreciate the theological legacy that they have bequeathed to subsequent generations. With this in place, the chapter will progress and build upon the reformers' insights about Christ with fresh advancements that flow from its
more recent tributary, dispensational theology.

15.1 The Reformers' View of Christ Alone—Biblically Grounded

When the reformers protested against the theological abuses of the
medieval Roman Catholic Church, thankfully they did not have to offer
correction regarding the basic understanding of the person of Christ regarding His eternality, full deity, full humanity, virgin birth or any other issue
that had been hammered out since Nicea.[3] The reformers had no need to

---

[1] For a full, book-length treatment of this vast subject, see the installment in The
5 Solas Series: Stephen Wellum, *Christ Alone* (Grand Rapids, MI: Zondervan, 2017). Of
course, that book is not intended to advance the dispensational perspective on the
issue.

[2] John F. Walvoord, *Jesus Christ Our Lord* (Chicago, IL: Moody Press, 1969), 122.

[3] An understanding of the Nicene Creed is foundational to understanding both
Christology itself as well as its historical development. Alister E. McGrath summarizes:
"The *Council of Nicea* (325) was convened by Constantine, the first Christian emperor,

break—and did not break—with the mother church in its understanding and acceptance of the orthodox view of the person of Christ, as articulated specifically in the Nicene Creed. [4]

That creed reads as follows regarding the Savior:

> I believe . . . in one Lord Jesus Christ, the only-begotten Son of God, begotten of the Father before all worlds; God of God, Light of Light, very God of very God; begotten, not made, being of one substance with the Father, by whom all things were made.

> Who, for us men for our salvation, came down from heaven, and was incarnate by the Holy Spirit of the virgin Mary, and was made man;

---

with a view to sorting out the destabilizing Christological disagreements within his empire. This was the first 'ecumenical council' (that is, an assembly of Christians drawn from the entire Christian world, whose decisions are regarded as normative for the churches). Nicea (now the city of Iznik in modern-day Turkey) settled the Arian controversy by affirming that Jesus was *homoousios* ('one in being' or 'of one substance') with the Father, thus rejecting the Arian position in favor of a vigorous assertion of the divinity of Christ. The *Council of Chalcedon* (451), the fourth ecumenical council, confirmed the decisions of Nicea, and responded to new debates which had subsequently erupted over the humanity of Christ." *Historical Theology: An Introduction to the History of Christian Thought* (Oxford, UK: Blackwell Publishers, 1998), 33. The Nicene Creed had also been reaffirmed with revisions and additions in 381 A.D. at Constantinople. Cairns wrote: "The Council of Constantinople in 381 stated in canon 1 of its decisions that the faith of the 318 fathers at Nicaea 'shall not be set aside but shall remain dominant.'" Earle Edwin Cairns, *Christianity through the Centuries: A History of the Christian Church*, rev. and enl. ed. (Grand Rapids: Zondervan, 1981), 134. He says that, "The present Nicene Creed . . . [was] approved at Chalcedon in 451." Ibid.

[4] Notice, for instance, the inclusion of the Nicene Creed on the official Vatican website: "Catechism of the Catholic Church," Second Vatican Council, August 15, 1997, accessed September 3, 2017, http://www.vatican.va/archive/ccc_css/archive/catechism/credo.htm. Note also this statement from the United States Conference of Catholic Bishops: "Catholic belief is succinctly expressed in the profession of faith or *credo* called the *Nicene Creed:*" "What We Believe," United States Conference of Catholic Bishops, accessed September 3, 2017, http://www.usccb.org/beliefs-and-teachings/what-we-believe/. The proper approach in witnessing to Roman Catholics, therefore, is to commend them for their doctrinal commitment to an accurate understanding of the person to Christ—then explain to them how their church's teaching misunderstands the true essence of His work and its centrality in gaining salvation.

and was crucified also for us under Pontius Pilate; He suffered and was buried; and the third day He rose again, according to the Scriptures; and ascended into heaven, and sits on the right hand of the Father; and He shall come again, with glory, to judge the quick and the dead; whose kingdom shall have no end.[5]

Moreover, the later-but-related Chalcedonian Creed states:

We, then, following the holy Fathers, all with one consent, teach men to confess one and the same Son, our Lord Jesus Christ, the same perfect in Godhead and also perfect in manhood; truly God and truly man, of a reasonable [rational] soul and body; consubstantial [co-essential] with the Father according to the Godhead, and consubstantial with us according to the Manhood; in all things like unto us, without sin; begotten before all ages of the Father according to the Godhead, and in these latter days, for us and for our salvation, born of the Virgin Mary, the Mother of God, according to the Manhood; one and the same Christ, Son, Lord, only begotten, to be acknowledged in two natures, inconfusedly, unchangeably, indivisibly, inseparably; the distinction of natures being by no means taken away by the union, but rather the property of each nature being preserved, and concurring in one Person and one Subsistence, not parted or divided into two persons, but one and the same Son, and only begotten, God the Word, the Lord Jesus Christ; as the prophets from the beginning [have declared] concerning Him, and the Lord Jesus Christ Himself has taught us, and the Creed of the holy Fathers has handed down to us.[6]

---

[5] "Nicene Creed," Christian Classics Ethereal Library, accessed September 3, 2017, https://www.ccel.org/creeds/nicene.creed.html. The space and scope of this chapter does not allow for a complete treatment of Christology or this creed. For further study, readers are encouraged to consult such excellent sources as *Jesus Christ our Lord* by Walvoord, as well as Robert G. Gromacki, *The Virgin Birth: Doctrine of Deity* (Grand Rapids, MI: Baker Book House, 1974).

[6] "Chalcedonian Creed (451 A.D.)," Christian Classics Ethereal Library, accessed September 5, 2017, https://www.ccel.org/creeds/chalcedonian-creed.html.

The mother church, corrupt and heretical as she was, taught this historic, orthodox view of the person of Christ.[7] Berkhof summarizes as follows: "The Reformation did not bring any great changes in the doctrine of the person of Christ. Both the Church of Rome and the Churches of the Reformation subscribed to the doctrine of Christ as it was formulated by the Council of Chalcedon. Their important and deep-seated differences lay elsewhere."[8] McGrath concurs when, in writing about "The filioque controversy" that led up to the Great Schism of A.D. 1054, he states, "One of the most significant events in the early history of the church was agreement throughout the Roman Empire, both east and west, on the Nicene Creed."[9] More recently, Wellum wrote:

> From the patristic through the Reformation eras, all segments of the church spoke in a unified voice regarding Christ's identity, namely, the same Nicene and Chalcedonian view that our Lord Jesus Christ is nothing less than God the Son incarnate, the only unique and exclusive Lord and Savior. This common christological orthodoxy is represented by the Chalcedonian Definition.[10]

The reformers' treatment of this issue is consistent with their overall purpose of calling the church back to the teachings of the apostles. They were not seeking novelty for novelty's sake, and their handling of Christology demonstrates that fact. What the reformers certainly did do was to offer

---

[7] John Theodore Mueller states: "Because the Church of Rome accepts the ancient confessions of the unadulterated Christian Church, we still consider it as being within the pale of Christendom. But it has hedged in these ancient creeds by later creeds whose tenor is antichristian and which actually make void what the ancient Christian confessions declare. Moreover, these specifically papistical creeds are in direct opposition to Holy Scripture, for they reject Scripture as the only rule of faith and flatly contradict its central doctrines." *Christian Dogmatics: A Handbook of Doctrinal Theology for Pastors, Teachers, and Laymen* (St. Louis, MO: Concordia, 1934), 61.

[8] Louis Berkhof, *Systematic Theology*, 4th rev. and enl. ed. (Grand Rapids, MI: Wm. B. Eerdmans, 1941), 308.

[9] McGrath, *Historical Theology*, 69. The *filioque controversy* split the eastern and western branches of the church with regard to the procession of the Holy Spirit—the western view being that He proceeds from the Father *and the Son* (*filioque*).

[10] Wellum, *Christ Alone*, 250, 251.

a much different emphasis upon Christ—indeed, *Christ alone*—than those in the prevailing church understood.

Luther referred to *Christ* specifically in ten of the *95 Theses*. Thesis seventy-nine states, "To say that the cross emblazoned with the papal coat of arms, and set up by the indulgence preachers is equal in worth to the cross of Christ is blasphemy."[11] The issue of *sola Scriptura* is called the *formal principle* of the Reformation, and the matter of *sola fide* is referred to as the *material principle* of the Reformation. Yet, at the center of all that the reformers taught is the truth of *solus Christus*.

Nathan Busenitz drills into the vital importance and centrality of this plank of the Reformation when he states:

> The five solas of the Reformation all flow out of that commitment that Christ is the head of the church—not the pope. If Christ is the head of the church—not the pope—then the Word of Christ is the authority for the church, not the teachings, traditions and musings of the pope, the magisterium, the cardinals or Catholic tradition. That principle is called *sola Scriptura*. Scripture alone is my authority because Christ alone is the head of the church. Now if Scripture is my ultimate authority, then the gospel that is taught on the pages of Scripture is the true gospel. . . . The true gospel is a gospel of grace alone—apart from works; through faith alone—apart from my own self-effort; based on the finished work of Christ alone—and not on anything that I can contribute. . . . And if all of those things are true, then the credit for my salvation—I can take none of that credit. . . . All of the credit, or all of the glory, goes to God. . . . So the five solas of the Reformation—those five Latin phrases that summarize Reformation teaching—those five solas all flow from that foundational commitment that Christ alone is the head of the church. His Word is the authority, and the gospel taught in that Word is the true gospel.[12]

---

[11] Martin Luther, "The 95 Theses," Martin Luther, accessed September 2, 2017, http://www.luther.de/en/95thesen.html.

[12] Nathan Busenitz, "Reformation Hardware" (sermon), Grace Community Church, July 16, 2017, 45:20, accessed August 22, 2017, https://www.gracechurch.org/sermons/13326.

15.2 The Reformers' Presentation of Christ Alone—Boldly Engaging

How did this focus upon *Christ alone* compare to the prevailing ideas of the day in which the reformers lived—both in the church and the world—as well as the Biblical realities behind it all? This section will investigate the answer to that question by presenting a series of contrasts that show the superiority of Christ, especially to various alternatives that clouded the minds of so many throughout the Dark Ages—and may continue to do so even now.

15.2.1 Christ, Not Adam

First and foremost, one of the most magnificent truths found in the New Testament is that Christ has come—as a descendant of Adam—to succeed where Adam failed. The Apostle Paul contrasts Adam and Christ in two major passages of the New Testament: Romans 5:12-21 and 1 Corinthians 15:21-22.

In Romans 5, Paul is showing the overwhelming difference in magnitude between the effect produced by the first Adam when contrasted with the "Second Adam from above," as Charles Wesley called Him in his glorious Christmas hymn, "Hark! the Herald Angels Sing." Although the fall had incredible consequences, they are infinitesimal in comparison to the redemption wrought by Christ and the blessings that it brings. The contrast between the two is so vast that Paul uses it to illustrate the immensity of the resurrection in his great chapter on that subject:[13] "For as in Adam all die, so also in Christ all will be made alive" (1 Cor 15:22).

Where Adam fell, Christ stood. Where Adam sinned, Christ obeyed. Where Adam died Christ lives and gives life to all who believe.[14] *In Adam,*

---

[13] A complete exposition of these passages is outside the realm of this chapter.

[14] This is not meant to convey agreement with the concept known as the *active obedience of Christ*. For a traditional dispensational perspective on that issue, see Myron Houghton, "The Active Obedience of Christ," Faith Baptist Theological Seminary, August 27, 2012, accessed September 3, 2017, https://www.faith.edu /2012/08/the-active-obedience-of-christ; Wellum, who agrees with the concept of *active obedience*, discusses the issue historically in *Christ Alone*, 265-266.

we can do nothing that would contribute to our own salvation—even utilizing any grace that God might impart or infuse to us.[15] The reformers came to understand and believe that. But they recognized that, *in Christ* and through His gospel, they had: "the power of God for salvation to everyone who believes, to the Jew first and also to the Greek. For in it *the* righteousness of God is revealed from faith to faith; as it is written, 'BUT THE RIGHTEOUS *man* SHALL LIVE BY FAITH'" (Rom 1:16-17).

This leads to another contrast that should be studied in order to see the glory of the Savior more clearly.

15.2.2 Christ, Not Mary

A multitude of things have transpired in the 500 years since Luther first nailed the *95 Theses* to the Castle Church door in Wittenberg, Germany, on October 31, 1517. If the reformers returned to earth today, they would surely be shocked to witness some of these developments. Among the things of an ecclesiastical nature that would distress them would be calls for ecumenism—especially in celebration of this 500th anniversary of the Reformation.[16]

At first glance, such efforts might give the reformers pause—causing them to wonder if the mother church had actually taken heed and begun to reform herself! But then, imagine their surprise when told that Rome had actually deviated *much further* from Biblical realities in the intervening centuries![17] For instance, the reformers would have been familiar with only

---

[15] Note the usage of the terms *impart* and *infuse*: Lutheran World Federation and the Catholic Church, "Joint Declaration on the Doctrine of Justification," Vatican, accessed September 6, 2017, http://www.vatican.va/roman_curia /pontifical_councils/chrstuni/documents/rc_pc_chrstuni_doc_31101999_cath-luth-joint-declaration_en.html.

[16] See, for an example, this web page of the Evangelical Lutheran Church in America, which is devoted to all things "ecumenical and interreligious." Evangelical Lutheran Church in America, "Ecumenical and Interreligious," Freed and Renewed in Christ: 500 Years of God's Grace in Action, Accessed September 4, 2017, https://www.elca500.org/resources/ecumenical-and-interreligious/.

[17] The line of reasoning in this section is inspired by Dr. James White in his radio debate with Peter D. Williams, "Unbelievable? The Reformation: Return to

two Marian dogmas:[18] (1) *Divine Maternity* (Council of Ephesus, 431 A.D.): This is a misunderstanding of Mary as the "mother of God" (*theotokos*). (2) *Perpetual Virginity* (Council of Constantinople II, 553 A.D.): This is a misunderstanding of the Biblical fact that Mary remained a virgin only until the birth of Jesus (cf. Matt 1:24–25).

Sadly, in the centuries since the Reformation, two more such misguided concepts have been defined as dogmas by the Roman Church. They are: (1) *Immaculate Conception* (defined by Pope Pius IX, 1854): This is the concept that Mary, much as in the Biblical picture of her Son, was born and lived without sin. (2) *Bodily Assumption* (defined by Pope Pius XII, 1950): This is the concept that Mary's body, possibly upon her death,[19] ascended directly to heaven.

The issues currently before the Roman Church have pushed well past these dogmas to discussion over the potential of a fifth Marian dogma—one that would proclaim her to be "Coredemptrix, Mediatrix, and Advocate of the people of God."[20] But the truth that the reformers came to see is that Scripture nowhere hints at any of these ideas. Mary was a godly young

---

Truth or Tragic Mistake? James White vs Peter D Williams" (podcast), Premier Christian Radio, April 22, 2017, accessed September 5, 2017, https://www.premierchristianradio.com/Shows/Saturday/Unbelievable/Episodes/Unbelievable-The-Reformation-return-to-truth-or-tragic-mistake-James-White-vs-Peter-D-Williams.

[18] This information is found concisely in: Brian Kelly, "Four Great Marian Dogmas," Catholicism.org, July 12, 2016, accessed September 4, 2017, http://catholicism.org/four-great-marian-dogmas.html. In the interest of fairness, however, it should be noted that this is not a mainstream Roman Catholic website—although the information referenced here is part of the mainstream Roman Church. For a concise evangelical response with documentation from primary sources, see Matt Slick, "What Are the Four Marian Dogmas?" Christian Apologetics and Research Ministry, September 28, 2014, accessed September 4, 2017, https://carm.org/what-are-the-four-marian-dogmas.

[19] "Note that the issue of whether Mary died a natural death is left unanswered: some say she did, some say she didn't." James R. White, *Mary—Another Redeemer?* (Minneapolis, MN: Bethany House, 1998), 52.

[20] Ibid., 117. Though copied from White, his book offers an outstanding treatment of this subject, these terms are used regularly in primary sources. See, for instance, "Why a New Marian Dogma?" Fifth Marian Dogma, accessed September 4, 2017, http://www.fifthmariandogma.com/.

woman, but also a common sinner, who could cry out: "My spirit has re-joiced in God my Savior" (Luke 1:47).

15.2.3 *Christ, Not the Saints*

Proceeding from the previous category, the next logically follows. Many are familiar with the fact that the story of the Reformation is often told from the point of Luther's cry in a thunderstorm, in 1505, to his fam-ily's patron saint—St. Anne—the mother of Mary and the patron saint of miners, such as Martin's father Hans. It was this incident that led Luther into the Augustinian monastery at Erfurt, Germany, a short time later.[21]

On Wednesday, October 31, 1517, the Reformation story would begin to come full circle, as it was in preparation for All Saints' Day, and the crowd that would be gathered for it at the Castle Church, that Luther nailed his *95 Theses* to the church door. The world of the Dark Ages was a fanciful one—filled with belief in spirits and legends. Into such darkness came the light of the Reformation—based not on fear, but faith. As the Apostle Paul states in Colossians 2:18-19:

> Let no one keep defrauding you of your prize by delighting in self-abasement and the worship of the angels, taking his stand on *visions* he has seen, inflated without cause by his fleshly mind, and not hold-ing fast to the head, from whom the entire body, being supplied and held together by the joints and ligaments, grows with a growth which is from God.

Luther, by his own testimony, is well-known to have been as fully de-voted as anyone ever was to all the intricacies of the Roman system—and it led him to a sense of fear and dread. But that darkness was lifted when he came to understand the power of *Christ alone*.

James Swan offers the following quote from Luther to show how, over time, "Luther's thinking was transformed by a Christ centered hermeneu-tic."[22] Luther said:

---

[21] Martin Luther, "Introduction: The Catechism and the Bible," in *Doctor Martin Luther's Small Catechism*, ed. by C. Gausewitz (Milwaukee, WI: Northwestern Publishing House, 1956), 25.

[22] James Swan, "Martin Luther Believed in Devotion to Mary?" Alpha and

No one can deny that by such saint worship we have now come to the point where we have actually made utter idols of the Mother of God and the saints, and that because of the service we have rendered and the works we have performed in their honor we have sought comfort more with them than with Christ Himself. Thereby faith in Christ has been destroyed.[23]

White's words offer a fitting conclusion to this segment:

The Reformers insisted not only upon *sola scriptura* (the Scriptures as the sole infallible rule of faith for the church) and *sola fide* (we are justified by faith alone, not by any other work or merit) but upon another phrase as well: *solus Christus*, Christ alone. This, along with the phrase *soli Deo gloria* (to God alone be the glory), spoke to the fact that in Roman Catholic piety, one's pure and singular devotion to Christ is distracted by the intrusion of numerous intermediaries—Mary, saints, and angels. Nothing has changed since the Reformation, at least as far as this issue is concerned. What was important then is still important today.[24]

15.2.4 Christ, Not the Pope

There are thirty-four references to the *pope* in the English version of Luther's *95 Theses*.[25] Luther's clashes with the earthly head of the church he once loved became progressively more intense and are a huge part of his legend and his legacy. Luther became famous following his conversion for his utter castigation of the pope—considering him to be no less than the antichrist himself.

Spitz tells the most famous tale of Luther's animosity for the pope:

Omega Ministries, October 17, 2013, accessed September 4, 2017, http://www.aomin .org/aoblog/2013/10/17/martin-luther-believed-in-devotion-to-mary/.

[23] Martin Luther, WA, 11:415; cf. Ewald Plass, *What Luther Says*, vol. 3 (St. Louis: Concordia Publishing House, 1959), 1254; quoted in Swan, "Martin Luther Believed in Devotion to Mary?" n11.

[24] White, *Mary—Another Redeemer?*, 84.

[25] Luther, "The 95 Theses."

On June 15, 1520, Leo had published the bull *Exsurge domine*, citing forty-one heresies in Luther's writings, giving him sixty days in which to recant, and demanding that his books be burned. ... In retaliation the Wittenberg University faculty and students gathered on December 10, 1520, outside the Elster gate to build a bonfire and burn copies of scholastic writings and the canon law. Luther, shaking with emotion, stepped out of the crowd and threw upon the flames the papal bull, saying softly, "Because you have destroyed God's truth, may the Lord destroy you today in this fire." Luther had spoken his final farewell to Rome.[26]

For Luther, there was only one true head of the church, and that was Jesus Christ (cf. Eph 1:22, 4:15, 5:23; Col 1:18, 2:10, 19). Speaking to this point, White states: "The person who is subject to the authority of the Word of God cannot be subject to the Pope, having seen that the Papacy as an institution has no real basis in the Scriptures."[27] Thus, Luther spoke these very words before the Diet of Worms, "Unless I am convicted by Scripture and plain reason—I do not accept the authority of popes and councils, for they have contradicted each other—my conscience is captive to the Word of God."[28]

15.2.5 Christ, Not Priests or Sacraments

It is well-known how Luther trembled at the thought of his own elevation to the priesthood in 1507. His view of the concept of that priesthood would change radically, however—due in part to the corruption that he witnessed in Rome in 1510. The Luther of the Reformation renounced the very concept of priestly powers and emphasized the priesthood of all believers, as espoused in 1 Peter 2:9-10:

---

[26] Lewis W. Spitz, *The Renaissance and Reformation Movements*, vol. 2, *The Reformation*, rev. ed. (St. Louis, MO: Concordia, 1987), 338, 340.

[27] James R. White, *The Roman Catholic Controversy* (Minneapolis, MN: Bethany House Publishers, 1996), 124.

[28] Roland H. Bainton, *Here I Stand: A Life of Martin Luther* (New York: Mentor, 1950), 144, quoted in Erwin W. Lutzer, *Rescuing the Gospel* (Grand Rapids, MI: Baker Books, 2016), 82.

But you are A CHOSEN RACE, a royal PRIESTHOOD, A HOLY NATION, A PEOPLE FOR God's OWN POSSESSION, so that you may proclaim the excellencies of Him who has called you out of darkness into His marvelous light; for you once were NOT A PEOPLE, but now you are THE PEOPLE OF GOD; you had NOT RECEIVED MERCY, but now you have RECEIVED MERCY.

Concerning this, Erwin Lutzer writes:

In the Catholic tradition of the time, the ordination of priests was also a sacrament, a ritual that elevated them above the common people. Luther maintained that such an act simply recognized the freedom of the minister to perform the duties of his office, but it didn't give him a higher character or make him exempt from the jurisdiction of the civil courts; nor did it give him a special right to perform the sacraments unless it was understood that every Christian had such a right. Gone was the tradition of an exalted priesthood. Ordination vows, Luther said, do not give the priests magical powers to dispense salvation.

In fact, as far as Luther was concerned, ordination as practiced resulted in a "detestable tyranny" of the clergy over the laity. Their vestments and rituals were used to intimidate the common worshipers, causing them to think that their salvation rested in the hands of men who were separated from them as far as heaven is from the earth.[29]

Certainly, Luther continued to be a sacramentalist following his conversion and subsequent proclamation of reformation. But he became fully convinced that it was the sacrifice of Christ on the cross, not the sacrifice of the Mass, that saves. Wellum observes this point when he writes: "Rome confessed the exclusivity of Christ, but it lacked an equal emphasis on the sufficiency of his work, especially Christ *alone* as the *sole ground* of our justification which we receive through faith alone (*sola fide*), apart from works."[30]

---

[29] Erwin W. Lutzer, *Rescuing the Gospel* (Grand Rapids, MI: Baker Books, 2016), 64–65.

[30] Wellum, *Christ Alone*, 257.

Although Luther modified his view of the number of sacraments—maintaining only baptism and the Lord's supper—and adopted a radically new understanding of them (especially by rejecting transubstantiation and adopting his doctrine of the *real presence*[31]), he did not go far enough for many, including Ulrich Zwingli at the 1529 Marburg Colloquy, and certainly not far enough to please the modern-day dispensationalist or baptistic believer.

Yet Luther still achieved something radical through his modified presentation of the sacraments—he broke the stranglehold of the medieval priesthood and turned the focus back upon Scripture and *Christ alone.*[32]

In arguing for Luther's specific approach to the sacraments (with which this author does not agree), Mueller offers an interesting insight showing how Luther's theological spade cut to the root of the authority of the priesthood—and, in its place, offered the authority of *Scripture alone* and *Christ alone.* Mueller states, regarding the Lord's supper: "This doctrine is Scriptural; for neither the faith of man (Reformed) nor the power of the priesthood (Romanists) nor any magic influence of the spoken word makes the eating or drinking a Lord's Supper, or Sacrament, but only Christ's institution and command: 'This do ye.'"[33]

The Reformed understanding of the office of priest or the value of sacrifice must ultimately rest on the reformers' firm belief in *Christ alone* as the believer's great high priest (cf. Heb 2:17, 3:1, 4:14, 15, 5:5, 10, 6:20, 7:26, 8:1, 3, 9:11, 13:11, 12). Steven Lawson offers a fitting summary on this point.

> In this polemic [*The Babylonian Captivity of the Church*] Luther attacked the jugular vein of the Roman Catholic Church. He attacked the

---

[31] Martin Luther, *Doctor Martin Luther's Small Catechism*, 221.

[32] Many non-Lutherans fail to understand the distinctions that Lutherans make regarding the sacrament of baptism, surmising that their version of baptismal regeneration means simply that being baptized yields salvation. In actuality, confessional Lutheranism teaches that, "Baptism as a means of grace works faith in us, and through faith we have forgiveness of sins, deliverance from death and the devil, and eternal salvation." Luther, *Doctor Martin Luther's Small Catechism*, 198; answer to question no. 343.

[33] Mueller, *Christian Dogmatics*, 529.

priesthood. He attacked the sacramental system by which Rome brings every person's act under the power of the priest. The sacerdotal system Luther represented as the Babylonian Captivity of the church, and Rome as the whore of Babylon. Rome had established seven sacraments by which God's grace—God's favor, God's merit—was earned. And the one who would have favor from God must participate in these various sacraments. . . . And each of these were viewed as means of grace—means by which saving grace would come from God to the sinner. . . . Each of these were seen and viewed as conveying grace, and Luther attacked the very evil of the priesthood. And he attacked the corruption of the gospel of Christ in this. Luther studied the Bible and said, "No." All saving grace comes directly through Christ alone independent of the priesthood, and independent of the sacerdotal system, and independent of all rites and rituals. Saving grace comes directly through Christ alone. Luther said, "The Cross alone is our theology."[34]

15.3 The Dispensational View of Christ Alone—Ever Reforming

Just as the reformers continued in their agreement of the orthodox view of Christ that was taught by the Roman Catholic Church, so dispensational theologians continue their agreement with this position that was handed to them by the reformers and their successors.[35] In fact, there is no

---

[34] Steven Lawson, "The Five Solas of the Reformation" (podcast), SermonAudio, October 30, 2005, accessed August 21, 2017, http://www.sermonaudio.com/sermoninfo.asp?SID=29102136270.

[35] It must be noted that Luther and his successors actually did deviate from standard orthodoxy regarding the person of Christ in one aspect—although it could be argued that the unique Lutheran position on *ubiquity* offered an incomplete correction to a far greater inconsistency in Roman Catholic theology. The issue relates to whether Christ's human body can presently be, in some sense, omnipresent—which has implications for the Lutheran view of the *real presence* in the Lord's Supper. *Luther's Catechism* explains this view: "In, with, and under the earthly elements, as we eat the bread and drink the wine, Christ gives us His body and blood. His body, given into death for us, is present with the bread; His blood, which was shed for us, is present with the wine. Hence this sacrament is also called 'Holy Communion.'" Luther, *Doctor Martin Luther's Small Catechism*, 221; answer to question no. 399. See an extended discussion on this

aspect of dispensational theology that should alter one's view of the essence of the Godhead, the nature of the Trinity or the person of Christ (or His hypostatic union), as opposed to the view of a covenant theologian, a Lutheran or, arguably, even an orthodox Roman Catholic theologian.

This does not mean, however, that there is nothing more to be done with the type of information that has been surveyed in this chapter.[36] One question that remains is: How then does a proper understanding of dispensational theology affect, aid or enhance one's view of *Christ alone*, in particular, and Christology or theology proper in general? The following two proposals are offered to the reader.

First, the dispensationalist's commitment to literal, grammatical-historical hermeneutics—based on an unyielding commitment to the inspiration, inerrancy, authority and sufficiency of Scripture—should drive him to seek the greatest possible understanding of these issues, and to express them with the greatest clarity. Christians do not need any new or novel interpretations or eccentric explanations of the nature of God or the person of Christ that are unique to dispensationalism. This is the stuff of which cults

---

matter in Mueller, *Christian Dogmatics*, 509–520. Displaying the depth of the division over this issue since the time of the Reformation, Mueller states: "Calvin, on the one hand, condemned the Lutheran doctrine as an 'incantation of Satan' . . ." (519). He goes on to quote Melanchthon as saying of Calvin and Zwingli, "'Although they condemn us (as false teachers), they nevertheless desire that we should regard them as brethren.' (St. L., XVII, 1956)" (519). Berkhof responds to this issue (308–309), referring to it as "one peculiarity of Lutheran Christology." *Systematic Theology*, 308. Seeing the level of dissention that this understanding caused very early following the beginning of the Reformation, we may legitimately argue that the Lutheran view of *ubiquity* is not inherent to the basic teachings of the Reformation or the five solas—and that it certainly is not immune from refinement in the light of further study and theological development. Walvoord also responds to this view, calling it, "a significant variation" (115–116).

[36] It will not be the author's purpose here to go into aspects of application of the doctrine of *Christ alone* to the contemporary culture—based on a model offered by the reformers. For a thought-provoking treatment of this subject, however, the reader is encouraged to consult Wellum's chapter 11, "The Loss of Christ's Exclusivity: Our Current Challenge," and chapter 12, "Reaffirming Christ Alone Today," in *Christ Alone*, 275–310.

are made—not the basis for building up or building out the system of dispensational theology in the tradition of the Reformation.

Second, however, dispensationalists—being those who purportedly possess the fullest and most accurate literal understanding of the sacred text—may place a unique emphasis upon some truths about Christ that others in the theological stream flowing from the Reformation may miss. When dispensationalists place such a distinct emphasis upon a particular aspect of the person or work of Christ, they do so with historical precedent—indeed, with the very stamp of the reformers themselves. One has sufficient cause to be alarmed, however, if those conclusions do not, upon further examination, appear to be even more biblical extensions of the reformers' very own teachings.

Are there any such unique emphases that dispensational theology contributes to a biblical understanding about the second person of the Godhead? The following section will offer two that are worth examining—and they hinge on two very key prepositions.

15.3.1 Christ for the Believer

It is true that traditional dispensationalists are divided on matters of soteriology and, in particular, the *ordo salutis* (order of salvation). Some very clearly hold to positions consistent with Reformed soteriology—such as maintaining that regeneration must precede faith. For instance, MacArthur and Mayhue state: "Significant disagreement surrounds the relationship between regeneration and faith, yet Scripture seems to clearly present faith as the consequence of the new birth."[37]

---

[37] John MacArthur and Richard Mayhue, ed., *Biblical Doctrine: A Systematic Summary of Bible Truth* (Wheaton, IL: Crossway, 2017), 569. Interestingly, MacArthur and Mayhue go on to state later, "The distinction between regeneration and faith is to be defined not in terms of time but in terms of logical causality. ...most have clarified that they are speaking of logical, not chronological, order. From a temporal perspective, regeneration and faith occur simultaneously; in the exact moment that man is born again, he repents and believes the gospel" (585; see also 567n84). By contrast, Myron Houghton states: "In this discussion of justification and regeneration, we recognize the special work of God that precedes faith and is the cause of faith. That work has often been described as the 'effectual calling' and is what enables us to trust Christ. ...God's

Noted dispensational theologian Dr. Myron Houghton follows a different line of thought when he points out the following:

> Scripture, however, seems to teach that although both justification and regeneration occur when we trust Christ as Savior, justification logically precedes regeneration. Notice how Paul described these two benefits of salvation in Colossians 2:13. "And you, being dead in your trespasses and the uncircumcision of your flesh, He has made alive together with Him, having forgiven you all trespasses." Being made alive is regeneration and is dependent upon having forgiveness, which is justification.[38]

Houghton calls justification "the primary benefit of salvation," and goes on to offer this explanation, which highlights the difference between the Reformed view and his understanding:

> When confronted with the Catholic view of justification and grace, the Reformed faith clearly sides with the Biblical view. But when some of the Reformed leaders insist that regeneration precedes faith and is the cause of faith, they come dangerously close to agreeing with the Catholic view that grace is a God-given ability to do good works which is infused in a believer! Isn't that what regeneration is? Romans 8:13, for example, states, "For if you live according to the flesh you will die; but if by the Spirit you put to death the deeds of the body, you will live." And just a few verses earlier Paul said, "But you are not in the flesh but in the Spirit, if indeed the Spirit of God dwells in you. Now if anyone does not have the Spirit of Christ, he is not His" (Rom 8:9).
> Regeneration is one of the benefits of salvation but it is not the

---

effectual calling precedes faith and is its cause" Myron Houghton, "The Importance of Justification," Faith Baptist Theological Seminary, August 27, 2012, accessed September 3, 2017, https://www.faith.edu/2012/08/1893/. In this light, note again MacArthur and Mayhue: "Finally, there is good reason to believe that calling and regeneration speak of two aspects of the same reality, namely, the summons to spiritual life on the one hand and the impartation of spiritual life on the other" (570). They continue in the footnote: "Thus the effectual call ought to be identified with regeneration" (570n89).

[38] Houghton, "Importance of Justification."

primary benefit or the basis of our salvation. Christ FOR us, i.e., Christ's death and resurrection for us, is the basis of our salvation.[39]

This author's view is that this emphasis upon *Christ for us* (as opposed to *Christ in us*) is the more consistent dispensational understanding. While this emphasis may not be uniquely dispensational, it is certainly distinctive from Reformed theology and is derived solely from attention to Biblical detail—rather than theological, logical or historical arguments. Furthermore, it ties to dispensationalism by drawing its support primarily from the epistles—as opposed to the gospels—for teaching on soteriology and, in particular, the doctrines of justification and regeneration.

Nevertheless, this view also takes the Reformed emphasis on justification by grace alone, through faith alone, to its logical, Biblical fulfillment. It offers a complete disconnect with Roman Catholic teaching and precludes any possibility of influence by priests or sacraments in producing salvation in the life of an individual. Indeed, the only means that the believer has available to bring about such life is the gospel itself: "So faith *comes* from hearing, and hearing by the word of Christ" (Rom 10:17). Emphasizing the work of *Christ for the believer*, then, is one way in which dispensationalists can build upon their Reformed legacy.

15.3.2 The Believer in Christ

Even those dispensationalists who may disagree with the previous point will likely find agreement here: The dispensational emphasis upon the believer's place *in Christ* is very distinctive. While opposed at points by the reformers, it is actually, arguably, the logical extension of their early attempts to understand the unique role of the church's position under *Christ alone*—free from the tyranny of popes and kings.

How is this different from the understanding of the reformers or modern-day covenant theologians? To find the answer, one need only think through the traditional covenantal understanding of the definition of the church. Berkhof offers that as follows: "For both Luther and Calvin the Church was simply the community of the saints, that is, the community of those who believe and are sanctified in Christ, and who are joined to Him

---

[39] Houghton, "Importance of Justification."

as their Head."[40] This statement is ambiguous with regard to the beginning of the church, and demands clarification. Berkhof offers that when he states:

> The New Testament Church is essentially one with the Church of the old dispensation....The representation given in the preceding proceeds on the assumption that the Church existed in the old dispensation as well as in the new, and was *essentially* the same in both, in spite of acknowledged institutional and administrative differences. This is in harmony with the teachings of our confessional standards. . . . The Church is essentially, as was pointed out in the preceding, the community of believers, and this community existed from the beginning of the old dispensation right down to the present time and will continue to exist on earth until the end of the world. On this point we cannot agree with those Premillenarians who, under the influence of a divisive dispensationalism, claim that the Church is exclusively a New Testament institution, which did not come into existence until the outpouring of the Holy Spirit on the day of Pentecost and will be removed from the earth before the beginning of the millennium.[41]

With this theological context as their backdrop, one can surmise—at least to some extent—why the reformers were unable (and also unwilling) to disentangle themselves from the governmental power structures of their world. After all, if the church existed in, and derives at least a portion of its authority and direction from, the Old Testament, then it would be logical to conclude that it should be doing the types of activities that are found in the Old Testament—including operating a national government that functions with the full force of a theocracy.

More recently, Millard J. Erickson has offered a mediating position which, nevertheless, ends in a similar place: "We conclude that the church originated at Pentecost. . . . those who were part of Israel prior to Pentecost have been incorporated into the church. . . . Israel was not, then, simply succeeded by the church; rather, Israel was included within the church. The

---

[40] Berkhof, *Systematic Theology*, 564.
[41] Ibid., 571.

people of God are truly one people; the body of Christ is truly one body."[42]

Ryrie reiterates the covenantal understanding of the church, stating: "The covenant theologian denies the distinctiveness of the church to this present age. His viewpoint is based on his premise that God's program for the world is the salvation of individuals; therefore, the saved people of God in all ages may be called the church."[43]

The dispensational understanding of the unique position of the church age believer is quite different, indeed. Berkhof, perhaps without realizing the full force of his statement, points out the key to this discussion when he states: "They [dispensationalists] like to define the Church as 'the body of Christ,' which is a characteristically New Testament name."[44]

Indeed, "Having been justified by faith" (Rom 5:1), the believer receives certain benefits of salvation—a topic that was introduced in the previous point. One of the most notable of these benefits is that of receiving a place in the body of Christ.[45] The believer is bound intimately to Christ as a member of His body (cf. Rom 12:5; 1 Cor 10:17, 12:12-13, 27; Eph 1:22-23, 3:6, 4:12, 5:23; Col 1:18, 24, 3:15).

Membership in the body of Christ is a blessing that is completely unique to New Testament church age believers. Scripture makes this point certain in several places. For instance, Paul describes it as a μυστήριον (*mysterion, mystery*) in Ephesians 3:3-6:

By revelation there was made known to me the mystery, as I wrote

---

[42] Millard J. Erickson, *Christian Theology* (Grand Rapids, MI: Baker Book House, 1985), 1048-49. Erickson displays his view of dispensationalism when he writes: "In some cases, the deemphasis of the visible church may stem from a dispensational view which regards the church in general as a parenthesis in God's plan, a virtual afterthought" (1046).

[43] Charles Caldwell Ryrie, *Dispensationalism*, rev. and exp. ed. (1995; repr., Chicago, IL: Moody, 2007), 150.

[44] Berkhof, *Systematic Theology*, 571.

[45] It is ironic that the Roman Catholic focus on the body of Christ in the Mass—as well as the Lutheran focus on the *real presence* of the body of Christ in the Lord's Supper—both effectively serve to obscure the amazing Biblical reality of the believer's actual membership and participation in the body of Christ as it is presented in the passages under discussion.

before in brief. By referring to this, when you read you can understand my insight into the mystery of Christ, which in other generations was not made known to the sons of men, as it has now been revealed to His holy apostles and prophets in the Spirit; *to be specific*, that the Gentiles are fellow heirs and fellow members of the body, and fellow partakers of the promise in Christ Jesus through the gospel.

McClain defines a *mystery* as follows: "The word does not necessarily mean something incomprehensible to the human mind, but rather that which has hitherto been unrevealed."[46] The nature of the mystery in Ephesians 3 is not merely the inclusion of the Gentiles into an already existent Jewish body; rather, it is the very creation of an altogether new body. Ice states: "After having explained to the Ephesian Christians how God has taken elect Jews and Gentiles and placed 'the two into one new man' (Eph. 2:15), he proceeds in chapter three to describe how this truth was a mystery, never before revealed in the Old Testament."[47] If this point is not self-evident in Paul's language to the Ephesians, Peter's direct claim that the baptism of the Holy Spirit at Pentecost marked "the beginning" could not be any more explicit: "And as I began to speak, the Holy Spirit fell upon them [the Gentiles] just as *He did* upon us [Jews] at the beginning [Day of Pentecost]. And I remembered the word of the Lord, how He used to say, 'John baptized with water, but you will be baptized with the Holy Spirit'" (Acts 11:15–16).

Believers during this age, then, are placed into that body by the baptizing work of the Holy Spirit. First Corinthians 12:13 states: "For by one Spirit we were all baptized into one body, whether Jews or Greeks, whether slaves or free, and we were all made to drink of one Spirit."

Houghton argues that this body must be universal—because Paul was not baptized in water at Corinth (cf. Acts 9:18)—and invisible, because there is no visible church structure or organization found in the New Testament outside of the local church. The one performing the baptism is the Holy

---

[46] Alva J. McClain, *The Greatness of the Kingdom* (Winona Lake, IN: BMH Books, 1974), 324.

[47] Thomas Ice, "The Uniqueness of the Church," Pre-Trib Research Center, accessed September 7, 2017, http://pre-trib.org/articles/view/uniqueness-of-church.

Spirit and the baptism is Spirit baptism—not water baptism. [48] John 14:20 states: "In that day you will know that I am in My Father, and you in Me, and I in you."

According to Houghton, "that day" is the Day of Pentecost, when the Holy Spirit began to relate to Jesus' disciples in the new way that He described in John 14:16-18; and "you in Me" is a reference to membership in the body of Christ.

Houghton also believes that the phrase *in Christ* (variations of which are found roughly ninety-two times in the New American Standard Bible) is a technical term that signifies membership *in the body of Christ*. Thus, reasoning from the greater to the lesser, everyone who is *in the body of Christ* is, first of all, *in Christ*.

This unique dispensational emphasis on the believer today being *in Christ* signifies a distinctively new relationship that the church age believer has with all three members of the Godhead. It is based on the completed earthly ministry of Christ and, subsequently, God's unique program for this age—which involves a new emphasis upon the work of the Holy Spirit within each individual believer. That means, of course, that every church age believer is the recipient of all the benefits and blessings of being *in Christ*. Cataloging all of those benefits would involve investigating the scores of New Testament references that deal with the phrase, *in Christ*.

It also means that every believer participates in all of the *mysteries* related to the New Testament church age—not merely the concepts revealed in Ephesians 3. Furthermore, it means that every church age believer:

- Goes to "be with Christ" at death (Phil 1:23);
- If dead, will be resurrected to be "with Him" at the rapture (1 Thess 4:14);
- "Shall always be with the Lord" following the rapture (1 Thess 4:17);
- Will enjoy participation in *the marriage supper of the lamb* and the final return of Christ to Earth (Rev 19:1-16);
- "Will reign with Him for a thousand years" (Rev 20:6); and

---

[48] Myron J. Houghton, "Systematic Theology IV" (notes from class lectures, Faith Baptist Theological Seminary, Ankeny, IA, Spring 1996).

- Will experience the immediate presence of God for all eternity (Rev 21:1-4).

Ryrie's words serve as a summary to this entire section when he states:

The distinct character of the church is rooted in its unique relationship to the living Christ as the body of which He is the Head....

The distinctiveness of the character of the church as the body of Christ is twofold. It is distinct because of who are included within that body (i.e., Jews and Gentiles as fellow heirs), and it is distinct because of the new relationship of being in Christ and of Christ's indwelling the members of that body. Both of these distinctives are unique with the church and were not known or experienced by God's people in Old Testament times or even during the earthly lifetime of our Lord.[49]

Sadly, there have been real consequences to the reformers' lack of understanding on this point—and they continue down to the present day. Ronald Diprose's warning should suffice in speaking to this point: "Replacement theology and its corollary—the Church's self-understanding as the true Israel—are historically linked with overt contempt for Israel. This is evident both in the *Adversus Judaeos* [*Against the Jews*] tradition and in the anti-Semitic thought and practice of Post-Reformation Europe."[50]

15.4 Conclusion

Having been raised a confessional Lutheran, I have always been fascinated with the history of the Reformation. Truly, these people and events were used of God to reshape the world—and the truths that they restored have shaped my own life and thinking in incredibly profound ways. I believe that, now as a dispensationalist, I can see much more clearly how the truths rediscovered by Luther and the reformers fit into God's progressively revealed Word—and into the church's continuing ability to understand that Word more and more through the centuries.

---

[49] Ryrie, *Dispensationalism*, 144.

[50] Ronald E. Diprose, *Israel and the Church: The Origin and Effects of Replacement Theology* (Rome: Istituto Biblico Evangelico Italiano, 2004), 134. Diprose offers an extended explanation of "The *Adversus Judaeos* writings" in the endnotes for chapter 3, 209-10n13.

I pray that the Lord will be pleased to use this multi-author volume, done on the occasion of the 500ᵗʰ anniversary of the first Reformation Day, to once again call the church back to *Christ alone.*

As Luther stated in the "Preface to the Catechism": "Christ Himself will be our Reward if we labor faithfully. To this end may the Father of all grace help us; and to Him be praise and thanks forever, through Christ, our Lord! Amen."[51]

Soli Deo Gloria — To God Alone Be Glory!

---

[51] Martin Luther, "From Luther's Preface to the Catechism," *Doctor Martin Luther's Small Catechism,* ed. C. Gausewitz (Milwaukee: Northwestern Publishing House, 1956), n.p.

Bibliography

Bainton, Roland H. *Here I Stand: A Life of Martin Luther*. New York: Mentor, 1950. Quoted in Erwin W. Lutzer, *Rescuing the Gospel*. Grand Rapids, MI: Baker Books, 2016.

Berkhof, Louis. *Systematic Theology*. 4th rev. and enl. ed. Grand Rapids, MI: Wm. B. Eerdmans, 1941.

Busenitz, Nathan. "Reformation Hardware" (sermon). Grace Community Church. July 16, 2017. Accessed August 22, 2017. https://www.grace church.org /sermons/13326.

Cairns, Earle Edwin. *Christianity through the Centuries: A History of the Christian Church*. Rev. and enl. ed. Grand Rapids: Zondervan, 1981.

"Chalcedonian Creed (451 A.D.)." Christian Classics Ethereal Library. Accessed September 5, 2017. https://www.ccel.org/creeds/chalcedonian-creed.html.

Diprose, Ronald E. *Israel and the Church: The Origin and Effects of Replacement Theology*. Rome: Istituto Biblico Evangelico Italiano, 2004.

Erickson, Millard J. *Christian Theology*. Grand Rapids, MI: Baker Book House, 1985.

Evangelical Lutheran Church in America. "Ecumenical and Interreligious." Freed and Renewed in Christ: 500 Years of God's Grace in Action. Accessed September 4, 2017. https://www.elca500.org/resources/ecu menical-and-interreligious/.

Gromacki, Robert G. *The Virgin Birth: Doctrine of Deity*. Grand Rapids, MI: Baker Book House, 1974.

Houghton, Myron. "The Active Obedience of Christ." Faith Baptist Theological Seminary. August 27, 2012. Accessed September 3, 2017. https://www.faith.edu/2012/08/the-active-obedience-of-christ.

Houghton, Myron. "The Importance of Justification." Faith Baptist Theological Seminary. August 27, 2012. Accessed September 3, 2017. https://www.faith.edu/2012/08/1893/.

Ice, Thomas. "The Uniqueness of the Church." Pre-Trib Research Center. Accessed September 7, 2017. http://pre-trib.org/articles/view/uniqueness-of-church.

Kelly, Brian. "Four Great Marian Dogmas." Catholicism.org. July 12, 2016. Accessed September 4, 2017. http://catholicism.org/four-great-marian-dogmas.html.

Lawson, Steven. "The Five Solas of the Reformation" (podcast). SermonAudio. October 30, 2005. Accessed August 21, 2017. http://www.sermonaudio.com/sermoninfo.asp?SID=29102136270.

Luther, Martin. *Doctor Martin Luther's Small Catechism.* Edited by C. Gausewitz. Milwaukee, WI: Northwestern Publishing House, 1956.

———. "The 95 Theses." Martin Luther. Accessed September 2, 2017. http://www.luther.de/en/95thesen.html.

Lutheran World Federation and the Catholic Church. "Joint Declaration on the Doctrine of Justification." Vatican. Accessed September 6, 2017. http://www.vatican.va/roman_curia/pontifical_councils/chrstuni/documents/rc_pc_chrstuni_doc_31101999_cath-luth-joint-declaration_en.html.

Lutzer, Erwin W. *Rescuing the Gospel.* Grand Rapids, MI: Baker Books, 2016.

MacArthur, John, and Richard Mayhue, ed. *Biblical Doctrine: A Systematic Summary of Bible Truth.* Wheaton, IL: Crossway, 2017.

McClain, Alva J. *The Greatness of the Kingdom.* Winona Lake, IN: BMH Books, 1974.

McGrath, Alister E. *Historical Theology: An Introduction to the History of Christian Thought.* Oxford, UK: Blackwell Publishers, 1998.

Mueller, John Theodore. _Christian Dogmatics: A Handbook of Doctrinal Theology for Pastors, Teachers, and Laymen._ St. Louis, MO: Concordia, 1934.

"Nicene Creed." Christian Classics Ethereal Library. Accessed September 3, 2017. https://www.ccel.org/creeds/nicene.creed.html.

Ryrie, Charles Caldwell. _Dispensationalism._ Rev. and exp. ed. 1995. Reprint, Chicago, IL: Moody, 2007.

Second Vatican Council. "Catechism of the Catholic Church." Vatican, August 15, 1997. Accessed September 3, 2017. http://www.vatican .va/archive/ccc_css/archive/catechism/credo.htm.

Slick, Matt. "What Are the Four Marian Dogmas?" Christian Apologetics and Research Ministry. September 28, 2014. Accessed September 4, 2017. https://carm.org/what-are-the-four-marian-dogmas.

Spitz, Lewis W. _The Renaissance and Reformation Movements._ Vol. 2, _The Reformation._ Rev. ed. St. Louis, MO: Concordia, 1987.

Swan, James. "Martin Luther Believed in Devotion to Mary?" Alpha and Omega Ministries. October 17, 2013. Accessed September 4, 2017. http://www.aomin.org/aoblog/2013/10/17/martin-luther-believed-in-devotion-to-mary/.

Walvoord, John F. _Jesus Christ Our Lord._ Chicago, IL: Moody Press, 1969.

Wellum, Stephen. _Christ Alone._ The 5 _Solas_ Series. Grand Rapids, MI: Zondervan, 2017.

"What We Believe." United States Conference of Catholic Bishops. Accessed September 3, 2017. http://www.usccb.org/beliefs-and-teachings/what-we-believe/.

White, James R. _Mary–Another Redeemer?_ Minneapolis, MN: Bethany House, 1998.

———. _The Roman Catholic Controversy._ Minneapolis, MN: Bethany House Publishers, 1996.

"Why a New Marian Dogma?" Fifth Marian Dogma. Accessed September 4, 2017. http://www.fifthmariandogma.com/.

Williams, Peter D. "Unbelievable? The Reformation: Return to Truth or Tragic Mistake? James White vs Peter D Williams" (podcast). Premier Christian Radio. April 22, 2017. Accessed September 5, 2017. https://www.premierchristianradio.com/Shows/Saturday/Unbeliev able/Episodes/Unbelievable-The-Reformation-return-to-truth-or-tra gic-mistake-James-White-vs-Peter-D-Williams.

Soli Deo Gloria
[To the Glory of God Alone]

16

SOLI DEO GLORIA AS PINNACLE OF DISPENSATIONALISM'S SINE QUA NON

Christopher Cone
Calvary University

16.0 Introduction

In 1957, Charles Ryrie wrote an article published in *Bibliotheca Sacra*, entitled, "The Necessity of Dispensationalism."[1] In the article, Ryrie emphasized the concepts he later referred to as the *sine qua non* of dispensationalism,[2] and in particular he focused on the goal of history as being centered on God's glory: "the differing dispensations reveal the glory of God as He shows off His character in the different stewardships culminating in history with the millennial glory."[3] Ryrie's later iteration of the *sine qua non* (without which not) culminated with "the underlying purpose of God"[4] as "the total program of glorifying Himself."[5] Despite Ryrie's emphasis on the centrality of God's doxological purpose, few later dispensational thinkers have echoed the doxological purpose as a necessary and distinctively dispensational theme. It is not unusual for dispensational thinkers to acknowledge God's

---

[1] Charles C. Ryrie, "The Necessity of Dispensationalism," *Bibliotheca Sacra* 114, no. 455 (July 1957): 243–254.

[2] Charles C. Ryrie, *Dispensationalism Today* (Chicago, IL: Moody Press, 1965), 43.

[3] Ryrie, "Necessity of Dispensationalism," 248.

[4] Ryrie, *Dispensationalism Today*, 46.

[5] Ibid., 46.

glory as the highest end, yet Ryrie stands nearly alone in his assertion of God's glory as *uniquely necessary* for dispensational thought.

It seems clear enough that the consistent application of the literal grammatical-historical hermeneutic would uncover both the Israel-church distinction *and* the centrality of the doxological purpose. If this be the case, then the significance of including the two conclusions as part of the *sine qua non* is based not on their methodological usefulness, but rather on their explanatory value. The three elements are not altogether methodological. In fact, only one of the three components is methodological. In addition to that methodological factor, one is theological, and the other is teleological.[6] The *methodological* distinctive of dispensational thought is a hermeneutic one (the literal grammatical-historical hermeneutic consistently applied). The *theological* distinctive (the Israel-church distinction) is an explanatory litmus test so significant in its practical implications that there may be no single greater theological difference between the dispensational and re- formed systems. It is, however, the *teleological* distinctive that undergirds the theological distinctive. Recognizing the doxological purpose through exeget- ical examination (governed by literal grammatical-historical hermeneutics) highlights a number of theological keys, including the demand for the Israel- church distinction. If Ryrie is correct, the dispensational order of process would follow this pattern:

1. Exegete the Scriptures applying a consistently literal grammatical- historical hermeneutic.

2. Recognize the glory of God as God's highest end, and that end which governs all other ends.

3. Understand key theological distinctions (including the notable Is- rael/church distinction) observable through the application of a literal grammatical-historical hermeneutic and *confirmable* in light of the doxological purpose which permeates Scripture.

---

[6] The order of the three elements were not particularly important in Ryrie's thinking. In a private conversation he confirmed verbally to me that there was no par- ticular reason he listed them in the order he did. Inclusion of the three were vital, as was their flow, but the order (in which they were listed) was not.

The three elements of Ryrie's *sine qua non* flow from methodological, to teleological, to theological, and ultimately from methodological to explanatory. The flow of these three is sufficient to draw a fairly comprehensive and definitive contrast between dispensational and Reformed thought.

While there is a rich heritage in Reformed theology of acknowledging the centrality of the doxological purpose, there has also been a subtle drift toward a more soteriological focus. In contrast to Ryrie's brand of *sine qua non* based dispensational thought, modern day Reformed theology seems practically centered on a redemptive purpose rather than on a doxological one. It is within the distance covered by this drift that Ryrie finds perhaps the greatest contrast *in conclusions* between dispensational and Reformed understanding: dispensational thought sees God's glory as *necessary* for understanding the different administrations and economies described in Scripture, while the Reformed understanding of Scripture is simply not dependent on the doxological theme. In Ryrie's estimation, simply recognizing a literal grammatical-historical hermeneutic and thus arriving at a complete distinction between Israel and the church is not sufficient to distinguish between dispensational and Reformed thought. The great theme of *soli Deo gloria* (to God [be the] glory) is a pivot point that underscores the contrast between the two systems. In light of the reformers' emphasis on *soli Deo gloria* and subsequent drift toward a more soteriological center, if Ryrie is correct about the necessity of the doxological center and its uniqueness to the dispensational understanding, then when it comes to *soli Deo gloria*, dispensationalism is the truer descendant of the Reformation heritage. In this, the 500th anniversary of the Reformation, that implication is a significant reminder of the orthodoxy and value of dispensational thought to Christian understanding.

16.1 *Soli Deo Gloria* in the Biblical Data

Cataloging the activities of God as recorded in Scripture provides perspective on God's purpose in engaging those activities:

> The major works of God revealed in Scripture all serve the doxological purpose...This doxological purpose is at the center of God's revelation

to man, and there is therefore no higher purpose for man but to glorify God...this doxological purpose is not only man's highest calling, but is the intended design of all that is...The aim, therefore, of Biblical theology is to communicate the truth about God, to the extent to which God has revealed Himself in Scripture, and for His own doxological purpose. Rightly understanding then the primacy of the doxological design is a necessity without which no consistent and coherent theology can result.[7]

David ascribes to God greatness of deeds, and recognizes that all the nations will worship Him (Ps 86:9-10). John narrates a still-yet-future song that will celebrate all the nations fearing Him and glorifying His name (Rev 15:4). In a general sense, God's identity and His deeds are worthy of praise. His glory is well deserved. Still, Christians are not left with only a general understanding of His doxological purpose as His highest end, as the Scriptures provide numerous specific examples. In each of these activities of God, His own glory is identified as the highest purpose.

God predestines and calls for the purpose of His glory (Eph 1:4-6). In fact, it was through His glory—or as an expression of it, that He calls believers to salvation (1 Pet 1:3). The ministry of Christ was for His glory and the Father's (John 13:31-32). The earthly ministry and plan of salvation executed by Christ was for His and the Father's glory (John 17:1-5). God is glorified in fulfilling His promises to His people (2 Cor 1:20). Jesus is glorified in the equipping of His people (Heb 13:21). Creation itself declares His glory (Ps 19:1-6). One of the reasons given for the worthiness of God to receive glory is that He is the Creator (Rev 4:11). God is glorified by His truth (Rom 3:7). His name is glorified in saving, helping, and forgiving His people (Ps 19:9). God is glorified in Christ's accepting of His people (Rom 15:7). He is glorified in His entire plan (Rom 16:25-27). Christ redeems for His glory (Eph 1:7-12). The Holy Spirit seals for His glory (Eph 1:13-14). The demonstration of mercy unto salvation is for His glory (1 Tim 1:15-17). He is glorified in His people's sanctification (2 Tim 4:18). His

---

[7] Christopher Cone, *Prolegomena on Biblical Hermeneutics and Method*, 2nd ed. (Fort Worth, TX: Tyndale Seminary Press, 2012), 15-16.

strengthening of His people is for His glory (Jude 24-25). He is to be glorified in all the actions of His church (1 Cor 10:31). Thankfulness for grace is purposed for the glory of God (2 Cor 4:15). The fruit of righteousness is for the glory of God (Phil 1:11). His working in His people is for His glory (2 Thess 1:11-12). He is glorified before all time, now, and forever (Jude 24-25). He is glorified in the suffering of His people (1 Pet 4:16). He is glorified when His disciples bear fruit (John 15:8). He will be glorified when every tongue confesses that Jesus Christ is Lord (Phil 2:11). He is glorified in illness (1 Sam 6:5; John 9:1-3). He is glorified in healing (Luke 17:11-18). He is glorified in death (John 21:19). He is glorified in resurrection (John 11:4). He is glorified in judgment (Rev 14:7). He is glorified in the deliverance of Israel (Isa 60:21, 61:3). He is glorified in the fulfilling of His covenants and the summing up of all things (Isa 25:1-3, 43:20; Luke 2:14; Rom 4:20, 15:8-9; 2 Cor 1:20; 2 Pet 1:3-4; Rev 19:7). And in case these specific statements are not convincing enough, Peter states that God is glorified in all things (1 Pet 4:11). Inarguably, through the lens of the literal grammatical-historical hermeneutic, the doxological purpose is central in Scripture, as Ryrie suggests.

16.2 *Soli Deo Gloria* in Other Notable Dispensational Perspectives

While Ryrie does not specifically spell out the primacy of the doxological purpose in his *Basic Theology* to the extent he did in *Dispensationalism Today*, he does note that one of the four primary purposes of the knowledge of God (theology) is "to generate true worship of God (Rom 11:33-36)."[8] Of course, many other dispensational thinkers agree with Ryrie that God's primary revealed focus is doxological, but few suggest that the idea is central to dispensational theology.

One who agreed with Ryrie regarding the import of *soli Deo gloria* was John Walvoord, who critiques Reformed/Covenant theology as "unduly restrict[ing] the larger purpose of God to soteriology."[9] Walvoord adds his own understanding that,

---

[8] Charles C. Ryrie, *Basic Theology* (Wheaton, IL: Victor Books, 1982), 26.

[9] John F. Walvoord, "A Review of 'Crucial Questions About the Kingdom of God,' by George E. Ladd," *Bibliotheca Sacra* 110, no. 437 (January 1953): 3.

a more tenable position is that the larger purpose of God is the manifestation of His own glory. To this end each dispensation, each successive revelation of God's plan for the ages, His dealing with the none-
lect as with the elect, and the glories of nature combine to manifest
divine glory. There is provided a unity to the plan of God which does
not require merging Israel and the church or the present form of the
kingdom of God with the future Messianic kingdom.[10]

Walvoord focuses on the unity of the Scriptures through the doxological purpose, rather than through artificial relationships necessitated by a
particular understanding of the redemptive center. Walvoord's simple explanation underscores an aspect of necessity for the doxological purpose in
dispensational understanding that is not present in Reformed thought—it
provides the unifying theme of the Bible.

In contrast to Walvoord's understanding of unification, Lewis Sperry
Chafer suggests that "the true unity of Scripture is not discovered when one
blindly seeks to fuse these opposing principles [Law and grace, as in the
theological covenants of Covenant theology] into one system, but rather it
is found when God's plain differentiations are observed."[11] For Chafer, it
is the dispensations themselves that unify Scripture. Chafer also recognizes
that any "plan of interpretation, which in defense of an ideal unity of the
Bible, contends for a single divine purpose, ignores drastic contradictions
and is sustained only by occasional or accidental similarities—is doomed to
confusion when confronted with the many problems which such a system
imposes on the text of Scripture."[12]

In this context, Chafer is not supportive of a grand narrative or singular purpose of God, though he does acknowledge that in this age, God's
divine purpose is "a complete demonstration of grace."[13] Further, Chafer
suggests that "the dispensationalist believes that throughout the ages God
is pursuing two distinct purposes: one related to the earth with earthly peo-

---

[10] Walvoord, "A Review of 'Crucial Questions,'" 3–4.
[11] Lewis Sperry Chafer, *Dispensationalism* (Fort Worth, TX: Exegetica, 2015), 51.
[12] Ibid., 52.
[13] Ibid., 70.

ple and earthly objectives involved, which is Judaism; while the other is related to heaven with heavenly people and heavenly objectives involved, which is Christianity."[14] Chafer does not discuss the doxological purpose or the glory of God as His end, and in most of the discussion regarding purpose and objectives, either salvation or the kingdom are in view. Chafer provides evidence that even prominent dispensational thinkers sometimes were not focused on *soli Deo gloria*.

Citing George Peters' recognition of a kingdom center,[15] Dwight Pentecost views the unifying purpose of God in Scripture as pertaining to the kingdom,[16] specifically fulfilled in Christ: "Thus the ages are the time periods within which God is revealing His divine purpose and program as it centers in the Lord Jesus Christ."[17] Pentecost follows Chafer in considering that "the divine purpose in the outcalling of the church is to display the infinity of His grace."[18] Pentecost also agrees with Chafer in expressing concerns regarding improperly identifying a unity in God's purpose: those who "emphasize the unity of God's purpose from the fall of man until the eternal state...fail to make any distinction between God's program for Israel and that for the church."[19] Like Chafer, and unlike Ryrie, Pentecost does not sense a need to identify a unified purpose of God in Scripture. Instead, the distinct and diverse aspects of God's kingdom plan[20] as expressed in Christ are thematically unified enough to make Scripture cogent. Pentecost does not ignore the doxological purpose entirely. He quotes Dennett in recognition of God's achieving His glory in the pursuance of His purposes.[21] Pentecost identifies those purposes specifically as realizing redemption and

---

[14] Chafer, *Dispensationalism*, 103.

[15] George N. H. Peters, *The Theocratic Kingdom* (Grand Rapids, MI: Kregel, 1952), 1:176, quoted in J. Dwight Pentecost, *Things to Come* (Grand Rapids, MI: Zondervan, 1965), 49.

[16] Pentecost, *Things to Come*, 484.

[17] Ibid., 130.

[18] Ibid., 133.

[19] Ibid., 139.

[20] Ibid., 142.

[21] Edward Dennett, *Daniel the Prophet* (London: G. Morrish, 1919), 9, quoted in Pentecost, *Things to Come*, 316.

manifesting His sovereignty.[22]

Clarence Larkin in *Dispensational Truth* primarily refers to *glory* as it relates to Christ, and not in any sense of doxological purpose. While the subtitle of Larkin's work is *God's Plan and Purpose in the Ages*, there is virtually no discussion of any particular purpose. Larkin does recognize that without the Fall, "the Universe would never have had the supreme spectacle of His forgiving love and redemptive grace as revealed on Calvary."[23] Larkin identifies God's purpose in this dispensation as "to gather out a 'People for His Name,' called THE CHURCH, composed of both Jew and Gentile."[24] For Larkin it seems that a unified purpose is elusive, as he points to the future "ages of the ages," and admits that "What the 'Ages of the Ages' shall reveal of the Plan and Purpose of God we do not know, but if we are His we shall live to know, and possibly take part in their development."[25] Larkin also acknowledges that it is "the purpose of God to set up a Kingdom on this earth."[26] Larkin seems to associate God's purpose with Christ and His kingdom, without specifically identifying any preeminent and overarching purpose of God.

C. I. Scofield in *Rightly Dividing the Word of Truth* does not discuss glory in the context of God's purpose, and his limited discussion of purpose is reminiscent of Chafer's in that statements of purpose are related to salvation, especially. Scofield notes that, "God's purpose in promising to reward with heavenly and eternal honors the faithful service of His saints is to win them from the pursuit of earthly riches and pleasures, to sustain them in the fires of persecution, and to encourage them in the exercise of Christian virtues."[27]

Early French theologian and contemporary of John Nelson Darby,

---

[22] Pentecost, *Things to Come*, 370.

[23] Clarence Larkin, *Dispensational Truth or God's Plan and Purpose in the Ages* (Glenside, PA: Clarence Larkin, 1918), 68.

[24] Ibid., 84.

[25] Ibid., 92.

[26] Ibid., 178.

[27] C. I. Scofield, *Rightly Dividing the Word of Truth* (Charleston, SC: Armor of God Ministries, 2010), 48, accessed August 1, 2017, http://www.armorofgodbooks.com/books/scofield/Rightly_Dividing_the_Word_of_Truth.pdf.

Emile Guers (1794–1882), underscores three components of his theology, not vastly dissimilar to Ryrie's. As Mike Stallard puts it, Guers agrees with Ryrie directly on the two points of literalism and diversity of classes and privileges in the entire body of the redeemed (Guers' third point is the literal value of the word *day* in prophecy).[28] However, Guers does not identify God's purpose as doxological. Still, Stallard recognizes that, "The fact that Guers has written a book on the future of national Israel shows that he believes that God is doing more in history than individual redemption."[29]

John Nelson Darby addresses the purpose of God being manifest in the heavenly glory of the church and the earthly glory of Israel.[30] Rather than a precisely doxological purpose, Darby observes a more Christological expression of doxology: "The good pleasure of the Godhead was that all its fullness should dwell and manifest itself in Christ. Such was the purpose of God...."[31] Still, God's glory is ultimately displayed in Christ through the church: "For it [the church] will be the sphere and means of the display of the glory and blessing of Christ."[32]

Charles Baker, who advocates for a mid-Acts dispensationalism,[33] argues for the eternal purpose of God, and specifies that "God's purpose and decrees are all just and good and that when the final decree is carried out all of God's creation will unite in giving all glory and honor to God. God's decrees, while they concern man, do not find their end in man, but in God. Whatever He has decreed, He has decreed for His own glory."[34]

---

[28] Mike Stallard, "Emile Guers and Charles Ryrie: A Case Study of Continuity in the History of Dispensationalism Concerning Literal Interpretation" (paper presented at the Council on Dispensational Hermeneutics, Grace Theological Seminary, Winona Lake, IN, September 14, 2016), 6–7.

[29] Ibid., 6–7.

[30] J. N. Darby, "The Purpose of God," in *The Collected Writings of J. N. Darby*, vol. 30, *Prophetic 1* (Addison, IL: BibleTruth Pulblishers, n.d.), accessed August 1, 2017, http://bibletruthpublishers.com/the-purpose-of-god/john-nelson-darby-jnd/collected-writings-of-j-n-darby-prophetic-1/la62216.

[31] Ibid., 468.

[32] Ibid., 484.

[33] Charles Baker, *A Dispensational Theology* (Grand Rapids, MI: Grace Bible College Publications, n.d.), xii.

[34] Ibid., 156–158, 162.

Henry Thiessen recognizes the centrality of the doxological purpose, saying,

> Though God sincerely seeks to promote the happiness of his creatures and to perfect the saints in holiness, neither of these is the highest possible end. The end is his own glory. All his works in creation (Ps. 19: 1-6; Prov. 3:19), preservation (Neh. 9:6; Rev. 4:11), providence (Ps. 33:10f.; Dan. 4:35; Eph. 1:11), and redemption (1 Cor. 2:7; Eph. 3:10f.) have this end in view.[35]

Thiessen is consistent in his application of the doxological purpose even in practical matters. In discussing, for example, the existence of evil, he asserts that God overrules evil for His purpose and glory, and exhorts his readers that "the fact that God has turned evil into good ought to induce his children to trust him to do the same with the evil of the present generation."[36] While he makes no statement regarding the uniqueness of the centrality of doxological purpose to the dispensational understanding, Thiessen demonstrates that the doxological purpose of God matters in the believer's practical application of Scriptural truth.

Arno Gaebelein suggests that, "All the glorious manifestations of Jehovah recorded in the Word of God are the manifestations of 'the Lord of Glory'...the focus of His Glory is the cross."[37] Gaebelein does not identify an overarching purpose in this context other than to recognize, "What a stupendous thought that He came from Glory to die for us so that He might have us with Him in Glory!"[38] He adds that "the revelation of His eternal purposes...locates His kingdom on earth after...the judgment of His second coming...."[39] Gaebelein's focus is Christological, with a view to His second

---

[35] Henry Thiessen, *Lectures on Systematic Theology*, rev. ed. (Grand Rapids, MI: Eerdmans, 1979), 82.

[36] Ibid., 125.

[37] Arno C. Gaebelein, "The Lord of Glory," in *The Lord of Glory: Meditations on the Person, the Work and Glory of Our Lord Jesus Christ* (New York, NY: Publication Office "Our Hope," 1910), accessed August 1, 2017, http://www.wholesomewords.org/etexts /gaebelein/lordof1.html.

[38] Ibid.

[39] Arno C. Gaebelein, "The Biblical Logic of Premillennialism," in *Meat in Due Season: Sermons, Discourses and Expositions of the World of Prophecy* (New York: Arno C.

coming and the culmination of His kingdom.

As evidenced in the particular perspectives highlighted above, there has historically been diversity in the viewpoints of dispensational thinkers as to whether there is actually a meta-narrative, and if so, whether it is Christological, soteriological, theocratic, or doxological. Ryrie's particular conclusions seem nearly unique, echoed only by Walvoord—that there is an overarching purpose, and that purpose is the glory of God. In fact, Ryrie's perspective is so unique among dispensationalists, that Craig Blaising critiques Ryrie's view because of its uniqueness, first observing that the doxological purpose was not "a particularly distinctive feature of earlier dispensationalism."[40] Blaising observes—as has been catalogued above, that, "Other dispensationalists used salvation and redemption as unifying themes but defined them to include national and political salvation and even the redemption of the entire creation."[41] While Blaising correctly notes that "Ryrie distinguishes dispensationalism from covenantalism as the difference between a doxological versus a soteriological perspective,"[42] Blaising misses a key point when he counters that, "Most evangelicals, especially among the Reformed, would have agreed on the comprehensive doxological purpose of God."[43] Blaising is correct, yet he does not address the aspect of the *necessity* of the doxological purpose as central in the theological systems, nor does he address the practical departure of Reformed thinkers from the doxological center in favor of a soteriological one, as Ryrie underscores.

In short, dispensationalists have been inconsistent in articulating this point. This may be at least partly due to their building on the Reformed redemptive platform and in some cases even the Reformed theological methodology. Such inconsistency could have been avoided had dispensational thinkers built their system exclusively from the exegetical data (as

---

Gaebelein, 1900), accessed August 1, 2017, http://www.wholesomewords.org/etexts/gaebelein/meat4.html.

[40] Craig Blaising, "Dispensationalism: The Search for Definition," in *Dispensationalism, Israel, and the Church*, ed. Craig A. Blaising and Darrell L. Bock (Grand Rapids, MI: Zondervan, 1992), 27.

[41] Ibid.

[42] Ibid.

[43] Ibid.

Ryrie prescribes) rather than utilizing an integrative method of building on existing Reformed doctrine with a dispensational eschatological and ecclesiological perspective.

The lesson we learn from Ryrie is to allow the text to direct us to the purpose of God as revealed within, and to rely on that same text to provide the theological particulars. If we do that, our theology will resemble Ryrie's far more than it will that of the other dispensationalists to whom Blaising refers, and will be arguably much more biblical. Ryrie's doxological recognition challenges exegetes to be consistent in their hermeneutic, and to consider how applying the interpretive method consistently will unveil God's remarkable purpose and plan. Ryrie's *sine qua non* is a lesson in reform for dispensational thinkers, first and foremost, as Blaising's accusations of inconsistency ring true (even if his thesis falls flat). Still, the Reformed camp is not without its own consistency problems. In fact, it is by borrowing from Reformed methodology that dispensationalists have found inconsistency so comfortable.

16.3 *Soli Deo Gloria* in Contemporary Reformed Theology

Charles Hodge recognizes the glory of God as the great end of all things,[44] saying that, "the Bible declares the glory of God, an infinitely higher end, to be the final cause for which all things exist,"[45] but in practice he seems to elevate the redemptive plan to a nearly equal height. Hodge notes that

> all the works of God declare his wisdom. They show, from the most minute to the greatest, the most wonderful adaptation of means to accomplish the high end of the good of his creatures and the manifestation of his own glory. So also, in the whole course of history, we see evidence of the controlling power of God making all things work together for the best interests of his people, and the promotion of his kingdom upon earth. It is, however, in the work of redemption that

---

[44] Charles Hodge, *Systematic Theology* (Grand Rapids, MI: Eerdmans, 1940), 1:425.

[45] Ibid., 1:423.

this divine attribute is specially revealed.[46]

Louis Berkhof explains that the wisdom of God "implies a final end to which all secondary ends are subordinate; and according to Scripture this final end is the glory of God."[47] He adds that, *"The final aim is the glory of God.* [author's emphasis] Even the salvation of men is subordinate to this. That the glory of God is the highest purpose of the electing grace is made very emphatic in Eph. 1:6,12,14."[48] Berkhof is adamant that,

> The supreme end of God in creation, the manifestation of His glory, therefore, includes, as subordinate ends, the happiness and salvation of His creatures, and the reception of praise from grateful and adoring hearts....His declarative glory is intrinsically of far greater value than the good of His creatures....The glory of God is the only end that is consistent with His independence and sovereignty.[49]

Still, in acknowledging this, Berkhof closely connects the glory of God with the soteriological purpose—nearly equating the two in practice: "The social gospel of our day likes to stress the fact that man is elected unto service. In so far as this is intended as a denial of man's election *unto salvation and unto the glory of God*, it plainly goes contrary to Scripture."[50] He speaks of "the great redemptive purpose of God,"[51] and later refers to "the grace and glory of God in Christ."[52] (It is worth noting that in the eight scriptural instances in which the two words *grace* and *glory* appear in close context [Ps 84:11; John 1:14; Rom 5:2; 2 Cor 4:15; Eph 1:6; Heb 2:9; 1 Pet 5:10; and 2 Pet 3:18], they are not so closely related as to be interchangeable, except in Psalm 84:11, where God is giving grace and glory, rather than describing His own grace and glory. In Ephesians 1:6, for example, the two are distinct,

---

[46] Hodge, *Systematic Theology*, 1:394.

[47] Louis Berkhof, *Systematic Theology* (Grand Rapids, MI: Banner of Truth, 1965), 74.

[48] Ibid., 125.

[49] Ibid., 148.

[50] Ibid., 125; emphasis mine.

[51] Ibid., 167.

[52] Ibid., 278.

though one leads to another.)[53]

Berkhof tightly connects the purposes of election, noting that it "calls man to a certain end: *the great goal to which the Holy Spirit is leading the elect, and consequently to the intermediate stages on the way to this final destiny.* It is a calling to the fellowship of Jesus Christ, I Cor. 1:9; to inherit blessing, I Pet. 3:9; to liberty, Gal. 5:13; to peace, I Cor. 7:15; to holiness, I Thess. 4:7; to one hope, Eph. 4:4; to eternal life, I Tim. 6:12; and to God's kingdom and glory, I Thess. 2:12."[54] Notice, in this context, while Berkhof has previously established the priority of the doxological purpose, the teleological priority becomes somewhat unclear, as Berkhof closely connects God's glory to aspects of the redemptive plan. Still, Berkhof repeats, even after this context, the primacy of God's glory and the redemptive plan's subjectedness to it: "Whatever their proximate aim may be, their final aim is not the welfare of man, but the glory of God, which is the highest conceivable aim of man's life...."[55] But on the other hand, Berkhof notes that good works are necessary "as required by God...as the fruits of faith...as expressions of gratitude...unto the assurance of faith...and to the glory of God."[56] While he periodically reminds the reader of the primacy of the doxological purpose, in other contexts that primacy is not so clear. In the body of Christ, Berkhof sees the glory of God "as manifested in the work of redemption."[57] While the redemptive purpose is subject to the doxological one, in practical terms so much focus is on the redemptive aspect that the doxological focus is sometimes lost.

Now, it is important not to be unfair to Berkhof and present him as equating the glory of God with His other attributes and activities—Berkhof is clear in his assertions that he does not equate God's glory with anything else. However, Berkhof illustrates the very subtle *practical* equating of God's

---

[53] This is a maneuver not unique to Reformed theologians, as Chafer, for example, also focuses on the church as displaying "His glory and grace." Lewis Sperry Chafer, *The Kingdom in History and Prophecy* (Chicago, IL: Moody Publishers, 1915), 115.

[54] Berkhof, *Systematic Theology*, 521.

[55] Ibid., 602.

[56] Ibid., 604.

[57] Ibid., 625.

glory with God's redemptive activities to the extent that the redemptive purpose is read back into passages, leading to supersessionism, for example. Some of these passages, which, if allowed to stand alone without the redemptive-priority theological lens, would contradict supersessionism and instead favor the Israel/church distinction.

Berkhof describes dispensational premillennialism as "a new philosophy of the history of redemption, in which Israel plays a leading role and the Church is but an interlude."[58] It is notable that Berkhof sees the primary distinction between the two systems as found in their respective philosophies of redemption. He adds, "in reading their descriptions of God's dealings with men one is lost in a bewildering maze of covenants and dispensations...Their divisive tendency also reveals itself in their eschatological program...there will also be two peoples of God."[59] In speaking of the eschatological aspect of the millennium as a literal expression of the kingdom of God, Berkhof asserts that, "The theory is based on a literal interpretation of the prophetic delineations of the future of Israel and of the Kingdom of God *which is entirely untenable* [emphasis mine]."[60] Berkhof cites a number of writers (Fairbairn, Riehm, Davidson, Brown, Weldgrave, and Aalders), and notes that "the books of the prophets themselves already contain indications that point to a spiritual fulfillment."[61]

In raising this argument against dispensational premillennialism, it is worth noting that Berkhof states an antithesis to Ryrie's *sine qua non*: the overarching principle is in the redemptive philosophy of history—the literal interpretation of Old Testament prophecy is untenable—and the distinction between two peoples of God (Israel and the church) is not scriptural. Recall Ryrie's implied process as discussed earlier:

1. Exegete the Scriptures applying a consistently literal (grammatical historical) hermeneutic.

2. Recognize the glory of God as God's highest end, and that end which governs all other ends.

---

[58] Berkhof, *Systematic Theology*, 787.
[59] Ibid.
[60] Ibid.
[61] Ibid.

3. Understand key theological distinctions (including the notable Israel-church distinction) observable through the application of a literal (grammatical-historical) hermeneutic, and *confirmable* in light of the doxological purpose which permeates Scripture.

Berkhof's flow of the three concepts would be as follows:

1. Understand the redemptive philosophy that governs the narrative.

2. Discover key theological concepts and relationships (including the theological covenants and the singular people of God).

3. Acknowledge a sometimes literal, sometimes allegorical hermeneutic that supports the redemptive philosophy and its specific findings.

In Berkhof's model, the teleological *is* the methodological which drives the hermeneutical and supports the theological. In Ryrie's model there is a stated attempt at applying the hermeneutic method and allowing the exegetical results to stand on their own merit. In Berkhof's model, the hermeneutic model is subject ultimately to the meta-narrative of the redemptive plan.

Kevin DeYoung takes Berkhof's approach to its logical conclusion. In his article entitled "Your Theological System Should Tell You How to Exegete," he suggests that, "No Christian should be interested in constructing a big theological system that grows out of a shallow and misinformed understanding of the smaller individual passages."[62] While few would disagree with such a pointed statement, the implications of what DeYoung means in his elaboration of that statement might be more problematic. DeYoung adds, "We come to the exegetical task...with a way of looking at the world, with a system."[63] He further explains how Christians can avoid the error of being "misinformed" when approaching the individual passages:

---

[62] Kevin DeYoung, "Your Theological System Should Tell You How to Exegete," The Gospel Coalition, February 23, 2012, accessed August 1, 2017, https://blogs .thegospelcoalition.org/kevindeyoung/2012/02/23/your-theological-system-should-tell-you-how-to-exegete/.

[63] Ibid.

Without a systematic theology how can you begin to know what to do with the eschatology of Ezekiel or the sacramental language in John 6 or the psalmist's insistence that he is righteous and blameless? As a Christian I hope that my theology is open to correction, but as a minister I have to start somewhere. We all do. For me that means starting with Reformed theology and my confessional tradition and sticking with that unless I have really good reason not to.[64]

Essentially, in order to approach the individual passages correctly—such as Ezekiel's eschatological pericopes, or John 6, or assertions of good and evil in the Psalms—a person must begin with Reformed theology and the confessional tradition (i.e., the *Westminster Confession*). In beginning with a system of theology and then working toward exegesis, DeYoung is modeling Berkhof's three-step process of starting with the grand teleology, moving to the theological particulars, and then applying hermeneutic methodology. DeYoung illustrates this specifically in his handling of the 144,000 in Revelation 7:4:

The 144,000 are not an ethnic Jewish remnant...[they] represent the entire community of the redeemed,"[65] because "...it makes sense that God would seal all of His people, not just the Jewish ones...the 144,000 are called servants of God. There is no reason to make the 144,000 any more restrictive than that...the 144,000 mentioned later in chapter 14...is generic, everybody kind of language...Are we to think that the 144,000 refers to a chosen group of celibate Jewish men? It makes more sense to realize that 144,000 is a symbolic number that is described as celibate men to highlight the group's moral purity and set-apartness for spiritual battle...the number itself is stylized. It is not

---

[64] DeYoung, "Your Theological System."

[65] Kevin DeYoung, "Theological Primer: The 144,000," The Gospel Coalition, April 28, 2017, accessed August 1, 2017, https://blogs.thegospelcoalition.org /kevindeyoung/2017/04/28/theological-primer-the-144000/; Kevin DeYoung, "Who Are the 144,000 in Revelation?" The Gospel Coalition, January 17, 2012, accessed August 1, 2017, https://blogs.thegospelcoalition.org/kevindeyoung/2012/01/17 /who-are-the-144000-in-revelation/.

to be taken literally...144,000 is God's way of saying all of God's people under the old and new covenant...The bottom line is that the number and the list and the order of the tribes are all stylized to depict the
totality of God's pure and perfectly redeemed servants from all time
over all the earth. That's what Revelation means by the 144,000.[66]

DeYoung's approach is not an anomaly/exception; but is emblematic of
contemporary and accepted Reformed methodology: his blogs are hosted
by The Gospel Coalition, "a fellowship of evangelical churches in the Reformed tradition,"[67] and his hermeneutics book, *Taking God at His Word*,
published by Crossway, is endorsed by David Platt, D.A. Carson, Matt
Chandler, and John MacArthur.

In considering contemporary Reformed methodology and the tension
between doxology and redemption that results, one might wonder if these
are inherited from the Reformation or if they are later additions. If they are
organic to the Reformation, then it might be fair to recognize contemporary
Reformed theology and covenantalism as a true inheritor of the Reformation legacy. On the other hand, if the reformers prescribed something
altogether different, we may discover that contemporary Reformed theology
is a departure from, rather than descendant of the Reformation.

16.4 *Soli Deo Gloria* in the Reformation

Leading up to the Reformation, Thomas Aquinas had been the most
influential theological voice, representing the Roman Catholic worldview
in an intricate balancing act with Aristotelian philosophy. In the hundreds
of references to *purpose* in his *Summa Theologicae*, he sparingly refers to God's
purposes. He acknowledges "the purpose of God to Whom it pertains to
measure grace,"[68] and occasionally refers to "the purpose of the grace of

---

[66] DeYoung, "Who Are the 144,000."

[67] The Gospel Coalition, "Preamble," accessed August 1, 2017, https://www.the
gospelcoalition.org/about/foundation-documents.

[68] Thomas Aquinas, *Summa Theologicae*, trans. Fathers of the English Dominican
Province, 3.7.11. Micro Book Studio software. The numbers refer to the Part, Question, and Article.

God."[69] He recognizes that "God gives to each one according to the purpose for which He has chosen him."[70] While Aquinas affirms that "God and nature do nothing without a purpose,"[71] he identifies only the purpose for the universe but says nothing specifically of *God's* purpose: "the entire universe, with all its parts, is ordained towards God as its end, inasmuch as it imitates, as it were, and shows forth the Divine goodness, to the glory of God."[72]

Aquinas adds a notable practical application that later appears in the *Westminster Confession,* "Now our end is God towards Whom our affections tend in two ways: first, by our willing the glory of God, secondly, by willing to enjoy His glory. The first belongs to the love whereby we love God in Himself, while the second belongs to the love whereby we love ourselves in God."[73] Aquinas' including the prescription of enjoying God and His glory underscores that the relational and human aspect of doxological purpose was not a Reformation development, but was plainly stated prior. Initially, *soli Deo gloria* in the Reformation seemed more about departing from Catholic venerations and returning the focus to God, rather than seeking out a metanarrative. Still, the centrality of God's doxological purpose was evident in the reformers—especially in John Calvin.

John Calvin states early on in his *Institutes* that, "the mark of sound doctrine given by our Saviour himself is its tendency to promote the glory not of men, but of God."[74] He adds that, "the world...was made to display the glory of God."[75] Calvin asserts not only doxological purpose, but acknowledges God's sovereignty in setting the parameters for the execution of that purpose, noting that, "it belongs to God to determine what is most conducive to His glory."[76] Calvin recognizes that the salvific plan is part of that doxological focus: "the purpose of the Lord in conferring righteousness

---

[69] E.g., Aquinas, *Summa Theologicae,* 3.6.3, ad. 3 (reply to objection 3).

[70] Ibid., 3.27.5, ad. 1.

[71] Ibid., 3.36.4, arg. 2, and 3.65.4, arg. 1.

[72] Ibid., 3.65.2, arg. 3, co. (I answer to that).

[73] Ibid., 2-2.83.9, arg. 5, co.

[74] John Calvin, *Institutes of the Christian Religion,* trans. Henry Beveridge, Christian Classics Ethereal Library, accessed August 1, 2017, https://www.ccel.org/ccel/calvin/institutes.ii.viii.html.

[75] Ibid., 1.5.5. The numbers refer to the book, chapter, and section.

[76] Ibid., 3.9.4.

upon us in Christ, was to demonstrate his own righteousness."[77] Calvin views God's glory as such a preeminent concept, that "we never glory in him until we have utterly discarded our own glory."[78] While salvation is a great means of demonstrating the glory of God, Calvin suggests that the condemnation of sinners shows His glory also.[79] So pervasive is the doxological theme in Calvin's understanding, that he proclaims, "God as the Lord and governor of nature who...at his pleasure, makes all the elements subservient to his glory."[80] Christ exhibits glory in His resurrection, in His kingdom, and shares it with His Father.[81] It is not until Calvin's final mention of glory in *The Institutes* that he identified any concept as remotely equal to the purpose of God's glory. In that context he says that all articles of faith "must be directed to the glory of God and the edification of the Church."[82] In light of the many contexts and oft repeated theme of doxological preeminence, it is unlikely that Calvin is in this last reference equating the edification of the church and the glory of God. On the contrary, to that point Calvin is unwavering throughout *The Institutes* regarding God's glory as central. While he does not discuss the doxological center as *necessary*, he states it repeatedly as factual.

Martin Luther's primary focus in his *95 Theses* was to challenge the prevailing culture of indulgences as a means of remission for sin. Luther's document left little doubt as to the prominence of God's glory in Luther's theological understanding. The sixty-second thesis celebrated the true treasure of the church as being the gospel of the glory and grace of God.[83]

Despite the pronouncements of both Calvin and Luther regarding the lofty ranking of God's glory, it is fair to recognize there is a hint in both Luther and Calvin of equating the means (the intermediary purposes of God) and the end (the final purpose of God). Luther does not engage the

---

[77] Calvin, *Institutes*, 3.13.1.

[78] Ibid., 3.13.1.

[79] Ibid., 3.24.14.

[80] Ibid., 4.14.18.

[81] Ibid., 4.17.17.

[82] Ibid., "One Hundred Aphorisms," in *Institutes*, 4.76.

[83] Martin Luther, "95 Theses (1517)," Martin Luther, accessed August 1, 2017, http://www.luther.de/en/95thesen.html.

topic as comprehensively as Calvin, and thus his allowance seems a bit more liberal, whereas Calvin's strong stance up until his final mention might cause one to read charitably and suggest there is in fact no hint of conflating the means with the end. It is evident—especially in Calvin's case—that the doxological purpose was recognized as preeminent by the time of the Reformation's apex. Calvin might even be read to view God's glory as a unifying principle of history, as he repeated the theme of all things serving the doxological purpose.

After Luther and Calvin, *The Shorter Catechism of the Westminster Confession of Faith* declared in 1647 that the chief end of man was "to glorify God, and to enjoy Him for ever."[84] While the Catechism did not address the chief end of God, the *Westminster Confession* of 1646 noted that,

> God the great Creator of all things does uphold, direct, dispose, and govern all creatures, actions, and things, from the greatest even to the least, by His most wise and holy providence, according to His infallible foreknowledge, and the free and immutable counsel of His own will, *to the praise of the glory of His wisdom, power, justice, goodness, and mercy"* [emphasis mine].[85]

The Shorter Catechism is in this subject matter more reminiscent of Thomistic theology than of Calvin's, as it primarily reflects the end of man, rather than the end of God, whereas Calvin speaks a great deal more to the issue of God's own end. In light of this, it seems that the key contribution of the Reformation in regards to *soli Deo gloria* was a return to an idea not prominent in Catholic thinking— that it was not only the highest end of all creation to glorify God, but that it *was God's own purpose* to glorify Himself. The other aspects of universal highest ends and human doxological ends, including the prescription of man's enjoyment of God and his glory, were all carryovers from earlier theologies. The real Reformation heritage was in

---

[84] "Westminster Shorter Catechism (1647)," Christian Classics Ethereal Library, accessed August 1, 2017, https://www.ccel.org/ccel/anonymous/westminster1.i.i .html.

[85] "The Westminster Confession of Faith (1646)," 5.1, The Center for Reformed Theology and Apologetics, accessed August 1, 2017, http://www.reformed .org/documents/wcf_with_proofs/.

the recognition of God's own doxological metanarrative as central.

16.5 The *Soli Deo Gloria* Exchange and the Reformed Legacy Revitalized in Dispensational Thought

If there has been historically in Reformed thought such a high view of God's doxological purpose, then how did the redemptive center gain such prominence to the point that Ryrie would view God's doxological purpose as one of only three definitive distinctives of dispensational thought differentiating it from Reformed understanding?

Jonathan Edwards helps us understand how the move from God's glory as the highest end to a greater focus on the redemptive center is possible within a theological framework claims to position the doxological purpose as the ultimate one. Edwards asserts the glory of God is the supreme and ultimate end of all of God's works.[86] Yet, importantly he understands that *part of the glory of God* is God's manifesting of that glory. Edwards writes:

> [The glory of God] includes the *exercise* of God's perfections to produce a proper *effect,* in opposition to their lying eternally dormant and ineffectual: as his power being eternally without any act or fruit of that power; his wisdom eternally ineffectual in any wise production, or prudent disposal of anything, etc. The *manifestation* of his internal glory to created understandings. The *communication* of the infinite fullness of God to the creature. The creature's high *esteem* of God, love to him, and complacence and joy in him; and the proper *exercises* and *expressions* of these. [87]

It is in this point that Edwards begins to combine the end with the means. He recognizes that these means (exercise, manifestation, communication, and expressions, for example) seem to be a plurality, yet he explains how they are actually part of the singular primary goal. He carefully considers that, "These at first view may appear to be entirely distinct things: but if

---

[86] Jonathan Edwards, "The End for Which God Made the World," in *Works of Jonathan Edwards*, vol. 1 (Carlisle, PA: The Banner of Truth Trust, 1974), Christian Classics Ethereal Library, accessed August 1, 2017, http://www.ccel.org/ccel/edwards/works1.iv.html.

[87] Ibid., 5.2.7. The numbers refer to the part, chapter and section.

we more closely consider the matter, they will all appear to be one thing, in a variety of views and relations. They are all but the *emanation of God's glory.*"[88] Edwards does this by distinguishing between God's internal, external, and essential glory, but yet by asserting that in order for one to be fulfilled they must all be fulfilled. Consequently, the means of God's glorification *is* part of God's glorification, and thus seems to have equal import as part of the end itself. Edwards notes that,

> What has been said may be sufficient to show, how those things, which are spoken of in Scripture as ultimate ends of God's works, though they may seem at first view to be distinct, are all plainly to be reduced to this *one* thing, *viz. God's internal glory or fullness existing in its emanation.* And though God in seeking this end, seeks the creature's good; yet therein appears his supreme regard to himself.[89]

In God's seeking His own glory He must seek His creature's good. Thus, Edwards' idea can be understood to convey that redemption *is in a sense equated to* the glory of God:

> But if strictness of union to God be viewed as thus infinitely exalted; then the creature must be regarded as nearly and closely united to God. And viewed thus, *their interest must be viewed as one with God's interest*; and so is not regarded properly with a disjunct and separate, but an undivided respect...if by reason of the strictness of the union of a man and his family, their interest may be looked upon as one, how much more so is the interest of Christ and His church...? (emphasis mine).[90]

Simply put, Edwards understands that God's and His people's interests are so aligned as to be one and the same. Thus, it can be said that the chief end of man is to glorify God, and it could also be said that God's chief end is His redemptive purpose—as the two purposes (doxological and redemptive) are essentially synonymous.

Martin Luther's summary of his own encounter with salvation shows

---

[88] Edwards, "End for Which God Made," 5.2.7.
[89] Ibid.
[90] Ibid.

a view similar to Edwards', even if not as precisely explicated. Luther re-counts that in his study of Scripture he found that "other terms had analo-gous meanings, e.g., the work of God, that is, what God works in us; the power of God, by which he makes us powerful; the wisdom of God, by which he makes us wise; the strength of God, the salvation of God, the glory of God."[91] In this narrative statement, Luther conveys that he views salva-tion as analogous to the glory of God. The two are at least so interrelated that they can be understood conceptually as one. What Luther hints at even during the Reformation, Edwards provides and explains thoroughly.

Edwards' and Luther's redempto-centric maneuver show how the Reformation heritage of *soli Deo gloria* could be gently reconfigured to deem-phasize (at least in a practical sense) the doxological purpose as central in God's plan. In that reconfiguration there is a return to a more Thomistic approach of emphasizing the salvific purpose of God, certainly not in con-tradiction of God's doxological purpose, but perhaps in ignoring it. Thus, within the Reformation there was present the seedling that would soon overshadow the newly refined doxological understanding that Calvin had so effectively elucidated. Edwards especially shows that the newly reempha-sized redemptive approach was more theologically rooted in Aristotelean thinking than in exegetical discovery. This departure from Calvin's Refor-mation legacy, especially, would leave a gap in Reformed thinking that would later be filled by a renewed emphasis on *soli Deo gloria* by Ryrie and other similarly inclined thinkers.

16.6 Conclusion

Ryrie's recognition of the primacy of God's doxological purpose as a central and necessary tenet of orthodox theology represents a brilliant re-turn to a vital principle that was understood well by the reformers, but in practice was quickly relegated to a status secondary to the redemptive pur-pose of Thomism. The Reformation heritage of *soli Deo gloria* invites

---

[91] Martin Luther, "Preface to the Complete Edition of Luther's Latin Works," trans. Andrew Thornton, from the "Vorrede zu Band I der Opera Latina der Witten-berger Ausgabe. 1545," in *Luthers Werke in Auswahl*, ed. Otto Clemen, 6th ed., (Berlin: de Gruyter. 1967), 4:421–428, accessed August 1, 2017, https://www.iclnet.org/pub/resources/text/wittenberg/luther/preflat-eng.txt.

Protestants to follow the doctrine to its logical conclusion—a conclusion that Ryrie recognized and reinvigorated by his inclusion of God's doxological purpose in the *sine qua non*: God does all things for the expression of His own glory and demands that His creation does the same.

Once the importance of the literal grammatical-historical hermeneutic is understood as first principle, the centrality of *soli Deo gloria* may be perceived with clarity in Scripture, and therefore, the centrality of *soli Deo gloria* in faith and practice. While the consistent application of the literal grammatical-historical hermeneutic is the methodological necessity of the *sine qua non*, and the distinction between Israel and the church is a premiere theological distinctive discernible from that hermeneutic method, it is the centrality of the doxological purpose that is indeed the philosophical pinnacle of the dispensational triad.

Soli Deo Gloria

Bibliography

Aquinas, Thomas. *Summa Theologicae*. Translated by Fathers of the English Dominican Province. Micro Book Studio software.

Baker, Charles. *A Dispensational Theology*. Grand Rapids, MI: Grace Bible College Publications, n.d.

Berkhof, Louis. *Systematic Theology*. Grand Rapids, MI: Banner of Truth, 1965.

Blaising, Craig. "Dispensationalism: The Search for Definition." In *Dispensationalism, Israel, and the Church*, edited by Craig A. Blaising and Darrell L. Bock, 13–34. Grand Rapids, MI: Zondervan, 1992.

Calvin, John. *Institutes of the Christian Religion*. Translated by Henry Beveridge. Christian Classics Ethereal Library. Accessed August 1, 2017. https://www.ccel.org/ccel/calvin/institutes.

Chafer, Lewis Sperry. *Dispensationalism*. Fort Worth, TX: Exegetica, 2015.

————. *The Kingdom in History and Prophecy*. Chicago, IL: Moody Publishers, 1915.

Cone, Christopher. *Prolegomena on Biblical Hermeneutics and Method*. 2nd ed. Fort Worth, TX: Tyndale Seminary Press, 2012.

Darby, J. N. "The Purpose of God." In *The Collected Writings of J. N. Darby*. Vol. 30, *Prophetic 1*, 468–484. Addison, IL: BibleTruth Pulblishers, n.d. Accessed August 1, 2017. http://bibletruthpublishers.com/the-purpose-of-god/john-nelson-darby-jnd/collected-writings-of-j-n-darby-prophetic-1/la62216.

DeYoung, Kevin. "Theological Primer: The 144,000." The Gospel Coalition. April 28, 2017. Accessed August 1, 2017. https://blogs.thegospelcoalition.org/kevindeyoung/2017/04/28/theological-primer-the-144000/.

DeYoung, Kevin. "Who are the 144,000 in Revelation?" The Gospel Coalition. January 17, 2012. Accessed August 1, 2017. https://blogs .thegospelcoalition.org/kevindeyoung/2012/01/17/who-are-the-144000-in-revelation/.

——. "Your Theological System Should Tell You How to Exegete." The Gospel Coalition. February 23, 2012. Accessed August 1, 2017. https://blogs.thegospelcoalition.org/kevindeyoung/2012/02/23/yo ur-theological-system-should-tell-you-how-to-exegete/.

Edwards, Jonathan. "The End for Which God Made The World." In *Works of Jonathan Edwards*. Vol. 1. Carlisle, PA: The Banner of Truth Trust, 1974. Christian Classics Ethereal Library. Accessed August 1, 2017. http://www.ccel.org/ccel/edwards/works1.iv.html.

Gaebelein, Arno C. "The Biblical Logic of Premillennialism." In *Meat in Due Season: Sermons, Discourses and Expositions of the World of Prophecy*. New York: Arno C. Gaebelein, 1900. Accessed August 1, 2017. http://www.wholesomewords.org/etexts/gaebelein/meat4.html

——. "The Lord of Glory." In *The Lord of Glory: Meditations on the Person, the Work and Glory of Our Lord Jesus Christ*. New York, NY: Publications Office "Our Hope," 1910. Accessed August 1, 2017. http://www .wholesomewords.org/etexts/gaebelein/lordof1.html.

Hodge, Charles. *Systematic Theology*. Vol 1. Grand Rapids, MI: Eerdmans, 1940.

Larkin, Clarence. *Dispensational Truth of God's Plan and Purpose of the Ages*. Glendale, PA: Clarence Larkin, 1918.

Luther, Martin. "95 Theses, 1517." Martin Luther. Accessed August 1, 2017. http://www.luther.de/en/95thesen.html.

——. "Preface to the Complete Edition of Luther's Latin Works." Translated by Andrew Thornton, from the "Vorrede zu Band I der Opera Latina der Wittenberger Ausgabe. 1545." In *Luthers Werke in Auswahl*, edited by Otto Clemen. Vol. 4. 6th ed. Berlin: de Gruyter. 1967. Accessed August 1, 2017. https://www.iclnet.org/pub /resources/text/wittenberg/luther/preflat-eng.txt.

Pentecost, J. Dwight. *Things to Come*. Grand Rapids, MI: Zondervan, 1965).

Ryrie, Charles C. *Basic Theology*. Wheaton, IL: Victor Books, 1982.

———. *Dispensationalism Today*. Chicago, IL: Moody Press, 1965.

———. "The Necessity of Dispensationalism." *Bibliotheca Sacra*, 114, no. 455 (July 1957): 243–254.

Scofield, C. I. *Rightly Dividing the Word of Truth*. Charleston, SC: Armor of God Ministries, 2010. Accessed August 1, 2017. http://www.armor ofgodbooks.com/books/scofield/Rightly_Dividing_the_Word_of_T ruth.pdf.

Stallard, Mike. "Emile Guers and Charles Ryrie: a Case Study of Continuity in the History of Dispensationalism Concerning Literal Interpretation." Paper presented at the Council on Dispensational Hermeneutics, Grace Theological Seminary, Winona Lake, IN, September 14, 2016.

Thiessen, Henry. *Lectures on Systematic Theology*. Rev. ed. Grand Rapids, MI: Eerdmans, 1979.

Walvoord, John F. "A Review of Crucial Questions About the Kingdom of God, by George E. Ladd." *Bibliotheca Sacra* 110, no. 437 (January 1953): 1–10.

"Westminster Confession of Faith, 1646." The Center for Reformed Theology and Apologetics. Accessed August 1, 2017. http://www.reformed.org /documents/wcf_with_proofs/.

"Westminster Shorter Catechism, 1647." Christian Classics Ethereal Library. Accessed August 1, 2017. https://www.ccel.org/ccel/anon ymous/westminster1.i.i.html.

17

SOLI DEO GLORIA
REVEALED THROUGHOUT BIBLICAL HISTORY

Luther Smith
Calvary University

17.0 Introduction

As it has been demonstrated in this work, thus far, the five *solas* of the Reformation are at the heart of the system of dispensationalism. In all the divine economies of God, one is saved by faith alone (*sola fide*)—salvation is only found when one places faith in Christ alone for salvation (*solus Christus*). The believer's salvation in Christ is received as a gift from God, not as a work earned (*sola gratia*), and this divine salvific plan of God is only revealed in the Scriptures, which is the highest authority for the Christian (*sola Scriptura*). However, what is the *motive* or *purpose* of God in His overall plan for mankind? Here the fifth, and final, *sola* of the Protestant Reformation is highlighted: the glory of God (*soli Deo gloria*).

It has been argued by some theologians that dispensationalism is a new development in theology, and thus it is alien to a historic Christian faith. Speaking to this point, dispensationalist Henry Ironside comments:

> In fact, until brought to the fore, through the writings and preaching of a distinguished ex-clergyman, Mr. J. N. Darby, in the early part of the last century, it is scarcely to be found in a single book or sermon through a period of 1600 years! If any doubt this statement, let them search, as the writer has in a measure done, the remarks of the so-

called Fathers, both pre and post-Nicene, the theological treatises of the scholastic divines, Roman Catholic writers of all shades of thought; the literature of the Reformation; the sermons and expositions of the Puritans; and the general theological works of the day. He will find the "mystery" conspicuous by its absence.[1]

This point of view has been the prevalent thought among many theologians who have been critical of dispensationalism. However, those who find this system unfavorable have neglected to observe that the fifth *sola* (i.e., the glory of God), which has been a cornerstone of the Reformation, has been a seminal component of dispensationalism. It seems necessary to support this claim by giving a brief historical survey on the importance of the glory of God throughout the Reformation, and how it has been one of the significant and essential qualities in dispensational thought.

17.1 Martin Luther: The German Reformer

As noted throughout the previous chapters in this book, Martin Luther was extremely influential in promoting the biblical position of faith in Christ alone (*sola fide*), and Scripture alone (*sola Scriptura*). Cairns notes this as follows:

> A reading of Romans 1:17 convinced [Luther] that only faith in Christ could make one just before God. From that time on justification by faith and *sola scriptura*, the idea that the Scriptures are the only authority for sinful men in seeking salvation, became the main points of his theological system.[2]

This was in sharp contrast to the teachings of the medieval Roman Catholic Church, which taught a person was righteous by faith in addition to the good works that were completed. The Roman Catholic Church also

---

[1] H. A. Ironside, *The Mysteries of God* (Whitefish, MT: Kessinger, 2009), 50.

[2] Earle E. Cairns, *Christianity through the Centuries*, 2nd ed. (Grand Rapids, MI: Zondervan, 1967), 314.

instructed people that authority was found in Scripture,[3] Tradition,[4] and the Roman Catholic Church.[5] Due to the writing and the translation of the *95 Theses* into the German language, Martin Luther's ideas took hold of Germany.[6] Luther's influence continued to spread throughout Germany, even after he had been excommunicated from the Roman Catholic Church in 1520. It was not until 1530, in what became known as the Diet of Augsburg, that Philip Melanchthon, a dedicated student of Martin Luther, and a prominent scholar of the biblical languages, documented what became known as the *Augsburg Confession*. This document, presented at the Diet, solidified the beliefs of Lutherans, and became the official confession of the Lutheran tradition. The confession even underscored the doctrine of justification by faith:

> Also [the Scriptures teach] that men cannot be justified before God by their own strengths, merits, or works., but are freely justified for Christ's sake, through faith, when they believed they are received into favor, and that their sins are forgiven for Christ's sake, who, by His death, has made satisfaction for our sins. This faith God imputes for righteousness in His sight.[7]

The influence of Martin Luther spread beyond the borders of Germany to Scandinavia, where it had its greatest impact, and even further to Scotland. *Sola Scriptura* and *sola fide* became hallmarks of the sixteenth century Reformation.

17.1.1 Soli Deo Gloria and Martin Luther

Martin Luther never penned the words *soli Deo gloria* (to the glory of

---

[3] "Catholic Tradition," The Beginning Catholic's Guide to the Roman Catholic Church, accessed May 2, 2017, http://www.beginningcatholic.com/catholic-tradition.

[4] Ibid.

[5] Second Vatican Council, *Dei Verbum* [Dogmatic Constitution on Divine Revelation], Vatican, November 18, 1965, accessed May 26, 2017, http://www.vatican.va/archive/hist_councils/ii_vatican_council/documents/vat-ii_const_19651118_dei-verbum_en.html.

[6] Cairns, *Christianity through the Centuries*, 315.

[7] Martin Luther, *The Book of Concord* (St. Louis, MO: Concordia, 1952), 12–13.

God alone) in any of his writings, however the concept of *soli Deo gloria* was described implicitly when Martin Luther was explaining the various "offices" (i.e., vocations) mankind could occupy under heaven. Martin Luther strongly rebuked the traditions of the Roman Catholic Church on three distinct issues, insisting that: (1) The Magisterium, especially the Pope, were not the only people who could interpret the Scriptures;[8] (2) the only sacraments that were valid in the church were the Lord's Supper and Baptism;[9] and (3) the priesthood was not confined to a certain class of people among the laity, but that it was extended to all believers as a result of faith in Jesus Christ for the forgiveness of sins.[10] It was in these three areas that Luther could see God's work and glory as not only bestowed on the working positions within the church (such as pastors and laymen), but also in everyday tasks that believers accomplished. Church historian Gustaf Wingren has summarized Luther:

> God himself will milk the cows through him whose vocation that is. [A person] who engages in the lowliness of his work performs God's work, be he lad or king. To give one's office proper care is not selfishness. Devotion to office is devotion to love, because it is by God's own ordering that the work of the office is always dedicated to the well-being of one's neighbor. Care for one's office is, in its very frame of reference on earth, participation in God's own care for human beings.[11]

The work of God was expressed when a Christian would operate in his office, or vocation, by serving his neighbor. However, for Martin Luther, the glory of God was seen *explicitly* in the salvation of man, and being justified by Jesus Christ on the cross as a gift to the undeserving sinner. In short, *soli Deo gloria*, for Martin Luther, was exclusively *soteriological*.

---

[8] Cairns, *Christianity through the Centuries*, 316.
[9] Ibid., 316.
[10] Ibid., 317.
[11] Gustaf Wingren, *Luther on Vocation* (Philadelphia, PA: Muhlenberg Press, 1957), 8.

17.2 *Soli Deo Gloria* and John (Jean) Calvin

While Luther's influence in Germany had blanketed the nation, John Calvin (1509–1564), was seminal for his theological influence in Switzerland (specifically Geneva). There were many distinctions between Martin Luther and John Calvin, but one of the most important contrasts in their theology was how they saw the glory of God in relation to man. As Cairns notes:

> Luther and Calvin differed theologically as well as personally. Luther emphasized preaching; but Calvin was interested in the development of a formal system of theology. Both accepted the authority of the Bible; but Luther's main emphasis was upon justification by faith whereas Calvin stressed the sovereignty of God.[12]

Martin Luther emphasized that the glory of God was seen in the salvation of man by Jesus' death, burial, and resurrection (i.e., soteriological). John Calvin, due to his position of the *absolute* sovereignty of God, saw the glory of God in *all* things, not just the salvation of man, but in *all* of God's works: creation, justification, the good works which the believer accomplishes, suffering, the punishment of the wicked, etc. Calvin penned his apologetic for Christian theology, in his magum opus titled, *The Institutes of The Christian Religion.* His central defense for this theological system had God in all His works, not merely the salvation of man, as the centerpiece of the glory of God. Calvin, commenting in his *Institutes* on the Lord's Prayer, wrote,

> The next words are, WHICH ART IN HEAVEN. From this we are not to infer that he is enclosed and confined within the circumference of heaven, as by a kind of boundaries. Hence Solomon confesses, "The heaven of heavens cannot contain thee," (1Kn 8:27); and he himself says by the Prophet, "The heaven is my throne, and the earth is my footstool," (Isa 66:1); thereby intimating, that his presence, not confined to any region, is diffused over all space. But as our gross minds are unable to conceive of his ineffable glory, it is designated to us by "heaven", nothing which our eyes can behold being so full of splendor

---

[12] Cairns, *Christianity through the Centuries,* 334.

and majesty.[13]

This main theological theme Calvin expressed would be the bedrock of instruction in the Reformed (i.e., Calvinistic) tradition, as Cairns comments:

> Calvin's greatest contribution of the Reformed faith was his *Institutes*, which has been the authoritative expression of the Reformed theology. In this work he laid the foundation of the Reformed emphasis upon the importance of doctrine and the centrality of God in Christian theology.[14]

After he died in 1564, John Calvin's theology continued to spread throughout France, Germany, Hungary, Scotland, Ireland, and Holland. His work was paramount in continuing the five *solas* with the sovereignty of God, and the glory of God, anchored at the center of his theological system.

17.2.1 Soli Deo Gloria and the Long and Shorter Catechism

Due to the influence of Jean Calvin and Martin Luther, the instruction and ecclesiology of the Reformation was placed in the national spotlight. As a result, the conflicts between these particular theological doctrines moved to a political level.[15] Seeking to develop a national creed concerning the theological position and ecclesiology of the Church of England, the Long Parliament instructed the Westminster Assembly to create a document that would articulate these issues in 1643. The group consisted of over 150 English Puritans and 8 Scottish Presbyterians. They met from 1643–1649 at Westminster Abbey. The Westminster Assembly completed the *Westminster Longer and Shorter Catechism* without Scripture references in 1647, and added biblical citations two years later in 1649. In the *Catechism*, the teaching of mankind and the glory of God was explained as follows:

Q. 1. What is the chief end of man?

---

[13] John Calvin, *Institutes of the Christian Religion*, 3.20.40. Kindle ed.
[14] Cairns, *Christianity through the Centuries*, 338.
[15] Ibid., 354.

A. Man's chief end is to glorify God, and to enjoy him forever.[16]

These catechisms, enshrined the glory of God, which was to be seen in all the works of man that God gives him to complete. Thomas Vincent (1634–1678), expanding on the first question of the Long and Shorter catechism, comments:

> Men ought to have no other chief end than the glorifying of God, but they may have subordinate ends. Men ought to be diligent in their particular callings, for this end, that they may provide for themselves and their families. . . . Men may eat, and drink, and sleep, for this end, that they may nourish and refresh their bodies. It is lawful to design, and desire, and seek such things as these in such actions, subordinately, or less principally; but in these and all actions, men ought principally and chiefly to design and seek the glory of God. . . . Men may moderately desire and endeavour after the enjoyment of such a portion of the good things of the world as is needful and useful; but they ought to make choice of God for their chief good, and desire the eternal enjoyment of him as their chief portion.[17]

17.3 The Influence of *Soli Deo Gloria*

As the Reformation spread throughout Europe, many were influenced by the teaching of *soli Deo gloria*, specifically among musical composers. One such person was the famous composer Johann Sebastian Bach (1685–1750), who was a devout Lutheran, and used his talent of composing music to glorify God. He signed each of his completed musical pieces by writing "SDG" (*soli Deo gloria*).[18] George Frederic Handel (1685–1759), composer

---

[16] Westminster Assembly, "The Westminster Shorter Catechism," The Westminster Presbyterian, accessed May 12, 2017, http://www.westminster confession.org/confessional-standards/the-westminster-shorter-catechism.php.

[17] Thomas Vincent, "The Shorter Catechism of the Westminster Assembly Explained and Proved from Scripture," Encyclopedia Puritannica Project, accessed May 26, 2017, http://www.puritannica.com/front/demo/wk/VincentThomas /ShorterExplained/0013-0049.html#13.

[18] Calvin R. Stapert, "To the Glory of God Alone," *Christian History and Biog-*

of the famous musical piece *Messiah* would also place the initials "SDG" at the end of his sheet music.[19] Christoph Graupner (1683–1760), a German composer and devout Christian who worked with George Frederic Handel, also penned "SDG" at the end of his musical scores.[20] The teaching of *soli Deo gloria*, in addition to *sola fide*, and *sola gratia* were continuing to influence what people taught, proclaimed, and confessed.

17.3.1 Soli Deo Gloria and John Nelson Darby

One of the earliest theologians who systematized and strongly promoted dispensational theology, with its accompanying notion of the glory of God in all things, was John Nelson Darby (1800–1882).[21] Darby, concerning the purpose of the successive dispensations of God, noted:

> These differences of dispensation are the displays of God's glory; and therefore of all importance, and most essential, because a positive part of His glory. The law maintained His majesty, and title to claim obedience, as the gospel displayed His grace, and gave the obedience as a child. . . . Let us only remember that dispensations are necessary displays of God's glory[22]

In speaking against Covenant theology, which instructs that the salvation of the elect is where God receives His highest glory, Darby comments:

> The salvation of the elect is not the great end of any Christian's thoughts, but the divine glory; and that God has been pleased to glorify Himself, and display His character in these dispensations for the

---

raphy, no. 95 (Summer 2007), accessed May 15, 2017, http://www.christianityto-day.com/history/issues/issue-95/to-glory-of-god-alone.html.

[19] Davis Hunter, *The Lives of George Frideric Handel* (Woodbridge [Suffolk, England]: Boydell Press, 2015), 320.

[20] Ibid., 321.

[21] Larry V. Crutchfield, *The Origins of Dispensationalism: The Darby Factor* (Lanham, MD: University Press of America, 1992), 1.

[22] John Nelson Darby, *Collected Writings of J. N. Darby*, ed. William Kelly, vol. 8, *Prophetic* no. 3 (London: Stow Hill Bible and Tract Depot, n.d.), 26, quoted in Larry V. Crutchfield, *The Origins of Dispensationalism: The Darby Factor* (Lanham, MD: University Press of America, 1992), 61–62.

instruction of the church; and that if the church casts it aside, they are casting aside the instruction which God has afforded His ways. They are making themselves wise without God, and wiser than He, for He thought it fit for His glory to instruct us in these things.[23]

As demonstrated from this brief sampling, God's glory was at the heart of John Nelson Darby's theological writings. His significant influence paved the way for this system of theology to have an enormous impact in early American Evangelicalism.[24]

17.3.2 Soli Deo Gloria and C. I. Scofield

Another influential theologian who significantly contributed to dispensationalism was Cyrus Ingerson Scofield (1843-1921). Scofield would further popularize the system by embedding a framework of seven dispensations in what became known as the *Scofield Reference Bible* (1909). In this Bible Scofield marks the periods of the successive dispensations and their explicit locations throughout the Scriptures. In the introduction to his *Reference Bible*, Scofield does not mention the glory of God explicitly. However it is implicit that this is the underlying purpose in Scofield's work:

The Dispensations are distinguished, exhibiting the majestic, progressive, order of divine dealings of God with humanity, "the increasing purpose," which runs through and links together the ages, from beginning of the life of man to the end in eternity.[25]

---

[23] John Nelson Darby, *Collected Writings of J. N. Darby*, ed. William Kelly, vol. 1, *Ecclesiastical* no. 1 (London: Stow Hill Bible and Tract Depot, n.d.), 116, quoted in Crutchfield, *Origins of Dispensationalism*, 62.

[24] It should be noted that John Nelson Darby's theological background was from the Church of England. The Church of England had a government structure borrowed from Presbyterianism, which originated from John Calvin in his writings concerning church government. Although John Nelson Darby was disenchanted concerning the ecclesiological practices of the Church of England, he still retained most of the doxological aspects of Calvin's teaching.

[25] C. I. Scofield, *The First Scofield Reference Bible: Containing the Old and New Testaments* (Niagara-on-the-Lake, ON: Believers Bookshelf, 1986), iii.

17.3.3 Soli Deo Gloria and Charles Ryrie

Afterward, Charles Caldwell Ryrie (1925–2016) also did much to promote dispensationalism. Ryrie developed his notes on the Scriptures, which would further buttress dispensationalism in Christianity, by publishing the *Ryrie Study Bible* (1978). In addition, Ryrie introduced the *sine qua non* (without which not) of dispensationalism: (1) a consistent distinction between Israel and the church in people and program, (2) a consistent literal-grammatical hermeneutic, and (3) the glory of God. In contrast to the salvation of mankind being the single focus of God's glory, Ryrie, like John Calvin, recognized it is the glory of God in *all of His works* that is the central, unifying quality in dispensationalism:

> The dispensationalist sees a broader purpose in God's program for the world than salvation, and that purpose is His own glory. For the dispensationalist the glory of God is the governing principle and overall purpose, and the soteriological program is one of principal means employed in bringing to pass the greatest demonstration of His own glory. Salvation is part and parcel of God's program, but it cannot be equated with the entire purpose itself.[26]

17.4 *Soli Deo Gloria,* Dispensationalism, and the Reformation

Soli Deo gloria is at the center of the Reformation of Martin Luther and John Calvin, and this *sola* is highlighted nowhere more than in the dispensational system. Dispensationalism recognizes not only the glory of God in salvation, which is something that Martin Luther emphasized, but also God's glory in all of His works, which is what John Calvin underscored. From the time of John Nelson Darby forward, many dispensationalists were also very strong Calvinists who held a consistent literal grammatical-historical hermeneutic, and held the distinction between Israel and the church.[27] Dispensationalism was built and established on the very foundation of the

---

[26] Charles Caldwell Ryrie, *Dispensationalism Today* (Chicago, IL: Moody Press, 1979), 102.
[27] Thomas Ice, "The Calvinistic Heritage of Dispensationalism," Pre-Trib Research Center, accessed May 26, 2017, http://www.pre-trib.org/articles/view/calvinistic-heritage-of-dispensationalism.

five *solas*, with the glory of God (*soli Deo gloria*) being at the very core of the theological system.

17.4.1 Glory of God Defined

The word "glory" has significant importance in Scripture. The Hebrew word to describe the glory of God is כָּבוֹד (*kābôd*) which occurs over 190 times in the Old Testament (NASB). *Kābôd* can mean "heavy, or weight," and is often used as a vivid word picture associated with the character of God.[28] The Greek word associated with the glory of God is the word δόξα (*doxa*) which refers to God as "a transcendent being deserving of honor."[29] *Doxa* is translated "glory" 165 times in the New Testament (NASB), and is the dominant way of expressing faith, honor, and obedience to God. Trent Butler noted this quality of God:

> The weighty importance and shining majesty which accompanies God's presence...it is to recognize the importance of another, the weight another carries in the community. In the Psalms people give glory to God, that is they recognize the essential nature of His "godness" that gives Him importance and weight in relationship to the human worshipping community.[30]

God is glorified among men because He is the sovereign Creator and ruler of all things. For men to recognize this character of God, and His works in creation, and establish their life and deeds around this reality is to glorify God in all things.

---

[28] See Ludwig Koehler and Walter Baumgartner, "4134 כָּבוֹד [kâbôd]," in *Hebrew and Aramaic Lexicon of the Old Testament* (Leiden, The Netherlands: Brill, 2000), BibleWorks; and John N. Oswalt, "943 כָּבֵד [kābēd]," in *Theological Wordbook of the Old Testament*, ed. R. Laird Harris (Chicago, IL: Moody, 1981), 926–28.

[29] Fredrick W. Danker, ed., "2077 δόξα, [doxa]" *A Greek-English Lexicon of the New Testament and other Early Christian Literature*, 3rd ed. (Chicago, IL: University of Chicago, 2000), BibleWorks.

[30] Trent C. Butler, ed., *Holman Bible Dictionary* (Nashville, TN: Holman Bible Publishers, 1991), s.v. "Glory."

17.4.2 Soli Deo Gloria and God the Father

The triune God is a God of glory (cf. Ezek 10:4). It is this weighy attribute that characterizes the Godhead in the most brillian manner—and the
Scriptures are repleate with references to glory ascribed to each member of
the Trinity. For example, the glory of God is found in God the Father who
was glorious before the heavens and the earth were created (John 17:5). Paul
writes that God the Father is also the "Father of glory" (Eph 1:17). Peter
highlights that God the Father was the "Majestic Glory" when God the Father declared Jesus was His beloved Son on the Mount of Transfiguration
(2 Pet 1:17). It was also the Father who glorified Jesus Christ in all His works
at His first advent (John 8:54). The death of Christ on the cross also results
in the glory of God the Father (John 13:31–32). The glory of God the Father
is emphasized with Jesus Christ concerning His resurrection; moreover, the
resurrection of the church will also bring glory to God the Father (Rom 6:4–
5). The praise of Jesus Christ results in glorifying God the Father (Rom
16:27). In the future, when Christ returns, He will come in the glory of His
Father (Matt 16:27; Luke 9:26). Additionally, in the future Scripture declares that people will confess that Jesus is Lord, all to God the Father's
glory (Phil 2:11).

17.4.3 Soli Deo Gloria and God the Son

Glory is also associated with Jesus Christ. Jesus is the brightness of
God's glory and the exact representation of His nature (Heb 1:1–3). When
Christ is born into the world the angels give glory to God (Luke 2:14). John
recalled that he, and the other disciples, saw the glory of Jesus (John 1:14).
On the Mount of Transfiguration Jesus revealed His glory to Peter, James,
and John (Matt 17:2). The miracles that Jesus performed among His disciples displayed His glory (John 2:11), and His raising up of Lazarus from
death was a display of His glory (John 11:1–44). Stephen recounting history
to the Pharisees said that the "God of glory" appeared to Abraham, men-
tioning the pre-incarnate Christ (Acts 7:2). The glory of God is seen in all
the works of Jesus Christ in His perfect active obedience to the point of
death on the cross (Heb 2:9). Jesus prayed in the garden of Gethsemane that
His saints would see Him in all His glory in the future (John 17:24). Paul
described Jesus as the "Lord of glory" who was crucified (1 Cor 2:8). When

Christ ascended into heaven, Paul described Jesus as being taken up in glory (1 Tim 3:16). Jesus, in the future, will reveal Himself in glory to gather the church (1 Pet 4:13), but He will also return; not just in His Father's glory, but His glory (Luke 9:26). Even though the word "glory" is not explicitly used, the Lord will judge the wicked for their unbelief and cast them into the lake of fire before the start of the eternal age (Rev 20:11-15). It is clear the glory of God is expressed even in the judgment of the wicked at the conclusion of the millennial kingdom.

17.4.4 Soli Deo Gloria and God the Holy Spirit

Throughout Scripture there is an explicit association between the Holy Spirit and glory. Paul states that the ministry of the Holy Spirit is associated with even more glory than that of the glory of Moses' face (2 Cor 3:8). The Holy Spirit, who releases the sinner from darkness, also operates to transform that one into a saint from "glory to glory" (2 Cor 3:12-18). Peter wrote that those who were insulted for the name of Christ were blessed, because the "Spirit of glory" and God rested on them (1 Pet 4:14). The Holy Spirit has, and is, working to produce in the saints the glory of God to the nations.

17.4.5 Soli Deo Gloria in Creation

Even though the word *kābôd* is not used in the Genesis creation account, the glory of God was explicitly seen in His *work* concerning creation. Heaven, earth, and all that is made within the earth is a work of God (Gen 1:1-31). Mankind was also created for the glory of God (Gen 1:26-28, 2:1-25; and 1 Cor 11:7). David in the Psalms wrote the heavens reveal and declare the glory of God (Ps 8:1, 19:1). These are just some of the many instances where the Old Testament highlights God's glory in creation.

17.4.6 Soli Deo Gloria and the Condition of Man

Mankind's condition is measured against the glory of God (Rom 3:23). This is because the Gentiles who knew God and observed His attributes in creation, exchanged the glory of God for the creature and refused to give Him due praise for the creation that God had fashioned (Rom 1:21-

23). The Jews, who were given the Law of God, failed to glorify God because they violated the very Law that God had given them to glorify Him (Rom 2:17-24). The divine charge is that Gentiles and Jews are all under sin. This is seen in what one thinks, says, and does (Rom 3:9-18). The glory of God is the standard by which mankind is to live. However, due to man's sinful condition, the divine charge is that mankind continually falls short of the standard of God's glory (Rom 3:23).

17.4.7 Soli Deo Gloria and Israel

The glory of God was no less associated with Israel. For example, the ten plagues that were executed on Egypt before Israel's exodus (Ex 7:14-12:29; Num 14:22), the parting of the Red Sea for the Israelites to walk across (Ex 14:13-31), and the manna that was provided from God for the Israelite people were all an expression of God's glory (Ex 16:31-35).

The glory of God was seen when God revealed Himself to the Israelites on Mount Sinai (Ex 19:18-25; Deut 5:24). Moses was only allowed to see the backside of God's glory, because Moses would perish if he saw God's face (Ex 33:18-22). The glory of God was also seen resting on the tent of meeting (Ex 40:34-35). There were many times the glory of God would appear to judge and punish the people of Israel (Num 14:5-11, 16:12-22, 42-50), and the glory of God was proclaimed when one confessed his sin before God (Josh 7:19).

The glory of God was present among the nation of Israel. The glory of God was connected to the Ark of the Covenant that Israel possessed (1 Sam 4:21-22). The glory of the Lord filled the tent of meeting among the Israelites (Ex 40:35), and was associated with the sacrifices the priests were to give. For example, when Aaron gave the offering the Lord commanded, the glory of the Lord appeared before the Israelites (Lev 9:6). The prophet Samuel, who rebuked Saul, called God "the Glory of Israel" (1 Sam 15:29), underscoring that the glory of the Israel is God Himself. When Solomon dedicated the temple, the glory of God rested on the holy temple (1 Kings 8:11; 2 Chron 5:1-14, 7:1-3).

God, through the prophet Jeremiah, proclaimed that He personally wanted Israel for Himself, and for His glory (Jer 13:11). When the Lord punished Israel for their sin, the glory of Israel departed (Lam 2:1). Simeon, in seeing the Lord Jesus as a baby, declares that Jesus Christ is "the glory" of Israel (Luke 2:32). In the age to come, Scripture declares the glory of God will be seen in Israel by the kings of the nations (Isa 62:2). Peace and glory from the nations will be abundantly given and seen in Israel (Isa 66:12). The nations will bring their riches into Israel, which also highlights the glory of God (Hag 2: 7).

17.4.8 Soli Deo Gloria and the Church

God's glory is also featured as the centerpiece in the church. Paul told the saints in Rome they were to accept one another because God had accepted them, to the glory of God (Rom 15:7). The Christian's motive for all daily activities is to glorify God (1 Cor 10:31). The gospel the church proclaims throughout the world is to the glory of Christ Jesus (2 Cor 4:4; Col 1:27; 2 Thess 2:14; Eph 1:6). The persecution and various afflictions the church endures are also producing the glory of God in the saints (2 Cor 4:17; Eph 3:13). The Holy Spirit who indwells every believer is given as an inheritance to God's glory (Eph 1:14). The body of Christ awaits the blessed hope of the appearing and glory of Christ (Titus 2:13). The saints, by The Holy Spirit, are being transformed "from glory to glory" (2 Cor 3:18). Those who are elders in the church will receive a reward titled the "crown of glory" (1 Pet 5:4). Peter explained that God's glory and excellence were the reason why the saint was called by God (2 Pet 1:3). In the future, the body of Christ will be physically glorified by God (1 Cor 15:1-58; Phil 3:21), and at Christ's second advent, the saints will be revealed in glory with Him (Col 3:4).

17.4.9 Soli Deo Gloria and the Nations

Moreover, the glory of God was demonstrated among the nations. David decreed the glory of God should be proclaimed to all the nations (1 Chron 16:24), and the Psalms expressed that God's glory should be declared throughout the earth (96:3). Scripture reveals that in the future all nations will observe the glory of the Lord (Ps 102:15). The nations will not only proclaim the glory of God (Isa 66:19), but the nations will also see His glory in the judgment of Israel (Ezek 39:21). As the nation of Israel dwelled in the Promised Land, they were to declare and praise the glory of God, which was found among them, and not the false gods that the nations around them worshipped (Isa 42:8). In the future, the nations will know who God is, as they see His glory among them (Isa 66:18). Additionally, the nations will acknowledge and bless the Israelite people, who are also closely associated with His glory (Isa 49:22–23; Zech 8:22–23).

17.4.10 Soli Deo Gloria and the Seven Dispensations

Dispensationalism asserts that history is not only *soteriological*, as Martin Luther has emphasized, but *doxological*, as John Calvin described. However, how does dispensationalism underscore the glory of God throughout history? This writer is convinced there are three distinct areas where the glory of God is revealed in Scripture:

1. *The past, present, and future works of God:* All the works that God has done, past, present, and future are accomplished to show His glory. These include, but are not limited to, His establishing and sustaining creation, His work through the Patriarchs, the nation of Israel, His present work among the church, and His future eschatological works.

2. *The progressive revelation of God:* God's glory is observed in what is known as "progressive revelation." Ryrie offers an explanation:

   > Progressive revelation is the recognition that God's message to man was not given in one single act but was unfolded in a long series of successive acts and through the minds and hands of many men of varying backgrounds.[31]

   Since this work of God throughout history revealed aspects of His multifaceted plan to men (e.g., Adam, Noah, Abraham, Moses, Paul, etc.), this work was also to the glory of God. In addition, the prophecies of God throughout history that have been (and have yet to be) fulfilled reveal the glory of God.

3. *The judgments of God:* In each successive dispensation, God judges humanity due to its failure to acknowledge the glory of God. These judgments were, and are, meant to reveal the glory of God

---

[31] Ryrie, *Dispensationalism Today*, 33.

to those whom He has judged (c.f. Ezek 28:22, 39:13).

While some dispensationalists believe there are more, or fewer than seven distinct dispensations, this author considers *soli Deo gloria* through a dispensational scheme that consists of seven dispensations, in order to highlight how the third point of the *sine qua* non of dispensationalism is directly connected to the fifth *sola of the Reformation*. The seven dispensations and how they are connected to the glory of God in these three areas (*soli Deo gloria*) are described below.

17.4.10.1 Prologue: The Glory of God Before Creation

The glory of the Lord was present prior to creation and thus before any of the dispensations began. John wrote in the beginning was The Word, and the Word was not only with God, but was God (John 1:1-3). This Word also had glory with the Father (John 1:14). Jesus in the Garden of Gethsemane asked God to glorify Him with the glory that He had before the world was created (John 17:5). Glory is at the very center of God's nature and character, and since God creates and works from His own nature, all things God does past, present, and future are to this purpose and end.

17.4.10.2 The Glory of God, Creation, and the Dispensation of Innocence

The creation narrative is marked by God creating the heavens and the earth (Gen 1:1). God was at work creating land, seas, vegetation, and various creatures (Gen 1:1-25). The start of the Dispensation of Innocence was when God created mankind in His own image and likeness (Gen 1:26). They were told by God to bear children and fill the earth (Gen 1:22). Man also was to exercise dominion over the animals (Gen 1:26). God placed them in the Garden of Eden to cultivate it and keep it (Gen 2:15). They were also told not to eat from the Tree of Knowledge of Good and Evil, and the consequence would be death if they disobeyed (Gen 2:16-17). Because God told Adam and Eve what they were to do, in essence, they were to *glorify God* by obeying all that He had commanded them to do. They were to tend the Garden of Eden, bear children and multiply across the earth, care for creation, and not eat of the fruit of the tree of the knowledge of good and evil.

The serpent enticed Adam and Eve to eat the fruit from the tree they were commanded not to eat (Gen 3:1–13). This resulted in the failure of Adam and Eve to glorify God. In addition to spiritual death, the consequence included physical repercussions, including increased pain in childbearing for women (Gen 3:16), conflict between man and woman (Gen 3:16), increased toil and hardship in labor (Gen 3:18–19) and ultimately physical death (Gen 3:18).

The glory of God is observed in the Dispensation of Innocence not only with the punishment God placed on Adam and Eve, but also on His judgment of the serpent, who deceived Eve. God commanded the serpent to eat the dust of the earth all of his days (Gen 3:14), and promised to provide a Redeemer from the seed of the woman who would crush the head of the serpent (Gen 3:15). God's glory was also highlighted by making skins for Adam and Eve and personally clothing them (Gen 3:20).

In the first dispensation it is shown that God glorifies Himself in His works in creation, in His fashioning and instructing mankind, and in punishing Adam and Eve, and the serpent for their disobedience. God's glory is also seen by His judgment of the serpent, and proclaiming that the works of the serpent would be destroyed by the Seed that was to come.

17.4.10.3 The Glory of God and the Dispensation of Conscience

After the Fall of Adam and Eve, God drove man out of the Garden of Eden, away from the tree of life (Gen 3:23). The Dispensation of Conscience was marked by the fact that since Adam now had a conscience (i.e., knowing good from evil), it would now serve to govern him. In addition, the Holy Spirit was present at this time striving or ruling with men (Gen 6:3). God's glory is seen in both Cain and Abel offering a sacrifice to the Lord (Gen 4:1–4). Abel's offering was accepted, that is, it glorified God, because Abel brought an acceptable sacrifice to the Lord (Gen 4:4). Cain did not bring a sacrifice that glorified God, and his sacrifice was rejected (Gen 4:4). Cain, due to his jealousy over God accepting his brother's offering murdered his brother (Gen 4:8). Over time God observed mankind's continual wicked intent (Gen 6:5). Human beings, due to their corrupted and wicked heart, fell from how they were to glorify God.

The glory of God can be seen in several ways in the Dispensation of

Conscience. First, it is seen in the punishment of Cain, in as much as he would be unable to work the ground for food (Gen 4:12), as well as in the sparing of Cain's life after he murdered his brother, making him a wanderer on the earth (Gen 9:14-15). The glory of God is also seen with Noah, as God commanded him to build an ark to save himself, his family, and two of every kind of animal the Lord would bring to Noah (Gen 6:13-20). In addition, the glory of God was seen in the judgement of God on the earth due to the global flood by which God destroyed all flesh (Gen 6:7).

In this second dispensation God glorified Himself by judging Cain, preserving Noah, his family, and creation in the Ark (Gen 7:17-24), and punishing mankind in a flood—all for their failure to glorify God.

17.4.10.4 The Glory of God and the Dispensation of Human Government

After the flood, God established a third dispensation: one which would be marked by human government. God gave the same command to Noah that He gave to Adam and Eve in the Garden of Eden: to bear children in the earth (Gen 9:1). In addition, the animals were given to mankind for food (Gen 9:2-3), which was something that was not commanded by God in the previous two dispensations. Additionally, due to the murder of Cain, and the corruption of men's consciences, God explicitly forbade murder. Moreover, God instituted a system of capital punishment in the event that one would violate this command of God (Gen 9:6). The activity of capital punishment is found exclusively in the hands of governing authorities whom Paul wrote were ministers of God to "bear the sword" by bringing the wrath of God on those who participate in evil (Rom 13:1-5).

God had revealed to Noah that mankind was to *glorify* God through repopulating the earth and respecting the life-blood of every creature (Gen 9:1-5). Noah's descendants were to "populate the earth" (lit: "swarm the earth") while submitting to God in obedient faith (v. 7). Yet man failed to do this in the days of Babel, when Noah's descendants built a city and a tower, as a testament to their own strength and autonomy, thereby neglecting the command from God to multiply and fill the earth (Gen 11:4). The glory of God is observed when He confused the peoples' speech and scattered them across the entire earth (Gen 11:8-9) —a sad and ironic twist to the story as mankind was now *forced* to move about the planet they were once commanded to do so freely.

17.4.10.5 The Glory of God and the Dispensation of Promise

After God scattered the people all over the earth, in the Dispensation of Promise, He called Abram (later Abraham) out of the country of his father and into a land that God showed him (Gen 12:1). In this, the glory of God was revealed, not only in the calling of Abram to leave his home country, but also in the distinct, unconditional promises, which God gave to Abram: (1) God would produce through Abram a great nation; (2) God would bless Abram, personally, and cause his name to be a blessing; (3) God would bring blessings on as many as would bless Abram, as well as curses for those who curse him; and, (4) God would bless all of the nations through him (Gen 12:2-3).

In the Dispensation of Promise the glory of God is in full view since these promises are all dependent on God and His work for Abraham. The glory of God would be emphasized in the *personal* promise God made to Abraham concerning his life, the *national* promise concerning the nation that would come from him (i.e., Israel), and the *universal* promise that God made to Abraham concerning the families of the earth. These promises were repeated many times throughout Abraham's life (Gen 13:14-17, 17:1-22, and 22:16-18). God also to give Abraham a son while he and his wife Sarah were advanced in years (Gen 15:1-22). Afterward, many of these same promises were repeated to Abraham's son, Isaac (Gen 26:3-5, 24), as well as his grandson, Jacob (28:10-22).

Abraham failed to glorify God in this dispensation by not waiting for the fulfillment of the promised son (Gen 16:1-6). Abraham lied twice about Sarah not being his wife (Gen 12:17, 20:1-18). Later, Isaac followed this pattern and also lied concerning his wife Rebekah, committing the same error as his father (Gen 26:1-35). The Israelite people neglected the promise that was tied to the land their forefathers were given, and did not return back to the land, but decided to stay in Egypt, even beyond Jacob's and Joseph's deaths (Gen 50:1-26). This resulted in the harsh enslavement of the Jewish people (Ex 1:1-22). However, the sovereignty and the glory of God were seen clearly in this dispensation due to the fact that God foretold the Israelites they would be enslaved for 400 years, and that He would afterward judge the nation that enslaved them (Gen 15:12-14).

17.4.10.6 The Glory of God and the Dispensation of Law

After God miraculously delivered Israel from their Egyptian captors, He led them to Mount Sinai; it is here that the fourth Dispensation of Law begins (Ex 19:20). The glory of God is physically manifest before the nation of Israel, and they are terrified in the presence of God (Ex 19:18-25: Deut 18). God claimed the nation of Israel for Himself, out from all the nations, to keep the promise He had made to Abraham, Isaac, and Jacob (Deut 7:6-7). God gave the nation of Israel Ten Commandments written on two tablets of stone (Ex 34:28; Deut 4:13). In addition, there were 603 more laws the nation of Israel was supposed to follow. These laws concerned how they were to worship, make restitution, and conduct themselves in daily living. God glorified Himself by revealing in this dynamic way who He was to Israel. Moreover, God gave them these commandments by His very own finger (Ex 31:18; Deut 9:10). If Israel conducted themselves according to these 613 commandments and glorified God in the presence of the surrounding nations by observing these commands, then they would receive the blessings God had promised, in response to their obedience (Deut. 28:1-14). However, if they refused to glorify God, God would bring upon them all manner of curses on account of their disobedience (Deut 28:15-68).

The biblical account is clear; Israel failed to glorify God during their time in the Promised Land. They constantly glorified and praised false idols, instead of the true God. Beyond that, they repeatedly violated the Mosaic Law (Jer 31:32; Ezek 16). Because of their hardened hearts, they also refused to humble themselves and give God glory (Ezek 36:26; Zech 7:12).

Subsequently, the glory of God is seen in the judgment which God brought upon Israel as a nation. They were ejected from the Promised Land and carried away into captivity by the Assyrians in the Northern Kingdom (2 Kings 15:29, 17:3-6) and the Babylonians in the Southern Kingdom (2 Kings 24:1; Jer 51:12-13; Dan 1:1-4).

17.4.10.7 The Glory of God and the Dispensation of the Church

The Dispensation of the Church begins during Pentecost when the

Holy Spirit first descended upon those who were present at Jerusalem (Acts 2:1-41). On that occasion, Peter declared the Holy Spirit would be given as many as would believe in the Lord Jesus Christ (Acts 2:38-39). The glory of God is found in the proclamation of the gospel of Jesus Christ, which is now being preached throughout the nations. In effect, Jews and Gentiles are made an entirely new creation through the work and ministry of Christ and the Holy Spirit (Eph 2:11-22, 4:1-5). Where the glory of God was evidenced in the previous dispensation through Israel's adherence to the Law and the Prophets, the glory of God is seen in this dispensation as Jew and Gentile believe in the Messiah for the forgiveness of sins, and are made into one corporate body, with Christ as the head (Eph 5:23).

While 613 laws guided Israel in their conduct toward one another, the glory of God is seen in the Dispensation of the Church through how believers follow the "one another" commands (Rom 12:10, 12:16, 14:13, 14:19, 15:7, 15:14; 1 Cor 12:25; Gal 6:2; Eph 4:2, 4:25, 4:32, 5:19, 5:21; Col 3:13, 3:16; 1 Thess 4:9, 4:13-18, 5:11, 5:13; Heb 13:3, 10:24-25; James 4:11, 5:9, 5:16; 1 Pet 1:22, 4:8-10, 5:5; 1 John 3:11, 3:23, 4:7, 4:11-12; 2 John 1:5). Additionally, because God has done this work in the believer, and has prepared these deeds beforehand for the saint to accomplish, therefore, the believer's good works glorify God (Eph 2:8-10).

The glory of God is seen in the present dispensation in how God disciplines the church when they act unbecomingly. One example of this is seen in the church of Corinth, where due to believers' dishonoring the Lord's Supper, God caused the early death of those who refused to glorify Him (1 Cor 11:27-32). Elsewhere in Scripture He demonstrates the prerogative to remove churches which fail to glorify Him (Rev 2:5). He declares that in the future, He will remove the Restrainer of His wrath (1 Thess 2:6-7), at which time He will wipe out the apostate church (Rev 17:16), and He will completely crush the unbeliever (Rev 19:17-21).

The church will ultimately fail to glorify God in this dispensation. God will not receive the glory He is due inasmuch as so many Jews and Gentiles will not receive the forgiveness of sins. Despite the admonitions of Scripture, the visible and institutional church will refuse to rebuke false teachers and will fail to make disciples. Instead, the church will largely embrace those false teachers, and refuse to honor God's revealed Word (2 Tim

3:1–5, 4:3–4). Individually and collectively, people who are believers will choose not to pursue godly lives and not heed the "one another commands." In the end, Scripture anticipates that the apostate church will be in complete rebellion (2 Thess 2:1–2), and the unsaved will stage a massive revolt against God (Rev 16:13–16; Ps 2:1–3).

In all of this it may be seen that the glory of God is found in God's judgment concerning church discipline for personal matters between believers (Matt 18:15–20), as well as corporately, for egregious sins (1 Cor 5:1–13). One day, deceased and living believers will be gathered together by Christ (1 Thess 4:15–18), and will be judged according to how they glorified God before men with their deeds on earth (2 Cor 5:9–10).

17.4.10.8 The Glory of God and the Dispensation of the Millennium

Scripture reveals that the final Dispensation of the Millennium will begin at the second advent of Jesus Christ and will end after the release, revolt, and the ultimate defeat of Satan (Rev 19:11–21, 20:1–10). It details a state in which Christ will physically reign on earth as the sovereign ruler of Israel and the entire world (Isa 11:1–5; Zech 14:9, 10; Rev 20:1–7). Saints will rule with Christ in this age (Rev 20:4–7). The glory of God will be seen in the physical environment as the conditions on the earth will be radically restored to pre-fall conditions (Matt 19:28; Acts 3:19–21; Rom 8:18–23). Animals and vegetation will be plentiful and abundant (Ezek 36:11, 47:8–10; Ps 72:16; Isa 30:23–24; Jer 31:10–14; Ezek 34:25–30, 36:29–30; Joel 2:21–26; Zech 8:11–12). Sickness and illness will be nonexistent (Isa 29:18, 33:24, 35:5–6). Mankind will experience extended physical life (Isa 65:20–22). Hostility between the nations will be prohibited (Isa 2:4; Mic 4:3). Satan will not be able to deceive or incite the nations (Rev 20:1–3). Moreover, all of the promises concerning Israel and the Gentiles in the Old and New Testaments will be fulfilled at this time.

This is the time when the glory of God will be broadcast throughout the entire earth, and all will know of the glory of the Lord (Hab 2:14). His glory will be manifested through all activities and individuals. Nevertheless, even when mankind observes all of these changes on earth, he will still rebel against God. The nations will be deceived by Satan one final time in an attempt to overthrow Jesus Christ and His beloved saints (Rev 20:7–10).

The glory of God is also displayed in this dispensation through His judgment at this time. Those who oppose Jesus during the millennium will be strictly punished (Isa 11:3-4, 29:20-21; Jer 31:29-30). The nations who do not glorify God at the Feast of Booths will not receive rainfall with which to grow their crops (Zech 14:15-19). Moreover, the glory of God will be observed in the judgment of Satan being thrown into the lake of fire (Rev 20:10). Finally, as many as will not believe in Christ for the forgiveness of sins (i.e., those whose names will not be found written in the Book of Life) will also be judged and thrown in the lake of fire (Rev 20:11-15).

17.4.10.9 Epilogue: Eternal Age–The Glory of God in its Fullness

Even though the eternal state may not technically be a dispensation, it is worth noting that the glory of God is at its fullness at this point. Scripture reveals that the New Jerusalem, the great city of God, will physically shine with the glory of God (Rev 21:22). All of the nations will observe the glory of Lord, and walk by the city's glory (Rev 21:24). All inhabitants of this place will be so glorious there will be no need for a sun, neither will there be any night (Rev 21:24-25, 22:5). The overarching purpose of history will have been completed. The glory of God will no longer be rejected or minimized; therefore, judgments or punishments will no longer be instituted (Rev 21:27). God will at last dwell with all men and will reign for all eternity (Rev 21:22).

17.5 The Glory of God: The Major Point

Due to the lack of a soteriological focus, dispensationalism is accused of separating the glory of God from Christ's death on the cross. One such critic has commented:

> It does not matter, [dispensationalist] say, if God condemns us or saves us. He is glorified either way, and that is the point of it all. The strange and dangerous thing here is pitting these two things, God's glory and man's salvation, against each other. The Bible holds them together...[dispensationalism] drives a wedge between God's glory and

man's salvation.[32]

Paul wrote to the churches in Corinth that all of the promises of God in Christ are "yes" and "amen" (2 Cor 1:20). Without Christ, His active obedience, and the penal-substitutionary atonement on the cross for the sins of the world, *none* of the things that God promised eschatologically would come to pass. There would be *no* salvation for national Israel, *no* salvation for the universal church, and *no* blessing for the nations. Salvation *is* the means by which all of the promises of God are fulfilled, and God is glorified in dying for the sins of mankind. However, salvation is only *one* aspect of God's multifaceted plan that brings Him glory. A real problem arises when an individual makes salvation, rather than the glory of God, the *sine qua non*. One clear example of this is evidenced by the fact that, there are creatures God has created of whom Christ did not die for—namely angels. Yet, God no less has a distinct plan for them. Concerning this Ryrie comments:

> All theologians of whatever persuasion realize that God has a plan for the angels. It does not involve redemption, for the elect angels do not experience it and the non elect angels cannot. And yet for the angels God has a distinct program—a distinct purpose, and it is not soteriological.[33]

Scripture testifies that some angelic beings are awaiting final judgment for their sins (Jude 6). In addition, animals do not participate in God's plan of salvation. As Solomon put it: animals return to the dust of the earth (Eccl 3:21). It must be concluded that the glory of God is not limited to the soteriological work of God concerning man. *All* of God's revealed works—His work in creation, His progressive plan for mankind, His established dispensations, His subsequent judgments, the fulfilling of His past prophecies, and *all* of His future promises for Israel, the church, the nations, and even the condemnation of the wicked—display the glory of God. Ryrie echoes this point:

---

[32] Bryan Wolfmueller, *Has American Christianity Failed?* (St. Louis, MO: Concordia, 2016), 220.

[33] Ryrie, *Dispensationalism Today*, 103.

God does have various ways of manifesting His glory, redemption be-ing one—a principal one, but not the only one. The various economies with their stewardship responsibilities are not completely separated from each other but are stages in the progress of the revelation of the various ways in which God is glorified.[34]

17.6 Conclusion

The Reformation sought to return the church to the eternal truth of God's Word, with the heart of the Reformation being *soli Deo gloria*. Martin Luther observed the glory of God from a *soteriological* view. This view was not only promoted but was expanded by John Calvin, who had a *doxological* view. Martin Luther was accurate to observe the glory of God in the salva-tion of man by Christ alone, given the contentious battle around *sola fide* and *sola Scriptura* during the time of the Reformation. John Calvin, taking it a step further was also accurate in observing that the glory of God was not to be confined to the heavens, but was demonstrated in all things under heaven. The Calvinistic tradition has correctly observed the glory of God is to be properly manifested in a believer's life. However, it has largely ne-glected the observations of John Nelson Darby, C. I. Scofield, Charles Ryrie, and so many other dispensationalists who have rightly perceived that the glory of God was to be shown throughout all the works of God.

The fifth *sola* of the Reformation is the third *sine qua non* of dispensa-tionalism, and it is this particular *sine qua non* that guides dispensationalists' consistent literal grammatical-historical hermeneutic. Dispensationalism recognizes the glory of God as the motive for which God will fulfill His promises to Israel, the church, and the nations. In addition, dispensation-alism would expand the five *solas* beyond the work of God in salvation. All saints throughout each dispensation have been saved by grace, through faith, believing in what God revealed to them at that particular time in his-tory concerning a Deliverer who would one day usher in the glory of God throughout the whole earth.

Soli Deo gloria is, and always will be, at the center of dispensationalism. By limiting the glory of God to *only* the salvation of man, one fails to see all

---

[34] Ryrie, *Dispensationalism Today*, 104.

of the *solas* of the Reformation clearly, and fails to give God the praise and glory that is due Him alone. Amen.

Soli Deo Gloria!

Bibliography

Butler, Trent C., ed. *Holman Bible Dictionary*. Nashville, TN: Holman Bible Publishers, 1991.

Cairns, Earle E. *Christianity through the Centuries*. 2nd ed. Grand Rapids, MI: Zondervan, 1967.

Calvin, John. *Institutes of the Christian Religion*. Kindle edition.

"Catholic Tradition." The Beginning Catholic's Guide to the Roman Catholic Church. Accessed May 2, 2017. http://www.beginningcath olic.com/catholic-tradition.

Crutchfield, Larry V. *The Origins of Dispensationalism: The Darby Factor*. Lanham, MD: University Press of America, 1992.

Danker, Fredrick W., ed. *A Greek-English Lexicon of the New Testament and other Early Christian Literature*. 3rd ed. Chicago, IL: University of Chicago, 2000. BibleWorks.

Harris, R. Laird, ed. *Theological Wordbook of the Old Testament*. 2 vols. Chicago, IL: Moody, 1981.

Hunter, Davis. *The Lives of George Frideric Handel*. Woodbridge [Suffolk, England]: Boydell Press, 2015.

Ice, Thomas. "The Calvinistic Heritage of Dispensationalism." Pre-Trib Research Center. Accessed May 26, 2017. http://www.pre-trib.org /articles/view/calvinistic-heritage-of-dispensationalism.

Ironside, H. A. *The Mysteries of God*. Whitefish, MT: Kessinger, 2009.

Koehler, Ludwig, and Walter Baumgartner. *Hebrew and Aramaic Lexicon of the Old Testament*. 5 vols. Leiden, The Netherlands: Brill, 2000. Bible-Works.

Luther, Martin. *The Book of Concord*. St. Louis, MO: Concordia, 1952.

Ryrie, Charles Caldwell. *Dispensationalism Today*. Chicago, IL: Moody Press, 1979.

Scofield, C. I. *The First Scofield Reference Bible: Containing the Old and New Testaments*. Niagara-on-the-Lake, ON: Believers Bookshelf, 1986.

Second Vatican Council. *Dei Verbum* [Dogmatic Constitution on Divine Revelation]. Vatican. November 18, 1965. Accessed May 26, 2017. http://www.vatican.va/archive/hist_councils/ii_vatican_council/do cuments/vat-ii_const_19651118_dei-verbum_en.html.

Stapert, Calvin R. "To the Glory of God Alone." *Christian History and Biography*, no. 95 (Summer 2007), 8–14. Accessed May 15, 2017. http://www.christianitytoday.com/history/issues/issue-95/to-glory-of-god-alone.html.

Vincent, Thomas. "The Shorter Catechism of the Westminster Assembly Explained and Proved from Scripture." Encyclopedia Puritannica Project. Accessed May 15, 2017. http://www.puritannica.com/front /demo/wk/VincentThomas/ShorterExplained/0013-0049 .html#13.

Westminster Assembly. "The Westminster Shorter Catechism." The Westminster Presbyterian. Accessed May 12, 2017. http://www .westminsterconfession.org/confessional-standards/the-westminster-shorter-catechism.php.

Wingren, Gustaf. *Luther on Vocation*. Philadelphia, PA: Muhlenberg Press, 1957.

Wolfmueller, Bryan. *Has American Christianity Failed?* St. Louis, MO: Concordia, 2016.

CONCLUSION

18

SEMPER REFORMANDA:
Always Reforming

Christopher Cone
Calvary University

18.0 The Curious Case of Charlie Brown

Charlie Brown is really a decent guy. He takes care of his dog, is respectful to adults, cares for his friends, and is reliable and trustworthy. He's the kind of kid you might want to have a lemonade with at the end of a hard day of school or play. I suspect that there is a little Charlie Brown in all of us. But despite Charlie's well-deserved accolades, he has a problem. He believes something about human nature that isn't quite right. He seems an eternal optimist—which is what you want in a friend, but not in a worldview. He doesn't quite grasp that there is something fundamentally wrong with humanity. Yet, every time he attempts to kick a football, his worldview (or at least his anthropology) is proven wrong. Lucy is going to pull the ball away. That's what she does. For Calvinists who are reading this, you understand, of course, that this is that to which Lucy was called. She can do no other. She grabs hold of the football's irresistible lace, and Charlie Brown is on his backside yet again. For those readers less Calvinistically-inclined, Lucy is remarkably predictable in her choice. She could hold the ball steady if she really wanted to but, alas, she never seems to make that choice (except for one isolated occasion in 1979, when she is rewarded with a kick in the hands and the arm). Admittedly, the reasons for her transgressions are difficult to ascertain. Lucy herself clouds the issue by announcing a number of various reasons for her misdeeds.

Columnist Eric Schulmiller actually researched and wrote an article titled: "The Complete History of Lucy's Pulling the Football Away." [1] He catalogues her reasons, including a muscle spasm in 1966, an expression of the women's lib movement in 1971, my personal favorite—a 1980 misapplication of Ecclesiastes 3 ("to everything there is a season and a time to pull away the football"), and several others. Regardless of which theological system drives Lucy to misbehave, she provides occasion for us to acknowledge that Charlie Brown's worldview is in need of reform. In fact, we could argue hers is even *more* ripe for refinement. Still, let's not let Lucy's feminine complexity cause us to lose sight of the important theological issue: Charlie Brown needs a better anthropology—and these are no mere head games. Charlie Brown's errant optimism will likely lead to significant chiropractic costs, a total loss of trust in his fellow man, and even worse—higher dry cleaning bills. In the words of Richard Weaver, "ideas have consequences." [2] Charlie Brown's ideas about humanity have painful and tangible consequences. Charlie Brown needs a bit of reform, and there is a bit of Charlie Brown in all of us.

18.1 The Ongoing Need for Reform

Reformation is a difficult and often painful labor. Undoubtedly, through the centuries the labor of reform has been encountered at great cost. Perhaps in part due to that cost, we tend to prefer comfortable rather than sacred ground. We arrive at plateaus of consensus in our understanding. Like Charlie Brown, we dwell in those sympathetic confines perceiving our knowledge to be sufficient, our interpretations inerrant, and our conclusions immovable. We grow unwilling to change, hardened in views that

---

[1] Eric Schulmiller, "All Your Life, Charlie Brown, All Your Life: The Complete History Of Lucy's Pulling The Football Away," Slate.com, October 8, 2014, accessed June 14, 2017, http://www.slate.com/articles/arts/culturebox/2014/10/the_history _of_lucy_s_pulling_the_football_away_from_charlie_brown_in_peanuts.html.

[2] Richard Weaver and Ted J. Smith, III, *Ideas Have Consequences* (1948; repr., Chicago, IL: University of Chicago Press, 2013), xix.

are mere codified preferences and not demonstrably divine mandates. In our pride we stunt the growth for which we are intended. We must do better. We *can* do better. Not only do we need reform in our understanding, but we need an attitude of reform.

In the realm of business and organization, this attitude is often referred to as *agility*. It is the ability to manage change in such a way that the change doesn't govern the business or the institution, but rather the entity is able to grab hold of the change momentum and do something special with the opportunity. To reform is to move from one position or understanding to another. But to be *always reforming* is another thing altogether. *Always reforming* reflects a posture of inviting renewal and welcoming growth. It is not just having agility, but practicing it. This is what we are called to do.

Paul's mandate that we be μεταμορφοῦσθε (*metamorphousthe*, transformed) by the renewing of our mind is a present tense, passive, imperative (Rom 12:2). It is not something we are ever finished doing in this life. His Ephesians' exhortation to "be renewed [ἀνανεοῦσθαι, *ananeousthai*] in the spirit of your mind" (Eph 4:23) is a present passive infinitive. These are ongoing. These reflect a continual mentality prepared to be always reforming. Always reforming starts with a committed mindset, continues with learning and growth, and culminates with the practical *therefore* – actions and a life that reflect the grand calling to which the believer has been called (e.g., Eph 4:1, 25).

18.2 A Cloud of Witnesses

Hebrews 11 catalogues a cloud of witnesses who model for us how to conform our thinking to God's revealed Word. These men and women did extraordinary things, because they aligned their beliefs and their thinking with what God had communicated. They gained approval through their faith—they believed what God had said, and they trusted in Him. Even in that, the design is that we should join them in their faith, so that we can be completed together (Heb 11:39). These were incredible people who teach us how to fix our eyes on the Author and Perfecter of the faith, so that τρέχωμεν (*trechomen*, we might continually run, a present active subjunctive) the race set before us (Heb 12:1–2).

Abraham, for example, was always reforming. He believed in God (Gen 15:6). He obeyed when he was called and he looked for God to keep His Word (Gen 12:4; Heb 11:8, 19). Even when his own understanding was flawed, he was open to having his mind changed by God's Word. That was a vivid lesson he demonstrated on Mount Moriah (Gen 22:8, 14). And Abraham is not an exceptional case. Many are described in Hebrews 11 as doing incredible things based on how the Word of God changed their worldview. *Always be reforming.*

18.3 The New Birth of Martin Luther

Five hundred years ago God used a group of courageous leaders who showed by their example that there must be an unquenchable fire within us to be always reforming our perspectives and our understandings—to be ever more rooted in Scripture. On October 31, 1517, Martin Luther nailed his *95 Theses* to the Cathedral Church door in Wittenburg. His was a call for Christians to return to the Scriptures—to allow our thinking to be reformed by God's Word, and consequently, to act in a way that reflected biblical thinking. For Luther that moment was a practical *therefore* in his own personal journey. He had spent a decade in monastic service before arriving at the recognition that something wasn't quite right in the understanding and practice of the dominant church. As he interacted with Scripture he could no longer justify certain traditions.

His personal journey was hardly completed with his entering monastic ministry. There was more reforming to do. Luther himself needed to reform. As the word of God continued to shape his thinking, Luther came to understand the grace of God *a decade after he became a monk.* Luther described in detail his encounter with the gospel of righteousness in this way:

> I had dealt in university courses with St. Paul's Letters to the Romans, to the Galatians, and the Letter to the Hebrews. I had conceived a burning desire to understand what Paul meant in his Letter to the Romans, but thus far there had stood in my way, not the cold blood around my heart, but that one word which is in chapter one: "The justice of God is revealed in it." I hated that word, "justice of God," which, by the use and custom of all my teachers, I had been taught to understand philosophically as referring to formal or active justice, as

they call it, i.e., that justice by which God is just and by which he punishes sinners and the unjust.

But I, blameless monk that I was, felt that before God I was a sinner with an extremely troubled conscience. I couldn't be sure that God was appeased by my satisfaction. I did not love, no, rather I hated the just God who punishes sinners. In silence, if I did not blaspheme, then certainly I grumbled vehemently and got angry at God. I said, "Isn't it enough that we miserable sinners, lost for all eternity because of original sin, are oppressed by every kind of calamity through the Ten Commandments? Why does God heap sorrow upon sorrow through the Gospel and through the Gospel threaten us with his justice and his wrath?" This was how I was raging with wild and disturbed conscience. I constantly badgered St. Paul about that spot in Romans 1 and anxiously wanted to know what he meant.

I meditated night and day on those words until at last, by the mercy of God, I paid attention to their context: "The justice of God is revealed in it, as it is written: 'The just person lives by faith.'" I began to understand that in this verse the justice of God is that by which the just person lives by a gift of God, that is by faith. I began to understand that this verse means that the justice of God is revealed through the Gospel, but it is a passive justice, i.e. that by which the merciful God justifies us by faith, as it is written: "The just person lives by faith." *All at once I felt that I had been born again and entered into paradise itself through open gates. Immediately I saw the whole of Scripture in a different light.* I ran through the Scriptures from memory and found that other terms had analogous meanings, e.g., the work of God, that is, what God works in us; the power of God, by which he makes us powerful; the wisdom of God, by which he makes us wise; the strength of God, the salvation of God, the glory of God. I exalted this sweetest word of mine, "the justice of God," with as much love as before I had hated it with hate. This phrase of Paul was for me the very gate of paradise [emphasis mine].[3]

---

[3] Martin Luther, "Preface to the Complete Edition of Luther's Latin Works,"

Imagine if Luther had considered his transformation complete when he arrived at the status of "blameless monk." He would have never known what he refers to as *being born again* by receiving the grace of God through faith. He had spoken of *sola fide* and *sola gratia* in 1517, but just two years prior, he had no understanding of what those words really meant. *Always be reforming.*

18.4 The Reformer King

In addition to Hebrews 11's cloud of witnesses and the illustration of Martin Luther's new birth, we find in the pages of Scripture another personal journey of reform rooted in God's Word. It is a magnificent account of a youth whom God used to impact countless lives. The year was 640 B.C. An eight-year-old boy had just ascended to the throne of Judah following the assassination of his father (2 Kings 21:24-26). This boy would be one of the youngest kings in all of world history. The stakes were high. The times were turbulent. And God placed a child at the center of the world. The Southern Kingdom of Judah had been warned by one prophet after another that Judah's departure from God had not gone unnoticed, and would not go unanswered. Josiah's pedigree offered no indication that he would be a reformer. On the contrary, it seemed more likely that he would continue a longstanding legacy of rebellion. His grandfather was Manasseh, perhaps the most wicked of Judah's kings, and his father was Amon, another evil king whose reign was so inept that he was killed by his own servants in his own house (2 Kings 21:23). But Josiah was different. In 2 Chronicles 34:1-2 he is described in this way:

> Josiah *was* eight years old when he became king, and he reigned thirty-one years in Jerusalem. He did right in the sight of the Lord, and walked in the ways of his father David and did not turn aside to the right or to the left.

We are told what he did, the example he followed, and the degree to

trans. Andrew Thornton, from the "Vorrede zu Band I der Opera Latina der Wittenberger Ausgabe. 1545," in Luthers Werke in Auswahl, ed. Otto Clemen, 6th ed. (Berlin: de Gruyter. 1967), 4:421-428, accessed June 14, 2017, https://www.iclnet.org/pub/resources/text/wittenberg/luther/preflat-eng.txt.

which he was faithful. Righteous in God's sight, walking like David, and fully faithful in his leadership as king, Josiah became a historic reformer. But what was at the center of his reform? What set apart his life and ministry, that he could rise above his forefathers' failures? We read in 2 Chronicles 34:3 that "in the eighth year of his reign while he was still a youth, he began to seek the God of his father David;" and within four years his personal reform led to a great awakening that spread throughout all of Judah.

In the twelfth year of his reign (at age twenty) he began to remove all the idolatrous places and icons of worship (2 Chron 34:3-4). Josiah knew that God desired for all Israel to meet Him at the temple, and they should not make for themselves altars and sanctuaries in other locations (Lev 26:1, 30-31; 1 Kings 9:3-5). Josiah took that message seriously, and embarked on reform accordingly. Before he tore down the altars, he burned the bones of the false priests on those very altars. This violent irony sent a powerful message to all the people, and surely served as a reminder that God had chosen a specific tribe to minister in a specific location, and all else were counterfeits. In keeping with God's instructions, Josiah purged the land far beyond the borders of his own kingdom, as his reforms even reached Naphtali—one of the northernmost tribes (2 Chron 34:6). Once this preliminary work was accomplished, Josiah returned to Jerusalem (2 Chron 34:7).

In the eighteenth year of his reign (at age twenty-six), Josiah began a major temple-rejuvenation project. He used funds collected by the Levites, from the remaining remnant of Israel, and from the inhabitants of Judah, and put the money in the hands of the workers who were overseeing the temple. They administered the work and provided the resources to the carpenters and other craftsman, and the work of repair was underway (2 Chron 34:8-13). During the process, Hilkiah the high priest found the book of the law in the temple (2 Kings 22:8-10; 2 Chron 34:14-18). Shockingly, up to this moment Israel and Judah had been operating from memory and oral tradition. This state of affairs implies that the previous kings had not been faithful in personally reproducing a copy of the law in the presence of the Levitical priests as they had been commanded in Deuteronomy 17:18-20. This is, of course, not only a failure on the part of the kings, but also on the part of the Levites for letting it happen. God had prescribed this exercise specifically so that the king would fear the Lord, would be careful to obey

Him, would maintain humility, and would not turn aside from what God had commanded.

Without having this failsafe, it is quite remarkable that Josiah had the level of understanding that he did. Still, when the book of the law was read to him, he tore his clothes, as he realized the reality that God was pouring out His wrath on Israel and Judah just as He had said He would do if the nation failed to be faithful to Him and to His Word (2 Chron 34:19-20). Josiah immediately sought the Lord's guidance through Huldah the prophetess, who confirmed that judgment was assured because of Israel's and Judah's idolatry (2 Chron 34:21-26). Despite this tragic news, we learn in 34:27-28 how God viewed Josiah, the reformer:

> "Because your heart was tender and you humbled yourself before God when you heard His words against this place and against its inhabitants, and *because* you humbled yourself before Me, tore your clothes and wept before Me, I truly have heard you," declares the Lord. "Behold, I will gather you to your fathers and you shall be gathered to your grave in peace, so your eyes will not see all the evil which I will bring on this place and on its inhabitants."

God acknowledged Josiah here, allowing him to escape the coming judgment, not because of what he had done before, but because of how he responded to God *when he heard His Word*—both for his inward heart response of tenderness and humility and for his outward expressions. It is worth noting here, as a point of application, that reformed actions without tenderness of heart and humility toward God are not what He is looking for. Unfortunately, perhaps the greatest manifestation of our need for reform is our pride and our stubbornness in not responding properly to God's Word.

Josiah was a young man who was deeply committed to honoring God, and he was working with the limited knowledge that he had. He did good things with that, but just like all of us, he was in need of reform. When he was confronted afresh with God's Word he *reformed*. He responded personally to God, and he took the people with him in reformation:

> Then the king sent and gathered all the elders of Judah and Jerusalem. The king went up to the house of the Lord and all the men of Judah,

the inhabitants of Jerusalem, the priests, the Levites and all the people, from the greatest to the least; and he read in their hearing all the words of the book of the covenant which was found in the house of the Lord. (2 Chron 34:29-30)

It wasn't enough for him to hear the Word and proclaim it to all the people, he acted upon it. He was a doer of the Word:

Then the king stood in his place and made a covenant before the Lord to walk after the Lord, and to keep His commandments and His testimonies and His statutes with all his heart and with all his soul, to perform the words of the covenant written in this book. (2 Chron 34:31)

Josiah modeled tenderness, humility, respect for God's Word, and solemn commitment to walk with Him, and then he followed through.

Moreover, he made all who were present in Jerusalem and Benjamin to stand *with him*. So the inhabitants of Jerusalem did according to the covenant of God, the God of their fathers. Josiah removed all the abominations from all the lands belonging to the sons of Israel, and made all who were present in Israel to serve the Lord their God. Throughout his lifetime they did not turn from following the Lord God of their fathers. (2 Chron 34:32-33)

Not only did Josiah remove all the "abominations" from the land, but he "made all who were present in Israel to serve the Lord their God" (2 Chron 34:33). At first glance, this passage seems to imply that Josiah forced Israel to follow God, but the Hebrew verb translated *made* (עָבַד, abad) is in the hifil stem, which communicates causation. The phrase could be translated, "he *caused to be made* all who were present in Israel to serve the Lord their God." Especially in light of the next sentence, it appears that this was a result of his leading by example rather than a causation by force: "Throughout his lifetime they did not turn from following the Lord God of their fathers" (2 Chron 34:33).

Josiah's personal reform—his commitment to continual conformity in his own life to God's Word—was an example to the nation who followed him. The prophetess had spoken of God's impending judgment, and that it would be delayed because of Josiah's righteousness. In his own reform, Josiah carried the nation with him, and God delayed the most severe judgment on Judah (total exile) until twenty-five years after Josiah's death. The example of Josiah's life should encourage all of us to be always reforming, always pliable and tenderhearted *to align more closely with the Word of God.*

While Josiah's life offers much material for our own personal exhortation, he offered in death one final lesson. Just like Moses before him, Josiah had been a godly and a righteous man. But just as Moses had a lapse and failed to treat God as holy before the sons of Israel (Num 27:14), Josiah failed to recognize the Word of God as revealed through Neco, King of Egypt, and engaged in a battle that the Lord had not sanctioned. Josiah died on the battlefield, thus providing for us yet another reminder that we are all in need of reform, and that we must be always reforming (2 Chron 35:20–24). Still, even in spite of this failure, Josiah is characterized by the Chronicler as doing "deeds of devotion as written in the Law of the Lord" (2 Chron 35:26). Praise God for His mercy and His grace for allowing us to remember Josiah in this way.

18.5 Conclusion

Josiah, the cloud of witnesses, and the more recent examples of Martin Luther and John Nelson Darby as seen in this volume, all provide us with a grand parade which reminds us of our need for the continual guidance which God's Word provides. We must urge each other to be always reforming, always realigning, always growing in our understanding and application of His Word. Brothers and sisters ought not to let one another wander in ungrounded doctrine nor wobble in immature practice. We owe each other an immeasurable debt of love (Rom 13:8). That debt demands that we consider how to encourage one another to love and good deeds (Heb 10:24). Our source material remains, as always, *Sola Scriptura.* Nothing less, and nothing more.

Looking back on his own personal journey, Martin Luther challenges us all to learn from his example of violating that very principle of Biblical sufficiency for which he advocated. He warns,

From my case you can see how hard it is to struggle free from errors which become fixed by universal standard and changed by time-honored custom into nature. How true the proverb is: "It's hard to abandon customs" and "Custom is a second nature." How right Augustine was when he said, "Custom, if it is not resisted, becomes necessity."[4]

Luther's words strike fiercely at the core of all of us. Indeed, transformation, not custom, is our necessity. Truth is our aim, not errors which become fixed into nature. God's truth never changes, but we must change in conforming our hearts and minds to be more aligned with His own timeless truth.

Semper Reformanda, brothers and sisters. We must be *always reforming*.

We bow our knees before you, Father, from whom every family in heaven and on earth derives its name. That you would grant us according to the riches of your glory to be strengthened with power through your Spirit in our inner man, so that Christ may dwell in our hearts through faith, and that we, being rooted and grounded in love may be able to comprehend with all the saints what is the breadth and length and height and depth, to know the love of Christ which surpasses knowledge so that we may be filled up to all the fullness of God. Now to You who are able to do far more abundantly beyond all that we ask or think, according to the power that works within us, to you be the glory in the church and in Christ Jesus to all generations forever and ever. *Amen.*

---

[4] Luther, "Preface to the Complete Edition."

Bibliography

Luther, Martin. "Preface to the Complete Edition of Luther's Latin Works." Translated by Andrew Thornton, from the "Vorrede zu Band I der Opera Latina der Wittenberger Ausgabe. 1545." In *Luthers Werke in Auswahl*, edited by Otto Clemen. Vol. 4. 6th ed. Berlin: de Gruyter. 1967. Accessed June 14, 2017. https://www.iclnet.org/pub/resources/text/wittenberg/luther/preflat-eng.txt.

Schulmiller, Eric. "All Your Life, Charlie Brown, All Your Life: The Complete History of Lucy's Pulling the Football Away." Slate.com. October 8, 2014. Accessed June 14, 2017. http://www.slate.com/articles/arts/culturebox/2014/10/the_history_of_lucy_s_pulling_the_football_away_from_charlie_brown_in_peanuts.html.

Weaver, Richard, and Ted J. Smith III. *Ideas Have Consequences*. 1948. Reprint, Chicago, IL: University of Chicago Press, 2013.

SCRIPTURE INDEX

Old Testament
Genesis
1:1, *541*
1:1-25, *541*
1:1-31, *537*
1:4, 10, 18, 21, 25, *445*
1:22, *541*
1:26, *541*
1:26-28, *445, 537*
1:31, *233, 445*
1-3, *325*
2:1-25, *537*
2:2, *287*
2:8-10, *230*
2:15, *541*
2:16-17, *445*
2:16-17, *445*
2:16-17, *541*
2:18-25, *445*
3, *320*
3:1-13, *542*
3:14, 15, *542*
3:16, *542*
3:18-19, *542*
3:20, *542*
3:21, 22-24, *445*
3:23, *542*
4:1-4, *542*
4:4, *64, 542*
4:6-7, 8, *446*
4:8, *542*
4:12, *543*
4:15, *446*
4:20-22, *446*

5:1-2, *445*
5:5, *446*
6:3, *542*
6:5, *446, 542*
6:8, *384*
6:10, 18, *446*
6:13, *446*
6:13-20, *543*
6:19-20, *446*
6-9, *385*
7:2-3, *446*
7:17-24, *543*
8:15-17, 21, *446*
9:1, *543*
9:1-5, *543*
9:2-3, *543*
9:6, *543*
9:7, *543*
9:8-17, *446*
9:14-15, *543*
10:8-9, *118*
11:4, *543*
11:7, *447*
11:8-9, *543*
11:27-32, *447*
12:1, *544*
12:1-3, *181*
12:2-3, *447, 544*
12:3, *184*
12:4, *560*
12:17, *544*
13:14-17, *544*
15:1-22, *544*
15:6, *428, 560*
15:8, *447*

15:12-14, *545*
15:12-21, *181*
15:18, *182*
15:18-21, *181*
15, 17, *448*
16:1-6, *544*
17, *447*
17:1-22, *544*
17:3, *447*
17:11, *182*
17:17, *447*
19:19, *385*
20:1-18, *544*
22:8, 14, *560*
22:16-18, *544*
26:1-35, *544*
26:3-5, 24, *544*
28:10-22, *544*
33:5, *384*
33:11, *384*
43:29, *384*
49:10, *206*
50:1-26, *544*
Exodus
1:1-22, *544*
3:21, *384*
3-4, *449*
3-14, *385*
4:13-14, *449*
7:14-12:29, *538*
11:3, *384*
12:36, *384*
14:12, 16-31, *450*
14:13-31, *538*
15:24-26, *450*

569

16:3-35, *450*
16:31-35, *538*
17:2, 5-7, *451*
19, *447*
19:3-25, *433*
19:10-13, 16, *448*
19:18-25, *538, 545*
19:20, *545*
20:1-17, *448*
20:22-23:33, *448*
22:27, *384*
24:4-18, *448*
24:9-11, *449*
24:18, *449*
31:18, *545*
32:4, *448*
32:9-10, *451*
32:11-13, *451*
32:14, *448*
33:11, *449*
33:12-13, *384*
33:16-17, *384*
33:18-22, *538*
33:19, *384*
34:6, *384, 385*
34:6-7, *449*
34:9, *384*
34:28, *545*
34:29, *449*
39:42-43, *451*
40:34-35, *538*
40:35, *538*
Leviticus
9:6, *538*
26:1, *563*
Numbers
6:25, *384*
11:11, 15, *384*
13:26-33, *451*

14:5-11, *538*
14:11-12, *451*
14:13-16, *451*
14:17-19, *452*
14:22, *538*
14:37-38, 41-45,
    452
16:12-22, 42-50,
    538
27:14, *566*
Deuteronomy
1:3, *453*
2:7, *453*
4:13, *545*
5:24, *538*
7:6-7, *545*
7:6-8, *181, 211*
8:1-5, *453*
9:6, *211*
9:10, *545*
17:18-20, *563*
18, *545*
26:9, *195*
28:1-14, *545*
28:15-68, *200,
    211, 545*
29:2-6, *454*
29:9-15, *453*
29-30, *182*
32:39, *363*
Joshua
7:19, *538*
Judges
6:17, *384*
1 Samuel
4:21-22, *538*
6:5, *501*
15:29, *538*
2 Samuel
7, *182*

7:11-16, *181*
7:13, *208*
12:22, *384*
15:25, *384*
23:2-7, *207*
1 Kings
8:11, *538*
8:27, *529*
9:3-5, *563*
19:18, *130*
2 Kings
13:23, *384*
15:29, *545*
17:3-6, *545*
21:23, *562*
21:24-26, *562*
22:8-10, *563*
24:1, *545*
1 Chronicles
12:32, *111*
16:24, *539*
26:18, *28*
2 Chronicles
5:1-14, *538*
7:1-3, *538*
30:9, *384, 385*
34:1-2, *562*
34:3-4, *563*
34:6, 7, *563*
34:8-13, *563*
34:14-18, *563*
34:19-20, *564*
34:21-26, *564*
34:27-28, *564*
34:29-30, *565*
34:31, *565*
34:32-33, *565*
35:20-24, *566*
35:26, *566*

Nehemiah
3:1, *231*
3:26, *231*
3:29, *231*
3:3, *231*
5:15, *280*
9:6, *506*
9:17, 31, *384, 385*
Job
33:24, *384*
Psalms
1-150, *111, 183*
2:1-3, *547*
2:4, *184*
4:1, *384*
6:2, *385*
8:1, *537*
9:13, *385*
19:1, *537*
19:1-6, *500, 506*
19:9, *500*
22:22, *195*
33:10f, *506*
34:8, *126*
72:16, *547*
84:11, *384, 509*
86:15, *384, 385*
86:9-10, *500*
89, *182*
89:28-37, *411*
90:4, *287*
96:3, *539*
102:15, *539*
103:8, *384, 385*
110:1, *202*
111:4, *384, 385*
112:4, *384, 385*
116:5,, *384*
145:8, *384, 385*

Proverbs
3:4, 34, *384*
3:19, *506*
21:22, *115*
Ecclesiastes
3:7, *123*
3:21, *549*
Isaiah
2:1-4, *183*
2:2-4, *201*
2:4, *183, 547*
9:6-7, *183, 201*
11:1-5, *547*
11:3-4, *548*
11:4, *183*
11:6-9, *183*
11:9, *183*
14:1-2, *201*
14:3-6, *183*
19:23-25, *183*
25:1-3, *501*
29:18, *183, 547*
29:20-21, *548*
30:18-19, *385*
30:23-24, *547*
33:2, *385*
33:24, *547*
35:5-6, *183, 547*
42:6-7, *183*
42:8, *540*
43:20, *501*
44:5, *193*
49:22-23, *540*
53:10, *198*
60:21, *501*
61:3, *501*
62:2, *539*
65:20, *183*
65:20-22, *547*
66:1, *529*

66:12, *539*
66:18, *540*
66:19, *539*
Jeremiah
3:17, *201*
6:14, *75*
11:26a, *411*
13:11, *538*
14:7, *77*
30, *183*
30:7, *258*
30:7-9, *267*
30:9, *183*
30:24, *181*
31:2, *384*
31:10-14, *547*
31:29-30, *548*
31:31-34, *182, 300*
31:32, *545*
31:36, *207*
32:2, *195*
33:14-18, *201*
51:12-13, *545*
Lamentations
2:1, *538*
Ezekiel
10:4, *536*
16, *545*
18:5-9, *198*
28:22, *541*
34:23-24, *183*
34:25-30, *547*
36:11, *547*
36:26, *545*
36:29-30, *547*
39, *325*
39:13, *541*
39:21, *539*
40-48, *254, 255, 325*

46:1-15, 183
47, 183
47:8-10, 547
Daniel
    1:1-4, 545
    2:44, 250
    4:35, 506
    7:13-15, 183
    8, 368
    8:14, 369
    9, 283
    9:24-27, 267, 280
    9:27, 246, 280
    12:1, 267
    12:12, 287
Hosea
    1:1-2:13, 386
    2:14-23, 386
Joel
    2:13, 384, 385
    2:21-26, 547
Amos
    5:15, 385
    9:13-14, 183
Jonah
    2:9, 437
    4:2, 384, 385
Micah
    4:3, 547
    5:2, 322
Habakkuk
    2:14, 547
Haggai
    2: 7, 539
Zechariah
    2:8, 184
    7:12, 545
    8:3, 183
    8:4-5, 183
    8:11-12, 547

8:22-23, 540
10, 183
12:9-14:5, 267
12:10, 183, 384
14:1-9, 184, 201,
    252
14:4, 252, 255
14:6-9, 203
14:9, 10, 547
14:15-19, 548
14:20-21, 183
Malachi
    1:9, 385

New Testament
Matthew
    1:24-25, 473
    4:17, 54, 57, 119
    4:19, 71, 231
    7:3, 64
    7:14, 64
    8:11, 233
    10:34, 290
    12:31-32, 133
    13:24-30, 149
    13:25, 59
    16:16-19, 62
    16:19, 166
    16:27, 413, 536
    17:2, 536
    18:15-20, 547
    18:20, 137, 140
    19:28, 184, 202,
        228, 547
    20:26-28, 129
    22:30, 289
    24:4-8, 271
    24:8, 267
    24:13, 410
    24:14, 267

24:21, 267
24:27, 231
24-25, 270
25:37, 183
26:29, 228, 233,
    238
Mark
    13, 270
Luke
    1:47, 474
    1-2, 181
    2:14, 501, 536
    2:32, 539
    2:52, 386
    3:7-9, 211
    6:32, 33, 34, 386
    9:26, 536, 537
    13:29, 233
    17:9, 386
    19:11-27, 412
    19:17, 19, 228
    21:8-11, 25-27,
        270
    22:20, 300
    24:27, 45, 355
    24:44, 27
John
    1:1-3, 541
    1:12, 438
    1:13, 395
    1:14, 509, 536, 541
    1:16-17, 386
    1:17, 429
    1:29, 231, 435
    2, 323
    2:11, 536
    3:16, 442
    6:45, 115
    7:37-39, 231
    8:31-47, 211

8:54, *536*
9:1-3, *501*
11:1-44, *536*
13:31-32, *500, 536*
14:16-18, *487*
14:20, *487*
15:1, 5, *126*
15:8, *501*
16:33, *267*
17:1-5, *500*
17:5, *536, 541*
17:24, *536*
21:11, *323*
21:19, *501*

Acts
1:6, *202*
1:6-7, *185*
2, *136, 185*
2:1-41, *546*
2:38-39, *546*
2:47, *386*
3:19-21, *547*
4:27, *197, 198*
4:28, *198*
7:2, *536*
7:10, *386*
7:51, *134*
9:18, *486*
10-11, *234*
11:15-16, *486*
11:19, *132*
11:25, *228*
13:1-3, *228*
13:14, *150*
13:45, 48, *235*
14:21, *150*
14:22, *75, 267*
14:23, *150, 151, 173*
14:26, *228*

15:6-7, *150*
15:19-21, *150*
15:19-31, *148*
15:22, 23, *150*
15:35-41, *228*
16:31, *405*
17:26, *124*
18:22-23, *228*
20:7, *138*
20:17, 28, *148*
20:28, *148, 150, 173*
20:29-30, *230*
24:27, *386*
25:9, *386*

Romans
1-16, *111*
1:7, *51*
1:16-17, *390, 472*
1:17, *526*
1:21-23, *538*
2:1-3:20, *390*
2:17-24, *538*
3:7, *500*
3:9-18, *538*
3:21, *424*
3:21-24, *443*
3:21-4:5, *386-90*
3:23, *537, 538*
3:24-25, *388*
3:24-26, *427*
3:27, *390*
4:1-5, *389*
4:3, *428*
4:5, *393*
4:16, *386*
4:20, *501*
4:24, 25, *427*
5:1, *399, 485*
5:1-2, *388*

5:2, *386, 509*
5:3, *267*
5:12-21, *471*
5:20b, *386*
6:4-5, *536*
6:14, *386, 393*
6:17, *386*
6:23, *443*
7:1-2, *60*
7:25, *386*
8:9, *482*
8:13, *482*
8:18-23, *547*
9, *200*
9:3-4, *196*
9:4, *183, 196*
9-11, *32, 193, 196*
9:13, *114*
9:16, 31-32, *211*
10:17, *425, 483*
11, *294*
11:1, *196, 200*
11:6, *386, 393, 397, 414*
11:13, 17-21, *235*
11:15, 26, *31*
11:25, *35*
11:25-27, *228, 292*
11:29, *411*
11:33-36, *501*
11:35, 36, *442*
12:2, *57, 559*
12:3, *386*
12:5, *485*
12:6, *386*
12:10, *546*
12:12, *267*
12:16, *546*
13:1-5, *543*
13:1-7, *73*

13:8, *121, 566*
14:7–8, *122*
14:10–12, *412*
14:13, 19, *546*
14:17, *238, 289*
15:7, *500, 539*
15:7, 14, *546*
15:8–9, *501*
15:15, *386*
16:25–27, *500*
16:27, *536*
1 Corinthians
1:4, *386*
1:9, *510*
2:7, *506*
2:8, *536*
2:14, *439*
3:9–15, *412*
3:10, *386*
4:7, *442*
5:1–13, *547*
5:4–7, *148*
6:6, *392*
6:19, *122, 148*
7:15, *510*
9:17, *23*
9:19, *121*
9:24–27, *412*
10:17, *485*
10:30, *386*
10:31, *501, 539*
11:7, *537*
11:20–23, *138*
11:27–32, *546*
12, 115, *122*
12:7, 11, *148*
12:12–13, 27, *485*
12:12, 27, *148*
12:13, *174, 486*

12:18, 20, *129*
12:25, *546*
12:28, *72*
14:29–32, *116*
14:33, *134*
14:36, *116*
14:40, *148*
15:1–58, *539*
15:10, *386*
15:21–22, *471*
15:57, *386*
2 Corinthians
1:20, *500, 501, 549*
2:14, *386*
3:8, 12–18, *537*
3:18, *539*
4:4, *539*
4:15, *386, 501, 509*
4:17, *539*
5:9–10, *547*
5:10, *412, 413*
5:20, *442*
5:21, *104*
6:17, *118*
8:4, *386*
8:6, 7, 19, *386*
8:16, *386*
9:15, *386*
11:3, *465*
12:14, *71*
Galatians
1–6, *111*
1, *149*
1:6, *386*
1:8–9, *438*
2:11–3:14, *393*
2:21, *386*
3:15–20, *448*
3:21–22, *428*

3:7-9, *447*
5:4, *386*
5:13, *122, 510*
6:2, *546*
6:5, *77*
Ephesians
1:4–6, *500*
1:6, *509, 539*
1:6, 12, 14, *509*
1:7–12, 13–14, *500*
1:10, *23*
1:11, *506*
1:14, *539*
1:15–23, *391*
1:17, *536*
1:22, *148, 476*
1:22–23, *391, 485*
2:1–10, *386, 390–
93*
2:8, *425*
2:8 9, *424*
2:8–10, *423, 390–
93, 546*
2:8–9, *211, 443*
2:11–22, *391, 546*
2:15, *486*
2:20, *150*
3, *487*
3:10f, *506*
3:13, *539*
3:2, *23*
3:2, 7–8, *386*
3:3–6, *485*
3:6, *485*
4, 122, *137*
4:1, 25, *559*
4:1–5, *546*
4:2, *546*
4:3, *136*

4:4, *510*
4:7, *386*
4:11, *148*
4:12, *485*
4:15, *148, 476*
4:23, *559*
4:25, 32, *546*
5:19, 21, *546*
5:23, *476, 485, 546*
Philippians
1:1, *150*
1:7, *386*
1:11, *501*
1:23, *487*
2:11, *501, 536*
3:21, *539*
Colossians
1:18, *476*
1:18, 24, *485*
1:25, *23*
1:27, *539*
2:10, 19, *476*
2:13, *482*
2:18-19, *474*
3:4, *539*
3:13, 16, *546*
3:15, *485*
1 Thessalonians
2:6-7, *546*
2:12, *510*
4:7, *510*
4:9, 13-18, *546*
4:14, *487*
4:15-18, *547*
4:17, *136, 487*
5:11, 13, *546*
5:19-20, *355*
5:21, *149*
2 Thessalonians
1:11-12, *501*

2:1-2, *547*
2:4, *246*
2:14, *539*
1 Timothy
1:12, *386*
1:14, *386*
1:15-17, *500*
3:1-2, *148*
3:8ff, *150*
3:16, *537*
5:8, *67*
5:17, *148*
6:12, *510*
2 Timothy
1:3, *386*
1:9, *386, 443*
2:13, *411*
3, *88*
3:1-5, *547*
4:3-4, *547*
4:18, *500*
Titus
1:2, *411*
1:5, *148, 173*
1:5, 7, *173*
1:6-9, *148*
2:13, *539*
3:4-7, *386*
Hebrews
1:1-3, *536*
1:1-4, *465*
2:9, *509, 536*
2:17, *478*
3:1, *478*
4:9, *287*
4:14, 15, *478*
5:5, 10, *478*
6:18, *412*
6:20, *478*
7:26, *478*

8:1, 3, *478*
8:7-12, *300*
9:7, *388*
9:11, *478*
9:11-14, *388*
10:24, *566*
10:24-25, *546*
11, *559*
11:1-2, 6, *454*
11:1-40, *437*
11:6, *435*
11:8, 19, *560*
11:39, *559*
12:1-2, *559*
13:3, *546*
13:9, *386*
13:11, 12, *478*
13:21, *500*
12:23, *149*
12:28, *386*
James
2:14-26, *116*
4:11, *546*
5:9, 16, *546*
1 Peter
1:3, *500*
1:10-12, *435*
1:22, *546*
2, *115*
2:5, *120*
2:5-9, *116*
2:9-10, *476*
3:9, *510*
3:15, *466*
4:8-10, *546*
4:11, *501*
4:13, *537*
4:14, *537*
4:16, *501*
5:1-4, *148*

576

5:2, *148, 150, 173*
5:2-3, *150*
5:2-4, *148*
5:4, *123, 539*
5:5, *546*
5:10, *509*
2 Peter
  1:3, *539*
  1:3-4, *501*
  1:10, *403*
  1:17, *536*
  3:8, *287*
  3:18, *509*
1 John
  2:2, *387*
  2:22, *233*
  2:27, *116, 122*
  3:9, *396*
  3:11, 23, *546*
  4:7, 11-12, *546*
  4:20-21, *210*
2 John
  1:5, *546*
Jude
  1:1, 3, *149*
  1:3, *149*
  1:6, *549*
  1:24-25, *501*
Revelation
  1-22, *488*
  1, *115*
  1:1, *253*
  1:3, *253*
  1:6, *120, 242*
  1-11, *279*

2:5, *546*
2:25, *149*
2-3, *137*
3:10, *275*
3:11, *253*
3:21, *413*
4:11, *500, 506*
5, *115*
5:10, *183, 228*
6:4, *253*
6:9-11, *267*
7:1-17, *267*
7:4, *513*
7:4-8, *324*
9:15, *253*
11:2-14, *267*
12:7-12, *267*
12:13-17, *267*
12-19, *279*
13:7, *267*
14:1-5,12-13, *267*
14:7, *501*
15:1, *267*
15:4, *500*
16:1-21, *267*
16:13-16, *547*
16:18, *253*
16:3, *253*
17:16, *546*
19:1-6, *267*
19:1-16, *487*
19:7, *501*
19:11-21, *547*
19:15, *267*
19:17-21, *546*

20, 34, 115, 277,
  279, 296, 325
20:1-3, *237, 293,*
  547
20:1-7, *184, 547*
20:1-10, *228, 245,*
  547
20:2-7, *202, 203*
20:4, *183, 237, 267*
20:4-6, *237, 295*
20:4-7, *547*
20:6, *487*
20:7-10, *547*
20:10, *548*
20:11, *413*
20:11-15, *413,*
  537, 548
21:16, *254*
21:22, *548*
21:24, *548*
21:24-25, *548*
21:27, *548*
21-22, *254, 255*
22:5, *548*
22:6-7, *253*
22:10, *253*
22:12, *253, 413*
22:20, *253*

SUBJECT INDEX

Albury Conferences, 96, 282
Alexandrian School, 24-27, 45, 198,
    230-33, 238
Amillennialism, 238, 247, 277, 287
Anabaptists, 162, 285, 291, 313
Anderson, Robert
    interpretation
    literal, 257
Antiochene School, 24-27, 45, 200,
    228, 230, 257
Anti-Semitism, 185-87, 488
    historical development, 179n1,
    194-201
Aquinas, Thomas
    purpose of God, 514-15
    writings
        Summa Theologica, 6, 514-15
Augsburg Confession, 527
Augustine
    amillennialism, 238, 278
    grace (theology), 393-97, 397
    interpretation
        allegorical, 233, 323
    writings
        City of God, 234, 236
Beza, Theodore
    sola gratia, 401
Bible
    translations
        English, 33, 242
        Geneva Bible, 31, 35
        German, 103, 242
        Vulgate, 239
Bible conferences, 299

Bible school movement, 140, 299
Blackstone, William Eugene
    interpretation
    literal, 257
Brethren, 99-101, 132n62, 297, 371
    origins, 92-95
Brookes, James Hall, 169, 299, 407
    ecclesiology, 171-72
    influence on
        C. I. (Cyrus Ingerson) Scofield,
        97
    local church autonomy, 170
Bullinger, E. W.
    writings
        Figures of Speech Use in the Bible,
        318n17
Calvin, John
    anti-Semitism, 250
    ecclesiology, 147, 157-62
    interpretation
        allegorical
            rejection, 312
        selective literalness, 244-47
    on interpretation, 31, 240
    sola gratia, 395
    sola Scriptura, 355n8
    soli Deo gloria, 515-17, 529-30
    writings
        Institutes of the Christian Religion,
        The, 157-62, 515-17
Calvinism, 37, 38
Chafer, Lewis Sperry, 372
    ecclesiology, 172-74
    faith, 438

577

interpretation
    literal, 257
    law and grace, 430–34
Chiliasm. See Millennialism
Christian Reconstructionist, 210
Church
    local autonomy, 141, 148–50, 164,
        172
        England, 163
        Switzerland, 163
    soli Deo gloria, 539
Church and state, 155–57, 156–57,
    166, 168, 169
    Investiture Controversy, 157n40
Church councils
    Chalcedon, 467n3, 468–69
    Constantinople, 467n3, 473,
        376n85
    Nicaea, 117n22, 155, 466n3, 467
Church of England and Ireland. *See*
    Established Church
Clement of Alexandria, 25, 198, 232
    writings
        Instructor, The, 198
Cocceius, Johannes, 271n14, 287
Congregationalism, 164, 165
Constantine I (Roman Emperor),
    153, 155, 235
Covenant theology, 320–21
    church and state, 484
    hermeneutics, 321–22
    Israel and the church, 484
Cyprian of Carthage, 276
    on church authority, 146, 152–54,
        159n52, 160
Cyril of Alexandria, 200
Dallas Theological Seminary
    doctrinal statement, 435, 447
Darby, John Nelson, 297, 371
    clergyman, 86–88, 127–29

early background, 84–85, 124–27
ecclesiology, 130–32, 371
faith, 440
influence of, 101–2, 138–41
influence on
    C. I. (Cyrus Ingerson) Scofield,
        84n5
    Dwight L. Moody, 97
    F. F. (Frederick Fyvie) Bruce,
        84n5
    Harry H. Ironside, 97
    James H. Brooks, 97
interpretation
    literal, 37, 257
Irish reformer, 82–83
law and grace, 429
parallels to Martin Luther, 125n43
priesthood of believers, 128, 134–
    35, 141
separation from the Established
    Church, 88–91, 128–29
sola Scriptura, 129, 131, 141
soli Deo gloria, 532–33
tombstone inscription, 104
writings
    Nature and Unity of the Church,
        91, 130–32
    Notion of a Clergyman, 91, 132–
        35
    On the Formation of Churches,
        135–38
Darbyites, 90
Didache, The, 151
Diet of Worms, 336–37, 476
Diodore of Tarsus, 200
Dispensation
    defined, 23
Dispensationalism, 35, 36–39, 425
    classical, 300, 372
    defined, 20–24

doxological priority, *409-11*, *497-99*, *501-3*
faith, *436-43*
grace (biblical doctrine), *409*
hermeneutics, *213*, *257*, *316*, *373-75*
mystery, *485-86*
progressive, *183n4*, *300*, *372*
revised, *300*, *372*
salvation, *426-36*
sine qua non, *9*, *70*, *257*, *316*, *497-99*, *508*, *534*
soli Deo gloria, *503-8*, *534*, *548-50*
Dispensations, *447*
soli Deo gloria, *540-48*
Dispensationslists
beliefs, *22*
Early reform movements, *20*, *81*
Eastern Orthodox Church, *19*
Edict of Milan, *153*, *155*, *235*
Edwards, Jonathan, *35*, *296*, *405*
interpretation
historicist, *270*
soli Deo gloria, *518*
Epistle of Barnabas, *185-86*, *195*
Established Church, *86*, *88*, *124*, *134*, *162*
Eusebius, *237*, *289n58*
Five *Solas*, *20*, *243*, *313*
Free grace-Lordship controversy, *436n41*
Glory of God
defined, *535*
Grace (biblical)
doctrine, *406-14*
New Testament, *386-93*
Old Testament, *384-86*
Hus, John, *20*, *46*, *243*
Hypplolytus of Rome, *199*
writings

Expository Treatise Against the Jews, *199*
Indulgences. *See* Roman Catholic Church, indulgences
Interpretation, *29*
"woodenly" literal, *317*, *320*, *366*
allegorical, *27*, *185-87*, *195*, *210*, *230-37*, *239*, *245*, *322-25*
eschatology, *252-56*, *283-91*, *287*
Christological/Christocentric, *27*, *344-48*
futurist, *36*, *37*, *267*, *278-81*, *297*
historica sentential, *201*
historicist, *35*, *37*, *267*, *268-72*, *279*, *287*, *293-96*, *296*
idealist, *267*
literal, *36*, *256*, *314*, *315*, *318-20*
literal (grammatical-historical), *35*, *70*, *313*, *325*, *341-43*, *373-75*, *480*
preterist, *253*, *267*, *278-81*, *297*
Irenaeus
interpretation
futurist, *36*
interpretation
literal, *203*, *289n59*
Ironside, Henry Allen
interpretation
literal, *257*
Irving, Edward, *96*, *282n40*
Israel, *34*, *181-85*, *195-96*, *211*
prophecies, *183-85*, *201-3*
soli Deo gloria, *538-39*
Israel and the church, *33*, *37*, *214*, *249*, *258*
Jerome, *237*, *239*
Jerusalem Council, *150*
Josiah (King of Israel)
biblical reformer, *562-66*
Justification by faith, *386-90*

Justin Martyr
  writings
    Dialogue with Tryho, a Jew, 196,
      228
Louis Berkhof
  soli Deo gloria, 509–14
Luther, Martin
  amillennialism, 286
  anti-Semitism, 187–92, 205–9, 249
  early background, 47–50, 110–11
  ecclesiology, 162
  eschatology, 285
  influence of
  five *solas*, 526–27
  interpretation
    allegorical, 180, 205–9, 284–87
    rejection, 312, 343–44
    Christological/Christocentric,
      344–48
    literal, 285, 341, 374n82
    selective literalness, 244–47
  justification by faith, 50–52, 560
  letter to Albrecht of Brandenburg
    (Archbishop of Mainz), 55
  on interpretation, 30, 240, 343
  parallels to John Nelson Darby,
    125n43
  priesthood of believers, 114, 116,
    118–21, 141, 187, 476–79
  repentance, 57, 63–65, 119n27
  Romanist walls, 114–17
  sola gratia, 395
  sola historica sentential, 194
  sola Scriptura, 112, 141, 187, 215,
    335–40, 355n8
  soli Deo gloria, 516–17, 527–28
  writings
    95 Theses, 3–4, 56–77, 355n8,
      470
    Against the Sabbatarians, 207

*Babylonian Captivity of the
  Church, The*, 117–20, 398,
  478
Catechism, 479n35
Disputation of Scholastic Theology
  (97 Theses), 4 n1, 115n14
*Explanations of the Ninety-Five
  Theses*, 55, 76–77
Freedom of the Christian, The,
  121–22
On the Jews and Their Lies, 189–
  92, 250
On the Last Words of David, 207
*Open Letter to the Christian
  Nobility*, 113–14
That Jesus was Born a Jew, 189,
  205
Three Treatises, 112, 122–23
Lutheran tradition
  sola Scriptura, 363–66
  Millennialism, 31, 34, 35, 38, 201,
    203, 228, 229, 237, 257, 265n1,
    267, 289n59, 291, 297
  rejection of, 287–91
Miller, William, 271, 366–70
Millerite tradition
  hermeneutics, 367–70
  sola Scriptura, 366–70
Millerites
  origins, 366
New Covenant, 181–84
Nicene Creed, 155, 466n3, 467,
  467n3
Novatians, 146
Origen
  interpretation
    allegorical, 25, 26, 27, 198, 233,
      236, 241, 276, 278
Pentecost, J. Dwight, 372
Perkins, William

sola gratia, 403
Peter's Indulgence, *53-55, 75, 239*
Poiret, Pierre, *287, 300*
Pope Gelasius I, *156*
Pope Gregory VII, *157*
Pope Leo X, *53-55, 121n35, 336, 475*
   papal bull, *75*
Postmillennialism, 277
Posttribulationism, 276, 277
   Powerscourt Conferences, 95-97,
      99n54, 283
Powerscourt, Lady Theodosia, *95, 282*
Premillennialism. *See Millennialism*
Pretribulationism, 257, 277
Priesthood of believers
   literacy, 242
Puritan theologians
   belief in millennialism, *32, 296*
Puritans (Separatists), *163-64*
Reformation
   five *solas*, 313
   sola Scriptura, 334-35
   soli Deo gloria, 514-18
Reformed theology
   hermeneutics, *251, 360-63*
   Scripture
      perspicuity, *361-63*
   sola Scriptura, 360-63
   soli Deo gloria, 508-14
Replacement theology, *37, 195, 197,
   201, 488*
Roman Catholic Church, *239*
   Counter Reformation, 272
   indelible character of priests, 120
   indulgences, *53-77, 239*
   intercession of the saints, 474-75
   Jesuit
      interpretation, 272-82
   Mariology, 472-74
   sacramental system, *119n28,477-*
      79
   seven sacraments, *118n26, 398*
   writings
      Catechism, 6
      Summary Instruction, 54, 60-61,
         67, 68-69, 75
Ryrie, Charles C., *23, 372*
   faith, *438*
   on dispensations, 447
   salvation, 434-36
   soli Deo gloria, 534
Salvation (biblical)
   Old Testament, *443-54*
Savoy Declaration, 164
Scofield Reference Bible, The, *97, 316,*
   372
Scofield, C. I. (Cyrus Ingerson)
   influence on
      Lewis Sperry Chafer, 97
   interpretation
      literal, 257
   soli Deo gloria, 533
Scripture
   perspicuity, *339-40, 357-58*
   sufficiency, *337*
Sensus plenior, *28n26, 358n18*
Seventh-day Adventism, 367-70
   interpretation
      historicist, *269, 270*
Sine qua non. See Dispensationalism,
   sine qua non
Sola fide, *423-26*
Sola gratia, *393-414*
Sola Scriptura, *283, 313, 333-35, 354-*
   58, 373-75
Soli Deo gloria
   biblical, 499-501
   creation, *537*
   influence of, *531-32*
   man, condition of, *537*
   nations, 539

Trinity, *535–37*

Solus Christus, 465–81

State or national church, *136, 140, 162*

Supersessionism. *See* Replacement theology

Tertuallian, 276

Tetzel, Johann, *53–55, 60–61, 60, 63, 66, 239, 336*

Thornwell, James Henley
   local church autonomy, *168–69*

Tyndale, William, *240, 243*

Ursinus, Zacharius
   sola gratia, 402

Walvoord, John F., *372*
   ecclesiology, *172–74*
   prophecy, 297

Westminster Confession of Faith, The, 147, 164, 169, 320, 356, 403, 517 n14, *271*

Westminster Longer and Shorter Catechism
   soli Deo gloria, 530–31

Wycliffe, John, *20, 46*

CPSIA information can be obtained
at www.ICGtesting.com
Printed in the USA
LVHW080833220223
740023LV00027B/1358